Writings on the Spiritual Life

VICTORINE TEXTS IN TRANSLATION
Exegesis, Theology and Spirituality from the Abbey of St Victor

4

Grover A. Zinn
Editor in Chief

Hugh Feiss OSB
Managing Editor

Editorial Board
Boyd Taylor Coolman, Dale M. Coulter,
Christopher P. Evans, Franklin T. Harkins,
Frans van Liere

In the twelfth century the Augustinian canons of the Abbey
of St Victor in Paris occupied a critical position between
traditional, meditative theology and emerging scholasticism.
In a series of thematic volumes, this collaborative effort will
make available in new, annotated English translations many
of their most important and influential works, as well as other
Victorine works that deserve to be better known.

Writings on the Spiritual Life

A Selection of Works of Hugh, Adam, Achard,
Richard, Walter, and Godfrey of St Victor

New City Press
of the Focolare
Hyde Park, New York

Published in the United States by New City Press
202 Comforter Blvd., Hyde Park, NY 12538
www.newcitypress.com
©2014 Brepols Publishers, Turnhout (Belgium)

Cover design by Leandro de Leon

Library of Congress Cataloging-in-Publication Data:

Trinity and creation / Boyd Taylor Coolman, Dale M. Coulter, eds.
p. cm. — (Victorine texts in translation : exegesis, theology and spirituality from the Abbey of St. Victor ; 1)
Contains translations from selected members of the Abbey of St Victor.
Includes bibliographical references and indexes.
ISBN 978-1-56548-373-6 (pbk. : alk. paper)
1. Trinity—History of doctrines--Middle Ages, 600-1500. 2. Creation—History of doctrines—Middle Ages,
600-1500. I. Coolman, Boyd Taylor, 1966- II. Coulter, Dale M. (Dale Michael), 1970- III. Hugh,
of Saint-Victor, 1096?-1141. Selections. English. IV. Adam, de Saint-Victor, d. 1192. Selections. English.
V. Richard, of St. Victor, d. 1173. On the Trinity. English. VI. Saint-Victor (Abbey : Paris, France)
BT109.T77 2011
231'.04409021—dc22 2011009585

ISBN 978-1-56548-504-4

Printed in the United States of America

For Elizabeth, Lauren, Andrew, and Matthew Evans

TABLE OF CONTENTS

The Spirit and Prayer

Mary

PREFACE

The Abbey of Saint Victor at Paris was one of the major centers for biblical interpretation, theological reflection, spiritual guidance, and liturgical practice and innovation in the twelfth century. The Editorial Board of this series, *Victorine Texts in Translation*, is pleased to present this fourth volume in a continuing series of ten volumes offering English translations (often for the first time) of a wide range of writings by authors resident at or formed at the abbey.

The past several decades have seen a renaissance in the study of the Victorines, with a number of recent studies, the inception of a French translation series, a dedicated monograph series published with Brepols, the establishment of the Hugo von Sankt Viktor Institut, and a Colloquium in Paris celebrating the 900th anniversary of the founding of the abbey. The translated texts presented in this series form an American counterpart to these initiatives. Our series aims to make Victorine texts more accessible to a wider English speaking audience. Where possible, *Victorine Texts in Translation* uses the latest critical Latin texts published, for example, in the *Corpus Christianorum: Continuatio Medievalis*; where no critical edition exists, translations have been have been produced using the Latin published in Migne's *Patrologia Latina*, corrected where necessary. Introductions to each volume and each work translated give the intellectual and historical background for understanding the work. Each text is also annotated, and each volume contains a bibliography.

The planning and execution of this project have been a community effort from the beginning. Our plans crystallized at a meeting hosted by the late Rabbi Michael Signer at the University of Notre Dame. The members of editorial board have shared the decisions regarding what to translate, produced some of the translations, and reviewed the translations. We have been joined by a number of other scholars engaged in Victorine studies who have offered translations, introductions, and helpful suggestions.

The subtitle of this series, *Exegesis, Theology and Spirituality from the Abbey of Saint Victor*, uses categories developed in the centuries following the flourishing of Victorine thought. However, these categories indicate well the breadth of the Victorines' interests. For them and for their predecessors, what is today understood as "theology" often occurred in the context of scriptural interpretation and was intertwined with spirituality and liturgy. This integrated vision stands as an important contribution that the Victorines can make to modern readers.

This volume is the first in this series to be devoted entirely to works that fall in the category of "spirituality." The term as used here has a wide field of reference, spanning texts ranging from sermons to devotional exercises, a treatise on the nature of prayer to exposition of the Lord's Prayer, and a treatise examining the fallen state of human beings to a collection of tropological interpretations of Psalms passages. Most of the works in this volume are relatively short and reflect a Victorine characteristic, namely, the abundance of shorter works addressing a variety of topics in spirituality.[1] The fruitful intersection of various dimensions of the life of Victorine canons can be seen in several ways. Hugh's analysis (using classical rhetoric) of the nature of prayer and the relation of personal affective states to the language of the Psalms as prayers reveals both the scholar analyzing experience and the canon at prayer. The sermons, of which there were many at St Victor, show reflective piety at work in liturgical settings, while sequences (a special development at St Victor) and a single hymn show poetic creativity in the service of spirituality. An exegetical starting point and framework can be found in Richard's treatise, *On the State of the Interior Man*, while the collection of his Psalms tractates shows his virtuosity as an expositor of the tropological (moral and spiritual) meaning of biblical materials. Several works reflect the twelfth-century flowering of devotion to the Virgin Mary and to the Holy Spirit who gifts give impetus to the spiritual life of Christians. The variety of topics and genres found in the works translated in this volume is but a sampling of the rich, creative and influential spirituality of the Victorine canons. The next volume in this series will again be devoted to spirituality. It will present several well-known longer Victorine spiritual works, including Hugh's *On the Ark of Noah* and *Little Book on the Construction of Noah's Ark* and Richard's *On the Ark of Moses*, as well a commentary on the Song of Songs by the less-known Thomas Gallus.

Grover A. Zinn, Editor in Chief
Oberlin College

---

[1]   For Hugh and Richard of St Victor, see Rudolph Goy's surveys of the surviving manuscripts of their writings. See bibliography, *ad nomen*.

ACKNOWLEDGEMENTS

I am grateful to all of the members of the editorial board for their cooperation, dedication, and perseverance in completing this fourth volume of the series, *Victorine Texts in Translation*. All of the members contributed to the painstaking task of vetting the translations and introductions. I am grateful to Franklin T. Harkins, Joshua C. Benson, and Vanessa Butterfield who graciously produced translations. Fr. Hugh Feiss and Frans van Liere also produced translations and more than what was expected of them, so I am especially appreciative for their efforts. I am also indebted to Dale Coulter for taking on a short introduction and to Grover Zinn and Fr. Hugh Feiss for their excellent feedback on and corrections to the general introduction.

I am also grateful to Brepols for its continued interest in this series and to Luc Jocqué, our Editor at Brepols, for his support and help in dealing with dilemmas that a volume like this inevitably entails.

The Hill Monastic Manuscript Library (St John's University) and the Vatican Film Library (St Louis University) were instrumental in making accessible and providing microfilm copies of many manuscripts used in this volume.

I am thankful to the Faculty Development Committee at the University of St Thomas (Houston, TX) for awarding me a research grant to hire a copyeditor, Kerry J. MacArthur. His careful attention to detail was invaluable.

Finally, I am most grateful to my family for their constant support and encouragement of my research.

Christopher P. Evans
University of St Thomas (Houston, TX)
Feast of St Pulcheria 2012

ABBREVIATIONS

General Abbreviations

ACW	*Ancient Christian Writers* (Westminster, MD/New York, NY: Newman/Paulist Press, 1946–).
AHDLMA	*Archives d'histoire doctrinale et littéraire du moyen âge* (Paris: J. Vrin, 1927–).
Arsenal	Bibliothèque de l'Arsenal.
BAV	Biblioteca Apostolica Vaticana.
BGPTMA	*Beiträge zur Geschichte der Philosophie und Theologie des Mittelalters* (Münster: Aschendorff, 1891–).
BL	British Library.
BM	Bibliothèque municipale.
BML	Biblioteca Medicea Laurenziana.
BnF	Bibliothèque nationale de France.
BV	Bibliotheca Victorina (Turnhout: Brepols, 1991–).
CCCM	*Corpus Christianorum, Continuatio Mediaevalis* (Turnhout: Brepols, 1967–).
CCL	*Corpus Christianorum, Series Latina* (Turnhout: Brepols, 1954–).
CS	*Cistercian Studies* (Kalamazoo: Cistercian Publications, 1970–).
CSEL	*Corpus Scriptorum Ecclesiasticorum Latinorum* (Vienna: Tempsky, 1866–).
Denz.-Schön.	H. Denzinger, *Enchiridion Symbolorum, Definitionum et Declarationum de Rebus Fidei et Morum*, 36th ed., ed. A. Schönmetzer (Freiburg: Herder, 1976).
Denz.-Hün.	*Kompendium der Glaubensbekenntnisse und kirchlichen Lehrentscheidungen. Lateinisch-Deutsch: Enchiridion Symbolorum, Definitionum et Declarationum de Rebus Fidei et*

	Morum, 3rd edition, ed. and tr. Peter Hünermann (Freiburg: Herder, 2009).
DS	*Dictionnaire de spiritualité: ascétique et mystique, doctrine et histoire*, 16 vols. (Paris: G. Beauchesne et ses fils, 1932–1995).
Loeb	Loeb Classical Library (London: William Heinemann; Cambridge, MA: Harvard University Press, 1912–).
MA 1	*Miscellanea agostiniana; testi e studi, pubblicati a cura dell'Ordine eremitano di s. Agostino nel XV centenario dalla morte del santo dottore*, vol. 1 (Rome: Tipografia Poliglotta Vaticana, 1930).
Mazarine	Bibliothèque Mazarine.
Oeuvre 1	*L'œuvre de Hugues de Saint-Victor*, vol. 1, Latin text by H. B. Feiss and P. Sicard, tr. (French) D. Poirel, H. Rochais, and P. Sicard, intro., notes, and appendices D. Poirel, Sous la Règle de saint Augustin (Turnhout: Brepols, 1997).
Oeuvre 2	*L'œuvre de Hugues de Saint-Victor*, vol. 2, intro., tr., and notes by B. Jollès, Sous la Règle de saint Augustin (Turnhout: Brepols, 2000).
ONB	Osterreichische Nationalbibliothek.
PL	*Patrologiae cursus completus sive bibliotheca universalis, integra, uniformis, commoda, oeconomica, omnium ss. Patrum, doctorum scriptorumque ecclesiasticorum qui ab aevo apostolico ad Innocentii III tempora floruerunt . . . series Latina*, ed. J. P. Migne, 221 vols. (Paris, 1844–1864).
PG	*Patrologiae cursus completus . . . series graeca*, ed. J. P. Migne (Paris 1857–1876).
RBen.	*Revue Bénédictine* (Maredsous, 1885–).
RTAM	*Recherches de théologie ancienne et médiévale* (Louvain, 1929–), now *RTPM: Recherches de théologie et philosophie médiévales.*
SC	*Sources Chrétiennes* (Paris: Éditions du Cerf, 1942–).
SB	*Spicilegium Bonaventurianum* (Grottaferrata: Editiones Collegii S. Bonaventurae, 1963–).
SBO	*Sancti Bernardi Opera*, ed. J. Leclercq, C. H. Talbot, and H. Rochais, 9 vols. (Rome: Editiones Cistercienses, 1957–1977).

Schmitt	*Anselmi Opera Omnia*, ed. F. S. Schmitt (Edinburgh: Thomas Nelson, 1938–1968). Reprinted with Spanish translation in *Obras completas de San Anselmo*, ed. Julian Alameda, 2 vols. (Madrid: Biblioteca de Autores Cristianos, 1951–1953).
TPMA	Textes philosophiques du Moyen Age (Paris: J. Vrin, 1958–).
UB	Universitätsbibliothek.
VTT	Victorine Texts in Translation (Turnhout: Brepols, 2010–).
WSA	The Works of Saint Augustine: A Translation for the 21st Century (New York: New City Press, 1990–).

VICTORINE AUTHORS[1]

ACHARD OF SAINT VICTOR

Discretione	*De discretione animae, spiritus et mentis*, ed. G. Morin, "Un traité faussement attribué à Adam de Saint-Victor," *Aus der Geisteswelt des Mittelalters*, BGPTMA, Supplement-band 3/1 (1935), 251–62; ed. N. Häring, "Gilbert of Poitiers, Author of the 'De discretione animae, spiritus et mentis' commonly attributed to Achard of Saint Victor," *Mediaeval Studies* 22 (1960): 148–91; tr. H. Feiss, *On the Distinction of Soul, Spirit and Mind*, in *Achard of Saint Victor: Works*, CS 165:353–74.
Serm.	*Sermons inédits*, ed. J. Châtillon, TPMA 17 (1970); tr. H. Feiss, *Sermons*, in *Achard of Saint Victor: Works*, CS 165:59–351.
Unitate	*De unitate Dei et pluralitate creaturarum*, ed. E. Martineau (Saint-Lambert des Bois: Authentica, 1987); tr. H. Feiss, *On the Unity of God*, in *Achard of Saint Victor: Works*, CS 165:375–480.

[1]   An asterisk (*) indicates doubtful authenticity.

Adam of Saint Victor

Sequentiae — *Sequentiae*, ed. J. Grosfillier, *Les sequences d'Adam de Saint-Victor: Étude littéraire (poétique et rhétoriue). Textes et traductions, commentaires*, BV 20 (2008), 252–481; ed. E. Misset and P. Aubry, *Les proses d'Adam de Saint-Victor, texte et musique* (Paris: H. Welter, 1900); ed. Guido Maria Dreves and Clemens Blume, *Analecta Hymnica Medii Aevi* 54–55 (Leipzig: O. R. Reisland, 1922); ed. B. Jollès, *Quatorze proses du xiie siècle à la louange de Marie*, Sous la Règle de saint Augustin 1 (Turnhout: Brepols, 1994); tr. D. Wrangham, *The liturgical poetry of Adam of St. Victor*, 3 vols. (London: Kegan Paul, Trench, & Co., 1881).

Godfrey of Saint Victor

Microcosmus — *Microcosmus*, ed. Ph. Delhaye (Lille: Facultés catholiques, 1951); partially tr. H. Feiss, *Microcosm (par. 203–27)*, VTT 2.301–41.

Fons — *Fons philosophiae*, ed. P. Michaud-Quantin, Analecta mediaevalia Namurcensia 8 (Louvain: Nauwlaerts/ Namur: Godenne, 1956); tr. E. Synan, *The Fountain of Philosophy* (Toronto: Pontifical Institute of Mediaeval Studies, 1972); partially tr. H. Feiss, VTT 3.389–416.

Sermo gen. cap. — *Sermo in generali capitulo*, ed. H. Riedlinger, *Die Makellosigkeit der Kirche in den Lateinischen Hoheliedkommentaren des Mittelalters*, BGPTMA 38/3 (1958), 188–93 (*Sermon at a General Chapter*).

Hugh of Saint Victor

Adnot. in Pent. — *Adnotationes elucidatoriae in Pentateuchon*, PL 175.29–114 (*Notes on the Pentateuch*).

Archa Noe — *De archa Noe* (*De arca Noe morali*), ed. P. Sicard, CCCM 176 (2001), 3–117; tr. a Religious of C.S.M.V., *Ark of Noah*, in *Hugh of Saint-Victor: Selected Spiritual Writings* (New York: Harper and Row, 1962), 45–153.

Arrha	*De arrha animae*, ed. K. Müller, *Hugo von Sankt Viktor, Soliloquium de arrha animae und De vanitate mundi,* Kleine Texte für Vorlesungen und Übungen 123 (Bonn, 1913), 1–26; ed. and tr. P. Sicard *et al., Oeuvre* 1:226–83; tr. H. Feiss, *Soliloquy on the Betrothal-Gift of the Soul,* VTT 2.183–232.
Assumpt.	*Pro assumptione Virginis,* ed. B. Jollès, *Oeuvre* 2:112–61 (*Assumption of the Virgin*).
BM Virg.	*De beatae Mariae virginitate,* ed. B. Jollès, *Oeuvre* 2:182–253 (*Virginity of Mary*).
Cant. BM.	*Super canticum Mariae,* ed. B. Jollès, *Oeuvre* 2:24–91; tr. F. Harkins, *Exposition on the Canticle of Mary,* VTT 4. 427–52.
Decalogum	*Institutiones in Decalogum,* PL 176.9–15 (*Instructions on the Decalogue*).
Didasc.	*Didascalicon,* ed. C. H. Buttimer (Washington: The Catholic University Press, 1939); tr. J. Taylor, *The Didascalicon of Hugh of St. Victor* (New York: Columbia University Press, 1991); tr. F. Harkins, *Didascalicon on the Study of Reading,* VTT 3.81–183.
Egredietur	*Super "Egredietur uirga,"* ed. B. Jollès, *Oeuvre* 2:270–86 (*A Shoot Will Come Forth*).
Eulogium	*Eulogium sponsi et sponsae* (*De amore sponsi ad sponsum*), PL 176.987–94; tr. H. Feiss, *The Praise of the Bridegroom,* VTT 2.113–36.
In hier. cael.	*Commentariorium in hierarchiam caelestem,* PL 175.923–1154 (*Commentary on the Celestial Hierarchy*).
In Eccl.	*In Salomonis Ecclesiasten homiliae,* PL 175.113–256 (*Homilies on Ecclesiastes*).
Inst. nov.	*De institutione novitiorum,* ed. P. Sicard, *Oeuvre* 1:18–114 (*Instruction of Novices*).
Lament.	*Super Lamentationes,* PL 175.255–322 (*On Lamentations*).
Laude car.	*De laude caritatis,* ed. P. Sicard, *Oeuvre* 1:182–207; tr. F. Harkins, *On the Praise of Charity,* VTT 2.149–68.
Libellus	*Libellus de formatione arche* (*De arca Noe mystica*), ed. P. Sicard, CCCM 176 (2001), 121–62; tr. J. Weiss, "*A Little Book about Constructing Noah's Ark,*" in *Medieval Craft of Memory,* ed. M. Caruthers and J. Ziolkowski

(Philadelphia: University of Pennsylvania Press, 2002), 41–70.

Meditatione De meditatione, ed. R. Baron, *Six opuscules spirituels*, SC 155 (1969), 44–59; tr. F. van Liere, *On Meditation*, VTT 4. 387–93.

*Misc. Miscellanea, PL 177.469–900. Many are not authentic; those by Hugh of Saint Victor are concentrated in Books I and II, PL 177.469–588 (*Miscellanea*).

Orat. dom. De oratione dominica, PL 175.774–89 (*On the Lord's Prayer*).

Quat. volunt. De quatuor voluntatibus, PL 176.841–46 (*The Four Wills of Christ*).

Quid vere Quid vere diligendum sit, ed. R. Baron, *Six opuscules*, 94–99; tr. V. Butterfield, *What Truly Should be Loved?*, VTT 2.169–82.

Quinque sept. De quinque septenis, ed. R. Baron, *Six opuscules*, 100–19; tr. J. Benson, *On the Five Sevens*, VTT 4. 361–68.

Sac. dial. De sacramentis legis naturalis et scriptae dialogus, PL 176.17–42 (*Dialogue on the Sacraments*).

Sacr. De sacramentis christianae fidei, ed. R. Berndt, *Hugonis de Sancto Victore: De sacramentis Christiane fidei* (Münster: Aschendorff, 2008); PL 176.173–618; tr. R. Deferrari, *On the Sacraments of the Christian Faith (De sacramentis) of Hugh of Saint Victor* (Cambridge, MA: The Mediaeval Academy of America, 1951).

Sapientia De sapentia Christi, PL 176.845–56 (*The Wisdom of Christ*).

Script. De scripturis et scriptoribus sacris, PL 175.9–28; tr. F. van Liere, *On Sacred Scripture and its Authors*, VTT 3.213–48.

Sent. div. Sententiae de divinitate, ed. A. Piazzoni, "Ugo di San Vittore 'auctor' delle 'Sententiae de divinitate,'" *Studi medievali*, 3rd series, 23 (1982): 861–955; tr. C. Evans and H. Feiss, *Sentences on Divinity*, VTT 1.111–77.

Sent. quest. O. Lottin, "Questions inédits de Hugues de Saint-Victor," *RTAM* 26 (1959): 177–213; *RTAM* 27 (1960): 42–60.

Septem donis De septem donis Spiritus sancti, ed. R. Baron, *Six opuscules*, 120–33; tr. J. Benson, *On the Seven Gifts of the Holy Spirit*, VTT 4. 375–80.

Subst. dilect.	*De substantia dilectionis*, ed. R. Baron, *Six opuscules*, 82–93; tr. V. Butterfield, *On the Substance of Love*, VTT 2.137–48.
Tribus diebus	*De tribus diebus*, ed. D. Poirel, CCCM 177 (2002), 3–70; tr. H. Feiss, *On the Three Days*, VTT 1.61–102.
Vanitate	*De vanitate mundi*, PL 176.703–39; tr. A Religious of the C.S.M.V., *The Vanity of the World*, in *Hugh of Saint-Victor: Selected Spiritual Writings*, 157–82.
Verbo Dei	*De Verbo Dei*, ed. R. Baron, *Six opuscules*, 60–81 (*The Word of God*).
Virtute orandi	*De virtute orandi*, ed. H. Feiss, *Oeuvre* 1:126–61; tr. H. Feiss, *On the Power of Prayer*, VTT 4. 331–47.
Virtutibus	*De virtutibus et vitiis*, ed. R. Baron, *Ètudes sur Hugues de Saint-Victor* (Paris: Desclée de Brouwer, 1963), 250–55 (*On Virtues and Vices*).

RICHARD OF SAINT VICTOR

XII patr.	*De duodecim patriarchis (Benjamin Minor)*, ed. J. Châtillon, *Les douze patriarches ou Beniamin minor*, SC 419 (1997); tr. G. Zinn, *The Twelve Patriarchs*, in *Richard of Saint Victor, The Twelve Patriarchs, The Mystical Ark, Book Three of the Trinity*, Classics of Western Spirituality (New York: Paulist, 1979), 51–147.
*Abdiam	*In Abdiam*, PL 175.371–406 (*On Obadiah*).
Adnot. Ps.	*Mysticae adnotationes in Psalmos* (= *Tractatus super quosdam Psalmos*), PL 196.265–404.
Apoc.	*In Apocalypsim*, PL 196.683–888 (*On the Apocalypse*).
Ad me clamat	*Ad me clamat ex Seir*, ed. J. Ribaillier, *Opuscules théologiques*, TPMA 15 (1967), 256–80 (*He Calls to Me from Seir*).
Arca Moys.	*De arca Moysi (De arca mystica; Benjamin major)*, ed. M.-A. Aris, *Contemplatio: Philosophische Studien zum Traktat Benjamin Maior des Richard von Sankt Victor. Mit einer verbesserten Edition des Textes*, Fuldaer Studien 6 (Frankfurt am Main: Josef Knecht, 1996); tr. G. Zinn, *Twelve Patriarchs*, 149–343.

*Cant.

In Cantica Canticorum explanatio, PL 196.405A–534A (*Explanation of the Song of Songs*).

Carb.

Carbonum et cinerum, ed. J. Châtillon, *Trois opuscules spirituels de Richard de Saint-Victor* (Paris: Études augustiniennes, 1986), 253–63 (*Coals and Ashes*).

Causam

Causam quam nesciebam. ed. J. Châtillon, *Trois opuscules*, 201–21 (*A Cause I Did Not Know*).

Comp. Christi

De Comparatione Christi ad florem et Mariae ad virgam, PL 196.1031–32 (*Comparing Christ to a Flower and Mary to a Branch*).

Decl. nonn. diff.

Declarationes nonnullarum difficultatum Scripturae, ed. J. Ribaillier, *Opuscules théologiques*, 201–14 (*Resolutions of Some Difficulties in Scripture*).

Diff. pecc.

De differentia peccati mortalis et venialis, ed. Ribaillier, *Opuscules théologiques*, 291–93 (*The Difference between Mortal and Venial Sin*).

Diff. sac.

De differentia sacrificii Abrahae a sacrificio Beatae Mariae Virginis, PL 196.1043–60 (*The Difference between the Sacrifices of Abraham and Mary*).

Emman.

De Emmanuele, PL 196.601–66 (*On Emmanuel*).

Erud.

De eruditione hominis interioris, PL 196.1229–1366 (*Instruction of the Interior Person*).

Exterm.

De exterminatione mali et promotione boni, PL196.1073–1116 (*On Exterminating Evil and Promoting Good*).

Gem. pasch.

Sermo in die pasche, PL 196.1059–74 (*Twofold Pasch*).

Illa die

In illa die, ed. J. Châtillon, *Trois opuscules*, 123–52 (*On That Day*).

LE

Liber exceptionum, ed. J. Châtillon, *Liber exceptionum*, TPMA 5 (1958) (*Book of Notes*).

*Misc.

Miscellanea 4.43–47, PL 177.721–25; *Miscellanea* 4.52, PL 177.726–27; *Miscellanea* 5.4, PL 177.753–54; *Miscellanea* 6.14, PL 177.817–19; *Miscellanea* 6.27, PL 177.826–27; *Miscellanea* 6.28, PL 177.827–30; *Miscellanea* 6.33, PL 177.831–36 (*Miscellanea*).

Misit Her.

Misit Herodes rex manus, PL 141.277–306 (*Herod the King*).

Missione

De missione Spiritus sancti sermo, PL 196.1017–32 (*Sermon on the Sending of the Holy Spirit*).

*Pascha	Sermo in die Pascha, PL 196.1067–74 (Sermon On Easter).
Pot. lig.	De potestate ligandi et solvendi, ed. J. Ribaillier, Opuscules théologiques, 77–110 (The Power to Bind and Loose).
Quat. grad.	De quatuor gradibus violentae caritatis, ed. G. Dumeige, Ives, Épître à Séverin sur la charité; Richard de Saint-Victor, Les quatre degrés de la violente charité, TPMA 3 (1955), 126–77; tr. A. Kraebel, On the Four Degrees of Violent Love, VTT 2.261–300.
Quomodo Christus	Quomodo Christus ponitur in signum populorum, PL 196.523–28 (How Christ Is a Sign for the Peoples).
Ramis	Sermo in ramis palmarum, PL 196.1059–67 (Sermon on Palm Sunday).
Serm. cent.	Sermones centum, PL 177.899–1210 (One Hundred Sermons).
Sp. blasph.	De spiritu blasphemiae, ed. J. Ribaillier, Opuscules théologiques, 121–29 (On the Spirit of Blasphemy).
Statu	De statu interioris hominis post lapsum, ed. J. Ribaillier, AHDLMA 42 (1967): 61–128; tr. C. Evans, On the State of the Interior Man, VTT 4. 251–314.
Super exiit	Super exiit edictum sive De tribus processionibus, ed. J. Châtillon and W.-J. Tulloch, Sermons et opuscules spirituels inédits: L'édit d'Alexandre ou Les trios processions (N. pl.: Desclée de Brouwer, 1951) (On the Three Processions).
Tract.	Tractatus super quosdam Psalmos (= Mysticae adnotationes in Psalmos), PL 196.265–404; B. Hauréau, Notices et extraits de quelques manuscripts latins de la Bibliothèque Nationale, 5 vols. (Paris: C. Klincksieck, 1890–1893), 1:112–14 (Tract. on Post sex annos), 116 (Tract. on Tolle puerum... proles [incomplete]), 116–17 (Tract. on Apprehendet messis), 118–19 (Tract. on Quid eis dabis); tr. C. Evans, Tractates on Certain Psalms, VTT 4. 147–240.
Trin.	De Trinitate, ed. J. Ribaillier, TPMA 6 (1958); ed. G. Salet, La Trinité, SC 67 (1959); tr. C. Evans, On the Trinity, VTT 1.209–382.
Tribus per.	De tribus personis appropriatis in Trinitate, ed. J. Ribaillier, Opuscules théologiques, 182–87 (On Trinitarian Appropriations).

Verbo Eccl.　　　*De illo verbo Ecclesiastici "Eleemonsina patris non erit in obliuionem,"* ed. J. Ribaillier, *Opuscules théologiques,* 295–96 (*The Alms of the Father*).

Verbis ap.　　　*De verbis apostolicis,* ed. J. Ribaillier, *Opuscules théologiques,* 314–17 (*The Words of the Apostle*).

Vis. Ezek.　　　*In visionem Ezechielis,* ed. J. Schröder, *Gervasius von Canterbury, Richard von Saint-Victor und die Methodik der Bauerfassung im 12. Jahrhundert,* Veröffentlichung der Abteilung Architekturgeschichte des Kunsthistorisches Instituts der Universität zu Köln 71 (Cologne: Kleikamp, 2000), 2:372–553; PL 196.527–606 (*The Vision of Ezekiel*).

ROBERT OF MELUN

Sent.　　　*Sententiae* I.1.1–6, ed. R. Martin, *Oeuvres de Robert de Melun,* Tome III.1–2, Spicilegium Sacrum Lovaniense 21, 25 (Louvain: "Spicilegium Sacrum Lovaniense" Bureaux, 1947–1952); tr. N. van Baak, *Sentences (selections),* VTT 3.445–72. *Sententiae* I.2.1, 5–8, 16–37, ed. R. Heinzmann, *Die Unsterblichkeit der Seele und die Auferstehung des Leibes,* BGPTMA 40.3 (Münster: Aschendorff, 1965), 86–102. *Sententiae* I.2.9–15, ed. Raymond Martin, "L'immortalité de l'âme d'après Robert de Melun," *Revue néo-scolastique de philosophie* 41 (1934): 139–45.

Quaest.　　　*Quaestiones de epistolis Pauli,* ed. R. Martin, *Oeuvres de Robert de Melun,* Tome II, Spicilegium Sacrum Lovaniense 18 (Louvain: "Spicilegium Sacrum Lovaniense" Bureaux, 1938).

WALTER OF SAINT VICTOR

Serm. ined.　　　*Sermones inediti triginta sex,* ed. J. Châtillon, CCCM 30 (Turnhout: Brepols, 1975).

Contra quat.　　　*Contra quatuor labyrinthos Franciae de Gauthier de Saint-Victor,* ed. P. Glorieux, *AHDLMA* 19 (1953): 195–334 (*Against the Four Labyrinths of France*).

Writings Associated with St Victor

Liber ordinis   *Liber ordinis Sancti Victoris Parisiensis*, ed. L. Jocqué and L. Milis, CCCM 61 (1984).

Sent. divinit.   *Sententiae divinitatis*, ed. B. Geyer, *Die Sententiae divinitatis. Ein Sentenzenbuch der gilbertschen Schule, aus den Handschriften zum ersten Male herausgegeben und historisch untersucht*, BGPTMA 7/2–3 (1967).

Summa sent.   *Summa sententiarum*, PL 176.41–174.

Other Authors

Augustine of Hippo

Civ. Dei   *De civitate Dei*, ed. B. Dombart and A. Kalb, CCL 47–48 (1955); tr. H. Bettenson, *The City of God* (New York: Penguin, 1986); tr. R. W. Dyson (New York: Cambridge, 1998).

Conf.   *Confessiones*, ed. L. Verheijen, *Confessionum Libri XIII*, CCL 37 (1990), 1–273; ed. J. J. O'Donnell, *Confessions*, vol. 1 (Oxford: Clarendon, 1992); tr. Maria Boulding (Hyde Park, NY: New City Press, 1997); tr. H. Chadwick (New York: Oxford, 1991).

En. Ps.   *Enarrationes in Psalmos*, ed. E. Dekkers and J. Fraipont, CCL 38–40 (1956); tr. M. Boulding, 6 vols. (Hyde Park, NY: New City Press, 2000–2004).

Gn. litt.   *De Genesi ad litteram*, ed. J. Zycha, CSEL 28.1 (1894); tr. E. Hill, *The Literal Meaning of Genesis in On Genesis* (Hyde Park, NY: New City Press, 2002), 155–506.

Jo. ev. tr.   *In Johannis evangelium tractatus*, ed. R. Willems, CCL 36 (1954); tr. J. Rettig, *Tractates on the Gospel of John*, FOC 78, 79, 88, 90, 92 (Washington, DC: The Catholic University of America, 1988–1995).

Lib. arb.   *De libero arbitrio*, ed. W. Green, CCL 29 (1970); tr. M. Pontifex, *The Problem of Free Choice*, ACW 22 (1955).

Serm.   *Sermones*, PL 38–39; tr. E. Hill, *Sermons*, 11 vols. (Hyde Park, NY: New City Press, 1990–).

Trin.   *De Trinitate*, ed. W. J. Mountain and F. Glorie, CCL 50, 50A (1968); tr. E. Hill, *The Trinity* (Hyde Park, NY: New City Press, 1991).

BERNARD OF CLAIRVAUX

Consid.   *De consideratione libri v*, SBO 3:393–493 (1963).

Dilig.   *De diligendo Deo*, SBO 3:119–54 (1963).

Gradibus   *De gradibus superbiae et humilitatis*, SBO 3:13–59 (1963).

Gratia   *Liber de gratia et libero arbitrio*, SBO 3:165–203 (1963). Tr. D. O'Donovan, *Bernard of Clairvaux: On Grace and Free Choice* (Kalamazoo: Cistercian Publications, 1988).

Laud. BVM   *Homiliae super 'Missus est' (In laudibus Virginis Matris)*, SBO 4:13–58.

SCC   *Sermones super Cantica Canticorum*, SBO 1–2 (1957–1958); tr. K. Walsh and I. Edmonds, *On the Song of Songs*, Cistercian Fathers Series 4, 7, 31, 40 (1971–1983).

GREGORY THE GREAT

Hom. ev.   *Homiliae in Evangelia*, ed. R. Étaix, CCL 76 (1999).

Mor.   *Moralia in Iob*, ed. M. Adriaen, CCL 143, 143A, 143B (1979–1985).

ISIDORE OF SEVILLE

Etym.   *Etymologiarum sive Originum Libri XX*, 2 vols., ed. W. M. Lindsay (Oxford: Clarendon Press, 1911); tr. S. Barney *et al.*, *Etymologies* (New York: Cambridge University Press, 2006).

JEROME

Heb. nom.   *Liber interpretationis Hebraicorum nominum*, ed. P. de Lagarde, CCL 72 (1969), 58–161.

Peter Lombard

Sent.

Sententiae in IV Libris Distinctae, ed. I. Brady, SB 4–5 (1971–1981); tr. G. Silano, *Sentences*, 4 vols. (Toronto: Pontifical Institute of Mediaeval Studies, 2007–2010).

Thomas Aquinas

ST

Summa theologiae, ed. P. Caramello, 3 vols. (Taurin: Marietti, 1952–1956); tr. Fathers of the English Dominican Province, *St. Thomas Aquinas Summa Theologica*, 5 vols. (New York: Benziger Bros., 1948).

William of St Thierry

Natura

De natura corporis et animae, ed. P. Verdeyen, CCCM 88 (2003).

GENERAL INTRODUCTION

Christopher P. Evans

beatus vir cui est auxilium abs te ascensiones in corde suo disposuit

Psalms 83:6 (Vulg.)

The twelfth century is often singled out as a spiritual awakening,[1] a century which Jean Leclercq calls "the highpoint of the Middle Ages from the point of view of spirituality."[2] Jean Châtillon considers it the birth of what is sometimes called "affective spirituality" that often characterizes Victorine approaches to the spiritual life.[3] If extensive dissemination of medieval manuscripts is any indication of success, then the spiritual writings of Hugh and Richard of St Victor were among the bestselling books, so to speak, in the Middle Ages. Scholarship today continually substantiates their influence on subsequent theologians, both scholastic and contemplative. The intellectual fervor and acute sense of systematization of the time also inspired a class of theologians like Achard of St Victor and Robert of Melun who desired to build upon past accomplishments and open the way to further synthesis. Given the attention these authors gave to the spiritual life, a volume dedicated to Victorine spirituality can only offer a sampling of that vast library.

The choice of Victorine writings selected for a volume on the spiritual life needs some explanation. Classifications of their writings are notoriously difficult. Exegesis and theology are all entwined in their writings, so criteria based on thematic genres can be artificial at times. Nevertheless, as a matter of convenience, a writing—whether a treatise,

---

[1] S. Chase, *Contemplation and Compassion: The Victorine Tradition*, Traditions of Christian Spirituality Series (Maryknoll, NY: Orbis Books, 2003), 17–23.

[2] *Bernard of Clairvaux: Selected Works* (New York: Paulist Press, 1987), 13.

[3] J. Châtillon, "*Cor et cordis affectus*," in *DS* 2.2 (1953), 2291. É. Gilson agrees. "Rightly seen," he says, "the Cistercians gathered around St Bernard, the Victorines around Hugh and Richard, the Franciscans around St Bonaventure represent the affective life of the mediaeval West at its most intense and its most beautiful" (*The Philosophy of St. Bonaventure* [Paterson, N.J.: St. Anthony Guild Press, 1965], xii).

sermon, letter, hymn, or poem—that is not explicitly dogmatic or exegetical usually falls under the rubric of a spiritual writing. Spirituality, moreover, as an experience with Christ through the Spirit within the regular canonical life and/or Church and as an examination of that experience, is a broad term open to many considerations and emphases. Love and contemplation are prominent themes that often characterize Victorine spirituality and so are edification by word and example, disciplines of regular canonical life, and the soul's religious and moral progress or ascent.[4] As such, all of the volumes in this series contribute to an overall portrait of Victorine spirituality. Volumes two and five, for example, contain or will contain writings notable for their teaching on love and contemplation; volumes three and six contain or will contain writings on reading, one of many important spiritual exercises at the Abbey of St Victor; and volumes eight and nine will contain key writings on the liturgy and regular canonical life. The purpose of this volume is to incorporate assorted writings during the period from Hugh up to Godfrey of St Victor (*ca.* 1130s to 1180s) that speak directly on prayer and Mary as well as other writings that offer reflections on the spiritual life in general, especially its interior dimensions. This volume is thus arranged into three parts: The Trajectory of the Christian Journey, The Spirit and Prayer, and Mary.

The first part offers comprehensive reflections on the spiritual experience. The *Tractates on Certain Psalms* is, in the estimation of J. Leclercq, remarkable for the psychological considerations that Richard gives to the spiritual life.[5] In it he provides a miscellanea of reflections on the various virtues and vices, illicit thoughts, different kinds of demonic temptations, spiritual warfare, human freedom, nature and grace, contemplation, divine justice, and so on. In his *On the State of the Interior Man* he provides his most mature reflection on

---

4. E.g, see J. Leclercq, "La spiritualite des chanoines reguliers," in *La vita commune del clero nei secoli XI e XII: atti della Settimana di studio, Mendola, settembre 1959* (Milan: Società editrice Vita e pensiero, 1962), 1:136–40; J. Châtillon, "La crise de l'Église aux XIᵉ et XIIᵉ siècles et les origines des grandes fédérations canoniales," *Revue d'histoire de la spiritualite* 53 (1977): 45–46; C. W. Bynum, *Docere Verbo et Exemplo: An Aspect of Twelfth-Century Spirituality* (Missoula, MT: Scholars Press, 1979), 9–93; Ibid., *Jesus as Mother: Studies in the Spirituality of the High Middle Ages* (Los Angeles: University of California Press, 1982), 22–58; G. Zinn, "The Regular Canons," in *Christian Spirituality: Origins to the Twelfth Century*, ed. B. McGinn and J. Meyendorff (New York: Crossroad, 1996), 218–27; Chase, *Contemplation and Compassion*, 13–14.

5. J. Leclercq, "Les psaumes 20–25 chez les commentateurs du haut moyen âge," in *Richesses et déficiences des anciens psautiers latins*, Collectanea Biblica Latina 13 (Rome: Libreria Vaticana, 1959), 225.

the sickly condition of human nature after the Fall and its spiritual healing. Also included here is Achard's *Sermon 13* which J. Châtillon calls his "most curious and most interesting" sermon.[6] In it he utilizes an architectonic scheme that integrates dogmatic and moral themes to depict the spiritual journey.

The second part offers writings that exemplify the Christian life based on the spiritual exercises of regular canonical life and the virtues. Hugh, for example, enumerates five steps (*gradus*) of those exercises in which and through which the "life of just people" (*vita iustorum*) is trained (*exercetur*) and lifted to the future perfection: reading or teaching (*lectio sive doctrina*), meditation (*meditatio*), prayer (*oratio*), work (*operatio*), and contemplation (*contemplatio*).[7] Among the writings of his vast corpus, Hugh wrote the *Didascalicon* for instruction on reading (the topic of VTT 3), and this volume contains the two writings that provide his instruction on the second and third exercises, namely, *On Mediation* and *On the Power of Prayer* (the writings on contemplation will be provided in VTT 5).[8] Also featured here is Hugh's very famous *On the Five Sevens* in which he integrates a spiritual program with the seven petitions of the Lord's Prayer, the seven gifts of the Spirit, the seven beatitudes, and the seven virtues and vices. Of importance in these regards is also Hugh's *On the Seven Gifts of the Holy Spirit* and Richard's *Exposition on the Lord's Prayer*.

The third part offers a commentary, a sequence, hymns, and sermons on the Blessed Virgin Mary. The twelfth century is often considered the golden age of Marian faith and devotion.[9] This is especially true at the Abbey of St Victor where, according to their Ordinary, they even celebrated the Feast of the Conception (Dec. 8) at a time when it was not universally recognized.[10] Insofar as she is the

---

[6]   J. Châtillon, *Achard de Saint-Victor: Sermons inédits*, TPMA 17 (Paris: J. Vrin, 1970), 131.

[7]   Hugh of St Victor, *Didasc.* V.9 (Buttimer, 109; tr. Harkins, VTT 3.161); cf. also *Meditatione* (Baron, 46; tr. Van Liere, VTT 4. 387); Richard of St Victor, *Serm.* 44 (PL 177.1017D); *Erud.* I.7 (PL 196.1242C). Naturally this list can be abridged; e.g., 1) *lectio, meditatio, contemplatio*; see Hugh of St Victor *Archa Noe* II.7 (Sicard, 45); Richard of St Victor, *Arca Moys.* I.3 (Aris, 8–9; tr. Zinn, 155–56); 2) *cognitio, meditatio, contemplatio*; see Hugh of St Victor, *Libellus* (Sicard, 146); *In Eccl.* (PL 175.116D, 118A); Richard of St Victor, *Serm.* 72 (PL 177.1131A). See also P. Sicard, *Hugues de Saint-Victor et son école: introduction, choix de texte, traduction et commentaires* (Turnhout: Brepols, 1991), 199–230.

[8]   See Sicard, *Hugues de Saint-Victor et son école*, 203.

[9]   L. Gambero, *Mary in the Middle Ages*, tr. T. Buffer (San Francisco: Ignatius Press, 2000), 105.

[10]   Paris, BnF lat. 14506, fol. 266v (sec. xiii). Of course this is not an explicit acceptance of the immaculate conception, an issue that lacks clarity in Victorine writing. In the late twelfth century Stephen Langton attests to its infrequent celebration in his *Glossa super maior glos-*

"star of the sea" by which the spiritual journey is navigated Mary's intercession is instrumental in the Christian life. Given the Victorine interest in the interiorization of the spiritual life, not surprisingly Mary's exemplary experience with Christ provides occasions for further reflections on the spiritual life.

The general introduction offers readers a summary of a Victorine theological anthropology with a heavy focus on Robert of Melun. This also requires some explanation. Short introductions accompany all the translations, so specific topics like prayer and Mary are summarized there. Rather than repeat that information, the general introduction provides a theological contextualization for their diverse reflections on the spiritual life. After all, the interior dimensions, both cognitive and affective, of that life are an obvious interest of all the authors in this volume. Themes directly related to it—the parts of the soul, human freedom, nature and grace, and moral development—thus underlie these spiritual reflections. Robert of Melun, who studied theology with Hugh and Peter Abelard, is of particular interest here for several reasons.[11] While some like A. Landgraf stress the Abelardian influence on Robert's theology, he is, as R. Heinzmann rightly notes, thoroughly Victorine in his anthropology;[12] there is no doubt today that he belongs to the closest circle of Victorine theologians. Moreover, unlike the propensity of some early scholastic theologians for succinctness and subtlety, Robert strives in his major writing, *Sentences*,[13] for exhaustive descriptions and critical expositions of all known positions at the time

---

satura Lombardi (Paris, BnF lat. 14443, fol. 271va; Salzburg, Stiftsbibliothek a.X.19, p. 26b): "Tercio subtilius sic: tres fuerunt status in beata Virgine in illo instanti in quo anima infusa sit corpori, rea fuit originalis peccati sicut et alie anime, demum in utero materno fuit mundata a reatu originalis peccati sed non a fomite. Si enim Ieremias mundatus est ab originali in utero et Iohannes Baptistus et quidam alii sancti multo magis sacta Dei genitrix. Libet non legatur, potuit tamen peccare quia fomitem habuit. Cum ergo habuit originale, si celebretur festum de conceptionem ipsius ratione instantis in quo anima est infusa corporis, hereticum est; si ratione illius instantis in quo anima est mandata a reatu originali peccato, bonum est. Sed tamen istud festum non est generaliter ab ecclesia institutum, et ideo non generaliter celebratur." On the spread of this feast in the Middle Ages, see C. Bouman, "Immaculate Conception in the Liturgy," in *The Dogma of the Immaculate Conception*, ed. E. D. O'Connor (Notre Dame, IN: University of Notre Dame Press, 1958), 135–40.

[11] D. Coulter provides an excellent introduction to Robert's life and works in VTT 3.429–43.

[12] See A. Landgraf, *Introduction à l'histoire de la littérature théologique*, tr. A.-M. Landry (Paris: J. Vrin, 1973), 89; R. Heinzmann, *Die Unsterblichkeit der Seele und die Auferstehung des Leibes; eine problemgeschichtliche Untersuchung der frühscholastischen Sentenzen- und Summenliteratur von Anselm von Laon bis Wilhelm von Auxerre*, BGPTMA 40.3 (Münster: Aschendorff, 1965), 117 n. 67.

[13] See n. 54 below.

(late 1150s). Consequently, Robert offers us one of the most thorough theological anthropologies in the twelfth century. And because his *Sentences* remain mostly unedited, many of the descriptions and citations are presented here for the first time.[14]

SPIRITUALITY: THE HUMAN SPIRIT AND ITS ASCENTS

The Latin adjective *spiritualis* ("spiritual") and adverb *spiritualiter* ("spiritually") in their broadest senses refer to what pertains to the spirit (*spiritus*) or even to the soul (*anima*) when it is used interchangeably with spirit.[15] "Spiritual" can also be contrasted with *animalis* ("animal") derived from the noun *anima* ("soul") or with *corporalis* ("corporeal") derived from *corpus* ("body").[16] These

---

[14] As a general rule for the footnotes, I provide Latin citations for all unedited materials or edited materials that I corrected with one or more medieval manuscripts. These citations are untranslated in the footnotes, although they are often paraphrased in the body of the text. Edited material that I did not correct with the medieval manuscripts will be translated into English mostly without the Latin in order to conserve space. All English translations in the general introduction are mine.

[15] For studies on the word "spirituality" and its variants in the Middle Ages, see L. Tinsley, *The French Expressions for Spirituality and Devotion: A Semantic Study*, Studies in Romance Languages and Literatures 47 (Washington, DC: Catholic University of America Press, 1953); J. Leclercq, "Spiritualitas," *Studi medievali* 3 (1962): 279–96; W. Principe, "Toward Defining Spirituality," *Studies in Religion* 12/2 (1983): 127–41; A. Solignac, "Spiritualité," in *DS* 14 (1990), 1142–60. See also L. Bouyer, *The Spirituality of the New Testament and the Fathers*, tr. M. Ryan (New York: Desclee Company, 1963), x; P. Sheldrake, *Spirituality and History* (New York: Crossroad, 1992), 34–36; D. Marmion, *A Spirituality of Everyday Faith: A Theological Investigation of the Notion of Spirituality in Karl Rahner* (Louvain: Peeters Press, 1998), 4–28.

[16] E.g., Hugh of St Victor, *Cant. BM* (Jollès, 44; tr. Harkins, VTT 4.434), where *anima* is used with respect to the body and *spiritus* with respect to the rational spiritual substance; Achard of St Victor, *Serm.* 13.34 (Châtillon, 168; tr. Feiss, VTT 4.117): "We glorify and carry God in our body; there he dwells as though bodily, but in our spirit spiritually, and in our mind intellectually" ("Glorificatus et portatus a nobis Deus in corpore nostro, ibi habitat quasi corporaliter, in spiritu autem nostro spiritualiter, in mente vero nostra intellectualiter"). See also Achard, *Sermo* 14.22 (Châtillon, 194; tr. Feiss, 289); *Sermo* 15.12 (Châtillon, 213; tr. Feiss, 314); *Discretione* 53 and 55 (Häring, 186; tr. Feiss, 369 and 370), where *spiritualis* means *in spiritu*, and an *anima sine spiritu* are *brutis animalis* that lack memory. See also Robert of Melun, *Quaest.* on Rom. 1:9 (Martin, 20). In *Exterm.* III.18 (Paris, BnF lat. 17469, fol. 72ra; PL 196.1114B–C) speaking about the division of "soul" and "spirit" (*divisio animae et spiritus*) Richard says: "Quid, queso, uspiam creaturarum hac diuisione mirabilius cernitur, ubi id quod essentialiter unum est atque indiuiduum in seipsum scinditur, et quod simplex in se et sine partibus constat a seipso diuiditur atque separatur? Neque enim in homine uno alia essentia est eius spiritus atque alia eius est anima, sed prorsus una eademque simplicisque nature substantia. Non enim in hoc gemino uocabulo gemina substantia intelligitur. Sed

distinctions are frequently understood within a Pauline dualism of the flesh and spirit (Gal. 5:17; Rom. 7:15), the internal and external man (2 Cor. 4:16), and the "animal man" (*animalis homo*), who does not see the things of God, contrasted with a spiritual person who judges all things (1 Cor. 2:14–15; 15:46). What is contrasted here is a life in the Spirit as opposed to a carnal life resistant to the Spirit's work. But in the twelfth century the dualism also indicates the natural parts of a person, that is, what is internal, incorporeal and invisible as opposed to what is external, corporeal and visible. Of course these various nuances are not mutually exclusive and are often entwined to make intelligible spiritual experiences.[17]

cum ad distinctionem ponitur gemina uis eiusdem essentie, una superior per spiritum, alia inferior per animam designatur. In hac itaque diuisione anima et quod animale est in imo remanet, spiritus autem et quod spirituale est ad summa euolat." In other words, the distinction of faculties is purely extrinsic (i.e., based on the object of perception) not substantial. When directed to the corporeal objects, this is called the lower power of the soul or the animal part; and when directed to spiritual objects, this is called the higher part. Cf. J. Ebner, *Die Erkenntnislehre Richards von St. Victor*, BGPTMA 19.4 (Münster: Aschendorff, 1917), 22–23.

17   Credit for the transmission of the various nuances of what is spiritual should be given in part to the *Media glossatura* of Gilbert of Poitiers (i.e., his commentary on the Psalms and Pauline Epistles) which was widely used not only to aid classroom lectures but also biblical exegesis. The following citations are noteworthy: Gilbert of Poitiers, *Com. in epist. Pauli* on 1 Cor. 3:1 (Lisbon, Biblioteca Nacional *Fundo Alcobaça* XCVII/178, fol. 31va–b): "Eosdem dicit carnales a carne quos dixerat animales ab anima. Per utrumque nomen uolens intelligi homines. Nam et eosdem inferius uocat homines;" Gilbert of Poitiers, *Com. in epist. Pauli* on 1 Cor. 2:14 (Lisbon, Biblioteca Nacional *Fundo Alcobaça* XCVII/178, fol. 31rb–va): "Homo dicitur animalis siue spiritualis uita uel animi sensu. Vita animalis, uerbi gratia, dicitur qui fertur dissoluta lasciuia anime sue quam intra naturalis ordinis metas spiritus rector non continet, eo quod et ipse se Deo regendum non subicit. Anime uero sensu dicitur animalis qui de Deo uel eius in humano genere facta gratia iuxta corporam fantasiam uel legis litteram uel rationem philosophicam iudicat. Et ideo uel se ab ecclesia segregat superbus inperditis conputandus, uel in eius unitate remanet paruulus propter sacramentorum sanctitatem saluandus. Spiritualis autem est uita qui, spiritu Deum habente rectorem, animam regit. Animi uero sensu spiritualis est qui etsi ex parte et per speculum uidet, tamen de Deo uel eius gratia nec imagines corporum nec legis litteram nec humanam philosophiam secutus sed Spiritui Dei subiectus certissime sentit ea que animalis homo non percipit" (cf. also Peter Lombard, *Collectanea in Pauli epist.* on I Cor. 2:14 [PL 191.1552C–1553A]); Gilbert of Poitiers, *Com. in epist. Pauli* on 2 Cor. 4:16 (Lisbon, Biblioteca Nacional *Fundo Alcobaça* XCVII/178, fol. 57va): "Attende quod quamuis dicat 'is et is homo,' non tamen duo sunt homines sed unus qui dicitur 'exterior' non tantum secundum corpus sed etiam secundum animalem uitam exterius sentiendi, memoria remiscendi, conducibilia appetendi, incommoda fugiendi. Idem uero dicitur 'interior' secundum illam uim mentis qua et de corporalibus ipsius, que per sensum corporis traxit, secundum sempiternas iudicat rationes et ad celestia cognoscenda se subleuat, secundum quod etiam idem unus homo ad imaginem Dei dicitur factus. Hic totus, idest et interiore et exteriore sui parte, uetus est propter peccatum qui quantum ad corpus et ad uitalem conpagem uel etatum mutationibus uel morborum

Sometimes Hugh speaks of the two parts of a single person, that is, the body and spirit that have "two lives" (*duae vitae*): the "spiritual life" and the "carnal life."[18] The carnal and temporal life need not be a hindrance to the spiritual life and is often regarded as necessary first step for a spiritual ascent.[19] Even the carnal life has its goods that foster healthy living,[20] but both lives also have their evils that can corrupt and disorder. To preserve what is right and beneficial for both lives, external powers (*potestates*) were instituted, so that just as the temporal goods necessary for the health of the carnal life are entrusted to secular powers, the highest of which is the king, so the spiritual goods necessary for the health of the spiritual life are entrusted to ecclesiastical powers, the highest of which is the Pope.[21] Needless to say, according to this usage of the word "spiritual," Hugh envisions an exclusively Christian

inequalitatibus et uariis afflictionibus semper corrumpitur, donec ultima corruptione, que dicitur mors, ipse deficiat. Proportione uero collata dum secundum exteriorem ita corrumpitur, secundum interiorem idem unus renouatur; non quod uno momento hec renouatio fiat sed in baptismo omnium peccatorum remissione quantum ad reatum iustificatur, quantum uero ad actum quia uita humana temptatio est super terram non iustificabitur in conceptu eius omnis uiuens; tamen 'de die in diem,' concupiscentiarum motibus temperatis, boni mores augentur et roborantur. In fine uero et corpus resurrectione reformabitur, et uisione Dei interioris imaginis similitudo perficietur, ut sicut uetustatis terminat defectu consuptio, ita nouitatis profectum terminet consummatio."

18   See Hugh of St Victor, *Sacr.* II.2.4 (Berndt, 338; PL 176.418A; tr. Deferrari, 256). Psalm 6, the first penitential Psalm, is a common occasion to discuss these "two lives," which seems to have first been inserted into the *Media glossatura* of Gilbert of Poitiers (see n. 31). See *Com. in Ps.* 6 (Cambridge, Queens' College 5, fol. 11va; Valenciennes, BM 44, fol. 8ra; Vorau, Stiftsbibliothek 261, fol. 6v): "Vel ideo dicitur 'octauus' quia due uite sunt. Vna pertinet ad corpus qui est uetus homo, cui et uetus datum est testamentum in qua regnauit mors. Altera pertinet ad animam qui est nouus homo regeneratus per Christum. Ad corpus autem pertinet quaternarius, quia et ex quatuor elementis constat et quatuor afficitur qualitatibus (sicca, humida, calida, frigida) et quatuor ministratur temporibus (uerno, estate, autumno, hieme). Ad anima uero pertinet ternarius, scilicet diligere Deum ex toto corde et ex tota anima et ex tota mente. Peractis igitur hic que ad corpus pertinent et que ad animam, quasi transacto septenario numero ueniet octauus dies iudicii, ubi cuique pro meritis reddetur, unde timens ecclesia orat hic." See also Peter Lombard, *Com. in Ps.* 6 (PL 191.103C–D), where the ternary that pertains to the soul is changed to the triple power (*vis*) of the soul, that is, the rational, irascible, and concupiscible.

19   E.g., Hugh of St Victor, *Sacr.* I.6.6 and 27 (Berndt, 141 and 159; PL 176.267B and 280C; tr. Deferrari, 98 and 113); Richard of St Victor, *LE* II.10.2 (Châtillon, 377); *Trin.* Prol. (Ribaillier, 82–83; tr. Evans, VTT 1.210–11); *Erud.* II.25 (PL 196.1324C).

20   See, e.g., Hugh of St Victor, *In Eccl.* 13 (PL 175.210A); *In Eccl.* 16 (PL 175.226A). For a definition of both spiritual and carnal goods, see Hugh of St Victor, *Misc.* I.1 (PL 177.473A–475C).

21   In *Sacr.* II.2.4 (Berndt, 339; PL 176.418C; tr. Deferrari, 256) the "spiritual person" (*spiritualis*) who judges all things but is judged by no one (1 Cor. 2:15) refers to the Pope, the supreme spiritual power, who judges all things, including temporal powers, but is only judged by God.

spirituality that is alive when in communion with the Church that has
the Pope as her head.

This dualism however is commonly understood in a psychological
sense. The external or carnal self is the natural lower powers associated
with sensual perception and appetite for sensual and visible things (i.e.,
the part of a human person that is common to irrational animals); the
internal or spiritual self is the highest and noblest part of a person and
thus the locus of spirituality, that is, the higher faculties of the soul that
bear the image and likeness of God. And so, unlike animals, humans
have a spiritual capacity or a higher faculty (spirit) that tends towards
loftier invisible truths and holy desires.[22] Thus, according to Achard,
someone is called "spiritual" whose higher powers in the soul rule the
other faculties subject to it.[23] Of course, after the Fall the soul suffers
from a weakened state that is usually made intelligible by combining
the Pauline imagery of the adversity between flesh and spirit (e.g., Gal.
5:17) with a penetrating human psychology. The soul's faculties have
been disordered, so that, as common experience attests, those baptized
in faith in Jesus Christ still feel the propensity or kindling of sin as the
residual effect of the original sin that was cleansed at baptism (see
discussion below). In this post-lapsarian state people are called
"spiritual" who desire and think about spiritual things and resist carnal
things (carnal here in the moral-religious sense of impure or illicit).
But this is always depicted as a gradual transition. "You start to be
spiritual," Richard says, "when you start to pursue spiritual speculations,
to ascend through a consideration of your spirit to a contemplation of
spirits, and to compare spiritual things with spiritual things (cf. 1 Cor.
2:13)."[24] For Richard this is the transition from what the Apostle Paul
calls the "animal person" (homo animalis) to a "spiritual person" (1 Cor.
2:14).[25] But this designation entails not just a cognitive perception of
spiritual things but especially the desire for them. As Achard succinctly

---

[22] E.g., according to Robert of Melun, Sent. I.2.173 (Innsbruck, UB 297, fol. 125ra; Abbrev. 598
      [London, BL Royal 7.F.XIII, fol. 99vb]), man has two senses (sensus): an external sense and
      internal sense. The internal sense is called reason. Robert also calls this the spiritual sense
      (spiritualis) as opposed to the animal sense (animalis). By this spiritual sense alone man
      knows God in visible things, which are subjected to the senses, and in invisible things which
      transcend the senses.

[23] Achard of St Victor, Discretione 64 (Häring, 189; tr. Feiss, 372).

[24] Richard of St Victor, Arca Moys. III.5 (Aris, 62; tr. Zinn, 228). See also Arca Moys. III.8
      (Aris, 65; tr. Zinn, 233); Tract. on Ps. 2.8 (PL 196.271A; tr. Evans, VTT 4.152).

[25] Cf. also Richard of St Victor, Arca Moys. II.13 (Aris, 35; tr. Zinn, 191).

states: "Spiritual delights make a life spiritual, and carnal delights make a life carnal."[26] Or, according to Richard,

> In the [post-lapsarian] state some people are called "carnal" and others "spiritual." . . . Carnal people are said to walk after their lusts and are subject to carnal desires. Spiritual people are those who strongly resist carnal desires and vehemently strive after spiritual pursuits. To feel and consent to carnal lusts pertains to the carnal. To feel carnal lusts does pertain to the spiritual but not to consent to them, but rather to resist, fight and mortify them.[27] But, compared to the pre-lapsarian state, we are carnal for the reason that we feel the carnal lusts and the unclean and disordered delights.[28]

The attention that spiritual writers give to the ordered steps of this assent arose in part because of a need to make clear a measurable progress in a spiritual itinerary. In accordance with the general outlook of the twelfth century,[29] a dynamic vision of the ordered and hierarchical universe, society, and man would have naturally fostered a view of the spiritual life that consisted of polarities with a perpetual movement of ascent and descent. Or, as Achard put it, "human beings never remain in the same state but are always advancing and declining: advancing when they ascend in their heart by walking from virtue to virtue until they see the God of gods in Zion (Ps. 84:5, 7)."[30] An early twelfth-century attestation of this is found in the *Media glossatura* of Gilbert of Poitiers,[31] which was found on the shelves of many medieval libraries (the Abbey of St Victor owned at least two copies).[32]

---

26 *Serm.* 13.3 (Châtillon, 137; tr. Feiss, 210). Cf. also Richard of St Victor, *Trin.* VI.10 (Ribaillier, 239; tr. Evans, VTT 1.328).

27 Cf. Richard of St Victor, *Statu* 13 (Ribaillier, 77; tr. Evans, VTT 4.263).

28 Richard of St Victor, *Verbis ap.* 4 on Rom. 7:14 (Ribaillier, 327). Cf. also Richard of St Victor, *Tract.* on Ps. 84 (PL 196.328D; tr. Evans, VTT 4.175); *Tract.* on Ps. 139 (PL 196.378B; tr. Evans, VTT 4.210); Ps-Richard of St Victor, *Abdiam* (PL 175.383C): "Just as there are two natures in us: spirit and flesh, so there are two motions (*motus*) by which each nature is moved . . . From this virtues and vices are born. If it is motion of the spirit, then virtue. The motion of flesh is nothing but the motion of the mind not obeying the spirit. The spiritual motion makes us spiritual; a carnal motion makes us carnal. The first motion is called 'spirit', the second 'flesh'."

29 See M.-D. Chenu, *Nature, Man, and Society in the Twelfth Century* (Chicago: The University of Chicago Press, 1968), 4–18, 24–37, 80–88.

30 *Serm.* 2.3 (Châtillon, 39; tr. Feiss, 152).

31 For a study on the dates of these commentaries, see T. Gross-Diaz, *The Psalms Commentary of Gilbert of Poitiers: From* Lectio Divina *to the Lecture Room*, Brill's Studies in Intellectual History 68 (New York: E. J. Brill, 1996), 27–35.

32 Paris, BnF lat. 14418, fols. 1–123 (sec. mid-xii) and Paris, BnF lat. 14419, fols. 1–239 (sec. xiii). On Richard's use of Gilbert's commentaries, see my introduction below to the *Tractates on Certain Psalms*.

Hence it is clear that in this context the steps signify those who ascend. Who, where, from where, on what route, to what place do they ascend? We learned this in Psalm 83 in which it is said: *In the heart of a blessed man God has arranged the ascents in the valley of tears, so that the blessed man may go from virtue to virtue into the place which God has arranged* (cf. Ps. 83:6–7 [Vulg.]). Notice that in these words all the steps are evident and comprehended. Who ascends? A blessed man. Where are the ascents? In the heart. From where? From the valley of tears. On what route? From virtue to virtue. Into what place? Into the place that God has arranged. [The Psalmist] does not limit with boundaries into what place [the blessed man ascends], but he says without limits *in the place which God arranged*, as if to say: in that place which *eye has not seen or ear heard* (2 Cor. 2:9). Nor did [the Psalmist] set limits on what virtue. The ascent to Christ, the power of God, is a progress from lesser to greater virtues or from fewer to more virtues. One ascends by faith, hope, and love and by all the virtues joined to these. Because, among these virtues, love alone moves the foot, one who loves more ascends more. So that we may be able to ascend, there occurred a descent to us. For the *Word was made flesh* (Jn. 1:14) and, drinking the chalice of passion (cf. Mt. 20:21–22), he became for us a valley of tears. And he who remained what he was with respect to his divinity became for us a mountain of ascension. Great people, who ascend up Jacob's ladder to advance in spiritual understanding, descend down the same ladder, while they say what children are able to grasp.[33]

---

[33] Gilbert of Poitiers, *Com. in Ps.* 83 (Valenciennes, BM 44, fol. 148vb; Vorau, Stiftsbibliothek 261, fol. 211r; Cf. Augustine, *En. Ps.* 119.1–2 [CCL 40.1776–78]): "Vnde manifestum est quod gradus hoc loco significant ascendentes. Qui et ubi et unde et qua et quo ascendant? Docemur in Psalmo 83 in quo dicitur: *Disposuit in corde beati uiri ascensiones in conualle plorationis, ut de uirtute in uirtutem eat beatus in locum quem disposuit Deus.* Ecce his uerbis totus horum graduum manifestus est intellectus. Quis enim ascendit? Beatus uir. Vbi sunt ascensiones? In corde. Vnde? A conualle plorationis. Qua? De uirtute in uirtutem. Quo? In locum quem Deus disposuit. Nulla diffinitione terminat 'in quem locum' sed indefinite ait 'in locum quem disposuit,' tamquam si diceret: In illud quem *oculus non uidit nec auris audiuit* etc. Nec etiam diffiniuit de qua uirtute. De minoribus enim ad maiores uel de paucioribus ad plures prouectus in Christum Dei uirtutem ascensus est. Ascenditur enim fide, spe, caritate et omnibus, que his sunt adiuncte, uirtutibus. In quibus tamen, quia sola caritas mouet pedem, qui plus diligit plus ascendit. Vt autem possimus ascendere, descensum est ad nos. Nam et *Verbum factum est caro* et bibens calicem passionis factus est nobis conuallis plorationis; qui quantum ad diuinitatem mansit quod erat mons ascensionis. Et magni, qui in scala Iacob ad intellectum spiritualium proficientes ascendunt, descendunt in eadem, dum que paruuli possint capere dicunt." Cf. Peter Lombard, *Com. in Ps.* 119 (PL 191.1133D–1134A). See also John Cassian, *Collationes* XIV.2 (Petschenig, 399): "For whoever wants to arrive at contemplation there are certain ordered and distinct steps that makes possible for human humility to ascend to the top."

Or as Hugh states it:

> When we say that something is the highest in spiritual and invisible realities, we do not mean that this would be spatially located at the top or highest point in heaven, but we mean the inmost of all realities. To ascend to God is to enter into oneself, and not only to enter into oneself but also in some ineffable manner to transcend even oneself to the inmost depths. Therefore, the one who enters deep within oneself, so to speak, and, penetrating deeply, transcends oneself, truly ascends to God.[34]

The interior spiritual progress—from the outside to the inside, from the inside to the center, or from the center to the summit—is somewhat fluid.[35] The Ps-Dionysian division "purgation–illumination–union"[36] provides a foundation for subsequent modifications, and often it gives way to a great variety of degrees of ascents and descents based on a tropological-anagological interpretation of the Bible: Jacob's dream (Gen. 28:12–13); the three chambers and stories of Noah's Ark (Gen. 6:16); the six steps of Solomon's throne (1 Kings 10:19); Ezekiel's vision of the Temple (Ez. 40:26); the Sermon on the Mount and the Beatitudes (Mt. 5–7); Jesus' Transfiguration (e.g., Mt. 17:1–9); Paul's rapture to the third heaven (1 Cor. 12:2), and so on. These images can also derive from the sacred liturgy like the translation from the "region of dissimilitude" (*regio dissimilitudinis*) where disordered desires rule.[37]

---

[34] Hugh of St Victor, *Vanitate* II (Douai, BM 364, fol. 91ra–b; Douai, BM 366, fol. 9ra; Grenoble, BM 390, fol. 151rb; Laon, BM 463, fol. 75v; Paris, Mazarine 717, fol 127vb; Paris, BnF lat. 14506, fol. 116r; PL 176.715B): "In spiritualibus ergo et inuisibilibus cum aliquid supremum dicitur, non quasi localiter supra culmen aut uerticem celi constitutum sed intimum omnium significatur. Ascendere ergo ad Deum, hoc est intrare ad semetipsum, et non solum ad se intrare, sed ineffabili quodammodo in intimis etiam seipsum transire. Qui ergo seipsum, ut ita dicam, interius intrans et intrinsecus penetrans transcendit, ille ueraciter ad Deum ascendit." See also Hugh of St Victor, *Unione* (Piazzoni, 884): "Minds ascend through contemplation from the lowest to the highest, from the body to the spirit through the mediation of sense and sensuality, from spirit to God through the mediation of contemplation and revelation." Cf. Augustine, *Trin.* XII.8.13 (Mountain and Glorie, 368; cited by Peter Lombard, *Sent.* II.24.5.4 [SB 4:454]): "As we ascend inward through the parts of the soul by certain steps of consideration . . ."

[35] See, e.g., E. Bertaud and A. Rayez, "Échelle spirituelle," in *DS* 4 (1960), 62–86.

[36] See, e.g., Walter of St Victor, *Serm.* 6 (Châtillon, 47; tr. Butterfield, VTT 4.539).

[37] The phrase is found in Augustine, *Conf.* VII.10.16 (Verheijen, 103). The canons at the Abbey of St Victor would have chanted the following first response in the first nocturn of Matins for the Feast of St Augustine: "Augustine found himself far from God in the region of dissimilitude" ("Inuenit se Augustinus longe esse a Deo in regione dissimilitudines" [Paris, BnF lat. 14506, fol. 314r]). That response was the sacred text that was commented upon in sermons preached on that feast day, see Achard of St Victor, *Serm.* 9 (Châtillon, 101–107

Often such imagery can be adopted to depict a multifaceted spiritual itinerary that integrates the classifications of virtues and vices, gifts of the Spirit, and degrees of love and contemplation. Thus, for example, Hugh develops a complex architectonic scheme found in his *On Noah's Ark* and *A Little Book about Constructing Noah's Ark* that integrates the many facets of the interior spiritual life. There are four ascents up the house-mountain of the Ark each with three rooms that total twelve "ladders" or steps.[38] The first ascent is from the cold northeast (i.e., pride) by the affects fear, sorrow, and love; the second is from the hot southwest (i.e., carnal concupiscence) by patience, mercy, and compunction; the third is from the cold northwest (i.e., ignorance) by the spiritual disciplines of thinking, meditation, and contemplation; and the fourth is from the hot southeast (i.e., spiritual fervor) by the virtues of temperance, prudence, and fortitude. Achard maps out the spiritual journey similarly but adopts the biblical theme of being led by the seven gifts of the Spirit into seven deserts of the interior man (Mt. 4:1): (1) desertion of mortal sin led by the spirit of fear; (2) desertion of the world led by the spirit of piety; (3) desertion of the flesh led by the spirit of knowledge; (4) desertion of one's own will led by the spirit of fortitude; (5) desertion of reason led by the spirit of counsel; (6) the desert of union with God led by the spirit of understanding, and at this point "[the sojourner] has," Achard says, "truly become spiritual" so that he or she can see the things of God (cf. 1 Cor. 2:14);[39] (7) the desert of serving others in conformity to Christ and led by the spirit of wisdom.[40] In *On Exterminating Evil and Promoting Good* Richard gives a tropological interpretation of the crossing of the Jordan (*transitus*

[esp. 99 n. 3]; tr. Feiss, 65–70]); Anon., *Serm.* 7 (Châtillon, CCCM 30, 276–82). See also Achard of St Victor, *Serm.* 15 (Châtillon, 199; tr. Feiss, 299); Richard of St Victor, *Exterm.* I.1 (PL 196.1073D); *LE* II.7.33 (Châtillon, 228); *Tract.* on Ps. 28 (PL 196.313B); *Tract.* on Ps. 84 (PL 196.328D; tr. Evans, VTT 4.175); G. Dumeige, *Richard de Saint-Victor et l'idée chrétienne de l'amour* (Paris: Presses universitaires de France, 1952), 49–50; R. Javelet, *Psychologie des auteurs spirituels du XIIᵉ siècle* (Epinal, Vosges: Javelet, 1959), 11–19.

38 See Hugh of St Victor, *Archa Noe* II.7 (Sicard, 42–43, 45; tr. Squire, 83–84, 85–86); *Libellus* 4–6 (Sicard, 141–51; tr. Weiss, 57–63). Cf. also G. Zinn, "*De gradibus ascensionum:* The Stages of Contemplative Ascent in Two Treatises on Noah's Arch by Hugh of St. Victor," *Studies in Medieval Culture* 5, ed. J. Sommerfeldt (Kalamazoo, MI: Publications of the Medieval Center, 1975), 61–79; B. McGinn, *The Growth of Mysticism: Gregory the Great through the 12ᵗʰ Century*, The Presence of God: A History of Western Christian Mysticism 2 (New York: Crossroad, 1994), 376–82, esp. the diagram on page 377; P. Sicard, *Théologies Victorines: Études d'histoire doctrinal médiévale et contemporaine* (Paris: Parole et Silence, 2008), 62–85.

39 *Serm.* 15.34 (Châtillon, 237; tr. Feiss, 345).

40 *Serm.* 15 (Châtillon, 203–43; tr. Feiss, 303–51). For an analysis see the introduction of Châtillon (196–99) and Feiss (291–97).

Jordanis).[41] The journey has three main steps. The first is to depart from Egypt,[42] that is, to forsake the world; the second is to depart from the desert, that is, to leave oneself; the third is to enter into the Promised Land, that is, union with God.

Examples also abound on how the spiritual exercises are used in the mapping of the spiritual life. Hugh, for example, regards reading and mediation as the principal ways of advancing in the cognitive ascent,[43] but, as he relates elsewhere, the rational soul is not available for such exercises until after the carnal appetites are quenched through abstinence.[44] On a number of occasions Richard mentions that he seeks refuge from aroused sensual appetites in work and prayer.[45] In *The Twelve Patriarchs* work, reading/meditation, and prayer are symbolized by the three disciples that Christ took up with him on the Mount of Transfiguration (cf. Mt. 17:1–5).[46] "One who seeks," Richard says, "to have Christ as a guide for the journey and a leader of the ascent joins the effort of work and prayer to the effort of reading."[47] All these spiritual exercises are required of those who want to learn divine truths; prayer in particular provides occasions for being instructed in ways that transcend work and reason.

The number of possible spiritual itineraries structured on sacred images is limited by an ingenuity which Victorine authors did not lack. But, as even they would admit, they are groping in these writings to describe a spiritual experience or an interior encounter with Christ that is sometimes elusive and vibrant. There is a reason why, for example, a subtle thinker like Richard often complains of the poverty of words. Nevertheless, the classifications of the soul in, for example, Hugh's *Union of Spirit and Body* and Achard's *On the Distinction of Soul, Spirit,*

---

41   *Exterm.* I.6 (PL 196.1077B). See Dumeige, *Richard de Saint-Victor*, 51–53; D. Coulter, *Per visibilia ad invisibilia: Theological Method in Richard of St. Victor (d. 1173)*, BV 19 (Turnhout: Brepols, 2006), 30–34.

42   See also Richard of St Victor, *Tract.* on Ps. 80:6 and 80:11 (PL 196.325C–326D and 325D–327C; tr. Evans, VTT 4.172 and 173); *Tract.* on Ps. 113 (PL 196.335C–D; tr. Evans, VTT 4.185); *Tract.* on Mt. 2:13–15 (tr. Evans, VTT 4.222–25); *Tract.* on "Egypt is the Life" (tr. Evans, VTT 4.229).

43   Hugh of St Victor, *Didasc.* Pref. (Buttimer, 2; tr. Harkins, VTT 3.81); cf. Hugh of St Victor, *In hier. cael.* II.1 (PL 175.950C); *Misc.* I.142 (PL 177.559B); Richard of St Victor, *Arca Moys.* IV.14 (Aris, 104; tr. Zinn, 282).

44   E.g., Hugh of St Victor, *Archa Noe* II.7 (Sicard, 45).

45   E.g., Richard of St Victor, *Tract.* on Ps. 25 (PL 196.282B; tr. Evans, VTT 4.162); cf. also *Erud.* I.8 (PL 196.1244A); *Erud.* I.11 (PL 196.1246B–C).

46   Richard of St Victor, *XII patr.* 79 (Châtillon, 318–20; tr. Zinn, 136–37).

47   Richard of St Victor, *XII patr.* 79 (Châtillon, 318; tr. Zinn, 37).

and Mind provide a framework to make that encounter more comprehensible.

TAXONOMY OF THE SOUL

The intellectual currents of the twelfth century were ripe for psychological speculations that would provide a descriptive basis for an ascent to God and map out its various stages.[48] Such a program, however, required a taxonomy of the different parts or powers of the soul.[49] Thus, either in a treatise on the soul or in occasional treatments within a larger text,[50] the speculative mystics, as Gilson calls them,[51] sought methodically to enumerate and describe the powers and faculties of the soul in light of their spiritual program. This focus on

---

[48] For an historical overview of the traditions that influenced twelfth century anthropology, see L. Reypens, "Ame (son fond, ses puissances, et sa structure d'après les mystiques)," in *DS* 1 (1937), 433–41; the introduction by B. McGinn in *Three Treatises on Man*, CS 24 (Kalamazoo, MI: Cistercian Publications, 1977), 2–19; R. Dales, *The Problem of the Rational Soul in the Thirteenth Century* (Leiden: E. J. Brill, 1995), 4–12. For the different systematic schemes of the soul in the twelfth century, see P. Michaud-Quantian, "La classification des puissances de l'âme au XIIᵉ siècle," *Revue du moyen âge latin* 5 (1949): 15–34. For a helpful study on different meanings of *spiritus*, see M.-D. Chenu, "*Spiritus*: Le vocabulaire de l'âme au XIIᵉ siècle," *Revue des sciences philosophiques et théologiques* 41 (1957): 209–32.

[49] The interest in the soul in the twelfth century has long been documented among modern scholars. See, e.g., P. Delhaye, *Le Microcosmus de Godefroy de Saint-Victor* (Lille: Facultés catholiques, 1951), 137–44; Chenu, *Nature, Man, and Society*, 24–37.

[50] For treatises on the soul by Victorine authors, see Hugh of St Victor, *Unione* (Piazonni, 861–88); Achard of St Victor, *Discretione* (Häring, 148–91; tr. Feiss, 353–74); and for Robert of Melun see n. 56 below. Richard's *On the State of the Interior Man*, translated in this volume, also offers a penetrating psychological analysis. For Cistercian authors, see William of St Thierry, *De natura corporis et animae* (Verdeyen, 103–33; tr. Clark, *Three Treatises on Man*, 103–52); Isaac of Stella, *Epistola de anima* (PL 194.1875B–1890A; tr. McGinn, *Three Treatises on Man*, 155–77); Alcher of Clairvaux, *De spiritu et anima liber unus* (PL 40.779–832; tr. Leiva and Ward, *Three Treatises on Man*, 181–288); Aelred of Rievaulx, *Dialogus de anima* (Talbot, 685–754); There are also other currents of interests from the physicists from Chartres. See, e.g., William of Conches, *Dragmaticon philosophiae* VI.18–26 (Ronca, 239–70; tr. Ronca and Curr, *William of Conches: A Dialogue on Natural Philosophy* [Notre Dame, IN: University of Notre Dame Press, 1997], 154–73); Bernard of Silvestre, *De mundi universitate* (ed. C. S. Barach and J. Wrobel, *Bernardi Silvestris De mundi universitate libri duo* [Frankfurt a.M.: Minerva, 1964]). See also Adelard of Bath, *Quaestiones naturales* (ed. and tr. C. Burnett, *Adelard of Bath: Conversations with his nephew, On the same and the different, Questions on natural science, and On birds* [Cambridge: Cambridge University Press, 1988]). On the various treatises on the soul in the twelfth century, see E.-H. Wéber, *La personne humaine au XIIIᵉ siècle* (Paris: J. Vrin, 1991), 48–61.

[51] É. Gilson, *History of Christian Philosophy in the Middle Ages* (New York: Random House, 1955), 164–71.

the interiorization of the spiritual ascent also brought an influx of Latin words and symbols to depict its various cognitive and affective dimensions. Latin terms like senses (*sensus*), soul (*anima*), will (*voluntas*), sensuality (*sensualitas*), affection (*affectio*) evoke a complex psychological construct that at times is difficult to discern due to the fluid nature of these words. Thus a primer on a Victorine theological anthropology will help in the interpretation of their sundry reflections on the spiritual life. Attention will be focused on the various writings of Hugh,[52] Achard,[53] Richard,[54] Godfrey,[55] and Robert of Melun.[56]

---

[52] See, e.g., H. Ostler, *Die Psychologie des Hugo von St. Victor*, BGPTMA 6.1 (Münster: Aschendorff, 1906); J. Kleinz, *The Theory of Knowledge of Hugh of St. Victor* (Washington, D.C.: The Catholic University of America Press, 1944); M.-D. Chenu, "*Imaginatio*: note de lexicographie philosophique," *Miscellanea Giovanni Mercati* II, *Studi e Testi* 22 (Vatican City: Biblioteca Apostolica Vaticana, 1946), 593–602; E. Bertola, "Di alcuni trattati psicologici attribuiti ad Ugo da San Vittore," *Rivista di Filosofia Neoscolastica* 51 (1959): 436–55; R. Baron, "La situation de l'homme d'après Hugues des St. Victor," *L'homme et son destin d'après les penseurs du Moyen Age* (Louvian: Nauwelaerts, 1960), 431–36; Ibid., "Spirituelle médiévale: le traité de la contemplation et ses espèces," *Revue d'ascétique et de la mystique* 39 (1963): 137–51; R. Heinzmann, *Die Unsterblichkeit der Seele*, 75–82; P. Sicard, *Hugues de Saint-Victor et son École: Introduction, choix de texte, traduction et commentaries* (Turnhout: Brepols, 1991), 199–251; D. Poirel, *Hugues de Saint-Victor* (Paris: Cerf, 1998), 113–32. Closely connected to Hugh is the *Summa sent.* which was likely composed after Peter Abelard's condemnation in 1141. For an overview of the historical complexities and different views, see D. Luscombe, *The School of Peter Abelard* (Cambridge: Cambridge University Press, 1970), 198–213.

[53] J. Châtillon, *Théologie, spiritualité et métaphysique dans l'œuvre oratoire d'Achard de Saint-Victor*, Études de philosophie médiévale 58 (Paris: J. Vrin, 1969).

[54] J. Ebner, *Die Erkenntnislehre Richards von St. Victor*, BGPTMA 19.4 (Münster, 1917); E. Ottaviano, *Riccardo di San Vittore, la vita, le opere, il pensiero* (Rome: Dott. Giovanni Bardi, tipografo della R. Accademia nazionale dei Lincei, 1933), 453–66; J. Robilliard, "Les six genres de contemplation chez Richard de Saint Victor et leur origine platonicienne," *Revue des sciences philosophiques et théologiques* 28 (1939), 229–33; G. Dumeige, *Richard de Saint-Victor et l'idée chrétienne de l'amour* (Paris: Presses universitaires de France, 1952); R. Javelet, *Psychologie des auteurs spirituels du XIIᵉ siècle* (Epinal, Vosges: Javelet, 1959); Ibid., "Thomas Gallaus et Richard de Saint-Victor mystiques," *RTAM* 29 (1962): 206–33; *RTAM* 30 (1963): 88–121; P. Delhaye, "Les perspectives morales de Richard de Saint-Victor," *Mélanges offerts à René Crozet* (Poitiers: Société d'Études Médiévales, 1966), 855–61; H. Feiss, "Learning and the Ascent to God in Richard of St. Victor" (STD diss., Rome: Pontifical Athenaeum of Sant' Anselmo, 1976), chap. 3 "Christian Anthropology;" N. Den Bok, *Communicating the Most High*, BV 7 (Turnhout: Brepols, 1996), 375–429; I. van 't Spijker, "Exegesis and Emotions: Richard of St. Victor's *De Quatuor Gradibus Violentae Caritatis*," *Sacris erudiri* 36 (1996): 147–60; S. Knuuttila, *Emotions in Ancient and Medieval Philosophy* (Oxford: Clarendon Press, 2004), 201–205.

[55] P. Delhaye, *Le Microcosmus de Godefroy de Saint-Victor* (Lille: Facultés catholiques, 1951).

[56] See Heinzmann, *Die Unsterblichkeit der Seele*, 84–117; and O. Lottin, *Psychologie et morale aux XIIᵉ et XIIIᵉ siècles* (Gembloux: J. Duculot, 1957), 1:31–37. Unfortunately, much of Robert's teachings are too little studied because his magnus opus, *Sententiae*, remains mostly unedited. Martin's critical edition covers fewer than thirty percent of book one and none of book two. A critical edition of the entire *Sent.* is currently underway (Matthias Perkams is

Following the Augustinian tradition twelfth-century authors regard
the soul as an immortal spiritual substance that is simple, and yet we
also find attempts to make a real distinction of "virtual parts" in the
soul when referring to the unfolding of its activities or motions.[57] These
authors are aware of several classifications—for example, the Platonic
distinction of the rational, concupiscible and irascible powers, the
Aristotelian distinction of the sensitive, vegetive, and rational souls,
and the Boethian cognitive distinction of sensual perception,

responsible for book one and I for book two). Robert's teaching on the soul is found in
two places: his treatment on man (*Sent.* I.2.1–184) and his treatment on the Incarnation
where Christ's soul is discussed (*Sent.* II.2, passim); for the list of questions, see Martin,
Oeuvres 3.1 (1947), 94–106, 146–56. For book one I rely on Innsbruck, UB 297 (shortly before
the submission of this volume, M. Perkams graciously allowed me to consult his edition of
Sent. II.2. I found no variant worth indicating in my transcriptions that I provide in the
footnotes). I also make reference to the *Abbreviationes* of Robert's *Sent.*, and for it I rely on
London, BL Royal 7.F.XIII. Transcriptions of selected chapters from *Sent.* I.2 can be found
in Heinzmann, *Die Unsterblichkeit der Seele*, 86–102 (based on Brügge, Bibliothèque de la
ville 191); R. Martin, "L'immortalité de l'âme d'après Robert de Melun," *Revue néo-scolastique
de philosophie* 41 (1934), 139–45; citations are also found in Lottin, *Psychologie et morale*,
1:131–37. For a complete list of manuscripts of the *Sentences* and *Abbreviation*, see Martin,
Oeuvres des Robert de Melun 1 (1932), xv–xvii (*Sent.*), xviii–xix (*Abbrev.*); *Oeuvres* 3.1 (1947),
vi–viii (*Sent.*).

57 The reconciliation of the soul's simplicity with the multiplicity of its acts was often discussed in the twelfth century (cf. Ostler, *Die Psychologie des Hugo von St. Viktor*, 89–96).
In 1159 John of Salisbury, former student of Robert of Melun, mentions two views: one that
makes no distinction of powers in the simple soul and one that make a qualitative distinction (*Metalogicon* IV.9 [Hall, 148; tr. McGarry, 217–18]). Of course, Robert of Melun knows
very well that the soul is not composed of formal parts: "We know this with an undeniable
testimony of Augustine, because he said that although the soul and reason are the same in
essence, they differ in property. He said: 'reason thinks, soul lives, and they are the same' (cf.
Peter Damian, *Ep.* 81 [Reindel, 4/2:423]; cited also by Isaac of Stella, *Epistola de anima* [PL
194.1877A]). This cannot be true if reason is the form of the soul" (*Sent.* I.2.80 [Innsbruck,
UB 297, fol. 108vb]: "Quod etiam ipsius Augustini testimonio indubitanter cognoscimus,
quia animam et rationem proprietate differre dicit, quamquam in essentia idem sint. Ait
enim 'ratio sapit, anima uiuit, et tamen anima et ratio idem sunt'. Quod uerum esse non
potest, si ratio anime forma est"). Thus while the soul and reason are one, one can speak
of them as distinct subjects of activities. Achard also holds that the soul is essentially one
and the immediate principle of its various activities; nevertheless, he also speaks of "virtual
parts" (*partes virtuales*) based on the modes of operations (*exercitia sive officia*) (*Discretione* 1 [Häring, 174; tr. Feiss, 357]; cf. Richard of St Victor, *Tract.* on Ps. 113 [PL 196.338C;
tr. Evans, VTT 4.187]; *Exterm.* III.18 [PL 196.1114B–C], cited in n. 16). Whenever the soul
acts (or perhaps 'affects') it is also affected, and Achard regards these various "affections" (*affectiones*) that occur in the soul as certain qualities that variously "inform" the soul, so that
its potencies are distinguished formally, not essentially; consequently, words like "reason"
and "will" are not interchangeable since distinct activities are predicated of them (*Discretione* 16–18 [Häring, 177; tr. Feiss, 360]; cf. Hugh of St Victor, *Sacr.* I.3.16, 25 [PL 176.222B–C,
227B; tr. Deferrari, 47, 53]).

imagination, reason, intelligence—[58] and they appropriate one or more of these classifications in various contexts. The classification discussed here divides the inner self into three basic faculties of ascending or descending hierarchical orders based on the external or internal object.[59] Generally these faculties are of two types, affective or cognitive. Thus they provided a number of different spiritual itineraries depending on the biblical symbols being adapted, on whether they want to discuss the reality of the descent and/or ascent, on whether they focus on the affective and/or cognitive dimensions of that journey, or on whether they encompass the whole trajectory (e.g. from the very bottom to the top) or just one specific course (e.g., within the highest parts of the soul). But again all these parts are discussed in Victorine spiritual writings of the twelfth century, and often a reader's knowledge of them is presumed.

It is a basic anthropological principal in the twelfth century that a human being (*homo*) is composed of a body and soul, a corporeal substance and an immaterial or spiritual substance. As Robert of Melun articulates this, the nature of human beings is caught between two different natural forces of attraction, the spiritual and worldly.[60] The dualism here creates the problem for understanding not only the union between body and spirit but also the connection between the physical and spiritual worlds.[61] There are two Victorine treatises in particular that addressed this: *The Union of Spirit and Body* by Hugh (before

---

[58] Boethius, *De consolatione philosophiae* V, prosa 4 (Bieler, 97). On the number of cognitive powers in Hugh's writings and/or the twelfth century, see Ostler, *Die Psychologie des Hugo von St. Viktor*, 95–96; Kleinz, *The Theology of Knowledge*, 23–26; M.-T. d'Alverny, *Alain de Lille: Textes inédits* (Paris: J. Vrin, 1965), 163–83; E. Bertola, "Di una inedita trattazione psicologica intitolata: *Quid sit anima*," *Rivista di Filosofia Neo-Scolastica* 58 (1966): 573–77.

[59] The tripartite division of man is also found in Isaac of Stella, *Epistola de anima* (PL 194.1878A; tr. McGinn, 159) and Alcher of Clairvaux, *Liber de spiritu et anima* 34 (PL 40.803; tr. Leiva and Ward, 232).

[60] Robert of Melun, *Sent.* I.2.1 (Heinzmann, 86; Innsbruck, UB 297, fol. 93va; *Abbrev.* 479 [London, BL Royal 7.F.XIII, fols. 94rb–95va]): "Factus est itaque homo ex duabus substantiis: una scilicet corporea et altera incorporea. In quantum ex corporea est, cum ceteris animalibus communis nature habet participationem, sed in forme compositione ad alia animantia differentiam habet. Nam illa formam ad terram inclinatam habent et pronam. Ex quo significatur preter ea, que terrena sunt, ab eis nulla esse appetenda. Hominis uero forma in altum erigitur et sursum eleuatur, qui et preter cetera animantia rectum habet incessum et ad superna aspectum, quo liquide declaratur eum illa que sursum sunt sapere debere et tota mentis intentione illuc tendere [cf. Ovid, *Metamorphosen* I.1.84–86], ubi Christus sedet ad dexteram Dei Patris. Sic ergo homo ex corporis forma ammonetur in appetitu bonorum a ceteris differre animantibus, quamquam cum eis corporis habeat communem naturam."

[61] This paragraph and the next are based on Hugh of St Victor, *Unione* (Piazzoni, 885–88.82–156).

ca. 1130)—what Bernard McGinn says is "perhaps the most important twelfth-century treatment"[62] on this issue—and *On the Distinction of Soul, Spirit and Mind* by Achard (before *ca.* 1160).[63] Hugh's solution, followed by Achard, is to unite the two extremities through a medium (the faculty of imagination),[64] and consequently Hugh accepts a tripartite division of the interior man.[65]

[62] McGinn, *Three Treatises*, 88.

[63] All we know of Achard's dates is that he was the abbot of St Victor from 1155 to 1161, that he was appointed bishop of Avranches in 1161, and that he died in 1170 (see Feiss, *Achard of Saint Victor: Works*, 20–24). It seems likely that Magister Udo was aware of Achard's *Discretione* (see n. 72), so this dates Achard's treatise before *ca.* 1160 when Magister Udo's *Sententie* is usually dated. Note also that some scholars today regard the authenticity of this treatise as controversial (e.g., McGinn, *Three Treatises*, 66). N. Häring, who re-edited the work in 1960, argues that Gilbert of Poitiers is the author. Four years later, J. Châtillon defended Achard's authorship. See Häring, "Gilbert of Poitiers, Author of the 'De discretione animae, spiritus et mentis' commonly attributed to Achard of Saint Victor," *Mediaeval Studies* 22 (1960): 148–57; Châtillon, "Achard de Saint Victor et le 'De discretione animae, spiritus et mentis," *AHDLMA* 31 (1964): 7–35.

[64] See Ostler, *Die Psychologie des Hugos von St. Viktor*, 67–89; C. H. Talbot, *Ailred of Rievaulx: De Anima* (Nendeln/Liechtenstein: Kraus Reprint, 1976), 40–44. Ostler lists three solutions in the writings of Hugh of St Victor that were drawn from Augustine and Boethius. The first is a union through harmonic relation of numbers, for which he lists as examples Hugh of St Victor, *Didasc.* II.4, 12 (Buttimer, 27–28, 32–33; tr. Taylor, 64–65, 69 [esp. n. 26, 29]); Richard of St Victor, *Statu* 34 (Ribaillier, 101–102; tr. Evans, VTT 4.282). The second is a union through a physical medium for which Hugh's *Unione* is the classical example. The third is a personal union that Hugh works out in Christological contexts (e.g., *Sacr.* II.1.11 [Berndt, 323–28; PL 176.405A–409D; tr. Deferrari, 242–47]). The three solutions are not mutually exclusive and are often found together in the same work; e.g. Isaac of Stella, *Epistola de anima* (PL 194.1881B–1882C; tr. McGinn, 164–66). The imagination is used extensively in the writings of Achard and Richard, but Robert of Melun makes no use of it. Robert does however offer the most extensive treatment on a personal union. It is commonly held that the constitution of a *homo* is comprised of soul and body, but, following Hugh and Achard, Robert also argues that this union does not constitute a "person" (*persona*), because the soul is the person; though the union does constitute a *homo*. Thus, according to Robert, "souls are *human* persons when clothed with flesh. For the soul confers its distinction of person to the body conjoined to it" (*Sent.* I.2.34 [Heinzmann, 101; Innsbruck, UB 297, fol. 100vb; *Abbrev.* 498 (London, BL Royal 7.F.XIII, fol. 97ra–b)]: "Quod quia indubitanter verum est et absque omni dubitatione affirmandum est et animas humanas quando carne erant indute personas fuisse. Anima enim corpori sibi coniuncto suam confert persone discretionem"). And elsewhere he defines this "personal union" (*personalis unio*) as "the soul having a human body conjoined to itself in its identity of person" (*Sent.* I.2.32 [Heinzmann, 100; Innsbruck, UB 297, fol. 100va; *Abbrev.* 497 (London, BL Royal 7.F.XIII, fol. 95ra)]). Obviously, this anthropology is the basis of a Christology unique to Victorine authors that is usually called today the Homo-Assumptus Theory. Victorine Christology and its underlying anthropology will be the theme of VTT 7.

[65] Hugh's predecessor, William of Champeaux, makes no use of the imagination per se but like Hugh makes use of a tripartite division of man. According to William of Champeaux (and Anselm of Laon who teaches something very similar) the soul is composed of two natures or powers, sensuality and rationality. Anselm calls them the sensual soul (*anima sensualis*)

With an emphasis on the cognitive distinction Hugh adopts a Boethian division: sensual perception (*sensus*), imagination (*imaginatio*), reason (*ratio*), and intelligence (*intelligentia*).[66] Achard's taxonomy is more complete because it includes the cognitive and affective faculties (*perceptio* and *affectio*). And thus in addition to the Boethian division he also mentions the will (*voluntas*), sensual appetite (*sensualitas*), and memory (*memoria*).[67] In both authors the dissimilar extremities of body and soul or man and God unite in a medium that allows for the traditional tripartite division of the interior man: (1) the higher faculty which Hugh calls "reason" in the incorporeal soul and

and the rational soul (*anima rationalis*), while William refers to the soul and spirit (*anima et spiritus*) which compose the interior man ("spirit" here obviously refers to the rational part). Both regard sensuality as the lower power by which the body is given life and the five senses are managed. Reason or the spirit is the higher power by which good and evil are discerned and celestial truths contemplated (here is where William locates specifically the image of God). Moreover, each power is divided into three grades (*gradus*) based the extrinsic object. At the highest grade reason is focused only on celestial things, according to Anselm, or on God's essence alone, according to William. Both call this contemplation. The middle grade concerns both heavenly and earthly things, according to Anselm, or heavenly and spiritual things, according to William. The lowest grade concerns earthly things alone, or, as William specifies, the soul stoops to animal things in order to instruct and teach it and to arrange earthly things in a rational and honest way. This lowest grade of reason, according to both authors, converges with the highest grade of sensuality, whose highest function is to obey reason in the governance of temporal things (this duty was lost as a punishment after the Fall). Furthest removed from reason is the lowest grade of sensuality which is "to murmur back at spirituality" (*remurmurare spiritualitati*), according to Anselm, or to be completely involved with earthly delights, according to William. The middle grade of sensuality conjoins the two other designated grades. See Anselm of Laon, *Sententie diuine pagine* (Bliemetzrieder, 24); *Sent.* (Bliemetzrieder, 56 and 152); William of Champeaux, *Sent.* 244 (Lottin, 5.201); *Sent.* 253 (Lottin, 5.206). See also *Sententiae Atrebatenses* (Lottin, 5.405). The distinction between higher and lower parts of the rational soul is based on a rich tradition that goes back to Augustine; see R. Mulligan, "*Ratio Superior* and *Ratio Inferior*: the Historical Background," *The New Scholasticism* 29.1 (1955): 1–32.

66   E.g., Hugh of St Victor, *Unione* (Piazzoni, 888.150–59). See Boethius, *De consolatione philosophiae* V, prosa 4 (Bieler, 97); *Commentarium in Isagoge Porphyrii* I.3 (Brandt, 8); cf. also Godfrey of St Victor, *Miscrocosmus* 19 (Delhaye, 46). See discussion in Delhaye, *Le Microcosmus*, 103; Kleinz, *The Theory of Knowledge of Hugh of Saint Victor*, 23–26.

67   E.g., Achard of St Victor, *Discretione* 17, 34 (Häring, 177, 181; tr. Feiss, 360, 364). His designation for the higher cognitive powers is fluid: *ratio* (20, 21), *intellectus, intelligentia*. In one instance he seems to distinguish *ratio* and *intelligentia*, thus presents us with the common fourfold scheme (55 [Häring, 187; tr. Feiss, 370]). The fourfold scheme is implied later but with the word *intellectus* which "not only surpasses the things subject to the senses and images, but even leaves itself behind to some extent and reaches above itself to contemplate the immense and incomprehensible majesty of the deity" (67 [Häring, 187; tr. Feiss, 370]). Needless to say, neither in Hugh's *Unione* nor Achard's *Discretione* is the five-fold scheme found that distinguishes *intellectus* and *intelligentia*. For a complete discussion on these schemes, see B. McGinn, *The Golden Chain: A Study in the Theological Anthropology of Isaac of Stella* (Washington, DC: Cistercian Publications, 1972), 197–227.

which Achard calls the "mind" (*mens*) where reason and will are located; (2) the lowest faculty which Hugh calls "sensual perception" (*sensus*) in the corporeal spirit and which Achard calls "soul" (*anima*) where sensual perception and sensual appetite (*sensualitas*) are located; and (3) the mediating faculty that unites the other two which Hugh calls imagination (*imaginatio*) in the corporeal spirit and which Achard calls "spirit" (*spiritus*) where imagination and its corresponding affection are located.[68]

The connection between sensual perception and imagination is clearly established in both authors, though Achard shows no interest in the physiological aspect of the senses. As we learn from Hugh, the sensual perception (*sensus*) is a "fiery power" that is first diffused outside the body through the individual senses, takes on the forms or shapes of present external objects that it contacts, and then brings back those forms into the brain where they are cleansed and purified before entering into the "phantasmal chamber" (*cella phantastica*), where they become the imagination (*imaginatio*).[69] In irrational animals this is where the ascending motion ends, but in human beings, capable of spiritual things, the imagination is purified to the extent of contacting the incorporeal substance of the rational soul that sets into motion the judgment of reason (*discretio*). As such, then, body and incorporeal spirit are conjoined in the imagination that has a likeness to both: it is a higher power in the body than the senses because it perceives the images of bodies and not the bodies themselves, and it is lower than reason because it is not incorporeal.[70] The upward progression from the body to the spirit via the imagination makes possible intellectual growth and ultimately spiritual growth as well. "Knowledge" (*scientia*) occurs as a result of the upward progression of imagination that "informs" reason from below, just "wisdom or understanding"

---

[68]   According to Achard (*Discretione* 48–49 [Häring, 184; tr. Feiss, 368]), the lower cognitive and affective powers of the "soul" (i.e., sensual perception and sensuality) have their imitation in the "spirit." Apparently, then, there is a third affective faculty in the interior man. Imagination is the cognitive faculty of the spirit, but Achard has no specific name for its affective counterpart other than the general designation of an "affection of the soul" (*ipsius affectio*). See n. 72 and n. 106 below.

[69]   Cf. William of Conches, *Dragmaticon philosophiae* VI.19 (Ronca, 243–44; tr. Ronca and Curr, 157); John of Salisbury, *Metalogicon* IV.17 (Hall, 155); Alcher of Clairvaux, *De spiritu et anima* 33 (PL 40.802–803; tr. Leiva and Ward, 230–31). See also Baron, *Science et Sagesse chez Hugues de Saint-Victor* (Paris: P. Lethielleux, 1957), 58–59, 194.

[70]   Writing some thirty years after the *Unione*, Isaac of Stella will provide a similar description in his *Epistola de anima* (PL 194.1881B; tr. McGinn, 164).

(*sapientia sive intelligentia*) occurs as a result of divine illumination descending into the soul and informing reason from above.[71]

According to Achard's tripartite division of the self, "the mind is on top, the soul at the bottom, and the spirit in the middle."[72] Based on the

71 For a discussion of the lower and higher cognitive powers in Hugh's *Unione*, see Kleinz, *The Theory of Knowledge*, 32–40, 66–81.

72 Achard of St Victor, *Discretione* 31 (Häring 181; tr. Feiss, 364): "Est enim mens in summo, anima in imo, spiritus in medio." Achard's classification finds its way into three influential *Sentences*: Magister Udo's *Sententes* (*ca.* 1165), the *Pseudo-Poitiers Gloss* and Peter of Poitiers's *Sententes* (the latter two are after *ca.* 1170). On at least one occasion Magister Udo mentions "Magister Achard," so perhaps he may have had direct contact with his writings or lectures; see *Sententie* I (Vatican City, BAV Pal. lat. 328, fol. 6va; Vienna, ONB 1050, fol. 120rb; *om.* Salzburg a.V.35): "Vnde sciendum est quod secundum magistrum Achardum non sequitur . . ."

Magister Udo summarizes Achard's classification in two places. The first is in *Sententie* I (Salzburg, Stiftsbibliothek a.V.35, fol. 9r–v; Vatican City, BAV Pal. lat. 328, fol. 5rb; Vienna, ONB 1050, fol. 119ra; cited by Lottin, *Psychologie et morale*, 6:12) which was copied in the *Pseudo-Poitiers Gloss* I.3.2.1 (Bamberg, Staatsbibliothek Msc. Patr. 128, fol. 32r–v; London, BL Royal 7.F.XIII, fol. 6vb; Naples, Biblioteca Nazionale, cod. VII C 14, fol. 6rb; Paris, BnF lat. 14423, fol. 45ra; partially cited in P. Moore, *The Works of Peter of Poitiers* (Notre Dame, IN: University of Notre Dame, 1936), 154–55 n. 21). The second summary is found in the second book of Magister Udo and the *Pseudo-Poitiers Gloss* (cited below). Note that the affective and cognitive faculties of the soul are preserved, but Magister Udo transposed their names. Of interest also is that Magister Udo and the *Pseudo-Poitiers Gloss* provide a name for the affective faculty of the spirit, namely *effectus* (see n. 68 above), but neither author speaks of the highest affective faculty, namely the will, at least in this context.

Magister Udo, *Sententie* II (Salzburg, Stiftsbibliothek a.V.35, fol. 68v [S]; Vatican City, BAV Pal. lat. 328, fol. 32vb–ra [P]; Vienna, ONB 1050, fol. 146va–b): "Est ergo diligenter attendendum quod interior homo, scilicet anima est imago et similitudo, et quasi quoddam exemplar exterioris hominis, scilicet corporis. Sicut enim ipsum corpus habet in se tres partes—infirmam scilicet que continet duos pedes, mediam scilicet uentrem que continet duas partes ante scilicet retro, et supremam partes scilicet caput que continet duos occulos—, sic ipse interior homo (scilicet anima) habet tres partes—scilicet infirmam que continet in se quasi duos pedes scilicet sensualitatem et sensum, et medium que continet spiritum et imaginationem et eius effectum, et supremam scilicet mentem que continent in se quasi duos occulos scilicet cognitionem et dilectionem. De his singulis ordine agendum est. Sensualitas ergo est potentia percipiendi res corporales in se<met>ipsis ut uidentes aliquam rem corporalem ipsam cognoscimus et percipimus. Sensus autem est potentia afficiendi ex rebus sensualite perceptis ut aliquam rem corporalem cognoscentes gaudio uel delectatione merore uel tristicia afficimur. Imaginatio autem est potentia percipiendi res corporales in imaginibus suis ut per somnum et huiusmodi. Effectus autem eius est potentia afficiendi ex rebus imaginatione perceptis ut per somnium aliquam rem corporalem uidentes afficimur gaudio et delectione tristicia et merore. Mens uero est omnium eorum que sunt in anima et dignitate sublimior et subtilitate interior affectu et effectu Dei naturaliter capax, habens Dei imaginem in potentia cognoscendi et eius similituindem in potentia diligendi. Qualiter distet inter sensualitatem et sensum et imaginationem et eius effectum [affectum *scr.* P S] et ipsam mentem superius dictum est."

Pseudo-Poitiers Gloss II.24.3.1 (London, BL Royal 7.F.XIII, fol. 24va; Naples, Biblioteca Nazionale, cod. VII C 14, fol. 28rb–va; Paris, BnF lat. 14423, fol. 72vb): "Sciendum est itque quod mens et spiritus et anima quandoque pro eodem accipiuntur, scilicet pro tota proper ordering whereby the higher power moves, affects, and regulates the lower, the immediate reception of God's grace—whether the inspiration of love (affective dimensions) or the illumination of truth (cognitive dimensions)—is located in the inmost core of man (the mind), and this creates a ripple effect that moves into the middle core (spirit) and through it into the soul.[73] Achard subdivides three virtual parts of the interior man into two faculties or powers of "perception" and "affection" (*perceptio et affectio*)[74] or simply the cognitive and affective powers of the mind, spirit, and soul. The cognitive power of the mind and soul is distinguished based on the object perceived, whether intellectual things (*intellectuales*) or corporeal things (*corporales*). Achard calls the first power "reason" (*ratio*) and the second "sensual perception" (*sensus*), that is, through the five senses. The affective power of both the mind and soul Achard calls the "natural affections" (*naturales affectiones*), which correspond to the Platonic distinction between the concupiscible and irascible appetite. Achard does not use these latter terms, but as defined later by Godfrey, "the human spirit without flesh is naturally concupiscible and irascible: with the concupiscible appetite seeking without deliberation what is beneficial, with the irascible appetite forsaking without deliberation

substantia interiori ex qua simul cum corpore constat homo, quandoque ab inuicem distinguntur ita aut mens accipiatur pro eo quod est superius in homine interiori. Est enim mens omnium eorum que sint in anima et dignitate prestancior et tenuitate interior, Dei intellectu et affectu naturaliter capax, habens imaginem Dei in potencia diligendi et uel magis in potencia cognoscendi. Est ergo ipsa mens quasi caput hominis interioris, occulte intelligencie et dilectionis perspicax. Est autem idem mens quod ratio. Ratio autem in duo partitur in sapientia et scientia. De quibus plene in littera agit. Sapientia est uis mentis ad superna contemplanda. Scientia in duabus consistit: in dispositione et ordinatione inferiorum. Prius enim disponimus, post actualiter ordinamus. Et est scientia uis mentis ad hec inferiora disponenda et ordinanda. Anima uero inferius est in homine continens in se quasi duos pedes hominis interioris: sensus et sensualitatem. 'Sensus est potencia percipiendi corporalia in se<met>ipsis. Sensualitas potentia afficiendi ex sic perceptis' (cf. Achard, *Discretione* 36 [Häring, 182]). Spiritus uero in medium est qui continet duas partes ymaginationis. Ymaginatio est potentia percipiendi corpora in ymaginibus suis. Vnde de re nunquam uisa, quandoque habemus ymaginationem, et tamen secundum alium effectum dicitur imaginatio potencia afficiendi ex rebus sic perceptis. Et sic distinguenda esse docet Apostolus dicens: *Animalis homo non percipit ea que Dei sunt*, et item *Psallam spiritu, psallam et mente*. Deinceps sequentia faciliora erit." Cf. Peter of Poitiers, *Sent.* II.20 (Moore, Garvin, and Dulong, 160–62); Magister Martin, *Conpilatio questionum theologie* II.25 (Paris, BnF lat. 14526, fol. 87va–b; Troyes, BM 789, fol. 42vb); Prepositinus, *Summa* II (Einsiedeln, Stiftsbibliothek 230, p. 82; London, BL Royal 9.E.XI, fol. 157ra–b; Paris, BnF lat. 14526, fol. 22va–b; Vienna, ONB 1501, fol. 30vb–31ra).

73   Cf. *Discretione* 30–32 (Häring, 180–81; tr. Feiss, 363–64).

74   E.g., *Discretione* 36 and 62 (Häring, 182, 188; tr. Feiss, 365, 371).

what is not beneficial."[75] Or, as Achard simply states: "people naturally love what is good for them and hate what is bad."[76] While these natural affections are the same in the mind and soul, they are distinguished based on the object of affection. The concupiscible or irascible appetite for intellectual or spiritual objects perceived by reason is called the "will" (*voluntas*), and the "sensual appetite" (*sensualitas*) is the concupiscible or irascible appetite for corporeal objects perceived by the sensual perception. The medium where the mind and soul converge is called the spirit.[77] The spirit is the virtual part of the interior man that perceives the images of visible things, which the soul perceives, by means of the faculty of the imagination (*vis imaginationis*).[78] As such, the spirit has a likeness to the soul because the perceived objects are the same (i.e., corporeal), but they are different in the mode of apprehension, that is, the soul perceives them by the sensory perception and the spirit by the imagination. The soul and spirit perceive the same object, but the soul sees the corporeal object in itself via the sensory organs (*sensus*) while the spirit sees the corporeal object in its image via the imagination (*imaginatio*).[79] The transition from spirit to mind is thus a transition to incorporeal objects which the spirit is not capable of perceiving.

Within these anthropological treatises then we have at least three cognitive faculties of ascending order, which corresponds exactly to a favorite Victorine metaphor of three eyes: of the flesh, of reason, of contemplation,[80] and two clearly distinguished affective faculties, will

---

[75] Godfrey of St Victor, *Microcosmus* I.28 (Delhay, 52). Cf. also Robert of Melun, *Sent.* I.2.147 (Innsbruck, UB 297, fol. 121ra): "Verum sensualitatis appetitus tripartitus esse uidetur. Nam sensualitate ad ea appetenda movemur, in quibus temporalis commoditas consistit, et ad ea uitanda, quorum incommoditatem formidamus. Iocunda etiam et suavia ex affectu sensualitatis desiderantur, et austera et amara spernuntur."

[76] E.g., Achard of St Victor, *Discretione* 38 (Häring 182; tr. Feiss, 365).

[77] Achard of St Victor, *Discretione* 41–49 (Häring 183–85; tr. Feiss, 366–68).

[78] Achard of St Victor, *Discretione* 41 and 49 (Häring 183 and 184–85; tr. Feiss, 366 and 368).

[79] Achard of St Victor, *Discretione* 56 (Häring 187; tr. Feiss, 370). The collection of these images of corporeal objects is retained in the soul's memory, what Achard calls the *imaginaria memoria*. Because the spirit cannot perceive what the mind perceives, Achard also speaks of a memory in the mind.

[80] E.g., Hugh of St Victor, *Misc.* I.1 (Grenoble, BM 390, fol. 20rb–va; Heiligenkreuz, Stifts-bibliothek 235, fol. 46v; Paris, Mazarine 717, fol. 157va; Paris, BnF lat. 14303, fol. 107ra; PL 177.471C): "Qui enim uidet oculo contemplationis uidet Deum et ea que in Deo sunt. Qui uidet oculo rationis uidet animum et ea que in animo sunt. Qui uidet oculo carnis uidet mundum et ea que in mundo sunt. Qui autem uidet ea que uidentur oculo contemplationis uidet et ea que uidentur oculo rationis et ea que uidentur oculo carnis, quia in superioribus inferiora cognoscuntur. Qui autem uidet oculo rationis ea que uidentur oculo carnis uidet;

and the sensual appetite. Such classifications thus provide our spiritual authors with a psychological framework within which to develop their biblical reflections on the spiritual life. Greater attention must now be given to the higher faculties of the inner self; here freedom is found that is so important for their spiritual teaching.

FREEDOM AND SPIRITUAL WARFARE

Because reason and will, which conjoined together comprise free choice, are the highest cognitive and affective powers of the soul that reflect the image and likeness of God, it is here that one finds the a locus of salvation and spirituality. According to Hugh, nothing but reason and will can compose and increase faith;[81] and, as Achard suggests, nothing but the mind can receive God's illumination and inspiration.[82] With regard to free choice, Robert considers it one of two dogmas on the soul that must be believed for human salvation (the other is its eschatological salvation or damnation based on personal merit or the merit of others).[83] The freedom of judgment is for Richard the very image of eternity and the divine majesty.[84] Bernard of Clairvaux

---

sed non similiter ea que uidentur oculo contemplationis uidet. Qui uero oculo carnis uidet ex eo nec ea uidet que uidentur oculo contemplationis, nec ea que uidentur oculo rationis. Propterea igitur *spiritalis diiudicat omnia* (1 Cor. 2:15), quia sicut per oculum contemplationis ea uidet que in Deo sunt, ita per oculum rationis contemplatione illuminatum ea uidet que in animo sunt, et per ea et in eis ea quoque que in mundo sunt. Qui ergo omnia uidet, de omnibus iudicare potest, quia nichil ab eius iudicio subtrahitur a cuius cognitione nichil occultatur." See also Hugh of St Victor, *Sacr.* 1.10.2 (Berndt, 225; PL 176.329C; tr. Deferrari, 167). On the three eyes see D. Lasić, *Hugonis de S. Victore theologia perfectiva* (Rome: Pontificium Athenaeum Antonianum, 1956), 125–35; P. Sicard, *Diagrammes médiévaux et exégèse visuelle: Le Libellus de formatione arche de Hugues de Saint-Victor*, BV 4 (Paris: Brepols, 1993), 187–92.

[81] E.g., Hugh of St Victor, *Sacr.* I.10.3, 4 (Berndt, 227, 229; PL 176.331B, 332B; tr. Deferrari, 169, 170).

[82] E.g., Achard of St Victor, *Discretione* 30–32 (Häring, 180–81; tr. Feiss, 363–64), where the mind is the immediate receptor of God's love.

[83] Robert of Melun, *Sent.* I.2.67 (Innsbruck, UB 297, fol. 106ra–b): "Prius ergo ostendendum est, quid de anima humana credere teneamur. Hoc enim primum in ordine enumerationis proposite tenet locum. Tenemur ergo credere animam substantiam creatam esse rationalem et inmortalem, et pro meritis bonis vel malis dampnandam esse uel saluandam que per se uel per alios facit . . . Eam etiam liberum arbitrium habere credendum est per quod libere et bene et male uelle potest atque operari. Hec sunt que de ipsa anima credere tenemur. Sine enim fide istorum nemo que salutis sunt operari potest."

[84] Richard of St Victor, *Statu* 3 (Ribaillier, 66; tr. Evans, VTT 4.254). See Dumeige, *Richard de Saint-Victor*, 45.

probably captured this tradition best when he wrote: "Take away free choice and there will be nothing to be saved. Take away grace and there will be no means of salvation . . . None but God can give it, nothing but free choice can receive it."[85] The significance of this for the spiritual life is also highlighted in a popular Augustinian dictum: "A man can do other things unwillingly, but he cannot believe unless willingly;" the point here, Robert argues, is not that the will is lacking in reluctant actions, but to highlight the fact that even the gift of faith is not formed except in the will.[86] A reluctant action is not really involuntary; it proceeds from the will though it is not preferred.[87] For Augustine such actions are not truly meritorious.[88] Thus, in good Augustinian fashion, the spiritual life is a voluntary and free relationship with Christ in the Spirit and this presupposes faith and grace.

Free Choice

Though no theologian in the twelfth century denies free choice, its definition is another matter. In his usual clarity and thoroughness Robert enumerates and analyzes all the current definitions and as such provides the first critical exposition of the definitions in circulation at the time (only the Anselmian definition as preservation of uprightness for its own sake is not discussed).[89] The refutations also provide useful descriptions of his anthropology and provide a headway to other themes pertinent to the spiritual life.

---

[85] Bernard of Clairvaux, *Gratia* 1.2 (SBO 3:166).

[86] Robert of Melun, *Sent.* I.2.124 (Innsbruck, UB 297, fol. 117va; *Abbrev.* 559 [London, BL Royal 7.F.XIII, fol. 97vb]): "Libera est ergo uoluntas omnis et nulla omnino ui necessitatis pressa. Per hoc enim quod scriptum est 'cetera potest homo nolens, credere non potest nisi uolens' (Augustine, *Jo. ev. tr.* 26.2 [Willems, 260]), non uoluntas omnis a ceteris tollitur que facit homo, sed in quo fides consistat intimatur idest in voluntate et non in exteriore operatione."

[87] Robert of Melun, *Sent.* I.2.124 (Innsbruck, UB 297, fol. 117rb; *Abbrev.* 559 [London, BL Royal 7.F.XIII, fol. 97vb]): "Ex quo certum est uoluntatem cogi non posse, quamquam uere dicatur quosdam inuitos et quasi nolentes quedam uelle. Quod, ut dictum est, et ideo uerum est et uere dicitur, quia causa, propter quam uoluntatem talem habent, nec placita nec accepta est."

[88] Augustine, *Conf.* I.12.19 (Verheijen, 11): "Nemo enim invitus bene facit." See discussion in R. Saarinen, *Weakness of the Will in Medieval Thought: From Augustine to Buridan* (Leiden: E.J. Brill, 1994), 31–37.

[89] See Lottin, *Psychologie et morale*, 1:31–38.

(1) "Free choice is the power of discerning between good and evil;"[90] or "free choice is the power to turn to good or to evil."[91]

(2) "Free choice is the discernment of good and evil with the election of the good and detestation of evil."[92]

(3) "Free choice is a voluntary appetite."[93]

(4) "Free choice is a free judgment concerning the will."[94]

The first definition is found in the *Summa sententiarum* and was utilized by Peter Lombard's *Sentences* published before 1157: "Free choice is a faculty of reason and will by which the good is chosen with the aid of grace or evil is chosen without the aid of grace."[95] The second definition is attributed to Augustine. The third definition belongs to Hugh and the fourth to Boethius.

Robert has no sympathy for the first definition and in his analysis spanning twenty-four chapters he provides an arsenal of refutations from authorities and reason.[96] The problem is that it allows for a

---

90   Robert of Melun, *Sent.* I.2.92 (Innsbruck, UB 297, fol. 111va; *Abbrev.* 535, fol. 96vb): ". . . potestate inter bonum et malum discernendi." Cf. Peter Lombard, *Sent.* II.7.2 (SB 4:359).

91   Robert of Melun, *Sent.* I.2.93 (Innsbruck, UB 297, fol. 111va; *Abbrev.* 535 [London, BL Royal 7.F.XIII, fol. 96vb]): ". . . potestas et ad bonum et ad malum deflectendi."

92   Robert of Melun, *Sent.* I.2.122 (Innsbruck, UB 297, fol. 116vb; *Abbrev.* 557 [London, BL Royal 7.F.XIII, fol. 97vb]): "Discretio boni et mali cum electione unius, idest boni, et detestatione alterius, idest mali."

93   Robert of Melun, *Sent.* I.2.121 (Innsbruck, UB 297, fol. 116vb; *Abbrev.* 556 [London, BL Royal 7.F.XIII, fol. 97vb]): "Liberum arbritrium appetitus est uoluntarius."

94   Robert of Melun, *Sent.* I.2.125 (Innsbruck, UB 297, fol. 117va; *Abbrev.* 559 [London, BL Royal 7.F.XIII, fol. 97vb]): "Liberum arbitrium est iudicium de voluntate liberum." In the same chapter Robert also lists a variant of this definition: "Free choice is a free judgment having power of willing those things that can be done freely or not done freely from free choice" ("liberum arbitrium iudicium liberam potestatem habens uoluntatum illarum rerum que ex libero arbitrio libere fieri possint et libere dimitti"). The idea here, as Robert explains, is that some acts occur without the cooperation of free choice, like reaching puberty. Thus the definition is an attempt to specify the scope of the freedom of will by limiting it to only future contingencies that are not impossible. A version of this teaching is found in Hugh of St Victor, *Sacr.* I.5.22 (Berndt, 125–26; PL 176.256A–C; tr. Deferrari, 71), but Robert specifically has Peter Lombard in mind (*Sent.* II.25.1.3 (SB 4:461–62; on this point see Lottin, *Psychologie et morale*, 1:35 n. 1). Robert thinks that this limits the scope of the will's freedom too much, because someone like Lucifer merited punishment when he willed the impossible (e.g., to be like the Most High), but according to Lombard's definition this will would not fall under the power of free choice. For a discussion of and citation of relevant passages in Robert's *Sent.*, see Lottin, *Psychologie et morale*, 1:34–37.

95   Peter Lombard, *Sent.* II.24.3 (SB 4:452): "Liberum arbitrium est facultas voluntatis et rationis qua bonum eligitur gratia assitente uel malum eadem desistente." Cf. *Summa sent.* III.8 (PL 176.101C), which speaks of *habilitas* rather than *facultas*.

96   Robert of Melun, *Sent.* I.2.92–120 (Innsbruck, UB 297, fols. 111va–116vb; *Abbrev.* 535–56, fols. 96vb–97vb).

positive acceptance of sin through free choice, but Robert is adamant that the power of sinning is not an integral part of human nature,[97] and neither is it a part of free choice.[98] To sin "from free choice" simply means "not from coercion."[99] As such sin is a corruption of nature and defect of power, and human freedom is truly realized only when one turns toward the good.

The third definition is attributed to Augustine. Robert regards it as true but not specific enough. He argues as follows: election of the good happens in two ways, by judgment and by act; that is, either the power to prefer good to evil through the practical discernment of judgment, or the power to do the good and to detest evil by forsaking it. Now the

[97] An important motivation for this anthropology is Christological; e.g., Robert of Melun, *Sent.* I.2.112 (Innsbruck, UB 297, fol. 115ra–b): "Si enim esset potentia peccandi de substantia rationalis creature et pars quedam substantialis esset liberi arbitrii uel potestas ipsum liberum arbitrium continens, homo a Verbo Dei assumptus potestatem peccandi habuisset. Nam in ipso tota integritas humane nature fuit. Quod alia ratione uel auctoritate non oportet probare quam fide ecclesie catholice que omnia etiam que nostra sunt preter peccatum a Christo assumpta esse credit et predicat. Si ergo potestas peccandi de integritate nature humane est atque substantie, aut ipsa in Christo fuit aut Christus humane nature integritatem non assumpsit. Sed quia hoc falsum esse nemo dubitat qui de humana natura a Christo assumpta sane sentit, idest integritatem humane nature et totam ueritatem a Christo non esse assumptam, nemo de natura humana a Christo assumpta sane sentiens postestatem peccandi de integritate humane nature esse arbitratur, eo quod tota integritas nature humane atque ueritas in Christo fuit, in quo potestas peccandi non solum non fuit, sed nec etiam esse potuit. Hec itaque sunt et alia huiusmodi quibus firmissime atque uerissime ostendi potest potestatem peccandi potestatem nullam esse, nec partem liberi arbitrii esse credendam uel dicendam." Cf. also Anselm of Laon, *Sententie diuine pagine* (Bliemetzrieder, 28).

[98] Cf. Anselm of Canturbery, *De libertate arbitrii* 1 (Schmitt, 1:207–208).

[99] Robert of Melun, *Sent.* I.2.95 (Innsbruck, UB 297, fol. 111vb; *Abbrev.* 537 [London, BL Royal 7.F.XIII, fol. 96vb]): "Quid enim arbitrium aliud est uel esse potest quam potestas discernendi, que rationabiliter facienda sunt et que ommittenda?;" *Sent.* I.2.95 (Innsbruck, UB 297, fol. 112ra; *Abbrev.* 537 [London, BL Royal 7.F.XIII, fol. 96vb]): "Vnde constat arbitrium liberum tanto liberius esse, quanto a peccato remotius est;" *Sent.* I.2.102 (Innsbruck, UB 297, fol. 113rb; *Abbrev.* 543 [London, BL Royal 7.F.XIII, fol. 97ra]): "Nam nichil aliud est ex libertate arbitrii et uelle peccare et peccare quam nulla cogente causa et uoluntatem peccandi habere et ipsam operis actu implere. Quod quando fit, non ex potentia fit, sed ex potentie defectu. Et ideo, quamquam ex libertate arbitrii voluntas peccandi haberi dicatur et actu compleri, non tamen potentia peccandi pars erit libertatis arbitrii, sed, ut dixi, ipsius quidam defectus ac velut impotentia quedam. Vnde possibilitas peccandi non proprie potentia dicitur, que rectius impotentia posset appellari;" *Sent.* I.2.102 (Innsbruck, UB 297, fol. 113va; *Abbrev.* 544 [London, BL Royal 7.F.XIII, fol. 97ra]): "Quod ex huius vocis 'peccatum' significatione manifeste sciri potest. Peccatum enim nature corruptio est. Vnde et qui peccat bonum quod ex Deo est corrumpit, et ideo potentia peccandi aliud esse non uidetur quam potentia quod bonum est corrumpendi. Que quia potentia non est, idest potentia corrumpendi quod bonum est, sed impotentia quedam, nec potentia peccandi potentia est, sed indubitanter impotentia summa."

Augustinian definition calls free choice the "discernment of good and evil," which pertains to judgment. Thus the "election of the good and detestation of evil" must pertain to the act.[100] Therefore, if Augustine intended that free choice is sufficient for the election of the good (i.e., to do the good and to detest evil by forsaking it), then he excludes grace from the cause of human salvation, because free choice will be sufficient without supervenient grace to merit salvation. In other words, this Augustinian definition could be interpreted in a Pelagian manner and hence it is not without its ambiguity. This, I think, highlights how sensitive he is to any hint of Pelagianism and how much grace is on the forefront of his mind when discussing human freedom.

The second definition derives from Hugh.[101] In a somewhat gentle rebuttal Robert argues that the second definition "does not seem to be suitable." Appetite pertains to the will not reason, thus the definition is tantamount to calling free choice a voluntary will.[102] As is clear

---

[100] Robert of Melun, *Sent.* I.2.119 (Innsbruck, UB 297, fols. 116vb–117ra): "Verum hec <diffinitio>, etsi uera sit, non perfecte liberi arbitrii substantiam uidetur explicare. Non enim ostendit cuiusmodi bonum liberum arbitrium debeat eligere nec cuiusmodi malum detestari. Non uero habet arbitrium liberum potestatem quodlibet bonum eligendi. Nam si hoc haberet, et ad salutem absque gratia sufficeret. Quid uero per electionem boni uult Augustinus intelligere? An illam que fit iudicii discretione, an eam que fit boni operatione, idest an hoc quod liberum arbitrium potens sit iudicio preferre bonum malo, an hoc quod potens sit ipsum bonum operari et malum dimittendo detestari? His namque duobus modis solet dici electio boni fieri, idest iudicio uel operatione. Sed ea que per iudicium fieri solet in primo diffinitionis uerbo est designata. Dicit enim, quod 'liberum arbitrium est discretio boni et mali', in quo iudicium ostenditur, et iccirco per 'electionem boni et detestationem mali' non illa electio uel fuga intelligenda que iudicii sit, sed operationis que salutem confert et periculum aufert ... Si ergo uult Augustinus liberum arbitrium sufficiens esse ad boni electionem, idest ad bonum operandum et ad malum detestandum, idest ad malum dimittendum, a nostre salutis causa gratiam excludit, eo quod liberum arbitrium sine superueniente gratia ad salutem promerendam erit sufficiens."

[101] Hugh of St Victor, *Sacr.* I.5.21 (Cambridge, Trinity College West 363, fol. 35rb; Cambridge, Trinity College West 1478, fol. 38r; Douai, BM 361, fol. 28vb; Douai, BM 362/I, fol. 44va; New Haven, Library T.E. Marston 248, fol. 23va; Berndt, 125; PL 176.255C–D; tr. Deferrari, 85): "Quoniam spontaneus motus uel uoluntarius appetitus liberum arbitrium est: liberum quidem in eo quod est uoluntarius; arbitrium uero in eo quod appetitus." See also *Sacr.* I.6.4 (Berndt, 139; PL 176.265C; tr. Deferrari, 96).

[102] Robert of Melun, *Sent.* I.2.121 (Innsbruck, UB 297, fol. 116vb): "Dicunt enim quod liberum arbitrium appetitus est uoluntarius. Per appetitum rationem intelligunt, per uoluntarium uoluntatem que libera est. Sed nec hec diffinitio liberi arbitrii esse uidetur conuenienter assignata, eo quod differentiam pro genere habet et genus pro differentia. Appetere enim rationi non conuenit sed solum discernere. Vnde nec ipsa appetitus dici debet nec in aliqua scriptura tali uocabulo uel in aliquo usu loquendi appetata inuenit. Nam omnis scriptura et omnis discrete loquentium usus rationi discretionem assignare et uoluntari appetitum. Et ideo ad rationem pertinet discretio et ad uolutnatem appetitus. Ex his ergo constat non recte ita diffinit liberum arbitrum: liberum arbitrium est uoluntarius appetitus, eo quod appetitus

elsewhere, Robert does not seem to oppose the priority of the will made explicit in Hugh's definition, but Robert also insists on a place for reason in any definition of free choice.

The Boethian definition is accepted "nearly by everyone" (*ab omnibus fere*) because it accounts for the two constituents of free choice: the first, as suggested by the term "judgment" or "choice" (*arbitrium*), is the discernment of reason concerning what must be done or avoided, and the second, suggested by the term "free" (*liberum*), is the free consent of will to the discernment of reason. Or as Robert states it:

> The perfection of free choice consists in two things: reason and will. There is no judgment without reason, and there is no freedom without the will. Reason discerns and the will freely consents to or dissents from what reason discerns to be done or to be avoided.[103]

But the "duties" (*officii*) of reason and will and their relationship in the spiritual and moral life are, Robert notes, a source of "great confusion."[104] As such he spends the remainder of his treatment on issues involving the higher faculties in the spiritual and moral life.

Duties of Reason and Will in the Spiritual Life

Spiritual writers of the twelfth century spend a great deal of time with issues related to will, freedom, and power because it is here in part that the spiritual life—its battles, its moral movements, its balance of will and reason, its current state, etc.—is made intelligible within their psychological constructs. The higher cognitive and affective faculties—

---

idem est quod uoluntas. Vnde aliud non uidetur dici quando dicitur 'liberum arbitrium est uoluntarius appetitus' quam si diceretur liberum arbitrium uoluntaria uoluntas quod genus locutionis nugatorium et friuolum solet appellari. Vicio ergo non uacat predicta diffinitio liberi arbitrii et ideo ea liberum arbitrium non conuenianter explicatur."

103   Robert of Melun, *Sent.* I.2.123 (Innsbruck, UB 297, fol. 117rb; *Abbrev.* 558 [London, BL Royal 7.F.XIII, fol. 97vb]): "Duo utique sunt, in quibus liberi arbitrii perfectio consistit, idest ratio et uoluntas. Nam sine ratione arbitrium esse non potest nec absque uoluntate libertas. Est enim rationis discernere et uoluntatis libere eis consentire uel ab eis dissentire, que per rationem discernuntur facienda esse uel fugienda." See also *Sent.* I.2.119 (Innsbruck, UB 297, fol. 116va; *Abbrev.* 556 [London, BL Royal 7.F.XIII, fol. 97ra–b]): "Habet tamen, ut mihi uidetur, liberum arbitrium partes duas, idest potentiam declinandi a malo et potentiam faciendi bonum . . . Que quia duo sunt, et duplex potentia libero arbitrio est data, una qua ad malum uitandum idoneum esset et altera qua ad bonum faciendum promptum fieret." However, cf. Hugh of St Victor, *Sent. quest.* 57 (Lottin, 63).

104   Robert of Melun, *Sent.* I.2.129 (Innsbruck, UB 297, fol. 117vb; *Abbrev.* 564 [London, BL Royal 7.F.XIII, fol. 98ra]), cited in n. 152.

reason and will—stand out in these writings; in fact, they provide Hugh with a summary of his entire psychology:

> There are two things in which the whole nature of a rational soul is assigned: cognition and will, that is, wisdom and love . . . Therefore, the whole substance of the rational soul is ruled by these two: cognition and will, so that it may find truth through wisdom and embrace virtue through love.[105]

Robert of Melun, who prefers to distinguish will from sensual appetite,[106] enumerates three "properties" of the soul (*proprietas ipsius*

---

[105] Hugh of St Victor, *In Eccl.* 2 (Grenoble, BM 247, fols. 136v–137r; New Haven, Library T. E. Marston 248, fol. 237rb; Oxford, Bodleian Library, Laud. Misc. 370, fols. 183v–184r; Troyes, BM 496, fol. 79rb–va; Troyes, BM 1388, fol. 64ra; PL 175.141B–C): "Duo quippe sunt quibus anime rationalis natura tota disponitur, uidelicet cognitio et affectus, idest sapientia et amor. Que duo si anima perfecte optineat et legitime disponat, beata est. Si uero uel in his quantum natura expetit optinendis deficiat uel optenta contra naturam peruertat, in ea procul dubio parte qua uel defectum uel confusionem horum patitur, misera necesse est efficiatur. Tota ergo anime rationalis substantia his duobus regitur, idest cognitione et affectu, ut per sapientiam quidem ueritatem inueniat, per amorem autem amplectatur uirtutem." Cf. also Hugh of St Victor, *In hier. cael.* VII (PL 175.1065B); Richard of St Victor, *Serm. cent.* 53 (PL 177.1050B); *XII patr.* 5 (Châtillon, 100; tr. Zinn, 57), where the two primary powers are *ratio* and *affectio*; *Tract.* on Ps. 121 (PL 196.363B; tr. Evans, VTT 4.196), where he speaks of cognition, reason and intellect (*ratio, intellectus, cognitio*) and affection, affect and love (*affectio, affectus, dilectio*). See also Peter Lombard, *Sent.* II.24.3–5 (SB 4:452–54), who simply mentions *sensualitas* and the higher and lower parts of *ratio*. Magister Udo's commentary uses Achard of St Victor to expand on this section in Lombard's *Sentences* (see n. 72 above); Peter the Chanter, *Distinctiones Abel*, a late twelfth-century theological dictionary perhaps intended for spiritual exegesis (Graz, UB 724, fol. 9r; Vatican City, BAV Vat. lat. 1003, fol. 5rb; Vatican City, BAV Vat. lat. 1004, fol. 9r): "Anima causa doctrine dicitur habere duas partes potenciales: [1] superiorem, scilicet rationem, que duas habet partes: scilicet sapientiam de superius que non potest uelle nisi bonum quam contemplamur Deum, et scientiam inferiorem que sic conuersatur in mundo ut uiuat sine querela nisi corrumpatur per Euam, idest per carnem, [2] et inferiorem, scilicet sensualitatem, que similiter duas habet partes: superiorem de licitis et necessariis ut conuenire et bibere, et inferiorem de illicitis ut fornicari et huiusmodi, et hec dicitur serpens que suggerit Eue."

[106] The vocabulary for the affective faculties is very fluid in the twelfth century. In his treatment on the soul Robert of Melun occasionally pauses to mention the customary interchangeability of key terms for the affective faculties like *appetitus, affectus, sensualitas*, and *voluntas* (*affectio* is not attested in his treatise). While they all can designate an affective faculty, nevertheless in practice Robert only uses *voluntas* ("will") for the highest affective faculty where freedom lies and *sensualitas* ("sensual appetite") for the lowest affective faculty. Thus, for example, in *Sent.* I.2.146 Robert says that the *voluntas* can freely accept or forsake the *affectus* or *appetitus nature* or *sensualitatis motus* (see citation below). In Achard's *Discretione* we noted the same distinction between *voluntas* of the mind and *sensualitas* of the soul, but he also speaks of a third affective faculty, the *affectio* of the spirit or what Magister Udo calls the *effectus* (perhaps a variant for *affectus*); see n. 68 and n. 72 above. Because *voluntas*, as discussed below, is the mediating part between *ratio* and *sensualitas*, Peter Lombard will speak of a "will of reason" and a "will of sensuality" (*Sent.* III.18.2.1, regarding the two wills

anime): reason, will, and the sensual appetite (*ratio, voluntas, et sensualitas*).[107] Each have what is generally called their "duties" (*officii*) in Christian perfection that serve as a basis for making intelligible the nature of the Fall and the subsequent spiritual battles that everyone feels within.

With regard to the duties of reason and will, Robert reiterates a common psychological ordering when he writes: "the will stands between reason and the sensual appetite."[108] Reason has a twofold duty or office of moral discernment and instruction. It distinguishes not only what is true and false or good and evil but also what is expedient or not. The second office is to instruct the will on what it should seek

in Christ [SB 5:106]: "Humana voluntas est affectus rationis uel affectus sensualitatis").

Here are the relevant citations of Robert's vocabulary: *Sent.* I.2.121 (Innsbruck, UB 297, fol. 116vb): "Appetitus idem est quod uoluntas;" *Sent.* I.2.132 (Innsbruck, UB 297, fol. 118vb; *Abbrev.* 566 [London, BL Royal 7.F.XIII, fol. 98rb]): "Affectum uoluntatem uocat;" *Sent.* I.2.146 (Innsbruck, UB 297, fol. 121ra): "Solet uero iste affectus quandoque uoluntas etiam appellari. Vnde et dici solet quia uoluntati, qua ea uolumus que caro desiderat, non semper est consentiendum sed resistendum;" *Sent.* I.2.158 (Innsbruck, UB 297, fol. 122va; *Abbrev.* 584 [London, BL Royal 7.F.XIII, fol. 99rb]): "Affectus quo vellet homo id facere;" *Sent.* I.2.160 (Innsbruck, UB 297, fol. 122vb): ". . . de ipso sensualitis appetitu, qui nonnunquam nomine voluntatis appellatur, cui sepe iudicio rationis resistitur."

Affectus, like the other terms of affectivity, is often used in a generic sense of desire or a faculty of desire, but it can also designate one of four principal affects: love (*amor*), fear (*timor*), joy (*gaudium*), and sorrow (*tristitia* [or *moeror*]). As Magister Udo described it (see n. 72 above), the faculties of desire, whether the will or sensual appetite, are the "power[s] of being affected (*potentia afficiendi*) from the things perceived" by the cognitive powers, whether the sensual perception (e.g., fear at the sight of something frightful) or the imagination (e.g., fear of hell, often called "servile fear"). In *Statu* 9 Richard lists the typical four affects—*amor, timor, spes, dolor* (Ribaillier, 72; tr. Evans, VTT 4.258)—, but in *XII patr.* 7 he lists seven: *spes, timor, gaudium, dolor, odium, amor, pudor* (Châtillon, 108; tr. Zinn, 60); cf. also Hugh of St Victor, *Virtute orandi* 14 (Feiss, 154; tr. Feiss, VTT 4.341); PL 176.985); Godfrey of St Victor, *Microcosmus* II.105 (Delhaye, 116–17).

For good studies on the vocabulary of affectivity, see I. Choquette, "Voluntas, Affectio and Potestas in the *Liber De Voluntate* of St. Anselm," *Mediaeval Studies* 4 (1942): 61–81; J. Châtillon, "Cor et cordis affectus," DS 2.2 (1953): 2288–2300; Dumeige. *Richard de Saint-Victor*, 38–39; M. Casey, *Athirst for God* (Kalamazoo, MI: Cistercian Publications, 1988); P. F. Sirovic, *Der Begriff "Affectus" und die Willenslehre beim Hl. Bonaventura: Eine analytische-synthetische Untersuchung* (Mödling bei Wien, Druck: Missionsdruckerei St. Gabriel. 1965); E. A. Dreyer, "Affectus in St. Bonaventure's Description of the Journey of the Soul to God" (Ph.D. Dissertation. Marquette University, 1982), a summary of Sirovic's main conclusions of *affectus* is on page 15; T. Dixon, *From Passions to Emotions: The Creation of a Secular Psychological Category* (Cambridge: Cambridge University Press, 2003), 26–61; Knuuttila, *Emotions in Ancient and Medieval Philosophy*, passim.

107 Robert of Melun, *Sent.* I.2.141 (Innsbruck, UB 297, fol. 120ra; *Abbrev.* 573 [London, BL Royal 7.F.XIII, fol. 98va]); *Sent.* I.2.147 (Innsbruck, UB 297, fol. 121ra).

108 Robert of Melun, *Sent.* I.2.147 (Innsbruck, UB 297, fol. 121ra): "Inter rationem et sensualitatem uoluntas media est."

and forsake.[109] This corresponds roughly to Richard's distinction between the discernment of judgment and prudential counsel or deliberation.[110] Very often reason is regarded as a ruler over the will and the sensual appetite.[111] Robert makes a threefold division of the sensual appetite (*sensualitatis appetitus*). First, the sensual appetite "moves" someone to seek temporal benefits (*temporalis commoditas*), which is usually called the concupiscible appetite, or it moves someone to forsake what is harmful (*incommoditatem*), which is usually called the irascible appetite. When someone desires what is pleasant and attractive in this life or hates what is unpleasant and harsh, these motions occur naturally from the sensual appetite.[112] Because the will stands between reason and the sensual appetite, it sometimes consents to reason (i.e., an ordered motion), and sometimes it subjects itself or stoops to sensuality against reason (i.e., a disordered motion). The will's consent to reason can be meritorious but never culpable, whereas its consent to sensuality, understood here as an illicit motion, is always culpable and never meritorious.[113]

---

109   Robert of Melun, *Sent.* I.2.147 (Innsbruck, UB 297, fol. 121ra): "Quid uero rationis sit, ex his que ante dicta sunt, satis euidens est. Est autem, ut dictum est, rationis officium discernere inter bonum et malum, et bonum et bonum, et malum et malum, atque docere que appetenda sunt et que fugienda sunt et que magis appetenda sunt et que magis et que minus et que equaliter et que magis fugienda sunt et que minus."

110   See, e.g., Richard of St Victor, *Statu* 28–29 (Ribaillier, 94–96; tr. Evans, VTT 4.276–78).

111   E.g., Robert of Melun, *Sent.* I.2.131 (Innsbruck, UB 297, fol. 118va; *Abbrev.* 565 [London, BL Royal 7.F.XIII, fol. 98rb): ". . . quia debet ratio sensualitatem regere eique preesse ut uir mulieri. Vnde et sensualitas rationi obtemperare debet atque obedire et non ratio sensualitati;" *Sent.* I.2.141 (Innsbruck, UB 297, fol. 120ra; *Abbrev.* 573 [London, BL Royal 7.F.XIII, fol. 98va]): "Sensualitatis uero officium est illa appetere quibus sustentari et foueri possit uita temporalis que uictu atque uestitu indiget." See also Achard of St Victor, *Serm.* 13 (Châtillon, 143; tr. Feiss, VTT 4.95–96); Richard of St Victor, *Tract.* on Ps. 121 (PL 196.363A–364A; tr. Evans, VTT 4.196); *Status* 6 (Ribaillier, 68–69; tr. Evans, VTT 4.255–56).

112   Robert of Melun, *Sent.* I.2.147 (Innsbruck, UB 297, fol. 121ra): "Verum sensualitatis appetitus tripartitus esse uidetur. Nam sensualitate ad ea appetenda mouemur, in quibus temporalis commoditas consistit, et ad ea uitanda, quorum incommoditatem formidamus. Iocunda etiam et suauia ex affectu sensualitatis desiderantur, et austera et amara spernuntur."

113   Robert of Melun, *Sent.* I.2.141 (Innsbruck, UB 297, fol. 120ra; *Abbrev.* 573 [London, BL Royal 7.F.XIII, fol. 98va]): "Ante uero, quam homo peccasset, hec rationi perfecte obtemperabant. Nam et uoluntas ipsius iudicium semper sequebatur et sensualitas, quando uolebat et quomodo uolebat et quantum uolebat, ea appetebat que uite temporali erant necessaria. Sed postquam peccauit homo, hanc dignitatem potestatis amisit. Nunc enim illarum contradictionem sentit atque rebellionem, idest uoluntatis et sensualitatis, que ante pecccatum in nullo ei resistere poterant;" *Sent.* I.2.147 (Innsbruck, UB 297, fol. 121ra): "Inter rationem et sensualitatem uoluntas media est que quandoque rationi consentit et aliquando sensualitati se subicit. Quando uero rationi consentit, aliquando meritum habet et nunquam culpam. Sed quando sensualitati consentit, quandoque culpam habet, et nunquam ideo premium."

The Fall and Its Effects

Such classifications can be used to make intelligible the psychological effects of the Fall and the Pauline dualism of the flesh and spirit. The corruption of ignorance and lust is an Augustinian theme that naturally follows from the aforementioned emphasis on reason and will in Hugh's anthropology.[114] Building upon Hugh's teaching, Richard teaches that the image of God is located in the higher cognitive parts of the self: reason (ratio), knowledge of truth (cognitio veritatis), and understanding (intellectus). The similitude of God is located in the higher affective parts: love (dilectio), love of virtue (amor virtutis), and desire (affectus).[115] These goods became corrupt by the three principal evils: ignorance, concupiscence, and weakness (ignorantia, concupiscentia, and infirmitas).[116] And so, in Sermon 70 Richard teaches:

---

[114] See, e.g., Hugh of St Victor, Sacr. I.7.28 (Berndt, 184; PL 176.299A; tr. Deferrari, 134); Sent. quest. 56 (Lottin, 61–62); Misc. I.103 (PL 177.535C); see also Richard of St Victor, Decl. (Ribaillier, 213); LE X.2.11 (Châtillon, 398).

While there is no consistent Victorine opinion on what constitutes original sin, they all agree that ignorance and concupiscence afflict all of humanity after the Fall. As summarized by Lottin (Psychologie et morale, 4.1:12–29, 272–75), three views on original sin circulated in the twelfth century. First, Peter Abelard defined original sin not as a sin in a strict sense (since there is only personal sin, i.e., an act of the free will of which infants are incapable) but only in the broader sense of a penalty that makes everyone liable to eternal punishment. Second, Anselm of Laon and William of Champeaux bear witness to the predominate Augustinian theory that original sin is concupiscence of the lower sensual faculty inclining the will toward evil. Hugh of St Victor and the Summa Sententiarum argue that original sin consists of both concupiscence and ignorance (see Lottin, Psychologie et morale, 4.1:65–76). See, e.g., Hugh of St Victor, Sacr. I.7.28 (Berndt, 184; PL 176.299A; tr. Deferrari, 134), where the original corruption is the ignorance of mind and concupiscence of the flesh. Third, Anselm of Canterbury regards original sin as a privation of original righteousness or as a loss of the rectitude of the will, the effect of which is concupiscence of the sensual appetite. This view was virtually ignored until after 1225.

Robert of Melun rejects Hugh's opinion that original sin is ignorance, though he does regard it as an effect of original sin (see R. Martin, "Les idées de Robert de Melun sur le péché originel," Revue des sciences philosophiques et théologiques 7 [1913]: 700–25 [esp. 704]; Lottin, Psychologie et morale, 4.1:76–88). Achard departs from both Hugh and Robert and follows the view of Anselm of Canterbury (see Serm. 2.1 [Châtillon, 44; tr. Feiss, 112]; Lottin, Psychologie et morale, 4.1:81, 87; Châtillon, Théologie, 167–68). Richard of St Victor seems to remain faithful to Hugh's teaching, while Walter of St Victor seems to follow Achard; see, e.g., Richard of St Victor, LE X.11 (Châtillon, 398); Walter of St Victor, Serm. 1.5 (Châtillon, 14); cf. also Anon., Expositio in epist. Pauli on Rom. 5:18 (Peppermüller, 113–14) which also follows Achard. But again all would agree that the afflictions (incommoda) of human beings are twofold: concupiscence and ignorance; e.g., Hugh of St Victor, Sacr. I.7.11–22 (PL 176.291–97); Achard of St Victor, Serm. 1.3 (Châtillon, 30; tr. Feiss, 100); Walter of St Victor, Serm. 18.3 (Châtillon, 151); see also Châtillon, Théologie, 170 n. 67.

[115] Richard of St Victor, LE 1.1.1 (Châtillon, 104); Sermo 70 (PL 177.1119C).

[116] Richard of St Victor, LE 1.1.3 (Châtillon, 105). See also Sermo 70 (PL 177.1120B).

Humanity was despoiled and wounded—despoiled of the good and wounded by evil—, and left half-alive (*semivivus*), since even though the divine similitude, which is in love, can be totally corrupted in human nature, yet the divine image, which is in reason, cannot be totally erased. For, although humanity can be afflicted with wickedness so great that nothing of the good is loved, yet humanity cannot be blinded with ignorance so great that nothing of the truth is known . . . Therefore, it is rightly said that humanity is half-alive, since even though it was corrupted in part by the primordial evils, yet it was not totally blind . . . Therefore, the sword of the enemy did not totally kill humanity, when it could not completely erase the dignity of the natural good in it.[117]

This weakened condition left human beings in a state of internal disarray. Before the Fall the proper ordering of the soul's faculties was perfectly maintained. Man, as Robert argues, consented to God perfectly even in the lower powers of the soul (external man), that is, body and sensual appetite, over which reason ruled freely and directed most easily to all that it willed. The will always followed the judgment of reason, and sensuality always desired only what was necessary for the temporal life. Despite that, Adam exalted himself in disobedience against his superior (God)—a disobedience that mirrors the stooping of the rational soul to the sensual appetite—, and the internal opposition of his lower faculties is felt throughout.[118]

From the moment man defiantly exalted himself against his superior, he felt the contradiction of his inferiors: "because Adam did not want not to sin when he was able, the inability not to sin has been inflicted upon him when he wants not to sin."[119] and, as the Prophet said, *his entire bed was turned into weakness* (Ps. 40:4 [Vulg.]). For the mind

---

117   Richard of St Victor, *Sermo* 70 (PL 177.1120B–1121B).
118   Robert of Melun, *Sent.* I.2.192 (Innsbruck, UB 297, fol. 127rb; *Abbrev.* 607 [London, BL Royal 7.F.XIII, fol. 100rb]): "Cuius rei causa penes deum tota consistebat qui et hominem, dum sibi obediebat, in anima et in corpore contra omnem aduersitatem muniebat eique in suum inferius omnimodam concedebat potestatem, idest in hominem exteriorem, hoc est corpus et sensualitatem quibus ratio ante culpam liberrime imperabat et ad cuncta que uoluit facillime flectebat. Ex quo uero ipse se contra suum superiorem contumaciter extulit, et ipse sui inferioris contradictionem sensit."
119   A dictum that is found in Gilbert of Poitiers, *In epist. ad Rom.* 7:14 (Lisbon, Biblioteca Nacional *Fundo Alcobaça* XCVII/178, fol. 14vb): "Si quis autem querat unde michi huius contractus necessitas, respondeo quia *venundatus* sum in primo parente qui pro cibi uetiti uoluntaria concupiscencia huic concupiscendi necessitati se subdidt. Quia namque continere cum posset noluit, inflictum est ei non posse cum uelit;" see also Peter Lombard, *In epist. ad Romanos* 7:14 (PL 191.1422B).

was covered with the darkness of ignorance and deprived of much of its power that it had over its lower self, because it often fails in its discernment and judgement by accepting something false as true and by rejecting something true as false, by detesting the good as if it were evil, and by commending evil as if it were good. In this way, therefore, the mind of man was turned into weakness because of the first guilt. But his lower self is completely enflamed with the flame of the original kindling. In this life no surge from the gift of any grace happens upon a man to extinguish this flame. It endures and always goads the sensual appetite against reason, as the Apostle said: *the flesh always lusts against the spirit* (Gal. 5:17), and the spirit of lust is always in resistance based on something . . . And thus man always suffers the guilt of his disobedience both in his reason and in his inferior part, that is, the sensual appetite.[120]

In other words, viewed in terms of a disordering of the psychological balance that was enjoyed before the Fall, now the sensual appetite has become inordinate and the will's resistance of it has become difficult. Reason is confronted with a contradiction and rebellion of sensuality and the will. And the will stands on the battleground of two often competing powers: reason and sensuality, the higher and lower parts of the soul, spirit and the flesh. The intensity of this battle is different in different people. In the few sensuality is so subdued that the will is rarely drawn to its consent. In imperfect and very evil people the will consents easily to sensuality.[121]

---

120 Robert of Melun, *Sent.* I.2.192 (Innsbruck, UB 297, fol. 127rb; *Abbrev.* 607 [London, BL Royal 7.F.XIII, fol. 100rb]): "Ex quo uero ipse se contra suum superiorem contumaciter extulit, et ipse sui inferioris contradictionem sensit, et 'quia noluit non peccare cum potuit, inflictum est ei etiam non posse, cum uellet' (see n. 119) et, ut ait Propheta: *stratum eius totum in infirmitatem uersatum est* (Ps. 40:4 [Vulg.]). Nam et mens ipsa caligine ignorantie est obducta et potestate quam in suum inferius habebat ex magna parte priuata, quia in discretione rerum atque iudicio sepe fallitur falsum pro uero recipiendo et uerum pro falso negando et bonum, quasi malum, detestando et malum, quasi bonum sit, commendando. Sic ergo mens hominis pro prima culpa in infirmitatem est uersata. Eius uero inferius flamma fomitis originalis radicitus est incensum. Vnde nulla unda alicuius doni gratie eam in uita presenti contingit in homine extingui. Manet enim semper sensualitatem aduersus rationem instimulans, ut Apostolus ait dicens *caro semper contra spiritum concupiscit* (Gal. 5:17), et spiritus concupiscentie secundum aliquid semper resistit. Sicut idem apostolus alibi ait de spiritu et concupiscentia loquens: *hec sibi aduersantur, ut non quecumque uolumus faciamus* (cf. Gal. 5:17), spiritum et concupiscentiam intelligens quorum consensus per omnia concors in uita presenti esse non potest. Et ita semper luit homo inobedientie sue culpam tam in ipsa ratione quam in eius inferiori, idest sensualitate." See also Hugh of St Victor, *Sent. quest.* 56 (Lottin, 61–62); *Sent. quest.* 57 (Lottin, 63).

121 Robert of Melun, *Sent.* I.2.148 (Innsbruck, UB 297, fol. 121vb; *Abbrev.* 578 [London, BL Royal 7.F.XIII, fol. 99ra]): "Facile autem sensualitati consentitur, postquam homo per culpam

In the spiritual and moral life progress depends on the will. As Robert says in his usual clarity:

> To consent to reason is nothing other than to will what reason judges should be willed or done or not to will what reason judges should not be willed or done. To consent to sensuality is to will what is desired by the sensual appetite, and not to consent to sensuality is not to will that toward which the sensual appetite is drawing.[122]

The "first motion" (*primus motus*) of any sin surges from the sensual appetite enticing the will to something illicit.[123] The duty of reason is

a suo creatore recessit. Vnde lucta nunc est et semper erit inter hominis inferius et eius superius, idest inter rationem et sensualitatem. In quibusdam uero hec pugna maior est, in quibusdam minor. Est enim in quibusdam sensualitas adeo debilitata atque edomita, ut uoluntatem raro in consensum suum trahat uel trahere possit. De quibus Apostolus loquitur dicens: *Iam non est nobis colluctatio* etc. Verum hec perfectio admodum paucorum est, idest solum perfectorum. In aliis uero, idest in imperfectis et penitus malis, sensualitati facile uoluntas consentit." Cf. also William of Champeaux, *Sent.* 253 (Lottin, 206–207).

122 Robert of Melun, *Sent.* I.2.148 (Innsbruck, UB 297, fol. 121ra–b; *Abbrev.* 577 [London, BL Royal 7.F.XIII, fol. 98vb]): "Interius uero attendenti nichil aliud consensus apparebit quam uoluntas quam mediam diximus esse constitutam inter sensualitatem et rationem, neque consentire aliud esse uidebitur quam uelle. Quid enim aliud est rationi consentire quam id uelle quod ratio iudicat esse uolendum uel faciendum, uel id non uelle quod ratio iudicat non esse uolendum uel non faciendum? Quo etiam modo monstrari potest, quid sit sensualitati consentire uel non consentire. Est enim sensualitati consentire id uelle quod affectu sensualitatis appetitur, et ei non consentire est id non uelle ad quod ipsa trahit. Hec ergo considerans inuenio consensum nichil aliud esse quam uoluntatem;" *Sent.* I.2.149 (Innsbruck, UB 297, fol. 121rb): "Consensus est uoluntas qua iudicio rationis obedimus uel appetitui sensualitatis succumbimus."

123 The sensual motion inclining the will toward sin arises from three causes: the kindling from original sin, imbalanced complexion (i.e., mental disorders), and a condemnable habit (*fomes originalis, infirmitas complexionis, consuetudo dampnabilis*). The motion from the kindling of original sin is a mortal sin in the unbaptized regardless whether there is consent or not (*Sent.* I.2.162 [Innsbruck, UB 297, fol. 123ra]). In the baptized Robert seems to regard it as uncontroversial that the first motion is a venial sin even when the will does not consent to it, a common teaching in the twelfth century (*Sent.* I.2.161 [Innsbruck, UB 297, fol. 123ra]: "Qui motus ante consensum ueniale est, sed si ei consentitur, mortale esse dicitur"). However, at least in *Tract.* on Ps. 28 (PL 196.310C) Richard seems to suggest otherwise. Based on an allegory of Noah's Ark containing inside it clean and unclean irrational animals, the human person (i.e., Noah's Ark) has within natural sensual appetites that can be good or bad. A person is judged to be just or unjust only when one consents or does not consent to the desire in accordance with the judgment of reason. See also Richard of St Victor, *Statu* 39 (Ribaillier, 110; tr. Evans, VTT 4.289–90).

In terms of the early-scholastic discussions of his day, Richard is making a distinction between *propassio* and *passio*, which is often discussed in Christological context where questions on Christ's psychological weaknesses are discussed; e.g., Peter Lombard, *Sent.* 3.15.2.1–2 (SB 5:98–99); Alan of Lille, *Regulae* 105 (Häring, 210); Simon of Tournai, *Institutiones in sacram paginam* VII.43 (Burgo de Osma, Biblioteca de la Catedral de Osma, cod. 147, fol. 37va; London, BL Royal 9.E.XII, fol. 33ra; Oxford, Merton College 132, fol. 141va; Paris, only to judge the motion unfitting for consent.[124] Faced with competing motions the locus of all merit and demerit lies in the will. Its consent to the illicit motion of sensuality only brings guilt and punishment, but its consent to reason is never sinful and in matters pertaining to human salvation such a consent is the basis for human merit and reward.[125] Of course the power actually to accomplish this must be attributed first to the working of the Spirit.

GRACE AND THE SPIRIT

The absolute necessity and priority of divine grace in the spiritual life is one of the more obvious teachings of twelfth-century theologians. Quite simply, Robert states, "a person merits nothing that he does not merit through a free choice that grace precedes and follows."[126] And,

Arsenal 519, fol. 47va; Paris, BnF lat. 14886, fol. 45va): "Infirmitas duplex est. Vna mouens illecebras, ut uoluptatem; alia mouens angustias, ut dolorem. Vtriusque autem est duplex effectus. Primus dicitur propassio, secundus passio. Est autem propassio cum in homine ex infirmitate mouetur uoluptas uel angustia citra turbationem rationis. Et dicitur propassio, idest protopassio, idest prima-passio. Passio uero est cum in homine ex infirmitate mouetur uoluptas uel angustia turbans rationem. Tunc enim efficaciter homo dicitur 'pati', quando turbatur eius ratio." For an overview of the first motion in the twelfth century, see Lottin, *Psychologie et morale*, 6:493–520; Knuuttila, *Emotions in the Ancient and Medieval Philosophy*, 178–88.

[124] Robert is quite emphatic and devotes a number of chapters to the fact that in a sinful act reason does nothing culpable (*Sent.* I.2.129–38 [Innsbruck, UB 297, fols. 118ra–119vb]). In other words, the basis for merit and demerit is in the will. See also Achard of St Victor, *Serm.* 1.3 (Châtillon 30; tr. Feiss, 101). "Reason never sins, but the will does. In the will lies all merit, whether good or evil. If reason is sometimes said to sin, it is to be understood that a person sins knowingly." See also n. 152. To account for why the authorities sometimes attribute good and evil to reason, Robert explains that a building is usually attributed to an architect even though the workers construct it (*Sent.* I.2.132 [Innsbruck, UB 297, fol. 118vb]). The same argument finds its way into Prepositinus' famous *Summa* at the end of the twelfth century (Einsiedeln, Stiftsbibliothek 230, p. 80–81; London, BL Royal 9.E.XI, fol. 156vb–157ra; Paris, BnF lat. 14526, fol. 22ra–b; Vienna, ONB 1501, fol. 30rb–va).

[125] Robert of Melun, *Sent.* I.2.148 (Innsbruck, UB 297, fol. 121rb–vb; *Abbrev.* 578 [London, BL Royal 7.F.XIII, fols. 98vb–99ra]): "Quod fieri non potest, idest quod rationi consentiamus in his que ad salutem sunt et meritum habent, absque gratia Dei qua consensus preuenitur et per quam subsequentem remunerabilis efficitur. Quando uero sensualitati consentimus in illicitis motibus eius, culpam tantum habet sensualitas et penam. Tunc enim a gratia recedit ab ipsaque deseritur. Et iccirco in culpam dampnabilem uel uenialem labitur." See also *Sent.* I.2.151 (Innsbruck, UB 297, fol. 121va): "Est autem, ut dictum est, consensus per quem iudicio rationis obtemperamus. Quod cum fit, nunquam peccamus, licet non semper mereamur. Iudicium enim rationis non solum in his est que meritum habent, verum etiam in multis que et sine culpa et sine merito fieri possunt."

[126] Robert of Melun, *Sent.* I.2.127 (Innsbruck, UB 297, fol. 117vb): "Nichil namque meretur

according to Richard who reiterates a common theme that grace provides the ability (*posse*) lost in the Fall, "with the help of God human free choice begins to have power to do what it cannot do on its own; and the capacity for good that it now lacks by nature it receives through grace."[127] Achard also repeats the traditional teaching that Christ's grace actually makes a soul righteous and that this is a work "in us, not without us" (*in nobis non sine nobis*).[128] In other words, grace that arises as God's gift is a kind of first movement toward the good,[129] just as the kindling of sin that arises in the sensual appetite is the first movement toward sin. The terminology for the different kinds of graces varies in the twelfth century, but two kinds were typically seen as means to avoid two ancient heresies: Manicheanism that denied human merit in salvation and Pelagianism that denied divine grace in human salvation.[130] Operative or prevenient grace (*gratia operans vel*

homo quod per liberum arbitrium non mereatur, gratia ipsum precedente vel sequente;" see also *Sent.* I.2.145 (Innsbruck, UB 297, fol. 120vb; *Abbrev.* 575 [London, BL Royal 7.F.XIII, fol. 98vb]): "Nullus uero Pelagiano errori hoc consentire estimet quod nunc de uoluntate naturali ipsius mentis humane dictum est. Ille enim de uoluntate locutus est, qua mentitur hominem gratiam absque gratia mereri et sine gratia dignus gratia effici. Ista uero de qua nunc agimus nichil homo meretur, nisi et ipsa gratia adiuuetur. Nulla quippe ratio est, quare tali uoluntate homo aliquid mereatur. Nam non magis ei naturale est cibum et potum appetere quam uoluntate de qua nunc agimus bonum uelle. Vnde sicut nichil meretur homo cibum et potum naturaliter appetendo, ita nichil meretur ista uoluntate qua naturaliter bonum affectat."

127 Richard of St Victor, *Statu* 16 (Ribaillier, 80; tr. Evans, VTT 4.265); see Dumeige, *Richard de Saint-Victor*, 65.

128 Achard of St Victor, *Serm.* 3.1 (Châtillon, 44; tr. Feiss, 122); cf. Augustine, *Jo. ev. tr.* 72.2 (Willems, 508). Achard summarizes his teaching on grace in *Serm.* 11.3 (Châtillon, 44; tr. Feiss, 89–90) and 3.1 (Châtillon, 44; tr. Feiss, 112–13). See discussion in Châtillon, *Théologie*, 230–32.

129 Cf. *Summa sent.* III.17 (Douai, BM 363, fol. 34va–b; Douai, BM 364, fol. 33va–b; Klosterneuburg, Stiftsbibliothek 312, fol. 49r; PL 176.114D): "Inter dona autem et uirtutes hec est differentia quod dona sunt primi motus in corde, quasi quedam semina uirtutum iacta super terram cordis nostri; uirtutes quasi seges que ex ipsis consurgunt. Sunt enim effectus donorum et quidam habitus boni iam confirmati. Et dicuntur septem dona, septem spiritus. Vnde in Apocalipsi: Vidit Ioannes septem spiritus discurrentes ante thronum Dei (Rev. 1:4). Spiritus dicuntur aspirationes que precedunt uirtutes; et sunt dona solummodo et non merita. Virtutes sunt et dona et merita. In illis operatur Deus sine nobis; in istis operatur nobiscum;" Robert of Melun, *Sent.* I.2.164 (Innsbruck, UB 297, fol. 125vb): "Motus uero illi, qui mentem ad bonum mouent, quidam ex naturali affectu procedunt, quidam ex interna gratie inspiratione absque adhibitione cause extrinsece, quidam uero per ministerium predicationis uel exempli ammonitione innascuntur, diuina tamen gratia hoc totum inspirante." See also Richard of St Victor, *Arca Moys.* II.21 (Aris, 48.12–13; tr. Zinn, 209).

130 Anon., *Quaestiones in epist. Pauli* q. 113 on Rom. (PL 175.460A–B); Anon., *Expositio in epist. Pauli* on Rom. 4:8 (Peppermüller, 92); Peter Lombard, *Sent.* II.26 (SB 4:470–80). See A. Landgraf, *Dogmengeschichte der frühscholastik* I/1 (Regensburg: Friedrich Pustet, 1952), 119–36.

preveniens), as Achard calls it, works before the will in order to heal it. After the will is healed, cooperative or subsequent grace (*gratia subsequens vel cooperans*) works with the will to love and accomplish good works. In other words, this operation can either precede the deliberation of the will or cooperate with it, the results of which are union with Christ, an ordered or good will and good works.[131] As Hugh succinctly states:

> The Holy Spirit first works a good will in these virtues, which arise through the restorative grace; then He cooperates with the good will that is moving itself and working. The Holy Spirit first inspires a good will so that it may exist, and he then inspires it so that it may move and work lest it be idle. The Holy Spirit first works it, then He works through it.[132]

Or according to Richard:

> God requires voluntary consent in the work of our justification . . . It is clear then that this work, in which God cooperates with his creatures, is accomplished by two. In this work there is a need for one's own effort and divine grace . . . Our justification is accomplished by our own deliberation and divine inspiration.[133]

Whenever divine grace is treated in relation to the higher cognitive and affective faculties, its psychological impact is very often considered as the divine operations of illumination of the mind and inspiration of the will. According to Hugh,

> They are called people of the natural law who walk according to the concupiscence in which they were born . . . People of grace are those

---

[131] E.g., Hugh of St Victor, *Archa Noe* Prol. (Sicard, 3–4); Achard of St Victor, *Sermo* 5.4 (Châtillon, 72); Richard of St Victor, *LE* II.12.2 (Châtillon, 461–2); *Arca Moys.* II.21 (Aris, 48; tr. Zinn, 209); *Arca Moys.* III.16 (Aris, 74; tr. Zinn, 244); *Arca Moys.* III.24 (Aris, 83–4; tr. Zinn, 256).

[132] Hugh of St Victor, *Sacr.* I.6.17 (Cambridge, Trinity College West 363, fol. 44va; Cambridge, Trinity College West 1478, fol. 46r; Douai, BM 361, fol. 35ra; Douai, BM 362/I, fol. 55va–b; New Haven, Library T. E. Marston 248, fol. 29va; Berndt, 150; PL 176.274B; tr. Deferrari, 105): "Sed in his uirtutibus que per gratiam reparatricem sunt primum Spiritus sanctus bonam uoluntatem operatur; deinde bone uoluntati mouenti se et operanti cooperatur. Primum bonam uoluntatem aspirat ut sit, deinde bone uoluntati inspirat ut moueatur et operetur ut uacua non sit. Primum operatur eam, deinde operatur per eam." See also *Misc.* I.164 (PL 177.559D); and Anon. *Summa sent.* III.7 (PL 176.99D).

[133] Richard of St Victor, *Arca Moys.* III.16 (Aris, 74). See also Hugh of St Victor, *Misc.* II.77 (PL 177.631A); Richard of St Victor, *Arca Moys.* III.24 (Aris, 83–4; tr. Zinn, 256); see also *Misc.* IV.107 (PL 177.742C).

who, having been inspired through the inspiration of the Holy Spirit, are illuminated to know the good that must be done and inflamed to love and strengthened toward perfection.[134]

And very often these divine operations are depicted as unpredictable, spiritual visitations:

> Christ comes to souls often and in many different ways. He comes through the contemplation of creatures; he comes through the reading of Scripture, he comes through the working of miracles, he comes through the preaching of his precepts; he comes through internal inspiration. He comes through adversity; he comes through prosperity. He comes with the threat of evils; he comes with the promise of goods. Christ comes to the soul spiritually by visiting it. He is made its guest by justifying it. Sometimes he passes by the soul by removing grace. Sometimes he removes grace partly so that the mind may be made humble which thinks too highly of itself. But Christ returns again when he infuses it again.[135]

Divine illumination occurs whenever the Spirit is present to the rational soul in such a way that it aids both the perception of spiritual truths and the discernment of the good. Not surprisingly then such illumination in the higher cognitive faculty is often likened to the sun, light, and physical sight, and contemplation or eyes of contemplation as a highest kind of spiritual vision. What is perceived here is what Richard calls intellectible truths, that is, invisible things that reason cannot understood without grace, as opposed to sensible truths perceived by the senses or intelligible truths perceived by reason. After such truths are illumined, reason can then affirm and the authority of divine Scripture sanction the intellectible truth infused into the soul.[136] Even discernment of moral truths requires the Spirit's illumination. What Hugh calls the "precept of nature" (*praeceptum naturae*) is the

---

134 Hugh of St Victor, *Sac. dial.* (Berlin, Staatsbibliothek Preussischer Kulturbesitz Lat. 744, fol. 91ra; Florence, BML S. Marco 476, fol. 5rb–va; Grenoble, BM 390, fol. 92ra; Laon, BM 463, fol. 83r; Paris, BnF lat. 14303, fol. 167rb–va; PL 176.32B): "Similiter tria sunt genera hominum, idest homines naturalis legis, homines scripte legis, homines gratie. Homines naturalis legis dici possunt qui sola naturali ratione uitam suam dirigunt, uel potius homines naturalis legis dicuntur qui secundum concupiscentiam in qua nati sunt ambulant. Homines scripte legis sunt hi qui exterioribus preceptis ad bene uiuendum informantur. Homines gratie sunt hi qui per aspirationem Spiritus sancti afflati et illuminantur ut bonum quod faciendum est agnoscant et inflammantur ut diligant et corroborantur ut perficiant."

135 Richard of St Victor, *Serm. cent.* 90 (PL 177.1182A). See also *LE* II.7.23 (Châtillon, 330–31).

136 Richard of St Victor, *Arca Moys.* I.7 (Aris, 14; tr. Zinn, 165); see also *XII patr.* 81 (Châtillon, 326, 328; tr. Zinn, 138–39).

natural moral law inspired into the soul at original creation.[137] Robert regards this as an indelible "natural affect by which the rational mind always desires and strives toward the good,"[138] or what is commonly called sinderesis especially after 1170.[139] Despite this natural inclination, the judgment and discernment of reason has still sustained moral blindness as a result of the Fall and hence needs the Spirit's illumination.[140]

Divine inspiration is the salvific operation of the Spirit in the higher affective faculty of the soul (i.e., the will) that usually entails the infusion and arousal of love or the desire for good. What God specifically inspires or infuses into the soul varies depending on the context. Sometimes the soul is infused with the seven gifts of the Spirit in order to heal the seven wounds (cf. Isa. 11:2–3), thus empowering it for virtue.[141] Sometimes the soul is infused with a steady peace to counter the great vicissitude in the human heart.[142] Sometimes divine inspiration pours into the soul an unaccustomed sweet joy, in comparison to which the bitterness of its sinful condition is very apparent.[143] And sometimes compunction and consolation are inspired.[144] However, the infusion of love is the common descriptor of volitional inspiration (cf. Rom. 5:5).[145] According to one source, "the grace of God is defined as 'God giving

---

[137] Hugh of St Victor, *Sacr.* I.6.7 (Berndt, 143; PL 176.268C; tr. Deferrari, 99); *Sacr.* I.6.28 (Berndt, 160; PL 176.281B; tr. Deferrari, 114); cf. also *Sacr.* I.4.25 (Berndt, 110–11; PL 176.245C; tr. Deferrari, 73); Anon., *Summa sent.* III.4 (PL 176.95D).

[138] Robert of Melun, *Sent.* I.2.143 (Innsbruck, UB 297, fol. 120rb-va; *Abbrev.* 574 [London, BL Royal 7.F.XIII, fol. 98vb]): ". . . naturali affectu quo mens rationalis semper appetit bonum et ad illud bonum tendit cuius in se imaginem gerit."

[139] See, e.g., Alexander Neckam (d. 1217), *Speculum speculationum* IV.13 (Thomson, 405), where he cites Robert's definition without attribution. For a study of synderesis in the twelfth century, see Lottin, *Psychologie et morale*, 2:103–22.

[140] See Richard of St Victor, *Statu* 28, 30, 31 (Ribaillier, 95–96, 97–98; tr. Evans, VTT 4.276–77, 278–80).

[141] E.g., Hugh of St Victor, *Septem donis* 2.3 (Baron, 124, 126; tr. Benson, VTT 4.376); Richard of St Victor, *Tract.* on Ps. 134 (PL 196.368D; tr. Evans, VTT 4.206); *LE* II.7.24 (Châtillon, 332); *Erud.* I.27 (PL 196.1276B–C). See also Anon., *Summa sent.* 3.17 (PL 176.114D).

[142] E.g. Hugh of St Victor, *Archa Noe* Prol. (Sicard, 3–4); Richard of St Victor, *Diff. Sac.* (PL 196.1054C); see also *Misc.* III.50 (PL 177.669A–B).

[143] E.g. Hugh of St Victor, *Archa Noe* 3.3 (Sicard, 57); *Archa Noe* III.6 (Sicard, 67); *Misc.* II.5 (PL 177.590C).

[144] E.g. Richard of St Victor, *Erud.* I.22 (PL 196.1268D); *Erud.* II.25 (PL 197.1325B); Hugh of St Victor, *Misc.* I.109 (PL 177.538D); *Misc.* I.147 (PL 177.553B); cf. also *Misc.* IV.6 (PL 177.705B); *Misc.* IV.28 (PL 177.711A).

[145] E.g. Hugh of St Victor, *Libellus* 5 (Sicard, 134–5); *Sacr.* I.8.11 (Berndt, 203; PL 176.313A; tr. Deferrari, 149); *Misc.* II.36 (PL 177.607A); Richard of St Victor, *Trin.* VI.14 (Ribaillier, 245–6; tr. Evans, VTT 1.334); *Sp. blasph.* (Ribaillier, 123); *Erud.* I.34 (PL 196.1289B); *Erud.* II.9 (PL 196.1309A); *XII patr.* 3, 4 (Châtillon, 96, 98, 100); *XII patr.* 29 (Châtillon, 170); *Diff. sac.* (PL 196.1058B); *Tract.* on Ps. 121 (PL 196.364D; tr. Evans, VTT 4.198).

freely' (*Deus gratis dans*) the grace—that is, divine inspiration or operation of God—by means of which the mind is moved to love God and neighbor."[146] And, based on John 20:22, this infusion of love is the reception and participation with the Holy Spirit, who is given by the Father and Son. Richard explains:

> What is the gift or infusion of the Holy Spirit, except the infusion of an owed love? Therefore, the Holy Spirit is divinely given to humans at the moment when the owed love of deity is inspired into a human mind. For when the Holy Spirit enters the rational mind, he ignites its affection with the divine flame and transforms it to the similitude of his property, so that it may present to its Author the love which it owes . . . For, in consequence of the infusion of such a fire, the human mind gradually removes all blackness, coldness, and hardness; and the whole mind changes into the similitude of him who inflames it. The whole mind becomes white-hot from the igniting of the divine fire; it flares up and, at the same time, liquefies in the love of God (cf. Rom. 5:5) . . . Thus we are certainly conformed to the property of the Holy Spirit to the same extent that we return an owed love to our Creator. In fact, the Holy Spirit was given to humans and inspired in them for this reason: that they may be conformed to him insofar as it is possible for them. This gift is sent, or this mission is given, at the same time and in the same way both from the Father and from the Son.[147]

CONCLUSION

The Victorine spiritual journey is, as Fr. Sicard notes, one of integration and deepening. It is an ascent of continuity.[148] The spiritual progresses depicted as ascents are symbolic expressions not intended to be understood linearly as if one must leave behind the lower stage for a higher one. On the contrary, with regard to the cognitive ascent, Hugh says that

> just as a spiritual person sees the things that are in God through the eye of contemplation, so, after having been illumined in contemplation, he sees the things that are in the mind through the eye of reason, and he also sees the things that are in the world through all things and in

---

[146] Anon., *Quest. ad Cor. II* 3 (PL 175.514A–B).
[147] Richard of St Victor, *Trin.* VI.14 (Ribaillier, 245–6; tr. Evans, VTT 1.334): see also *Trin.* VI.10 (Ribaillier, 239; tr. Evans, VTT 1.328).
[148] Cf. Sicard, *Hugues de Saint-Victor*, 201–202.

all things. Therefore, a spiritual person, who sees all things, can judge all things, because nothing is removed from his judgment, and nothing is hidden from his knowledge.[149]

Hugh hardly regards contemplation as making reason and sensual perception irrelevant. The same can be argued about the necessary relationship between knowledge and love in the spiritual ascent.[150] Someone like Robert of Melun, for example, is particularly keen on avoiding any kind of confusion between the cognitive and affective activities in his moral and spiritual theology, but this psychological compartmentalizing should not be regarded as an exclusion. Robert argues, for example, that in this life the discerning power of reason is not greater than the power of the will.[151] Their proper ordering and cooperation with grace are necessary for the spiritual journey. Richard is most emphatic on this point when, commenting on reason and will symbolized as Adam and Eve,[152] he teaches:

---

[149] Hugh of St Victor, *Misc.* I.1, cited in n. 80.

[150] Endre von Ivánka finds in Richard's spirituality a continuous ascent of the cognitive and affective powers, as opposed to Thomas Gallus in the early thirteenth century who places a radical division between the two powers and sees a break of the *principalis affectio* with the cognitive powers, a division that so characterizes mysticism in the late Middle Ages. Von Ivánka also argues that this division was first introduced by Isaac of Stella, a thesis that Bernard McGinn rejects. See, Von Ivánka, "Zur Überwindung des neuplatonischen Intellektualismus in der Deutung der Mystik: intelligentia oder principalis affectio," *Scholastik* 30 (1955): 186–87, 192; McGinn, *The Golden Chain*, 150–52.

[151] E.g., Robert of Melun, *Sent.* II.2.144 (Innsbruck, UB 297, fol. 120va–b; *Abbrev.* 575 [London, BL Royal 7.F.XIII, fol. 98vb]): "QVOD NON MAGIS RATIONIS EST BONVM A MALO DISCERNERE QVAM NATVRALIS VOLVNTATIS BONVM APPETERE. Nec mirum quia non magis potentia discernendi de substantia anime est quam potentia uolendi. Et ideo sicut naturale anime est bonum a malo discernere, ita et ei naturale est bonum uelle atque ad id naturaliter tendere. Quod et semper facit, si inde fructum meriti nullum habet, quia et hoc, ut superius dictum est, in quantocumque crimine sit agit, idest naturaliter bonum vult et naturaliter amat."

[152] The stages of sin are often depicted in a popular allegory of the serpent, Eve, and Adam who symbolize the sensual appetite, the will, and reason. Thus the serpent suggests, the will eats and gives the forbidden fruit to reason that also eats (e.g., see Peter the Chanter, *Distinctiones Abel* cited above in n. 105). Robert objects to this allegory, because it seems to relate judgment to the will and consent to reason, neither of which is the proper duty (*officia*) of these faculties or parts of free choice. See also Achard, *Serm.* 13 (Châtillon, 143; tr. Feiss, VTT 4.95–96); Richard of St Victor, *Tract.* on Ps. 121 (PL 196.363A–364A; tr. Evans, VTT 4.196). Robert of Melun, *Sent.* I.2.129 (Innsbruck, UB 297, fol. 117vb; *Abbrev.* 564 [London, BL Royal 7.F.XIII, fol. 98ra]): "Vnde non parum admiror quare rationi consensus bonus uel malus attribuatur. Hoc nempe uoluntatis est, idest consentire. Magna ergo fit confusio in partibus liberi arbitrii, quia id, quod uoluntatis est tantum, rationi ascribitur, idest consensus. Nam cum sint hec tria in anima humana (idest sensualitas, uoluntas et ratio), sensualitas suggerit, uoluntas mouet, ratio discernit. Hec sunt tria que in peccato primo sunt designata: serpens suggerit per que sensualitas est figurata, mulier comedit per quam uoluntas est designata, uiro dedit qui et comedit per quem ratio est intelligenda. Voluntas

Brother, you must pay careful attention to this and especially commit it to memory: it is not very praiseworthy for Adam to want to enter [into the house of the Lord] without Eve, and it is absolutely impossible for Eve to be able to enter without Adam. What profit is it to know eternal things and not to love eternal things? But if you do not first know eternal things, then you absolutely do not love them. To have only eternal things before one's eyes, to cling only to eternal things is for Adam and Eve to be together in some way within the house of God.[153]

However, in terms of sequence reason comes before the will. In the same allegory cited above Richard also argues that "Adam was created first, and Eve was created later from Adam ... Therefore, let the knowledge of truth come first and let the love of justice follow."[154] But in terms of acquisition and effect the will is often highlighted in Victorine reflections on the spiritual life. This intense focus on love is after all in keeping with a rich spiritual tradition captured by an Augustinian dictum that circulated in the earliest gloss traditions of the twelfth century: "Because love alone moves the feet, he who loves more ascends more."[155] Robert highlights the urgency of love when he argues that "the power of love is not as easily realized (*efficax*) in a rational creature as the power of knowledge is," that is, the love of God does not come as naturally for a human being and hence has a greater need for grace.[156] Though more

---

ergo sensualitati suggerenti consensit; ratio, ut dicunt, uoluntati obedit. Quod quare dicatur non uideo, cum nec ad rationem pertineat consensus nec ad uoluntatem iudicium. Sicut ergo non recte officia parcium liberi arbitrii distingueret qui uoluntati iudicium assignaret et rationi uelle, ita nec recte rationis officium discernunt qui ei consensum ascribunt."

[153] Richard of St Victor, *Tract.* on Ps. 121 (PL 196.366C–D; tr. Evans, VTT 4.200). See also Hugh of St Victor, *Sent. quest.* 55 (Lottin, 60–61), where love and intellect together constitute contemplation in the third heaven.

[154] Richard of St Victor, *Tract.* on Ps. 121 (PL 196.363B; tr. Evans, VTT 4.196); see also *Tract.* on. 134 (PL 196.368b; tr. Evans, VTT 4.206): "But we know that all affection arises from cognition, since the mind is never affected by something, unless the object itself is first perceived through cognition."

[155] Gilbert of Poitiers, *Com. in Ps.* 83 (Valenciennes, BM 44, fol. 148vb; Vorau, Stiftsbibliothek 261, fol. 211r; Cf. Augustine, *En. Ps.* 119.1–2 [CCL 40.1776–78]; *En. Ps.* 120.5 [CCL 40.1789]): "In quibus tamen, quia sola caritas mouet pedem, qui plus diligit plus ascendit." See n. 33 above for full citation.

[156] Robert of Melun, *Sent.* I.2.182 (Innsbruck, UB 297, fol. 125vb; *Abbrev.* 602 [London, BL Royal 7.F.XIII, fol. 100ra]): "Non enim potestas diligendi ita efficax in creatura rationali est sicut potestas cognoscendi. Cuius rei argumentum non aliunde sumere oportet quam ex nobis ipsis. Nam pauci sunt adulte etatis et sane mentis qui cognitionem Creatoris aliquam non habeant, licet perrari sint qui Creatoris dilectionem habeant. Si enim ita naturale anime esset atque substantiale diligere, sicuti cognoscere est, sicut semper Deum cognoscit, ita semper Deum diligeret. Quod quia non fit, patet quia non est ita naturale atque substantiale

difficult, there is also greater merit in the affective spiritual life,[157] but also greater risk: the affective connection is stickier, that is, as Hugh argues, bodily delights are like the adherence of skin that is peeled off only with pain.[158] All of these sentiments are sometimes expresses by the perceived juxtaposition of the "very many" who know God and the "very few" of them in their day who actually love God.[159] Thus if Victorine spirituality is intensely affective in orientation, this in part is because this is what they perceived as the greatest need of their day. And perhaps Victorine reflections on this matter within the regular canonical life of the twelfth century is equally relevant for our day as well.

Deum diligere sicuti cognoscere." The question here is whether Adam before the Fall needed divine grace to love and know God. Robert position is that Adam's natural cognitive powers were sufficient to know God to some extent, or, as Robert states it: "from the very nature of his creation man had the power to know whatever was necessary to know for salvation" ("Ex ipsa enim natura creationis sue potens erat cognoscere quicquid ei ad salutem scire fuit necessarium" [*Sent.* I.2.181 (Innsbruck, UB 297, fol. 125vb)]). However, Adam's natural affective powers were insufficient and needed grace. Of course, after the Fall neither natural faculty is sufficient without grace, though the cognitive ascent is still much easier than the affective ascent.

[157] E.g., Hugh of St Victor, *Sacr.* I.10.4 [Berndt, 229; PL 176.332C; tr. Deferrari, 170): "the affective power in faith is more praiseworthy than the cognitive power" ("affectum magnum in fide magis laudabilem esse quam cognitionem magnam"); Robert of Melun, *Sent.* I.2.184 (Innsbruck, UB 297, fol. 126ra): ". . . in a [rational creature] love is to be rewarded more than knowledge" ("dilectio in ea magis esset remuneranda quam cognitio").

[158] Hugh of St Victor, *Unione* (Piazzoni, 887.124–37).

[159] Richard of St Victor shares this perception in his very interesting *Tract.* on Hosea 9:14 (tr. Evans, VTT 4.227); see also Robert of Melun, *Sent.* I.2.182, cited in n. 156.

ACHARD OF ST VICTOR

SERMON 13: ON THE DEDICATION OF A CHURCH

INTRODUCTION AND TRANSLATION
BY HUGH FEISS OSB

INTRODUCTION

Fr. Jean Châtillon, whose edition[1] and study[2] of Achard's sermons brought them to the attention of modern scholars, judged this discourse given on the Feast of the Dedication of a Church to be the most interesting of Achard's fifteen surviving sermons. Châtillon concluded that it was most likely composed for the Feast of the Dedication of the Abbey Church at St Victor in Paris (June 5) and delivered to the abbots of the Order of St Victor, assembled for a general chapter.[3] The sermon speaks of a triple dwelling that Christ builds in the Christian. These three nested dwellings are a participation in three divine attributes, and so Achard is led to discuss participation, Trinitarian appropriations, and the form that sharing in Christ's grace impresses on the soul of Christians. On this theological basis, Achard unfolds the stages or components of the building of the house of God by Christ in the souls of Christians and the responsibilities of abbots to foster the process.

OUTLINE OF THE SERMON

I. Introduction (1–5)

(A) On earth, building rather than dedication (1).
(B) Christ's power, wisdom and anointing; capability, know-how and will to build a house for himself and for human beings (2).
(C) Trinitarian appropriations: power/love (*virtus*), wisdom/contemplation, anointing/delight = way, truth, and life (3).
(D) Seven columns hewn by virtue, wisdom, and anointing are participations (4).

[1] Achard of St Victor, *Sermons inédits*, ed. J. Châtillon, TPMA 17 (Paris: J. Vrin, 1970).
[2] J. Châtillon, *Théologie, spiritualité et métaphysique dans l'œuvre oratoire d'Achard de Saint-Victor*, Études de philosophie médiévale 58 (Paris: Vrin, 1969).
[3] Châtillon, *Sermons*, 36, 131. The Order of Saint Victor and its general chapters have not been studied much. For some information see F. Bonnard, *Histoire de l'abbaye royale et de l'ordre des chanoines réguliers de St-Victor de Paris. Première période (1113–1500)* (Paris: Arthur Savaète, 1904), 141–89; H. Feiss, "The Ordo of St. Victor in Ireland," *Ordo Canonicus*, series altera, 4 (Neustift: Studium Vitae Canonicae, 1988), 56–87.

(E) Purposes of columns: solidity, illumination, beauty. Power, wisdom and anointing are formally distinct, causally one; three and one. House of grace built in human beings, but not without them (5).

II. Builders (6–9)

(A) Consider who, of what, and how. Who: Solomon the peacemaker; Christ the peacemaker between heaven and earth; prelates as peacemakers (6).
(B) Peace with God and neighbor (7).
(C) Peace within oneself among reason, will and flesh (8–9).

III. Materials and Manner and Building (10–33)

Introduction (10)
(A) Stone House (power/virtue)
    (1) White and black
        (a) Squared stones from Lebanon (whitening) for building (11).
        (b) Christ is white in three ways: whiteness by divinity, white in his mind, whitened in his risen flesh (12).
        (c) Two blacknesses (13).
    (2) Grace
        (a) In Christ the head, participated in by his members (14).
        (b) Justification: Christ's justice is the form, human being the matter; kindness (*pietas*) is God's motive (15).
        (c) God's kindness is God; God's kindness to us, forming the deformed (16).
    (3) Stones' fourfold form (17)
        (a) Cardinal virtues (18).
        (b) Four beatitudes (19).
        (c) Meek and humble; an easy yoke, a light burden (20).
        (d) Fourfold love of God and neighbor (21).
        (e) Love of God and love of self (22).
        (f) Bound by worldly prospects, pleasures of the flesh, stubbornness of mind, affection for others (23).
    (4) Axe and hammer (faith and reason) are needed to form square stones (24).
        (a) Tools used in chapter meeting by abbey officials (25).
        (b) Used by abbots on themselves as well as on others (26).
        (c) Subjects use axe and hammer on themselves and in limited way on others (27).

(d) Hammer and axe fall silent when liberty of spirit is obtained. Six arms of love and root of charity = seven columns of virtue/power (28).

(B) Cedar House (anointing, delight, life)
    (1) Love of the good (justice, cleanness) in itself, rather than as one receives or has it (29–30).
    (2) Seven Joys (31).

(C) Golden House (wisdom, contemplation; truth)
    (1) Seven contemplations and participations (32).
    (2) From delight (Holy Spirit) to contemplation (Christ) and back (33).

IV. Summary and Conclusion—Stone: discipline, virtue, love, way; cedar: goodness, joy of anointing, delight in life; golden: knowledge, light of wisdom, contemplation of truth. Work of the Trinity. The work of Christ's flesh, spirit, and divinity in building House of God in human beings. Concluding prayer to Christ (34).

Occasion and Literary Form

The Dedication of the House of God

According to Châtillon, at St Victor the only feast of the dedication of a church was held on June 5 to commemorate the dedication of the church of St Victor.[4] Two sermons of Achard on the feast or its octave survive. Here our concern is with Sermon 13. The other, Sermon 2, is much shorter.[5] In it Achard speaks of Christ, the Son of Justice, in whose gifts the just participate. In them Christ dwells through knowledge and love. Here below Christ dwells in a tent, because the Christian sometime advances, sometimes goes back. In heaven God will erect a permanent dwelling, a temple, and give the blessed the fullness of knowledge and love along with bodily immortality.[6]

Hugh of St Victor devotes chapter four of the second book of his On the Sacraments to the "sacrament" of the dedication of a church.[7]

---

4   Châtillon, Sermons, 36 n. 2.

5   Châtillon, Sermons, 37–41; tr. Feiss, 147–54.

6   These are the three goods (bona) that God gave to the first human beings. Christ came to remedy the damage caused them by sin. See, e.g., Hugh of St Victor, Didasc. VI.14 (Buttimer, 130.17–23; tr. Harkins, VTT 3.178–79); Richard of St Victor, LE I.1.1–4 (Châtillon, 104–105; tr. Feiss, VTT 3.299–301).

7   Hugh of St Victor, Sacr. II.5.1–3 (PL 176.439–442C). This chapter is preceded by treatments

His treatment falls into three chapters. In the introductory chapter, Hugh explains that he put the dedication of the church before baptism and the other sacraments, since the rest of the sacraments are cele-brated in the church. The church is baptized first; then the faithful are baptized within it and become members of Christ through the grace of a new birth. What is expressed visibly in this house of prayer is ex-pressed through invisible truth in the faithful soul. The virtues form a structure of spiritual stones: faith is the foundation, hope is the walls, and charity is its final completion. Hence, Hugh's second chapter con-cerns the things visibly done in the dedication by the bishop, and his third chapter concerns the mystery contained in them, because "the house to be dedicated is the soul to be sanctified."[8] For example, Christ is the altar upon which we make the offering of our devotion to the Father. The bishop goes around the altar and sprinkles the whole church with holy water, as though "extending his care to all and pre-senting himself to all in common by word and example."[9]

The notion of the house of God is pervasive in the Bible, and the texts that refer to it were used in the liturgy for the feast of a dedication of a church. In the Old Testament the "house of God" is preeminently the temple, less often Jerusalem or Palestine, where the temple was located, and once the universe.[10] God dwells with his people.[11] In the New Testament Jesus refers to the temple as his Father's house,[12] yet God does not dwell in a house made by man.[13] Both the Christian com-

---

of Christ, the Church, the orders of clergy, and sacred vestments. It is followed by treat-ments of Baptism, Confirmation, Eucharist, and so forth. It was only shortly after the time of Hugh's death, in the mid-twelfth century, that the number of sacraments became fixed at seven.

[8]   Hugh of St Victor, *Sacr.* II.5.3 (PL 176.441A): "Domus dedicanda, anima sanctificanda est."

[9]   "Circuit pontifex altare, et ecclesiam totam aspergendo, quasi omnes lustrando et curam im-ponendo omnibus verbo et exemplo communem se praebens universis" (442B). On Hugh's treatment of the Dedication of a Church see H. Neuheuser, "Domus dedicanda, anima sanctificanda. Rezeption des Ivo von Chartres und Neuprägung der hochmittelalterliches Kirchweihtheologie durch Hugo von St. Viktor," *Ecclesia Orans* 18 (2001), 373–96; 19 (2002), 7–44. A. Meyer, *Medieval Allegory and the Building of the New Jerusalem* (Rochester, NY: D. S. Brewer, 2003), 91–94 treats briefly of the dedication liturgy in Richard of St Victor, *Serm. cent.* 3 and in the *Speculum ecclesiae*.

[10]   For this paragraph, see J. Gaillard, "*Domus Dei,*" *DS* 3 (1957), 1551–67. For God's throne as Palestine, see Hos. 8:1; 9:8.15; Jer. 12:7; Zach. 9:8; as the universe, see Bar. 3:24.

[11]   Gen. 28:16–22; Isa. 57:1; 66:1–2.

[12]   Matt. 21:13; Mark 11:17; Luke 19:46, citing Jer. 7:11 and Isa. 56:7.

[13]   Acts 7:44–50; 1:24; Mark 14:58.

munity[14] and the individual Christian are the house of God.[15] Among the Fathers of the Church the House of God is Christ himself, the Church, life in heaven with God, the individual Christ, or Mary. Typical of medieval authors is Warner (Garnier) of St Victor's entry regarding the term 'House":

> The noun "house" designates the heavenly church, as Solomon, when he was building the temple indicated where it is written: *When the house was being built, it was built of dressed and perfect stones. And hammer and saw, and all other irons tools were not heard in the house while it was being built* (1 Kings 6:7). "House" designates the Body of Christ, as Solomon says: *Wisdom built a house for itself* (Prov. 9.1). Wisdom established a house for itself when the only-begotten Son of God through the mediation of his soul created a human body for himself within the womb of the virgin. As the body of the Only-Begotten is called the house of God, and as it is also called a temple, so also one and the same Son of God and man is he who indwells and he who is indwelt.
>
> The noun "house" also designates the conscience, as Ezekiel says: *Enter and close yourself in the middle of your house* (Ezek. 3:24) . . .
>
> "House" designates the abode of heaven, as it is said: *The sparrow has found a home for herself* (Ps. 84:4 [Vulg.]).
>
> "House" designates the structure of the virtues, as Solomon says: *Carefully work your field, and afterwards you will build your house* (Prov. 24:27).[16]

---

[14] 1 Cor. 3:9–13; 2 Cor. 6:16; Eph. 2:19–22 (which uses six terms derived from the Greek word for house, *oikos*); 1 Tim. 3:15; 1 Pet. 2:5; 4:14.

[15] Rom. 8:9, 11; 1 Cor. 3:1; 6:19; 2 Tim. 1:14.

[16] Warner of St Victor, *Gregorianum* XIII.6 (PL 193.395A–396A): "Domus nomine coelestis Ecclesia designatur, sicut Salomone templum aedificante aperitur cum dicitur: *Domus autem cum aedificaretur, de lapidibus dolatis atque perfectis aedificata est. Et malleus, et securis, et omne ferramentum non sunt audita in domo cum aedificaretur* (1 Kings 6:7). Domus corpus Christi designat, sicut *Salomon dicit: Sapientia aedificavit sibi domum* (Prov. 9:1). Sapientia quippe sibi domum condidit, cum unigenitus Dei Filius in seipso intra uterum virginis, mediante anima, humanum sibi corpus creavit. Sic namque corpus unigeniti domus Dei dicitur, sicut etiam templum vocatur, ita vero ut unus idemque Dei, atque hominis filius ipse sit qui inhabitat ipse, qui habitatur. Domus nomine conscientia designatur, sicut ad Ezechielem dicitur: *Ingredere et includere in medio domus tuae* (Ezek. 3:24) . . . Domus coeli habitaculum designat, sicut dicitur: *Passer invenit sibi domum* (Ps. 84:4 [Vulg.]). Domus virtutum fabricam designat, sicut Salomon dicit: *Diligenter exerce agrum tuum, ut postea aedifices domum tuam* (Prov. 24:27)."

It is striking how Warner, who seems to have been a contemporary of Achard, cites the same texts to roughly the same purpose as Achard. They shared a common religious and biblical culture and celebrated the same liturgy. The one difference is Warner's tropological develop-ment of the "house of conscience," which he uses to admonish preach-ers to self-scrutiny and all people to avoid wandering out through external desires and thoughts about gaining glory. In his sermon, Achard certainly includes moral application and exhortation, which he roots directly in the theology of grace. For him, the Christian life is a participation in Christ's grace, which leads one to share in the very life of God.

Interpreting the Bible

The text here translated is the polar opposite of a brief text message; instead of condensing his message to 140 characters, Achard expands on a single sentence of the Bible for 14,000 words. The text from which he begins is Proverbs 9:1: *Wisdom has built a house for herself; she has hewn out seven columns.* Achard mulls each of the principal words in the text, drawing on other occurrences of the word throughout the Bible. If asked whether this was an arbitrary (mis-)use of the text, Achard would have answered, "No." He begins with the *historia,*[17] the words and narrative of the text he is explaining. He even notes a textual variant.[18] As Hugh of St Victor and his other Victorine successors taught, Achard looks at the meaning of the *res,*[19] that is, the persons, places, number and qualities to which those words and narratives refer, using the rest of the Scriptures and philosophy to elucidate their mani-fold meanings.

Sermon

It is doubtful that Achard gave this exact sermon to the abbots as-sembled in the chapter room of St Victor. Very likely he expanded and polished the text of his address when he prepared it for written circula-tion. It is one of three very long sermons, numbers 13–15 in Châtillon's

---

[17]   See par. 10–11 in the translation below.
[18]   See par. 34 in the translation below.
[19]   For the notion that the words of Scripture refer to things which in their turn have multiple meanings, see the texts translated in VTT 3, e.g., Hugh of St Victor, *Didasc.* V.3 (Buttimer, 96–97; tr. Harkins, VTT 3.151–52; tr. Taylor, 121–22); *Sacr.* I.Prol.5 (PL 176.185A–C; tr. Evans, VTT 3.264).

numbering, that sometimes circulated together or alone apart from the rest of Achard's sermons.[20]

Audience

Beginning from the Scripture passages about Solomon's building of the temple, Achard asks who the builder of the temple was and is. As Solomon built the house of God in Jerusalem, so Christ both is and constructs the house of God among all people everywhere. Abbots and the officials who assist them are also "Solomons" who are entrusted by Christ with building the temple in the religious entrusted to their care. As Solomon was by name a "peacemaker," so Christ made peace between earth and heaven, and abbots should bring genuine and wholesome peace within and among the members of their community and within themselves.[21]

It is possible that Achard adapted a sermon he had at hand to fit the audience of abbots he was addressing, but the exhortations to the abbots are so integral to the text that it seems likely that he composed his discourse with the abbots as the intended audience. In any case, the sermon as we have it is a treatment of the trajectory of Christian life, situating that life on solid theological foundations: Creation, Trinity, Christ, and the grace of Christ.

THEOLOGICAL FOUNDATIONS

Created Participation

The idea of God as the only complete and true being was essential in the development of Christian metaphysics, for which there is an unfathomable distance between the infinite, eternal God and the finite, changeable being of everything else. All else must have its existence from God, who is the Creator of the universe. All that is not God is

---

[20] The sermon was inserted by Frowin of Engelberg (d. 1174) in his *De laude liberi arbitrii*. See J. Châtillon, "The *De laude liberi arbitrii* of Frowin of Engelberg and Achard of St. Victor," *American Benedictine Review* 35 (1984): 314–29; H. Feiss, "Three Victorine Texts in Frowin of Engelberg's *De laude liberi arbitrii*," *Studia Monastica* 50 (2008): 203–19.

[21] See par. 6–9 in the translation below.

inherently contingent, given out of love as a gift,[22] and a starting point from which human beings can come to know their maker.[23]

In the sermon Achard thinks about the relationship between created things and their creator in terms of a metaphysics of participation. Something is good, just, or white by participation in Goodness, Justice or Whiteness. Goodness grants a share in Itself to whatever is good, without Itself being diminished. Achard suggests we think of this as being like sunlight which is not diminished by shining on a field. In his philosophical understanding, Justice imposes the form of justice on finite things, which express justice in their finite ways.[24]

Trinitarian Appropriation

The Christian God is Trinitarian, one God in three persons. When God builds a house for God in human beings, all three persons do the work of building, yet "it is customary to attribute some of the works to the Father," and others to the Son or Holy Spirit.[25] Achard here makes use of the notion of Trinitarian appropriations pioneered by Hugh of St Victor and refined by Achard's contemporary, Richard of St Victor.[26] The Father to whom are attributed virtue, power and love, works first in time, though not in dignity to build the house of virtue in us. Thus, Virtue (the Father) formally brings about virtue in human beings, but because Father, Son and Holy Spirit are one substance, causally all three persons effect all participations in divine being, and each effects all. Moreover, what Virtue effects does not lack Delight and Illumination

---

22   É. Gilson, *The Spirit of Medieval Philosophy*, tr. A. H. C. Downes (New York: Scribner, 1940), 42–107; H. Heimsoeth, *The Six Great Themes of Western Metaphysics*, tr. R. Betanzos (Detroit: Wayne State University Press, 1994), 44–46; C. Glacken, *Traces on a Rhodian Shore* (Berkeley: University of California Press, 1973), 150–68. For a study of Achard's views on creation, which turn on the relation of the One and the many, see M. Ilkhani, *La philosophie de la création chez Achard de Saint-Victor* (Bruxelles: Ousia, 1991).

23   Rom. 1:20, which is cited by Hugh of St Victor, *Tribus diebus* I.1 (Poirel 3; tr. Feiss, VTT 1.61); *Sent. div.* Prol. (Piazzoni, 928; tr. Evans, VTT 1.129); 3 (Piazzoni, 950; tr. Evans, VTT 1.156); Achard of St Victor, *Unitate* I.37 (Martineau, 106–107; tr. Feiss, 407); II.4 (Martineau, 148–49; tr. Feiss, 441); Richard of St Victor, *Trin.* I.8 (Ribaillier, 93; tr. Evans, VTT 1.218), I.10 (Ribaillier, 95; tr. Evans VTT 1.219); V.6 (Ribaillier, 201; tr. Evans VTT 1.297); VI.1 (Ribaillier, 228; tr. Evans VTT 1.319); VI.15 (Ribaillier, 247; tr. Evans, VTT 1.335); VI.17 (Ribailler, 251; tr. Evans, VTT 1.338).

24   See par. 4 in the translation below.

25   See par. 3 in the translation below. The Latin text reads: "Sic namque et opera Trinitatis, licet sunt indivisa, quedam tamen specialiter solent Patri attribui" (Châtillon, 136).

26   See Coolman, VTT 1.28–35, 55–58 and the passages cited there.

which are formally attributed to divine Anointing (the Holy Spirit) and divine Wisdom (the Son).

Grace of Christ

The Son or Wisdom of God came from God to be the tenting place of God with and within human beings. The house he builds on earth is heavenly. When the time comes it will be taken up to heaven and amalgamated with the house that divine Wisdom built in the angels.[27]

In his divinity, Christ is brilliant whiteness. When he took up a human nature, that nature was created white from the first moment of its existence; its mind was always free from sin and the impulse to sin. However, in his flesh he took up the darkness of suffering and death; his flesh was whitened at his resurrection. In accepting death, he accepted the penalty of death, but not the guilt of sin that caused it. In his soul and mind, Christ enjoyed glory, while at the same time experiencing the blackness of temptation and suffering which humankind experienced as a penalty for sin.[28]

The whiteness that filled Christ's divinity by nature filled his humanity with the fullness of grace in all its kinds. The members of Christ's body participate in His fullness of grace. They receive whiteness not directly from Christ's divinity, but through the mediation of his humanity. They receive grace from Christ's fullness and on account of his merits. Participation in Christ's grace is for them justification and reformation. By his grace they are formed and squared into living stones.[29] Divine Justice forms rational nature according to Itself, which presupposes that human nature is capable of justification. The matter formed by divine grace is the good of human nature. Only the grace of Christ could reform human nature defaced by sin. Grace drew reformed nature toward heaven. Such is divine loving-kindness, which showed mercy and impressed itself on fallen nature, as form on matter.[30]

---

[27] See par. 6 below.
[28] See par. 13 below.
[29] See par. 14 below.
[30] See par. 15–16 below.

The Way to Truth and Life

Virtue

The spiritual journey begins with conversion from the false goods of the world—prospects for success and fleshly pleasures—and from one's own hardness of heart and carnal attachments to people.[31] Such conversion requires a change of perception, which only grace can effect.[32] This conversion is a response to a call from Christ to his beloved, and takes the convert to Christ's humanity and then to his divinity. To move from love of worldly delusion, to accept the form of Christ is possible only through grace, which Christ, moved by loving-kindness, bestows on sinners. Through his grace, Christians are conformed to him in spirit, and at the resurrection they will be conformed to him in body as well.[33]

The pattern to which the Christian is to be reformed is given in the Gospels and the rest of the Scriptures, which tell that Christ redeemed us through his suffering and death, sanctified us through Baptism, gave us justice through Confirmation and wisdom through the Eucharist, in which we savor the Lord, knowing him sapientially.[34] Christ, the Wisdom of God, teaches us prudence, temperance, justice, and fortitude, as well as the Beatitudes.[35] He tells us to learn from him because he is meek and humble of heart; his burden of love of the Lord is easy for the humble person and his yoke of love of neighbor is light for those who are patient.[36] The Christian is to love God with his whole heart, mind, soul and strength—fervently, wisely, perseveringly, and abundantly—with the love of God which the Spirit pours into our hearts.[37] To love God is to love oneself, for whoever does not love God loves evil and so hates himself. To love oneself is to love God with one's whole heart, mind, soul, and strength, and to love one's neighbor is to wish

---

[31] See par. 11, 23 below.

[32] See par. 9, 11 below.

[33] See par. 11, 15, 16 below. The use of "form" and compounds like "conform," "deform" and "reform" is a favorite Victorine topos. For Hugh's use of it, see B. Coolman, *The Theology of Hugh of St. Victor: An Interpretation* (New York: Cambridge University Press, 2010). See also the index to Achard, *Sermons inédits*, ad loc. "forma," "formare," "formatio," "formator," "deformis," "deformare," "deformitas," "conformare," "conformis," "reformare," "reformatio."

[34] See par. 17 below.

[35] See par. 18, 19 below.

[36] See par. 20 below.

[37] See par. 20, 21 below.

that he may love God in a similar way or because he does love God thus, and can know the expanse of God's love.[38]

To separate oneself from the impediments to loving God and neighbor, one needs to use tools of faith and reason to show the threat of punishment and the filth of sin. The process of purification through the grace of the Holy Spirit is lifelong.[39] However, it is possible to reach a state of interior quiet and liberty of spirit, to be a cheerful giver, to be afire with the Spirit and so act out of love rather than fear, to rejoice in the advance of others and to feel compassion for their troubles as though they were one's own. Thus, the house of virtue is built of seven pillars: the love of God and the love of neighbor shown in obedience, care, shared joy, compassion, imitation and exhortation.[40]

Delight and Contemplation

Having reached this point, the Christian delights in Christ and the Holy Spirit and in the testimony of his own conscience. He tastes and sees the sweetness of the Lord, and he rejoices not just because he experiences that sweetness, but in the sheer fact of God's sweetness. In heaven, the saints each have their own portion of joy, but each rejoices in the joy of the others as though it were his own.[41] Similarly, one comes to delight not over the habit of justice or cleanness that one has, but in justice or cleanness itself, loved for its own sake. One prefers to be perfectly blessed in order to be perfectly just, rather than the other way around.[42] There are, then, seven joys that arise from the sevenfold Spirit of charity. They arise from the habit of cleanness, the habit of justice, the certain hope of final beatitude, the foretaste of divine sweetness, the nature of the sweetness of which one has a foretaste, the beauty and form of justice, and the beauty of spiritual cleanness.[43]

The final stage of the spiritual journey is wisdom or the contemplation of truth, whether in physical or spiritual creatures, which participate in the Supreme Good, God the Creator. Spiritual creatures participate in God because they are created in God's image and likeness, by justification that realizes their capacity to understand and love

[38]   See par. 33 below.
[39]   See par. 24, 27 below.
[40]   See par. 28 below.
[41]   See par. 29 below.
[42]   See par. 30 below.
[43]   See par. 31 below.

Goodness, and by beatitude that includes contemplation and delight. Beyond these four are contemplation of the eternal arrangement of things, of the predestination of the saints, and finally of the unity and trinity of God.[44]

Delight and contemplation nurture each other. Their mutuality reflects the interaction of Christ and the Spirit. The Son was conceived by the Spirit, then the Son sent out the Spirit who leads into all Truth.[45] Thus, the summit of the spiritual journey is in the Trinity, where it began. In the end, Christians become the House of God, in body, spirit and mind. God dwells in their bodies in an imitable way, in their spirit in a way that brings delight, and in their minds as available for contemplation. They reach this fulfillment by discipline of their flesh, by the goodness of their spiritual nature, and by wisdom in their mind as it contemplates the Truth. Achard ends his sermon with a prayer that Christ may dwell in him and he in Christ, that Christ and he may indwell and belong to each other, and that Christ may be praised not just by all that Achard is, but by His entire heavenly court.[46]

The translation that follows is based on the latin text in J. Châtillon, *Sermons inédits*, 134–68. An earlier translation can be found in *Achard of St Victor: Works*, translated by H. Feiss, 207–53.

---

[44]   See par. 32 below.
[45]   See par. 33 below.
[46]   See par. 34 below.

SERMON 13: ON THE DEDICATION OF A CHURCH

I.

1. *Wisdom has built a home for herself; she has hewn out seven col-umns.*[1] I have proposed a theme about building, not about dedication. I am not unaware that the feast celebrated today is not one of building, but of dedication. However, I also know something that I think I should follow, namely, that what is required of us is not the dedication, but the building of the true and interior house, namely, the house of God. It is still the time for it to be built in us, not dedicated. For what is not completely built cannot yet be dedicated. The dedication of a house usually occurs, and should occur, not when it is begun, nor when it is being built, but only when it is completed.

The distance between the building of God's house and its dedication does not span just a few things nor is it short. The two differ in place, time, quality of things, and quality of persons. Look at the many things that separate them. See how far apart they are in each of these. In place, how great is the distance between this house to be built on earth and its dedication in heaven. In time, how great is the distance between what is to be built in this life and what will be dedicated in another; it is to be built in time, but dedicated in eternity. In quality of things, how great is the distance, because building now must really take place, but in the meantime[2] the dedication cannot occur except in hope. The building is in virtue (*virtute*); the dedication will be in beatitude. The building occurs from (*ex*) grace through justice; the dedication will happen from justice through glory. Building is merit; dedication will be the reward. There is a great difference in the quality of persons doing the building and those dedicating. Human beings cooperate with God in building, but God alone will be at work in the dedication,

Therefore, since it belongs to God alone to dedicate his house, let him speak of the dedication of his house, and let those also speak who have the spirit of God,[3] who clinging to God are one spirit with him.[4] To them God has revealed through his Spirit[5] the uncertain and hidden things of his wisdom,[6] which God has prepared for those who love him.[7] But it is enough for me to speak of the building of the house of God. Would that I were up to speaking of it as I ought. Therefore, because obedience requires that I offer my brothers some word to build them up,[8] let me speak to them a word about building. If they are not built up by it, let them at least learn how it should be built in them, or how they are to build.

2. Let me, therefore, return to the theme I proposed regarding the building of the house of God: *Wisdom has built a home for herself; she has hewn out seven columns.*[9] Christ is the power[10] of God and the wisdom of God. He is Christ, that is, anointed. The Spirit of God is upon him, for the Spirit has anointed him.[11] God anointed him with the Holy Spirit more than all his companions,[12] with an overflowing abundance of graces, giving him the Spirit without measure.[13] By this anointing poured upon him superabundantly, he is completely gentle and pleasant, totally merciful and kindly. Hence, he is pleased to join us to some participation in his anointing, though without any lessening of his fullness, and through our anointing to build his house in us. Although this house is his, although he also builds it to dwell in it, nevertheless we also dwell there with him. He does not need it; only we need it. Therefore, he wishes to build his house in us only by that grace with which he abounds, the effervescent, superabundant anointing in him, that is, only because he himself is the Christ, because God superabundantly anointed him. However, because he is also wisdom, he knows how to build it as he wants; because he is virtue itself, he can also build it as he wants and knows how. Where these three things, that is, will, know-how, and possibility,[14] come together regarding anything to be built, nothing can block the realization of the work and the achievement of the result.

3. Although these work together in the building of the house of God, there is a house which virtue builds for itself, and one that Christ, that is, the "Anointed" or "His very unction," builds for himself, and there is one that wisdom builds for itself. Although the works of the Trinity are undivided, it is customary to attribute some especially to the Father, others especially to the Son, and others especially to the Holy Spirit.[15] However, as will be clear in the following when the building of the houses is discussed, the house that power (*virtus*) builds for itself, for us and in us, is first in time though not in dignity. The house that anointing builds for itself follows second; and the house that wisdom builds for itself comes third after these two. The house that power (*virtus*) builds for itself is the house of virtue (*virtus*); the house that anointing builds for itself is the house of anointing; the house that wisdom builds for itself is the house of wisdom.

To refer to the same three by other names which pertain to the same distinction among them, the first house is the house of love; the second house is the house of delight; and the third house is the house of contemplation: for virtue is in love, anointing in delight, wisdom in contemplation. The first house is also the house of the way; the second is the house of life; the third is the house of truth. Christ is, as he himself said, the *way, the truth and the life.*[16] Christ is the way because he is power. One does not go to anointing and delight, or to wisdom and contemplation, or for that matter to eternal beatitude, except through virtue and love. Christ is the truth, because he is wisdom itself. Christ is life because he is anointed and he is our anointing. The anointing and delight of the spirit is in a way his life; good delight is a good life; bad delight is a bad life; spiritual delight makes a spiritual life; carnal delight makes a carnal life.

4. As wisdom hews seven columns in her house,[17] so virtue hews seven columns in its house, and anointing hews the same number in its house. In each house there are a total of seven columns, because each and all are spiritual. Not only do power (*virtus*), anointing, and wisdom set up columns in their own houses, but they also cut out columns as from themselves. The columns in their houses are participations in them; all participations are a kind of cutting from the plenitude of things in which they participate. In the house of virtue the columns are also virtues. In the house of anointing, too, the columns are spiritual anointings or delights. In the house of wisdom or contemplation, the columns are also of the same kind, that is, contemplations. The virtues, anointings, and contemplations of creatures are nothing else than participations and, as it were, emanations of divine power, anointing, and wisdom.[18] In their houses, the columns are cut out from them in such a way that nothing is subtracted from them. For the sun pours and spreads out rays from itself in manifold ways, but it undergoes no lessening of its brightness.

5. In material buildings the material columns usually are made in a material way for three causes: in some places they are made so that the buildings are firm and solid; in others so that they are charming and pleasant; in others so that they are open and well lit. For this third reason, sometimes in buildings columns are put in place of walls so that the interior will be bathed in greater light. Likewise, for the same reasons, each of the three houses, though spiritual, has, so to speak, spiritual columns in it hewn from itself. In the house of virtue, the columns are for solidity; in the house of anointing, they are for delight;

and in the house of wisdom, for illumination. Virtue builds itself a solid house; anointing builds itself a pleasant house; wisdom builds itself a well-lit house. For virtue makes solid, anointing gives delight, and wisdom enlightens.

Formally it is as though each makes these singly, but insofar as they are a single substance causally each effects all of them and all effect each.[19] Power is the cause not only of solidity, but also of delight and illumination as well. Similarly, anointing is the cause not only of delight, but also of illumination and solidity. Wisdom is also the cause not only of illuminating but also of solidity and delight. However, insofar as they are distinct from each other by what is proper to each (*proprietatibus*) as though by certain forms, it pertains to the form or property of power to solidify, to the form and property of anointing to delight, and to the form and property of wisdom to illumine.[20] In line with this, therefore, the foregoing distinction of the houses stands and is understood, according to which the house of power is said to be solid, the house of anointing is said to be pleasant, and the house of wisdom to be well-lit. Nevertheless the house of power does not lack its delight and light, nor the house of anointing lack its light and solidity, nor the house of wisdom lack its solidity and delight. In its substance and nature power is not only solid, but also delightful and luminous; anointing is not only delightful, but also luminous and solid; wisdom is not only luminous, but also solid and delightful, so that, as was said, each befits itself, as it were, formally, still all befit all and each both substantially and causally.

Since these three house are built in one heart, there they are joined as though into one house, so that in some way they are both three and one. Three in one, and one in three, a house one and threefold, as the house of God, one and three, one house and nevertheless, like the ark of Noah, distinct in a threefold way.[21] This house, which is built in us, is not built without us. We must cooperate with God[22] to build his house in us.

II.

6. However, the house of God cannot be built in a random and disorderly fashion by just anyone, or from just anything, or in just any way. One must take into account the workers, the material for the work, and the manner of working. Therefore, regarding the house of God,

one needs to consider by whom, from what, and in what way it should be built. Perhaps it is to be built by people like Solomon, who built the house of God, from the sort of materials with which he built, and how he built, so that what we carry out spiritually will correspond to what Solomon did materially. Regarding the kind of person Solomon was, it is enough now to speak only about what may be gathered from the meaning of his name. "Solomon" is translated as "peacemaker," and in accord with his name he was a peacemaker.[23] God's own statement to David through Nathan the prophet presented this as the reason why, for the building of His house, he preferred Solomon to David, the father of Solomon.[24] In this regard those who want to imitate Solomon in building the house of God should be like him.

Such, to be sure, was he who came from the bosom of the Father[25] to us in order to build the house of God in us, so that he would be the tabernacle of God with men, and would dwell with them,[26] but also in them: with them because among them, in them because within them; with them *because he was found in the likeness of a human being*,[27] in them because *he did not think it robbery* but nature *to be God's equal.*[28] Who, then, is this heavenly carpenter of the house of God, and not just its carpenter, but also its inhabitant? The carpenter through whom the entire structure of the world was created and subsists is the son of a carpenter.[29] This artisan is the Wisdom that built and still builds a house for herself. The house that Wisdom builds for herself[30] is the house of God. So Wisdom, the builder, herself is God and the Son of God. Although while in the form of God he had built himself a home in the heavens, he also took up the form of a servant to build a home on earth.[31] First he had built the house of God in the angels. Afterwards, he also came to build the house of God in human beings. This house, although meanwhile it is built on earth, is not itself earthly, but heavenly. Hence, when at the proper time it is to be taken across into heaven and united and amalgamated by God with the angelic house, and so there these will be not two houses, but one house. The builder of both houses is Solomon, but also someone more than Solomon.[32] He brings peace to all things *whether in heaven or on earth.*[33] *He is our peace, who makes one out of both*,[34] and the discipline of our peace is upon him.

Ministers who wish to cooperate with this teacher and primary artificer must in their way be such artisans. This artisan does not want to have collaborators who are not imitators of him.[35] Otherwise, they do not build, but tear down, and they do not collect with him, but scatter without him and against him.[36]

7. *Blessed are the peacemakers for they will be called children of God.*[37] It belongs to the children of God to build the house of God with the Son of God. All sons of God are peacemakers. Let them be peacemakers so they can build the house of God. Let them be peacemakers even *with those who hate peace.*[38] This is incumbent most of all on those who undertake to build the house of God not only in themselves, but also in others, for *his place is made in peace.*[39] The house of God is made in peace, though not in the peace of the world, but in the peace of God himself, in that peace which does not belong to the impious[40] but only to *people of good will.*[41] *The peace that surpasses all understanding*[42] is in God, so God wants peace to be in his house and in those who build his house. If it is not yet possible that *the peace which surpasses all understanding* be in them, at least let there be in them peace which is not against, but in accord with understanding, not according to the understanding of the flesh, but according to the understanding of reason. For the peace in them must be spiritual, not carnal. They must have peace, both in relation to the one who is above, and one who is next to them: peace toward God and peace toward neighbor.

It was for the sake of these two kinds of peace that our Solomon, the Author and Lover of peace, said, *I leave you peace, my peace I give you.*[43] Because Christ is God and man, the peace that he says is his is to be understood as the peace between God and humankind: the peace that he left us is to be understood as the peace of human beings with each other. The former is higher, the latter is lower; only grace leads to the former, but to the latter our common nature invites us and in some fashion draws us. Hence, he gives us the former as from a superior, as from what is his; he leaves us the latter as from something lower, and in what is ours. However, what is ours cannot suffice for the latter without what is his. The peace of humankind in relation to God is that it is good for human beings to cling to God,[44] so that clinging to Him they may become one spirit with him.[45] The peace of one human being to another is that they may have *one heart and one soul,*[46] and be *anxious to preserve the unity of the Spirit in the bond of peace.*[47] Human beings should not only be at peace with God and neighbor, but also with themselves.

8. But it cannot happen that one has peace in relation to the one above and in relation to one's neighbor unless one also has peace in oneself. In oneself there must be peace between reason and will and peace between the will and the flesh so that the will submits to the reason, and the flesh to the will.[48] Whatever one may think about peace

between the reason and the will, in this life there cannot be perfect peace between the will and the flesh. There cannot be between them peace devoid of struggle, at least if that peace is to be a good peace.

At first, there is between them peace, but a mere peace, an evil peace, even the worst peace: a bad peace according to the flesh, a worse peace according to the will, the worst peace according to the will and flesh together. There it is bad because the flesh entices the will and worse because the will freely consents to the flesh; and worst is the pact that is made by the attraction of the flesh and the consent of the will. After this mere and worst peace there sometimes follows a mere but good (but not entirely good) struggle. It is good that the will fights the flesh, bad that the flesh assails the will. Next follows peace and war together: peace approaches, but war does not immediately cease. War is lessened, but not eliminated. Both of these are good, but peace is better than war. Peace is good in both respects, but war is good only with respect to the will. Finally, but only after this life, there will be a peace that is not partial, but full, not good in only one respect, but best in both respects.

As I said, in the first, at first there is mere peace, peace of the worst kind, when the will acquiesces to flesh and blood in everything, when it approves nothing except what flesh and blood have revealed to it,[49] when it has no taste for anything except what the wisdom of the flesh, which is an enemy to God,[50] has told it. O perverse peace, confused peace, disordered peace, confusing and perverting the order of things, subordinating the mind and imposing the flesh, trampling on the image of God and enthroning the beast![51] O peace that is not peacemaking, but assails nature and disturbs the whole person! O harmony that is not harmonious, but discordant from the heart of God and deprived of all reason,[52] a filthy, rotten pact, a dirty partnership, a love hateful to chaste love and a peace that actually rebels against peace. In this peace, the more the will agrees with the flesh, the more it joins the flesh in deserting all reason and decency.

9. Sometimes, however, reason meets with will and reproaches it about this sordid peace. It brings it to will's attention that will owes more to reason than to the flesh, indeed, that it owes to the flesh nothing that is contrary to reason, but only what is in accord with reason. It calls attention to the ancient and divinely established ordinance that will ought to be in the power of reason and not in the power of the flesh, so that not the flesh, but reason rules over it. Woman is the image of man, and Eve was made as a help for Adam, not as assistance to the

serpent.[53] Therefore, let her help Adam against the serpent, not the serpent against Adam. Adam is reason; the serpent is the flesh; Eve is between Adam and the serpent; the will is between reason and the flesh, below reason and above the flesh. Because will is made as a help to reason and not to the flesh, let it be subject not to the flesh, but to reason, so that along with reason it may rule the subjugated flesh. Meanwhile, the will, thus taught and corrected by reason, understands the truth and resolves to follow what it has understood.

Alas, the miseries of human beings, the wretched state of sinners. Alas, those who commit sin are made slaves of sin.[54] They do not know this when they do it, because they delight in doing it. However, they know it when they regret the deed and try to escape. Because the will, having served the flesh for a long time, longs for its liberty and tries to return to reason, the flesh comes against it as against a fugitive slave, raises objections, and completely opposes it. Hence, for a time there arise between them a fierce struggle and a serious fight. The weak will loses this conflict and is conquered, unless the strong hand of God rescues it.[55] Helped through grace by God's power, it prevails and conquers; chastising the flesh, it reduces it to the servitude that it owes.[56] Its members that earlier displayed the arms of iniquity on behalf of sin now display the arms of justice for God.[57] Thus, not only the spirit, but also the body is made a temple of the Holy Spirit. Hence, between the will and the flesh there is a certain peace and spiritual harmony, though not without some struggle. The flesh often mutters complaints and secretly raises its heel against its Lord.[58] *I take delight in the law according to the interior man; but I see another law in my members, fighting against the law of my mind.*[59] See, there is still a fight. *The flesh desires in opposition to the spirit, and the spirit in opposition to the flesh.*[60] See, a fight that is still more evident. When then is there peace? *My soul thirsted for you, as did my flesh in so many ways.*[61] *My heart and my flesh exulted in the living God.*[62] See, here is peace. The more this peace increases, the more that fighting decreases. However, no matter how much the fighting diminishes, as long as *the corruptible body weighs down the soul,*[63] it will not be completely ended. But when this corruptible thing has put on incorruptibility, when death has been absorbed into victory,[64] when the body itself is spiritual, not by crossing over into the nature of spirit, but by subjecting itself completely and inseparably to reason and the will of the spirit, then there will be in us *the peace which surpasses all understanding,*[65] peace *in itself,*[66] the best peace, peace in every respect, eternal peace. O lovable peace, O desirable peace! Who will grant me that I who work in myself may go across from myself and rest in you?[67] Who will grant me that in the meantime (*interim*) I may fight for you against myself, so that conquering myself I may finally be crowned in you?

III.

10. These things have been said about peace and peacemakers for the sake of the builders of the house of God, who ought to be like Solomon in virtue. However, because we said that not only should they be like Solomon, but they should also build of similar materials and in a similar way, therefore we need to consider from what materials and in what way Solomon built the house of God. If we look to the historical meaning regarding these things and inquire about the material and the manner of building, it answers us that the materials there were of three kinds: squared stones, cedar wood and purest gold. There it describes the manner of building as follows. First Solomon built the house of squared stones.[68] Secondly, he paneled the interior of the whole house with cedar wood.[69] He did this in such a way that, in effect, the wood walls were within the stone walls, as though there were a wooden house within a stone one. Thirdly, he covered the entire interior with purest gold; everywhere he attached an overlay of gold to the cedar wood with golden nails.[70] He did this in such a way that there were, so to speak, golden walls within the cedar walls, and a golden house within the cedar house. Therefore, he made it in such a way that it was like one house in three and three in one: a stone exterior, a cedar interior, and deep inside a golden one. Also it seems to have pertained to the manner of building that when the house of God was being built, no hammer or axe was heard.[71] They were not heard there then because earlier they had been heard enough elsewhere.

So, that is how many, from what, and in what order and manner Solomon built the material and figurative house of God materially and figuratively. Therefore, let us, too, observe Solomon in his threefold material and his order and manner of building, and, so to speak, draw from him exteriorly a kind of form and example for the work of our Solomon, namely Christ. And if we, too, are Solomons, that is, peacemakers, let us build the spiritual and true house of God within *in spirit and in truth*[72] spiritually and truly.

A.

11. The first house, or the first part, we meet is the house to be constructed from squared stones.[73] Where, then, are there squared stones for us? Perhaps from the place whence Solomon had them. And where was that? From Lebanon. Read the history and consider, and you will find that then they were taken from Lebanon.[74] Lebanon is a large mountain, and it has not yet been consumed or stripped. Let us, therefore, following in Solomon's footsteps, go to Lebanon, from which we may take as many as we need of the stones we seek. There are two qualities in squared stones: one is that for which they are called stones; and the other is that for which they are called squared. They are called "stones" with respect to their matter, "squared" with respect to their form. They are stones by what they are naturally; squared by what they have accidentally.[75] In both respects, however, according to what they are by nature and according to what they are accidentally, they are from Lebanon. They are from Lebanon both in matter and form. However, the matter is from one Lebanon, the form from another.

Lebanon is translated as "whitening."[76] These two Lebanons are two whitenings: the whitening of truth and the whitening of vanity; the Lebanon of Christ and the Lebanon of the world: regarding the Lebanon of Christ: *The just one will flourish like a palm tree; like a cedar of Lebanon he will thrive in the house of the Lord*[77]; regarding the Lebanon of the world: *The Lord will shatter the cedars of Lebanon.*[78] The Lebanon of Christ has true whiteness; the Lebanon of the world has a shadowy whiteness. The whitening of Christ lies more within and still remains hidden; the whitening of the world is completely exterior and appears on the surface. So, the world is like a wall painted white outside, but inside completely dirty and unclean. The whitening of Christ consists of true and spiritual goods; the whitening of the world consists of carnal and false goods. Hence, the whitening of Christ nurtures and enlightens spiritual eyes; the whitening of the world deludes, tears out and blinds carnal eyes.

With respect to these two whitenings, these two Lebanons, the bridegroom says to the bride in the Song of Songs: *Come from Lebanon, my bride, come from Lebanon, and you will be crowned.*[79] First, she is called from Lebanon to Lebanon to be a bride; secondly, because she is a bride, from Lebanon she is called above Lebanon to be crowned. The first calling is from Lebanon to Lebanon, from one whitening to another whitening, from the imaginary to the genuine, from the exterior to the interior, from the carnal to the spiritual, from the whitening of the world to that of Christ. The second calling is from Lebanon to above Lebanon, that is, from the whitening to whiteness itself, from the whitening of Christ to the whiteness of God, from the whitening of the humanity of Christ to the whiteness of the divinity of Christ himself. For although Christ is white according to his divinity and according to his humanity, according to his humanity he is white as whitened, whereas according to his divinity he is not whitened, but only white, or rather whiteness itself, the whiteness of eternal light.[80]

12. There are three whitenings in Christ according to his humanity. For our common nature is whitened in Christ in one way, his special nature, that is, his singular humanity, in another way. However, since his humanity consists in two things, that is, his mind and his flesh, there is one whitening there with respect to his mind, and another with respect to his flesh. Our common nature is whitened in him in such a way that it changes from black to white. Before this common nature was in him, it had been black in everyone else by the rust and stains of sins. However, through grace it happened that this nature, which was black in others, in him became white immediately from the moment when it began to be, so that in him it was never black, but always white. It was taken up by the Word in such a way that it was without any wicked impulse (*vitio*) and sin.[81] Therefore, the mind of Christ is not whitened by being changed from black to white, for it never was black, either there or elsewhere. For before it was there, it was nowhere else, because before there it was nothing. There, from the time when it was, it could not be black, because it inhered to the Word himself instantly, perfectly and personally. The blackness of original sin was not there, because this man was conceived from (*ex*) the Holy Spirit and by (*ab*) the Virgin.[82] The blackness of actual sin was not there, because *he committed no sin, nor was deceit found in his mouth*.[83] However, the flesh of Christ was whitened from the blackness that he had in it at first and later set aside.

13. There are two blacknesses, one of guilt, the other of penalty.[84] To these are opposed two whitenesses, one of justice, the other of glory. The blackness of guilt and the whiteness of justice cannot coexist in the same person, if the justice is consummate and perfect as it was in Christ. Likewise the blackness of punishment and the whiteness of glory cannot coexist in the same person in the same respect. Although they coexisted in Christ, it was not in the same way. The whiteness of glory was with respect to his mind, the blackness of penalty with re-

spect to his body, in such a way that the flesh did not then share in this whiteness, nor did the mind ever share in this blackness, nor at any time was there punishment in the mind of Christ, and as long as there was present punishment in the flesh of Christ, glory was not yet found there.

The blackness of guilt and the whiteness of glory are never in the same person, whether in the same regard or not. However, it does happen that the blackness of punishment and the whiteness of justice are in the same person. Hence the bride in the Song of Songs says, *I am black, but beautiful*:[85] *black* because of punishment, *beautiful* because of justice. On account of this whiteness and this blackness, the bridegroom was also *comely above the sons of men*,[86] and according to the pronouncement of another prophet, *there was no comeliness or beauty in him*.[87] *God sent his Son in the likeness of the flesh of sin*:[88] because he was sent in the likeness of the flesh of sin pertains to blackness; what is not in that flesh belongs to whiteness. He was tempted *in all things on account of the likeness, but without sin.* That he was tempted *in all things on account of the likeness* [to human beings] pertains to the blackness, but *without sin* pertains to whiteness.[89] Because of this whiteness and this blackness, the bride says of him, *My beloved is white and ruddy.*[90] In the Scriptures, "ruddy" and "black" usually have the same force and signify both guilt and penalty. Regarding guilt, it is said, *If your sins are red like scarlet*;[91] and regarding punishment, in the person of angels Christ is addressed: *Why is your clothing red, and your clothes like theirs who tread in a winepress?*[92] He responds to them: *I have trod the winepress alone, and I have stained all my garments.*[93] He says his garments are stained in his passion and the shedding of his blood. Earlier his flesh had been black through its capacity to suffer and die; then it became blacker through his passion and death; afterwards it was whitened through his resurrection. There he put on beauty and strength.[94] There Christ's clothes, which previously had been stained, became white as snow,[95] and even whiter than snow. There as he came out of his tomb *like a bridegroom emerging from his marriage chamber*,[96] he was glorified (*clarificatus*) by the Father with the brilliance (*claritate*) that he had with the Father in his predestination before the world was.[97]

14. Therefore, according to his humanity Christ is whitened; according to his divinity he is whiteness; in both respects he is white. In the divinity of Christ, there is whiteness according to the fullness of nature; in the humanity of Christ, whiteness is according to the fullness of

grace; in both instances whiteness is according to the fullness of glory. The fullness of glory in Christ's divinity is from that full nature; the fullness in his humanity is from fullness of grace in all its kinds. The whiteness in the members of Christ is not according to nature but according to grace, not as in Head according to the fullness of grace, but according to some participation in that fullness. The members do not have their own whiteness immediately from his divinity, as does the humanity of the Head, but through the mediation of the humanity of their Head and by participation in his fullness. We, who are his members, *have all received from the fullness* of the Head,[98] not from the fullness of nature, which belongs to the divinity alone, but from the fullness of grace, which belongs only to the humanity of Christ. Therefore, the Evangelist, to attest that we participate by grace and not by nature, went on to add: *And grace for grace,*[99] that is, a participation of grace from the fullness on account of that plenitude. So we not only have received from his grace, we have also received on account of his grace, not only from his fullness, but also on account of his fullness.[100] The grace that the humanity of Christ had with God has merited for us the participation that we have in him. For God *has graced (gratificavit) us in his beloved Son;*[101] that is, God has graced us in Christ. What is this gracing of us in Christ if not a participation by us in the grace of Christ on account of Christ? This participation of ours in grace is our justification. Our justification[102] is our reformation;[103] and our reformation is the forming and squaring of living stones.

15. Now if justification is their formation, justice is also their form. If their form is justice, what will be their matter, if not the rational nature itself, which is capable (*capax*)[104] of justification? The matter is the good of human nature; the form is the gift of divine grace.[105] But however good human nature may be, it is primitive and unformed matter, unless it is formed by supervenient grace. Moreover, although the hand of God had formed this matter in us, it was deformed in us and by us by our hand, which we stretched out wickedly to what was forbidden. No power (*virtute*) or merit of ours could or can reform it; it is to be reformed only through the grace of Christ by the power of him by whom it was formed. For Christ is the upper Lebanon, from whom form is to be hoped and asked for; the world is lower Lebanon, where material is abundant enough. Before the upper Lebanon came down to the lower Lebanon, before Christ came into the world, matter and form were separated far from each other. Matter was below on the earth; form was above in heaven; matter was in human beings, form

was only in God by nature and in angels by grace. Matter, inasmuch as it was earthly, heavy, and weighty, could not ascend into heaven to form, and so form needed to descend to earth to matter in order to imprint itself on matter. So it formed matter according to itself, and what it then had formed according to itself it drew into heaven after and to itself. Once form had come to matter graciously and freely given (*gratis*) and had informed it with its own imprint, but ungrateful matter disdained the form of grace, threw off grace, and freely deformed itself against the will of form. Thus, there was nothing in it whence it could require the coming of form; on the contrary, there was reason why form rightly would not come to it after that. However, although form was justice, it was not without loving-kindness (*pietate*). In fact not only was it not without loving-kindness, but it was also full of loving-kindness. In form itself was complete loving-kindness; for loving-kindness and justice are the same in God. So, loving-kindness conquered justice. Indeed, because justice was itself loving-kindness, in a way it conquered itself.[106] For it did not shut up *its mercies in its anger*,[107] but as though forgetful of the earlier injury and unmindful of the early rejection, it eventually descended to matter even lower than before and impressed itself on it more deeply, and formed it according to itself, indeed, reformed it. Form also wanted to be for a time with matter in the region of matter, so that matter could afterwards be for eternity with form in form's own region.

16. O kindly (*pia*) justice, O form truly divine! It is supremely fitting that God supreme should be most kindly just as he is most just. It is also certainly most just that he, as God, be most kindly. However, when will you come to understand how kindly he is in himself, if you are not able to do so even when you want to think about how kindly he is toward you? For who may think worthily of the great regard that divine loving-kindness shows toward us who are so unworthy? From loving-kindness alone did form so beautiful unite itself with matter so unformed, and not just unformed (*informi*) but misshapen (*deformis*), and not just misshapen, but misshaped (*deformate*), and misshaped not by any necessity but only by the voluntary perversity of self-will. I am saying that the divine form freely came to humankind, freely deformed; grace came graciously to one ungrateful for grace; medicine not asked for came to the sick, strength to the weak, wisdom to the foolish, holiness to the unclean, truth to the liar, mercy to the merciless, peace to the rebel, piety (*pietas*) to the impious, love (*caritas*) to the enemy, justice to the unjust, not to judge and condemn humanity according

to His own justice, but to justify humanity from its injustice, and form it according to Himself, and once formed according to Himself to glorify it in Himself. Thus, the form of God came into the flesh to conform to himself, first in spirit, and afterwards even in the flesh, those whom God *foreknew and predestined to be conformed in the image of his Son*.[108] Thus, we who bore the image of the earthly might also bear the image of the heavenly. That form is God's and ours: God's because it is from God, ours because it is in us. It is expressed by God, and it is impressed on us by Him.

17. This form is square,[109] because it is stable and firm. Alternatively, it is square because it is found in four places: the divinity of Christ, the humanity of Christ, in angels, and in us. Again, it is square because it is presented to us in the four gospels, or rather because Christ is our form, who, as the Apostle formed by him shows, has become a spiritual square for us. For, according to the word of the Apostle, *Christ is made wisdom for us by God, and justice, and sanctification, and redemption*.[110] See a vital and heavenly square! Come and receive it, as living stones, whereas without it you are dead and earthly. In it you are made squared, and thus from being dead you will be made alive and from being earthly you will be made heavenly.

In listing these four things, which the one Christ became for us, the Apostle follows the order of dignity, not the temporal order. From a temporal perspective, redemption occurred for us first, sanctification second, justice third, and wisdom fourth. He became redemption for us when he gave himself as our price (*premium*). He became sanctification for us in the remission of sins, justice for us in the bestowal of gifts, and wisdom through contemplation in a kind of present reward (*remuneratione*) of merits, which merits of ours are his gifts.[111] He became redemption for us through the sacrament of his suffering and death, sanctification through the sacrament of baptism, justice through the sacrament of confirmation, wisdom through the sacrament of the altar. It is this sacrament that is referred to in the prophetic invitation: *Approach him, and be enlightened*,[112] that is, *Taste and see that the Lord is sweet*.[113] Approach to taste, and so to be enlightened to see! In taste is the savor of interior sweetness, in sight is the splendor of knowledge. Wisdom consists of these two things, that is, savory knowledge. No knowledge is really savory except knowledge about God; nor is knowledge about God ever without savor. Only God is known with true savor, and He is never truly known without savor. The one who does not savor God does not experience (*noscat*) it, because he does not know God.[114]

18. In many passages in the Scriptures there occur (*occurrunt*) many squares, but they all come together (*concurrunt*) in this one square, which is Christ. *God has made* Christ *wisdom for us.*[115] He is the wisdom of God; he is that universal (*generalis*) wisdom by which all know wisely (*sapiunt*). All men or angels who know wisely do so by participation in him. In the book of Wisdom the wise man says of wisdom: *She teaches moderation and prudence (sapientia), justice and fortitude (virtus), than which nothing is more useful to people in life.*[116] Surely this is a good square, if in people's lives nothing is more useful than it is. Moreover, wisdom is also life in people, life not of the flesh, but of the spirit. This is certainly a useful life and much more useful than the life of the flesh. These are the four principal virtues: for here he designates temperance by the word "moderation," prudence by "wisdom," justice by its own name, and fortitude by "power." Through prudence good is distinguished from evil, through temperance evil is rejected, through justice good is chosen, through fortitude the good is implemented and maintained.

19. Elsewhere Wisdom proposes to us this same square and its usefulness, speaking in the flesh: *Blessed are you poor, because yours is the kingdom of God. Blessed are you who are now hungry, because you will be satisfied. Blessed are you who are now weeping, because you will laugh. Blessed will you be, when people hate you, and exclude you, etc., because of the Son of Man.*[117] Notice that there are four: poverty, thirst, weeping, and bearing persecution. Poverty pertains to temperance, thirst to justice, weeping to prudence, and bearing persecution to fortitude. Poverty is of the spirit when, even if the riches and luxuries of the world are plentiful (*affluant*), still the heart is not set on them,[118] but restrains itself from them. Matthew says this about thirst: *Blessed are those who hunger and thirst for justice.*[119] Solomon says of prudence: *Because in much wisdom there is much upset, and whoever gathers knowledge gathers sorrow as well.*[120] What in this life is wiser than for a person to weep continuously, both because of this life's abundance of evils and because of a lack of the goods of the other life?[121] These are the lower and higher pools of water.[122]

20. In another place of the gospel, where Christ, who both forms us and is our form, invites us to become conformed to him; he says, *Learn from me, because I am meek and humble of heart.*[123] Notice that there are two things: the virtue of meekness and humility of heart. However, so that there not be a duality, but a square, he adds two other things: his *yoke is easy and* his *burden light.*[124] The easy yoke of Christ is the

love of God, through which we are gently joined (*copulamur*) to him. The light burden of Christ is love of neighbor, through which we freely and so easily act on our neighbor's behalf. To this pertains what the Apostle says: *Bear one another's burdens, and so you will fulfill the law of Christ*.[125] Therefore these two are joined to the two previous ones, because in some way they follow from them. Indeed, *the love of God is poured into our hearts through the Holy Spirit*, that is, through the Spirit of God, who is given to us.[126] When God says, *My Spirit rests on him*,[127] whom does he mean if not the humble person? Notice that the love of God is based on humility. And the love of neighbor, especially love of an enemy, which is a more perfect love, proceeds from patience, that is, from meekness. For if anyone is not yet up to loving his enemy as he should, let him only bear with him patiently. God will grant him enough grace and charity to be able to bear with him, even easily. Moreover, through the patience he shows toward his enemy, God will quickly expel enmity from his heart.

21. Also, in just the love of God, a square is proposed and imposed for us to receive. We are commanded to love God *with (ex) our whole heart*, that is, fervently, and *with our whole mind*, that is, wisely, *and with our whole soul*, which signifies our life, that is, perseveringly, and *with all our strength*,[128] that is, abundantly. *With our whole soul*, that is, indefatigably, *with our whole strength*, that is, sufficiently. The love of God is indefatigable when it is not ended or interrupted; it is sufficient when nothing that pertains to it is neglected or left out. Through this square in its structure the spiritual house is firmly conjoined to Christ. Where, however, is the square through which it is firmly attached also to the neighbor? For not only ought it cohere there to the corner stone[129] but also to the stones on each side of it (*collaterali*), not only to the stone of life, but also to the living stone, not only to the one squaring, but to the one squared.

Pay attention to what follows in the command of love of neighbor and learn if by chance there is a square there also. As you know, that command is presented in these words: *Love your neighbor as yourself*.[130] But what will we do? There does not seem to be evidence of a square here. However, look more closely. Perhaps even here there is the impress of a square, although less expressly. What does the phase *as yourself* call for? Why and how does God teach you to love your neighbor as yourself, if you have not yet learned to love yourself? Where has he taught you this, if not where he taught you to love God?

22. No prescription about love preceded, but none was necessary. To love God in truth, that is, in God himself, is to love oneself; that is, to put it otherwise, not to love God is to hate oneself. Whoever does not love God loves iniquity: *Whoever loves iniquity hates his soul.*[131] Therefore, if by the very fact that you love God you also love yourself, by loving God in the four ways mentioned, you also love yourself in four ways. For you love yourself in loving God *with your whole heart*, and in loving Him *with your whole mind*, and *with your whole soul*, and *with all your strength.*[132] Therefore, when you are commanded to love your neighbor as yourself, this is enjoined on you in such a way that as you must love yourself in order to have these four, or you love yourself in these four which you already have, so you may love your neighbor as you love yourself, for the sake of these same four or in them. For you must love your neighbor to this end, that he love God or because he loves God fervently; and that he may love or because he does love God wisely; and that he may love or because he does love God indefatigably; and that he may also have, or because he has, love of God sufficiently.

See, then, the pervasive squaring in the twofold command. And as the Lord says the two commands are similar,[133] so there is also found in them a square that is not dissimilar. If anyone is looking for a more explicit square in the love of neighbor, let him take up what the Apostle expounds and enjoins: *Correct the restless, console the faint-hearted, support the infirm, and be patient toward all.*[134] This square pertains especially to prelates. Someone who has received squares of this kind will arrive through them to a higher square, so that he can *comprehend with all the saints what is the breadth and length and height and depth:*[135] how great the width, namely, the width of God in love, and how great the length in eternity, how sublime in power, and how deep in wisdom.[136]

23. Notice how from and in the higher Lebanon, that is, from and in Christ, living stones are squared and shaped. As long as they are held back on the lower Lebanon, as long as they are stuck in love of the world, people are far from this squaring and forming. While they bear the form of the world, to which the Apostle forbids us to be conformed,[137] they are not formed but unformed, not beautiful (*formosi*) but misshapen (*deformes*). The form of the world, *which is under the power of the evil one*,[138] is formlessness and deformity. The order of the world, toward which his stones are directed, is enormity; the beauty of the world is filth. The order of the world, which is *in revelries and drunkenness, and promiscuities and impurities, in wrangling and jeal-*

ousy,[139] and in other similar things, is not order, but just confusion and disorder. The equality of the world is inequality. It is necessary, then, that someone who conforms himself to the equality and measure of one who is dedicated to the world *be wavering in all his ways*[140] and never remain in the same state. Therefore, to receive the beautiful form of higher Lebanon, one certainly must put away this deformed form of lower Lebanon. For these two forms, which are so different from each other, cannot be in the same subject at the same time. As the one who was beloved of Christ said, *If anyone loves the world, the love of the Father is not in him.*[141] And, according to the testimony of Truth himself, *no one can serve two masters.*[142]

Hence, for stones to be formed in the higher Lebanon, they must first be taken out of the lower Lebanon; to be formed in the love of God, they must first be dug from the love of the world. To draw and extract them from there is very difficult. As the natural world is composed of four elements,[143] so these are bound in a kind of world of vanity as though by four chains. What was on Mount Lebanon detains them there because the world shines and smiles on them and flatters them, because they prosper in its ways,[144] and because perhaps they have been raised or hope to be raised there to some pinnacle of honor. Their own weight, that is, the pleasure of their flesh, also detains them, as does their hardness, that is, the stubbornness of their mind. Moreover, their connection with other stones, that is, the carnal affection that they have toward others and that others have toward them, holds them back. Thus, *the members of his household are his enemies.*[145] They neither want to enter into the spiritual building, nor do they permit others in the household to enter. These are the scales pressing on each other, from which, as God told Job, the body of Leviathan was composed.[146]

24. Here, certainly the hammer and axe are necessary. Here they should be used and heard, if by their blows on the stones, the form of Lebanon, which glitters in them can be destroyed, their bulk lessened, their hardness broken, and their connections dissolved so that they can be distinguished in this way from the mass of perdition and separated from the lower Lebanon. Once separated they can be removed, polished and squared and formed on the higher Lebanon and so inserted into the structure of the spiritual house. They are to be struck sometimes by faith, and sometimes more aggressively by reason: for less learned people faith should be used more; for those who are wiser and more skilled in reasoning reason should be used. For in the latter, as in a square[147] or weight of reason, that is, by the evident and irrefutable

light of truth, error should be attacked, conquered and overthrown. It is an axe when someone agrees by faith, a hammer when someone agrees by reason. The filth of sin and the harshness of punishment are also to be presented to them. However, because the carnal mind abhors the harshness of punishment more than the filth of sin, the axe is employed when the filth of the sin is exposed, and the hammer when the harshness of punishment is presented. But also, in a different way, with regard to sins the axe is the exposure of the filth in venial sins, while the hammer is the exposure of the filth in mortal sins. Also, in punishments the axe is the threat of the miseries of the present life, and the hammer is the threat of the miseries of the life to come. The axe can be assigned solely to present miseries, when someone is afraid of the loss of his things or the persecution of his friends; the hammer, when he is frightened by the affliction in his own person. In regard to future tortures only, the axe can be taken to be the fear of purgatorial fire, the hammer the fear of eternal fire.

By such axes and hammers, with the cooperation of the grace of the Holy Spirit, sometimes it happens that some stones are extracted from the quarries of lower Lebanon, that is, from the desire of the world and from a worldly and carnal way of life. Will these ever cease, so that then hammer and axe will not be heard? Certainly not yet, for their use is still necessary. The stones are still rough; more of the form of the world still needs to be put off than has already been removed. The old is not so much stripped off as still to be stripped off. Only a beginning has been made, not a perfect consummation. Many deformities and enormities and much unevenness are still apparent in them. The greater vices in them should be pounded off immediately as if with a hammer; the lesser ones are to be shaved off little by little as though with an axe. Former habits and perverse actions are to be destroyed in them immediately and completely; little by little their feelings and thoughts are to be polished, so that they change from carnal to spiritual. Whatever is illicit is to be eliminated immediately; even some licit things are to be cut off little by little.

25. The workshop in which the hammer and axe are principally heard among us is this house of discipline, the chapter room I am pointing out, in which we are now assembled.[148] Here the prior and the subprior and the circator, with undaunted zeal for the order,[149] strike transgressors of the rule with the hammer of fraternal charity, pursuing not the people involved, but for their sake pursuing the transgressions in them, in order to drive out not injuries to themselves but to the order

and religious life. Because of their office it is their duty to act strictly and vigorously to pursue disorderly things that need to be detected and checked.[150] It is enough for the others to take the axe and touch, rather than beat, the things that are to be corrected. However, the abbot, who in all matters sits as judge, and to whose judgment all things are referred,[151] inasmuch as the keys of the kingdom of heaven are handed over to him, brandishes the hammer with one hand and the axe with the other. It is his task to correct all things and to return them to the rule of reason. Let him take the hammer against major offenses and the axe against lesser ones. With the hammer let him rebuke more sharply, and with the axe let him reproach more gently. Let him impose more serious discipline with the hammer, and lighter discipline with the axe. Let him use the hammer on the obstinate and rebellious, the axe on the humble and cooperative. It is necessary to use the hammer against those who sin habitually, deliberately or from perversity of mind. It is enough to apply the axe to those who are surprised by a fault or fail from ignorance or weakness. However, if there are some who are so obstinate that neither the hammer nor the axe can govern their stiff necks, let them be thrown out as dirty rocks, which are not only useless but also harmful. Otherwise they will corrupt the other stones by being mixed with them and disturb and disfigure the whole house.

26. Let abbots remember to carry a hammer and an axe not just for others, but also for themselves, so that when they have preached to others they themselves do not become reprobates.[152] Far from us be those builders *who bind up heavy and unbearable burdens* on the shoulders of others, *but do not want to move a finger themselves*.[153] Indeed, not only must they bear all things as do the rest, but also as much as possible they ought to precede others, as the leaders on the way, in all the rigor, austerity and discipline of the order. They must be a pattern for their flock,[154] forming those committed to them more by their life than by their tongue, by deed rather than talk.[155] Let them carry around in their bodies[156] the dying (*mortificationem*) of Jesus, mortifying their *members which are upon the earth*,[157] so that each of them can say what the Apostle said: *Be imitators of me, as I am of Christ* Jesus.[158]

It is their task to receive into themselves the rule (*regulam*), according to which the stones are to be squared by the Cornerstone himself and to direct others according to it.[159] They are obligated on behalf of themselves and others; they will have to give an accounting for both.[160] Thus, there will be a very exacting judgment for those who preside. As here they are not like other people,[161] so there also they will not be like others. As here they are not equal in status to others, so then they will be superior to others in glory or inferior to them in reproach. Thus, they are going to receive either a double crown or a double punishment. Therefore, let them now strive to have double merits, so that *all have twin offspring*.[162] Let them carry the hammer and axe not only for reproaching and correcting others, but also for disciplining their own body and humbling their own heart.

27. For their part, let subjects not be content with the hammer and axe of their prelates, but let each one carry for himself an axe in compunction of heart and a hammer in affliction of the flesh. However, let the subject be careful not to presume to raise the hammer of rebuke or the axe of correction against his prelate, but also let him not dare to offer a reminder except with the fear of God, humility and all restraint[163] and reverence. And let brother use the hammer on a brother not at all, and the axe only rarely. It is the role of an equal to offer a reminder to an equal, and the role of prelates to rebuke and admonish. We require an everyday hammer in the struggle *against flesh and blood*, while an axe is needed in the struggle *against the spiritual forces of wickedness in the heavens*.[164] Also, when there are battles outside and mutinies within, the axe is exterior persecution by visible enemies; the hammer is interior persecution by false brothers.[165] For no plague is more adept at doing harm than an enemy within the household.[166]

By hammers and saws of this sort, by shearings and pressures of this kind, stones polished and squared pass over in a suitable and proper way into the spiritual building, are fitted into their places by the hand of the artisan,[167] and arranged to remain in sacred buildings. After they have been so shaped, the hand of God, the artisan, locates them in the structure of his spiritual house, placing some above, some below, some inside, some outside, some to the right, some to the left, depending on their shape and how they fit with the others as required by the harmony (*congruentia*) of his whole house. All of them, wherever they are placed in the building, he joins firmly into one with spiritual cement, the cement of the Holy Spirit, that is, the glue of perfect charity, teaching them *to preserve the unity of the Holy Spirit in the body of peace*.[168] The Son of God himself is the mason; the Holy Spirit is the cement.[169]

28. At this point the hammer and axe are now silent.[170] It is enough to have heard them until now; henceforth it is not necessary to hear or use them. Those who are of such perfection that they are suitable for placing in the building of God advance *in all the justifications of God*

without complaining.[171] They conduct themselves without offense toward those within and those without. They do not need to be rebuked or censured or even reminded. They are established in liberty (*libertate*) of spirit and as cheerful givers they offer a voluntary sacrifice,[172] or rather a holocaust. Afire with the Spirit,[173] they are sons, not servants; they do all things from love, and nothing from fear. As though it were a hammer, perfect love casts out of them the fear of incurring damnation, and, as though it were an axe, it expels the fear of losing beatitude.[174] Previously, it was as though there was a hammer, when they were forced by others to do good contrary to their desire (*voluntatem*) to act disobediently, and it was like an axe when they forced themselves to do so. Now, however, without any constraint, from others or themselves, they are so ready for any good that so habitual has doing good become for them that it seems innate. O how much someone like this adds to the beauty of God's house! How beautiful and ordered he is there! How regulated in himself, how harmonious with others, how seemly for the whole house. He reverences his superiors like parents. If any are subject to him he looks out for them as though they were his children. He rejoices with spiritual joy for those who are advancing on the right, as if their grace were his own. He feels compassion for those on the left who are in some difficulty, whether it be some temptation or some trouble of mind or body, just as if he himself were suffering it. He regards the bad and good things of others as his own; hence he knows how *to rejoice with those who rejoice, and to weep with those who weep.*[175] Those who are ahead of him he aims to imitate, not envy; those who follow he does not disdain, but challenges and urges them to better things.

Thus, paralleling the six surfaces of a squared stone, as though with six arms of charity spread into the whole earth, he is joined above to living stones through obedience, below through providing, on the right through shared joy, on the left through compassion, in front through imitation, and from behind through exhortation. These are, so to speak, the six arms of brotherly love, by which in parallel to the works of the six days he reaches out in good works toward his neighbor.[176] However, love of God[177] remains simple and undivided within in the root of the heart.[178] These seven distinctions among the virtues (*virtutes*) are the seven columns which power (*virtus*) carves out in its house.[179] This is the house of power, the house of the way, the house of love. Because of the more difficult material, it was necessary to delay for a longer time over this house to locate, extract, hew, and square stones. After this, we need to proceed to the second house, as though to enter it through this first one.

B.

29. After the outer, stone house, there follows the inner, cedar house, that is, after the house of power comes the house of anointing, after the house of the way comes the house of life, after the house of love comes the house of delight. The entrance to the second is through the first. If for someone in the first house the *yoke* of Christ is made *gentle and his burden light*[180] by perfect love of God and neighbor, he delights more in Christ the less he delights in the world. Having turned from carnal joy he rejoices in the Holy Spirit. Because he does nothing for empty glory but does everything with a solid conscience, he glories and delights in the testimony of his own conscience.[181] He delights because he is not aware of any evil demerit, and because he is conscious of good merit, and because from the present good merit he is aware of a future reward for himself. He rejoices because he has a clean conscience, because he has a just life, and because he awaits a crown of glory. He delights and rejoices because he has a clean heart, because he has a full heart, and because he hopes to be filled even more excellently. He has a heart clean both from the inclination toward (*affectu*) sin and guilt from (*reatu*) sin. He has a heart full of flowers of virtues and fruits of good works. He hopes it will be filled with an abundance and consummation of heavenly joys. He has a heart full of the good things not of the world, but of the mind. He waits for it to be filled with the good things of God. He believes that *he will see the good things of the Lord in the land of the living.*[182]

Meanwhile (*interim*)[183] he perceives certain first fruits of future beatitude; he now perceives in part what afterwards he is going to perceive perfectly. He tastes and sees *how sweet the Lord is.*[184] By tasting how sweet God is to him, he sees and understands how sweet the Lord is in himself. He says, "How sweet in Himself is he who is so sweet in his gift! How sweet he is in His substance who is so sweet in his grace. How sweet he is in his fullness who is so sweet when he is participated." First he rejoices because he senses how sweet God is, then because God is much sweeter than he can sense. First he rejoices because he has such in part; then, because such is what he has thus. It is one thing to rejoice over something because one has it; it is another to rejoice in the quality of what one has. A person rejoices over his enemy because he has him in prison, but he does not rejoice in the enemy whom he has there. Thus many rejoice over the knowledge that they have because they have it, but they do not rejoice in the very knowledge that they have. They do not love knowledge for the sake of knowledge, but because of something else that they have or wish to have through it.

In accord with these two kinds of joy, the saints of the other life have one joy that is equal and one that is unequal. Consider two of them, of whom one has there more than the other. The one who has more rejoices and delights more in that of which he possesses more. The one who has less rejoices less in the quality of the thing of which he has less. However, the inferior rejoices that his superior has what the superior has and he himself does not have, as much as he would rejoice to have it if he had it. Thus, everyone there rejoices over the good of the other as if over his own, although not equally as in his own, nor equally as in God, the common good of all. According to these two ways or causes of rejoicing, he, regarding whom these examples have been adduced, both rejoices, as I said, that he has a foretaste of how sweet God is in the present, and he rejoices because God, of whom he has a foretaste, is so sweet. To rejoice in this latter way is much more perfect, for the one who rejoices that God is sweet to him to some extent restricts his joy to himself, while the one who rejoices that God is so sweet in himself, indeed that He is sweetness itself, pours back his joy into God himself. The former rejoices over his own special good; the latter rejoices over the common and general good of all the saints.

30. In accord with this latter way of rejoicing and delighting there follows another joy regarding justice. The one who first was delighted by the habit of justice afterwards delights in the very beauty and elegance of the justice that he has. Now he no longer rejoices that he has justice, but that the justice he has is so beautiful in itself, and because it would be no less beautiful in itself even if neither he nor anyone else possessed it. He does not love justice only because through it he will come to the crown, but he loves it for its own sake. For even if he hoped to gain nothing from it, he is still of a mind to embrace and love it. It can even happen that he progresses so far that he prefers to be perfectly blessed in order to be perfectly just, rather than to be perfectly just in order to be perfectly blessed.[185] To prefer this seems to be more perfect and more just. All people want to be blessed, but not all want to be just. Also, the one who wants to be perfectly blessed surely wants his will to be perfectly fulfilled in God and by God; the one who wishes to be

perfectly just wants very much that the will of God be perfectly fulfilled in him and by him. Who can doubt that in all things he should prefer the fulfillment of the divine will to the fulfillment of his own will?

In accord with this same manner of rejoicing a second rejoicing over cleanness (*munditia*) of heart then follows from the first. Not only does he rejoice that he has cleanness of heart, but he rejoices also in the very purity (*puritate*) of that cleanness, whether he or another has it, a purity that cleanness would have in itself even if no one had it. He loves cleanness not only because through it he may or will avoid punishment, but also for cleanness' own sake, that is, because it is so beautiful in itself that it should be loved for itself. Hence, even if he were not going to avoid punishment through it, he would still wish to pursue and guard it as much as he could. Sometimes he also advances so far in love of it that, if it were necessary to choose, he would prefer to become wretched rather than impure. In fact, he regards uncleanness as the supreme misery.[186]

31. These are the seven joys, seven holy and spiritual delights that come forth from the sevenfold spirit, from perfect charity.[187] The first delight is from the habit of cleanness, the second from the habit of justice, the third from a sort of certainty about having beatitude in the future, the fourth from a foretaste of divine sweetness, the fifth from the quality and fullness of sweetness of which one meanwhile has a foretaste, the sixth from the beauty and form of justice, the seventh from the purity and beauty of spiritual cleanness. These are seven delights, seven anointings of the spirit, seven columns cut out in the house of anointing.[188]

There are other delights also, but for the present it is sufficient to have enumerated and, as though by cutting them out, extracted and explained as many as correspond to the number of the columns. Joys of this kind are the cedar boards in the second house. Who does not know that wood is softer than stones? In the building or preparation of the first house there was much hardness and roughness in preparing, exercising and perfecting virtues, but here there are only softness and gentleness, only sweetness and joy. Also, in the same way that cedars are tall in height and by nature free of rot, so to delight in the good and rejoice in the Holy Spirit the heart also stretches upward and guards itself unharmed from the rot of vices. The cedar boards are attached to and rest on the squared stones, because it is impossible to know these kinds of delights where the virtues are not present. Also, the cedar house is inside, the stone house outside, because of the way the virtues advance through the exercise of external activity, whereas these delights consists solely in interior goods.

C.

32. After the first and second house there comes a third; after the exterior house and the interior house, there comes the inmost house; that is, after the stone house and the cedar house comes the golden house; that is, after the house of virtue and the house of anointing comes the house of wisdom; after the house of the way and the house of the life comes the house of the truth; after the house of love and the house of delight comes the house of contemplation. The contemplation of truth is gold.[189] If some falsity is added to gold it is impure. Such gold is found among heretics and secular philosophers. However, contemplation of truth without any admixture of falsity is gold, even pure gold. This kind of contemplation even of a bodily creature[190] is pure gold, but of a spiritual creature it is purer gold, and when contemplation of the Creator Himself is attained it is the purest gold.

There are many ways of contemplating the Creator, either in some participation in Him, or outside of and beyond all participation.[191] The Creator is the Highest Good, and without participation in him whatever else is good is not good. Physical creation has the lowest and, as it were, external and only general participation in the Highest Good, namely that according to which it is said of every creature *all things that he had made were very good*.[192] However, in the spiritual creation participation in the highest good is not only general, but also special, higher and more interior than the general participation, not simple, but multiple; that is, not one, but three. In this case, participation by creation, by justification, and by beatitude are distinct.[193] For the spiritual creature, the first participation in the highest good is according to its creation, because it is made to the image and likeness of God himself, insofar as it can love and understand that very Goodness. A second participation occurs by justification, because not only can it understand and love Goodness, but also it actually does understand and love it. The third participation is according to beatitude, when Goodness, perfectly understood and loved, is perfectly enjoyed by contemplating it perfectly and delighting in it perfectly. In these four participations in the Highest Good, one in bodily things, and three in spiritual ones, four contemplations of God are formed in those who participate in

Him. Beyond these occurs a fifth contemplation in the eternal arrangement of all things,[194] but also a sixth, still higher and as it were more interior, in the special predestination of the saints.[195] The seventh, highest and most interior, without any reference to a creature, simple and absolute, occurs in the unity and trinity of the godhead.[196] These seven kinds of divine contemplation are perhaps the seven columns which wisdom carves out in her house.

33. The gold plates can be understood as the single,[197] that is, singular and individual, contemplations in each kind of contemplation. The golden plates are fittingly applied to the cedar boards because contemplations of God need to be founded in and rest upon spiritual delights. Delight raises the mind into contemplation and sustains it in contemplation once it is raised there; otherwise, the mind cannot rise or remain there. The golden nails, by which the gold plates are attached to the cedar boards,[198] are back and forth movements from delight to contemplation and from contemplation to delight. Delight leads to contemplation, and contemplation pours back into greater delight. Greater delight leads back again to more comprehensive contemplation.

This ordering is kept and represented in the Son and the Holy Spirit. First the Son was conceived from the Holy Spirit; then the Son sent out the Holy Spirit; and finally it is said that the Holy Spirit is going to lead into all truth, as into the fullness of the Son. However, as the contemplation of truth is referred to the Son, so spiritual delight is referred to the Holy Spirit. O how happy, how bright is this passing over and back, how pleasant and beautiful this moving back and forth from the Holy Spirit to the Son, and from the Son to the Holy Spirit, from the gentleness of delight to the brightness of contemplation, and from the brightness of contemplation to the gentleness of delight! Therefore, because both delights—here those from contemplation, there, as was earlier shown, those from virtues—flow into the spirit from both sides, rightly is the cedar house located in the middle between the exterior stone house and the interior gold house.

IV.

34. These three houses set forth above are now finally expounded according to our capacity, although not according to theirs. The first is the house of virtue, the house of the way, the house of love; the second

is the house of anointing, the house of life, the house of delight; the third is the house of wisdom, the house of truth, the house of contemplation. O lovable house, O house to be enjoyed, O house to be contemplated. O house one and three, all of which is built upon a single rock.[199] If there is anyone of you who dwells in a mud house,[200] if anyone of you has built your house on sand,[201] where you waver and become embittered and gloomy, look here and see a solid house, a pleasant house, a brightly lighted house. Look and long, behold and want, consider and desire, desire and hasten, hasten and enter, enter and inhabit. Inhabit and love, inhabit and delight, inhabit and contemplate. Love that you may be solid, delight that you may rejoice, contemplate that you may be illumined. Be solid so that you may become eternal; rejoice that you may become blessed; shine so that you may become glorious. Cling to God the Father through the solidity of eternity; cling to the Holy Spirit through the joy of beatitude; cling to the Son through the light of glory.[202]

Although the Son is said especially to build the house of God, he does not build it for himself alone, but for the whole Trinity together. For this reason he builds not only a single, but also a threefold house. Just as the one person of Christ consists of three essences, that is of flesh, spirit and divinity,[203] so the first house pertains in some fashion to his flesh because of the power which he exercises through the flesh, the second to his spirit because of his spiritual anointing, the third to his divinity because of divine contemplation.[204] When these three houses are built in us, we also are completely made into a house of God. For our body is made into God's house because of the first house, our spirit because of the second, our mind because of the third. We glorify and carry God in our body;[205] there he dwells as though bodily,[206] but in our spirit spiritually, and in our mind intellectually.[207] He dwells in our flesh as if through his flesh, in our spirit through his spirit, in our mind through his beauty (*speciem*). He dwells in our flesh through the working of power and love in imitation of his flesh; in our spirit through the delight of unction or the unction of delight in the pouring in of his Spirit; in our mind through the contemplation of wisdom or the wisdom of contemplation from some showing of his beauty.

So, he dwells in our flesh in an imitable way; in our spirit in a way that can bring delight; in our mind as available for contemplation. In power and love by his flesh he leads us through himself, the Way; in anointing and delight he feeds us with the Holy Spirit through himself, the Life; taking us in wisdom and contemplation from the way by his beauty and perfecting us in life, he enlightens us through himself, the Truth. Therefore, in accord with those three things that David asked for himself and proposed that we ask for,[208] God dwells in our flesh through discipline, in our spirit through goodness, and in our mind through knowledge. To discipline pertain exercise of virtue and love on the way. To goodness (which another translation calls "sweetness") belong the joy of anointing and delight in life and refreshment. To knowledge belong the light of wisdom and the contemplation of truth.

Accordingly, Christ, Good Teacher, *teach me your goodness, discipline and knowledge,*[209] so that through these three you may dwell in me completely and I may dwell wholly in you, and I may be completely yours and you may be completely mine, drawing me completely to you and filling me completely in you, and not otherwise than from you. Thus, in all of me, and not only by all of me, but also by your entire heavenly house you may be praised without end for all of me who am in you. Amen.

NOTES

1 Prov. 9:1. Cf. Hugh of St Victor, *Sapientia* (PL 196.851 D–852B). Throughout, biblical references are to the numbering of the Latin Vulgate Bible (*Biblia sacra*, ed. R. Weber *et al.*, 4th ed. [Stuttgart: Deutsche Bibelgesellschaft, 1994]). Unless otherwise indicated, all translations are mine, even if a reference to a published English translation is provided.

2 "interim": meanwhile, in the meantime, for the time being. The word is often used for the present time, which lies between the first and final coming of Christ, the time of "already but not yet." See the very helpful article of F. Châtillon, "Hic, ibi, interim," *Revue d'ascetique et mystique* 25 (1949): 194–99; Châtillon, *Théologie*, 278–81; Feiss, *Achard of St. Victor: Works*, 208 n. 17. See par. 9 and 29 below.

3 See Rom. 8:9; 1 Cor. 7:40.

4 1 Cor. 6:17; Achard of St Victor, *Serm.* 2.3 (Châtillon, 39–40; tr. Feiss, 151–53); *Serm.* 15.34 (Châtillon, 237–39; tr. Feiss, 344–46).

5 See 1 Cor. 2:10.

6 See Ps. 50:8.

7 See 1 Cor. 2:9.

8 "edificationis": "of building, of edification." Achard is punning. He is supposed to edify by speaking a word about edification/building, but if his listeners are not edified, they can at least learn how to be built/edified or how to build/edify.

9 Prov. 9:1.

10 "virtus": this word means both power and virtue. It was translated "virtue" in the first paragraph. It will be translated according to context in what follows, but if it seems helpful the Latin word will be indicated in parentheses. See 1 Cor. 1:24.

11 See Luke 4:18; Isa. 61:1.

12 "participibus suis": see Ps. 44:8; Heb. 1:9.

13 John 3:34. Achard of St Victor, *Serm.* 4.5 (Châtillon, 59–61; tr. Feiss, 131–33).

14 "velle, scire et posse": This triad corresponds to the wisdom, anointing and power (*virtus*) that Achard finds in Christ, and which he will develop throughout the sermon. Elsewhere, Achard speaks of understanding, love and action or fruition. Human beings, as God's image and likeness, share in these attributes: *Serm.* 9.4 (Châtillon, 105–106; tr. Feiss, 68); see also Richard of St Victor, *Tract. on Luke* 13:34 (*Sex sunt dies*; tr. Evans, VTT 4.227–28). This triad also corresponds to the power, wisdom and goodness of Hugh of St Victor's *On the Three Days* (VTT 1.49–102). As Châtillon points out (*Théologie*, 160), Achard thus locates the image and likeness in the soul rather than in the human being, and so espouses a form of dualism that was common in the Middle Ages. In his *Discretione* 1–2 (Häring, 174; tr. Feiss, 357–58), Achard writes of the "interior substance" of the human being, which is distinct from the body. Godfrey of St Victor will reject such a dualism; see Feiss, VTT 2.309–10.

15 Achard here makes use of the theological theory of appropriations in the development of which Hugh and Richard of St Victor played an important role. See Châtillon, *Sermons*, 136 n. 14; Coolman, VTT 1.23–48; Feiss, VTT 1.55–58; Richard of St Victor, *Trin.* VI.15 (Ribaillier, 247–48; tr. Evans, VTT 1.335–36 = *Tribus per.* [Ribaillier, 182–83]); Godfrey of St Victor, *Microcosmus* III.227 (Delhaye, 248; tr. Feiss, VTT 2.335–36, 340–41 n. 89).

16 John 14:6.

17 Prov. 9:1.

18 Achard says something very similar in *Unitate* 2.3 (Martineau, 144; tr. Feiss, 439): "Virtutes autem creaturarum quas per gratiam accipiunt [sancti], quaedam sunt illarum quae in Deo omnes et totae et simul et semper sunt virtutum primarum et summarum participationes quae omnes substantialiter ibi una sunt virtus, nec ipsa aliud nisi ipse Deus; item creaturarum beatitudines nonnisi beatitudinis summae quae in Deo et Deus est quedam sunt derivationes, et utraeque non aliud sunt nisi creaturae ratonalis ad creatorem suum tanquam imaginis ad unitatem connexiones, quae et ipsae connexionis summae, quae inter personas Triniatatis

est, videntur esse quaedam ymagines" ("Now the virtues of creatures which the saints receive through grace are certain forms of participation in those first and supreme virtues that are all, wholly, simultaneously, and always, in God. These are all substantially one virtue, which is not other than God himself. Likewise, the beatitudes of creatures are only certain derivatives of the highest beatitude that is in God and is God. Both [virtues and beatitudes] are nothing other than connections of the rational creature to its Creator, of the image to Unity; they also seem to be certain images of that supreme connection which exists between the persons of the Trinity"). In *Serm.* 4.1 (Châtillon, 54–56; tr. Feiss, 125–27) Achard calls these three participations the virtual (powerful), intellectual and spiritual bodies of Christ.

19   Achard here balances what he has said about the activities appropriated to each of the persons of the Trinity "formally" by restating that all three are one in effecting the results. See Châtillon, *Théologie*, 227–29.

20   Using this same terminology in *Discretione* 16–22 (Häring, 177–79; tr. Feiss, 360–62), Achard says that the essence of the soul is one but multiplied formally into various powers. All the various powers are in essence one power, but formally distinct from each other.

21   The Victorines loved lists and divisions of three. For example, in his *De archa Noe*, Hugh of St Victor distinguishes three words (II.3), three decks (II.5), three books (II.10, 13), three words (II.11, 14), three woods (II.12, 15), three fears (III.11), three kinds of people (IV.8) and so forth, and in the *Libellus de formatione arche* he distinguishes three eras (3).

22   Cf. 1 Cor. 3:9; 3 John 1:8; Achard of St Victor, *Serm.* 15.22 (Châtillon, 225; tr. Feiss, 328–30).

23   Cf. 1 Chron. 22:9.

24   Cf. 2 Sam. 7:1–17; 1 Chron. 22:7–10.

25   Cf. John 1:18.

26   Cf. Apoc. 21:3, a verse read as the capitulum for Sext in the office for the Dedication of a Church.

27   Phil. 2:7.

28   Phil. 2:6.

29   Cf. Matt. 13:55.

30   Cf. Prov. 9:1.

31   Cf. Phil. 2:6–7.

32   Cf. Matt. 12:42.

33   Col. 1:20.

34   Eph. 2:14.

35   Cf. Eph. 5:1.

36   Luke 11:23. The word "gather" ("colligunt" from "colligere," "collectus") had many meanings and connotations: to collect, read, reckon up, collect oneself, summarize, garner. In his *Confessions* X.11.18, in which he collects the fragments of his life into a narrative whole, Augustine, speaking of the act of memory, writes: "velut ex quadam dispersione conligenda, unde dictum est cogitare" ("as though to be collected together from their scattered state, whence it is called thinking" [O'Donnell, 1:126; tr. Chadwick, 189]). Hence, the idea of a "collect" prayer. O'Donnell (*Confessions*, 3:182) sees here an echo of Isa. 11:12, which speaks of God collecting the dispersed of Judah. For references elsewhere in the Bible, in the *Confessions*, and in Plotinus, see O'Donnell, *Confessions*, 2:21, commenting on *Conf.* I.3.3. For a classic Victorine use of the image of gathering the dispersed fragments, see Hugh of St Victor, *Libellus* 5 (Sicard, 149–50; PL 176.696D–697B): "Someone runs out of a cave with his face covered, and tripping on a rock breaks the bowl he is carrying. This expresses the ignorance that through various errors scatters the unity of the soul . . . Meditation . . . collects the pieces of the broken bowl. Contemplation, like a workman, fires these fragments, liquefying them in such a way that the liquid . . . seems to run through a pipe . . . into a mold. This symbolizes the following mystery: the unity of the soul, which ignorance scatters, is found by knowledge, and collected by meditation. Contemplation liquefies it through the fire of divine love, and pours it into the mold of the divine likeness to be reformed" ("Quidam de caverna obvoluta facie prodiens

corruit, et in lapidem offendens vas quod portat confringit ad exprimendam ignorantiam que per varios errores anime *integritatem dissipat . . .* meditatio *. . . colligens fragmenta vasis fracti.* Contemplatio formatur ad similitudinem fabri conflans eadem fragmenta, ita ut ipsa liquefactio . . . quasi per fistulam . . . in monetam currere videatur. Propter hoc mysterium: quia integritatem anime, quam ignorantia frangit, cognitio invenit, *meditatio colligit,* contemplatio per ignem divini amoris liquefaciendo in monetam divine similitudinis reformandam fundit"). For other examples of the Victorine use of the topos of scatter (outside) and gather (inside), see Hugh of St Victor, *Misc.* I.6 (PL 177.482AD), a text which considers the various sorts of peace and struggle that Achard treats in this sermon; *Misc.* 1.55 (PL 177.501D–502B); *In hier. cael.* 7 (PL 175.1054B); *Archa Noe* III.12 (Sicard, 56; PL 176.648A); Richard of St Victor, *Apoc.* I.1 (PL 196.690A–B; tr. Kraebel, VTT 3.344).

37 Matt. 5:9.
38 Ps. 119:7.
39 Ps. 75:3.
40 Ps. 48:22.
41 Luke 2:14.
42 Phil. 4:7. The Latin word translated "understanding" in this paragraph is "sensus."
43 John 14:27.
44 Cf. Ps. 72:28.
45 Cf. 1 Cor. 6:17. See Achard of St Victor, *Serm.* 2.3 (Châtillon, 40; tr. Feiss, 153 with n. 5); *Serm.* 13.1 (Châtillon, 134–35; tr. Feiss, 208); *Serm.* 15.34 (Châtillon, 237; tr. Feiss, 344). On "unitas spiritus" in medieval authors, see B. McGinn, *The Growth of Mysticism: Gregory the Great through the 12th Century,* The Presence of God, A History of Western Christian Mysticism 2 (New York: Crossroad, 1994): 213–16 (St Bernard of Clairvaux), 243–44, 263–67 (William of St Thierry), 417–18 (Richard of St Victor).
46 Acts 4:32.
47 Eph. 4:3.
48 Cf. *Serm.* 2.2 (Châtillon, 38–39; tr. Feiss, 150–51); *Serm.* 9.1–2 (Châtillon, 101–104; tr. Feiss, 65–66).
49 Matt. 16:17.
50 Rom. 8:6–7.
51 Apoc. 17:17.
52 "O concordia non concors, sed a corde Dei discors et universe rationi exsors": harmony is a recurrent theme in Victorine writings. See, e.g., the entry "harmony in nature" in VTT 1.420 (esp. the notes on page 97), and those to "harmony" among and within human beings in VTT 2.388. Adam of St Victor in particular emphasizes unity among persons. From an early twenty-first-century perspective, harmony seems to suggest a concord of different voices and instruments, which is enriching, whereas unity might imply uniformity (see M. R. Miles, "Leaning toward Enlightenment," *Harvard Divinity Bulletin* [Winter/Spring, 2010]: 67–68). To some extent, the implications of the metaphor, at least in Adam of St Victor, may depend on whether the music was strictly monophonic. One might then think about whether the apparent emphasis on uniformity in earlier medieval monasticism gave way to greater diversity, individuality or individualism in later medieval monasticism, and whether there were differences between those who followed the *Rule of Benedict* and the canons regular who followed the *Rule of St Augustine.*
53 Cf. Gen. 2:18, 20–25.
54 Cf. John 8:34.
55 Cf. Neh. 1:10; Bar. 2:11 *et al.* See Godfrey of St Victor, *In Cant. BVM* 10 (Gasparri, 69; tr. Feiss, VTT 4.522).
56 Cf. 1 Cor. 9:27.
57 Cf. Rom. 6:13.
58 Cf. Gen. 3:15.

59 Rom. 7:22–23.
60 Gal. 5:17.
61 Ps. 62:2.
62 Ps. 83.3.
63 Wisd. of Sol. 9:15.
64 Cf. 1 Cor. 15:53–54.
65 Phil. 4:7.
66 Ps. 4:9. On the connotations of "in idipsum" in Christian Latin, see Feiss, VTT 2.182 n. 5.
67 Cf. Augustine, *Conf.* I.1.1 (O'Donnell, 1:3; tr. Chadwick, 3).
68 Cf. 1 Kings 5:17; 6:7. "Quadratos": squared-off, foursquare, hewn, suitable. I will translate the word consistently as "squared."
69 Cf. 1 Kings 6:15, 17.
70 Cf. 1 Kings 6:20–22.
71 Cf. 1 Kings 6:7.
72 John 4:23.
73 Cf. 1 Kings 5:17.
74 Cf. 1 Kings 5:14.
75 The form impresses on matter or substance a quality that is only accidental. Achard makes the same distinction in *Discretione* 3 (Häring, 174; Feiss, 358) and *Unitate* II.13 (Martineau, 172; tr. Feiss, 460) regarding light, but without specifying that the quality is given by the form accidentally.
76 On Lebanon, see Jerome, *Heb. nom.* (*De Regnorum Lib. III*) (De Lagarde, 111.18; PL 23.865–66); Hugh of St Victor, *Assumpt.* (PL 177.1222D); Achard, *Serm.* 14.3 (Châtillon, 175; tr. Feiss, 263). There are additional references in Hugh of St Victor, *Eulogium* 11 (PL 176.990C; tr. Feiss, VTT 2.128 and 134 n. 75). In this discussion of "Lebanon" Achard, like Hugh before him, uses a number of related words that I have tried to translate consistently: "candor" (whiteness), "candidatio" (whitening), "candidus" (white), "candidatus" (whitened). "Whiteness" and "blackness" are not usual words in English parlance, but they convey something of the "Platonism" of Achard's thought-world.
77 Ps. 91:13–14.
78 Ps. 28:5.
79 Song of Songs 4:8.
80 Cf. Wisd. of Sol. 7:26.
81 Cf. Achard of St Victor, *Serm.* 3.3 (Châtillon, 49–50; tr. Feiss, 116–17).
82 Cf. Achard of St Victor, *Serm.* 3.3 (Châtillon, 48; tr. Feiss, 115–16).
83 1 Pet. 2:22; cf. Isa. 53:9.
84 "culpa": guilt, sin, crime, failure, defect; "pena": punishment, satisfaction, penalty, torment. It is difficult to cover these ranges of meanings with a single English word. I have chosen "guilt" and "punishment."
85 Song of Songs 1:4.
86 Ps. 44:3.
87 Isa. 53:2.
88 Rom. 8:3.
89 Heb. 4:15. The Latin reads: "Temptatus est 'per omnia pro similitudine, absque peccato.'"
90 Song of Songs 5:10.
91 Isa. 1:18.
92 Isa. 63:2.
93 Isa. 63:3.
94 Ps. 92:1.
95 Cf. Matt. 17:2.
96 Ps. 18:6.
97 Cf. John 17:5.

98   John 1:16.
99   John 1:16.
100   The meaning of these sentences hinges on the two prepositions "de" (from) and "pro" (in front of, on account of, in place of, for the sake of, by virtue of).
101   Eph. 1:6.
102   Achard here uses some terms freighted with theological connotations and history. "Justificatio": a word that in the Latin of the Vulgate Bible occurs about 40 times in the OT, 25 times in Rom., Gal., and 1 Cor., and about 15 times elsewhere in the NT. One way to approach its meaning is the Vulgate rendering of Wisd. of Sol. 6:11: *Qui enim custodierint justa juste, justificabuntur* ("Those who have kept the holy ordinances in holiness, shall be made holy" [tr. D. Winston, *The Wisdom of Solomon*, Anchor Bible (Garden City, NY: Doubleday, 1979), 151]). That is, those who justly abide by the things that are just are justified (= they are found just, juridically or in fact, by God most importantly). In short, those who do what is right in the right way are upright. Châtillon explains that in Achard's writings "original justice" is the state of the newly baptized, that is, their participation in the merits or grace of Christ. Once a person reaches the age of personal responsibility, he must cooperate with grace to act justly; then he has "actual justice." Original justice is the result of grace acting in us, but without us; actual justice is the result of grace acting within us, but not without us. Actual justice is maintained or regained in the course of a lifelong struggle to overcome inclinations toward sin and to achieve transformation (see Châtillon, *Théologie*, 230–32).
103   "reformatio": re-formation. Again, as Châtillon explains (*Théologie*, 158–65), Achard distinguishes three ways or regions in which human beings resemble God: creation, justice (grace), and glory. Likeness according to justice consists in using the power of knowing and loving. Likeness in glory consists in the full beatitude of heaven. Because humankind fell into a region of unlikeness, reformation is the lifelong struggle, empowered by grace, to regain likeness to God through "actual justice." Coolman's book, *Theology of Hugh of St. Victor*, explores the central place of formation, deformation, reformation and transformation in the theology of Hugh of St Victor.
104   "capax": capable of. Augustine, *Trin.* XIV.8.11 (Mountain and Glorie, 436; tr. Hill, 379): "Eo quippe ipso imago eius est quo eius capax est eiusque esse particeps potest" ("It is His image insofar as it is capable of Him and can be a sharer in Him"). Protestant theologians sometimes advance the proposition, "Finitum non capax infiniti" ("The finite is not capable of the infinite"). See n. 155 below.
105   Achard's Latin reads: "Materia est bonum humane nature, forma est donum divine gratie."
106   This tussle between "pietas" and "justitia" recalls the theme, widespread in the Middle Ages, of the conflict of four daughters of God, which are allegorized in Ps. 84:11: *Misericordia et veritas obviaverunt sibi: iustitia et pax osculatae sunt* ("Mercy and truth have met; justice and peace have kissed"). The virtues ("the daughters of God") argue over the fate of humankind; justice requires humankind to remain in bondage to the devil, but mercy urges that humankind be redeemed. These themes appear often in the Victorines: Hugh of St Victor, *Sacr.* I.8.1, 4 (PL 176.305C–D, 308A–B); *Misc.* II.63 on Ps. 84:11 (PL 177.623B–625D); *Misc.* III.29 (PL 177.651AC); Richard of St Victor, *Ad me clamat* (Ribaillier, 267); *Apoc.* IV.2 (PL 196.801C, 802B). See J. Rivière, *Le dogme de la rédemption au début du moyen âge* (Paris: J. Vrin, 1934), 309–62; J. Leclercq, "Nouveau témoin du 'conflit des filles de Dieu'," *RBen.* 58 (1948): 110–24; M. Fumagalli, *Le Quattro sorelle, il re e il servo. Studio sull'allegoria medievale del ps. 84, 11* (Milan: Cisalpino-Goliardica, 1981); M. Ralson, "The Four Daughters of God in *The Castell of Perseverance*," *Comitatus: Journal of Medieval and Renaissance Studies* 15 (1984): 25–44; and introduction to and selection from a Middle English translation of Robert Grosseteste's *Le Château d'Amour* in G. Shuffelton, *Codex Ashmole 61: A Compilation of Popular Middle English Verse* (Kalamazoo: Medieval Institute Publications, 2008).
107   Ps. 76:10; cf. Achard of St Victor, *Serm.* 3.3 (Châtillon, 48; tr. Feiss, 115); *Serm.* 15.1 (Châtillon, 200; tr. Feiss, 299).

[108] Rom. 8:29.

[109] In what follows Achard will look for fours (and also for sixes, because of the six sides of a cube). Such inquiries did not end with the Middle Ages. See N. Hance, "Cosmic Connections," *Way* 50/3 (July 2011): 97–107, where he draws parallels between the four forces of the universe—gravitational, weak, electromagnetic and strong—and C. S. Lewis' four loves—charity, affection, friendship and eros.

[110] 1 Cor. 1:30.

[111] Here, as is usual, Achard is very careful to attribute any human merits to God's grace that comes through Christ. In this, he anticipates the teaching of the Council of Trent formulated in answer to Luther. On this, see J. O'Malley, *Four Cultures of the West* (Cambridge: Harvard University Press, 2004), 58–60, 109–113.

[112] Ps. 33:6.

[113] Ps. 33:9.

[114] The last few lines of this paragraph turn on the words "scientia" and "sapientia," a contrast that provided the title for R. Baron's study of Hugh of St Victor, *Science et sagesse chez Hugues de Saint-Victor* (Paris: P. Lethielleux, 1957). See, e.g., Hugh of St Victor, *Didasc.* I.2 (Buttimer, 6–7; tr. Harkins, VTT 3.84–85; tr. Taylor, 48); *Archa Noe* III.6 (Sicard, 63–66; PL 176.651D–652A); Achard of St Victor, *Serm.* 13.34 (Châtillon, 168; tr. Feiss, 252); Richard of St Victor, *Apoc.* IV.l (PL 196.798C); V.Prol. (PL 196.818D–819A); *LE* II.10.10 (Châtillon, 395.21–24 = *Serm. cent.* 10; PL 177.920C); *Arca Moys.* III.21 (Aris, 80; PL 196.130D–131A; tr. Zinn, 251–52); *Emman.* II.18 (PL 196.653BC); Pseudo-Richard of St Victor, *Cant.* 1 (PL 196.41BC), 5 (PL 196.420B–C); Walter of St Victor, *Serm.* 8.1 (Châtillon, 63); Anonymous of St Victor, *Serm.* 7.2 (Châtillon, *Sermones inediti*, 277). Often, "scientia" and "sapientia" are used interchangeably, but there are times when the Victorines, like other medieval authors, make a distinction. A good example is Walter of St Victor, *Serm.* 3.3 (Châtillon, 29), the gist of which is as follows: "Knowledge which does not have the seasoning of divine love is not savory but tasteless, inflating not upbuilding, and therefore unworthy of the name of wisdom . . . Knowledge of the truth reforms in us the image of God; love repairs in us the likeness of God" ("Scientia enim quae non habet condimentum divinae dilectionis non est sapida sed insipida, inflans non aedificans, ideoque indigna nomine sapientiae . . . Cognitio veritatis reformat in nobis Dei imaginem, dilectio reparat in nobis Dei similitudinem"). Sometimes the distinction is made in the light of the belief that Christ is the Wisdom of God; at other times, as in the passage just quoted, the distinction turns on whether knowledge is suffused with love. Another factor in the distinction is that for these authors philosophy (and Christianity is the true philosophy) is love of wisdom, not just seeking knowledge. Thus, wisdom (*sapientia*) is knowledge (*scientia*) seasoned (*saporata*) with love, that is sap[or + sc]ientia. On the background for this distinction and terminology in Augustine and Gregory the Great, and some examples of it in twelfth-century authors, see A. Solignac, "Sagesse," *DS* 14 (1990): 103–107.

[115] 1 Cor. 1:30.

[116] Wisd. of Sol. 8:7. As Achard goes on to show, the author of *Wisdom* is enumerating the four cardinal virtues of Greek philosophy, though the Latin of the Vulgate somewhat obscures that.

[117] Luke 6:20–22.

[118] Cf. Ps. 61:11.

[119] Matt. 5:6.

[120] Eccl. 1:18.

[121] Achard here draws on the theology of compunction, which was a central component in Gregory the Great's legacy to medieval Christianity. See, e.g., McGinn, *The Growth of Mysticism*, 48–50. For compunction, see Richard of St Victor, *LE* II.10.15 (Châtillon, 405 = *Serm. cent.* 10; PL 177.929BC); Anonymous of St Victor, *Serm.* 1.4 (Châtillon, 243); Richard of St Victor, *Super exiit* 4 (Châtillon, 86–88); *Tract.* on Ps. 28 (PL 196.303D–304B). Achard's reference to the upper and lower pools comes from Gregory the Great, *Dialogues* III.34.3–4 (De Vogüé,

402). See Hugh of St Victor, *Adnot. in Pent.* (*In Librum Judicum* 1) (PL 175.87A); Pseudo-Hugh of St Victor, *Speculum ecclesiae* 4 (PL 177.347C); Walter of St Victor, *Serm.* 11.5 (Châtillon, 97.160–66); Anonymous of St Victor, *Serm.* 4.6 (Châtillon, 260). For other medieval uses of the text, see A. Blaise, *Lexicon latinitatis medii aevi*, CCCM (1975), 510. In *The Power of Prayer* (VVT 4.317–48) Hugh of St Victor assigns "devotio" a central role in "oratio," so Richard of St Victor sometimes assigns "devotio" a central role in "compunctio," see *Erud.* I.18 (PL 196.1259A–B); *Adnot. Ps.* 136 (PL 196.375A); *Pot. lig.* 25 (Ribaillier, 110).

122 Cf. Judg. 1:15.
123 Matt. 11:29.
124 Matt. 11:30.
125 Gal. 6:2.
126 Rom. 5:5.
127 Cf. Isa. 11:2.
128 Mark 12:30; Luke 10:27; Matt. 22:37; Deut. 6:5.
129 Cf. Eph. 2:20.
130 Matt. 22:39; Lev. 19:18; Mark 12:31; Luke 10:27.
131 Ps. 10:6.
132 Mark 12:30; Luke 10:27; Matt. 22:37; Deut. 6:5.
133 Cf. Matt. 22:39; Mark 12:31.
134 1 Thess. 5:14.
135 Eph. 3:18.
136 Cf. Pseudo-Richard of St Victor, *Quaest. in epist. Pauli, In epist. ad Eph.*, q. 17 (PL 175.572A).
137 Rom. 12:2. See Châtillon, *Théologie*, 237–38.
138 1 John 5:19.
139 Rom. 13:13.
140 James 1:8.
141 1 John 2:15.
142 Matt. 6:24.
143 See *Serm.* 15:8 (Châtillon, 209; tr. Feiss, 309); Châtillon, *Théologie*, 241–43.
144 Cf. Ps. 36:7.
145 Matt.10:36.
146 Job 41:6.
147 The manuscripts have "quadam," which Châtillon corrects to "quadra": a square of parchment, area around a castle ("the castle quarter"), which overlaps with the masculine, "quadrus": stone block, frame, a fourth share of an inheritance, measure of land and "quadrum": fourth. If Châtillon's conjecture is correct, I wonder if Achard isn't referring to some kind of carpenter's square.
148 This statement makes clear that Achard delivered this sermon in a chapter room. There during the chapter of faults the abbot assigned penances for those who transgressed the rule. Religious could accuse themselves or be accused by their fellow religious or by the abbey officials mentioned in the next line. See the description in the customary of St Victor, *Liber ordinis* 33, "De hora capituli" (CCCM 61.153–63).
149 "zelo ordinis:" "ordo" refers both to the daily round of the monastery and to the congregation of monasteries following that "ordo," which was spelled out in the *Liber ordinis*.
150 The duties of the prior and subprior include watching over the proper behavior of the community (see *Liber ordinis* 5, 8 [CCCM 61.26, 29–30]). The *circator* was an official specifically appointed to make the rounds (*circas*), to correct anything amiss, and to report transgressions in the chapter meeting (*Liber ordinis* 41 [CCCM 61.194–96]). On the office of *circator* at St Victor, see H. Feiss, "*Circatores* in the *Ordo* of St. Victor," in *The Medieval Monastery*, ed. A. McLeish, Medieval Studies at Minnesota 2 (St. Cloud: North Star, 1988), 53–58, and more generally H. Feiss, "*Circatores* from Benedict of Nursia to Humbert of Romans, *American Benedictine Review* 40 (1989): 346–79. S. Bruce, "'Lurking with Spiritual Intent': A Note on

the Origin and Functions of the Monastic Roundsman (Circator)," *RBen.* 109 (1999): 75–89, faults the previous article for giving an "idealized image of the disciplinary integrity of some large monasteries in the central Middle Ages." L. Kornexl, "Ein benedikitinischer Funktion-sträger und seine Name: Linguistische Überlegungen rund um den *circa*," *Mittellateinisches Jahrbuch* 31 (1996): 39–60, studies the use in Anglo-Saxon monasteries of "circa," a shortened form of "circator."

151   *Liber ordinis* 33 (CCCM 61.167–71); cf. Châtillon, *Théologie*, 76–78.

152   Cf. 1 Cor. 9:27. The Vulgate here uses "reprobi" (false, spurious), which by Achard's time had become a quasi-technical word for "damned." See also 2 Tim. 3:8. This passage and what follows makes it quite certain that Achard is addressing a group of abbots, most likely those of the Order of St Victor gathered in their general chapter. The chapter on the lifestyle of the abbot (*Liber ordinis* 4 [CCCM 61.21–25]) begins: "The abbot should see to it that by his good way of life he is an example of discipline for all. He should not abuse the power he has received, but all the more restrain himself under all the discipline, insofar as he has no one above him by whom he can be restrained" ("Providendum est abbati, ut bona conversatione sua omnibus exemplum disciplinae fiat, nec accepta abutatur potestate, sed tanto magis se ipsum in omni disciplina cohibeat, quanto alium supra se nullum habet, a quo cohiberi posit"). This sentence is suggestive of a lack of power of the Victorine general chapter over individual abbots. This was probably one reason that the order was not very cohesive.

153   Matt. 23:4.

154   Cf. 1 Pet. 5:3.

155   "Forma . . . informare": The notions of form, in-forming, re-forming the deformed, and transforming are important in Victorine thought. See Richard of St Victor, *Quat. grad.* 43 (Dumeige, 171; tr. Kraebel, VTT 2.293–94); *Pot. lig.* (Ribaillier, 99); Walter of St Victor, *Sermo* 9.7 (Châtillon, 79–81). See n. 103 above.

156   Cf. 2 Cor. 4:10.

157   Col. 3:5.

158   1 Cor. 11:1.

159   Cf. Eph. 2:20.

160   Cf. Heb. 13:17; 1 Pet. 4:5.

161   Cf. Luke 18:11.

162   Cf. Song of Songs 4:2.

163   Cf. 2 Tim. 2:25.

164   Eph. 6.12.

165   Cf. 2 Cor. 7:5; 11:26.

166   This is a proverb widely quoted in the Middle Ages. See, e.g., Boethius, *De consolatione philosophiae* III.5 (Stewart and Rand, 252.41–42); Bernard of Clairvaux, *Ep.* 330 (SBO 8.267.7–8). For other references see S. Signer *et al.*, *Thesaurus proverbiorum medii aevi* (Berlin: De Gruyter, 1996), 3:191–201.

167   Achard's Latin here is as follows: "hujusmodi tonsionibus et pressuris lapides expoliti atque quadrati convenienter et condigne in edificium transeunt spirituale, suisque aptantur locis per manum artificis, disponuntur permansuri sacris edificiis." He is incorporating a stanza from the hymn, "Urbs Ierusaelm beata," used for the office of the dedication of a church: "Tunsionibus, pressuris / expoliti lapides / suis coaptantur locis / per manum artificis; / disponuntur permansuri / sacris aedificiis" (*Liturgia horarum iuxta ritum romanum* [Vatican City: Libreria Editrice Vaticana, 1977], 1:1011).

168   Eph. 4:3.

169   On the Holy Spirit as the cement of the Church, see Richard of St Victor, *LE* 2.10.1 (Châtillon, 375.11–13 = *Serm. cent.* 1; PL 177.901B).

170   1 Kings 6:7.

171   Luke 1:6. Achard quotes the Vulgate ("in omnibus . . . justificationibus Domini sine querella"). It is hard to know what Achard thought it meant, so I have translated it literally. The New

American Bible translates: "observing all . . . ordinances of the Lord blamelessly." See above n. 102.

172 Cf. Ecclus. 35:11; 1 Cor. 9:7.

173 Cf. Rom. 12:11.

174 Cf. 1 John 4:18. On this theme of "love casts out fear," see Feiss, VTT 2.60 n. 113–15 (Augustine); 74 n. 212 (Adam of St Victor); 106 n. 389 (Thomas Aquinas); Hugh of St Victor, *Archa Noe* 54 (Sicard, 266; tr. Feiss, VTT 2.221); Adam of St Victor, *Simplex in essentia* 5, 9 (Grosfillier, 342.25–30, 343.5–56; tr. Mousseau, VTT 2.241); Achard of St Victor, *Serm.* 12.5 (Châtillon, 128–30; tr. Feiss, 195). The "libertas" spoken of earlier in this paragraph is the state of freedom and ease in doing good that occurs when love has replaced fear as a motivation for virtuous action.

175 Rom. 12:15.

176 The Victorines often make comparisons between the six days/works of creation, the six ages of the world, the six ages of a human being, and so forth. See Feiss, VTT 2.174 and 305; Hugh of St Victor, *Quid uere* 7 (Baron, 98; tr. Butterfield, VTT 2.180); Godfrey of St Victor, *Microcosmus* III.212 (Delhaye, 232–33; tr. Feiss, VTT 2.322).

177 "caritas autem divina": Achard speaks next of seven different virtues or columns, so here he has in mind love for God, rather than God's love for creatures, or charity as the root of all the other virtues.

178 Cf. Eph. 3:17.

179 Cf. Prov. 9:1.

180 Matt. 11:30.

181 Cf. 2 Cor. 1:12.

182 Ps. 26:13.

183 See n. 2 above.

184 Ps. 33:9. See Châtillon, *Théologie*, 256–57.

185 See Achard, *Serm.* 9.6 (Châtillon, 107; tr. Feiss, 69–70); Châtillon, *Théologie*, 257–58.

186 "Cleanness" ("munditia") and "purity" ("puritas") seem to be synonyms, which Achard uses for literary effect. The two nouns do not appear often in the Vulgate, but the related adjectives are used frequently, especially with reference to clean hands as a metaphor for uprightness. Prov. 22:11 refers to purity of heart: *Qui diligit cordis munditiam* ("Whoever loves purity of heart"). For Christians a key text is the beatitude in Matt. 5:8: *Beati mundo corde quoniam ipsi Deum videbunt* ("Blessed are those with a pure heart for they will see God"). On "purity of heart," see VTT 2.122 n. 20. The term means freedom from all that is incompatible with holiness, and so has a much wider application than the word "purity" has in contemporary English. The phrase occurs fairly frequently in Victorine writings; e.g., Hugh of St Victor, *Eulogium* 4 (PL 176.988C; tr. Feiss VTT 2.126); Adam of St Victor, *Gratulemur ad festivum* 5.17–18 (Grosfillier, 264.18, 266.57–62; tr. Mousseau, VTT 2.237, 239); Godfrey of St Victor, *Microcosmus* 207 (Delhaye, 228.28; tr. Feiss, VTT 2.319); Walter of St Victor, *Serm.* 1.5 (Châtillon, 15.124); *Serm.* 11.9 (Châtillon, 100.269–74, 101.297–98); Anonymous Victorine, *Serm.* 7 (Châtillon, 281.201). See the anonymous, late fourteenth-century, Middle English poem that begins with the word "Cleanness" (http://rpo.library.utoronto.ca/poem/22.html).

187 There are here references to two ideas of medieval Christian thought: (1) the seven gifts of the Holy Spirit, a list derived from the Vulgate rendering of Isa. 11:1–3: *Et egredietur virga de radice Iesse et flos de radice eius, ascendet et requiescet super eum spiritus Domini, spiritus sapientiae et intellectus, spiritus consilii et fortitudinis, spiritus scientiae et pietatis, et replebit eum spiritus timoris Domini* ("And a shoot will go out of the root of Jesse and a flower will ascend from his root, and upon him the Spirit of the Lord will rest: a spirit of wisdom and understanding, a spirit of counsel and fortitude, a spirit of knowledge and piety, and the spirit of fear of the Lord will fill him"). See, e.g., Hugh of St Victor, *Septem donis* (Baron, 121–33; tr. Benson, VTT 4 369–80); *Quinque sept.* 1.3 (Baron, 102, 110–19; tr. Benson, VTT 4 349–68); Adam of St Victor, *Iubilemus Salvatori / quem* (Grosfillier, 278.39); Richard of St Victor, *LE*

II.10.11 (Châtillon, 398–99 = *Serm. cent.*11; PL 177.923C); *LE* II.24.11 (Châtillon, 507); Walter of St Victor, *Serm.* 8.1–3 (Châtillon, 63–65); for bibliography see Y. Congar, *I Believe in the Holy Spirit* (New York: Crossroad, 1997) 2:134–41; (2) charity is the root of form of the virtues; see VTT 2.54–55, 69, 78, 89. 97, 106, 257–58 n. 26, 311 n. 29.

188   Cf. Prov. 9:1.

189   On gold as a symbol of wisdom and contemplation, see Gregory the Great, *Mor.* XVIII.26.39 (Adriaen, CCL 143A.910; PL 76.58; tr. Library of Fathers, *Morals* 2/2:343); *Hom. ev.* 10.6 (PL 76.1113); Pseudo-Hugh of St Victor, *Misc.* III.39 (PL 177.660B).

190   "Creatura": here and in the next paragraph this word can be translated as "creature" or "creation."

191   Hugh of St Victor, *In Eccl.* 1 (PL 175.117B); Richard of St Victor, *Super exiit* 3 (Châtillon, 76.20–78.2, and lxxi–lxxiii): "Speculativos hoc loco volumus intelligere qui . . . sine rerum corporalium similitudine nesciunt in rerum spiritualium intelligentiam assurgere. Contemplativos vero dicimus, qui faciem revelatam habent et veritatem nude et aperte et absque involucro vident" ("In this context we wish to understand by 'speculatives' . . . those who do not know how to arise to the understanding of spiritual things without the likeness of bodily things. However, by 'contemplatives' we mean those who have their faces unveiled and see the truth plainly, openly and without any covering"); *Arca Moys.* V.14 (Aris, 143; PL 196.187A–B; tr. Zinn, 335–36); *Diff. sac.* (PL 196.1055A); *Trin.* I.10 (Ribaillier, 95.12–15; tr. Evans, VTT 1.219); *Ad me clamat* 17 (Ribaillier, 280); *Tract.* on Ps. 113 (PL 196.342; tr. Evans, VTT 4.192); S. Pinckaers, "Recherches de la signification veritable du terme 'speculatif,'" *Nouvelle Revue Théologique* 81 (1959): 673–95; J. Leclercq, *Études sur le vocabulaire monastique du moyen âge*, Studia Anselmiana 48 (Rome: Herder, 1961), 82–87; G. R. Evans, *Old Arts and New Theology: The Beginnings of Theology as an Academic Discipline* (Oxford: Clarendon, 1980), 91–100.

192   Gen. 1:31.

193   Châtillon (*Sermons*, 165 n. 75–78) observes that these three modes of participation correspond to the three regions of likeness according to nature, justice and beatitude, which Achard distinguishes in *Serm.* 9.4–6 (Châtillon, 105–107; tr. Feiss, 67–70). Achard makes a similar distinction in *Serm.* 1.3 (Châtillon, 28–31; tr. Feiss, 99–100), where he distinguishes the natural image, which consisted in the possibility of knowing, loving, and enjoying God, and the image from grace which consists in actually knowing and loving.

194   According to Châtillon (*Sermones*, 165–66 n. 79), "the eternal arrangement of all things" seems to correspond to the formal causes or reasons that are the object of contemplation described in *Serm.* 14.20 (Châtillon, 92–193; tr. Feiss, 286). Whereas *Serm.* 12.8 (Châtillon, 129–30; tr. Feiss, 199) assigns contemplation of the formal causes of the archetypal world to the blessed in heaven, *Serm.* 13 and *Serm.* 14 indicate that spiritual people can contemplate something of them while still on earth. See Hugh of St Victor, *Sent. div.* 2 (Piazzoni, 936–38; tr. Evans, VTT 1.140–44 with n. 152 and 156); *Sacr.* I.2.2–3 (PL 176.206D–208A); Achard of St Victor, *Unitate* (Martineau; tr. Feiss), passim.

195   On the predestination of the saints see also Hugh of St Victor, *Sent. div.* 2 (Piazzoni, 939; tr. Evans, VTT 1.144 with n. 166–68); *Sacr.* I.2.21 (PL 176.213D–214A); Achard of St Victor, *Serm.* 14.20 (Châtillon, 192; tr. Feiss, 285–86); *Unitate* 2.3 (Martineau, 142–47; tr. Feiss, 440–41). For background in John Scotus Eriugena, see Châtillon, *Sermons*, 166 n. 80; and Châtillon, *Théologie*, 286 n. 42–43.

196   See *Serm.* 14.22 (Châtillon, 193–94; tr. Feiss, 288–89).

197   Cf. 1 Kings 6:35.

198   Cf. 1 Kings 6:21.

199   Cf. Matt. 7:24–25; Luke 6:48.

200   Cf. Job 4:19.

201   Cf. Matt. 7:24–25; Luke 6:48.

202   See Ps. 35:10; Apoc. 22:5; Thomas Aquinas, *ST* I.12.5 (Caramello, 1:55–56); Council of Vienne

(1312) (Denz-Schön., 895; tr. *Decrees of the Ecumenical Councils*, ed. N. Tanner [Washington, DC: Georgetown University Press, 1990], 1:383–84).

203 See Hugh of St Victor, *Sapientia* (PL 176.847C).

204 Achard's treatise, *Discretione* (Häring, 148–91; tr. Feiss, 353–74), explores the distinction between spirit and mind.

205 Cf. 1 Cor. 6:20.

206 Cf. Col. 2:9.

207 See Achard of St Victor, *Serm.* 4.1 (Châtillon, 54–56; tr. Feiss, 125–27); *Serm.* 14.22 (Châtillon, 193–94; tr. Feiss, 288–89).

208 See Ps. 118:66: *Bonitatem et disciplinam, et scientiam doce me* ("Teach me goodness, and discipline, and knowledge").

209 Ps. 118:66.

RICHARD OF ST VICTOR

TRACTATES ON CERTAIN PSALMS

INTRODUCTION AND TRANSLATION
BY CHRISTOPHER P. EVANS

INTRODUCTION

The *Tractates on Certain Psalms* consist of twenty-eight tracts that often read like snippets, much like the notes found in the *Miscellanea* (PL 177.469–900). Some, like the tracts *Egyptus est uita* and *Aufer a me* (Ps. 118:22, 62, 175), seem to have been taken, as it were, from a note-book in which Richard jotted down ideas while reflecting on a sacred text. Others, like the tract *Iudica me* (Ps. 25:1–6), are lengthier and more developed treatises. Another tract on the *Afferte domino* (On Ps. 28) is a polished and very lengthy sermon addressed to a specific group within the community, namely, the novices ("Vobis dicitur, nouitii"). The various tracts feature tropological interpretations of a sacred text, and as such readers are presented with a wide array of spiritual and moral teachings from one of the more famous contemplative theologians in the twelfth century.

Although the original occasion of the tracts and their gathering is unknown, the external evidence suggests a composition and compilation date before 1159 when Richard flourished as a teacher at St Victor. "Magister" ("teacher") is the only title attested in the rubricated attribution of the manuscripts, and several of these manuscripts were written in a Protogothic minuscule that points to a date closer to mid-century. The manuscript tradition thus suggests that the individual tracts were composed, gathered into a collection (the *Tractates*) and circulated sometime in the 1150s.

It is doubtful that Richard provided a title to this collection of writings, but of the two copies preserved at the Abbey of St Victor—Paris, Mazarine 769 (*ca.* 1200) and Paris, BnF lat. 14514 (sec. xii)—only the former supplies a title: *Defloraciones quedam de libro psalmorum.*[1] A long title is preserved in several independent, twelfth-century manuscripts particularly of French origin: *Tractatus super quosdam psalmos et quorumdam sententias scripturarum.*[2] A shorter title (*Tractatus super*

---

[1]   The same title is found in two other manuscripts that were copied from Paris, Mazarine 769, Paris, BnF lat. 15733 (Sorbonne; sec. xiii) and Mâcon, BM 84 (Cluny; sec. xiii).

[2]   E.g., Dijon, BM 42 (24); Laon, BM 25; Paris, Arsenal 327; Paris, BnF lat. 15732; Paris, BnF lat. 16379; Troyes, BM 302 (H 77).

quosdam psalmos) is widely attested particularly among Germanic manuscripts.[3] Because *Tractates on Certain Psalms* (*Tractatus super quosdam psalmos*) is the best attested title in the Middle Ages, it will be retained in this volume. Needless to say, the title supplied by later printed editions (*Adnotationes mystice in psalmos*) has no support in the Middle Ages, and also noteworthy for the genre is the fact that no twelfth-century scribe designated the *Tractates* as a sermon collection (see below).

The content and unity of the *Tractates* is strongly attested among the manuscripts with the exception of the Germanic manuscripts which omit the tract *Afferte domino* (no. 3 in Figure 1).[4] Aside from this variant, the content and ordering of the *Tractates* is as follows (the incipits of the Psalm are the titles of the individual tracts):

1. Quare fremuerunt (Ps. 2:1–4)
2. Iudica me (Ps. 25:1–6)
3. Afferte domino (Ps. 28:1–11)
4. Homo pacis mee (Ps. 40:10)
5. Astitit regina (Ps. 44:10)
6. Quia calix in manu (Ps. 74:9)
7. Cum exiret de terra (Ps. 80:6)
8. Dilata os tuum (Ps. 80:11)
9. Iustitia et pax (Ps. 84:11)

15. Letatus sum (Ps. 121:1)[5]
16. Omnia quecumque (Ps.134:6–9)
17. Qui producit uentos (Ps. 134:7)
18. Imperfectum meum (Ps. 138:16)
19. Eripe me domine (Ps. 139:2–3)
20. In medio annorum (Hab. 3:2)
21. Post sex annos (Lev. 25:4)[6]
22. Tolle puerum (I) (Matt. 2:13)[7]
23. Tolle puerum (II) (Matt. 2:13)[8]

---

[3]   E.g., Admont, Stiftsbibliothek 82; Erlangen, UB Erlangen-Nürnberg 226; Bamberg, Staatsbibliothek Msc. Patr. 130.2 (B.IV.29). Other notable twelfth-century witnesses include Paris, BnF lat. 2590 and Oxford, Bodleian Library Digby 200.

[4]   The manuscripts from Austrian and German monastic libraries all share distinctive variant readings which suggest a common exemplar and thus a sophisticated network of distribution from Paris to those libraries. Admont, Stiftsbibliothek 82, which contains the *Tract.* without the *Afferte domino*, was copied in a clear Protogothic minuscule and thus must be dated closer to mid-century. Admont, Stiftsbibliothek 82 is not the main exemplar for the Germanic textual family, so the circulation of the *Tract.* without the *Afferte domino* appears to be early. Moreover, the circulation of *Afferte domino* independent of the *Tract.* is very well attested in these monastic libraries in Austria and Germany. Admont, Stiftsbibliothek 142 was written in a similar hand as Admont 82 and at a similar date, so the independent dissemination of the tract *Afferte domino* appears to be deliberate.

[5]   After the tract *Letatus sum* the tract *Cum dederit dilectis* (Ps. 126:2–3) is attested in two independent manuscripts (Paris, Mazarine 770 [sec. xii]; St Omer, BM 118 [sec. xv]). Goy, who presumes its authenticity, lists it among Richard's "sermons" (Nr. 112); see *Die handschriftliche Überlieferung der Werke Richards von Sankt Viktor im Mittelalter*, BV 18 (Turnhout: Brepols, 2005), 361.

[6]   Goy, *Die handschriftliche*, 361 (Nr. 101). Ed. Hauréau, *Notices et extraits*, 1:112–14. His edition is based on seven manuscripts of which he was aware.

[7]   Goy, *Die handschriftliche*, 361 (Nr. 105).

[8]   Goy, *Die handschriftliche*, 360 (Nr. 102). Partially edited by Hauréau, *Notices et extraits*, 1:116.

10. Moyses et Aaron (Ps. 98:6)
11. Cum essent (Ps. 104:12–15)
12. Montes exsultauerunt (Ps. 113:4)
13. Vox exsultationis (Ps. 117:15)
14. Aufer a me (Ps. 118:22)

24. Apprehendet messis (Lev. 26:5)[9]
25. Quid eis dabis (Hos. 9:14)[10]
26. Sex sunt dies (Luke 13:14)[11]
27. Santificamini hodie[12]
28. Egyptus est uita[13]

Figure 1: Content of *Tractates*

In addition to the *Tractates* another independent collection of ten sermons and sentences circulated out of St Victor:

1. Scuto circumdabit (Ps. 90)[14]
2. De quatuor gradibus caritatis[15]
3. Geminum pascha colimus[16]
4. In pace in idipsum (Ps. 4:9)
5. Spiritus Domini repleuit orbem[17]

6. Benedictus dominus (Ps. 143:1)
7. Illumina faciem (Ps. 118:135)
8. Exitus aquarum (Ps. 118:136)
9. Descendet sicut pluuia (Ps. 71:6)
10. In salicibus in medio (Ps. 136:2)

Figure 2: Content of *Sermones et Sententie*[18]

The manuscripts at the Abbey of St Victor preserve these writings in a larger collection of sermons. The earliest attestation of the collection is found in Troyes, BM 259 (Cîteaux), where it is entitled *Sermones et Sententie*.

An important manuscript at the Abbey of St Victor (Paris, Mazarine 769),[19] dated sometime in the late twelfth or early thirteenth century, bears witness to the first conflation of the *Tractates* with the *Sermones*

A short conflation of the two tracts on Matt. 2:13 (no. 22 and 23) is found in *Misc.* VI.28 (PL 177.827C–830A).

[9] Goy, *Die handschriftliche*, 360 (Nr. 104). Ed. Hauréau, *Notices et extraits*, 1:116–17.
[10] Goy, *Die handschriftliche*, 361 (Nr. 108). Ed. Hauréau, *Notices et extraits*, 1:118–19. This tract is also found in *Misc.* IV.52 (PL 177.726D–727B).
[11] Goy, *Die handschriftliche*, 361 (Nr. 109).
[12] Goy, *Die handschriftliche*, 361 (Nr. 110).
[13] Goy, *Die handschriftliche*, 361 (Nr. 111).
[14] Or *De septem generibus temptationum*.
[15] ed. Dumeige; tr. Kraebel, VTT 2.261–300.
[16] Or Sermo in ramis pal*marum*
[17] Also titled *Sermo in die pentecostes* or *De missione spiritus sancti*.
[18] This collection is found in 50 total manuscripts as a complete or partial collection. The most important twelfth-century manuscripts are Troyes, BM 259 (Cîteaux); Paris, BnF lat. 14809 (St Victor); Paris, BnF lat. 14957 (St Victor); Paris, BnF lat. 14590 (St Victor); Paris, BnF lat. 15082 (St Victor); Charleville, BM 184 (Signy); Paris, Mazarine 771 (Unknown); Cambria, BM 259 (Cambria).
[19] Paris, Mazarine 769 is part of a textual family that includes Paris, BnF lat. 14517 (St Victor; sec. xii) and Paris, Mazarine 770 (Unknown; sec. xii). The conflation did occur at the Abbey of St Victor well after Richard's death, but it was rarely copied. To date I have located only two thirteenth-century manuscripts that have reproduced the conflated collection: Paris, BnF lat. 15733 (Sorbonne; sec. xiii); Mâcon, BM 84 (Cluny; sec. xiii).

et Sententie.[20] The result of the conflation was twofold. First, sermons
no. 21–28 in Figure 1, not based on a Psalm, were omitted from the
Tractates; although, it is unclear why the tract *In medio annorum* (Hab.
3:2) was not omitted. Second, with the exception of the sermon *Scuto
circumdabit* (Ps. 90), the sermons based on a Psalm in the *Sermones et
Sententie* (no. 4, 6–10 in Figure 2) were incorporated into the *Tractates*
in the proper sequence.[21] The first printed edition of Richard's *Omnia
opera* (Paris, 1518)[22] was clearly dependent upon Paris, Mazarine 769 at
least for the *Tractates*.[23] As such, the 1518 edition omitted tracts no. 21–
28 in Figure 1 and included sermons from the *Sermones et Sententie*,
but it also introduced the following changes for unknown reasons:
(1) the editor changed the name of the *Tractates* to *Mistice Annotationes
quamplurimorum versuum psalmorum David*; (2) he changed the order
of the sermons to make them out of sequence;[24] and 3) he adds the
sermon *Scuto circumdabit* (Ps. 90; no. 1 in Figure 2) at the end. Between
1534 and 1650 four more editions of the *Opera omnia* were published
but the *Tractates* was a simple reproduction of the 1518 edition.[25] Finally,

20   Sometimes the *Tractatus* and certain sermons of the *Sermone et Sententie* can be found in
      the same manuscript but as separate works. E.g., in Oxford, Bodleian Library, Digby 200
      (sec. xiii) sermons no. 7 and 8 from Figure 2 are included after the end of the *Tractatus*;
      and in Mâcon, BM 84 sermons no. 21–28 from Figure 1 are placed before the incipit of the
      Tractatus.
21   Cf. also Hauréau, *Notices et extraits*. I.112–20; Ottaviano, *Riccardo di S. Vittore*, 423–25, 432,
      434, 437; Châtillon, *Trois opuscules spirituels*, 38–40; Ibid., "Richard de Saint-Victor," DS
      13 (1987), 618–20; P. Cacciapuoti, *Deus existentia amoris: Carità e Trinità nell'itinerario teo-
      logico di Riccardo di San Vittore (d. 1173)*, BV 9 (1998), 61–62, 74–75.
22   *Richardi sancti uictoris doctoris preclarissimi omnia opera in unum volumen congesta solerti
      cura ac diligentia emendata atque nunc primum parrisiis impresa*. Tenundantur in edibus
      Joannis Petis sub lilio aureo vici diui Jacobi (Paris, 1518). The very first printed edition of
      Richard's writings was not complete and did not include the *Tractates*; see *Opera uenerabilis
      et eximii doctoris Ricardi de sancto victore* (Venice, 1506).
23   The 1518 edition in Paris reproduced the key variants only found in Paris, Mazarine 769,
      as well as Paris, BnF lat. 15733 and Mâcon, BM 84. For example, the extended ending only
      found in these three manuscripts was reproduced in the 1518 edition; see n.43 below.
24   That is, he inserted the tract *In medio annorum* (Hab. 3:2) after the tract *Quia calix in manu*
      (no. 7 in Figure 1); and he inserted the tract *Descendet sicut pluuia* (Ps. 71; no. 9 in Figure 2)
      at end of the *Adnotationes*, that is, after tracts *Eripe me* (Ps. 139) and *Benedictus dominus* (Ps.
      143).
25   *Richardi sancti victoris . . . omnia opera in unum uolumen contexta, dunuo quantum fie-
      ri potuit accuratissime prealis ascita*. Prostant Lugduni: Apud Vincentium de Portonariis
      (Lyon, 1534); *Richardi sancti victoris Scoti . . . Opera que hactenss apparuere omnia, in duas
      partes diuisa, vnicumque in Volumen congesta*. Apud Ioannem Baptisam Ciottum & Soclos.
      (Venice, 1592); *Richardi sancti victoris Scoti . . . Opera . . . Nunc primum in Germania correc-
      tius edita*. Apud Ioannem Gymnicum sub Monocerote (Cologne, 1621); M. *Richardi sancti
      victoris . . . opera ex manuscriptis eiusdem operibus quae in Bibliotheca Victorina sueruantur*,

in 1855 Migne published the edition on which all scholarship since has relied (PL 196.265–402). His edition is a reproduction of the 1650 edition but the following changes were introduced: (1) Migne revised the title to the shorter *Mysticae Adnotationes in Psalmos*; and (2) he moved the tract *In medio annorum* (Hab. 3:2) to the very end.

The *Tractates* enjoyed good success throughout the Middle Ages particularly in monastic and religious communities. It is preserved in 121 manuscripts: 30 of these manuscripts contain it as a complete work; 59 manuscripts contain only the sermon *Afferte domino* (Ps. 28);[26] and the remaining manuscripts preserve only one or more of the tracts.[27] The dissemination of these manuscripts is widespread, but they are generally preserved in monastic libraries (Benedictine and Cistercian). Moreover, as the dissemination indicates, the *Tractates* received good attention in the twelfth century (13 manuscripts) but its reception gradually waned in subsequent centuries, unlike the sermon *Afferte domino* (Ps. 28) whose popularity increased throughout the centuries. In comparison to Richard's other major writings like *On the Trinity* and *Ark of Moses* (each between 70–100 manuscripts), *Book of Notes* (over 100 manuscripts), and *The Twelve Patriarchs*—Richard's most famous work with nearly 250 manuscripts—, the *Tractates* as a complete work received moderate attention with fewer than 40 manuscripts (much like *On the Apocalypse*). Obviously, this says nothing about the importance of this treatise at the Abbey of St Victor or for understanding Richard's theology.

The literary genre and purpose of the *Tractates* is a bit unclear. With the exception of the tract *Afferte domino* (Ps. 28)[28] the *Tractates* in its

accurate castigata et emendata; cum uita ipsius ante hac nusquam edita; studio et industria Canonicorum Regularium Regalis Abbatiae Sancti Victoris Parisiensis. Rothomagi: Sumptibus Ioannis Berthelin (Rouen, 1650).

[26] This is the only sermon in the collection that comments on every verse of the Psalm in question and is thus the longest sermon in the *Tractatus*. In fact this one sermon consists of 35.5% of the forthcoming critical edition of the *Tractatus*. It is also the only sermon addressed to a specific audience in the community, that is, the novices; see n. 28 below.

[27] Cf. Goy, *Die handschriftliche*, 305–25. He attributes more popularity to the *Tractatus* than the evidence warrants, primarily because he does not account for the conflation of the *Tractatus* with the *Sermones et Sententie*, and he treats the tracts no. 21–28 in Figure 1 as independent sermons. In other words, he relies entirely on Migne's version of the collection. See my review in *Manuscripta* 50.2 (2006): 317–22.

[28] The *Afferte domino* (Ps. 28) is likely a sermon(s) preached publically. The personal address at the beginning suggests this (e.g., "this is spoken to you, novices" ["Vobis dicitur, nouitii"]), as does the conclusion of the "sermon": "But at last let this lengthy sermon make peace its end. It is good that we are here, and it is not expedient for us to exceed the limits of peace. Therefore, let us end our sermon in the contemplation of this peace and the peace that will

present form does not belong among the sermon collections of Richard.[29] When compared, for example, to the twenty-seven diverse sermons published in the *Book of Notes*,[30] the *Tractates* lacks certain oratory clues like the vocative "fratres carissimi" ("dear brethren"), and the use of the second person plural to address listeners is lacking (though Richard does not seem consistent with the latter convention). Nevertheless, many of the tracts could have derived from his preaching.[31] He uses the second person plural throughout in the tract *Sanctificamini hodie* (no. 27 in Figure 1), and sporadic use of this address is found in the tracts *Qui producit* (Ps. 134:7) and *Tolle puerum . . . mater mentis* (Matt. 2:13). Also, in the Ordinary of St Victor the *Sanctificamini hodie* is a responsory on Christmas Eve and Matt. 2:13 was a reading for the Vigil of Epiphany,[32] so these sacred texts are fitting passages for

have no end (cf. Isa. 9:7). May he, *who is our peace* (Eph. 2:14), deign to give to us this peace through the endless ages. Amen" ("Sed tandem prolixus sermo ponat fines suos pacem. Bonum est enim nos hic esse nec expedit nobis fines pacis excedere. Finiatur ergo sermo noster in contemplatione huius pacis et pacis cuius nullus erit finis quam nobis donare dignetur *qui est pax nostra* per infinita seculorum secula. Amen" [PL 196.322B]). However, a 14627-word sermon is a "lengthy sermon" indeed, one that would have taken at least two hours to preach. If this seems a bit unusual, then a possible solution is to regard the present form of *Afferte domino* as a conflation of sermons. After all, about a quarter into the sermon Richard seem to announce an end: "It still remains at the end of our sermon to learn what is the difference between the cedars of Lebanon and the calf of Lebanon" ("Restat illud adhuc addiscere in finem sermonis nostri: que sit differentia inter cedros Libani et uitulos Libani" [PL 196.295C]), after which he discusses the differences (this apparent conclusion goes up to Ps. 28:5). Nevertheless, nowhere in the manuscript tradition does the sermon end here, and the internal referencing suggests a unity at least in its present form; e.g., a reference is made near the end of the sermon to a verse discussed at the beginning: ". . . he sung with confidence what we read above in this same Psalm: *The voice of the Lord . . .* (Ps. 28:4)" ("quod superius in hoc eodem Psalmo legimus, fiducialiter psallebat: *Vox Domini*" [PL 196.319D]).

29   At least the *Tract.* is never circulated as a collection of sermons. In the two twelfth-century manuscripts from the Abbey of St Victor, Paris, BnF lat. 14517 contains the *Tract.* along with *Super exiit*, and Paris, Mazarine 769 contains the *Arca Moys.*, *Statu*, *Trin.*, and *Tract.* Outside St Victor the *Tract.* is most commonly preserved with *Acra. Moys.*, *Statu* and/or *Erud.*; the most common variations are found in the following twelfth-century manuscripts: *Arca. Moys.*, *Statu*, *Tract.*, *Erud.* (Paris, BnF lat. 15733); *Statu*, *Erud.*, *Tract.* (Bamberg, Staatsbibliothek Msc. Patr. 130.2); *Arca. Moys.*, *Tract. Erud.* (Erlangen, UB Erlangen-Nürnberg 236; Paris, Arsenal 327); *Erud.*, *Arca. Moys.*, *Tract.*, *Carb.* (Dijon, BM 42; Paris, BnF lat. 15732); *Tract.*, *Illa die*, *Causam*, *Statu*, *Erud.* (Laon, BM 25); *Illa die*, *Tract*, *Exterm.*, *Erud.* (Paris, Mazarine 770). Such a grouping of writings in these late twelfth-century manuscripts may give us clues with regard to genre, but to use it for determining dating of a particular writing is not cogent.

30   Richard, *LE* X.1–27 (Châtillon, 375–438).

31   E.g., in the tract *Omnia quecumque* (Ps. 134:6–9) Richard seems to address listeners: "as you can hear in this verse" ("sicut hic audire potes"), but in the tract *Quid eis dabis* (Hos. 9:14) he seems to address readers: "you must read this" ("debes legere").

32   Paris, BnF lat. 14506, fol. 270r and 273v.

preaching and exposition. Whatever the occasion, the *Tractates* offers verse-by-verse, tropological annotations over selected passages for the spiritual edification of readers at St Victor and beyond. Some tracts are uniform and long; others are miscellaneous spiritual notes on a particular verse. None, in my opinion, are extemporaneous, and they often betray Richard's ingenuity and education. The tracts *Quare fremuerunt* (Ps. 2:1–4) and *Omnia quecumque* (Ps. 134:6–9) are offered here as examples.

By the time Richard flourished as a teacher, certain materials have been compiled to aid lectures, namely, the glosses which included the biblical text along with a patristic exposition. By mid-century the following glosses on the Psalms (and the Pauline Epistles) circulated widely: *Parva glossatura* (or *Glossa ordinaria*) of Anselm of Laon, the *Media glossatura* of Gilbert of Poitiers, and the *Magna glossatura* of Peter Lombard.[33] To some extent these glosses standardized, but did not exhaust, certain literal interpretations of the Psalms. In treating Psalms 2:1–2,[34] for example, a lecturer and student in the early twelfth century would have likely noted that David, a prophet, was speaking in the person of Christ.[35] This literal voice would then situate the Psalm within a specific socio-historical situation, namely, the crucifixion. The "nations" or "gentiles" mentioned in the Psalm would be the brutish

---

[33] For Anselm's *Parva glossatura* I have consulted Florence, Biblioteca Medicae Laurenziana, Plut. 17.4 (sec. xii), and the first printed edition: *Biblia Latina cum Glossa ordinaria: Facsimile reprint of the editio Princeps Adolph Rusch of Strassburg 1480/81*, vol. 2 (Turnhout: Brepols, 1992). For Gilbert's *Media glossatura* I have consulted Cambridge, Queens' College Ms 5 (sec. xii); Vorau, Stiftsbibliothek 261 (sec. xii); and Valenciennes, BM 44 (sec. xii). Peter's *Magna glossatura* is found in PL 191.55A–1296C. Additionally there are a number of early twelfth-century commentaries on the Psalms. There is an obvious connection among these commentaries and glosses, but their relations can be very difficult to decipher. See, e.g., D. van den Eynde, "Literary Note on the Earliest Scholastic *Commentarii in Psalmos*," *Franciscan Studies* 14.2 (1954): 149–54; Ibid., "Complementary Note on the Early Scholastic *Commentarii in Psalmos*," *Franciscan Studies* 17 (1957): 121–72.

[34] "Why have the nations growled and the people meditated on inane things? The kings of the earth stood up, and the princes met together" ("*Quare fremuerunt gentes et populi meditati sunt inania? Astiterunt reges terre, et principes conuenerunt in unum.*").

[35] Gilbert of Poitiers, *Com. in Ps.* (Cambridge, Queens' College Ms 5, fol. 5ra; Valenciennes, BM 44, fol. 4va): "[The Prophet] is speaking in the person of Christ" ("loquens in persona Christi"); Peter Lombard, *Com. in Ps.* (PL 191.69C): "loquitur Christus vel Propheta." Cf. also Pseudo-Remi d'Auxerre, *Expositio psalmorum* (PL 131.793A–B; *ca.* mid-twelfth according to D. van den Eynde, "Complementary Note," 166–71): "in voce Christi legitur;" Pseudo-Bruno, *Expositio in Psalmos* (PL 152.643D; after 1140 according to D. van den Eynde, "Complementary Note," 164–66); Pseudo-Hymo, *Glossae psalterii continuae* (Troyes, BM 904, fol. 2vb–3ra [sec. xii]; PL 116.201A): "Here Christ is speaking about himself as if about a third person" ("hic uero Christus de seipso quasi de tercia persona loquitur").

Roman soldiers standing at the cross; the "people" would be the Jews thinking inane thoughts, that is, that Christ will stay dead or that he is not the Messiah; the "kings" would be Herod and Pilate; and the "princes" would be the high priests, Annas and Caiphas. Such identifications, moreover, have the support of authorities like Augustine and above all Acts 4:25–27.[36]

With regard to the common literal interpretation of Psalm 134:6,[37] a lecturer and student would have likely interpreted the Psalmist as praising God's sovereign will and goodness, an interpretation that goes back to Augustine.[38] Here the glosses also provide a spiritual interpretation based on the meaning of heaven, earth, sea, and abysses. For example, in the *Ordinary Gloss* of Anselm "heaven" and "earth" are spiritual and carnal members of the Church, the "sea" is seething unbelievers, and the "abysses" are the hidden thoughts of men.[39]

---

36   See, e.g., Peter Lombard, *Com. in Ps.* (PL 191.644B), who reproduces and expands on Anselm of Laon, *Glossa ordin.* on Ps. 2 (Florence, Bilblioteca Medicea Laurenziana, Plut. 17.4, fols. 1v–2r; ed. princeps 2.459) and Gilbert of Poitiers, *Com. in Ps.* (Cambridge, Queens' College Ms 5, fol. 5ra; Valenciennes, BM 44, fol. 4va).

37   "The Lord has done whatever he wanted in heaven and on earth, in the sea and in all the abysses" ("*Omnia quecumque uoluit Dominus fecit in celo et in terra, in mari et in omnibus abyssis*").

38   Augustine, *En. Ps.* 134.6 (Dekkers and Fraipont, CCL 40.1945): "The cause of all that God makes is his will" ("causa omnium quae fecit, voluntas ejus est"); Anselm of Laon, *Glossa ordin.* on Ps. 134:6 (interlinear) (Florence, Bilblioteca Medicea Laurenziana, Plut. 17.4, fol. 183v; ed. princeps, 2.632): "The cause of all that God makes is his will, not necessity but goodness" ("Causa omnium que fecit uoluntas est, nulla necessitas sed bonitas"); Gilbert of Poitiers, *Com. in Ps.* 134:6 (Vorau, Stiftsbibliothek 261, fol. 224ra; Valenciennes, BM 44, fol. 156rb): "The cause of all things is only God's will. Necessity forces you to work for food and other such things, but God who lacks nothing does all things out of his goodness" ("Causa enim omnium est sola uoluntas. Te etenim ad operandum necessitas alimentorum aut huiusmodi cogit. Ille uero, qui nullo eguit, sola bonitate omnia fecit"); Peter Lombard, *Com. in Ps.* 134:6 (PL 191.1189A): "The cause of all things that God made is his will, not necessity" ("Causa enim omnium quae fecit voluntas ejus est, et nulla necessitas").

39   Anselm of Laon, *Glossa ordin.* on Ps. 134:6 (marginal) (Florence, Bilblioteca Medicea Laurenziana, Plut. 17.4, fol. 183v; ed. princeps, 2.632): "We can recognize these figuratively in human beings: heaven is spiritual people, earth is carnal people. The Church consists of both. God does whatsoever he wills in them and even in the sea, that is, in unbelievers in whom nothing happens without God's command. They do not rage without God's permission. The abysses are hidden thoughts of men hidden in the heart. Even there God does what he wills . . . ("Typice hec in hominibus [omnibus *scr. ed. princeps*] possumus agnoscere: celum spirituales, terra carnales. Ex his duobus constat ecclesia. In his facit quecunque uult et etiam in mari, idest in infidelibus in quibus nichil fit nisi iussu Dei. Non enim seuiunt nisi permittant a Deo [non – a Deo *om. ms*]. Abyssi latentia corda [profunda corda mortalium *add. ed. princeps*] profunde cogitationes hominum. Et ibi facit Deus quod uult. Interrogat iustum et impium; latet cor bonum, latet et malum et in utroque est abyssus, sed [latet² – sed *om. ms*] Deus hoc uidet quem nichil latet [quem – latet *om. ms*], hoc consolatur, illud torquet"); cf. Peter Lombard, *Com. in Ps.* 134:6 (PL 191.1190B–C) who reproduces Anselm. See also

When Richard composes his various notes on the Psalms, he does so with one eye on the literal interpretations standardized by the glosses, but his obvious focus is the spiritual and moral formation of his readers.[40] His handling of Ps. 2:1–4 is exemplary of his almost exclusive concern for tropology even when these verses are generally understood as Christ's words about himself. In this and other tracts Richard provides a somewhat self-contained treatment of each verse, and as such each verse offers similitudes that can take him in various directions even in the same verse.[41] The tract on Ps. 2:1–4 thus handles a wide array of spiritual lessons: the various virtues and vices, impure thoughts, different kinds of demonic temptations, spiritual warfare, nature and grace, contemplation, divine justice, and so on. The literal treatment of the glosses that identifies "gentiles" and "people" as Roman soldiers and Jews finds no place in Richard's spiritual treatment where "nations" instead refer to perverse thoughts and "people" to vain thoughts. Richard does, however, have the glosses in his purview when he notes that the murmuring or growling of the nations (*fremuerunt gentes*) is a quality of wilds beasts rather than humans,[42] which occurs,

Gilbert of Poitiers, *Com. in Ps.* 134:6 (Vorau, Stiftsbibliothek 261, fol. 224ra; Valenciennes, BM 44, fol. 156rb): "Typice celum spirituales, terra carnales. Ex his duobus constat ecclesia. In his ergo tamquam celo et terra omnia quecumque uoluit fecit, quia pro uoluntate fecit, ut et spirituales predicarent et carnales obsecundarent. Mare infideles seuientes qui etiam non seuiunt nisi permissi. Abyssi profunde cogitationes bone uel male, ubi Deus facit quod uult, qui consolatur bonum cor, malum torquet." Cf. also Pseudo-Remi d'Auxerre, *Expositio psalmorum* (PL 131.793A–B; *ca.* mid-twelfth according to Van den Eynde, "Complementary Note," 166–71); Pseudo-Bruno, *Expositio in Psalmos* (PL 152.1347C; after 1140 according to Van Den Eynde, "Complementary Note," 164–66).

[40]   J. Leclercq regards Richard as the most remarkable commentator on the Psalms because of the extent of the psychological consideration that Richard gives in the *Tract.*; see "Les psaumes 20–25," 225.

[41]   In this sense Richard is faithful to a hermeneutical principle mentioned in his *Vis. Ezek.* Prol. (Schröder, 372; PL 196.527A; cf. Smalley, *Study of Bible*, 108): "Mystical senses are drawn from and formed from a suitable similitude of the things contained in the letter" ("mystici sensus ex earum congrua rerum similitudine eruantur atque formantur, quae in littera proponuntur").

[42]   See Anselm of Laon, *Glossa ordin.* on Ps. 2 (Florence, Bilblioteca Medicea Laurenziana, Plut. 17.4, fols. 1v–2r; ed. princeps 2.459): "[*The nations*] growled like wild beasts without reason" ("*Fremuerunt*, ut fere sine ratione"); Gilbert of Poitiers, *Com. in Ps.* (Cambridge, Queens' College Ms 5, fol. 5ra; Valenciennes, BM 44, fol. 4va): "Fremuerunt ut fere agentes sine ratione;" Peter Lombard, *Com. in Ps.* (PL 191.644B): "To growl is characteristic of lions who are irrational" ("Fremere vero leonum est, qui irrationabiles sunt"). Cf. also Pseudo-Remi d'Auxerre, *Expositio psalmorum* (PL 131.155B; *ca.* mid-twelfth according to D. van den Eynde, "Complementary Note," 166–71); Pseudo-Haymo, *Glossae psalterii continuae* (Troyes, BM 904, fol. 2vb–3ra [sec. xii]; PL 116.201A).

Later in his tract when commenting on the distinction between the Lord's ridiculing and mocking (Ps. 2:4), the glosses again provide Richard with a helpful similitude for a moral lesson. See, e.g., Anselm of Laon, *Glossa ordin.* on Ps. 2 (Florence, Bilblioteca Medicea according to Richard's spiritual interpretation, whenever human appetite usurps reason. Nevertheless, Richard does divert, so to speak, the passage away from an understanding of Christ to discuss the internal spiritual self, and this may have inspired the later scribal insertion at the end of the tract: "Let no one be surprised, let no one scorn us if for the sake of edification we divert the things spoken of and understood about Christ according to the letter to his members according to the mystical understanding."[43]

In his tract on Ps. 134:6–9 Richard provides terse tropological notes, though elsewhere he is familiar with the literal interpretation found in the glosses.[44] In verse 6 the heaven-earth-sea-abysses sequence offers a multitude of spiritual meanings based on the similitude of the letter. As noted above, the *Ordinary Gloss* offers a popular interpretation that is attributed to the authority of Augustine.[45] Richard's spiritual interpretation here is based not on the glossed authority but on his own ingenuity and common Victorine teaching. The qualities of heaven, abysses, earth, and sea for him indicate certain moral qualities of the heart and mind:

Laurenziana, Plut. 17.4, fol. 1v–2r; ed. princeps 2.459): *"He will ridicule them*, as if with his cheeks, . . . *the Lord will deride them* with his nose (*"irridebit eos*, quasi buccis, . . . *Dominus subsannabit*, naso, *eos"*); Gilbert of Poitiers, *Com. in Ps.* (Cambridge, Queens' College Ms 5, fol. 5ra; Valenciennes, BM 44, fol. 4va): "The Prophet uses human likeness when he says that *he will ridicule* as if with cheeks, and *he will mock* as if with snubbed nose" ("utitur propheta humana similitudine cum dicit irridebit quasi buccis, et subsannabit quasi rugato naso"). Cf. also Peter Lombard, *Com. in Ps.* (PL 191.71A); Pseudo-Jerome, *Breviarium in Psalmos* (Troyes, BM 88, fol. 2ra [sec. xii]; PL 26.826A): "Subsannatio proprie rugata fronte, et contracto naso exprimitur;" Pseudo-Remi d'Auxerre, *Expositio psalmorum* (PL 131.155B; *ca.* mid-twelfth according to D. van den Eynde, "Complementary Note," 166–71): "Irrisio fit ore, subsannatio in rugas naso contracto."

43   "Nemo miretur, nemo indignetur, si ea, que de Christo dicuntur et intelliguntur iuxta litteram edificationis gratia deriuemus ad eius membra iuxta misticam intelligentiam." The addition is first found in Paris, Mazarine 769, a manuscript copied at St Victor (i.e., inserted by a Victorine scribe), and witnessed in subsequent manuscripts dependent upon Paris, Maz. 769, namely, Paris, BnF lat. 15733 and Mâcon, BM 84. The addition is also found in Migne's edition (PL 196.274A).

   Of course no early scholastic denies the tropological interpretation of the Psalms. As described by Gilbert of Poitiers, the subject matter (*materia*) of the Psalms is *Christus integer* or "the whole Christ," which includes both Christology and Ecclesiology, as when, e.g., the Psalmists speaks in the person of Christ or of his Church, whether perfect or imperfect members; see Gilbert, *Com. in Ps.* Prol. (Cambridge, Queens' College Ms 5, fol. 2ra; Valenciennes, BM 44, fol. 3ra; Vorau, Stiftsbibliothek 261, fol. 1r): "Christus integer, caput cum membris, est materia huius libri, de qua agit propheta hoc modo. Loquitur enim aliquando simul de toto, id est Christo et ecclesia, aliquando de singulis, idest Christo uel ecclesia . . . De ecclesia uero duobus modis: Aliquando secundum perfectos, aliquando secundum inperfectos."

44   E.g., Richard, *Erud.* II.46 (PL 196.1343C); *Erud.* III.19 (PL 196.1364C–D).

45   Cf. Augustine, *Serm.*56.8 (PL 38.380): "In the Church spiritual people are heaven and carnal people are earth" ("In Ecclesia spirituales coelum sunt, carnales terra sunt").

Geographic Location in v. 6:	Heaven	Abyss	Earth	Sea
External Quality:	Lucid	Dark	Solid	Slippery
Interior Man:	Heart	Heart	Mind	Mind
Interior Quality:	Understanding	Ignorance	Steadfastness	Lust

Figure 3: Chart of Tract on Ps. 134:6

From similitudes of the geographic locations Richard draws out the spiritual meaning of a clear and dark heart or a stable and slippery mind. Because "ignorance" contrasts better with "understanding," his tropological focus forced him to alter the Psalmist's sequence of geographic locations by placing "abyss" after "heaven" and thus associate "ignorance" as a corruption of the heart rather than the mind and "lust" as a corruption of the mind. Nevertheless, the corruption of lust and ignorance is an Augustinian theme that is common to Hugh's theology,[46] and so one can probably sense his influence here.

Of interest here as well is how Richard uses himself as a source in his sermons, as the following chart indicates.

Tract. Ps. 28 (PL 196.291D–292A)[47]	*Tract.* Ps. 134 (PL 196.365D)
Omnia ... in omnibus abyssis. Vbi inuenit cor intelligentia lucidum ut celum, ubi repperit mentem firmam ut terram, si uidit cor amarum et instabile ut mare, si aspexit animum tenebrosum ut abyssum, semper et ubique quidem *omnia ... in omnibus abyssis.*[48]	*Omnia ... in omnibus abyssis.* Si inuenit cor intelligentia lucidum ut celum uel e contrario ignorantia tenebrosum ut abyssum, item si repererit mentem constantia solidam ut terram uel econtra concupiscentia lubricam ut aquam, ubique quidem et semper *omnia ... in omnibus abyssis.*[49]

Richard often bookends his tropological notes with the biblical passage as he does in the tract on Ps. 134:6, which highlights the juxtaposition of the heart's understanding or ignorance and the mind's

---

[46] See, e.g., Hugh of St Victor, *Sacr.* I.7.28 (PL 176.299A); *Misc.* I.103 (PL 177.535C); see also Richard of St Victor, *Decl.* (Ribaillier, 213); *LE* X.2.11 (Châtillon, 398). Richard can also add a third corruption, weakness, depending on occasion or the similitude of the letter; e.g., *LE* I.1.3 (Châtillon, 105); *Statu* Prol. (Ribaillier, 61; tr. Evans, VTT 4.251).

[47] Cf. also *Misc.* IV.45 (PL 177.722B–C) which is an abridged version of the *Tract. on Ps. 28.*

[48] "*The Lord has done whatever he wanted in heaven and on earth, in the sea and in all the abysses.* Where he finds a heart lucid with understanding like the heaven, where he discovers a mind stable like the earth, if he sees a heart bitter and unstable like the sea, then always and everywhere indeed *all things, whatever he willed, God made in heaven and on the earth, in the sea and in every abyss.*"

[49] See translation below VTT 4.204.

steadfastness or lust. Subsequently, as I suggest, Richard inserts the tropological note into his sermon, but the context of the sermon requires the following adjustment:

Geographic Location:	Heaven	Earth	Sea	Abyss
External Quality:	Lucid	Solid	Bitter & Unstable	Dark
Interior Man:	heart	mind	heart	mind
Interior Quality:	Understanding	N/A	N/A	N/A

Figure 4: Chart of Tract on Ps. 28:5

In his sermon on Psalm 28 Richard interprets the fifth verse as the Lord breaking prideful minds ("animos elatos") and an arrogant heart ("cor arrogantia tumidum").[50] This, as he notes, is extremely difficult, if not impossible, for us to accomplish on our own, but nothing is impossible for God. To explain this Richard inserts the tropological note on Ps. 134:6, which, as he is well aware, is a common verse to discuss God's sovereign will at the literal level (see above). For Richard this still means God's works in hearts and minds, but the specific pairing of the internal quality is no longer instrumental for that interpretation and thus omitted.

Obviously this sampling of two notes does not offer an exhaustive analysis of what Richard's methods. To be sure, as I suggest, he was well imbued with the scholarly interpretations that disseminated in the famous glosses of the time and utilized them as he saw fit, and clearly, as the program at St Victor required, education is an important matter for reading sacred texts. But Richard also shows a clear preference for the moral interpretation, not because he is disinterested in scholarship but because he sees spirituality as of equal necessity for reading sacred texts.[51] For him this is not a matter of stressing external activities alone, as important as they are, but the internal imperatives that derive from the truths of the sacred text. In other words, it does not make much

---

50   On the possibility that the tract *Afferte domino* (Ps. 28) is a sermon, see n. 29 above.

51   E.g., Richard of St Victor, *XII patr.* 79 (SC 419.318): "O how many people do we see today who are so studious in reading, so slothful in work, tepid in prayer, and yet presuming that they can attain the peak of this mountain! But how, I ask, will they attain this when they do not have Christ as their leader? For, Christ does not lead them, since he does not want to ascend up the mountain without his three disciples. Therefore, let him, who seeks to have Christ as the guide of the journey and leader of the ascent, join the endeavors of work and prayer to the endeavor of reading." See also the tract on Lev. 26:5 below (VTT 4.226).

sense to learn of the Psalmist's experiences with Christ unless readers also learn to make those experiences their own. To facilitate this Richard wades through the many similitudes of the letter to thresh out as many spiritual truths as possible. Indeed, such a concern means at times that he must extend past the authorities to present a multiplicity of spiritual truths that cannot be exhausted. Thus if he wants to venture past the glossed authorities, it is not to contradict them but to broaden the application of moral and spiritual truths found in them. And if this comes across as a bold undertaking, Richard offers the following apology:

> I know that the Fathers neglected certain passages of Scriptures which they could easily have addressed . . . Therefore, let no one be scandalized if I say something different or say it differently than what is found in the glosses. Let no one scorn me for wanting to gather leftover grains. To the Fathers the divine command was given, to them it was divinely granted to fill the storehouses of so many books from the harvest of Scriptures. But it should come as no surprise that some of these grains escaped their notice or rather that they gladly left them for the poor. . . . Therefore, note carefully not whether I say something new but something true. I have no fear of saying something diverse provided that I say nothing perverse.[52]

Published here for the first time is the English translation of the *Tractates on Certain Psalms* as it would have been known to medieval readers.[53] The translation is based on my critical edition that will be published in CCCM (Brepols). The sermon *Afferte domino* (Ps. 28), addressed to novices, was left out of this volume and will be included in VTT 5. Whenever a title to an individual tract is ascribed, it is the incipit of the biblical passage. In the English translation I have provide

---

52 *Vis. Ezek.* 10 (Schröder, 460; PL 196.562A–B; cf. Smalley, *Study of Bible*, 109): "Scio quidem Patres quaedam Scripturarum loca quae facile possent penetrare negligenter tamen praeterire, dum invenisse desiderarent, atque gauderent quae juxta litteram stare non possent, ut per hoc saltem convincerentur homines allegoriam recipi debere, quam illis adhuc temporibus admodum pauci vix voluissent recipere. Neminem ergo scandalizet si quid dicimus aliud, vel aliter quam in glossis invenerit. Nemo dedignetur nos remanentes spicas velle colligere, nemo miretur illis elabi aliquas potuisse, vel illos potius pauperibus eas sponte reliquisse, quibus hoc divinitus praeceptum est, quibus divinitus datum est tot voluminum horrea de Scripturarum messe replesse. Sed tu vis honorare, et defendere veterum auctoritatem, sed nunquam verius honoramus veritatis amatores, quam quaerendo, inveniendo, docendo, defendendo, diligendo veritatem. Attende ergo non utrum dicam aliquid novum, sed verum. Parum timeo dicere aliquid diversum, dum tamen nihil dicam perversum."

53 I am grateful to Fr. Hugh Feiss for his careful reading of the translation and his helpful revisions.

titles based on the treated biblical verses. For example, the first tract *Quare fremuerunt* is given the English title *On Psalm 2:1–4*, which are the verses discussed in that tract.

TRACTATES ON CERTAIN PSALMS

ON PSALM 2:1–4

1. *Why have the nations growled and the people meditated on inane things?*[1] How else do we interpret the nations who do not know God and worship idols except as wicked and perverse thoughts? And how else do we understand the people who meditate on inane things except as vain and foolish thoughts? It is written about the one: *Perverse thoughts separate from God,*[2] and it is written about the other: *The Holy Spirit of discipline will flee from the deceitful and will withdraw from thoughts that are without understanding.*[3]

2. *From thoughts,* it says, *that are without understanding.*[4] If the Holy Spirit withdraws from thoughts that are without understanding, then what will happen regarding those thoughts that we can only admit with a base and illicit affect or those that we admit willingly only with some perverse consent? What one passage plainly calls "perverse thoughts," the other passage figuratively calls "nations," as people who are perverse and turned away from the true God. And what one passage wanted to call "thoughts without understanding" the other passage, unless I am mistaken, designated "people who meditate on inane things." Those thoughts that are not without wickedness are certainly worse than those thoughts that roam aimlessly without understanding. For that reason the passage calls the first kind of thoughts "nations" and the second kind "people." The nations are certainly damned by their perversity, but people, however faithful, are abased by their own ignobility. And so every vain or idle thought is worthless, but a wicked and perverse thought is absolutely detestable. Such are the kinds of thoughts the Prophet rebukes, or rather the kinds he mocks when he says: *Why have the nations growled and the people meditated on inane things?*[5]

We must note that growling is characteristic of beasts not humans. The growling of nations is the insurrection of wicked desires against reason. Whenever we criticize the just judgments of God and murmur against His punishments, we are transforming our human voice into growling. And whenever we follow appetite rather than reason, we imitate beasts, as if we were ashamed of being human. Therefore, the

Prophet first rebukes the growling of iniquity, and then he reproves the pursuit of vanity. He criticizes the pursuit of vanity when he says: *And the people meditated on inane things.*[6] And perhaps to think about inane things is venial, but to mediate on them is completely reprehensible, because it is one thing for us to experience something due to negligence or unwillingness, but it is another thing for us to be occupied willingly with a useless pursuit.

3. *The kings of the earth stood up, and the princes met together.*[7] Let us first ask about the identity of these kings and princes. The passage says "the kings" but specifies "the kings of the earth." It is said to a sinner: *You are the earth, and to earth you will return.*[8] On this earth demons, whom the Apostle calls the principalities of this earth and rulers of darkness,[9] have royal command and exercise dominion, while they push us toward unclean desires and distract us with worldly lusts. "King" derives from "ruling," and "earth" rightly indicates a heart that longs with earthly desires. And so those demons, who strive with fraud rather than virtue in subverting and subjugating people to themselves, are called "kings" in Sacred Scripture. The artifice of some demons is greater, but the audacity of others is more ferocious. The former are more covert in their temptation, but the latter are more vehement in their onslaught. The temptation of the former is deceptive, but the temptation of the latter is violent. The former deceive as if by consultation, but the latter bear down in some way with a very fierce attack. The former are understood through the word "kings," and the latter through "princes." The former take charge over people by ruling, the latter by dominating: they lure into iniquity people whom they have either artfully deceived or forcefully overthrown.

Let us see, therefore, what the Prophet says: *The kings of the earth stood up.*[10] I find in Sacred Scripture that one spirit is called the "spirit of fornication," and another is called the "spirit of pride."[11] The same can be understood with other vices. One spirit obtains a kingdom in self-indulgent people, and another in gluttonous people. One presides over greedy people, and another over angry people. This one rules over the envious, that one rules over the proud. And so what else does it mean that such kings stand together if not that one king helps another in assaulting people? While someone is being forced into some vice by one king, as a result he often finds himself to be weaker in resisting the others. Someone burdened with drunkenness is usually much more quickly and more easily inflamed with self-indulgence. And so the kings stand together when they work together in assaulting us.

4. *The princes meet together,*[12] because whatever part they play in our subversion, however diverse it may be, they nevertheless conspire together. Moreover, we are right to understand that not only do these kings and princes stand together but so do the nations and people, because, as long as our minds roam aimlessly with wicked and foolish thoughts, we provide an opportunity for deceptive spirits to tempt us. And so the kings are assisting and princes are meeting together with the growling nations and the people meditating on vain things. While our perverse and vain thoughts, which the nations or people signify, are making so much noise, malignant spirits are discovering the opportunity to tempt us and are receiving from the just judgment of God the permission to tempt us.

And yet we can understand these demons not only through the kings and princes but also through the nations and people. And we can make subtle distinctions among them based on these names. Consider now the great number of demons, or rather their innumerable multitude. Just as some of these demons are more subtle in nature than others, so have no doubt that some are bolder in their presumption and craftier in their deception. This produces a situation in which some demons rule over the weaker ones and freely dominate them, even though the weaker demons are more numerous. The more copious multitude of demons thus exists as inferior subjects, but the bolder and craftier demons exist as superiors. And this produces a situation in which the superior demons on account of their greater audacity exercise free reign over the inferior demons, and on account of their greater craftiness they prescribe endeavors or duties to the lower ones as they see fit.

Perhaps Sacred Scripture wanted to warn us about this when it identified some demons as kings or princes but designated other demons as nations and people. However, if we seek the difference between nations and people, then we will be able to distinguish one from another easily. Different customs and language distinguish one nation from another, and often one nation usually has many people. The Prophet thus indicates a diversity of customs in one nation and a multiplicity in another. Some nations are more notorious in certain vices, and others are more friendly or energetic than others. And so perhaps the Prophet mentioned the nations first and then the people, because he noticed diverse customs and pursuits as well as a countless multitude in each distinction. If therefore we have discernment of spirits,[13] if we pay careful attention to these differences, then we will be able to understand the different demons not only through the kings and princes but also through the nations and people.

Let him, therefore, who is able, think about how excellent, great and gifted with such excellent discernment and great virtue is the man against whom the nations and people have raged and against whom the kings and princes have conspired. If we knew that we could have resisted or can resist the ferocity and cunningness of any demon at all, then we would not only think that we accomplished something great, but we would also believe that we were no longer human but superhuman. That man, however, realizes that he is being attacked not only by a nation or king but also by nations, people, kings and princes, and he knows that he cannot be conquered. He then wrote about it and leaves it for future generation to read, so that he may put our pride to shame— we who are nothing—and yet our pride shames us not.

Now if someone wants to interpret the nations and people as thoughts and interpret the kings and princes as affections, then I easily grant it because I do not dispute the fact that the affections of the soul preside over the thoughts. Let us allow this meaning in such a way that we do not deny the earlier meaning because we do not doubt that the Sacred Scripture allows multiple interpretations. Let us, therefore, ascribe everything in this passage either to the vices of a soul or to demons, or, if this seems better, we ascribe it partly to immoral behaviors and partly to the instigators of vices. To overcome immoral behaviors or the instigators of vices is great, but the ability to resist both is even greater. Yet if the Prophet were unable to resist both, then he would not assault them with such great confidence when he says: *Why have the nations growled and the people meditated on inane things? The kings of the earth stood up, and the princes met together.*[14]

5. But if we pay careful attention to the words that follow, we will quickly discover the reason why he anticipates a victory over so many enemies. He says: *The kings of the earth stood up, and the princes met together.* But against whom? *Against the Lord,* he says, *and against his Christ.*[15] Thus he was anticipating a victory from Him who was tirelessly fighting in him against so many enemies. What else is the soul of David than a tower of God that the Lord—*as if a man of war, almighty is his name*[16]—defends against so many enemies for his own sake. David himself proclaims elsewhere about one of these towers: *Let peace be in your strength and abundance in your towers.*[17] The nations first attack this tower, which is mighty before all of the rest and unique among the mighty, and the people surround it with a siege. But because they could

not prevail, the kings finally stood up and the princes assembled together. But the tower remained unconquerable as the Lord was tirelessly defending it for his own sake. David stood safely among so many enemies on account of God's protection, and he will even triumph in the end over them through God's victory. Therefore, David was not afraid of insulting them because he noticed that they could not prevail over him, and he says: *Why have the nations grumbled and the people meditated on inane things? The kings of the earth stood up and the princes met together against the Lord and against his Christ.*[18]

6. *Against the Lord*, he says, *and against his Christ.*[19] The gifts of nature in us are different from the gifts of grace. Let us distinguish no less "the Lord" and "his Christ." Interpret "Lord" as "Creator" and "Christ" as "Savior." Sometimes the word "Creator" is used, and sometimes the word "Savior" is used. He is called "Creator," because he created what did not exist before. But thereafter he is called "Savior," because he restored what had been destroyed. And so the gifts of nature pertain to the Creator, and the gifts of grace seem to pertain especially to the Savior. We speak about the gifts of nature when we see some with a greater propensity toward compassion as a natural temperament and others more rigid in justice. Some are naturally more prudent, and others more simple (and any other dispositions which anyone who has them possesses naturally without any effort). We speak about gifts of grace, when someone tries to have through grace what he could not possess at all through nature. And so we receive the gifts of nature at first creation from the gift of the Creator, and we receive the gifts of grace at the proper time from the kindness of the Savior. Consequently, when we corrupt the gifts of nature, we, who are not afraid of destroying his work, sin against the Creator. However, when anyone destroys the gifts of grace, he specifically acts against his Savior who toiled to the point of death for our restoration. And because wicked morals or the instigators of vices (the demons) seek to subvert in us the goods of nature and the gifts of grace, the Prophet correctly portrays the nations and people as conspiring with the kings and princes not only against the Lord but also his Christ. As an affront to the Creator, they hasten to corrupt the work of creation in us, and, as an insult to the Savior, they strive to undo the work of redemption. Rightly, therefore, the Prophet says: *The kings of the earth stood up and the princes met together against the Lord and against his Christ.*[20]

7. *Let us break their chains and throw their yoke from us.*[21] By chains we are fettered so that we cannot go where we want to go. By a yoke we

are forced against our will to toil at something that we do not want to do. These are two great evils: being impeded from the good and being occupied in evil. The chains of lust call us away from the good, and the yoke of fear propels us toward evil. To break such chains and throw off this yoke is surely good advice from the Prophet. But perhaps you are seeking a method and desire to hear how this can be accomplished. Listen, but do not ignore. Do not *love the world nor the things that are in the world*,[22] and you have broken the bonds. Do not *fear those who kill the body and can do nothing to the soul*,[23] and you have thrown off the yoke. *Let us break their chains and throw their yoke from us.*[24]

8. *He who dwells in the heavens will ridicule them, and the Lord will mock them.*[25] Is it a great wonder why the Lord is said to dwell in heaven and not everywhere, if he is indeed present everywhere? Or if he is indeed in heaven alone, then why do we believe that he is everywhere? Common experience tells us that an object may be seen in the place where it is located, but it cannot be seen at all where it is not located. Scripture wanted to locate God, who is undoubtedly everywhere, in heaven in a special way. Thus God is said to be mostly there where he is constantly seen by all inhabitants, so that a person who desires to see him may ascend by means of merit to that place where he can be seen. God is indeed on the earth, and yet we who are on the earth cannot see him. Nor is God absent in hell, even though we do not believe that He can be seen by the inhabitants of hell. However, we have no doubt that God is in heaven and is seen in heaven.

One must know that God is seen in three different ways: by faith, contemplation, and sight. The difference between a believer and an unbeliever is the difference between heaven and earth. We can call anyone a perfect heaven on account of faith. And yet a second heaven is located above this first one, namely, the dignity of spiritual men (*virorum*). And above this is a third heaven, namely, the sublimity of angels.[26] And so we see God in the first heaven by faith alone, we see him in the second heaven by contemplation, and we see him in the third heaven face to face.[27] We see God by faith when we firmly believe those things that are written about him. We see him through contemplation when, after having been divinely inspired, we fix the eyes of understanding to what was first believed about him. And we see him by sight when we see him *face to face*,[28] *just as he is* in his own substance.[29] Nevertheless, in whatever way God is seen he is still seen only in heaven—in the first heaven by faith, in the second heaven by contemplation, and in the third by sight. He only dwells in these heavens by grace, even though he is located everywhere by the presence of his power or essence. And because the Lord dwells uniquely in the saints, the Scripture correctly designates him a special place in the heavens.

But if we interpret "earth" as flesh and "heaven" as the soul, then there is still another meaning in this verse that deserves our attention. One must know that the fleshly sense never enters into the mystery of divinity; corporeal sense is never admitted into those inmost secrets. Only the soul, which is made in its likeness,[30] can see the substance of the divine nature. But no one will desire to see the divine nature corporeally there, just as here no one strives to see his wisdom corporeally. And so, because only the soul is capable of the light of divine glory, to which the corporeal sense can never penetrate, God is correctly said to dwell in heaven, that is, in the soul, which rejoices forever in his presence and enjoys the vision of him. What wonder is it then if God defended the soul against its enemies for his own sake, because he chose to dwell in it for eternity, just as it is written: *This is my rest for ever and ever, here will I dwell, since I have chosen it?*[31] *And so I will act confidently and will not fear.*[32] If I have such a dweller and if I find such a protector, then I will be secure among my enemies until the end and will not be afraid to insult them by saying: *He who dwells in the heavens will ridicule them, and the Lord will mock them.*[33] May he who dwells in the heavens and loves to inhabit souls defend me for his own sake. May he repel my enemies, conquer them, and laugh at them.

9. *He who dwells in the heavens will ridicule them, and the Lord will mock them.*[34] There is a difference between ridiculing and mocking. Ridicule occurs when we praise something ironically, as when we ascribe to it something by exaggerating it beyond what it is, or when we exaggerate it by ascribing to it something that it is not at all. Mocking occurs when we change our face into some expression by means of a simulated grimace, and when we express with a feigned grimace what sort of person one is, or rather what sort of people one believes us to be. And even though mocking seems to be indicated specifically by a snub nose, we can still refer to any scornful contortion of the lips, nose, eyes, and face as mockery. Therefore, we simulate the beauty of another by ridiculing them, but in some way we dissimulate our beauty by mocking. Or rather we dissimulate the ugliness of another by ridicule, and we simulate our own non-existent ugliness by mocking. Such simulation or dissimulation makes another's deformity appear more deformed and makes our beauty stand out as more beautiful.

What else then does it mean that the Lord ridicules his enemies other than he lets them loose to accomplish mighty or even great deeds, in which they can temporarily appear glorious to themselves and other? And then, when he allows them to do something, he utters what sounds like their praises into their ears, and as a result their proud minds boast in vain. These are the kind of people whom the Prophet attacks when he says: *May the Lord destroy all deceitful lips and the boastful tongue. They have said: "We will magnify our tongue. Our lips are our own. Who is Lord over us?"*[35] And so ridicule occurs when God simulates the fortitude of his enemies. Mocking occurs when he dissimulates his power or righteousness. For he often permits the unjust to prosper in this life and the just to be afflicted, as if he could not resist wickedness or did not want to have pity on the innocence. At those moments when he does not seem powerful or just enough to perverse minds, what else is this other than that he contorts his straight facial features, so to speak, from their perspective? They do not believe that he, who is just, is just, as if they do not see the beauty of his face in its splendor.

It often happens that, while wicked people go unpunished for their evil deeds, they believe that God does not care at all about human activities. These are the kind of people whom the Prophet describes as saying: *The Lord will not see nor will the God of Jacob understand.*[36] Some of them *have said in their heart: "God has forgotten and turned away his face lest he sees to the end."*[37] These perverse people are ridiculed when they presume false and great things about themselves; and they are mocked when their insane minds imagine something profane and vain about the Lord. They hear what sounds like their praises, but these praises are false insofar as they believe great things about themselves that are not at all true. They regard the Lord as deformed as long as they think unworthy things about him.

But these opinions in particular seem to fit the malignant spirits against whom this passage seems to be directed. They exhausted David with their temptations and hastened to subvert him with their ambushes, but David, who was secure on account of the Lord's protections, confidently sang: *He, who dwells in the heavens, will ridicule them, and the Lord will mock them.*[38] God often permits malignant spirits to prevail over some of the elect for a time. Hence, it often happens that in resistance to God's ordination they strive to destroy those whom the Lord eternally protects for his own sake. But at those moments when the elect rise up after their fall even more steadfast and humble, what else is this other than malignant spirits with their attacks serving, although unwillingly, the advancement of the good.

See, if you can, how they are ridiculed. Notice how they are mocked. Nothing causes them more grief and nothing makes them groan more than our good and progress. They hate our good nearly more than their own torment; indeed they prefer to increase their torment daily rather than not diminish our good and merits. And even after so many attempts and such great crises they still achieve nothing more than making good people better each day. And so they are ridiculed when they boast that they can do something against the elect, and they are mocked when they think that they do something against God's ordination. Obviously every action of their hostile malice is set against the salvation of the elect. However, in its pitiful attempt to impede it, it is forced to fulfill God's ordination. The Prophet, therefore, is correct when he says that the Lord will ridicule and mock them.

On Psalm 25:1–6

1. *Judge me, Lord.*[39] I would like to know what sort of person I am, but I can hardly discern the truth about myself. The private love that I have for myself prevents me from making a true judgment about myself. Therefore, *judge me, Lord*, you who truly know me. You say this to me about yourself: *I am the Truth*,[40] and I know that *every person is a liar*.[41] Thus I give little credence to myself (that is, a liar) about myself, fearing that if I judge myself, my iniquity may lie to me. You, who speak the truth, accomplish this with more honesty. You, who are the Truth, can do this much better than I. Therefore, let the Truth come into my heart. Let him bear a true testimony against me. Let him speak a true judgment about me. Judge me, therefore, Lord. Judge for me, I pray Lord, what sort of person I am. Pronounce a true judgment about me, and I enforce the punishment on myself. Or if perhaps the guilt in me is absolved through penance, then show me what I am lacking still in perfect righteousness. You effectively judge me before myself, if you clearly indicate to me what sort of person I am before you.

2. *Judge me, Lord, because I have come in my innocence.*[42] You were inside, I was outside. And so I was not able to hear your voice. I used to be outside, while I was seeking and reflecting on exterior things. But now I have become one of those turning to the heart, and I have hastened to fulfill that precept which says: *Return, you sinners, to the*

heart.[43] And look, Lord, I am now inside! You who are inside, see that I have come in my innocence, so that I could hear you and speak with you. I have thus come to you. Now I am inside with you. Therefore, *speak, Lord, because your servant is listening.*[44] I am now ready to listen to what the Lord, my God, says in me.

Those, who are outside and still love exterior things and think about exterior things alone, cannot hear your voice. Some are outside on account of their thoughts and love, while others are outside on account of their thoughts alone. Similarly some are inside on account of their thoughts alone, while others are inside on account of their thoughts and love together. For those who think about and love vanity[45] are certainly outside on account of their thoughts and their love. Those who reluctantly supervise exterior things because of their occupation do not so much love this supervision of external things as much as they tolerate it. They are compelled to be outside through their thoughts, even though they are inside through love. Some seek the truth eagerly and carefully, but they still do not love the truth. These people study the truth as though they are inside, yet they are not inside through the love of the truth. But those who seek and love the truth are inside both through their thoughts and through love. Therefore, if I think only about internal things, Lord, if I love only internal things, then clearly I am no longer outside. Obviously, I am inside with you.

3. *Judge me, Lord, because I have come in my innocence.*[46] Undoubtedly if I were not innocent, I would not presume to have come to you, nor would I dare to appear in your sight. If I were not innocent, I would not be able to hear your voice of inspiration, or rather I would not dare to hear it. And thus I will guard myself from my iniquity, so that I may be able to hear your words, so that I may not fear to appear in your sight, and so that I may deserve to enjoy your conversation. Because I know that *you will not deprive those who walk in innocence of the good,*[47] I have come to you confidently in my innocence. I know that the corruption of the mind is greater and worse than the corruption of the body and that we are often being renewed inwardly while being afflicted outwardly.[48] I used to avoid harming souls, so that I might be truly innocent. I could harm the soul of another by setting a wicked example, and I could also harm my soul through a mere consent to perversity. But I strove to be innocent, so that I might come before your judgment with confidence. And now *judge me, Lord, because I have come in my innocence.*[49] Whatever evil I was able to discern in me with my own judgment I hastened to correct. But now you judge me, Lord.

No matter how innocent I seem to my own judgment, I dare not put much credence in my judgment about me, and thus I pray: *Judge me, Lord.* Make known to me what sort of person I am who lies hidden before you. In the meantime I have preserved my innocence as much as I could, but maybe this is my innocence, not yours. My innocence was based on my own judgment, but perhaps this was not a genuine innocence according to your judgment. And so, *judge me, Lord, because I have come in my innocence.*[50]

4. *And as long as I put my hope in the Lord, I will not be weakened.*[51] Adam was inside and healthy, but yet he was not able to keep his health. After he was weakened, he was not able to remain inside, because he did not put his hope in the Lord. But *as long as I put my hope in the Lord, I will not be weakened.* The devil was created not only in the inmost good but also in the highest good, and yet he was not able to keep for very long the strength of his health that he received at his creation, because he put his hope in his own strength, not in the loving kindness of the Lord. But *as long as I put my hope in the Lord, I will not be weakened.* Both were inside; both were healthy. Afterwards both became weak; afterwards both were cast outside—the one from heaven, the other from paradise. Both were confident in themselves. However, *I have come in my innocence, and as long as I put my hope in the Lord, I will not be weakened.*[52] I was outside; I was weak. But now I have come inside, and *as long as I put my hope in the Lord, I will not be weakened.* They were healthy; they were inside. I was outside; I was weak. But now *I will go into the place of the wonderful tabernacle, all the way to the house of God with the voice of exaltation and confession,*[53] and, after going inside, *I will not be weakened, as long as I put my hope in the Lord.*[54]

I am aware, Lord, how much work it is to remain inside and to endure in the interior. Nevertheless, I believe that *I will not be weakened, as long as I put my trust in the Lord.*[55] It was certainly difficult to draw my mind into interior things from exterior things and very hard to enter into invisible things from visible things, but perhaps it will be much more difficult to remain in interior things for a long time. Nevertheless, *I will not be weakened, as long as I put my trust in the Lord.*[56] The sons of Israel were barely able to enter the promise land after many years and hazards, and afterwards they could not keep it for themselves without a great deal of effort and strength. I have reached with difficulty the land flowing with milk and honey;[57] at a late hour I merited to taste the sweetness of contemplation, and now I see the envy of my enemies burning more vehemently again me. Nevertheless, I am certain that *I will not be weakened, as long as I put my hope in the Lord.*[58] *Those who hope in the Lord will renew their strength.*[59] How much more will they not fear weakness? Therefore, *I will not be weakened, as long as I put my hope in the Lord.*

5. *Inspect me, Lord, and test me.*[60] Two actions are [under evaluation]: doing good and avoiding evil. Therefore, inspect me, Lord, to see whether I am ready to do good, and test me to see whether I am careful to avoid evil. *Inspect me, Lord, and test me.* Inspect me through adversity, test me through prosperity. *Inspect me, Lord, and test me.* There are also two things that make people perfect: virtue and wisdom. I want both, because I long for perfection. *Inspect me, Lord, and test me.* Through inspection we advance toward virtue, through testing we are educated in truth. Our virtue is trained during the inspection, and our foresight is instructed during the tests. *Inspect me, Lord, and test me.*

6. *Burn my reins and my heart.*[61] I know that lust sometimes rises from carnal vice and sometimes descends from mental vice. *Burn my reins and my heart.* Burn my reins in order to extinguish my carnal itch, and burn my heart in order to extinguish my heart's desires. Burn my reins in order to consume my carnal itch, and burn my heart in order to dry up my mental flux. *Burn my reins and my heart.* Burn my flesh, burn my mind. Burn my flesh with the fire of tribulation, burn my mind with the heat of compunction. The flesh is bruised, and the heart feels remorse. The flesh is afflicted with toil, and the heart is affected with sorrow. Both are thoroughly burned, both are cleansed. *Burn my reins and my heart.*[62]

7. *Because your mercy is before my eyes, and I have been pleased with your truth.*[63] I put no trust in my strength but in your mercy, and I put no confidence in my wisdom but in your mercy, *because your mercy is before my eyes.* I know that my enemy is stronger than I. I know that he is more experienced than I. Nevertheless, I must not be afraid, *because your mercy is before my eyes.* Indeed I know that my enemy is more powerful and wiser than I, but *my eyes have looked down upon my enemies,*[64] *because your mercy is before my eyes.*[65]

Inspect me, test me, and burn my reins and heart. In all of this I fear nothing and dread nothing, *because your mercy is before my eyes.*[66] I know that *all things work together for good to them who love God, to them who are called holy according to his purpose.*[67] I also know that *God is faithful and will not allow us to be tested beyond what we can handle, but with the test he will also provide a way out, so that we may be able to bear it.*[68] Therefore, I am not going to flee the battle, because I expect to conquer, *because your mercy is before my eyes.*[69] Your mercy is before my eyes, because I see it. It is before my eyes, because I look to it. The eye of providence, the eye of understanding—both are directed toward you, both are fixed on you, *because your mercy is before my eyes.* Because I think about it, because I recognize it, *your mercy is before my eyes.* Because I put my hope in it, because I long for it, *your mercy is before my eyes.*

8. *Because your mercy is before my eyes, and I have been pleased with your truth.*[70] I have not been pleased with my power but with your truth, not with my goodness and holiness but with your truth. I put no confidence in my merits but trust in your promises, *because I have been pleased with your truth.* You have given me promises and predestined me from eternity.[71] You cannot lie,[72] because you are the Truth.[73] You can keep your promises, and you must accomplish what you have predestined, because you are true.[74] If I am the kind of person that I have been preordained to be from eternity, then I must be pleasing to you. Or rather I know that I am pleasing you, even though I am not yet that person; nevertheless, I am pleasing to you, because I will be that person, because *I have been pleased with your truth.* I am pleasing to you in your truth, and I am pleasing to myself in your truth, because I have been pleased with your truth both for you and for me. I have been pleased with myself not in the adulation of others, not in my own exultation, but in your truth. I have become pleasing to you not based on human opinion but in your truth. Not according to the mouth of those speaking wicked things, not according to the heart of those contriving false things, but *I have been pleased with your truth.* If I am chaste in body, if I am pure in heart, then I know that *I have been pleased with your truth.* If my works are just, if my desires are virtuous, then truly *I have been pleased with your truth.* If I please you internally, if I please you externally, then I am pleased with both and I am pleased in every way. The pagan philosophers worship virtue, but they do not believe things that are true. Even though their work is pleasing, their faith is displeasing; and, for that reason, those who despise the true faith cannot please you. False Christians have faith but not the works of faith.[75] In one sense they are pleasing, but in another sense they are displeasing; and, for that reason, not even they can please you. If I have both, then I truly know that I am pleasing to you. And yet I do not attain either through myself, I cannot have either from myself. But who taught me this if not your truth? And thus *I have been pleased with your*

truth. Your truth taught me that my good is your gift, my evil is my sin, and *I have been pleased with your truth.* Your truth has instructed me to ascribe my evil to me and to attribute my good to you, and, for that reason, *I have been pleased with your truth.* I have learned that I cannot rise up on my own. I have recognized that I cannot stand without you. I believe and profess that you are the one who worked in me both *to will and to accomplish according to your good will,*[76] and, for that reason, *I have been pleased with your truth.*[77]

9. *I have not sat with the council of vanity, neither will I enter with those performing iniquity. I have hated the assembly of the malignant, and with the wicked I will not sit.*[78] My soul has hated the first three evils, but it detests the fourth. Vanity, iniquity, malice—these three are very hateful, but my soul absolutely detests impiety, which is directed toward God. Vanity is harmful, iniquity is bad, malice is worse, but impiety is the worst. Vanity is contemptible, iniquity is hateful, malice is abominable, and impiety is detestable. Having excessive bodily concerns, nurturing the flesh in carnal desires, indulging in too much food or sleep, seeking ornate clothing—all this is vanity, because all this is vain. Greedily holding fast to one's own possessions, greedily seeking the possessions of others, reserving to one's own power what the Author of all things wanted to belong to all in common, refusing to do for others what we want them to do for us—this is certainly not fair at all, because all this goes against equity, because all this is iniquity. Retaining hatred in one's heart, seeking revenge on enemies, rejoicing in the destruction of an enemy, being consumed with envy in the possessions of others—all this is wicked, all this is malicious, and the reason why all this cannot please me is that it is all full of malice. Murmuring, blaspheming, reprehending the just judgment of God, lifting one's heart against God in pride, exerting one's own glory in light of God's gifts— all this is impious, and a pious heart cannot accept any of this because this is all impiety, and to think otherwise is both pious and good. We must therefore despise vanity, hate iniquity, condemn malignity, and detest impiety.

Excessive love of self prompts vanity, a disordered love of the world introduces iniquity, hatred of our neighbor generates malice, and contempt for God fosters impiety. To devote oneself to carnal concerns is vain, to desire to surpass others in worldly glory is wicked, to practice hostility toward our neighbors is malicious, and to become arrogantly insolent against one's Creator is impious. Gluttony and indulgence represent vanity, because what they seek is vain, what they love is vain, and because gluttony requires superfluous contrivances in the utilization of nature, and indulgence wastes away an inept mind in intemperance, laughing, and jokes. Greed arouses iniquity when people reserve to their own possession what the one Author intended to be common to all people. As long as people wrongly deny to others what they want others to do for them, they sin against equity. Anger and envy lead to malice and arouse malignity, because while anger rages in its own injury, envy burns at another's happiness. Both maliciously act with respect to what belongs to their neighbor: anger is fueled in evil, envy wanes at the good. Impiety is aroused by sadness or pride, both of which are guilty of diminishing divine goodness with a wicked audaciousness. Sadness often murmurs against the punishment of God, but pride usurps to its own glory whatever it receives from the gift of God. While being corrected by God, sadness tries to blame God's justice rather than its own conscience. Whatever God brings about for the sake of correction as a medicine for a spiritual illness, pride is not afraid to distort into an insult. What, I ask, is so impious? What is so foreign to true piety? Pride empties the glory of the Glorifier, while it attributes God's gifts to its own merits or virtues to the extent that it can. Who can really describe how impious this is? Desiring to avoid vanity, *I have not sat with the council of vanity;*[79] and because I strive to avoid iniquity, *I will not enter with those performing iniquity.*[80] I cannot love malignity, and, for that reason, *I have hated the assembly of the malignant.*[81]

I must admit that it is true that countless thoughts often come into my mind and that many affections rise up and agitate me with bodily concerns and suggest many things about necessary uses. They convene in my mind as if to offer counsel, but really they are there to deceive me. Many counselors and vain advisers, or rather true deceivers, are assembling, but they are assembling as if in one counsel and for obtaining good counsel. They make many decrees together, but they are useless and vain, because it is a council of vanity and their whole counsel is about vanity. They propose that I drink wine for the sake of my stomach, prolong sleep for the sake of my brain, nurture my flesh lest it deteriorates, rejuvenate my body lest it becomes weak, relax abstinence just a little, and indulge in idleness for a short time. In this way it is concerned with bodily care and superfluous care. Vain inquiry is ventilated by vanity and often an entire day is consumed with such useless business. But, after much experience, I have now learned not to believe the counsel of vanity, especially because I should not subject my heart to vain counsels.

I have not sat with the council of vanity.[82] Whenever I see such vain counselors convening, I neither sit nor remain inactive, but I examine my mind. I seek refuge sometimes in work sometimes in prayer, saying: *Avert my eyes lest they should see vanity. Send forth your light and your truth.*[83] And I do not stop praying until vanity fades away and truth shines forth. Therefore, it is good, Lord, not to sit with the council of vanity. And it is just as good not to enter with them but rather to avoid participation with iniquity. But if I do not first shun vanity, then I cannot avoid iniquity. A slave to gluttony will necessarily be a slave to greed, because a lover of pleasure wants wealth now. But if my mind occasionally gives into the love of money,[84] then I will quickly assent to unjust counselors and those performing iniquity and freely accept their suggestions. And then, all of a sudden, depraved thoughts surface and perverse affections flare up. They decide to increase wealth and seek revenue. They instruct me to enlarge my estate and erect a palace. They admonish me to solicit the contributions of kings, not to disdain the small gifts of the poor, to lay field to field and join house to house,[85] to have hands extended to receive and shut to giving,[86] to receive all things and pay nothing out, to hate hospitality and defraud alms. They admonish me to enlarge my fringes and make my phylacteries broad,[87] to disfigure my face,[88] to pray long prayers so that I may be seen by men and to preach public sermons so that I may be heard by those passing by,[89] to produce tears in public deceptively, as if to profit souls but in actuality to amass wealth. In this way a disgraceful combination of those doing unjust things and those speaking depraved words often occurs after a council of those seeking vain things. And often while I depart from the hidden recesses of internal tranquility, while I emerge from within to think about external matters, suddenly a copious multitude of such thoughts surround me, and I am not permitted to leave this symposium of such great iniquity, *until I go into the sanctuary of God and understand things in their ends.*[90] For these and other such reasons *I have not sat with the council of vanity.*

11. *I will not enter with those performing iniquity.*[91] Far be it from me to enter the courts of the Lord with such an assembly![92] Far be it, I say, that I enter with them *into the place of the wonderful tabernacle, even to the house of God!*[93] With such wicked people I absolutely *will not enter the altar of God, to God who gives joy to my youth!*[94] Only after they are shut out and removed, only then will I boldly go into the Holy of Holies. Sometimes I go inside the first veil to the secret place of prayer, and sometimes I go inside the second veil to the mystery of

contemplation. Therefore, let such fancies first be driven out, lest perhaps, after being admitted inside, they destroy prayer and hinder contemplation. Indeed they usually disturb prayer and obscure contemplation. Inside the first curtain we ask God for celestial goods. But how are we to receive them, if we deny earthly goods to our neighbor? It is very just that we do not hesitate to sow our carnal goods, if we desire to reap spiritual goods. Jesus said: *Give and it will be given to you.*[95] If we freely give, then we may boldly enter inside the first curtain and ask that it may be given to us. But let us enter inside the second curtain and it will be given to us. Like beggars at the door of divine refreshment, we ask for alms inside the first curtain. After we are admitted inside the second curtain, as if being received inside the porch of a rich man, we receive, as it were, some of the leftover food and taste a very small portion of the Lord's sweetness. And there are many even today who desire to receive a taste of divine sweetness, yet they refuse the kindness that they ought to extend to their neighbors. They want it to be given to themselves, yet they refuse to give it. And what, I ask, is more unjust? Therefore, *I will not enter with those performing iniquity,*[96] because I know that if I do not give to those who ask, then I am not going to receive when I ask. And so any thought or affection may urge me to long greedily for other people's possessions and greedily retain my own. I do not listen to them at all. If I do not shut them out and remove them, I will not enter the tabernacle of the Lord. Because what they urge is evil, *I will not enter with those performing iniquity.*[97]

12. But what should I say about the malignant, Lord? You know, Lord, that *I have hated the assembly of the malignant.*[98] If I cannot sit with them, how much less am I able to reach you with them? What wonder is it if I reject the councils of those whom I cannot love? The malignant are those who seek or desire evil against their neighbor. I call every desire wicked and judge it to be malicious that stirs me to harm my neighbor or inflames me to hate him. But you know, Lord, that, even after being tormented often with insults, I do not ponder revenge, and, even after being provoked often with taunts, I do not respond with cruelty, because *I have hated the assembly of the malignant,* and I judge it malicious to acquiesce to them.

I have not sat with the council of vanity. I have hated the assembly of the malignant.[99] O vanity, O malignity! Vanity suggests a superfluous love of myself. Malignity tries to remove love of my neighbor. Vanity still has some delight, although it is vain and inept. But malignity knows nothing except sorrow and bitterness. How do you think wrath torments the mind? How much, I ask, does envy torture the mind? What is more malignant than these two vices? What is more grievous? And so, malignity is both punishment and guilt. These two greatest evils easily convince me not to love malignity, or rather they compel me to hate malignity. Truly *I have hated the assembly of the malignant*, and I cannot love it any more. How do I now love something in which I offend God, hurt my neighbor, and torment myself? Surely if the concern of my neighbor does not affect me, do I spare myself in this? For malignity always torments the mind of its possessor, although often it cannot injure its neighbor against whom it rages. For such reasons, *I have hated the assembly of the malignant*.[100]

But even though all malignity is evil, the worst form of this evil is the one that administers its torments under the form of holiness. Often when a person rages against a neighbor because of the vice of anger or venom of envy, an idea forms in his head that he does this because of his zeal for justice. Anyone who has been injured by his neighbor cannot yet easily look at him with an innocent eye. He is displeased with whatever offense he thinks was done by his neighbor. At nearly every moment he accuses him in his private thoughts. Every day innumerable causes flood his mind that prove his neighbor's guilt, and many reasons come to mind that convince him that the guilty party must be punished. And often this evil grows in him to the point that he believes that he will be guilty before God unless he corrects his neighbor very severely and reproves his neighbor for his perversity. Malignant thinking like this says to itself: "How long do I tolerate such a person as this? If I do not correct him [for his offense], then I am proven to agree with him. But if I agree with him, then I offend God. Therefore, I will correct him, so that I do not offend God. I will do nothing at all for my sake but only for the sake of avenging God's injury; indeed in this way I will restore him to himself." What now? To correct his neighbor and to punish him is not a desire to harm his neighbor but to benefit him. Often malignant thinking reasons with itself in this way. Its malice has blinded it and it believes that its hatred is love and that it is administering justice in inflicting injury. And so, such malignant thoughts assemble from all sides in the mind and they believe that they are building an assembly (*ecclesiam*) and not gathering an army. They think that they are assembling in a service of God, not that they wish to act out their hatred. A person who prepares himself for avenging himself assembles an army, as it were. In a way a multitude of thoughts builds an assembly (*ecclesiam*), because it pretends that they are assembling in service of God. Yet now I easily ridicule such an assembly, because *I have hated the assembly of the malignant, and with the wicked I will not sit.*[101]

I admit that I have not yet advanced to the point of hating them as much as I indicated with regard to the assembly of the malignant. And yet I do what I can: I refuse their company, and from now on I will not sit with the wicked. I do not know why it is that nothing so delights the mind as its ability to be glorified, even though it is written: *I will not give my glory to another.*[102] Therefore, more than anything else the human mind usurps for itself only that which God reserves only for himself and is unwilling to give to anyone else. So many goods of nature and so many gifts of grace do not satisfy men, unless in addition they also plunder and despoil their Lord of his glory so that they may put on themselves.[103] This is the reason why people are always ready to make excuses for their sins and deflect the blame to their God. With Adam they tell God: *The woman, whom you gave to me, deceived me,*[104] thinking that all sins derive from a vice of the flesh and thus they look for its guilt in the Author who created such flesh. By contrast, they ascribe the gifts of God to their own merits and seek their own glory from them, not the glory of him whose gifts they are. What sort of person, I ask, is so wicked that he wants his own evils to be imputed to God and the gifts of God to be ascribed to himself? Who does not see how wicked and sinful this is? This is why I will not sit with the wicked from now on but will refuse their counsels. If only I had hated all my wicked thoughts as much as I have hated the assembly of the wicked! If only I had never desired to usurp God's glory to myself as much as I do not delight in my neighbor's evil!

But even if I am not yet unable to eradicate the love of vain praise from my affection to the extent that I believe to have advanced in the hatred of [the assembly of] the malignant, I will still do what I can: I will not sit with the wicked. But whenever they convene in my mind, I will drive them out immediately. I take action and drive them away from my mind with as much harshness as possible. Therefore, just as *I have not sat with the council of vanity, so I will not sit with the wicked.*[105]

13. But because it is not enough to reject evil unless we also add doing good works, *I will wash my hands among the innocent.*[106] Therefore, it is not enough for me, Lord, that *I have not sat with the council of vanity,*[107] that *I have hated the assembly of the malignant,*[108] that *I will not enter with those performing iniquity,*[109] and that *I will not sit with the wicked,*[110] since all this is simply avoiding evil. But in order that

I may be perfectly pleasing in your sight,[111] I will strive to devote myself to you in good works. Therefore, *I will wash my hands among the innocent*.[112] The two hands are two works: the work of justice and the work of mercy. I will train myself in both of these works, so that I may have hands that I can raise to you through my good intention. Even if some stain should happen to stick to these hands during its activity, as is often the case, and even if either the scum of pride or the dirt of vain glory should make them filthy, then I will certainly wash my hands among the innocent and strive to clean them as much as I can. As often as I weep in your sight over the filthiness of my works, I strive to wash the blemishes of my hands with the water of tears. Whatever is made filthy through guilt is quickly washed clean through the bath of compunction. Therefore, the person who wants to have clean hands should strive to wash them with assiduous tears. But because such cleaning occurs better among good people—by whose examples we are instructed, through whose teaching we are taught, and through whose prayers we are aided—, I will not wash my hands among just any people, but among the innocent. I know that these innocent exist, and they watch over true innocence. They neither harm their own soul through the consent of a depraved will, nor do they injure another person's soul through the example of perverse actions. Therefore, I strive to have such companions, because I desire to have clean works.

On Psalm 40:10

1. *The man of my peace, in whom I trusted, who ate my bread, has enlarged deceit upon me.*[113]

Man of my peace.[114] There is an exterior man and an interior man, although the Apostle does say: *Our exterior man is corrupted, yet the interior man is renewed day by day*.[115] Therefore, the interior man laments the exterior man when he says: *Man of my peace*. As long as the body is chastened and is not yet fully subjected to the spirit, they are at war with one another. But after the body is chastened and forced back into servitude, peace is restored because the flesh submits to the spirit. This man's peace belongs to the spirit not the flesh, just as that peace, by which the spirit obeys the flesh, belongs to the flesh. Therefore, this man finds his peace of spirit in his flesh, when his flesh does not oppose him in his good endeavors. For that reason he says: *Man of my peace*. But a man never trusts in the peace of his flesh, even though its stimulus is reposed. And even though it promises him full security, he is often mindful of what the Prophet said: *The man of my peace, in whom I trusted, who ate my bread, has enlarged deceit upon me.*[116]

2. *In whom I trusted,* the Prophet said.[117] The Scripture says: *Let us make him a help like himself.*[118] What wonder is it if Adam trusts his help? What wonder is it if our interior man trusts in the man of his peace? Therefore, let him say: *The man of my peace, in whom I trusted,*[119] and then add: *Who ate my bread.*[120] Elsewhere it is said: *My tears have been my bread day and night,*[121] and in another passage it is said: *Rise up after you have sat, you who eat the bread of sorrow.*[122] The spirit merits having such bread *in the valley of tears, in the place which he has set.*[123] When someone grieves over his sins but still desires them and is unable to weep, the spirit alone eats the bread of sorrow, but the flesh still rejects such bread. But when the exterior man weeps bitterly over what grieves the interior man, then both certainly eat the one bread of sorrow, and the spirit feeds the man of his peace with his own bread. Therefore, let him say: *The man of my peace, in whom I trusted, who ate my bread, has enlarged deceit upon me.*[124] He grieves or rather deplores the fact that after he offered peace to him, after he offered him a valid hope, after he partook the bread of his sorrow, once again the man of his peace unexpectedly rises up against him, or rather now casts him out of his state of tranquility.

3. *He has enlarged deceit upon me.*[125] We know that a sin committed after the vow of profession incurs greater guilt. Therefore, before the vow a person's flesh casts him into sin, as often as the flesh deceives him. But the flesh undoubtedly enlarges deceit upon him who is overcome by it after he made his vow. And so the flesh first deceived, and later it enlarged its deceit.

ON PSALM 44:10

The queen stood on your right hand in gilded clothing.[126] *The Lord of virtues,* as the Psalmist says, *is the king of glory.*[127] Hence the Prophet says: *The queen stood at your right hand.* Rightly the queen of virtues is believed to be love, because what does not serve love is not called virtue. Temporal goods are at the left hand of God, but eternal goods are at his right hand. Therefore, love is said to stand at his right hand, because it rests on eternal goods not temporal. Love reigns in them alone whom the love of eternal things inflames. People, who run after temporal things with all their might, often over-exert themselves even to the point of death. But people, who love themselves in God, lay down their lives for others when necessary.[128]

Therefore, Queen Love stood on his right hand but *in gilded clothing*.[129] Clearly she wants to be pleasing in the sight of the supreme king, so she strives to wear very precious clothing. The error of those who say that works do not matter at all, are rejected here in my opinion. "Love," they say, "and do what you will."[130] This is certainly true. Just as I willingly commit no evil while filled with love, so I easily overlook no good that leads to action. And this is certainly what Augustine means. He did not say this to make excuses for your negligence. The evidence of love is the demonstration of works. For the queen's clothes are good works.

In gilded clothing, the Prophet said.[131] Interpret the clothing as the works of righteousness and the gold as the clarity of wisdom. Gilded clothes are prudent works. Perhaps you perform all your work mightily, yet not sweetly, because you do not perform them wisely. You do in fact have clothes, but you do not have gilded clothes, because wisdom *reaches from end to end mightily and manages all things sweetly*.[132] Wisdom extends from start to end. You start off mightily, but you finish feebly. Why is this unless because you do not manage all things sweetly, nor do you know how to work wisely? You begin, you run, you sprint, you pant, you become exhausted, and then you stop. You do not even make it to the middle much less the end. Therefore, the love, which never moves away from the right hand of God, forges ahead, or rather gives aid, in gilded clothing.

Surrounded with variety.[133] It is surely fitting that the queen has numerous and various clothes. Some of you always want to be in contemplation, but, as I hear, you do not know how to be clothed with variety. Others constantly strive to be in prayer, and you disregard the fact that love wants to be adorned with variety. Whoever delights in any one garment, however precious it may be, is not adorned in the work of love which is clothed with variety.

On Psalm 74:9

1. *Because in the hand of the Lord there is a chalice of pure wine full of mixed wine, and he has tilted it from here to there, but its dregs are not emptied*.[134] If we pay careful attention to this verse, we notice three things in the Lord's chalice: pure wine, dregs, and mixed wine.

If dregs were not found in the chalice, then the Prophet would not have said "its dregs," that is, the dregs of the chalice. And it seems that a contradiction is found in this verse, or rather this verse seems to propose something that is completely impossible. If his chalice contains pure wine, how, I ask, does it contain dregs or mixed wine? If perhaps someone explains that the pure wine is at the top of the chalice, the dregs at the bottom, and mixed wine in the middle, then this still goes against what the Prophet says, that is, "full of mixed wine." But this statement about the Lord's chalice can be referencing a temporal distinction. The chalice did contain pure wine, and that is why the Prophet called it "a chalice of pure wine," in the same way that the Scripture usually says "a basket of dung"[135] or "a basket of unleavened bread"[136] with respect to what each basket usually contains in it. But because he does not say that the chalice is full of pure wine as later in the verse he says "full of mixed wine," we can correctly say that previously the chalice contained both pure wine and dregs together—the pure wine at the top of the chalice, and the dregs at the bottom. We see this everyday in wine vases. And so the Prophet says "a chalice of pure wine" in order to indicate its previous content, but he clearly indicates its current content later in the verse when he says that the chalice is full of mixed wine. The appropriateness of the phrase "its dregs" as opposed to the chalice of dregs is sufficiently clear in itself, despite the fact the verse first mentions a chalice of pure wine.

We have just discussed this verse according to its literal interpretation. Now let us seek what mystical meaning lies hidden in these words. The Lord's chalice is righteousness, pure wine is joyfulness alone, dregs are supreme bitterness, and the mixed wine joins both together and mingles good and evil. The pure wine is eternal happiness, dregs are eternal unhappiness, and the mixed wine is the inconstancy of temporal prosperity and adversity. All these are drunk from the Lord's chalice, because the just Creator does everything justly, and the just Ruler manages all things justly. And so the Lord holds this chalice in his hand, because he never exceeds the bounds of equity in his work. He is the Lord. Let no one dare to say to him: *Why are you doing this?* This is the chalice *from which my Lord drinks*[137]—this is not Joseph, the great prelate of Egypt, but the Lord to whom all power in heaven and on earth has been given.[138] The Lord drinks from this chalice because of its sweet taste. This chalice, which justice commends, brings him great delight. This is the chalice *in which he uses for divination*,[139] because he weighs our secrets with scales of his justice.[140] He holds this chalice in his hand, because he accomplishes his justice in his work. Others carry this chalice not in their hand but in a sack like Benjamin,[141] because they have knowledge of what is just, but they do not show in their work what they have in their memory.

Angelic nature was first inebriated after it was given a drink from the Lord's chalice, but human nature was to be inebriated at some future time. As discussed above, this chalice did contain both dregs and pure wine but not mixed wine. The pure wine was at the top, but the dregs at the bottom. Therefore, angelic nature was created and was given a drink from this chalice. Some angels fell through their guilt and have become fixed in their evil, other angels remained steadfast through grace and have become fixed in the good—both were given a drink from the one chalice of divine justice. But the former was sufficiently inebriated from the dregs, the later from pure wine. Afterwards human nature was created in a similar way, and it was about to be given a drink from the Lord's chalice. But because human nature fell through its guilt, it was not worthy enough to drink from the pure wine. What will the just and mild Lord do? He, of whose *wisdom there is no number*,[142] knows what must be done. Because human nature sinned, the Lord did not give it a drink of pure wine; but because at another's prompting human nature fell through negligence, the merciful Lord did not want it to be inebriated from dregs. Therefore, the Lord stirred the chalice and mixed the dregs with wine, and the chalice has since remained full of mixed wine. Thus man is still given a drink of this mixed wine. And *because in the hand of the Lord there is a chalice full of mixed wine*,[143] the fate of man is constantly varied with prosperity and adversity from the beginning until the end of time. However much someone is dejected in this life he is generally uplifted with some kind of consolation at some point in his life, *because in the hand of the Lord there is a chalice full of mixed wine*. And so if this alternation of vicissitudes continues in all until the end of time, it is clear how correctly the Lord's chalice is presented as full of mixed wine. If you are discouraged, then don't fall away! If you are encouraged, don't be secure!

2. *Because he has tilted it from here to there.*[144] Be mindful of the good in evil days, and you should be mindful of evil in good days,[145] *because he has tilted it from here to there.* I see a vessel of wrath filled from the Lord's chalice and replete with bitterness. The vase of wrath was emptied again of its entire content and a vase of mercy was filled

from it. Why is this, I ask, if not because the Lord, who holds the chalice, *has tilted it from here to there*? Again I see a vase of wrath filled with an oil of temporal happiness: One spends his days in good[146] and has in the meantime things that avail for his peace.[147] Suddenly that vase is tilted and is emptied of its entire content, and the vase of mercy is filled with the same oil of happiness: He who used to grieve rejoices, and he who used to rejoice is saddened. And this variety of alternating fates continues as long as the Lord, who holds the chalice, does not stop tilting it from here to there. There is no one even today who is inebriated in this life with pure wine from the Lord's chalice, *because in the hand of the Lord there is a cup full of mixed wine.*[148] Happiness is never alone in this life and sorrow is never alone in this life, because happiness and sorrow are mixed together either at the top or bottom of this chalice. Look at the fish in water disturbed by rain water. They either ascend or descend, up and down. They find nothing except turbidity; they drink nothing except murky water. In the same way humans ascend up to heaven and descend down to the abyss; everywhere they drink from impure wine, *because in the hand of the Lord there is a chalice full of mixed wine.*[149] The Lord's chalice is still in motion, and thus he cannot make it pure wine. As long as the cup is in motion, the dregs do not settle but are mixed, which thus results in mixed wine.

Do you want to know why this cup is in motion, so that it cannot offer pure wine to drink? Because some angels are fixed in the good and others in their evil, some angels drink unmixed, pure wine while others drink the dregs. And just as evil angels do not expect anything better, so good angels are not afraid of losing what they received once and for all. But because justice is not yet fixed in humans, either part of the chalice remains uncertain for either evil or good humans. The chalice is constantly in motion, because immobile justice is still not fixed in anyone. After all, an unjust person can be converted, and a just person can be perverted. Likewise a good person can become better, and an evil person can become worse. An unclean person can still become dirty, that is, he can descend to the bottom of the chalice. Similarly a just person can still be justified, that is, he can be raised up to the top of the chalice. As long as this is the case, humans drink only from impure wine, *because in the hand of the Lord there is a chalice full of mixed wine.*[150]

3. *But its dregs are not emptied.*[151] Although the dregs are currently mixed with pure wine and the chalice is full of mixed wine, still *its dregs are not emptied.* After all things are accomplished,[152] and after humans

will at last be fixed as the angels are now[153]—the just in good, the unjust in evil—, the chalice will stop moving and the dregs will descend to the bottom of the chalice. The pure wine will be at the top, and only the dregs will remain at the bottom, because *its dregs are not emptied.*[154]

4. *Every sinner of the earth will drink.*[155] All the angels, who have sinned in heaven, have already drunk from the dregs, as already discussed; but some day all the sinners of the earth, who are not afraid of persevering in their sins, will drink from the dregs. The good will also drink at that time from pure wine, and only the evil will drink only from the dregs, so that thereafter it will not go badly for any good person, nor will it go well for any evil person.

On Psalm 80:6

When [Israel] came out of the land of Egypt, he heard a language which he knew not.[156] If Egypt is interpreted as darkness, then what else does the departure from Egypt mean than fixing the eyes of understanding in the light of truth after the darkness of ignorance has been dissipated? As often as we leave Egypt, we, forgetful of temporal things, fix the rays of contemplation on eternity. But one who leaves Egypt immediately *heard a language, which he knew not,*[157] because when, having spurned all external things, we are free for divine contemplation, we perceive the secrets of wisdom at one moment from angelic revelation, at another moment from divine inspiration. Angelic revelation is an unfamiliar language, and divine inspiration is an unknown language. The Apostle said: *If I speak in the language of men and of angels.*[158] Just as there is a human language, so there is also an angelic language. They cannot hear that language who, oppressed with worldly cares, gaze at nothing but darkness. Therefore, those longing for the knowledge of celestial wisdom should forsake the darkness of the world. If we withdraw from exterior works through loving and thinking, more quickly do we hear the voice of internal inspiration, just as it was written about Israel: *When he came out of the land of Egypt, he heard a language which he knew not.*[159] The more frequently someone hears this language, the further he advances in the knowledge of celestial wisdom.

On Psalm 80:11

Open your mouth widely, and I will fill it.[160] This verse does not pertain to everyone but only to the one whom the Lord God brought out of Egypt.[161] This, I say, rightly pertains to that person: *Open your mouth widely, and I will fill it.*[162] If you still live in Egypt and love the darkness of this world, then it is better that you close your mouth tightly rather than open it widely, because you will not easily discover in Egypt something with which you can fill it. We certainly see many who have nothing with which to fill their stomach. But it seems like a great mystery if some poor little soul is so miserable that it has nothing with which to fill its mouth.

What, I ask, is being said here and is being promised as a great offer: *Open your mouth widely, and I will fill it?*[163] If we interpret this as the mouth of our interior man, then we more readily discover the answer to our question. Let us consider what the people in Egypt hunger and thirst after, and then we will see how poor they are and how much they are in need. None of them can find what can fill even one mouth. Those in Egypt only long for carnal things and desire only temporal things; just as those who have left Egypt only desire spiritual things and only long for celestial things. About them it is said: *Blessed are they that hunger and thirst after justice, for they will have their fill.*[164] They are truly blessed, because the Lord *will feed them with the bread of life and understanding and give them the water of wholesome wisdom to drink.*[165] This verse seems to pertain to the number of those to whom the Lord's voice says: *Open your mouth widely, and I will fill it.*[166]

But what else is this mouth of the interior man except the desire of the heart? All the pleasures of Egypt cannot fill this mouth, because all the wealth of the world cannot satisfy it with carnal desire. Consider how small a part of the human body the physical mouth is and how narrow its opening is. Who does not see how small it is that a single morsel of bread can fill it? And so what a single morsel is to the physical mouth, this is—or rather this is much less than—what the whole world is to the mouth of the heart. One morsel easily fills a physical mouth, but the whole world cannot satisfy the desire of the heart. Consider, if you can, how wide the heart must be if the whole world cannot fill its mouth. Consider how the Word of God despises the abundance of the world, in comparison to which he prefers a single morsel of celestial bread.[167] If, therefore, you have left Egypt and learned to hunger after spiritual food, then it is said to you: *Open your mouth, and I will fill it*,[168] and again: *Open your mouth widely, and I will fill it.*[169] Therefore, if your mouth is closed, then you are being ordered to open it. If your mouth is open, then you are being ordered to widen it. Open your mouth and widen your desire as much as possible. Widen it greatly, so that you may be able to receive much. The more susceptible you are to these commands, the happier you will be. Therefore, open your mouth widely and do not hold back.[170] And if you want to hold back, then you should be afraid of yourself, not of the commands. They do not know how to fail you, but you can fall short of them. Therefore, *open your mouth widely* as much as possible,[171] because you can never receive too much. Open your mouth and open it widely, and it will be filled. He who made the mouth can easily fill it. *He sends his crystal to it like morsels*,[172] so that he may fill it not once or twice but frequently, something that the whole world cannot do even one time. *He sends*, the Prophet says, *his crystal like morsels*. Not like a morsel but "like morsels," so that you may have something with which you may fill your mouth frequently.[173]

But what is this crystal bread, which is so hard and so pure? It is indeed beautiful to gaze at but hard to chew. This is the reason why nearly all desire the bread of celestial wisdom, but very few acquire it. *The little ones*, he said, *asked for bread, and there was no one to break it for them*.[174] This bread is wonderful which little ones desire but great people cannot break. But yet what wonder is it if little ones desire it because of its crystal beauty, or what wonder is it if great people cannot break it on account of its crystal hardness? For that reason, when the Lord wants to restore anyone with the bread of life and understanding,[175] he first divides his bread into morsels, and thus at last, when and to whom he wills, *he sends his crystal like morsels* through the ministry of angels.[176] But do you think that perhaps they are capable of eating crystal bread that was divided as if into morsels? Not at all in my opinion. The same one, who *he sends his crystal like morsels*,[177] *will send out his word and will melt them*.[178] When Christ comes to fulfill his promise and passes by, he will minister to them. And lest it seems that a drink is lacking, *his Spirit blows and the waters flow*.[179] You see how Christ ministers with the food, and the Holy Spirit ministers in offering a drink? O what a wonderful meal, where Christ is the waiter and the Holy Spirit is the cupbearer!

On Psalm 84:11

Justice and peace have kissed.[180] There is a peace before penance, when the spirit submits to the flesh. There is another peace after completed penance, when the flesh submits to the spirit. Peace does in fact exist when the flesh lusts and the spirit submits. But peace also exists when the spirit rules and the flesh obeys. With regard to the spirit's peace with the flesh, it is said: *But now these things avail for your peace, but the days will come and they will limit you on every side, and they will knock you down to the ground.*[181] And again: *Peace, peace, and there is no peace,*[182] because we must not call something peace that is not true peace. With regard to the flesh's peace with the spirit, it is written: *And may the peace, which surpasses all understanding, guard your heart and your intellect.*[183] Between the first and last peace disharmony is produced, war is waged, hatred is engaged, because *the flesh lusts against the flesh, and the spirit against the flesh,*[184] when the body is chastened and reduced to servitude. But after the battle is over and victory is gained, peace is restored, discord is quieted, and a transition occurs from peace to peace: from carnal peace to spiritual peace, from false peace to true peace, from evil peace to good peace. In the first peace the flesh rules and the spirit submits. In the second peace the spirit rules and the flesh submits. The first peace is accomplished in the region of dissimilitude,[185] where lust reigns. The second peace is found in the land of promise,[186] where justice has command. The transition [from one peace to another] is indeed difficult, since one is not permitted to pass *from nation to nation and from one kingdom and another people,*[187] unless *with a mighty hand and outstretched arm.*[188] What else does "from nation to nation" mean except from the desires of the flesh to the desires of the spirit? What else does "from kingdom to kingdom" mean except from the kingdom of iniquity to the kingdom of love?[189]

Distinguish three times here: first, when lust is gratified;[190] second, when penance is performed; and third, when justice is loved. As long as the flesh lusts and the spirit submits, then peace does in fact exist, but it is not good because it is not just. Thus justice scorns and detests such peace. Justice withdraws, and peace remains indeed, but it is alone.

Sometimes it happens that, after lust is gratified, the heart is prodded to penance and is converted to justice. Suddenly they—the desires of the spirit on one side, and the desires of the flesh on the other—rise up and become fervently inflamed. The spirit is indeed very desirous, but the flesh opposes it. Peace is chased away, justice is turned away, and a mighty battle begins. The spirit does not rest until it rightfully recovers its kingdom in its flesh and places the flesh in perpetual servitude. The flesh does submit, although unwilling at first, but willingly afterwards. When the conscience is purified, peace is also restored. In this way peace returns so that justice does not slip away. No longer do justice and peace merely tolerate one another, but they embrace one another very tenderly and make a mutual alliance with the kiss of love, just as it is written: *Justice and peace have kissed.*[191]

First, therefore, peace does exist but it is alone at the time when lust is experienced. Second, justice exists but it is alone at the time when penance is performed. Finally, both peace and justice exist together at the time when the conscience has been purified.

On Psalm 98:6

1. *Moses and Aaron are among his priests, and Samuel is among them who call upon his name.*[192] Did something new, I ask, happen [to Samuel]? What did the Prophet want to teach us? Who will be reckoned among the priests of God, if Moses and Aaron, from whom the entire priesthood assumed its beginning, are not reckoned among them? When Samuel was still a boy he stayed in the temple day and night, but how much longer did he stay there during the days of David when he had grown older? Why else was it necessary for him to work in the temple other than to serve and to call upon the Lord? Therefore, I do not think that anything new happened [to Samuel], so that the Prophet needed to say or write about him: *Moses and Aaron are among his priests, and Samuel is among them who call upon his name.*

2. But if we pay careful attention, we discover that Moses and Aaron died long before the time of Samuel, and maybe Samuel had died at the time when the Prophet was writing such things. What then is he saying? What did he want to teach us, when he said: *Moses and Aaron are among his priests* etc.[193] We know of a living temple of God if we believe what the Apostle of God wrote about it: *The temple of God,* he said, *is holy, which you are.*[194] We must never believe that this temple of God is without priests or ought to be without those who call upon the name of the Lord. O that Moses and Aaron would be among his priests, and Samuel among them who call upon his name![195]

3. Let us ask who Moses, Aaron, and Samuel are. The law was given through Moses. The priesthood started with Aaron. And the gift of prophecy was given to Samuel. And so the office of Moses is to prescribe what must be done and to forbid what must be avoided. The office of Aaron is to implore the help of the Lord for the things that Moses commanded and to restore transgressors to favor again with God through prayer and sacrifice. The office of Samuel is to foretell what reward the doers of the law ought to hope for and what punishment the transgressors of the law ought to expect.

If then you already have seen someone recently coming out of the world, who was very attentive to religious life all day long and occupied with it at every hour—namely, what he should do to satisfy for past offenses, how he may cautiously guard himself against future offenses, how he must conduct himself and in what order of conduct, how much and when he must persist in certain things—, then you should understand that Moses ascended in the heart of such a person, and, as it were, established some new law in some way. Once Moses is born and grown up [in him], he now orders his behavior and regulates his mode of life. He ponders how he must walk and how he must sit. He discusses with himself how he must control his expression and how he should skillfully order his demeanor and gesture. He prescribes what must be eaten, how much time he must be awake, how he should resist anger, how he should oppose gluttony, how he should stamp out pride, why he should quench indulgence, how ready he must be for obedience, and how patient he should be in enduring many other things that we learn better and retain more deeply by doing than by reading. And so, when you see someone prescribing rigorous precepts and inflicting strict punishment, then recognize Moses in those two signs.

After the law is given and received, a person begins to desire to carry out the law, but the ability to fulfill the law is not given to him, so that he can proclaim with the Apostle: *To will is present with me, but to accomplish I find not.*[196] Indeed his mind is still proud, because he presumes to do all things by his own effort rather than from God's grace. Having forsaken God, he is frequently left to himself to learn his own weakness by experience. He begins, he hustles, he grows tired, and he fails. But even in this failure he is not immediately restrained from his presumption and self-confidence (but only after much experience is he called back). He recovers his strength again and his hope is renewed. He becomes angry with himself and begins to resent himself. He rebukes himself; sometimes he blames himself for negligence, sometimes he accuses himself of imprudence. He avenges himself on behalf of himself and brings assaults on himself. Consequently, his vigils are extended, and his fasting is prolonged. His body is afflicted with cold and nudity, and his flesh is chafed with labor and a whip. Multiple sacrifices are offered on the altar that is still external (the slightest hint of an interior altar has not occurred to him yet). In this great bodily affliction, during which no rest is allowed and neither mode nor measure is maintained, his body is now failing and his mind grows weary. Now, at last, when he sees that he is failing with his body and wasting away in his heart, he returns to himself and remembers the words of the Apostle: *It is not of him who wills, nor of him that runs, but of God who shows mercy.*[197] And so, after he forsakes all hope in all his self-confidence, he is converted to God; and, after the fire of the external altar has been extinguished, he is hastened into the Holy of Holies, yet not without the blood of a calf. After he sacrifices the calf of pride and forsakes all presumption of his past arrogance, he now despairs of himself and begins to place his hope in the Lord's assistance. And after offering many sacrifices on the external altar, as we recounted, he now accustoms himself to offer sacrifices to the Lord on the internal altar—that is, groans, sighs, prayers, and tears.

The external altar is the physical senses. The internal altar is the affection of the heart. Therefore, groans, sighs, tears, and anything else that moves the heart's affection are offered on the internal altar, just as vigils, fasting, labor, hunger, and anything else that pertains to the physical senses are offered on the external altar. And yet the fire of this altar (i.e., the external one) is extinguished, when one hastens to the internal altar. The power of sorrow is brought from bodily affliction to the heart where the fire of compunction is later inflamed. And so, when you see these affections of the heart being enacted more frequently, do not doubt that a new priesthood is being initiated in Aaron. For, as we discussed previously, seeking the protection of divine atonement and restoring favor with God through oblations and prayers pertains to Aaron. And so that we may recognize the office of the priesthood more fully, there are two duties that seem to pertain especially to it: to instruct the people and to make the Lord look favorably on themselves and on the people. Moses fully accomplishes the first duty, and Aaron fulfills the second duty magnificently. Hence it is rightly said about them: *Moses and Aaron are among his priests.*[198]

4. And it is added: *And Samuel is among them who call upon his name.*[199] Previously we said that just as legislation and the priesthood

had become evident in Moses and Aaron, so the gift of prophecy stood out in Samuel. What does it mean when it is said of him: *And Samuel is among them who call upon his name*, since it seems that the Prophet should have said instead: "And Samuel is among his prophets"? So why "among them who call" and not rather among them who prophesy? But perhaps Samuel is freely prophesying among them, who call upon God, or maybe they, among whom Samuel is prophesying, are freely calling upon God? This is surely the case. We cannot be in doubt about this matter. Samuel's prophecy knows how to make them sincerely call upon God and pray in truth. The more fully someone knows what rewards are reserved in heaven for the just and what torments are reserved in hell for the depraved and the more frequently and the more attentively someone ponders this, then the more sincerely, I think, he calls upon God and the more attentively he prays. But if Samuel stops prophesying, then the priests quickly stop calling. And the more infrequent the contemplation of the future becomes, then the more halfhearted prayer become and the slower invocation rises to God. Therefore, in order for Moses to be strict in precept and for Aaron to remain devout in prayer, it is necessary for Samuel to persevere as one astute in contemplation.

There is still something more subtle that we should say about Samuel's office. We frequently see that someone at the beginning of his conversion is both eager to work and devoted to prayer, so that Moses and Aaron who especially seem to preside over these activities seem to be alive still. But since he believed that he had already made satisfaction for past offenses, and since he already regarded himself as some holy and great person, he again begins to be negligent and to wane in his former fervor. Indeed after the death of Moses and Aaron, the mind quickly grows lukewarm and plummets into a certain negligence or even contempt, according to Moses' opinion who said: *I know that after my death you will do wicked things;*[200] *while I am yet living you have always been rebellious.*[201] Moses' death is the decline of earnest solicitude. Aaron's death is the disruption of devoted prayer. Therefore, after Moses and Aaron die the mind begins to plummet into a certain negligence or it even goes all the way to contempt. Temptations surge from here and there, impure thoughts are ubiquitous in the mind, and suddenly base delights arise in the heart. The flesh is profoundly inflamed, the mind is burning, and the whole conscience is agitated and disordered. He then hastens back to prayer and rushes to work. Again he becomes devout in prayer, eager to obey, studious in reading, and fervent with compunction, and quick to work. He does not cease from his vehemence until he first rescues himself from impending danger and reforms and orders himself again to his former tranquility. And so his former tranquility returns after all things are made peaceful. Tranquility leads to security, security is accompanied by idleness, idleness produces curiosity, and curiosity sneaks in cupidity. As lust, which is the mother of all vices, seizes the pinnacle of the mind and penetrates with some violence all the way into the innermost parts of the heart, it easily invites a multitude of vices to itself and very quickly leads in, as it were, its own army. The treasure chamber of wisdom is plundered of its booty, and the people of virtue are led into servitude. Again the most recent state of that person is worse than the earlier ones. And again he flees to the assistance of divine propitiation. Prayers are poured out from his heart, and the enthusiasm of his former conversion is renewed. At last, divine benevolence is again placated and appeased, and the previous freedom is restored to man.

This alternation of vicissitudes—sometimes the oppression of vices, sometimes the succession of virtues—occurs for some time and frequently. People are often handed over to their enemies on account of their negligence, and often they are delivered again from their enemies by the mercy of God. This wonderful dispensation of divine benevolence brings it about that human weakness becomes known to a man through frequent falls, that the enemies' inimical artfulness is made known to a man through their multiple invasions and deceptions, and that divine kindness is revealed to man through constant rescues.

Let him, who wants to know these things more fully, read the book of Judges a little more carefully. He will undoubtedly find there how, after their transgressions, the sons of Israel are attacked and conquered by their enemies and led into slavery. After they are afflicted by their enemies, they appeal again to divine aid. They entreat, seek, and find his mercy, and they return to their previous freedom. What else, I ask, do the invasions of their enemies mean except some confrontation of a spiritual battle between vices and virtues? Depending on whether God is withdrawing support or offering protection, sometimes vices conquer and sometimes virtues conquer; sometimes vices are conquered and sometimes virtues are conquered. Just as the enemy is prompted by the sins of Israel to assault them, so a savior is prompted by the prayers of Israel to rescue them. In both instances we must pay careful attention and firmly hold fast to the fact that they are not always attacked by the same enemy, but they are assaulted by different enemies at different times, and they are afflicted by some enemies for a short time but by other enemies for a long time.

If we do not ignore the fact that this is a confrontation of a spiritual and internal battle, which is waged within us, then we quickly realize that this confrontation is actualized within us according to the dispensation of God. It happens that we are attacked by one particular vice for a very long time, until we fully learn all its strength, nature, and method of attack. After we conquer that vice, another vice rises up against us. And after we overcome that vice, another vice follows it in hostile pursuit against us. The more aggressive the vice is, the more hostile its pursuit against us becomes and the longer the battle wages. The reason why divine compassion desires that we be attacked by every vice and allows us to be trained by each vice for a long time is so that we may announce the triumph of victory over every vice and, as we have already discussed, may someday have full and perfect knowledge of the strength and nature of each vice and its method of attack.

For that reason the saviors of the Hebrew people are not called "kings" but "judges" in the book of Judges. It is the office of kings to command what they please according to their free will, but it is the office of judges to know the laws and examine cases. Some judge or jurist rises among us, so to speak, when our mind is fully educated about any vice through many proofs and after countless experiences and when it does not order with authority what it wants to happen like a king does, but it tries to accomplish with some prudence what experience taught it. Whenever a mind, which has been taught through many experiences, uses skill more than violence to rescue itself from danger, it is experiencing, as it were, the prudence of its judges as a result of God's gift.

And so one judge rises up after another, because the mind advances from the knowledge of one vice to the knowledge of another, so that at some point after all the other judges the last judge, Samuel, comes who is fully knowledgeable about every vice and about the snares of every temptation. At that time he not only begins to recognize all the subtleties of the deceiver[202] and the nature of all the vices, but he also begins to expose them clearly to others and prudently explain them. Often while he silently observes an expression, demeanor, and bodily gesture in others, he discerns which vice is attacking someone almost better than the one being tempted. Often he detects the deceits of the enemy at the critical moment of temptation, and he knows long in advance what sort of danger could result from such a temptation. And this judge is Samuel, to whom the gift of prophecy was given, as we discussed above, and about whom it is also written: *All Israel, from Dan to Bersabee, knew that Samuel was a faithful prophet of the Lord.*[203] Does it not seem as if the task of prophecy is to detect the mind's hidden passions, to detect the enemy's snares, and to foreknow and foretell future dangers long before they happen?

In order to summarize our broad discussions: to discern with prudence what must be done pertains to Moses, to implore the help of God with respect to those things that we cannot accomplish on our own pertains to Aaron, and to foresee carefully what sort of benefit or danger can arise from certain things pertains to Samuel. And so we interpret Moses as discernment, Aaron as devotion, and Samuel as circumspection. To order morals pertains to discernment, to beseech God humbly pertains to devotion, and to foresee future consequences pertains to circumspection. If then you discover that your mind is discreet in work, devout in prayer, and prophetic in circumspection, then you will also be able to sing with the Prophet: *Moses and Aaron are among his priests, and Samuel is among them who call upon his name.*[204] As clear reason demonstrated above, although to inform people of precepts and to please God with prayers pertains to priests, clearly they cannot fulfill the office of their priesthood without discretion and devotion, that is, as if Moses and Aaron were dead. But circumspection, like a Samuel, certainly makes them just as devout in prayer and just as diligent in their invocation to God as it makes them fearful of the future. Therefore, because you see that the priesthood is being administered worthily and that God is being invoked both frequently and humbly, know that in no way are these being actualized without Moses and Aaron or even Samuel. The Prophet rejoices that these offices are performed around him, and he humbly and truthfully confesses: *Moses and Aaron are among his priests* etc.[205]

On Psalm 104:12–15

1. *When they were small in number, very few, and foreign sojourners in it.*[206] We have, as it were, few, or rather very few, citizens, because we only possess those virtues without which we absolutely cannot have salvation. Faith, hope, and love are indeed small in number and can be numbered easily. And it is sufficiently clear that there is no real salvation without them, and it is certain that no one can perish with them.

Nevertheless, it seems surprising how a transition specifically *from tribe to tribe and from a kingdom to another people*[207] is accessible or granted to such a few in number, especially since they are passing through a foreign land to a remote region. Not only are they very few but they are also sojourners and foreigners. Indeed faith does not yet apprehend through understanding what it believes, the object of hope is not yet obtained, and love does not yet enjoy its desire as long as it sojourns on the earth far from the Lord. We can also say that the knights of virtues are still few, as long as they cannot fully abolish the hostile cohort of vices; and they are fewer when they cannot yet subject them or at least make them vassals; but they are the fewest when they cannot resist them and defend life without great effort and grave peril. Yet, with God taking the lead, such very few often pass *from tribe to tribe and from a kingdom to another people.*[208]

2. What does "from tribe to tribe" mean except from carnal lusts to the delights of the spirit? What does "from kingdom to kingdom" mean except from the kingdom of lust to the kingdom of justice? A person who makes such a transition is called a Hebrew, since "Hebrew" is interpreted as one who crosses over. Trampling lust and seizing justice, the Hebrews pass from kingdom to kingdom, or rather, as the Prophet put it, *from a kingdom to another people.*[209] Who lives without sin in this life? Who never feels carnal delight in this life? Therefore, elsewhere, not in this life, justice does have a kingdom, although even in this life it has another people very foreign to vices. Meanwhile the Hebrews are deferred from the kingdom of justice and are still making the transition *from a kingdom to another people.*[210] Passage is not allowed except through the middle of their enemies' swords. Yet, with God's protection, they penetrate and pass through the middle of their enemies.

3. *Because He allowed no man to hurt them and rebuked kings on their account.*[211] Among all the living beings only humans use reason; and among humans some rule as kings. And so, because the Prophet knew that some of our adversaries are cleverer than others, and some are more audacious than others, he rightly designated the former with the term "man" and the later with the term "kings." The former try to deceive us with trickery and snares, the latter rush forth with some kind of attack. The former are more crafty, and latter more ferocious. The former tempt us very cunningly; the latter pursue us very forcefully. The cleverness of the former educates our prudence; the forceful pursuit of the latter trains our fortitude.

Yet perhaps if we pay more careful attention, then we can understand those adversaries designated more correctly as "kings." They are
characterized by their cunning audacity and audacious cunningness,
so that their temptation is so impetuous that it is also deceitful. The
more difficult their persecution is, the more dangerous it becomes. And
yet, *he allowed no man to hurt them*, whom the eternal providence of
God ordained to preserve, but *he rebuked kings on their account.*[212] God
certainly reproves their enemies on their behalf.

4. *Do not touch my anointed and do not malign my prophets.*[213] The
anointed are those who have received unction, but the prophets are
those who make predictions by foreseeing the future. But we know that
the unction of God is the love of God. Therefore, those who receive
such unction, those who fervently love the things of God are the
anointed of God and can be called "anointed." Therefore, we rightly
interpret the anointed as vows of sanctity and heavenly desires that we
have recognized to blaze in the hearts of the saints through the unction
of divine inspiration. A prophet, as it was said, is usually defined as one
who can foresee the future. They are rightly called prophets who ponder the secrets of the divine nature, who contemplate celestial things,
who penetrate inmost truths, and who reveal the depths of mysteries.
And so the spiritual senses are, as it were, like prophets, since they often
deal with celestial secrets and fix their eye of contemplation on invisible
truths. Therefore, the desire of eternal things makes people anointed
ones, and the knowledge of hidden things makes people prophets. The
ardor of love inflames the anointed, and the subtlety of contemplation
illuminates the prophets. The anointed ones love much, and prophets
apprehend much. Therefore, on behalf of the anointed and prophets
the Lord justly rebukes kings or any of their enemies. *Do not touch my
anointed*, the Lord says, *and do not malign my prophets.*[214] Tepidity attacks the anointed, but error attacks prophets. It is easy for the ardor
of devotion to fail and fall into tepidity, and the intellect is often blinded
and plunges into error after wandering far away.

On Psalm 113:4

1. *The mountains leaped like rams and the hills like the lambs of
sheep.*[215] It is a great spectacle to see mountains leap like rams and hills
like the lambs of sheep. Such exultation of those leaping like this is not
found *in the land of those living pleasantly.*[216] "There is no rejoicing for

the wicked," says the Lord.[217] If there is no rejoicing for them, then how them much less is there no such leaping? In my opinion, such leaping usually occurs in the exodus of Israel from Egypt, and not in any place whatsoever but in the desert. To have to leave Egypt and to flee the world is particularly pleasing to those who obtain such a miracle. But so that we may admire this more fully and desire it more passionately, let us delve more deeply into that leaping: either what kind of leaping is described, or to whom it is ascribed.

2. *The mountains*, the Prophet said, *leaped like rams.*[218] Who are the leapers? Mountains and hills. What kind of joy do they have? It is like the joy of rams and lambs. I confidently affirm this one point: the leaping of rams and lambs is not associated with derision and jeering. Yet what sort of gestures do they usually make when they play, or how do we think that they usually express their joy? As we all know, rams and lambs usually make some kind of leap in their exultation, suspend their bodies on high, and poise themselves through the air. But surely we should not expect something like this from hills or mountains? It is truly a great and amazing miracle to see mountains and hills leap like rams and lambs. Who is not astounded, who should not be astounded if he happens to see the massive structure of the mountains being detached from the plain and being separated from solid ground[219] and to see land being cut out of land and a great massive structure being suspended even a little in the air? It is certainly said to sinful man: *You are earth and to the earth you will return.*[220] For that reason it is also said to him elsewhere in chastisement: *Why is earth and ashes proud?*[221] And so in some people this earth (that is, human nature) swells even beyond the level ground of its creation and creates a mountain or hill. But in others this earth is lowered to the bottom and is reduced into a valley. Mountains ascend, valleys descend, and the plains lie on level ground and hold the middle position. In the mountains human endeavor ascends beyond nature; in the valleys it descends below nature; and in the plains human endeavor, which can possess good things naturally, sustains and preserves good things.

3. The Prophet says: *The mountains ascend, and the plains descend into the place which you have established for them.*[222] Why does he not mention valleys? The reason he does not is that the valleys certainly descend but not to the place which the Lord established for it, but to the place which a perverted mind has chosen for itself. The plains descend not to the place that is below nature but that is below the excellence of the mountains. And so the plains are those who do not forsake

earthly things but still live sober, just, and devout lives in this world. Mountains or hills are those who seek only those things that are above.[223] And so the more ardently such mountains desire heavenly things, the more vehemently they long for eternal things; and the higher they ascend, undoubtedly the closer they then touch the heights of heaven.

But it is one thing for them to extend on high the peak of their height and to touch the summit of heaven as if it is nearby, and it is another thing for them, so to speak, to leap and exult like rams and lambs.

4. *The mountains leaped like rams and the hills like the lambs of sheep.*[224] In order for us to distinguish the mountains, hills, and plains with differences appropriate for them, we understand "mountains" to mean contemplative people, "hills" to mean speculative people, and "plains" to mean active people. Active people by no means forsake the plains of this life while they attend to earthly activities and like the plains they yield, as it were, certain fruits of the land for earthly gains to use in this life. Speculative people are those who are intent on heavenly things and see the invisible things of God through a mirror in an enigma.[225] They are called "speculative people" because they only see through a mirror and in an enigma. By contemplative people we should understand those to whom it was given to see face to face,[226] and who, by contemplating *the glory of the Lord with unveiled face,*[227] see the unveiled truth in its simplicity without a mirror and enigma. And so mountains and hills are those who are intent on celestial things. But speculative people in no way transcend the clouds of corporeal similitudes, because they cannot see the supreme truth in its purity. However, contemplative people, by transcending like mountains the cloudy heights of allegories and enigmas with understanding, touch the tranquility of the celestial region, the serene summit of the mountain.

With regard to such hills and mountains we understand this statement of the Prophet: *On that day the mountains will drop down sweetness, and the hills will flow with milk and honey.*[228] He says that the mountains will drop down sweetness, and yet he does not say what sweetness, nor does he indicate it through some kind of similitude. Why is this, I ask, unless because the sweetness was so great that it cannot be described appropriately with any similitude? Why is this, I ask, unless because the mountains draw in and pour out pure sweetness? But the sweetness of the hills is expressed through a similitude when the Prophet figuratively calls it milk or honey. Consider then the nature and extent of that sweetness that higher people experience, when that sweetness experienced by lower people is called milk and honey. And so it is necessary for the mountains to sprinkle drop by drop that ineffable sweetness that they draw in such great abundance, but not to pour it out in abundance. They must temper the measure of their flow according to the capacity of the lower people. *The mountains,* the Prophet says, *will drop down sweetness, and the hills will flow with milk and honey.*[229] Such sweetness causes the mountains and hills to sing before the Lord[230] and to resound the voice of exultation and confession in praising him.[231] Mountains and hills sing praise before the Lord. Such sweetness, I say, causes the mountains and hills to exult wondrously in the Lord.

5. *The mountains leaped like rams and the hills like the lambs of sheep.*[232] But if we reflect on these mountains and hills, then surely what we previously said about them in admiration ceases to be great and wonderful. Indeed what is so great about people exulting like rams and lambs and making some kind of leap similar to them? And so let us seek spiritual, not corporeal, leaps in this prophetic statement, the kind of leaps that were fitting for the Holy Spirit to teach and for the Prophet to describe.

A corporeal leap occurs when the whole body is suspended above the ground. A spiritual leap occurs when the spirit and all that pertains to the spirit forsakes earthly things. A corporeal leap occurs when the body completely loses touch with the ground and the members of the whole body are poised in the air. The spiritual leap occurs when the mind withdraws, leaves the lowest things at the bottom, and transcends all things in contemplation of invisible things.

Therefore, think about the virtual parts of the soul,[233] and in this way you will perhaps discover more easily how great it is or what it is like to suspend all such parts from contact with earthly things and to make spiritual leaps. Indeed, in order to make the kind of spiritual leap that we are discussing here, the corporeal sense is first put to sleep, the bestial appetite is obstructed, the memory of external things is suspended, affection is inebriated, reason is transformed, intellect is renewed, and the whole mind is alienated from itself. Therefore, consider, if you can, what kind of heartfelt rejoicing occurs and how passionate the exultation is that compels the mind to forsake familiar things and rise above itself, to become unaware of temporal things for awhile, and in the midst of the heart's exultations to make frequently repeated leaps, as it were, into supernal and eternal things in many wonderful and unfamiliar ways.

Perhaps you respond to this with the words of Nicodemus: *How can these things be done?*[234] Let us grant that the ability to do this is great, wonderful, and absolutely amazing; but complete inability to do this is all the more unfitting. Look how unfitting it would be that the exterior man can make its own leaps according to its own mode, but the interior man absolutely cannot make a leap of its own kind according to a mode fitting for it. Notice how absolutely amazing and completely surprising it is that the body, which was taken from the ground,[235] leaves the ground for some time by leaping and can rise above itself, but the spirit (a spiritual and incorporeal nature) cannot be separated from corporeal and earthly things even for a moment. Are you amazed that spiritual creatures can suspend themselves in spiritual things, but you are not amazed that the spirit cannot be separated from non-spiritual things? For one paying close attention it almost seems to be contrary to nature that the spirit is so firmly and nearly inseparably united to corporeal things that it cannot be separated from them even a little. Does this cease to be amazing in your eyes and yet you seem less and not at all amazed that incorporeal nature is incapable of what is judged according to nature, namely to return to itself from corporeal thing and to stand firm in its own kind, that is, in incorporeal things? But, in my opinion, you are not amazed at this, because you do not experience it at all in yourself. But if your spirit cannot yet return to itself, then when will it be able to rise above itself and transcend to divine things by making leaps the like of which is fitting for a spiritual nature? What else does it mean that an incorporeal spirit returns to itself or in itself except that it only has before its eyes an incorporeal creature and those things that pertain to it? What else does it mean that a spirit raises above itself as if by leaping except that it fixes its eye of contemplation on that creative nature of all things and those things that pertain to it? And so, when spiritual men happen to experience such ecstasy on account of the magnitude of their exultation, then the words of the Psalmist are fulfilled in them: *The mountains leaped like rams and the hills like the lambs of sheep.*[236]

The rational spirit was certainly created for contemplating divine things. Why then are we amazed if it can achieve that for which it was created? It seems that one should only be amazed if it cannot accomplish this. And yet both are amazing, namely the ability to accomplish and the inability to accomplish. But one pertains to carnal things, the other to spiritual things. The ability to accomplish is amazing, because *the corruptible body weighs down the soul, and the earthly habitation weighs down the mind that is thinking many things.*[237] The inability to accomplish is amazing, because *the Spirit aids our weakness.*[238] Therefore, be amazed that you are amazed since you are *carnal, sold under sin.*[239]

But, in order to understand more fully still how much you should marvel or how appropriate it is for you to be astounded, consider the ninety-nine sheep that the supreme shepherd left on the highest mountains of the eternal inheritance,[240] when he searched for and found the one lost sheep across the lands and carried it back on his own shoulders.[241] Consider of what great dignity or excellence it is that the land of our mortality has some kind of innate similitude in common with the flock of the heavenly herd on the mountains of their exultation. Consider, I say, how it is full of honor and grace that the weakness of human nature, perhaps in the higher parts of that nature, can make leaps of its delight according to the property of an angelic similitude. If you think about these things, then where, I ask, does the magnitude of your admiration lead you, unless to understand that you cannot be sufficiently astounded at these things?

6. *The mountains leaped like rams and the hills like the lambs of sheep.*[242] If it is proper to understand human nature through "earth" and angelic nature through the designated flock, then who does not see how it is delightful and sweet for the angelic hosts to wander around and recline on this earth and to satiate that appetite of their desires with the fruits of our virtues, since *they hunger and thirst after justice?*[243] *Are they not all ministering spirits,* said the Apostle, *sent to minister for them, who receive the inheritance of salvation?*

7. *The mountains leaped* etc.[244] We have already heard what the Prophet says about the mountains and hills. But why, I ask, does he remain silent about the plains and valleys? As we previously discussed, the valleys are those who descend to the bottom and below nature and corrupt the goods of nature with depraved morals. And so understand here devout people as the plains and mountains but impious people as valleys. In this passage then the Prophet was right to remain silent about valleys, because he undoubtedly knew that impious people cannot have true joy. *There is no rejoicing for the wicked,* says the Lord.[245] But if the plains are associated with the just, then why, I ask, is the Prophet silent here about their joy and exultation, since it was written: *The voice of exultation and salvation is in the tabernacles of the just.*[246]

It is one thing to rejoice a little or even a lot, but it is something completely different to transcend the limits of human possibility in the joys of their exultation, and in the playful manner of rams and lambs to make the kind of spiritual leaps that we described to you, and to transcend by going beyond the human mind. But because the plains do not transcend the flats of the active life in their manner of life, they do not merit to exceed the mediocrities of the human life in their manner of exultation. Such exultation is rightly attributed to the mountains and hills alone, the likes of which are being described here in mystical way when the Prophet says: *The mountains leaped like rams and the hills like the lambs of sheep.*[247]

8. As you hear, the Prophet mentions three animals here: rams, sheep, and lambs. Of these animals rams undoubtedly have the highest place, sheep the middle, and lambs the last. Let us then look carefully at the rams, sheep, and lambs on one side, and the mountains, hills, and plains on the other side; and we will discover that the three animals correspond with the three kinds of terrain on account of some similitude. In comparison to higher terrains plains are the lowest regions, just as hills are middle regions, and mountains the highest. When, therefore, the Prophet said that the mountains leap like rams, it would seem to follow that he would also say that the hills leap like sheep, since both hills and sheep have the middle place in their kind, just as lambs and plains have the last place. Why then did the Prophet say that the hills leap like the lambs of sheep and not like sheep? But if we want to understand better the reason for this statement, we must pay more careful attention to the property of the proposed similitude.

In my opinion, those animals represent the hierarchy of angels as described by the great theologian, blessed Dionysius the Areopagite. As we know, he divides the whole assembly of celestial spirits with nine distinct orders into three hierarchies and assigns three tiers to each. He assigns the first tier to seraphim, cherubim, and thrones; the second tier to dominions, virtues, and principalities, and the third tier to powers, archangels, and angels.[248] The principal and highest-of-all hierarchy of the celestial orders is understood through the rams, which, as we previously discussed, hold the highest place among the animals of their kind; the middle hierarchy is understood through the sheep; and the lowest hierarchy through the lambs. We call that hierarchy the highest-of-all, because it is immediately united to God and illuminates all other hierarchies. This hierarchy is illuminated by no other but only by the Creator of all. The middle hierarchy is that which both illuminates and is illuminated. The last of all the hierarchies is that which is only illuminated by the higher hierarchy and does not have lower hierarchies to illuminate. We have now heard what we must think about this flock and their different positions. Now let us look for the spiritual and supercelestial leaps in the spiritual and supercelestial flocks.

What else does it mean that these animals make a leap of their own kind, except that they rise above themselves and ascend by contemplation to the things that are above them? And so, when the orders of the highest hierarchy ascend above themselves in contemplation, they find nothing other than the Creator, that substance of all substances. It is as if they are making some kind of leap and see the magnitude of that highest essence in itself without any mirror. Both modes of contemplating this magnitude are found in them. In the first mode they see it through a mirror; in the second mode they see it without a mirror. They perceive now in itself and now in a subject creature how wonderful and absolutely incomprehensible it is. For them to see the divine power and wonderful wisdom in themselves is like walking through a plain; but for them to contemplate and to marvel by contemplating the mighty deeds of the same power and wisdom in the lower orders is like making a descent not a leap. From this we can clearly conclude that the leaps of rams in their exultation are nothing other than to see without a mirror, as we said, and to ascend up to a pure and simple theophany.

When the orders of the middle and the last hierarchy ascend above themselves, they can indeed utilize a mirror, because they discover above themselves the orders of a higher dignity from which they make a fitting ascent to the admiration of divine wisdom and power. However, they usually utilize simple contemplation, and this is more like flying than leaping. A person making a leap doesn't remove himself very far from where he is standing, and we know that this usually is not the case with flying. Therefore, because the orders of spirits, which are designated by the rams, only utilize simple contemplation in their leaps, as it were, and because the other orders, which are designated by the lambs and sheep, always utilize speculation in their leaps, the Psalmist correctly said: *The mountains leaped like rams and the hills like the lambs of sheep.*[249]

Indeed, as we previously discussed, we interpret "mountains" as contemplative men and "hills" as speculative men. Mountains leaping like rams are nothing other than contemplative men attaining the highest truth with a pure and unveiled vision through the ecstasy of mind and seeing, as it were, face to face.[250] Hills leaping like sheep and lambs are nothing other than speculative people ascending by speculation to the admiration of the same truth through speculation and the ecstasy of mind.

One must note that although there are two kinds of speculation—one which rises from the wonder at corporeal things, the other which rises from the wonder at spiritual things—, only this second kind of speculation imitates the leaps and exultation of other-worldly lambs and sheep. If in those hills we reflect on spiritual men, then for them to make spiritual leaps and exultations like intellectual lambs and sheep means nothing other than that they are concentrating on the supercelestial spirits, whom they truly perceive above themselves, and from this speculation through wonderful and unusual movements of their joy they ascend up to the admiration of divinity.

But given that both intellectual sheep and speculative lambs, so to speak, normally play by leaping, why, I ask, does the Prophet say that the hills leap like lambs and not like sheep, since this too could be correct? But consider how for a wonderful reason the Prophet said what he was able to say in truth about the comparison between mountains and rams and in turn remained silent about a comparison between hills and sheep. He was certainly correct in doing this for fear that someone would attempt to make such a comparison based on equality and not based on similitude alone and thus would assume that the first tier of men correspond equally to the first tier of angels and the second tier of men correspond equally to the second tier of angels. Therefore, the Prophet left out the omitted statement in order to remove the assumption of equality, so that one may understand the statement that he made based on the principle of similitude.

Briefly, if it is acceptable, let us summarize our lengthy discussion. We said that contemplative people are interpreted as mountains and speculative people as hills. We said that the seraphim, cherubim, and thrones are interpreted as rams, and the powers, archangels, and angels are interpreted as lambs. And so about such mountains and hills we sing: *The mountains leaped like rams and the hills like the lambs of sheep.*[251]

Let us ponder, if we can, what kind of prerogative and grace and how much excellence and glory does the effort of human weakness have in order to ascend to the heights of angelic joy based on the connection of some kind of similitude and to reach it—although rarely and suddenly and as if in the ecstasy of mind—with some kind of wonderful and momentary leap of contemplation or speculation. O blessed soul! O truly happy soul worthy of much glorification! It was allowed up above to associate even a little with the wonderful joys of cherubim and seraphim during the time of its pilgrimage, to taste the blessed delights of internal and eternal sweetness, and amid the weariness of this miserable flesh to receive some first-fruits from the fullness of immensity. The memory of this tasting should touch our heart, penetrate the depths of our mind, transfix our affection, captivate our desire, as we sing daily and ponder: *The mountains leaped like rams and the hills like the lambs of sheep.*[252] The desire of this expectation makes our heart ardent, makes our spirit incandescent, and kindles our soul when we pray and sing: *The mountains leaped like rams and the hills like the lambs of sheep.* O that as we sing frequently so we should wisely sing: *The mountains leaped like rams and the hills like the lambs of sheep.*

On Psalm 117:15

1. *The voice of exultation and of salvation is in the tabernacles of the just.*[253] When the Prophet said "the voice of exultation," he aptly and immediately adds "and of salvation." Even those *who are glad when they have done evil and rejoice in most wicked things*[254] have their joy, although a perverse joy. Look at those living perverse lives: some are rejoicing, others are mournful. A voice like this may either be a voice of joy or a voice of mourning; it is certainly not a voice of salvation but of perdition. Similarly among those living good lives one may see some rejoicing but others grieving and weeping. But why are they still empty and sorrowful, mourning and grieving, given that it is written: *The voice of exultation and of salvation is in the tabernacles of the just*? Perhaps they are still performing penance and have not yet cleansed their conscience and obtained justice. And so in the meantime they have a voice of mourning and salvation, but someday they will have a voice of exultation and salvation. If you are like this, then grieve and weep, since *your sorrow will turn to joy.*[255]

One should note these four voices and distinguish them from one another: the voice of exultation and of perdition in those rejoicing perversely, the voice of mourning and of perdition in those grieving banefully, the voice of mourning and of salvation in penitents, and the voice of exultation and of salvation in those living perfect lives. Therefore, the Prophet rightly said: *The voice of exultation and of salvation is in the tabernacles of the just.*

Woe to them who begin to weep in this life and never stop weeping in the future. Woe to them as well who rejoice at the moment, so that they may grieve in the future. Woe to them, I say, who do not know the joys of the present or future life. Woe to them even more who always mourn both the good, which they have lost in this life, and the evil, which they have lost here and found there. Happy are they who mourn at the moment in order to rejoice in eternity. And happy are they, or rather much happier are they, who have a foretaste in time of what they will enjoy eternally.

2. *The voice of exultation and of salvation is in the tabernacles of the just.*[256] *In the tabernacles*, the Prophet says. Therefore, the just dwell in tabernacles not houses, because they do not have here a lasting city but are seeking a future city,[257] and because they are mindful of the things that are above, not the things that are upon the earth.[258] We already know that tabernacles of soldiers are fortifications, and we, whose life upon the earth is a warfare,[259] must be soldiers not slackers in idleness.[260] How cautiously and strenuously we must fight, and how diligently we must be watchful! *Our conflict is not against flesh and blood but against the spirits of wickedness in the high places.*[261] Justice is a very precious thing, and it quickly excites the envy of our adversaries and fervently inflames their hatred against us. This is the reason for the battle; this is the cause of our victory. We fight against malignant spirits in order keep justice unharmed. They fight against us not to capture justice for themselves but to force it away from us. They easily presume victory for themselves on account of our weakness, because *we bear this treasure in earthen vessels.*[262] But perhaps they did not notice at all that we put no confidence in ourselves but in our helper, to whom we say: *Not to us, Lord, not to us, but to your name give the glory.*[263]

But perhaps you wonder, and rightly so, how war and joy, the voice of joy and the battle-cry, are harmonized or how they can be coupled. From what does such great joy derive unless from frequent victories? Therefore, *the voice of exultation and of salvation is in the tabernacles of the just.*[264]

If you are amazed, if you want to have something in which to be amazed, then be more amazed *how one pursued a thousand, and two would drive away ten thousand.*[265] Will you not sing to the Lord a new song[266] and will the voice of exultation and salvation not be heard in your tabernacle, given that the following promise of your God has begun to be fulfilled in you: *Two thousand will fall at your side and ten thousand at your right?*[267] Therefore, the *voice of exultation and salvation* is heard *in the tabernacles of the just.*[268] If they rejoice so much in a foreign land, then how much do you think they will rejoice in their homeland? If they are so excited in their exile, how much joy will they have in their home? If their joy is so exuberant in combat, then what will they do with the eternal tranquility in that life? Insofar as their great and abundant joy can no longer be held in silence and prevented from coming out into the open and bursting forth in their voice, they, like vases that cannot contain more liquid being poured into them, are pouring out far and wide what is being poured into them from above. Likewise when the oil of joy has so filled the small vessel of their heart, it pours itself out through their voice and immediately shouts out: *The voice of exultation and of salvation is in the tabernacles of the just.*

On Psalm 118:22, 62, 175

1. *Remove reproach and contempt from me.*[269] Reproach is guilt, and contempt is punishment. Guilt is iniquity, and punishment is mortality. Because of iniquity I am made worthy of reproach; because of mortality I am made worthy of contempt. Lust makes me detestable, and misery makes me vile. Therefore, *remove reproach and contempt from me.* If you are making me just, then you are removing my reproach; if you are making me blessed, then you are removing my contempt.

2. *About the judgments of your justification.*[270] There are some judgments of God that condemn reprobates; there are others that justify the elect; and there are others that bless the justified. The first pertains to reprobation, the second to justification, and the third to glorification. The judgments that are condemning are administered in hell; the judgments that are justifying are administered in the world; the judgments that are making blessed are administered in heaven.

3. *Your judgments will help me.*[271] There are judgments of retribution, judgments of correction, and judgments of remuneration. Through the judgments of retribution Judas was made reprobate;[272] through the judgment of correction Saul was made blind;[273] and through the judgment of remuneration the humble David was elevated to royal power.[274] The judgment of retribution imparts the fear of falling to those standing; the judgment of correction bestows the hope of rising to the fallen; and the judgment of remuneration confers the love of perseverance to

the perfect. If, therefore, the first judgment of God produces fear, then the second fosters hope, and the third enkindles love. Regarding these judgments the Prophet rightly said: *Your judgments will help me.*

ON PSALM 121:1

1. *I rejoiced at the things that were said to me: "We will go into the house of the Lord."*[275] Adam is speaking to Eve. He is consoling her here, when he says: *I rejoiced at the things that were said to me: "We will go into the house of the Lord."* Adam no longer has much interest in returning to his own house, since he does not say: "I rejoiced, because we will return to our house." But now after the hardships of a long exile he presumes that he will reach the house of the Lord. Do you want to know who this Adam is, or how to interpret his Eve? Interpret Adam as reason and Eve as affection. The two are understanding and desire. The two are called soul and spirit.[276] Indeed the two are not distinguished by essence but by function (*efficientiam*).[277] The soul lives, the spirit discerns. Love pertains to the soul, knowledge to the spirit. And so, you have Adam, and you also have Eve. Adam was created first, and Eve was created later from Adam. We should first decide wisely through reason what must be loved, and then based on that the judgment of choice we should love ardently what must be loved. Therefore, let the knowledge of truth come first and let the love of justice follow. Discernment is first, love is next. Let the discernment between good and evil happen first, and let the discernment between good and the best follow second, and then let us choose from among the best what we should embrace more through love, since we all cannot accomplish all things.[278] Do you not see how a certain small part, as it were, is selected from the whole of Adam and from that part Eve is formed? It is good to discern good and evil, but it is evil to love good and evil, or rather it is impossible to love both, yet it is praiseworthy to know both. But because all men cannot do all things,[279] a certain part is taken from the good, and this is why Eve is created for the assistance of Adam.[280] If Eve does not contradict Adam in the judgment of choice, then she makes him more efficacious in the knowledge of the truth. Knowledge profits from love, just as love grows stronger from knowledge. But if love does not support reason in the search for truth, then very quickly the eye of discretion become dark. And love's support of reason then turns into the opposite when, because of her reason, she is hurled into the darkness

of error. Every time that Eve throws Adam out of paradise into exile, affection entangles reason, deflated from the search for truth, in vain thoughts. O how often does Eve throw Adam out of his own house! O how often does Eve force him to serve in someone else's house![281]

The house of Adam is truth, the house of the devil is vanity, and the house of God is eternity, about whom it is said: *He dwells in eternity.*[282] Surely the Prophet is speaking about that house in that part of the verse where Adam is saying to Eve: *We will go into the house of the Lord.*[283] Adam returns to his own house when he gives up his pursuit for vanity and returns to the search for truth; but he enters the house of God when, after searching a long time for the truth and scarcely finding it, he is raptured to the contemplation of eternity through ecstasy. Where are you, Adam? Where are you looking? In paradise or in exile? Adam, I say, where are you? Consider what you are thinking, and you will discover where you are. If you are reflecting on vanity, then you are in vanity; if you love vanity, then you are vanity. No longer do I ask you: "Where are you, Adam?," but I ask: "Who are you, Adam?" I believe that you are confused and ashamed to admit it.

The Prophet is not flattering you, when he says: *All things are vanity, all living men.*[284] Not just vanity, but all vanity: vanity of mutability, vanity of mortality, vanity of iniquity, because *all things are vanity, all living men.* In this threefold vanity man serves as if in exile. In this threefold vanity the devil reigns as if in his own house. After the devil was thrown out of the house of eternity, he builds a dwelling for himself out of a variety of vanities. He stretches out a porch for himself out of the vanity of mutability; he builds a house for himself out of the vanity of mortality; and he constructs a bedroom for himself out of the vanity of iniquity.

If you still love vanity, then consider, O man, whose servant you are. Why are you making a home out of your exile? Why are you enjoying your prison like a home? *Bring my soul out of prison, Lord, that I may praise your name.*[285] *I implore you, Lord, take my life from me!*[286] For *my soul is weary of my life,*[287] because *all things are vanity, all living men.*[288] Therefore, Lord, as Tobit said, *it is better for me to die than to live,*[289] because *all things are vanity, all living men.*[290] It is not for your sake, Lord, that we are put to death all day long,[291] so that now at last we may die, because *all things are vanity, all living men*?[292] Therefore, I implore you, Lord, *let my soul die the death of the just,*[293] so that I may no longer be a living man, because *all things are vanity, all living men.*[294] In the meantime, Lord, bring me back to my house, so that you may at last bring me to your house. Fix me first in the love of truth, and afterwards lift me up to the joy of eternity. *Turn away my eyes, so that I may not see vanity*, and you snatch me away from a foreign house.[295] *Send forth your light and your truth*,[296] and I will be in my house. *Restore to me the joy of your salvation*,[297] and I am in your house. If in the meantime you send me back to my house, then I will hope that at some point I will enter your house, so that even I may be able to sing: *I rejoiced at the things that were said to me: "We will go into the house of the Lord."*[298]

2. *I rejoiced at the things that were said to me.* In my opinion he was still rejoicing in hope not yet in actuality. He does not say "at the things that were given to me," but rather "at the things that were said to me." *I will hear what the Lord my God will speak in me*,[299] if perhaps he speaks even to me, if perhaps he promises something like that even to me. Therefore, *speak, Lord, because your servant is listening.*[300] What are you saying to me, Lord? Your speaking is your inspiration. Therefore, I implore you Lord, inspire in me through your Holy Spirit the assurance about this, lest my spirit ascribes it to itself through pride. Speak this to me, and let me not make it up. And then even I will sing: *I rejoiced at the things that were said to me: "We will go into the house of the Lord."*[301]

3. *We will go.* Adam is speaking here and he did not want to say, "I will go." He is speaking to his Eve and he did not want to say, "you will go," but "we will go." Previously we said that reason is understood through Adam, affection through Eve, and eternity through the house of God. Knowledge pertains to Adam, and love pertains to Eve. If you think about eternal things but do not love them, then Adam is going but alone. If you know eternal things and desire them, then Adam is going but not alone. Both Adam and Eve are going together, when you know and love celestial things. Adam must contemplate; Eve must rejoice. If you see and rejoice, then Adam and Eve are together.

4. *I rejoiced at the things that were said to me: "We will go into the house of the Lord."*[302] The Apostle boasts that he was raptured up to the third heaven.[303] As you hear in this verse, Adam is hoping that he will go [into the house of the Lord]. The first heaven is the subtlety of understanding, the second heaven is the splendor of justice, and the third heaven is the sublimity of glory. Contemplation of truth occurs in the first heaven, love of equity in the second, and the fullness of eternal joy in the third. About the first and second heavens the Apostle says: *Our citizenship is in the heavens.*[304] He does not say "in heaven" but "in the heavens," lest we may understand this with regard only to one of the heavens. About the third

heaven he said: *I know a man who was raptured up to the third heaven.*[305] To be raptured and to be a citizen are completely different. Citizenship occurs in the first and second heaven, but rapture occurs in the third heaven. If a person were not in the first heaven, that is, in the certitude of truth, then he would not be Catholic. If a person were not in the second heaven, that is, in the solidity of justice, then he would not have been just. In the first heaven he agrees to be faithful; in the second heaven he works to become good; but in the third heaven at some time it will be given to him to remain blessed. In the first heaven ignorance is illuminated; in the second heaven lust is extinguished; in the third heaven misery is overcome. And so in the meantime a person can abide in the first and second heavens, and he can be raptured to the third heaven, but he cannot go there. Every time that we are admitted into the third heaven, we enjoy in part that internal and eternal sweetness through ecstasy of mind. The mind of someone perfect is raptured to the secrets of the third heaven when he is absorbed in the sea of that eternal happiness and becomes intoxicated with the torrent of supercelestial delight.[306] As a result not only does he become forgetful of all exterior things, but he also becomes forgetful even of himself, so that afterwards he returns to himself and he proclaims and says with the Apostle: *Whether in the body or out of the body I do not know; God knows.*[307]

Adam wants what the Apostle calls "the third heaven" to be understood as the house of the Lord, when he says: *We will go into the house of the Lord.*[308] But the Apostle is bearing witness to his rapture; Adam, as we said above, hopes and asserts that he will go [into the house of the Lord]. The ability to go [into the house of the Lord] by one's own self is far more excellent and far more worthy than being rapt and lifted up by someone else. The entry of one who is rapt by another, as long as it is not granted him to enter on his own, his entry, I say, depends not on the will of the one wanting to enter, but on the grace and beneficence of the one able to lift him. If then I can enter on my own, I will certainly enter whenever I want to. But the one who still needs to be carried by another often cannot enter when he wants but only when it pleases the one who does the carrying. How do we respond to this? Can it be that Adam was actually able to achieve something that the Apostle did not merit to achieve? The Apostle is rejoicing about a past experience, but Adam is talking about a future experience. The Apostle is boasting about something that happened; Adam is rejoicing in the hope of it. For that reason he said: *I rejoiced at the things that were said to me: "We will go into the house of the Lord."*[309]

Brother, if the light of truth shines around you, then you have reached the first heaven. If the flames of charity are setting you on fire, then you dwell in the second heaven. If you have enjoyed a small taste of internal sweetness, then you have been admitted into the third heaven. *If you have tasted that the Lord is sweet,*[310] so that you can proclaim with the Prophet: *How great is the multitude of your sweetness, Lord, which you have hidden for those who fear you.*[311] Notice what he said: *If you have tasted.* I believe that only some taste is given to those who are still raptured. They will be inebriated after they can go [into the house of the Lord] on their own. *They will be inebriated, Lord, with the abundance of your house, when you will give them a drink from the torrent of your desire.*[312]

Brother, there is a difference between tasting and drinking. We receive a taste for the experience of sweetness; we are offered a drink for the profusion of intoxication. If you received a taste, then you will confidently also expect a drink. And so you will sing with joy, and you can sing with confidence: *I rejoiced at the things that were said to me,* etc.[313]

Brother, you must pay careful attention to this and especially commit it to memory: it is not very praiseworthy for Adam to want to enter [into the house of the Lord] without Eve, and it is absolutely impossible for Eve to be able to enter without Adam. What profit is it to know eternal things and not to love eternal things? But if you do not first know eternal things, then you absolutely do not love them. To have only eternal things before one's eyes, to cling only to eternal things is for Adam and Eve to be together in some way within the house of God. In the meantime they are raptured for tasting, and at some time they will enter not for tasting but for inebriation, so that they may boldly hope and sing with confidence: *We will go into the house of the Lord.*[314]

On Psalm 126:2–3

1. *When he will give sleep to his beloved, behold the inheritance of the Lord, the reward of a son, the fruit of the womb.*[315] Elsewhere it is written about the reprobate: *They have slept their sleep, and all the men of wealth have found nothing in their hands.*[316] Therefore, when evil people fall asleep in death, they lose all their goods. But good people receive infinite good. The former lose what they possessed for some time; the latter

receive what they never possessed. The former even lose their temporal goods; the latter find the eternal good.

2. *When*, the Prophet said, *he will give sleep to his beloved ones, behold the inheritance of the Lord, the reward of a son, the fruit of the womb.*[317] We usually use "behold" as a demonstrative. We say "behold" with regard to something that we see happening suddenly and unexpectedly. Therefore, what else does it mean to say, *Behold the inheritance of the Lord*, if not to show clearly that the inheritance of the Lord suddenly appears before God's beloved ones sleeping in death and presents itself to them in order for them to enjoy whatever that inheritance may be. But we know that God loves all people and foreknows those who will be his own. And yet, not all receive this inheritance of the Lord immediately when they sleep in every death, that is, those who had something less of perfect justice. Clearly then those who are called "beloved" in this verse are designated with a certain expression as is customary in the sacred Scriptures, that is, those who love God more ardently than the others and are loved by God more than the others with a certain prerogative of love, just as we read in the Gospel about John: *Here is the disciple whom Jesus loved.*[318] Obviously this passage does not say that Jesus did not love other people, but that John was more intimately connected to Jesus more than others by a unique prerogative of love.[319]

Therefore, strive to love *your God with all your heart, with all your soul, and with all your mind.*[320] If you do not love God, then you will never receive his inheritance; or if you love tepidly, then you will receive it late. Therefore, cherish that you may be cherished. Love that you may be loved,[321] because *when he gives sleep to his beloved, behold the inheritance of the Lord, the reward of a son, the fruit of the womb.*[322] If you are a friend of the Bridegroom, then you truly love and are truly loved. If you are a son of God, then you truly love and are truly loved. If you are a bride of Christ, then you truly love and are truly loved, or you are beloved. Therefore, as a friend of the Bridegroom, you will possess the inheritance of the Lord. As a son of God, you will receive the reward of a son. As the bride of Christ, you will have the fruit of the womb. And so, such people truly love and are truly loved.

When, therefore, he will give much sleep to his beloved and much sleep to those who are to be loved, *behold the inheritance of the Lord, the reward of a son, the fruit of the womb.*[323] When he gives not death but sleep to his beloved, because he will give them the goal of their work and he will give them rest from their labors, behold he appears, behold he presents himself, behold he offers himself, *the inheritance of the Lord, the reward of a son, the fruit of the womb.*

But why do we promise an inheritance to a friend and not a son, and why do we promise a reward to a son and not a friend, not to mention to a worker or servant? Let us grant that on account of its supereminent dignity hired workers and servants are excluded from this gift that is owed only to lovers. But would it not be a much better distinction, if at least a reward were promised to a friend and an inheritance to a son, since an inheritance is owed to a son, not to a friend, on account of an owed merit? But this reward is promised to a friend in an inheritance, and it will be recompensed as well to a son as a reward, so that one may thus understand that a reward is always gratuitous and yet it is still obtained through merits. Indeed no merits are sufficient for obtaining the reward, and yet a person, who does not strive after it through his merits, cannot obtain it.

If then you are a friend, you can receive the inheritance from a friend, but you cannot demand it. Even if you believe that you are a son, still strive after it with your merits as much as possible, lest if you should be a slacker in idleness, then you would lose the inheritance that you could have had. Always remember that because you are a son (or if you are not yet a son, you can still be one), you have this certainly not by birth but through adoption, not by nature but by grace.

3. *When he will give sleep to his beloved, behold the inheritance of the Lord, the reward of a son, the fruit of the womb.*[324] Notice how one gift is designated in many ways, so that it may be better expressed with multiple designations and be more deeply impressed upon the human mind as a result of frequent repetition. If we prefer, then this gift is an inheritance; if we prefer, it is a reward; and if we prefer, then it is a fruit. The gift is called an inheritance, because once received it is possessed through an everlasting right. It is called a reward, because it is paid more to one and less to another based on their merits. It is called fruit, because nothing tastes sweeter than this fruit, just as no fruit is sweeter than the fruit of the womb. Therefore, this gift is an inheritance not of just anyone but of the Lord. And the reward is not merely of anyone but of a son, and the fruit is not merely any kind of fruit but the fruit of the womb. And the inheritance of the Lord is aptly named, because it is possessed only as a gift of the Lord. If then it is of the Lord, then it is the sort of inheritance that must be given by the Lord, not the Lord of these people or those people, but the Lord of all. It is the eternal

inheritance of the eternal Lord, the universal inheritance of the universal Lord, and the infinite inheritance of the infinite Lord.

But this is demonstrated more fully from the following. In the subsequent words [of this verse] there is not only a praise of the gift but also a praise of the recipient. The praise of the recipient is expressed in the fact that the gift is a reward of God. Just as it is great happiness to obtain such a reward, so it is great dignity to have merited such a reward. If someone were not rewarded for merits and according to merits, then it would not be called a reward. But the praise of the gift is expressed in the fact that "of a son" is added. If then this reward is of a son, then it is the sort of reward that a father should give to a son or that a son should receive from his own father. It is not called the reward of a worker but the reward of a son. A servant labors, a hired worker labors, and a son labors. But a servant labors out of necessity, a hired worker labors for profit, but a son labors freely and willingly. Therefore, this reward, which is called the reward of a son, is the sort of reward that necessary servitude cannot merit, needy servitude cannot merit, but gratuitous servitude can merit. Therefore, this reward is both the reward of a son and the sort of reward that a father should give not to a slacking son nor to a negligent son, but to a son who works hard and merits well. Thus it is a worthy reward of a worthy son, the optimal reward of a most-beloved son, and a full reward of a perfect son. And so the designation "inheritance" affirms the permanence of the gift; the designation "reward of a son" praises the dignity of the gift, just as the designation "fruit of the womb" expresses the pleasantness of the gift. For, as we previously discussed, nothing is sought more fervently than the fruit of the womb, nothing is embraced more dearly and nothing is possessed with more delight.

We recognize that these two affections are the principal and chief affections among all the natural affections: a spouse's affection for a spouse and the parent's affections for child. Marital love holds first place, and parental love holds second place. The first love is not made any less as a result of the second, but rather without any contradiction the greater the first love is, the stronger and more joyful the second becomes. Love and delight increases in both as a result of a division in both, something that is nearly impossible for everything else. In other things the more something is divided into parts, the less it becomes in individual parts. But this marital love undoubtedly increases as a result of parental love; it becomes stronger and is complete.

We have now discussed in a way that we were able, not in a way that we ought, what the inheritance of the Lord is, what the reward of a son is, what the fruit of the womb is, and what sleep the Lord will give to his beloved: *Behold the inheritance of the Lord, the reward of a son, the fruit of the womb.*[325]

On Psalm 134:6–9

1. *The Lord has done whatever he wanted in heaven and on earth, in the sea and in all the abysses.*[326] If the Lord has found the heart lucid like heaven on account of understanding, or conversely if he has found it dark like the abyss on account of ignorance, likewise if he has found the mind solid like the earth on account of steadfastness, or conversely if he has found it inconsistent like water on account of lust, then in all places and at all time *the Lord certainly has done whatever he wanted in heaven and on earth, in the sea and in all the abysses.*

2. *He brings the clouds from the ends of the earth.*[327] The ends of our earth are the vilest sins and wicked works. Clouds are produced from such ends, because the gloom of shame is generated from the recollection of our depravity. As long as such clouds darken our mind, they bring relief against the fervor of lust as if against the heat of the sun. A person, who is mindful of his sins, becomes ashamed of such sins. The more he grieves over the past, the more cautious he is of the future.

3. *He caused lightning to strike in the midst of rain.*[328] Clouds are produced before lightning, just as rain follows lightning. Clouds are the darkness of shame, lightning is the terror of [divine] majesty, and rain is the tears of compunction. And so, according to the arrangement of divine piety, the memory of our depravity is first brought before the eyes of our mind, and then in such recollection we are struck with the fear of divine terror, and finally, after we have been caught between shame and fear and finally grown weary, we become tearfully remorseful. I have seen a cloud over me whenever *the shame of my face has covered me.*[329] I am struck by lightning when *the terrors of the Lord wage war against me.*[330] And the rain comes down upon me whenever I have been able to water my couch with my tears.[331]

4. *He brings forth the winds from his treasury.*[332] Just as *the Spirit blows where he wants,*[333] so also he blows when he wants. But, as you can hear in this verse, the winds are produced after the rain, since *blessed are those who mourn, because they will be comforted.*[334] The spirit

of fear, the spirit of piety, and the spirit of fortitude do not blow in the same way.[335] The Lord brings forth such winds from his treasury,[336] when we examine the secrets of Divine Scripture and marvel at the treasures of celestial knowledge and wisdom.[337] But as long as our mind earnestly pursues with such admiration and pays very careful attention, then it is astonished and is struck at different moments with the spirit of wisdom, the spirit of understanding, the spirit of counsel, and the spirit of knowledge.[338]

5. *He slew the firstborn of Egypt from man to beast.*[339] *Pride is the beginning of all sin.*[340] The darkness of error begets such firstborn, because the spirit of the Devil is cast out by the Spirit of God, and the spirit of pride is thrown down by the spirit of meekness.[341] It is fitting that the firstborn of Egypt die after the winds are produced. The winds are divine inspiration, and the firstborn of Egypt are diabolical pride and human presumption. Some people are proud about corporeal things; others become arrogant over spiritual things. Truly an irrational and animal sense is active, when the mind, made in the image of God,[342] becomes proud over those things that it has in common with beasts. And so some people are proud about vanity, others about sanctity. The pride of vanity is the firstborn of beasts; the arrogance of sanctity is the firstborn of men. While the wind of the divine Spirit blows, the first born of Egypt from men to beast are slain. While the spirit of fear blows, every swelling of pride is easily cast down. How much easier does this occur with the various spirits blowing and following one after another at different times!

6. *He sent forth signs and wonders in your midst, o Egypt, upon Pharaoh and upon all his servants.*[343] We reside in Egypt, that is, in darkness, as long as we live in this world, where we do not see each other's conscience, or rather, what is worse, where we do not fully know ourselves. And so we must know that every plague, with which Egypt was slain by the Lord, is discerned by those who rightly understand them as some kind of omen of future evils. Not only do they signify the evils that remain only in the soul after death, but they also prefigure the evils that the reprobate feels in both body and soul after the final day of judgment.[344] And so they are signs, because they indicate the evils that will occur soon after the death of anyone. They are correctly called wonders and predictions of the distant future, because they indicate what remains for the reprobate after the judgment.

On Psalm 134:7

He brings forth the winds from his treasury.[345] This is because we perceive the breath of divine inspiration, when we examine while marveling and marvel while examining the treasury of celestial wisdom in Divine Scriptures. Regarding this treasury of wisdom the Apostle cried out and said: *O the depth of the riches of the wisdom and knowledge of God!*[346] Do you want to know what the winds are that God usually brings forth from such a treasury? They are the spirit of wisdom and understanding, the spirit of counsel and fortitude, the spirit of knowledge and piety, and the spirit of the fear of the Lord.[347] Four of these winds pertain to intellect, and three to affection. Wisdom, understanding, discernment, and knowledge pertain to intellect. Confidence, love, and fear pertain to affection. The spirit of wisdom and understanding, the spirit of counsel and knowledge correspond to the intellect; but the spirit of fortitude and piety and the spirit of fear correspond to the affection.

But we know that all affection arises from cognition, since the mind is never affected by something, unless the object itself is first perceived through the cognition. And so the three spirits, which, as we said, pertain to the affection, are usually moved by the other spirits which pertain to the intellect. It is clear that the human mind is moved to fortitude and strengthened in perseverance sometimes by the spirit of wisdom, sometimes by the spirit of understanding, sometimes by the spirit of counsel, and sometimes by the spirit of knowledge. The spirit of wisdom blows from the south, the spirit of understanding blows from the east, the spirit of counsel resounds from the north, and the spirit of knowledge thunders from the west. These are the four cardinal winds, at least when they inspire fortitude. And any one of the spirits has two supporters, one on each side, because at one moment they inspire piety, at another moment they inspire fear. From whatever region of heaven it blows, the spirit of fortitude is a cardinal wind and is located in the middle of its two supporters, with the spirit of piety on its right and the spirit of fear on its left.[348] And so the Lord himself, to whom the treasure belongs, brings forth these winds from his own treasury.

In order to limit our discussion of this very large and copious treasury, let us separate it into four treasury chambers. The first treasury is built in the western chamber out of the historical sense, the second is erected in the northern chamber out of the moral sense, the third is made out of the allegorical sense and is located in the eastern chamber, and the fourth is made out of the anagogical sense and is located in the southern chamber. The silver of eloquence is hidden in the western chamber. Various and innumerable gems of virtue are hidden in the northern chamber. Purple garments, fine linens, and other royal trappings pertaining to the various mysteries of the Church are stored in the eastern chamber. But the gold of celestial wisdom is preserved in the southern chamber. Faith is taught in the first chamber; work is taught in the second chamber; devotion is cultivated in the third chamber; and the contemplation of heavenly things is initiated in the fourth chamber.

We must note that the doors of the western and eastern chambers are facing opposite of one another, because whatever allegory teaches history shows it to have preceded figuratively. And thus as long as the two meanings are gazing at one another, they bear mutual witness to the firmness of truth. Similarly, the doors of the northern and southern chambers are facing opposite of one another, because as long as the reward for our labors is seen from one's region, one willingly exerts oneself in the exercises of virtues. And it is clear enough that the measure of labor and the quality of retribution correspond to one another like a balanced scale.

The northern and western chambers are joined, and the eastern and southern chambers are similarly joined. We must seek morality after we examine history; similarly after morality we advance to anagogy through the knowledge of allegory. Through history we learn what was done; through morality we learn what must be done; through allegory we understand the mysteries of the Church and how they were announced beforehand in the figures of things that occurred previously; and through anagogy we perceive the invisible things of God through those things which were made.[349]

Therefore, the breath of divine inspiration comes out of the hidden innermost parts of such chambers. This only happens at the command of him, *who brings forth the winds from his treasury.*[350] And three winds seem to proceed from each of the chambers. But because this is clear from the previous discussion, it is superfluous to designate here which wind comes from which chambers. These are the twelve winds that roam about and blow throughout the whole land of the living, all of your lands, O Emmanuel.[351] The different winds blow at different times, however, and whenever the King and Lord of the winds desires—not the fabled Aeolus,[352] but he who *ascended upon the cherubim and flew upon the wings of the winds.*[353]

ON PSALM 138:16

Your eyes have seen my imperfect one, and all will be written down in your book. Days will be formed, and no one in them.[354] Imperfection of form is one kind of imperfection; imperfection of stature is another. The first is an imperfection of quality; the latter is an imperfection of quantity. By one everyone is such as he should be according to nature; in virtue of the other imperfection everyone grows as tall as they should according to nature. The first is found in boys, the second in adults. When a boy has all his limbs, he is perfect in form but not in stature.[355] Monstrous children do not recover that perfection that is according to form, no matter how much they grow. Faith without good works, good works without faith, chastity with pride, humility with unchastity—all this makes a person monstrous, and no such person achieves Christian perfection. Such a person does not belong to Christ, nor can it be said about him: *Your eyes have seen my imperfect one.*[356] A person who has justice, however imperfect it may be, certainly belongs to Christ, even though he is not perfect yet. Christ rightly speaks to his Father about such a person: "Your eyes have seen not just any imperfect person but my imperfect person."

Although such people depart from the body, they are still in the purview of divine grace and divine mercy, because *your eyes have seen my imperfect one, and all will be written in your book.*[357] Who are the "all"? Clearly they are all of his own, all who belong to Christ.[358] If he says "my imperfect one," then how much more "my perfect one"? Therefore, you see all of mine, and all of mine will all be written in your book.

But let us ask: what is this book in which all of his own will be written? If we say that it is the book of the living, then not only his own but also those not his own have been written there. About them it says elsewhere: *Let them be deleted from the book of the living.*[359] If we say that this is the book of life,[360] then perhaps they are already written in it. Then why do they still need to be written in it, given that it says: *and all will be written in your book,*[361] unless perhaps the Prophet is using the future tense for a past event.

ON PSALM 139:2–3

1. *Deliver me, O Lord, from the evil man; rescue me from the unjust man.*[362] Diabolical temptation is sometimes unexpected, sometimes violent, and sometimes deceitful. Temptation is unexpected when it precedes the judgment of reason. It is violent when it surpasses the possibility of our virtue. And it is deceitful whenever it deceives an examination of discretion. And so the tempter often receives the property of the name based on the mode of his temptation. This is why Sacred Scripture sometimes calls demons, the instigators of vices, sometimes "birds" or "beasts" and sometimes "men" on account of some similitude.[363] The tempter comes unexpectedly like flying birds, when he seizes the mind before its deliberation. Often the mind falls into a depraved thought so quickly that it is carried off into delight before it can deliberate on it. Therefore, the tempter is like a flying bird, when he comes unexpectedly or without warning. But sometimes he rages like a lion,[364] when we experience his violent temptation. Our past guilt often provides him a later opportunity for a violent and wholly unbearable temptation. But when the malignant enemy does not receive permission to use force, he often resorts to deceit. And so, when he tries to overcome us through trickery, he is correctly called a "man" (*homo*). Among the animals only humans use reason, and, consequently, they rule even over those animals that are stronger than themselves on account of the uniqueness of their ingenuity. Therefore, the tempter is like humans, when he uses cunningness rather than strength, and when he acts skillfully rather than forcefully. The same Prophet laments such birds, when he testifies elsewhere saying: *They put out the dead bodies of your servants as food for the birds of the air.*[365] But about beasts the Prophet immediately adds: *the flesh of your saints for the beasts of the earth.*[366] Even then the Prophet feared the beasts, when he proclaimed elsewhere to the Lord in a prayer: *Deliver not to beasts the souls that confess you.*[367] In the present passage, because he is fighting against a cunning tempter, he calls his attacker a man, when he says: *Deliver me, O Lord, from the evil man; rescue me from the unjust man.*[368]

But lest you think that I have fabricated this interpretation, read the Gospel, and you will undoubtedly discover that it refers to demons sometimes as birds and sometimes as men. Regarding the seed that fell alongside the road you read there that *the birds of the air devoured it.*[369] And about the tares it says: *A hostile man did this.*[370] Now the Truth clearly declared with an added explanation that he intended the birds or men to refer only to demons. What is clearer and more obvious than what is said here: *The hostile man is the devil?*[371] The Prophet claimed that he was delivered from such a hostile man, unjust man, and evil man, when he said: *Deliver me, O Lord, from the evil man,*[372] as if he was clearly saying: "See that I am enduring such an enemy who is so clever that I seem like a brute animal in comparison to him. Because of the prerogative of reason humans surpass animals to the same extent that the greatness of the enemy's cunnings excels the paucity of our understanding. I barely notice his snare, I hardly recognize his trick. Therefore, *deliver me, O Lord, from the evil man.*"

Spiritual men are like those who easily recognize the deceit of evil men,[373] but carnal people and people like me are compared to animals,[374] like animals who seldom ever or never avoid their snares;[375] nevertheless *you will save men and beasts, O Lord. How you have multiplied your mercy, O God!*[376] If you are hardly worried that I am fighting like an animal against a man and that I am fighting like a brute against a cunning attacker, if then you are not worried that a man is my enemy, then at least it should worry you that this man is evil. Therefore, *deliver me, O Lord, from the evil man (homine).*[377]

2. And it follows: *Rescue me from the unjust man (viro).*[378] Perhaps the previous phrase is being repeated with different words, and perhaps "the evil man" (*hominem*) and "the unjust man" (*virum*) mean the same. However, let us see if by chance another meaning may be hidden here that might be useful for our edification. Being a man (*virum*) is more than being a human (*hominem*). Indeed, we use the generic word "humans" (*homines*) to speak of women and boys, but we know that men (*viri*) surpass women in strength, and men surpass boys in prudence and strength. And so, because the Prophet first perceived his cunning enemy, he called him a "human" with respect to the remarkable subtlety of his trickery. But because he later perceives him acting not only skillfully but also forcefully, he wanted to refer to him with a suitable term, that is, "man." The intensity of the fight and the weight of temptation usually increases so much that the temptation, which was only deceitful at first, later becomes violent as well and that the tempter finally conquers with an added vehemence because he was unable to prevail with deceitful tricks alone.

One may reflect upon both the loving kindness of the divine dispensation and the deceit of diabolical depravity in one and the same way of temptation. The deceitful enemy first assaults a man (*hominem*) with an easier temptation, so that if that man should happen to fall over with a soft push, then the easier his temptation was, the less excuse he would have. But when the enemy does not dislodge someone's mind from its way of life by means of lesser battles, he prepares himself at once for greater battles. And yet, based on a far different consideration, the divine dispensation allows the enemy to carry out his temptation, since God is always mindful of human salvation in all that he does. Indeed God first instructs man through a lighter battle, so that, after having been instructed, he may learn at last to obtain victory over more severe dangers. With regard to us the Lord does not allow something to be done or happen other than what he determines to be kind and just. This is why it is said: *The Lord is just in all his ways and holy in all his works.*[379] Conversely, the Prophet calls the evil and unjust devil "evil," because he always desires to do harm; and he calls him "unjust," because he often stretches the limit of his attack beyond the measure of equity. The devil is rightly called "evil" because of the intention of his depraved will, even when he does not exceed the measure of equity in our affliction. He first persecutes us to the extent that our guilt requires, but, when he sees that this cannot be sufficient for our destruction, he often exceeds the measure of equity. And yet one must know that divine goodness relaxes the reins of freedom for the devil, whenever he determines that the devil's attack can benefit man. Therefore, the Prophet calls our tempter "evil," because he sees that he only intends evil in everything that he does to us. But the Prophet calls him "unjust," because it is clear that he often exceeds the measure of equity in our affliction. And so, the Prophet says: *Deliver me, O Lord* etc.[380]

The Prophet wanted this to occur quickly, because he did not say "liberate me" but "deliver me." Perhaps also he believed that this needed to occur by force, since he prayed that he should be liberated with forcible deliverance rather than by a command, not that the Lord was unable to do this with a command, but so that, speaking in a human way, he might reveal the severity of the danger.

3. *Those, who have devised iniquities in their hearts, designed battles all the day long.*[381] There is a difference between thinking iniquity and speaking iniquity. What we think is still hidden only from others, but what we say begins to be made known even to others. Malignant spirits think iniquity before perfect men, because they hide as much a possible the guile of their deceitful persuasion. They want to persuade good men of evil things under the appearance of the good, because they cannot allure them to a blatantly evil act. And so what else does it mean for

them to think, not speak, their iniquity, except to conceal in deceit the evil that they intend?

Notice by what steps evil grows: first it is thought, next it is spoken, and finally it is shouted out, just as it is written: *They have thought and spoken wickedness; they have spoken iniquity on high.*[382] First they have thought it, next they have spoken it, and finally they have spoken it on high. "They have thought," this pertains to thinking. "They have spoken," this pertains to speaking. "They have spoken on high," this pertains to shouting. They think, not speak, evil, as it were, when they conceal that what they propose is evil. They speak evil but as if in secret, when they do not conceal evil but make excuses for it. They speak evil on high, when they freely command someone to do what is blatantly evil. Therefore, they think evil before those perfectly good, they whisper evil before those imperfectly good or bad, and they shout evil before those perfectly evil. They preserve this order in one and the same person, as they hasten to snatch him away to destruction. They first entice us with an evil hidden under the appearance of the good, next they entice us with a visible evil with an excuse, and finally they blatantly command us to commit a public evil.

Perhaps they had experienced this kind of temptation during the time of David, whom they were not able to entice openly with evil, and, for that reason, they presumed to think evil rather than speak it. About them it is said: *Who have devised iniquities in their hearts.*[383]

On Habakkuk 3:2[384]

1. *In the middle of the years you will make known.*[385] What the Apostle calls "the fullness of time"[386] the Prophet, Habakkuk, calls "the middle of the years." He is offering his opinion about the body of Christ in relation to a similitude of the human body, when he foresees what will happen or predicts when it will happen. We spend the first half of our years by growing both in height and virtue,[387] but we spend the remaining half of our years by decreasing little by little. Until the age of thirty or thirty-five a person daily grows greater than he was before, but after the age of forty he grows weaker in virtue and day by day becomes less than he was before. Unless I am mistaken, this happens in the body of Christ. He who considers this very carefully can easily see this.

I call the body of Christ the Head with his members.[388] At the beginning of the world, when, as it were, the body of Christ was still a boy,[389] it was enough for the faithful only to believe in God and please him with offering and sacrifices. But it reached adolescence, when it received the commandment of circumcision and the observances of the Law. However, it did not yet know how, or rather it was not yet able to forsake its own things for the Lord[390] or to lay down its life in death for Christ. But it received higher commands and fulfilled them magnificently, after the fullness of time came, after it reached full maturity, and after it completed the first half of its years, when, as we have said, its bodily stature was greater and its virtue stronger. Now it is told: *Love your enemies;*[391] *If you wish to be perfect, go, sell all that you have, and give it to the poor;*[392] *Whoever loves his life more than me is not worthy of me.*[393] But we know that *greater love no one has than to lay down his life for his friends.*[394] It is clear, therefore, that the body of Christ, which is the Church, reached full maturity and reached the first half of its years, when it was now able to love even its enemies for the Lord's sake and when it was able to love its Lord even to the point of death. Thereupon, therefore, that time of time, about which Habakkuk had foretold, was at hand.

2. *In the middle of the years you will make known.*[395] What is it that was going to be known in the future, which perhaps the Lord has already made known? What else, I ask, if not that mystery previously hidden,[396] which none of the princes of this world knew?[397] What else, I say, except the heights of the divine plan for the salvation of the human race? I assert confidently that until that time no one fully understood how much God desired the salvation of humankind. God *did not even spare his own son, but handed him over for us.*[398] Only at that time when humanity was able to despise all things of this world for the Lord's sake and above all to lay down its own life in death for the Lord, was it appropriate for God to have made known to humanity that he loved them even to the extent of [assuming] the distresses of human weakness and the disgrace of death and the cross.[399] But just as this mystery should not be revealed to humanity in the past when it was still in a weaker condition, so it was undoubtedly necessary that it not be hidden any longer.

Consider where now is the constancy of the martyrs and the abstinence of the confessors; all this is practically absent in these present times. Why is this, unless because the world, which has already lived half of its years, is already declining toward old age? Therefore, because the mystery of the divine plan could not be revealed to the world, which was still weak, as it were, before the middle of its years, and because it was not necessary to conceal this mystery beyond the middle of its years, when it was necessarily declining in virtue, it is rightly said now: *In the middle of the years you will make it known.*[400] But perhaps it will be more acceptable, if we say something about this according to the moral sense.

3. *In the middle of the years you will make known.*[401] This seems to describe some time when God chooses to reveal something great to whomever he pleases.[402] We find a certain amazing and ineffable sweetness often described in the Sacred Scriptures and frequently promised to us. The more urgently it is commended, the more ardently it is desired. In Moses this is understood as *the land flowing with milk and honey.*[403] In the Wisdom of Solomon this is described as the *food having within it every delight and all flavors.*[404] The Apostle describes it more clearly, and the Lord explicitly promises it in the Gospel. The Apostle says: *What eye has not seen nor ear heard, what has not arisen in the human heart.*[405] For all that anyone has left behind for love of him, our Lord promises one hundredfold in this world and eternal life in the future.[406] Do you not see how *in varied and many ways God spoke to the fathers in the prophets and apostles and is now speaking at last to us also in his Son*[407] and promises something new and something great that only those alone, who have deserved to experience it, can know what it is? It is hidden manna, as blessed John affirmed in the Apocalypse.[408] The Apostle Paul testifies that *it has not risen in the human heart.*[409] Moreover, he shows that it was revealed to him and to those like him when he says: *But God has revealed it to us through his Spirit,*[410] and our Lord explicitly promises one hundredfold in the present life,[411] so that people would not be waiting for it in the world to come.

Of course this promise will not be able to stand literally, since a husband, who left one wife, will not have one hundred wives in the world, but neither will he have even one wife in the future, where *they neither marry nor are given in marriage.*[412] But since Sacred Scripture customarily uses "one hundred" to signify something heavenly, by promising one hundredfold the Lord does indeed promise sweetness for sweetness, but a heavenly sweetness for carnal sweetness, spiritual sweetness for animal sweetness, angelic sweetness for earthly sweetness, divine sweetness for human sweetness.

But you say: "*Behold, we have left all things, what then will we have?*[413] Rather than what is promised, [we want to know] when it will be given to us? We now have no doubts about the promise, but we are still uncertain about the time. We are no longer asking what it is, which can only be known by him who receives it. Based on the witness of so many great men we have no doubts that the promise is going to be given. Just tell us when these things will happen and what will be the sign for when they will begin to happen."

It is not for me to know the times or moments,[414] and what I did not merit to know myself I could not reveal to others. But let Habakkuk, the Prophet, answer for me. Let him satisfy you on my behalf with his answer. He says: *In the middle of the years you will make known.*[415] What wonderful wisdom on the part of the Prophet. What he wanted you to know he did not want to tell you. If he were speaking to you, anyone could doubt. He spoke this to God, as if to one to whom he would not dare to lie. Therefore, he did not want to say, "In the middle of the years he will make it known," but he said, *in the middle of the years you will make known.*[416] Consider, therefore, you who want these things to be made known to you and you who want these things to be revealed to you; consider, I say, if you have already come to the middle of your years, if you have already arrived at the perfect age. As we all know, the stature of the body is greater and its virtue is stronger at the middle of its years. I believe that he has reached the middle of his years who could truly say: *God has revealed to us through his Spirit.*[417]

You say: "O how many there are who left all that was theirs for the sake of the Lord, but who never tasted these spiritual delights in the present world." I confidently say that they did not reach the halfway point of their years. They were still among those to whom the Lord gives milk to drink, not food.[418] Perhaps they were still like newborn infants[419] and quite unable to receive solid food. Moreover, some die in childhood; some are taken away in youth. Surely none of these could reach that time in their life about which the Prophet Habakkuk spoke: *In the middle of the years you will make known.* Nevertheless, I think that *the kingdom of heaven belongs to such,*[420] because of what is written: *Your eyes have seen my imperfect one, and in your book all will be written.*[421] Those who begin to live good lives here will in the future or in the future world sometime reach the midpoint of their years.

At some time divine grace will complete in him what he himself could not complete here, provided only that he passed from this life to that without any lethal wound. A fatal wound is a mortal sin. Whoever dies in mortal sin is not brought to the midpoint of his years either here or in the future. *Men of blood and frauds will not come to the middle of their days.*[422] When will those who never begin to grow in good come to the midpoint of years, that is, to the robust age of virtues? If you wish to attain these promises of the Lord, hasten to reach that robust age, the midpoint of your years. I am speaking of years of merits, not temporal years. The more you advance, the more you grow. The one who reaches the summit of virtue has completed the midpoint of years, because he has arrived, so to speak, at the robust years of merits.

One must be aware that negligence still plots against those who are growing, and pride has taken by surprise those who have reached a mature age. Now the more you are negligent, the more you decrease and, so to speak, go backwards. One who is caught in negligence is doubtless called back. So pray to the Lord and say: *Do not call me back at the midpoint of my days.*[423] So fear negligence, but detest pride. As soon as someone thinks he has grown to the summit of virtue, he exalts himself in pride. The higher someone raises himself above himself in pride, the more he is cast down beneath himself in guilt, as God forsakes him. Thus it is written: *They go up to the heavens, and they descend to the abysses.*[424] Hence, there is what Hezekiah said: *I said in the middle of my days, I will go to the gates of hell.*[425] The one who just moments ago was congratulating himself for having reached the heavens is surprised that he slipped back to the gates of hell after he completed half of his years, after by his merits he reached to the summit of virtue. There are two gates of hell that lead those who enter to all evil. One is ignorance of the good; the other is concupiscence for evil. He foresaw that he was going to descend to these gates of death, because he was aware that he was abandoned by God because of his haughty mind. But immediately he took refuge in prayer, and it was granted him not to die. What does it mean that King Hezekiah is sick, but by praying is snatched from death, if not that often after boasting the mind of one of the elect is carried away into pleasure, but then through prayer is caught short before the death of evil consent.

On Leviticus 25

After six years we observe the seventh which follows as festive, and we spend time in a kind of leisure when after completing an activity we are led to tranquility of mind and are occupied only with prayer and contemplation. We are commanded also to make a week of these weeks of years, that is, to multiply seven by itself. If we take seven times seven, we obviously make forty-nine.[426] By divine command this is observed as festive, and the one which follows is called a jubilee. "Seven" leads us to think of tranquility of mind, because we realize that the seventh day is assigned for rest. Likewise, because all time unfolds in seven days, the fullness or perfection of anything is often symbolized by the number seven. We read that the Holy Spirit gives a sevenfold gift. Hence, that is why "seven" often signifies spiritual grace. Therefore, seven is multiplied by seven when the mind possesses full and perfect rest, or seven sevens appear when, after reaching complete rest, someone's mind attains to spiritual grace. Someone who has already merited to possess spiritual grace with full inner peace seems, after seven years have gone by seven times, to have already reached the forty-ninth.

After these the fiftieth year follows, which is called a jubilee,[427] because once the wars of the flesh have been surmounted, after the charismas of the Holy Spirit have been received, when the mind remembers what it is and how it used to be, it exults with exceedingly great joy. In this year every possession returns to its proper Lord. In this year, the Hebrew slave is restored to his earlier freedom.[428] Then it was customary that the land observed a Sabbath, and that the people of the land devote themselves to leisure and feasts.[429] The land which is our flesh celebrates a Sabbath when carnal desires no longer wear it out, when out of long habit spiritual exercises now delight. Think about what kind of effort is involved in being burned by the fires of concupiscence and worn out by the torches of gluttony; how much work must he do who is solicited by greed, enflamed by wrath, and tortured by envy! Consider, I suggest, how much work it is to endure these things. Then you will be able to imagine by contrast what kind of Sabbath it is to be worn down by them no longer. For the land receives its Sabbath when in it every base urge is stilled and by long practice regular discipline has become pleasant to it.

Moses is commanded by the Lord concerning this land that it is to be divided into the possession of the sons of Israel. The Prophet recalls this when he enumerates God's benefits, saying: *And he cast out the nations from before their face and by lot divided the land among them by a line of distribution.*[430] He wished to signify vices by the nations and virtues by the people of God, for he frequently calls God "the Lord of virtues."[431] When the sons of Israel arrive, the nations lose the land that they had possessed, because when the vices are excluded, virtues take their places. When lust is excluded, chastity takes control of the sexual organs. When greed is extinguished, generosity controls the hands for its own purposes. When pride has been trampled on, humility bends the neck. When gluttony has been constrained, abstinence makes the palate subject. When quarrelsomeness is excluded, reverence governs the eyes. When cruelty has been overcome and falseness conquered, then charity fills the heart and truth dwells on the tongue. Do you not see how the valiant race of virtues receives as its inheritance this land of our flesh of which we spoke earlier, and how, lest any one of them possess the whole of it, they divide this land among themselves once the vices have been thrown out? The land of the body is really divided by the virtues when each is allotted the part which it should have and when each exercises control by its own right in that part of the body which befits it.

Therefore, it is right that if at some time any of the virtues holds less of its possession, it should at least receive it back by God's gift in the jubilee year. Its own possession is returned to each in order that a man's mind turned to ecstatic joy can be fully and perfectly rapt up in the praise of God. As we said, in the jubilee year a Hebrew slave returns to liberty, whereas until then he was unable to go out into freedom. Hebrew means "one crossing over," and whoever commits sin is bound to be a slave of sin.[432] When the affection of the mind crosses over from the concupiscence of the flesh to the concupiscence of the spirit, it is said to be and is a Hebrew. When it is no longer subject to base pleasure, it ceases to be a slave.

In the jubilee year the Israelites devote time to leisure and feasts, because given over to contemplation the mind has an eager foretaste of the delights of the spirit. We must sound trumpets in this year,[433] for we must cause eternal rewards and punishments to loom large by often thinking and speaking about them so that we can remain steadfast in our intention.

As soon as the mind is broken by the weight of the effort, it returns to the evil pleasures which it had left behind. It no longer recalls what rewards are stored up in the future for the good and what torments await the wicked. So it is as though we are sounding trumpet whenever we sound forth in praise the rewards of merits. The Lord commanded through Moses that *two silver trumpets of malleable metal be made*,[434] which the same divine authority consecrated for sounding the signal for certain activities and at specified times. They used trumpets to call the people together; they blew them in breaking camp; and they called out with them in assembling the people in battles. They blew horns when they were at their leisure at banquets and when they held solemn celebrations. However, it is clear that he makes music with two trumpets who knows how to endorse with worthy amplification first the promises of God and then his warnings. We have these silver trumpets when we say nothing about these matters except what we can prove by the authority of the scriptures. Hammered metal is produced by blows, and we are ordered to make trumpets of hammered metal, because we produce these things better in the ears of our listeners if we ourselves are first perfectly struck with compunction.

ON MATTHEW 2:13

Take the child and his mother, and flee to Egypt.[435] The mother is purity of mind; her son is truth. The mother is a clean heart. From such a mother the understanding of truth is born. From such a mother the knowledge of oneself and the knowledge of God are born. This is perfect understanding and full wisdom.

Do you want to know that such a son is born from such a mother, namely that knowledge of God is born from the purity of heart? *Blessed,* Jesus says, *are the clean of heart, because they will see God.*[436] What does "to see God" mean except "to know God"? Herod attacks such an infant, as long the infant is still small. Christ is wisdom, and Herod is pride. They always oppose one another; they attack one another. Christ flees as Herod rages, because truth recedes as pride grows. Jesus returns when Herod dies, because the light of truth is restored when pride is extinguished. Truth and humility are mutual friends; pride and falsehood gaze at one another. What else is pride but the incorrect belief that one is holy and great? What else is humility but a true acknowledgement of one's own weakness? And so truth grows to the extent that humility advances. The kingdom of humility is increased to the extent that the reign of Herod is restricted. Rightly, therefore, *Herod and all of Jerusalem with him were troubled* at the birth of Christ.[437] Herod does not want the small child who has been given to grow, or rather he ordered all the children to be killed together.

Why do you think Herod hates small children, unless because he walks in great and wonderful things that are above him,[438] and he cannot see anything except something lofty? What do you say, Christ, about small children? What, I ask, do you, a small child *who was given to us,*[439] say about small children? *Allow,* he said, *the children to come to me.*[440] Truly *the Lord is high and looks upon the lowly.*[441] Truly Herod is proud and despises the lowly. Therefore, Christ loves the small Jews, but Herod loves the great Jews.

You know well that "Jew" is interpreted as "one who confesses." Therefore, do you want to know what sort of confessors the proud King Herod loves or what sort of confessors the humble Christ loves? *I am not*, [the Pharisee] said, *like the rest of men, robbers, unjust, adulterers; I fast twice in a week; I give tithes of all that I possess.*[442] Unless I am mistaken, Herod loves such people. Listen to someone else: *I am the least of the apostles: I am not worthy to be called an apostle.*[443] Christ certainly loves such people.

Do you want to know the difference between "Herodians" and Christians, between small Jews and great Jews? The first humbly reproach their own evils; the second brazenly boast great things about themselves. These are the false Jews and true Herodians, and the first are Jews in name but Christians in actuality. We can correctly call both "Jews," because both confess what they believe themselves to be. But, like a small child, Christ embraces small children, and Herod persecutes them to death, so that Christ may be killed among them. Herod ordered that all the children to be killed from two years old and under.[444]

Do you want to know who these small children are, or how they are two years old? A humble confession makes one a Jew and a small child—a small child insofar as humility is concerned, and a Jew insofar as confession is concerned. But there is a confession of sin and a confession of praise. Perhaps you discover in yourself only evil. You are ashamed. You confess. Perhaps another person discerns something good in himself as well. He knows that he possesses this good from the gift of God not from his own merit; he ascribes it to the Lord not to himself. Both you and that person are a Jew and small in virtue of a humble confession, but you are one year old, he is two. The one-year-olds are those who have lived for one year, the two-year-olds are those who have completed two years. Those making confession before the Lord for their sins have reached their first year. Those making confession before the Lord for his gifts have attained their second year. The confession of sin makes a one-year-old, but the added confession of praise makes a two-year-old.

It is clear that either of these confessions makes one small not great, because both render the soul of the confessor humble. How small do you think these confessors are who know that whatever they discover in themselves derives either from their own weakness or from the goodness of another? Their evil derives from their weakness, and their good, if there is any, derives from the goodness of God. Therefore, how small do you think they are, how humble are they in your estimation who know nothing except misery and mercy?

There are some Jews who boast that they possess what they absolutely do not have,[445] and other Jews believe that they possess uniquely what they have received in common. Others do not doubt that they have received from God what they have, yet they try to ascribe the gifts of God to their own merits. Still others with greater wickedness think that their merits or good derives from themselves. All these people are reckoned among the false Jews or true Herodians, because they speak without shame and think great things about themselves and because they confess with their mouth what they believe in their heart about themselves.[446] Herod loves such confessors, because he looks with admiration upon great and prideful people, eager and ready not to praise God but to stone Stephen.[447] None of these people are numbered among the children of Christ, because they skip over not only the first year but also the second year of a humble and devout confession. The small Christ only embraces small children, but, as we have said, Herod persecutes them until death. He commanded that all children be killed from two years old and under.[448]

On Matthew 2:13–15

1. *Take the child and his mother, and flee to Egypt.*[449] The child born of the virgin mother is truth born from a pure heart. A pure heart is the land that stands firm forever, because what is pure does not know corruption, and what does not take on corruption certainly does not know how to pass away. The fruit of this land is truth, as it is written: *Truth arises from the land.*[450] But when the light of truth is born in the heart, [the mind] is very disturbed by a spirit of pride. It is easy for someone's mind to be proud on account of such a child, especially at the moment when the internal light first illumines it, when it raises the mind above itself, and when the mind, suddenly illumined with a new and unfamiliar light, sees very clearly what it could not even slightly imagine earlier.

This is the reason why King Herod pursues the boy Jesus after his birth and tries to kill him: Christ is wisdom, Herod is pride. Herod pursues the boy Jesus, because the mind is more severely tormented by the spirit of pride after receiving the understanding of truth.[451] But he, who humbly assents to the counsel of the angel, evades very quickly the hand of Herod.

2. *Take*, the angel said, *the child and his mother, and flee to Egypt.*[452] Egypt is interpreted as "darkness." And so we are commanded to go in order to consider our darkness when the spirit of pride torments us. About such darkness the Apostle said: *You were darkness at one time, but now you are light in the Lord.*[453]

When many people receive the understanding of truth, they forsake themselves and seek things above themselves. They do not know themselves, even though they know many other things. At one moment they examine the mystery of the Trinity and the mystery of the Incarnation, at another moment they investigate heavenly secrets and the charismas of the Holy Spirit. And it often happens that while they examine with impious audacity those things that are above them, they ignore their own weaknesses and forget that they are men. And after they are struck down by pride, they fall into error; and after they fall into error, they return to iniquity. About this it is said in the Song of Songs: *If you do not know yourself, O fairest among women, then go forth and go after the flocks of your companions and feed your goats.*[454] This soul is compelled to go out in order to feed the goats of its lust. After it gains an understanding of truth, it forsakes its inmost self and does not know itself. It then seeks to apprehend only the knowledge that puffs up.[455] Therefore, if one wants to escape Herodian impiety and to preserve himself in humility, then let him strive to submit humbly to the counsel of the angel.

3. *Take*, he says, *the child and his mother, and flee to Egypt.*[456] Sometimes the boy Jesus is in Egypt, and sometimes he is found in Judea. He is in Egypt when he teaches me how great my darkness is. He is in Judea when he shows me what the glory of his wisdom is. My lust, my ignorance, my weakness—these are indeed darkness, and they can be called "darkness." *But God is light, and there is no darkness in him,*[457] because the radiance of the glory of the eternal light is in him.[458] God then is light, but my conscience is night. This child is truth. He is in Egypt when he teaches me truth about myself, but he is in Judea when he shows me truth about God. He gives me knowledge of myself in Egypt, and he gives me knowledge of God in Judea, as it is written: *God is known in Judea.*[459]

4. *Take*, he said, *the child and his mother.*[460] "Take them both," he said, "flee with both of them. Do not remain in Judea for the sake of the child. Do not flee without them both for your sake. If you do not

flee, the child will die. Without both your flight will not be safe. If you do not escape Herod, the child is killed, because if you do not avoid pride, then the light of truth is extinguished. If you do not go with both, then you will not be safe. Do not go without the virgin mother. Do not go without the child of the virgin. If the virgin is the purity of heart, if her son is truth, then the trip to Egypt is dangerous. It is even more dangerous to travel without the mother as a companion and without the son as the leader. If you go without the mother, you are returning to lust. If you go without the son, you are falling into ignorance. You should not go unless purity accompanies you, and you should not go unless truth guides you. If you recall your past errors, if you recall your former pleasures, then in the meantime you are living in Egypt while you willingly occupy yourself with thinking about your darkness. But if you come to this place without purity, then you are dragged off into base pleasures. If truth is not with you, then you quickly fall into error. If you are looking with lust down the old paths of habituated pleasures, then you are traveling without the virgin. If you make excuses for your evil or ignore your evil, then you live in Egypt without the child. Therefore, *take the child and his mother, and flee to Egypt, and stay there until the time that I will speak to you.*[461]

"Just as you are not now departing based on your choice, so do not return without my counsel. I better than you discern the time for returning, and I give you more useful instruction on the way of returning. Do not rely on your prudence; be no less careful about the counsel of Satan. He usually *transforms himself into an angel of light*[462] and sows his erroneous counsel under the appearance of the good. If you return to Judea before [the right] time, then you are quickly returning to pride. If you remain in Egypt too long, then you are undoubtedly falling into despair. If you focus too much on your evil, then you are quickly falling into the pit of desperation. If you rely on the mercy of God before the right time or beyond measure, then you are no less establishing yourself on presumption. Did you not read, or perhaps you did not pay enough attention, that *all things have their time?*[463] And the departure or return to Egypt or Judea undoubtedly has its own time. I send you to this or that place only when the time and circumstance requires it. The angel of Satan sends you to either place only when he has seen that it does not benefit you. And so, when you are led to desperation because of the memory of Egypt, and when you are absorbed with sorrow because of the excessive consideration of your darkness, then you know that you are following the counsel of Satan, not my counsel. If you are removed from the inhabitance of Judea through vain delight and carried away to vainglory, then you may conclude that someone other than me detains you or sends you to Judea. And so everyone should conclude from the result what sort of spirit sends them to Egypt or Judea. Therefore, *flee to Egypt and stay there until the time that I will speak to you.*[464] If then you are wise, if you have the spirit of discernment,[465] if you rightly ought to be called 'Joseph,' then I forewarn you: assent to me. *Flee to Egypt, and stay there until the time that I will speak to you."*[466]

5. *Joseph arose and took the child and his mother at night and withdrew to Egypt, and he was there until the death of Herod.*[467] When many receive the spirit of counsel, they do not receive the spirit of fortitude and thus they cannot complete the good that they know.[468] Because Joseph received both, he magnificently completed through the spirit of fortitude what he knew from the spirit of counsel must be done. And so, arising and preparing himself for difficult things, he took the child and his mother at night and fled to Egypt.

Yet why did he want to flee at night, since that was not part of the counsel of the angel? Or if he was supposed to flee at night rather than during the day, then why did the angel not say so? Or perchance is something left to our discretion? To whom was the decision entrusted after that first nativity? Sometimes night signifies ignorance on account of its darkness, but sometimes it designates sadness on account of its coldness. And so a person, who looks at the ways of his old errors with grave sorrow, is traveling toward Egypt at night. For who gazes into the darkness of his conscience with eagerness, and who remembers his former evils with happiness? Who else is this other than a person returning to Egypt during the day? And consider how shameless it is to look at one's sins and not grieve, to see what should cause shame and not to be ashamed, to see what should cause sorrow and not to be sorrowful at all? Indeed one who, contrite in prayer, made his vow to the Lord decided to go to Egypt at night and not during the day. *I will recollect to you all my years in the bitterness of my soul.*[469] A person, who recollects his years in the pleasantness of his soul, recollects the years of his past life not to you, Lord, but to himself.

I will *recollect all my years in the bitterness of my soul* but not in the sweetness of my soul,[470] so that the sweeter your goodness is to me, the more bitter my iniquity becomes; and the more my misery displeases me, the more your mercy pleases me.[471] And so every time Herod persecutes me and every time my mind is afflicted with the spirit of pride, it is to my advantage to flee to Egypt and to inspect carefully the darkness of my weakness, so that my mind may not become puffed up. But woe to me if the child Jesus and his mother are not with me! *If I walk in the midst of the shadow of death, I will fear no evil,*[472] but only if both of them are with me. But I confess: often I wanted to turn away from the Herodian impiety but mentally I was afraid of going to Egypt. I hesitated and doubted what I would do. If I were to remain in Judea, then I would despair of evading the hand of Herod; and when I decided to flee him, I was afraid of the darkness of Egypt. And I said: "*Perhaps the darkness will tread upon me,*[473] if I go to Egypt. But because *night to night reveals knowledge*[474] only if the child Jesus and his mother are with me in Egypt, will I go with confidence." And I confess: "Because of the presence of my Lord Jesus, *night has become my illumination in my pleasures.*"[475] O good Jesus, how great and excellent is your sweetness, when night is turned into day, darkness into light, bitterness into pleasure, mourning into jubilation, ignorance into knowledge, imprudence into wisdom, sorrow into joy!

6. Therefore Joseph *fled to Egypt, and he was there until the death of Herod.*[476] Herod's death is the death of pride. When Jesus is brought to Egypt, Herod is immediately weakened. If Jesus stays in Egypt for a little while, then the impious Herod dies. Indeed a person advances in the knowledge of his weakness to the extent that his pride decreases. When he knows his darkness perfectly, undoubtedly all arrogance dies. After Herod dies it will be a time to return to the land of Israel.[477] Israel is interpreted as "a man seeing God." When someone's mind is elevated to the contemplation of God, that person is, as it were, in the land of Israel. But I am a man seeing my poverty, inasmuch as I still cannot think otherwise. Even until today I am in Egypt, because I see nothing but my darkness. But he who is elevated by the grace of contemplation sees the glory of God. He surely dwells in the land of Israel. If someone speaks wisdom among the perfect[478] and confesses with his mouth what he contemplates in his heart,[479] then such a person undoubtedly lives in Judea. Therefore, someone is in Egypt through consideration of the self, someone is in the land of Israel through the contemplation of God, and someone is in Judea through the edification of his neighbor.

On Leviticus 26:5

1. *The harvest will reach to the vintage, and the vintage will reach to the sowing time.*[480] We reap by reading and meditating; we harvest the grapes by praying and contemplating; and we sow by working and preaching.[481] This order is correct and suitable, so that we may first learn through reading and discern through meditation what we should do or avoid afterwards. But because we are not able on our own to fulfill the good that we know, we must first ask for divine help through profuse prayers, and then we hasten to do the good.

2. *The harvest will reach to the vintage.*[482] When we understand what we read and memorize it, we gather useful fruit in the barn of our conscience. When we squeeze pious affections and tears of compunction with the winepress of divine fear, we press the wine that intoxicates the mind. But when the sweetness of contemplation raptures us above ourselves, we become intoxicated, as it were, by drinking wine of wondrous sweetness, and we exceed our human senses and become alienated from ourselves in divine affection. We experience nothing more pleasant in this life than this sweetness, and we drink nothing more passionately—nothing so distances our mind more from the love of the world, nothing so strengthens our mind more against temptations. By such an intoxicating tasting a person is delighted at every work and every toil. He labors without becoming tired, he hastens without faltering, he is afflicted without feeling it, he is tormented without knowing it, and he is ridiculed without noticing it.

3. As we have said, we sow either by exhorting others to the good or by exercising good works. Good work is rightly compared to sowing, because a good work makes someone's mind fertile for knowledge of truth and love of virtue. We also say that a preacher of helpful words "sows," because the crop of virtues is made fruitful in the minds of listeners through his preaching.

4. *The harvest will reach to the vintage, and the vintage will reach to the sowing time.*[483] This occurs when reading provides the stimulus for contrite prayer in the mind of a reader, and afterwards profuse prayers provide the strength for work.

But one must note that the text does not say: "the vintage will follow the harvest," but "the harvest will reach to the vintage." This certainly occurs when every vintage becomes so full that one can hardly be filled before the next follows.

ON HOSEA 9:14

What will you give to them, Lord? A womb without children and dry breasts.[484] The womb is the desire to learn, the seed is truth, and a child is a good will. The reason why you must read and understand this is so that you may strive to fill [your womb]. You do have a womb, if you have a desire for learning. If you understood the truth, then you conceived a good seed. If you love the conceived truth and accomplish your work, then you are giving birth to children and breast-feeding them. Who do you think these children are? Good and ordered affections. I see many studious people, but I find few religious people. What this text says is thus fulfilled in them: I will give to them a womb without children.[485] Many love to read, but few love religion; in fact, they often fall into a hatred of religion on account of their love of reading. What else, I ask, does divine reading teach us except to love religion, to keep unity, and to have charity? But you read these things and do not accomplish them, because you were not yet able to arrive at childbirth, because you have a womb without children.[486] What is your purpose in reading, if you do not desire to accomplish what you have understood? Surely a person who studies many writings will observe them? But they say: "We desire to teach others, and we want to preach useful things to others." I hear you say that you want to be doctors and preachers, and you strive for the upper seats and salutations among the people.[487] But, in my opinion, you will be given dry breasts. Every word of a preacher should be used for explaining or for persuading—for explaining obscure things, and for persuading things that can be useful. These two goals are like two breasts: a breast of exposition and a breast of exhortation. And many people receive such breasts, swollen but dry. They apprehend the knowledge that puffs up and lack the love that edifies.[488] Their breasts are swollen through knowledge but are dry, because they do not have sweetness of spirit. Every day we see many people with boastful tongues, but rarely do we see people with sweet tongues.

ON LUKE 13:34

There are six days in which we ought to work.[489] The seventh day is the day of rest.[490] There are three things that make us perfect: power, knowledge, and will.[491] Without these nothing can arrive at its goal. If you have a good will and not good discretion, then this verse applies to you: *It is vain for you to rise before the light.*[492] If a person who correctly and rightly discerns has not received the possibility from the Lord, then let him listen to what is said: *Unless the Lord builds the house, they who build it labor in vain.*[493] After all, you do not even begin to do something that you do not want to do. And so, without these three something is started in vain, because without them nothing arrives at its goal. But so that your God may reveal to you, O man, that *you have nothing that you did not receive,*[494] he effectively bestows different things at different times. Sometimes he mercifully removes one, sometimes another. Sometimes he gives one of the three after removing two. But sometimes he grants two after only one of the three is removed, and sometimes all three are received together from the one giver of all good things.

And so the different varieties of divine giving are like the different varieties of spiritual days. Power alone brings about one day, knowledge alone brings about another day, and the will alone brings about a day different from the other two. These three days are followed by three other very bright days, when two of these three days are given and one is removed. When only power is removed, there is another day. When only knowledge is absent, there is another day. And when only the will is removed, there is another day. These six days are followed by the seventh day, which is completed after those three days are joined together. On this day we are instructed to keep the Sabbath and to celebrate.[495] On this day we are ordered to make sacrifices and to offer our sacrifices.[496] We cannot perform ceremonial acts on the other six days, because one of the three is absent, or two is missing at the same time. As long as we notice that we are missing any one of them, we should strive with all eagerness to merit to receive it. But the mind rightly rests from its labor only when it discerns that it has arrived at the goal of its desire, and there is nothing that should fatigue the mind when discretion is not out of tune with the will, and the ability to finish is harmonized with both. Rightly, therefore, we celebrate this day, and rightly on this day we offer a sacrifice of praise[497] to the Lord and we make a sacrifice of devotion.

ON "SANCTIFY YOURSELVES TODAY"

"Sanctify yourselves today, because tomorrow you will see the majesty of the Lord."[498] The first day is the day of sanctification; the second day is the day of glorification. On the first day we receive so that we may be just, and on the second day we receive so that we may be blessed. And so, in the meantime the day of our redemption, through which we are justified, occurs now, afterwards the day of retribution will begin to dawn when we are made blessed. If you want to be sanctified today, then tomorrow you will go out and see the majesty of God. Today you go in, and tomorrow you will go out. *Return sinners to your heart*,[499] and you are inside. At death you will go out from the world and see God's majesty.

In another sense the first day was faith and the expectation of the promised Incarnation, and the second day was the presence of the revealed humanity. The first day occurred when Christ was expected and when he, who was about to come, was anticipated. The second day occurred when Christ, who was present, was seen, and he was seen to be God. And they saw him at that time: they saw his humanity in appearance and his divinity by faith. But we are still promised that when we see him in his majesty, we will see him face to face.[500]

Likewise, "sanctify yourselves today, tomorrow you will go out and see the majesty of the Lord." The first day of man is knowledge of oneself; the second day is knowledge of God. On the first day we go in, on the second day we will go out. On the first day enter into yourself, on the second day rise above yourself. Today you behold your iniquity; *in the morning you will see the majesty of the Lord*.[501] People draw near to the knowledge of God to the extent that they advance in self-knowledge.

On "Egypt is the life"

Egypt is secular life, the desert is discipline of the cloister, and the land of promise is spiritual grace. The king of Egypt is the will of the flesh, the land of Canaan is tranquility of mind, and the desert is the vow of profession. The Egyptians are sins; the Canaanites are vices. First the Egyptians, who have been submerged all together and at once, died; afterwards some Canaanites cannot be rooted out with great labor, others after many things, others absolutely not. We cast away all damnable works on one day, if we want, but we are not totally able to root out our vices during our entire lifetime.

NOTES

1 Ps. 2:1.
2 Wisd. of Sol. 1:3.
3 Wisd. of Sol. 1:5.
4 Wisd. of Sol. 1:5.
5 Ps. 2:1.
6 Ps. 2:1.
7 Ps. 2:2.
8 Cf. Gen. 3:19.
9 Cf. Eph. 6:12.
10 Ps. 2:2.
11 For the spirit of fornication, see Hosea 4:12; Hosea 5:4. For the spirit of pride, see Augustine, *Serm.* 72A (ed. M. Denis, *Sermones*, MA 1:157; tr. Hill, WSA III/3, 282–83); *Serm.* 181 (PL 38.980); Gregory the Great, *Mor.* VII.5 (Adriaen, CCL 143.337); XXII.20 (Adriaen, CCL 143A.1094); XXIII.11 (Adriaen, CCL 143B.1159). It is not uncommon for Richard to regard the Bible and the Church Fathers as "sacred scripture."
12 Ps. 2:2.
13 Cf. 1 Cor. 12:10.
14 Ps. 2:1–2a.
15 Ps. 2:2.
16 Exod. 15:3.
17 Ps. 121:7 (Vulg.).
18 Ps. 2:1–2.
19 Ps. 2:2.
20 Ps. 2:2.
21 Ps. 2:3.
22 1 John 2:15.
23 Richard seems to be conflating Matt. 10:28 and Luke 12:4 here.
24 Ps. 2:3.
25 Ps. 2:4.
26 In 2 Cor. 12:2 Paul speaks of a "third heaven" which assumes a first and second heaven. On the three heavens, see Richard of St Victor, *Trin.* Prol. (Ribaillier, 82; tr. Evans, VTT 1.211, 355 note 38); *Quat. grad.* IV.35 (PL 196.1219D; tr. Kraebel, VTT 2.290); *XII patr.* 74 (SC 419.302–4; tr. Zinn, 132); *Arca Moys.* I.10 (Aris, 19; tr. Zinn, 170); III.4 (Aris, 61; tr. Zinn, 227); III.8 (Aris, 65–66; tr. Zinn, 233–34); V.19 (Aris, 148; tr. Zinn, 343). Richard also discusses the third heaven in *Tract.* on Ps. 121 (PL 196.365B; tr. Evans, VTT 4.198–99).
27 Cf. 1 Cor. 13:12.
28 1 Cor. 13:12.
29 1 John 3:2.
30 Cf. Gen. 1:16; 5:1.
31 Ps. 131:14 (Vulg.).
32 Isa. 12:2.
33 Ps. 2:4.
34 Ps. 2:4.
35 Ps. 11:4–5 (Vulg.).
36 Ps. 93:7 (Vulg.).
37 Ps. 9:32 (Vulg.).
38 Ps. 2:4.
39 Ps. 25:1 (Vulg.).
40 John 14:6.
41 Ps. 115:11 (Vulg.).

42 Ps. 25:1 (Vulg.).
43 Isa. 46:8.
44 1 Sam. 3:10.
45 Cf. Ps. 4:3 (Vulg.).
46 Ps. 25:1 (Vulg.).
47 Ps. 83:13 (Vulg.).
48 Cf. 2 Cor. 4:16.
49 Ps. 25:1 (Vulg.).
50 Ps. 25:1 (Vulg.).
51 Ps. 25:1 (Vulg.).
52 Ps. 25:1 (Vulg.).
53 Ps. 41:5 (Vulg.).
54 Ps. 25:1 (Vulg.).
55 Ps. 25:1 (Vulg.).
56 Ps. 25:1 (Vulg.).
57 Cf. Exod. 3:8 *et al.*
58 Ps. 25:1 (Vulg.).
59 Isa. 40:31 (Vulg.).
60 Ps. 25:2 (Vulg.).
61 Ps. 25:2 (Vulg.).
62 Ps. 25:2 (Vulg.).
63 Ps. 25:3 (Vulg.).
64 Ps. 53:9 (Vulg.).
65 Ps. 25:3 (Vulg.).
66 Ps. 25:3 (Vulg.).
67 Rom. 8:28.
68 1 Cor. 10:13.
69 Ps. 25:3 (Vulg.).
70 Ps. 25:3 (Vulg.).
71 Cf. Rom 8:30; Eph. 1:5, 11.
72 Cf. Heb. 6:18.
73 Cf. John 14:6.
74 Matt. 22:16.
75 Cf. 1 Thess. 1:3; 2 Thess. 1:11.
76 Phil. 2:13.
77 Ps. 25:3 (Vulg.).
78 Ps. 25:4–5 (Vulg.).
79 Ps. 25:4 (Vulg.).
80 Ps. 25:4 (Vulg.).
81 Ps. 25:5 (Vulg.).
82 Ps. 25:4 (Vulg.).
83 Ps. 42:3 (Vulg.).
84 Cf. Ecclus. 10:9; 1 Tim. 6:10.
85 Cf. Isa. 5:8.
86 Cf. Ecclus. 4:36.
87 Cf. Matt. 23:5.
88 Cf. Matt. 6:16.
89 Cf. Matt. 6:5.
90 Ps. 72:16 (Vulg.).
91 Ps. 25:4 (Vulg.).
92 Cf. Ps. 83:3 (Vulg.).
93 Ps. 41:5 (Vulg.).

94   Ps. 42:4 (Vulg.).
95   Luke 6:38.
96   Ps. 25:4 (Vulg.).
97   Ps. 25:4 (Vulg.).
98   Ps. 25:5 (Vulg.).
99   Ps. 25:4-5 (Vulg.).
100 Ps. 25:5 (Vulg.).
101 Ps. 25:5 (Vulg.).
102 Isa. 42:8; 48:11.
103 Cf. Gal. 3:27.
104 Cf. Gen. 3:12.
105 Ps. 25:5 (Vulg.).
106 Ps. 25:6 (Vulg.).
107 Ps. 25:4 (Vulg.).
108 Ps. 25:5 (Vulg.).
109 Ps. 25:4 (Vulg.).
110 Ps. 25:5 (Vulg.).
111 Cf. Gen. 30:27 *et al.*
112 Ps. 25:6 (Vulg.).
113 Ps. 40:10 (Vulg.).
114 Ps. 40:10 (Vulg.).
115 2 Cor. 4:16.
116 Ps. 40:10 (Vulg.).
117 Ps. 40:10 (Vulg.).
118 Gen. 2:18.
119 Ps. 40:10 (Vulg.).
120 Ps. 40:10 (Vulg.).
121 Ps. 41:4 (Vulg.).
122 Ps. 126:2 (Vulg.).
123 Ps. 83:7 (Vulg.).
124 Ps. 40:10 (Vulg.).
125 Ps. 40:10 (Vulg.).
126 Ps. 44:10 (Vulg.).
127 Ps. 23:10 (Vulg.).
128 Cf. 1 John 3:16.
129 Ps. 44:10 (Vulg.).
130 Augustine, *Tractatus in epistolam Ioannis* 7.8 (Agaësse, 328; PL 35.2033). Cf. Hugh of St Victor, *Sacr.* II.13.12 (PL 176.545D–546D, 548CD; tr. Deferrari, 397, 399); *Sacr.* II.14.6 (PL 176.561AD, 562BC; tr. Deferrari, 413, 414); G. Constable, *"Love and Do What You Will": The Medieval History of an Augustinian Precept*, Morton W. Bloomfield Lectures IV (Kalamazoo, MI: Medieval Institute Publications, Western Michigan University, 1999).
131 Ps. 44:10 (Vulg.).
132 Wisd. of Sol. 8:1.
133 Ps. 44:10 (Vulg.).
134 Ps. 74:9 (Vulg.).
135 Luke 13:8 (Old Latin Version).
136 Cf. Exod. 29:23; Lev. 8:26; Num. 6:15, 17.
137 Gen. 44:5.
138 Matt. 28:18.
139 Gen. 44:5.
140 Rom. 2:16.
141 Gen. 44:2, 12.

142 Ps. 146:5 (Vulg.).
143 Ps. 74:9 (Vulg.).
144 Ps. 74:9 (Vulg.).
145 Cf. Ecclus. 11:27.
146 Cf. Job 21:13.
147 Cf. Luke 19:42.
148 Ps. 74:9 (Vulg.).
149 Ps. 74:9 (Vulg.).
150 Ps. 74:9 (Vulg.).
151 Ps. 74:9 (Vulg.).
152 Cf. Luke 18:31.
153 Cf. Matt. 22:30; Mark 12:25.
154 Ps. 74:9 (Vulg.).
155 Ps. 74:9 (Vulg.).
156 Ps. 80:6 (Vulg.).
157 Ps. 80:6 (Vulg.).
158 1 Cor. 13:1.
159 Ps. 80:6 (Vulg.).
160 Ps. 80:11 (Vulg.).
161 Cf. Deut. 5:6; Ps. 80:11 (Vulg.).
162 Ps. 80:11 (Vulg.).
163 Ps. 80:11 (Vulg.); cf. Deut. 5:6.
164 Matt. 5:6.
165 Ecclus. 15:3.
166 Ps. 80:11 (Vulg.); cf. Deut. 5:6.
167 Cf. Ps. 104:40 (Vulg.); John 6:31–32, 50–51.
168 Cf. Ezek. 2:8.
169 Ps. 80:11 (Vulg.); cf. Deut. 5:6.
170 Cf. Isa. 54:2.
171 Ps. 80:11 (Vulg.); cf. Deut. 5:6.
172 Cf. Ps. 147:17 (Vulg.).
173 Ps. 147:17 (Vulg.).
174 Lam. 4:4.
175 Cf. Ecclus. 15:3.
176 Ps. 147:17 (Vulg.).
177 Ps. 147:17 (Vulg.).
178 Ps. 147:18 (Vulg.).
179 Ps. 147:18 (Vulg.).
180 Ps. 84:11 (Vulg.).
181 Luke 19:42–44.
182 Jer. 6:14; cf. Ezek. 13:10.
183 Phil. 4:7.
184 Gal. 5:17.
185 On the region of dissimilitude, see Augustine, *Conf.* VII.10.16 (Verheijen, 103); Richard of St Victor, *Exterm.* 1.1 (PL 196.1073D); *LE* II.7.33 (Châtillon, 228); *Tract.* on Ps. 28 (PL 196.313B).
186 Cf. Heb. 11:9.
187 Ps. 104:13 (Vulg.).
188 Ps. 135:12 (Vulg.).
189 Cf. below *Tract.* on Ps. 104 (PL 196.333D; tr. Evans, VTT 4.183).
190 Cf. Gal. 5:16.
191 Ps. 84:11 (Vulg.).
192 Ps. 98:6 (Vulg.).

193 Ps. 98:6 (Vulg.). The present tense of the verb is what concerns Richard here, because Moses, Aaron, and maybe Samuel were already dead during the composition of this Psalm. According to Richard, that they are alive today is a tropological symbol of the priesthood today, which is never lacking in the Church.

194 I Cor. 3:17; cf. I Cor. 6:19.

195 Cf. Ps. 98:6 (Vulg.).

196 Rom. 7:18.

197 Rom. 9:16.

198 Ps. 98:6 (Vulg.).

199 Ps. 98:6 (Vulg.).

200 Deut. 31:29.

201 Deut. 31:27.

202 Cf. Mark 12:15.

203 I Sam. 3:20.

204 Ps. 98:6 (Vulg.).

205 Ps. 98:6 (Vulg.).

206 Ps. 104:12 (Vulg.).

207 Ps. 104:13 (Vulg.).

208 Ps. 104:13 (Vulg.).

209 Ps. 104:13 (Vulg.).

210 Ps. 104:13 (Vulg.).

211 Ps. 104:14 (Vulg.).

212 Ps. 104:14 (Vulg.).

213 Ps. 104:15 (Vulg.).

214 Ps. 104:15 (Vulg.).

215 Ps. 113:4 (Vulg.). In Latin "exultare" can mean "to leap" or "to rejoice."

216 Job 28:13.

217 Isa. 57:21.

218 Ps. 113:4 (Vulg.). See also Richard of St Victor, *Arca Moys.* V.14 (Aris, 142; tr. Zinn, 334).

219 The manuscripts read "a solito" ("from usual ground"), but I have emended it to "a solido" ("from solid ground").

220 Cf. Gen. 3:19 (Old Latin Version).

221 Ecclus. 10:9.

222 Ps. 103:8 (Vulg.).

223 Cf. Col. 3:1.

224 Ps. 113:4 (Vulg.).

225 Cf. 1 Cor. 13:12.

226 Cf. 1 Cor. 13:12.

227 Cf. 2 Cor. 3:18.

228 Joel 3:18.

229 Joel 3:18.

230 Cf. Isa. 55:12.

231 Cf. Ps. 41:5 (Vulg.).

232 Ps. 113:4 (Vulg.).

233 On "virtual parts" of the soul, see Achard of St Victor, *Discretione* 1 (Häring, 174; tr. Feiss, 357).

234 John 3:9.

235 Cf. Gen. 3:19.

236 Ps. 113:4 (Vulg.).

237 Wisd. of Sol. 9:15.

238 Rom. 8:26.

239 Rom. 7:14.

240   Cf. Exod. 15:17; Heb. 9:15.
241   Cf. Matt. 18:11–14; Luke 15:4–7.
242   Ps. 113:4 (Vulg.).
243   Matt. 5:6.
244   Ps. 113:4 (Vulg.).
245   Isa. 57:21.
246   Ps. 117:15 (Vulg.).
247   Ps. 113:4 (Vulg.).
248   Cf. Ps-Dionysius, *De cael. hierarchia* VI.2 (PL 122.1049C–1050A; tr. Luibheid, 160–61); *Summa sent.* II.5 (PL 176.85C–D); Peter Lombard, *Sent.* II.9.1 (SB 4:370–71). Richard, however, transposes "virtues" and "powers."
249   Ps. 113:4 (Vulg.).
250   Cf. 1 Cor. 13:12.
251   Ps. 113:4 (Vulg.).
252   Ps. 113:4 (Vulg.).
253   Ps. 117:15 (Vulg.).
254   Prov. 2:14 (Vulg.).
255   John 16:20; cf. Ps. 29:12 (Vulg.).
256   Ps. 117:15 (Vulg.).
257   Cf. Heb. 13:14.
258   Cf. Col. 3:2.
259   Cf. Job 7:1.
260   Cf. Apoc. 3:16.
261   Eph. 6:12.
262   2 Cor. 4:7.
263   Ps. 113:9 (Vulg.).
264   Ps. 117:15 (Vulg.).
265   Deut. 32:30.
266   Cf. Ps. 95:1 (Vulg.); 97:1 (Vulg.) *et al.*
267   Ps. 90:7 (Vulg.).
268   Ps. 117:15 (Vulg.).
269   Ps. 118:22 (Vulg.).
270   Ps. 118:62 (Vulg.).
271   Ps. 118:172 (Vulg.).
272   Cf. Matt. 27:3; John 13:27.
273   Cf. Acts 9:8.
274   Cf. 2 Sam. 5:1–5.
275   Ps. 121:1 (Vulg.).
276   Cf. Richard of St Victor, *LE* II.1.9 (Châtillon, 227).
277   Cf. Richard of St Victor, *Exterm.* III.18 (PL 196.1114B–C).
278   Cf. Ecclus. 17:29.
279   Cf. Ecclus. 17:29.
280   Cf. Gen. 2:18.
281   On the allegory of Adam and Eve, cf. Augustine, *De Genesi contra Manichaeos* II.11.15 (Weber, 135–37; PL 34.204); *Glossa ordin.* on 1 Cor. 11:8–10 (ed. princeps 4.324); Hugh of St Victor, *Sacr.* I.8.13 (PL 176.315C–316A); Peter Lombard, *Sent.* II.24.7–8 (SB 4:455–56).
282   Cf. Ps. 2:4 (Vulg.); Isa. 57:15.
283   Ps. 121:1 (Vulg.).
284   Ps. 38:6 (Vulg.).
285   Ps. 141:8 (Vulg.).
286   Jon. 4:3.
287   Job 10:1.

288 Ps. 38:6 (Vulg.).
289 Tob. 3:6.
290 Ps. 38:6 (Vulg.).
291 Cf. Ps. 43:22 (Vulg.); Rom. 8:36.
292 Ps. 38:6 (Vulg.).
293 Num. 23:10.
294 Ps. 38:6 (Vulg.).
295 Ps. 118:37 (Vulg.).
296 Ps. 42:3 (Vulg.).
297 Ps. 50:14 (Vulg.).
298 Ps. 121:1 (Vulg).
299 Ps. 84:9 (Vulg.).
300 1 Sam. 3:10.
301 Ps. 121:1 (Vulg).
302 Ps. 121:1 (Vulg.).
303 Cf. 2 Cor. 12:2. On the three heavens, see above *Tract.* on Ps. 2 (PL 196.271A; tr. Evans, VTT 4.152).
304 Phil. 3:20.
305 2 Cor. 12:2.
306 Cf. Ps. 35:9 (Vulg.).
307 2 Cor. 12:2.
308 Ps. 121:1 (Vulg.).
309 Ps. 121:1 (Vulg.).
310 1 Pet. 2:3; Cf. Ps. 24:8 (Vulg.).
311 Ps. 30:20 (Vulg.).
312 Ps. 35:9 (Vulg.).
313 Ps. 121:1 (Vulg.).
314 Ps. 121:1 (Vulg.).
315 Ps. 126:2–3 (Vulg.): "Cum dederit dilectis suis sompnum, ecce hereditas Domini, filii merces, fructus ventris." The Douay-Rheims Bible will translate "filii" as a nominative plural, thus "behold the inheritance of the Lord are children: the reward, the fruit of the womb." Richard regards "filii" as a genitive singular, hence "the reward of a son."
316 Ps. 75:6 (Vulg.).
317 Ps. 126:2–3 (Vulg.).
318 John 21:7.
319 See Feiss, VTT 2.230 n. 22.
320 Deut. 6:5; Matt. 22:37; Mark 12:30; Luke 10:27.
321 "Dilige ergo ut diligaris. Ama ut ameris." This is a common didactic saying; cf. Dhuoda of Uzès, *Liber Manualis* III.10 (Riché, 176): "Love all that you may be loved by all; cherish that you may be cherished." ("Ama omnes ut ameris ab omnibus, dilige ut diligaris"); Godfrey of Winchester, *Epigrammata* 229 (Wright, 143): "Dilige nos omnes, ut ameris ab omnibus unus."
322 Ps. 126:2–3 (Vulg.).
323 Ps. 126:2–3 (Vulg.).
324 Ps. 126:2–3 (Vulg.).
325 Ps. 126:2–3 (Vulg.).
326 Ps. 134:6 (Vulg.).
327 Ps. 134:7 (Vulg.).
328 Ps. 134:7 (Vulg.).
329 Ps. 43:16 (Vulg.).
330 Job 6:4.
331 Cf. Ps. 6:7 (Vulg.).
332 Ps. 134:7 (Vulg.).

333 John 3:8.
334 Matt. 5:5.
335 Cf. Isa. 11:2–3; 2 Tim. 1:7.
336 In Latin "spiritus" can mean "spirit" or "wind."
337 Cf. Rom. 11:33.
338 Cf. Isa. 11:2.
339 Ps. 134:8 (Vulg.).
340 Ecclus. 10:15.
341 Cf. 1 Cor. 4:21.
342 Cf. Gen. 1:27.
343 Ps. 134:9 (Vulg.).
344 Cf. 2 Pet. 2:9.
345 Ps. 134:7 (Vulg.).
346 Rom. 11:33.
347 Cf. Isa. 11:2–3.
348 What Richard seems to say is that each of the intellectual spirits, which blow at different times from their particular regions, will always bring with it the spirit of fortitude, and this spirit is always accompanied by piety and fear. Hence, while different intellectual spirits blow, the affective spirits are always present.
349 Cf. Rom. 1:20.
350 Ps. 134:7 (Vulg.).
351 Cf. Isa. 8:8.
352 Aeolus was the ruler of the winds in Greek Mythology.
353 Ps. 17:11 (Vulg.); cf. 2 Sam. 22:11.
354 Ps. 138:16 (Vulg.).
355 Rather than "stature" (*staturam*) many manuscripts read "nature" (*naturam*).
356 Ps. 138:16 (Vulg.).
357 Ps. 138:16 (Vulg.).
358 Cf. 1 Cor. 15:23; Gal. 5:24.
359 Ps. 68:29 (Vulg.).
360 Cf. Ecclus. 24:32; Phil. 4:3; Apoc. 3:5 *et al.*
361 Ps. 138:16 (Vulg.).
362 Ps. 139:2 (Vulg.).
363 Cf. Ps. 78:2 (Vulg.); Ps. 139:2 (Vulg.); Apoc. 19:17–20.
364 Cf. 1 Pet. 5:8.
365 Ps. 78:2 (Vulg.).
366 Ps. 78:2 (Vulg.).
367 Ps. 73:19 (Vulg.).
368 Ps. 139:2 (Vulg.).
369 Luke 8:5; cf. Matt. 13:4; Mark 4:4.
370 Matt. 13:28.
371 Matt. 13:39.
372 Ps. 139:2 (Vulg.).
373 Cf. Prov. 24:1–2.
374 Cf. Ps. 48:13 (Vulg.).
375 Cf. Eph. 6:11.
376 Ps. 35:7–8 (Vulg.).
377 Ps. 139:2 (Vulg.).
378 Ps. 139:2 (Vulg.).
379 Ps. 144:17 (Vulg.).
380 Ps. 139:2 (Vulg.).
381 Ps. 139:3 (Vulg.).

382   Ps. 72:8 (Vulg.).

383   Ps. 139:3 (Vulg.).

384   This tract on Hab. 3:2 and the next on Lev. 25 was profited by a draft translated by Fr. Hugh Feiss.

385   Hab. 3:2.

386   Gal. 4:4; Eph. 1:10; cf. Mark 1:15.

387   The Latin "virtus" will be translated throughout as "virtue." It means strength and vigor as well. The English word "virtue" means moral excellence primarily, but one meaning of the word that seems to be fading most quickly is "effective power." For Richard the word means both bodily strength and good moral habit. For the Romans "virtus" stood for all they regarded as "manliness," as its derivation from "vir" (man) suggests.

388   Cf. Rom. 12:5. In this paragraph and the next, Richard uses some expressions which were commonly used in the Middle Ages and are benchmarks of the corporate, cosmic and Christological dimensions of medieval Ecclesiology: the Church is the body of Christ, head and members; it began with Abel and traverses history until the end of time; it is a single entity, yet made up of many. For these components and their place in medieval Ecclesiology, see H. de Lubac, *Catholicism: Christ and the Common Destiny of Man* (San Francisco: Ignatius, 1988).

389   The Latin word here is "puer" which means "boy," but is also used for "child." Throughout his text Richard uses male words where he might have used gender-neutral expressions. In the interest of accuracy, I have generally followed his lead in this translation, rather than try to translate them into our contemporary inclusive language.

390   Cf. Acts 4:32; 2 Cor. 6:10.

391   Matt. 5:44; Luke 5:27, 35.

392   Matt. 19:21.

393   Matt. 10:27.

394   John 15:13; cf. John 10:11, 15, 17; 1 John 3:16.

395   Hab. 3:2.

396   Cf. Col. 1:26.

397   Cf. John 14:30.

398   Rom. 8:32.

399   Cf. Phil. 2:8.

400   Hab. 3:2.

401   Hab. 3:2.

402   Cf. Matt. 11:27.

403   Deut. 6:3; 26:9; 27:3; cf. Exod. 3:8; Lev. 20:24; Num. 14:8 *et al.*

404   Wisd. of Sol. 16:20.

405   1 Cor. 2:9.

406   Cf. Matt. 19:29.

407   Cf. Heb. 1:1–2.

408   Apoc. 2:17.

409   1 Cor. 2:9.

410   1 Cor. 2:10.

411   Cf. Matt. 19:29.

412   Matt. 22:30; Mark 12:25.

413   Matt. 19:27.

414   Cf. Acts 1:7.

415   Hab. 3:2.

416   Hab. 3:2.

417   1 Cor. 2:10.

418   Cf. 1 Cor. 3:2.

419   Cf. 2 Pet. 2:2.

420 Matt. 19:14.
421 Ps. 138:16 (Vulg.).
422 Ps. 54:24 (Vulg.).
423 Ps. 101:25 (Vulg.).
424 Ps. 106:26 (Vulg.).
425 Isa. 38:10.
426 Cf. Lev. 25:8.
427 Cf. Lev. 25:11.
428 Cf. Lev. 25:10.
429 Cf. Lev. 25:2, 4.
430 Ps. 77:54 (Vulg.).
431 Ps. 23:10 (Vulg.) *et al.*
432 Cf. John 8:34; Rom. 6:16.
433 Cf. Lev. 25:9.
434 Num. 10:2.
435 Matt. 2:13.
436 Matt. 5:8.
437 Matt. 2:3.
438 Cf. Ps. 130:1 (Vulg.).
439 Isa. 9:6.
440 Mark 10:14; cf. Matt. 19:14; Luke 18:16.
441 Ps. 137:6 (Vulg.).
442 Luke 18:11–12.
443 I Cor. 15:9.
444 Cf. Matt. 2:16.
445 Cf. 1 Cor. 4:7.
446 Cf. Rom. 10:9–10.
447 Cf. Acts 7:57–59.
448 Cf. Matt. 2:16.
449 Matt. 2:13.
450 Ps. 84:12 (Vulg.).
451 Cf. Matt. 2:2–3.
452 Matt. 2:13.
453 Eph. 5:8.
454 Cf. Song of Songs 1:6–7.
455 Cf. 1 Cor. 8:1.
456 Matt. 2:13.
457 1 John 1:5.
458 Cf. Wisd. of Sol. 7:26.
459 Ps. 75:2 (Vulg.).
460 Matt. 2:13.
461 Matt. 2:13.
462 2 Cor. 11:14.
463 Eccles. 3:1
464 Matt. 2:13.
465 Cf. 1 Cor. 12:10.
466 Matt. 2:13.
467 Matt. 2:14–15.
468 Cf. Isa. 1:2.
469 Isa. 38:15.
470 Isa. 38:15.
471 On the juxtaposition of "misery" (*miseria*) and "mercy" (*misericordia*), see Poirel, *Oeuvres* 1:163 n. 11; Feiss, VTT 4.327.

472 Ps. 22:4 (Vulg.).
473 Ps. 138:11 (Vulg.).
474 Ps. 18:3 (Vulg.).
475 Ps. 138:11 (Vulg.).
476 Matt. 2:14–15.
477 Cf. Matt. 2:19.
478 Cf. 1 Cor. 2:6.
479 Cf. Rom. 10:9–10.
480 Lev. 26:5.
481 On this list of interconnected activities, see Feiss, VTT 2.87, 308–9 n. 20.
482 Lev. 26:5.
483 Lev. 26:5.
484 Hosea 9:14.
485 Cf. Hosea 9:14.
486 Cf. Hosea 9:14.
487 Cf. Luke 11:43; 20:46.
488 Cf. 1 Cor. 8:1.
489 Luke 13:34.
490 Cf. Gen. 2:2.
491 This discussion of three days recalls Hugh of St Victor's *On the Three Days*, in which he discusses the power, wisdom and goodness of God (see Feiss, VTT 1.49–102; VTT 2.134 n. 19, 337 n. 12, 340–41 n. 89). However, here Richard uses a slightly different triad: power, knowledge, and will (*posse, scire, velle*). See also Achard of St Victor, *Serm.* 13.2 (tr. Feiss, VTT 4.90, 119 n.14).
492 Ps. 126:2 (Vulg.).
493 Ps. 126:1 (Vulg.).
494 I Cor. 4:7.
495 Cf. Exod. 20:10–11; Deut. 5:12–14.
496 Cf. Exod. 20:24.
497 Ps. 49:14 (Vulg.); cf. Ps. 115:17 (Vulg.); Heb. 13:15.
498 In the Victorine ordinal the *Sanctificamini hodie* was the responsory on Christmas Eve (Paris, BnF lat. 14506, fol. 270r).
499 Isa. 46:8.
500 Cf. Gen. 32:30; 1 Cor. 13:12 *et al.*
501 Exod. 16:7.

RICHARD OF ST VICTOR

ON THE STATE OF THE INTERIOR MAN

INTRODUCTION
BY DALE M. COULTER

TRANSLATION
BY CHRISTOPHER P. EVANS

INTRODUCTION

Richard of St Victor describes *On the State of the Interior Man* as a short summa on the nature of the human person. While the treatise originated as a request to explain Isaiah 1:5–6, most likely from one of his students, Richard took the opportunity to offer a more expansive mystical interpretation of the passage in question. In an allusion to the brief nature of his exposition, Richard describes himself as a kind of peripatetic engaged in a walkabout rather than someone on a long journey. His summa is the result of brief contemplative incursions into the text, possibly taken as Richard was leisurely strolling along one of the many paths that must have surrounded the abbey during his time there. What emerges from these peripatetic musings is Richard's most extensive statement on human nature in its postlapsarian condition.

Context and Purpose

As with most of Richard's works, an exact date remains allusive. Nevertheless, there are strong hints that the work stems from the 1160s when Richard was moving from sub-prior (1159–1162) to prior (1162–1173) at the abbey. In his chronology of Richard's works, Cacciapuoti places *On the State of the Interior Man* during Richard's time as sub-prior because of its close association in some manuscripts with *On the Extermination of Evil and Promotion of Good*.[1] There remain good reasons, however, not to restrict the date to Richard's sub-priorate. Instead, it seems better to place the work in the first half of the 1160s and look there for its purpose and context.

During the latter half of the 1150s and the early 1160s, Richard was beginning to flex his muscles as a theologian at the same time that he

---

[1] Cacciapuoti, *'Deus existentia amoris'*, 82–83; see also J. Ribaillier, "Richard de Saint-Victor: *De statu interioris hominis*," *AHDLMA* 42 (1967): 10–11. Cacciapuoti's dating almost all of Richard's major spiritual writings (*On the Twelve Patriarchs, On the Extermination of Evil and Promotion of Good, On the Mystical Ark/Ark of Moses, On the State of the Interior Man, Instruction of the Interior Person*) to Richard's three and a half years as sub-prior strikes me as excessive and unnecessary.

was moving into administrative roles at the abbey. Richard's admission
to his reader that he was hindered from completing *On the State of the
Interior Man* on many occasions most likely reflects the increase of
administrative duties commensurate with becoming sub-prior and
then prior.[2] This is especially the case when considering that from 1159
to 1162 St Victor went through a complete administrative turnover, with
Achard's resignation from the abbacy and departure in 1161, followed
by Gunther's brief tenure before Ernis was elected as the fourth abbot
in 1162. Moreover, at least fourteen manuscripts simply attribute to
Richard the title *magister* with one manuscript designating Richard as
magister and prior and two others as brother and prior. The conflation
of administrative roles (sub-prior and prior) with ongoing duties as a
Parisian master (*magister*) fit the 1160s much better, in particular, the
first half of the decade before the conflict with Ernis of St Victor began
to intensify.[3]

The administrative transitions at St Victor mirrored larger transitions in the evolving Parisian circle of scholars and churchman. Peter
Lombard's death in 1160 resulted in Maurice of Sully's stepping down
as master of the cathedral school of Notre Dame to become the new
bishop of Paris. Robert of Melun's, Andrew of St Victor's, and Achard
of St Victor's departures from Paris between 1161 and 1163 meant that
most of the leading scholars from the third generation were no longer
teaching. Along with others such as Peter Comestor and Odo of Sois-
sons (later of Ourscamp), Richard stepped into the void left by the
transitions of the early 1160s and became one of the leading scholars of
the fourth generation.

Richard's treatises from the early 1160s form three broad, overlap-
ping trajectories within his thought. The first is his ongoing concern
with the canonical ideal as embodied in the balance of the active and
contemplative lives. One can see this concern in a number of works
devoted to various aspects of that ideal, not least of which is Richard's
trilogy on Israel's formation as the people of God (*On the Twelve Patriarchs*), her exodus from Egypt and entrance into the promised land

---

[2]   Richard's statement prompts Châtillon to date the work after 1162. See Châtillon,
      "Richard de Saint-Victor," *DS* 13 (1987), 613.
[3]   While problems with Ernis' abbacy emerged before 1165, it is clear that Alexander
      III's public reprimand of Ernis in April of 1165 marks an important turning point that
      intensified the issue and was the beginning of the end for Ernis. On the situation,
      see D. Lohrmann, "Ernis, Abbé de Saint-Victor (1161–1172)," in *L'abbaye parisienne de
      Saint-Victor au moyen âge*, ed. J. Longère, BV 1 (Turnhout: Brepols, 1991), 181–93.

(*On the Extermination of Evil and Promotion of Good*), and the construction of the ark of the covenant in the tabernacle (*On the Mystical Ark/Ark of Moses*). These treatises symbolically represent the passage of the canon regular from the world into the abbey, the cultivation of virtue through penance and the active life, and the passage from the active life into the contemplative life with its climax in ecstatic vision. They supply the overarching narrative rationale for the canonical life while Richard's *Questions on the Rule of St Augustine* address its more basic questions. A second trajectory is Richard's increasing intervention in a number of theological questions stemming from student queries surrounding Peter Lombard's theology as well as other debated ideas. Richard's answer to these questions take the form of short tracts or letters written in response to solicitations. Finally, Richard seemed somewhat preoccupied with the Book of Isaiah, composing a number of works on various passages. The second and third trajectories probably pose the most immediate context within which to situate *On the State of the Interior Man* and the agenda behind it.

In the late 1150s Richard had become embroiled in a debate with his confrère, Andrew of St Victor, over whether the Hebrew term for the woman mentioned in Isaiah 7:14 should be interpreted as "virgin" or simply "young woman." Andrew had opted for the latter in his commentary on Isaiah while Richard vigorously defended the former in *On Emmanuel* as part of an overarching interpretation of Isaiah 7–8. Since Andrew left St Victor to return to Wigmore Abbey by 1163 at the latest, the debate most likely occurred sometime before then. This debate also stimulated further teaching on Isaiah, which led to a number of works devoted to various Isaianic texts. In *He Calls to Me from Seir*, a treatise stemming from early in his priorate, Richard developed Anselm of Canterbury's understanding of satisfaction as part of his exploration of Isaiah 21:11–12.[4] Richard also composed *In That Day*, a short spiritual reflection on Isaiah 7:21–22 that allowed him the opportunity to explore further the canonical ideals of the active and contemplative lives. One must situate Richard's exploration of Isaiah 1:5–6 in *On the State of the Interior Man* as part of a larger project on the spiritual interpretation of the Book of Isaiah. These four treatises suggest that Richard remained preoccupied with this book long after the initial controversy with Andrew. They also suggest that while Richard com-

---

4   On the dating of *Ad me clamat*, see J. Ribaillier, *Richard de Saint-Victor: Opuscules théologiques*, TPMA 15 (Paris: J. Vrin, 1967), 9–23, 221–22.

posed *On the State of the Interior Man* in response to a request made by another, this request most likely originated from Richard's own focus on Isaiah in his teaching during this period.

The probability that *On the State of the Interior Man* was a response to a question generated by Richard's oral teaching increases when one considers that a shorter version of this treatise is found among the Victorine *Miscellanies*.[5] Châtillon speculates that the abridged version may have been a first redaction by Richard, which accords with its basic structure.[6] All of the fundamental divisions Richard employs in the longer recension are present along with scriptural references. The shorter work only lacks the fuller explanations he will provide, which suggests that it serves as an outline for ease of delivery. Since many of the *Miscellanies* represent notes related to the oral teaching at St Victor, it may also be the case that this first redaction represents notes from Richard's own lectures that prompted the request for a fuller explanation.[7]

In addition to his focus on Isaianic texts, Richard's short theological treatises from the 1160s also point toward a deep engagement with current theological debates. At the requests of others, in particular a master Bernard, Richard directly engages Peter Lombard's positions in several of these works (*On the Power to Bind and Loose, On Mortal and Venial Sin, On the Spirit of Blasphemy*, and *Explanations of Several Difficulties of Scripture*). What connects these smaller works is a concern to clarify pastoral questions about penance and the moral life. These issues also make their way into some parts of the larger treatise *On the State of the Interior Man*, suggesting that it may be the fruit of a longer process of teaching and reflection. In each of these works, Richard carefully defends positions stemming from Hugh, but modified in light of Robert of Melun's work, among others. Thus, Richard's work represents a more refined version of Victorine positions on a number of theological questions about the Christian life. Richard's conclusions highlight the ongoing centrality of the pastoral task for the vocation of the Augustinian canons and point the way toward the penitential manuals that Victorines such as Robert of Flamborough would compose in the early thirteenth century.

---

5   PL 177.831–36.

6   Châtillon, "Richard de Saint-Victor," 614.

7   On this point, see Coulter, "Introduction to Richard of St. Victor's *Book of Notes*," VTT 3.292–93.

As a summa of the human condition, Richard composed his *On the State of the Interior Man* in the midst of the challenges his new administrative posts presented. His work also represents the fruit of his own musings on Isaianic passages as part of this oral teaching at St Victor; musings no doubt sparked in part by the controversy with Andrew of St Victor. Yet, true to the Victorine ethos, Richard saw Isaiah as a springboard for his own engagement with the most pressing questions of his day regarding a pastoral approach to penance and the moral life. The shorter answers Richard offered in his theological responses required a more expansive treatment of the human condition to fill in the inevitable gaps left by their ad hoc nature. This is what Richard hoped to accomplish in *On the State of the Interior Man*.

STRUCTURE AND CONTENT

As Richard indicates in the prologue, he has decided to use the text of Isaiah 1:5–6 to structure his summa on the human condition. While Richard suggests, in good Victorine fashion, that there are nine aspects of the human condition present in this verse, in point of fact, he identifies twelve. After a general introduction to the passage, he structures the rest of the work around four sets of three traits that he explores in relation to human nature. The result is as follows:

General Introduction (chap. 1)

Section 1: The Principle Parts in Man and Their Corruption

>   *Part 1*: Three Principle Parts in Man or Head, Heart, and Foot (chap. 2–10)

>   *Part 2*: Three Troubles of Man or Faint Head, Mourning Heart, and Entirely Unsound Body (chap. 11–37)

Section 2: Three Sins in Man or Wound, Bruise, and Swelling Sore (chap. 38–44)

Section 3: Three Remedies for Man or Bandages, Treatments, and Fomentation (chap. 45–52)

Before turning to discuss the various features of human nature, Richard makes a methodological statement that reveals his deep commitment to Victorine exegesis. He states, "See how the state of the interior man is described to you according to the quality of the exterior man . . ." This brief claim echoes a basic principle Hugh had articulated in the 1120s, which was repeated both by Robert of Melun and Richard himself.[8] In the move from literal interpretation to spiritual interpretation, Hugh insisted that the interpreter must move from the literal referent identified by the terms on the page to another referent. In other words, one always draws analogies from one thing to another thing, not from a word to a thing. Hugh then suggested that these analogies could be drawn either on the basis of the external form or the internal nature of the authorial referent (what Hugh called "first things"). As an example, he indicated that one could draw an analogy from the whiteness of snow (an external quality) to the internal nature of the soul. This is exactly the method Richard employs in this treatise as he moves from the external qualities associated with head, heart, and the other "things" referred to by the words of the text to the internal condition of humans.

Having established his approach to the text and its relationship to the structure of the treatise, Richard launches into his subject matter. As one moves through Richard's text, it becomes clear that the most important part of the passage is the term "sanitas" (soundness/health). Richard uses the reference to a lack of soundness in the body to move between physical health and spiritual health. He draws upon ancient and medieval ideas about physical well being centered upon balance and harmony within the body to portray spiritual well being. He states, "Soundness (*sanitas*) is the natural integrity of the temperament and the proportional measure of all the humors. And infirmity is nothing other than the privation of this soundness and the corruption of this integrity."[9] This definition of physical health finds its analogue in the balance among the various affective and appetitive movements in the soul. In particular, Richard identifies love, joy, hate, and sorrow as four affective movements that must possess a "balanced order and measure;" otherwise sickness will ensue. Recovering spiritual well being involves a process whereby grace liberates free choice to cooperate in

---

8   See Hugh of St Victor, *Sent. div.* Prol. (tr. Feiss, VTT 1.119); Robert of Melun, *Sentences* I.6 (tr. Van Baak, VTT 3.453); Richard of St Victor, *LE* I.2.5 (tr. Feiss, VTT 3.312).
9   *Statu* 11 (Ribaillier, 76; tr. Evans, VTT 4.262).

the process of restoring balance to the disordered psychological movements of the soul.

By focusing on health as balance and symmetry, Richard directly
links this treatise to Hugh's definition of virtue as

> nothing else than an affection of the mind ordered according to reason.
> Because of the same mind's various inclinations, there are said to be
> many [affections], which, nevertheless possess one root and origin, the
> will. For the one will forms various affections as it inclines itself to
> diverse objects either by attraction or avoidance, and it receives differ-
> ent names according to these same affections even though all of them
> are in the same will and are the same will.[10]

Moreover, Richard had offered this same definition in the seventh
chapter of *On the Twelve Patriarchs* in which he likened the sons of
Leah to ordered affections that the canon regular must develop. Hugh
and Richard most likely borrowed the idea from Bernard of Clairvaux's
On Grace and Free Choice in which Bernard states, "For mere affections
live naturally in us, as of us, but those additional acts, as of grace. This
means only that grace sets in order what creation has given, so that
virtues are nothing else than ordered affections."[11] Richard's contribution was to fuse the idea of ordered affectivity with notions of physical
well being he found in other Cistercian writers, such as William of
St Thierry's *On the Nature of the Body and the Soul*.

This Cistercian undercurrent to Richard's treatise also emerges in the
prominent role he gives to free choice, which the head symbolizes. Like
a ruler, free choice must take command over the numerous movements
of thoughts, appetites, and affections that occur within the soul. In this
way, Richard also draws upon the ancient idea that humanity is a microcosm that embodies the macrocosm of creation. The dynamism present
in the movements of created bodies (rivers, wind, fish, birds, etc.) all find
their analogue in the movements of the heart. Part of restoring health is
to liberate free choice to make proper judgments about created goods so
that it can begin to shape these interior movements accordingly.

The focus on "sanitas" also allows Richard to utilize Hugh of St Victor's definition of vice as a weakness that emerges from internal corruption.[12] Hugh had indicated that "the rational soul in its health is a
solid and sound vessel having no corruption, and when vices come into

---

[10]   *Sacr.* 1.6.17 (PL 176.273B–C; tr. Deferrari, 105).
[11]   *Gratia* 6.17 (tr. O'Donovan, 72–3).
[12]   *Sacr.* II.13.1 (PL 176.525A). Hugh uses the phrase "infirmitas spiritualis corruptionis"
       whereas Richard has "infirmitas naturalis corruptionis."

this they vitiate and corrupt in this way."[13] To illustrate his point, Hugh described the seven capital vices in terms of immoderate appetitive movements. For his part, Richard describes a vice as a "depraved motion," and an "appetite for evil" that stems from disordered affective movements.[14] The three primary vices (impotence, ignorance, and concupiscence) Richard finds symbolically represented in a fainting head, mourning heart, and unsound body are nothing less than the corruption of the psychological integrity of the person. The impotence of free choice resides in the lack of control over affective and appetitive movements. In good Augustinian fashion, Richard sees these unbalanced interior movements as summarized by the term concupiscence, an affective longing for evil, which, in turn, causes one to misperceive the value of objects in the world thereby leading to ignorance about various kinds of goods. By focusing on "sanitas," Richard is able to show how all three primary vices are a privation, a form of corruption that emerges from the breakdown of the primordial wholeness of the human person and that finds concrete expression in disordered and unbalanced movements of emotion and desire.

In his summa of the human condition, Richard weaves together ideas from twelfth-century scholars with the text of Isaiah in order to address issues of his day. With Victorine exegetical theory firmly in hand, he offers a spiritual interpretation of Isaiah 1:5–6 that draws analogies from the literal referents of the text to the interior life of the human person. Central to this approach is Richard's focus on "sanitas" and its loss. Postlapsarian humanity was caught up in psychological disintegration manifested in disordered movements of emotion and desire. Through cooperation with grace, humans engage in a lifestyle that seeks to reorder and reintegrate these movements to restore the integrity lost. In this glimpse at the human condition, Richard has set the stage for the pastoral advice that confessors would give to those seeking penance.

The Latin text translated here for the first time can be found in J. Ribaillier's critical edition (*AHDLMA* 42 [1967]: 61-128). Most of the references in the footnotes are selected from the more extensive source apparatus of his edition. The footnotes here are limited to citations and allusions to the Bible and to the loci of the same topic in Richard's writings and in other influential authors like Hugh of St Victor and Bernard of Clairvaux.

---

[13]   *Sacr.* II.13.1 (PL 176.525D; tr. Deferrari, 375).
[14]   *Statu* 39 (Ribaillier, 110; tr. Evans, VTT 4.289–90).

ON THE STATE OF THE INTERIOR MAN

Prologue

I was late in sending what I promised at your request. But, most beloved man, it was out of necessity not intention that I did not finish earlier what I first intended. With many occasions interfering and hindering my plan, I was not able to complete your command. I have decided to compensate the expenses of my long delay at least with a higher interest of my debt, one that seemed to accrue after so much procrastination of my promise. In the meantime, my friend, allow me to reflect carefully on the mind of a friend, for whom I was pleased to persevere so long in the service of a pleasant friend and to continue to work diligently on my short work so that my labor might serve your desire even longer (I dare not say "your advantage"). And so, having accepted the occasion for writing or even the rules of speaking from the words of Isaiah,[1] which you asked that I explain as a gift to you, I have given very extensive consideration to certain issues on the state of the interior man. I have surveyed and admired with a curious leisure and leisurely curiosity not the charms of places but the profundity of words and the sublimity of sentences,[2] and, like a surveyor not a traveler, I have produced short cuts or short routes through the many by-paths.[3] Who does not rightly marvel at the state of our decrepitude comprehended fully under such compendious brevity of words?

Consider carefully, I ask, how vices and afterwards sins are mystically described in a suitable order and with wonderful reason where the contempt for remedies is also connected. In these three the sum of all spiritual corruption is comprehended: three vices, three sins, three remedies. Impotence, ignorance, concupiscence—these are the vices of the inner man that turn into sins when they allure consent.[4] There are thus three kinds of vices and three kinds of sins. There are some sins that we commit through weakness, and others that we commit through error. But there are other sins that we commit willingly out of a perverse will alone. We recognize three remedies in divine institutions, in divine warnings, and in divine promises. And so, in this same order and with supreme brevity these nine things, which are explained

more fully in their own places, are comprehended in the few words of
Isaiah and are indicated by a mystical description and with marvelous
reasoning. What has resounded from the mouth of God and what has
flowed from the divine oracle must be something truly great, truly
profound, and indeed most salubrious. Even if one scorns human
teaching, should he not give at least some regard to divine teaching?

When you read my work and find many reprehensible ideas, you
will easily grant me your pardon. If I have become a fool, you have
compelled me.[5] Grant your pardon, O reader! I have not presumed to
teach, but I wanted to satisfy the request of a friend.

Section One

Chapter One. The state of the interior man after the fall[6]

*Every head is faint and every heart is mourning. From the sole of the
foot up to the crown of the head, there is no soundness therein. The
wound, the bruise, and the swelling sore—they are neither bandaged, nor
treated with medicine, nor soothed with oil.*[7] The Lord knows his image,[8]
and the variety and magnitude of illnesses cannot escape the notice of
the supreme doctor. See how he describes to you the measure and
magnitude of your illness, so that you may know what you must mourn,
what you must care for, and why you must implore the Lord. *Every
head*, he said, *is faint and every heart is mourning. From the sole of the
foot up to the crown of the head, there is no soundness therein.* See the
innate evils! Yet listen to the other evils: *The wound, the bruise, and the
swelling sore.* See the inflicted evils! See the nature and extent of the
evils! Some are inborn; others are inflicted. We suffer some evils inwardly; we commit others externally. The latter evils are generated from
one's own corruption; the former evils are often inflicted by the persecution of another. Faintness, mourning, and infirmity come from
within. The wound, bruise, and swelling sore arise from without. Now
the contempt for remedies follows at the peak of evils, in which the
despair of the sick truly lies. *They are neither bandaged*, he said, *nor
treated with medicine, nor soothed with oil.*[9] See how we are weighed
down by so many evils and are oppressed daily by such annoyances.
Learn, O man, even if you are rejected by man; learn at least from him
who teaches man knowledge.[10] Learn, I say, grieve, and lament over such
great troubles and such misery. Consider and know the magnitude of

the disease, so that you may desire more anxiously, seek more diligently, and love more ardently the remedy of the doctor.

Therefore, see how the state of the interior man is described to you according to the quality of the exterior man, so that you may learn what you should fear from the interior evils through the exterior evils, the nature and size of which you are aware. Who does not see that one cannot linger entirely at the literal sense?[11] Has anyone ever seen or heard that the heads of all are faint or that hearts of all mourn? *Every head*, he said, *is faint and every heart is mourning. From the sole of the foot up to the crown of the head, there is no soundness therein.* Here certain body parts of the exterior man are designated by name, so that when we hear the words "head," "heart," or "foot" in relation to what we must understand concerning interior things, we may be compelled to derive from them some similitude to interior things.[12]

Chapter Two. On the three principal parts in man

We know that the head has the highest place in the human body, the foot has the lowest place, and the heart has the middle and inmost place. The head is free choice, the heart is counsel, and the foot is carnal desire. The head is above the whole body, and free choice presides over every action. The heart has the middle and inmost place, and with difficulty salutary counsel can be drawn from a hidden place and found in a secrete place. The foot lies at the bottom, and carnal desire clings to lowest things through the appetite.[13] Free choice presides over every action, even over the appetite, because even when *you perform an evil deed*, and when sin *is already present at the door*, yet *its desire will be under you, and you will rule over it.*[14] What else does "its desire will be under you" mean except "under your choice"? For no desire proceeds into act without the voluntary approval and consent of the will. Counsel is sought in a hidden place and is drawn from the inmost depths, because *wisdom is drawn from a hidden place.*[15] The lust of the flesh lies at the bottom, as long as *my soul clings to the ground*[16] and *as long as our stomach cleaves to the earth.*[17]

Chapter Three. On the dignity of free choice

Among all the goods of creation there is in man nothing more sublime and more worthy than free choice; nothing is more useful and more hidden than salutary counsel; and nothing is lower and weaker than carnal desire. What, I ask, can be found in man more sublime and

more worthy than what was made in the image of God?[18] The freedom
of choice certainly has the image not only of eternity but also of divine
majesty. How much closer before all else does free choice resemble this
immutable eternity, and how much clearer does it bear the image of
God in itself, given that no guilt or even misery will ever be able to
diminish, much less destroy, it?[19] Do you wish to see the likeness of
majesty in it and to understand how it is clearly stamped with God's
image? God does not have, nor can he have, a superior,[20] and free
choice does not endure, nor can it endure, dominion because it is not
proper or possible for the Creator or for a creature to inflict force on
it.[21] Let the whole underworld, the whole world, and the whole multitude of the heavenly angels agree and concur on this one point: the
consent of free choice cannot be coerced unwillingly in any matter
whatsoever.

CHAPTER FOUR. ON THE BENEFIT OF COUNSEL

Just as there is nothing in man more excellent than the freedom of
choice, so there is nothing more salubrious than prudent counsel and
consulted prudence. *Happy is the one who finds wisdom and abounds
in prudence. The acquisition of it is better than the merchandise of silver
and gold. It is more precious than all riches, and everything that is desirable cannot be compared with it.*[22] Now no possession is more useful
than this gift of wisdom, and nothing is more difficult to find. It is a
treasure hidden in a field,[23] because according to Isaiah *wisdom is drawn
from a hidden place.*[24] But what is this hidden place, or what do we call
this field that hides this treasure? *Where is wisdom found, and where is
the place of understanding?*[25] Let us search for the place of wisdom and
understanding with blessed Job, and we will find it with Solomon:
I, Wisdom, dwell in counsel, and I am present among learned thoughts.[26]
Therefore, let us seek her who dwells in counsel within our heart, which
we have already called "counsel."[27] All of you longing for this very desirable treasure *guard your heart with all diligence,*[28] lest if you refuse to
guard it, you may be forced to mourn and say with the Prophet: *My
heart has forsaken me.*[29] Thus you would grieve and mourn the fact that
in the meantime you do not have a place where you should seek this
treasure or a place where you can find it. In my opinion their hearts
had forsaken them, and every counsel had withdrawn from those to
whom the Lord said by way of reproof: *Ephraim is like a dove that has
been decoyed and has no heart.*[30] Rightly, therefore, this is said to them:

They are a nation without counsel and prudence. O that they would be wise and understand and that they would provide for their future![31] With such great caution we must guard our hearts where that treasure is found. No possession is richer and more secure than it. If, according to the testimony of Wisdom, *wisdom enters into your heart and knowledge pleases your soul, then counsel will watch over you and prudence will protect you.*[32]

CHAPTER FIVE. ON THE INFIRMITY OF CARNAL DESIRE

Just as nothing is more useful than prudent counsel, so nothing is lower and weaker than the carnal desire because according to its likeness to a foot it has the lowest place and clings to worldly things through carnal pleasure.[33] What, I ask, is weaker and more abject than when we do not completely withstand those pleasures that bring us shame? How much vileness or how much infirmity is there in consenting mentally to the law of God because it is good and yet seeing *daily another law in my members that opposes the law of my mind and holds me captive in the law of sin?*[34]

From the discussions thus far you notice how free choice is correctly understood through "head," how counsel is correctly understood through "heart," and how carnal desire is correctly understood through "foot."

CHAPTER SIX. THE PREEMINENCE OF FREE CHOICE

The whole body is guided by the head, vivified by the heart, and moved around by the feet. The head guides the whole, and free choice rightly assumes control of everything in man and the management of its condition. And just as free choice does not endure a dominion from anything outside man, so it rules over everything inside man on account of the dignity of its liberty. Even if some motion in man rises up against or contrary to the human will, then just as it only consents to the will by reason of its free choice, so it only comes forth into action by its permission. The sensual motion very often rules over the bodily motion,[35] and the affect of the soul frequently rules over both the senses and the appetites. Yet none of these motions achieves the outcome of their impulse unless at the approval and voluntary consent of free choice. And so voluntary consent of free choice rules over every motion,[36] because, according to the teaching of Wisdom, *another is higher than one who is high, and above them there are others higher still; the king rules over all the land subject to him.*[37] The king rules over all the land, because every motion through the other members of the body serves him at his will. And thus if something does not willingly obey him and often revolts against him in a major disagreement, then the king is able to restrain its impetuousness from action, strike its unruliness with severe retribution, and subdue and enervate the audacity of its animosity with strong castigation.[38] In this way then whatever shamelessly opposes and vigorously resists him does not completely escape his power. Rightly, therefore, in my opinion, free choice, which rules over every other motion, is compared to the head.

CHAPTER SEVEN. ON THE VIRTUE OF HELPFUL COUNSEL

The heart vivifies the very same body that, as was said, the head governs. In order to discuss this matter according to natural philosophy, just as the animal spirit is seated in the head and the natural spirit is seated in the liver, so the vital spirit chooses a seat in the heart. As the animal spirit controls and gives sensation to the body and as the natural spirit vegetates it, so the vital spirit vivifies it.[39] Hence, every feeling and voluntary motion derives from the animal spirit, vegetive power (*vegetatio*) derives from the natural spirit, and life derives from the vital spirit.

A body without life is like a work without good intention.[40] Any act, however good it appears, is regarded as dead unless it is alive to good intention through counsel. Just as life proceeds from the heart and spreads itself through out every member,[41] so good intentions rise from counsel and continually make works of virtues alive to the vegetation of merit. And so it is rightly ordered by Wisdom: *Guard your heart with all diligence, because life proceeds from it.*[42] Life proceeds from the heart when council corrects a depraved intention. Death rather than life proceeds from the heart when counsel corrupts a good intention. What does it benefit to beget a child of good works and then to kill him through a depraved intention?[43] And what will it be like, I ask, if our own conscience convicts us of killing our children? Some in proposing good works corrupt them by their evil intention; others after exercising virtues become void of their original intention at the offering of vain praise.[44] What else are the former doing except producing abortive fetuses, and what else are the latter doing except killing, as it were, children after they have already been born or even grown up? Is it not better not to give birth than to perform an abortion? And is it not more beneficial not to beget a child then to suffocate him in his sleep or to kill him by counsel?[45] Is it not better that I go without children than to sacrifice my sons and daughters to demons?[46] Is it not much happier to be barren and not beget children than *merciless murderers of their own children, eaters of human entrails, devourers of blood, and parents who murder helpless lives*?[47] Always remember that even if killing the living lies within your will, the resurrection of the dead is not equally within your power. He alone has this power who *is able to raise children of Abraham from stones*.[48]

At the prophecy of the Son of Man and at the command of the Lord unto the bones that are found dried up in the field, the spirit entered into them and they began to live.[49] What, I ask, do the dry bones—soulless and dead bones—mean except mighty works without good intention and, for that reason, rightly void of virtues and ineffectual for the recompense of a reward? Nevertheless, such bones receive the spirit at the command of the Lord and come to life again. And, after their intention is corrected at the grace of His inspiration, these bones grow strong again in the hope of the eternal reward. But because counsel makes the intention honest and good, the spirit proceeds, as it were, from the heart and extends out and spreads itself throughout all virtuous members in order to vivify the body. Rightly, therefore, counsel is indicated by the heart and imitates its similitude.

CHAPTER EIGHT. ON THE RESTLESSNESS OF CARNAL DESIRE

We easily show how what we have said about feet applies to carnal desire according to its affect or appetite.[50] As feet move the body around, so carnal desire arouses and leads the mind around. As long as the mind, enticed and dragged away by carnal desire, follows its affect at one time and the appetite at another time, it is never allowed to be tranquil and at rest.[51] As long as it lives as a *wanderer and fugitive on the earth*,[52] it runs after its own lusts every day. And as long as it always strives either to seize what it desires or to flee what it hates, it *is filled with many miseries and never remains in the same state*.[53]

CHAPTER NINE. ON THE RESTLESSNESS OF HUMAN AFFECT[54]

Who, I ask, can correctly explain in how many ways the human affect continually varies itself? It alters itself in many ways and unleashes its impulse through many and nearly countless ways based on every alternation of its variability: always striving from one thing to another, growing tired of one thing after another, and often returning even more greedily to what it had despised earlier. This is the reason why Solomon said: *The spirit encircling all things proceeds in a circuit and returns to its gyres.*[55] The spirit is rightly said to proceed in a circuit by encircling all things because, as it was said,[56] the affect of the heart is carried off through different things and is altered in many ways.[57] Nowhere does it find a satisfying delight, and, for that reason, it always strives from one thing to another. Now it loves this, now that. Now it desires this, now that. Again it despises what it had loved earlier. Again it grows tired of what it had so desired for so long. But often after this aversion it returns more eagerly to its pathetic lusts, and in this way it proceeds in a circuit and directs its course in a circle. Love, fear, hope, sorrow, and any other affect are thus led through diverse things and are varied in many ways.[58] But through every motion of its affects and through every way of its motions the mind always returns to its circle, as long as it is moved again in the same way around the same or similar object. It is not that remarkable that the spirit, having been aroused and urged in any one direction, is swept along through various things and carried away through various pleasures in order to satisfy its desires, and, after, so to speak, encircling the whole face of the earth, it returns again to its usual and former delights. But what is very remarkable and worthy of amazement is that, while being carried often and abruptly by contrary winds, the spirit sometimes moves in one direction and sometimes in the opposite direction, so that it later attacks with an insatiable hatred what it had passionately loved earlier.[59]

This element, which we call "breath" (*spiritum*) or "air," is more erratic than all other elements and is subjected to various passions. *In a moment, in the blink of an eye*[60] it becomes heated and then grows cold again with the same ease as the breath sometimes comes out warm and sometimes blows out cold at nearly the same moment when it is gently exhaled or forcefully blown out of a mouth. In this way the spiritual breath and passible affect is easily moved and changed into contrary passions through a slight alteration. Who does not know how a man is wholly inclined immediately toward goodwill at a gentle breeze of a favorable breath, and if at about the same time a gust of slander blows from the same mouth, then it immediately turns his affect in another direction and changes it into hatred and fury? It is certainly remarkable, or rather pathetic, that at a few words, at a gentle breeze and at the sound of the tongue and stroke of air a noble creature, which was created in the image of God and preferred over all of creation,[61] is forcefully driven, as it were, from its state of uprightness, dragged off to different places in a remarkable way, and spun into a rotation like a whirlwind.

Chapter Ten. On the restlessness of carnal appetite

The carnal appetite is also always in motion and transition, and it can never remain in the same state. It comes and goes. It increases and decreases. It always departs and decreases so that it may return and increase again. It always returns and increases so that it may depart and decrease again. Nevertheless, the appetite does not agitate and disturb the mind with the same circuit or equal impulse as an affect. It is not varied like the wind by daily alterations through multiple circuits, and it is not driven by successive changes in directions opposite to headwinds, but like a river it follows the channel of its impulse until it achieves the end of its desire. It does not change its channel through fleeting alternations of its habit so that it continually regrets its subsequent desires even before it embraces what it desires. It does not block the channel of its desire or divert it in the opposite direction until it satisfies its desire, as an affect does which assumes various moods at each moment and often immediately turns the wind of its impulse in an opposite direction while it changes its love into hatred sometimes at a remarkable speed. To seek various pleasures, as if moving from place to place, and then, after being satisfied, to grow tired of one pleasure after another, as if forsaking one place after another, is not the same as to turn one's channel in the opposite direction and, after flowing downward, to return to the mountains. Water can never do this, and the appetite usually does not do this. Yet it is always running and flowing, and it always returns to itself, as Solomon said: *Unto the place from where the rivers flow, they return in order to flow once again.*[62] The carnal appetite is that vast abyss from where so many rivers flow out and from where so many and such an endless number of desires surge.

Let us consider then the place from which such rivers flow out and the place to which their currents reach; and let us consider the channel on which they flow and the channel on which they return. Necessity is the place from where the outflow of carnal appetite discharges;[63] satiety is the place to which it reaches; pleasure (*voluptas*) is the channel on which it travels; and desire (*cupiditas*) is the channel on which it returns.[64] The damage of our defect is the place from which it flows out; pleasure (*oblectamentum*) is the place on which it flows down; disgust is the place to which it flows; and desire (*desiderium*) is the place on which it flows back. After much disgust at its satiety every appetite reverts back to its own place out of a great desire of its lust. This happens so that that appetite may flow out once again because the same necessity as before urges it to return to its gratifying delights in order to restore its bodily damages. And just as every watercourse flows on the earth's surface and through visible channels and returns again through underground and invisible channels, so every appetite gradually flows out through a visible action and the satisfaction of its desire and returns again to an innate reflux of its habit through some natural hidden operation and vegetive motions.

What kind of misery, I ask, and how miserable is it to be moved incessantly through this gyration and to be trapped always in this very troubling disturbance? How much should we strive after, or rather how much should we detest, the satisfactions of our desires that are always derived from a defect and turned into disgust! But why do we say, as Scripture attests, that what is known always to complete its course in bitterness ends in disgust? *All rivers*, Scripture says, *flow into the sea, but the sea does not overflow.*[65] We know that rivers make water sweet, just as the sea makes water bitter. What then does it mean that rivers flow into the sea unless every carnal desire ends in bitterness? Therefore, every river flows into the sea because *sorrow lies at the end of happiness.*[66] All sweet waters ending up in the sea turn bitter,[67] because *laughter is turned into sorrow.*[68] All rivers flow into the sea and all sweet waters turn bitter because all pleasures, as it was said, turn into disgust and all carnal desires end in bitterness. Indeed human depravity does not know how or disdains to use well its own goods, so whenever people sin through an unjust desire supernal justice later turns this into their whip. But *rivers flow into the sea, and the sea does not overflow,*[69] because divine equity preserves its measure throughout our sufferings and scourging and because it does not exceed the limits of justice whenever we are struck for the purpose of retribution or correction. Therefore, *the sea does not overflow*, because the extent of our wretchedness does not surpass what our wickedness deserves.

From this one may assess how those feet of concupiscence, about which we have already spoken,[70] pull us asunder either through affect or appetite, and at what end the extremes of its downward course conclude.

Chapter Eleven. On the Threefold Troubles of Man

I trust that what we should think about the head, heart, or foot was sufficiently explained above. Now let us see what we should think about the members of the interior man based on divine teaching: *Every head is faint and every heart is mourning; from the sole of the foot up to the crown of the head, there is no soundness therein.*[71] The head is faint, the heart mourns, and the foot suffers with the whole body, because *from the sole of the foot up to the crown of the head, there is no soundness therein.* As previously discussed, the head is free choice, the heart is counsel, and the foot is carnal desire.[72] Therefore, the head is faint because free choice is torpid with respect to every good. The heart mourns because it cannot ignore or hide the evil counsel that it endures. The foot suffers with the whole body because the evil of its lust is completely aroused. The one who said, *without me you can do nothing,* wanted to show us the faintness of our head.[73] What is weaker than the complete inability to regain even the slightest strength for any good on one's own? Indeed *it is not a matter of the will or one who runs, but of the mercy of God.*[74] The heart mourns because counsel teaches that *it is better to go to the house of mourning than to the house of feasting.*[75] Indeed the further people advance in counsel, the more they grow in sorrow, *because in much wisdom there is much displeasure; and the one who increases knowledge also increases sorrow.*[76] The better people know through counsel the evil that they mourn, the more vehemently they become displeased at their depravity. And the more clearly they see the evil that they endure, the more severely they are struck with the sting of sorrow. The foot suffers with the whole body because its own infirmity wrenches out sorrow in each of its members. As it was said, *from the sole of the foot up to the crown of the head, there is no soundness therein.* Therefore, because infirmity seizes the whole body, what wonder is it if sorrow is everywhere? *There is no soundness in my flesh,* the Prophet said, *nor is there peace in my bones because of my sins.*[77] How great is the attrition, I ask, where the flesh cannot have soundness nor the bones have peace? So also Job was struck with the worst sore,[78] so that there would be no soundness in him from the sole of his foot up to the top of his head. Who, I ask, boasts about the soundness of his body,[79] when the chief of the prophets bewails his own infirmity and that man, to whom no one on earth compares, is stricken with the worst sore?[80] For *each man is tempted when he is drawn away and enticed by his own lust.*[81] And temptation is *man's life on earth.*[82]

Faintness lies in the head, mourning in the heart, and sorrow in the whole body. *Every head is faint and every heart is mourning; from the sole of the foot up to the crown of the head, there is no soundness therein.* And so, let us consider, if you please, these three troubles that are placed in man: faintness, mourning, and the privation of soundness. Faintness is infirmity abiding in the whole body and weakening it. Mourning is the sorrow raging very severely on the inside and erupting through tears on the outside. Soundness is the natural integrity of the temperament and the proportional measure of all the humors.[83] And infirmity is nothing other than the privation of this soundness and the corruption of this integrity.

Chapter Twelve. On the Infirmity of Free Choice

Consider the extent or nature of the head's infirmity and how the Prophet compared it to faintness. For, as it was said, because faintness is infirmity abiding in the whole body and weakening it, why is the head said to be faint unless because its defect oppresses the whole body and cannot be fully healed until the end of life? How rightly is something said to be faint that never moves toward any kind of good on its own?[84] What sort of good does someone actually accomplish on his own given that he cannot even *say, "Jesus is Lord," except in the Holy Spirit*?[85] Indeed someone is often moved toward the good, yet always through the Holy Spirit. You have heard how extensively the infirmity spreads itself: it seizes and weakens the whole body. Do you want to hear how long the body must be consumed under that faintness and sustain the sentence of the curse? *Until you return to the earth from which you were taken.*[86] But how, you ask, is such great freedom consistent with such great infirmity or such great infirmity with such great freedom? Freedom is certainly different from strength. You can be free and sick at the same time, just as, on the contrary, you can be healthy and a slave at the same time. A healthy and strong person can do many great things, but a free person cannot be coerced into something unless through injustice.[87]

Chapter Thirteen. What is freedom and power?

We do not call human choice free because it has the ability at hand to do good or evil but because it has the freedom not to consent to good or evil.[88] The ability to do evil certainly pertains to infirmity, and the ability to do good pertains to power, but neither pertains to freedom.

What pertains to freedom is this: that the consent of human choice cannot be coerced or impeded. A person can consent or not consent to divine inspiration in the same way that he can also consent or not consent to diabolical suggestions. Both arise from freedom, but neither ought to arise from necessity.[89] And so having freedom is not the same as possessing power. That one cannot be forced to will anything pertains to freedom; that one is not sufficient to do something good pertains to the privation of power. By sinning one could lose the power to merit, but, as was said above,[90] one will never be able to lose or lessen the freedom of choice by any sin or punishment, because he always had and will always have the freedom of choice.[91] Thus people have lost their power but not their freedom.

But, you ask, what sort of power? Hear what sort of power someone received, and you will understand what sort of power he lost: *You have subjected all things under his feet, all sheep and oxen and, moreover, the beast of the field, the birds of the sky, and the fishes of the sea that pass through the paths of the sea.*[92] Now do you want to see how this statement is reversed and how this power is diminished and removed? Notice how humans are now oppressed by those animals over which they used to rule: *The birds will devour them with a most bitter bite, and I will send the teeth of beasts upon them with the fury of creatures trailing upon the ground and serpents.*[93]

Chapter Fourteen. On the power of free choice before sin

Search, I ask, into the microcosm (for even man is so called);[94] search into the microcosm, that is, into a smaller world; search into the human heart for what is made in the image and likeness of God,[95] what is preferred above all else on account of the privilege of its dignity, and under whose feet everything else is subjected. I think you will find nothing other than free and rational consent, about which this may be better understood.[96] Why is it not correctly said that consent was made in the image and likeness of God?[97] Consent was made in the image of God insofar as it is free; it was made in the likeness of God insofar as it is rational.[98] Before transgression this consent had all things subjected to it and found no resistance in them, as long as it willingly subjected itself to its superior. It received from its inferiors the obedience it owed to its superior. Nothing that was in man opposed its command. It used to govern all things, manage all things, and rule all things. Nothing used to move against its will or apart from its will.

Every corporeal motion, every sense, every appetite, every affect, and every thought used to be moved, ordered, checked, and restrained at its command.[99] O how sublime was its power! How powerful was its sublimity! To rule over and have under its power the beasts of the land, the birds of the sky, and the fish of the sea! O the dignity of its sublimity! O the sublimity of its power! To possess justly under its choice, to order according to its will, and to incline toward the command of its authority the numerous flights of birds, roaming of beasts, swimming of fishes in so many pursuits, exercises, and delights of sublime investigations, multiple affects, and various delights.

CHAPTER FIFTEEN. ON THE PRIVATION OF THE FIRST POWER

The transgressor already lost this servitude of such great obedience because he disdained to give the reverence of servitude owed to his Creator. The zeal of the Creator takes armor and armed creation in revenge on his enemies,[100] and the whole world fights against the unwise on his behalf.[101] Already *the roaring lion roams about seeking whom he may devour*,[102] *the young lions are roaring after their prey*,[103] and the snake is raging *with the fury of creatures trailing upon the ground and of serpents*.[104] Do you want to know how, according to the word of the Lord, the birds with a most bitter bite are now devouring justly the transgressor on account of his transgression?[105] *My thoughts*, the Prophet said, *are dissipated and tormenting my heart*.[106] The Prophet was afraid of the teeth of beasts when he prayed to the Lord on account of them: *Save me from the lion's mouth and my lowness from the horns of the unicorns*.[107] He certainly knew that *anger kills a fool and envy slays a little one*.[108] How much the savagery of such beasts should be feared certainly could not escape his experience. Elsewhere he said: *My eyes have been disturbed by rage*.[109] But in a wonderful way based on the custom of human effort the same Prophet used to tame beasts for hunting and, after these beasts had been completely tamed, he used to hunt untamed beasts to the death: *I roared with the groaning of my heart*.[110] See how the roaring of his groaning suffocated the roaring of his previous rage. See what kind of opposition and rebellion a transgressor finds in a kingdom that he once possessed in peace and tranquility. He could, therefore, destroy the original power and lose the kingdom that he received, but he could never regain or retain it unless from the gift of him who is able to *raise the needy from the earth and to lift the poor out of the dunghill, so that he may sit with princes and hold the throne of* glory.[111] Indeed *the kingdom is the Lord's, and he will have dominion over the nations.*[112] He understood this who said: "This is your power and kingdom, Lord."[113] The Prophet also knew that the Lord is the ruler and in his hand are honor and authority and that he will give authority to him whom he wills.[114] Therefore, the Prophet humbly prays to him that he may restore his kingdom to him when he says: *Give your servant authority.*[115]

CHAPTER SIXTEEN. ON THE RESTORATION OF THE FIRST POWER

In his elect the King of Kings restores this kingdom daily, gradually, and partially, but he never restores it in this life to the same peace or security that man had in paradise before sin,[116] because the faintness of the head cannot be fully healed and free choice could never restore the vigor of its first state. And so, human free choice, which can do nothing good on its own, begins to have power at the time and to the extent that he, who can do all things, has willed it. *What is impossible with men is possible with God.*[117] Therefore, with the help of God human free choice begins to have power to do what it cannot do on its own; and the capacity for good that it now lacks by nature it receives through grace. Every day it increases in good, and everyday it is made stronger against evil. It increases in good so that he, who is in a position of power and has soldiers under him, can now say to this one: *Go, and he goes; and to another: Come, and he comes; and to his servant: Do this, and he does it.*[118] In the same way human free choice is also made stronger against evil so that *sin no longer reigns in its mortal body*[119] and often to such an extent that it now believes what was said to it: *Without your command no one will move hand or foot in all the land of Egypt.*[120] And how great do we think it is that human free choice can restrain all the rebellious motions of the soul and repress them from action, even though it is not yet able to eliminate all of them completely and restore its kingdom to full peace? Although it cannot eliminate all the adversaries of peace nor cut off all their hands and feet, it will still be great if none of them is permitted to move hand or foot without its command. A person who has such command can truly sing: *But I am appointed by him king over Zion, his holy mountain.*[121] Therefore, in the meantime the free consent of the will—the commander and lord of all the land, that is, numerous thoughts, affects, appetites, and senses— cannot remove every scandal from its kingdom[122] nor will it be able to establish full and continual peace. But *when the perfect will come and the partial will be purged*[123] and when the final death will be swallowed up in victory,[124] at that time his command will certainly be multiplied beyond measure and his peace will have no end.[125] Then, finally, *will he rule from sea to sea, and from the river unto the ends of the earth.*[126] *In those days Judah will be saved, and Israel will dwell in confidence,*[127] *because there is no one to terrify them.*[128]

CHAPTER SEVENTEEN. ON THE DISTURBANCE OF INTERNAL PEACE AND THE STRUGGLE OF VIRTUES WITH VICES

As long as *the flesh lusts against the spirit, and the spirit against the flesh,*[129] the king, who ought to command and preside over both spiritual and carnal desires, cannot find total peace and perpetual security. This is why the ruler of the people,[130] that is, the free consent of the soul, discovers in its kingdom so many oppositions, rebellions, struggles, altercations: thoughts are countering thoughts, affects are resisting affects, opposing motions are resisting opposing motions, *nation is rising against nation, and kingdom against kingdom,*[131] the good often rise up against the evil, the evil against the good, and, what is greater still, the evil rise up against the evil. They are divided against themselves,[132] and the Lord sets *the Egyptians to fight against the Egyptians.*[133] But what is more remarkable than all these, the good rise up against good. *A man fights against his brother, and a man fights against his friend, city against city, kingdom against kingdom;*[134] and *every man will eat the flesh of his arm: Manasses Ephraim, and Ephriam Manasses, together they will fight against Judah.*[135]

CHAPTER EIGHTEEN. HOW VICE OPPOSES VICE

Who does not know how serious the frequent conflict between greed and gluttony often is and how extensive their altercation is (I say this not with respect to wealth but about one single cent, since one vice desires to be spent what the other vice orders to be saved)?[136] In the same way pride is often at odds with lust, and one vice vehemently attacks another. Many times the evil of lust is held in check so that the proud mind may have a reason for boasting.[137] How many vices are there that obstinacy prohibits, yet vain glory commands and has power over! And in all these instances kingdom is divided against kingdom,[138] but one should be more astonished when a kingdom is divided against itself. Yet who does not know how often it takes place that pride resists pride, one pride gives way to another pride, and even the very overcoming of pride is proven to serve pride? We thus often throw off the clothing of pride and become even more proud on account of our poor garment. The height of honor is despised in such a way that the more we are secretly exulted about our contempt for honor the higher we are lifted up. But when you notice that *the Egyptians are fighting against the Egyptians* in this way,[139] do not be amazed or afraid but *know that its desolation is at hand.*[140] *Every kingdom divided against itself will be brought to desolation, and house will fall upon house.*[141] Therefore, *when you hear of wars, rebellions, and rumors of wars do not be afraid.*[142] He who comes from heaven is mighty in valor,[143] and the king is mighty and powerful in battle.[144] He does not come to send peace upon the earth but a sword, and he comes to divide father against son and son against his father,[145] and justly indeed because a good father often gives birth to an evil son and many times a good son has an evil father. When a mind is confounded and humbled by base delight and humility is generated from such a parent, rightly such a child is divided against such a father. Similarly since chastity begets pride, rightly such a parent detests and hates his child and divides himself against him. In this way a man often fights against his brother and man against his friend, and *a man's enemies will be in his own household.*[146]

Chapter Nineteen. How virtue opposes virtue

A conflict occurs among the disciples,[147] the good are fighting against the good, and great opposition and vehement dispute arise among them. This approaches the pinnacle of a great and intense wonder and points to some great marvel, namely, justice often speaks of one thing and mercy of another.[148] What is said by one virtue is opposed by the other, and a heated conflict occurs among these fellow-citizens of heaven. Mercy often orders the forgiveness of the same guilt that justice orders to be punished. Very rarely does justice allow its rigidity to be loosened, and mercy almost never endures something to be removed from its leniency. Justice orders all to be punished, and mercy strives to forgive all. Every virtue crosses the boundary of its property and tries to occupy the estate of another. Contrary to the precepts of divine sanction and the rule of discernment, the virtues do not allow the land to be divided among them by a line of distribution.[149] In this way then the good are often divided against the good. Some of the good rise up against others, and the kingdom of Israel is split into two parts.[150] Battles and rebellions often stir up among them, and in this life secure peace and complete rest are never found in any condition or progress.

But what, I ask, is the reason for these various altercations and endless conflicts in the human heart unless the faintness of the head, the loss of original virtue, and the privation of the former power? Every head remains faint up to today,[151] and, although human choice is truly free, it nevertheless continues to be sick and cannot be completely healed until this mortal will have put on immortality and this corruptible will have put on incorruption.[152] How does our interior man not have a faint head that can never either lift itself up even a little or support itself for a short time, even when it was supported by the hand of divine aid? For a faint head rises to the good only with the hand of another, and it immediately falls back on itself or even under itself when the supporting hand is taken away.

CHAPTER TWENTY. ON NATURE AND GRACE

Surely, you ask, it was possible for man to do some good by himself even before sin and while he was still in paradise? However, what did he possess that he did not receive?[153] He certainly possessed nothing that he did not receive, and he absolutely could not do anything unless he accomplished it by means of and in accordance with what he received.[154] He could do some things by nature and other things by grace. The goods of nature are different from the gifts of grace,[155] yet both of these goods obviously derive from grace because nature itself certainly derives from grace. And so the first good comes from prevenient grace and the second from subsequent grace.[156] We can correctly call grace "prevenient" and "subsequent," yet the former is first grace and the latter second grace. But custom attributes the name they have in common specifically to one of them, restricts its meaning to just one of them, and in its usage calls the second grace "grace." We call the first grace "nature" rather than "grace." Therefore, when we say that man before sin had the ability to do some good on his own, we only mean that he could do this through the natural good. Likewise, when we say that man cannot do some good on his own, we mean that he no longer has the ability to do any good through the natural good alone.

But surely we are not saying that man could not do some good by nature (i.e., through first grace) before nature was corrupted? If he did receive the ability to do some good from the nature of his creation, then this was precisely what he lost by sinning. However, he lost the power not the freedom.[157] The power to do the good is truly a power, just as the inability to be coerced is truly a freedom. If man could be coerced by another to do good or evil, then he would no longer be free at all. And if he were able to do the good and refuse evil, then not only would he be free but also able. But even if we deny that man before sin had the ability to do some good without added grace, then we still cannot deny that sin destroyed the not insignificant ability of doing the good. He truly could do what he was capable of through grace, and that he was capable of great things through grace was a great capability.

CHAPTER TWENTY-ONE. ON THE FULLNESS OF GRACE BEFORE SIN

Pay attention to what kind of grace humans received and how much they could accomplish through it, and then you will understand what sort of power they lost. Without a doubt and without any contradiction, before sin they possessed grace sufficient not for doing all good but for absolving every debt and avoiding every evil.[158] How great was this power of doing good and avoiding evil, I ask, that people possessed through cooperative grace?[159] Who can boast that he has restored the fullness of this power, or who can presume that he has recovered it in this life? Who, I ask, boasts in accomplishing everything that is necessary or in avoiding everything that is unlawful?[160] When, I ask, will every debt be absolved by those who, according to the insight of Job, *cannot pay back one for a thousand*?[161] But we also understand this because *we have offended everyone in many ways,*[162] and *if we say that we have no sin, then we deceives ourselves and the truth is not in us.*[163]

Grace can be restored but freely. People can grow daily in this restored grace but they still cannot recover the fullness of the first power.[164] If they can recover a greater grace to some extent, they still will not be able to possess the fullness of it in this life. A boy once maimed can have a larger body, but he can never have a whole body. If people were competent enough to absolve every debt and avoid every evil, then they would truly have the fullness of grace. But, according to the insight of Solomon, *there is no one on earth who is righteous and does not sin.*[165] Thus, people cannot recover the fullness of grace, nor after the evil of their corruption can they advance to the fullness of the first power, because the head is faint and its infirmity does not receive a full cure.

CHAPTER TWENTY-TWO. ON THE STABILITY OF GRACE BEFORE SIN

I want to add here that the grace that humans received once before sin could not be taken away justly. Even if they had received grace beyond merit, they still would not be able to lose it without guilt. But today grace can be taken away justly at any moment because people can never be found without guilt.[166] As they cannot recover grace once lost by themselves, so once restored by grace they cannot even preserve it without the support of another. Therefore, notice how much difference lies between the first and second states, namely, between the first state that existed before sin and the second that existed after the fall of humanity. In the first state humans had a full and stable grace, but now grace is neither full nor stable. However, in the future life, after death will have been swallowed up in victory,[167] people will have not only a stable grace but an irremovable one as well.[168] They had a stable grace before sin because they could always preserve it once received, but they clearly did not have an irremovable grace given that it was lost afterwards. But they will possess it permanently at that time when they can no longer lose it. But as long as we live a mortal life now in this body of sin,[169] we cannot have a stable grace, not to mention an irremovable grace. Grace is often offered freely to those of us who are negligent and torpid, and it is often removed suddenly and unexpectedly from those of us who have many great undertakings. Therefore, as long as we are unable to restore this lost grace back to its former integrity and stability, we do not restore the power of the mind back to the strength of its former vigor, nor do we fully recover the power of the first ability for good. For the most part we inevitably endure faintness of the head however much we advance in virtue.

Weakness thus remains along with freedom and freedom along with weakness to such an extent that neither is detrimental to the other—neither weakness to freedom, nor freedom to weakness—, because weakness does not diminish freedom, nor does freedom remove weakness.[170] When you read or hear then that free choice is held captive,[171] take it to mean only this: free choice is weak and deprived of the strength of its original power. This is what the Prophet, who described this with a faint head, suggests to us. Otherwise, those people contradict themselves with opposing assertions when they call human choice "free" and also affirm its captivity. But maybe those who affirm its captivity intend their assertion to be understood in this way: human choice is partly free and partly held captive. But who does not know that if

I had a thousand lords and one of them were still ruling while all the others freed me, I would still have a lord and could not rightly be called free. Clearly then human choice cannot be called free if it has lost even part of its freedom.

CHAPTER TWENTY-THREE. ON THE THREE GRADES OF FREEDOM AND THAT HUMANITY HAS SUPREME FREEDOM[172]

If we pay careful attention, I think that we will find that humanity has not just freedom but great freedom, or rather supreme freedom. The first grade of freedom is being subjected to no compulsion, the second is the obligation of being subjected to no compulsion, and the third and highest is the ability to be subject to absolutely no compulsion at all. Therefore, how is it that human choice is not truly or supremely free given that no force or power can deprive it of its freedom? No creature can do this, and it is not fitting for the Creator to do it. How can the Creator do this, given that he can do nothing that is unfitting? If then no force can deprive human choice of its freedom, it clearly has supreme freedom. Nevertheless, as it was previously demonstrated,[173] the will opposes will, and the will resists the will. One will attacks another, and one will after another is taken captive. But in the struggle of this dispute just as the will is both the assailant and victim, so it is both the conqueror and conquered. The will still remains intact in all of this because it always triumphs. And so this freedom of choice is not greater in the good or less in the evil because it is neither diminished through sin nor augmented though merit. It maintains above all the supreme grade of freedom; it cannot grow inasmuch as it cannot decrease. But just as you should marvel at the inability of free choice to be coerced by another, so you should be absolutely horrified at the inactivity of its weakness toward all good. Therefore, because nothing among the natural goods in the interior man is more dignified and sublime than this freedom, it is rightly described as the head. And because every person lives and dies with this allotted infirmity, it is properly associated with feebleness.

CHAPTER TWENTY-FOUR. ON THE IGNORANCE OF GOOD AND EVIL

Every head is faint, the Prophet said, *and every heart mourns.*[174] This is certainly correct as long as every head is actually faint and every heart also mourns. The ache of the head is a sufficient cause of aching. If we have a heart, if we are not entirely without understanding, and if we are not destitute of every counsel, then we cannot, nor should we, conceal such great evil. As it was discussed, if counsel should be correctly understood by the word "heart,"[175] then people who have such a heart cannot be devoid of sorrow because the evil that they see in themselves is not sustained without sorrow. Indeed, the better they realize this and the more deliberately they act, then the more deeply they mourn. A person who increases knowledge also increases sorrow.[176] Our sorrow ought both to squeeze us very tightly on the inside and to manifest itself on the outside: inwardly in relation to a remedy and outwardly in relation to example. For, as previously discussed, grief is sorrow churning very intensely on the inside and erupting on the outside through tears. If then we are not like the *dove which was seduced and does not have a heart*,[177] and if we do not lack counsel and prudence, then let us demonstrate in our action how much we truly grieve in our hearts, and let what we suffer internally manifest itself externally.

So that I may relate my own thoughts on this matter, I think that the Prophet indicated the cause for the effect in this verse, although I think he subtly hinted at the effect from the cause when he said: *every heart mourns*. Whenever we find a cause used for an effect, we need to investigate what results from that which is indicated by the interpretation or definition rather than what it is. In light of this consideration, what else is mourning other than the outpouring of tears and blurriness of vision? A constant outpouring of tears obstructs the eye's sharpness of vision and quickly causes loss of sight. The Prophet then correctly said, *every heart mourns*, because the sharpness of reason becomes dulled to every counsel. This is the reason for the teaching or precept of Wisdom: *Do not rely on your own wisdom*,[178] because *people do not know what is profitable for themselves in this life: in the days of their pilgrimage and in the time that passes like a shadow*.[179] If the interior eye were not blinded, then it would undoubtedly never err at all in the judgment of truth. What, I ask, is the cause of so frequent contrary counsels and so diverse opinions (I am not talking about the opinions of diverse hearts but one and the same heart and nearly at the same time)? What, I ask, is the reason for this, unless the blindness of our hearts and the obscurity of truth?

Chapter Twenty-Five. On the twofold error of judgment

We sin in two ways in the examination of our judgment when we often make our way in the foggy conditions of such great ambiguity. Sometimes we err in discerning quality and sometimes in the examination of quantity. The person who calls good evil or evil good errs in the quality of things, and the person who regards the greater as less and the less as greater errs in quantity.[180] The quality of actions had certainly deceived the people whom the Prophet censured when he said: *Woe to you who call evil good and good evil, who regard darkness as light and light as darkness, and who describe something bitter as sweet and something sweet as bitter.*[181] An error in the judgment of quantity is found in the person whom the Prophet refuted when he said: *The sons of men are liars in the scales so that they may together deceive by vanity.*[182] Obviously something is weighed on the scales, so that a person may not be ignorant of its quantity. We seek the weight of gold and silver in this way so that we may accurately determine its value. But no one would be a liar in the scales if no one was deceiving and no one was deceived. This is the reason for the words of Wisdom: *Deceitful scales and differing weights are an abomination before the Lord.*[183] Against this practice it is commanded in the Law: *Let your bushel be just and the sextary equal.*[184] This is also why the sons of Israel, when they received their promised inheritance, divided among themselves their land by a line of right distribution,[185] so that every virtue may maintain a measure of lawful equality in its action and not exceed at all the boundaries of discernment.[186] Who can show me a person who never erred in the determination of quality or quantity and who is never beset *by the business which walks about in the dark*?[187] The most honest businessman is one who is unable to be deceived and never wants to deceive in determining the quality and quantity of things. But when would a person be capable of this while enveloped in darkness and dwelling *in the region of the shadow of death*?[188] As long as the darkness is upon the face of the abyss,[189] this is obviously impossible for any person until he, who told the light to shine out from the darkness and who emitted his light and truth,[190] begins to divide the light from the darkness,[191] and there is evening and morning.[192] After an understanding of truth is emitted and received, a person immediately begins to divide the light from darkness and to discern at first the good from the bad and the bad from the good, and later the good from the better and the bad from the worse, and finally the better from the best and the worse from the worst. In this way, according to the insight of Wisdom, *the path of the righteous goes forth like light and increases even up to full day;*[193] and what is said is fulfilled: *And he will lead your justice as the light and your judgment as the noonday.*[194] The light once received gradually proceeds and grows up to full daylight, when the understanding of truth once received gradually advances and whenever it arrives at the fullness of discernment. *One*, the Apostle said, *judges between day and day, and another judges every day.*[195] What sort of gift of God do you think it is to give to him who is the Son of man [the power] to make judgment?[196] And this is indeed the first step, that a person may know how to judge between day and night, but the last and highest step is that a person may know how to judge every day. And so we need to ascend up certain sure steps of knowledge if we desire to reach the highest peak of ascent from the lowest point.

Chapter Twenty-Six. On the five grades of discernment

The first grade, as we already stated,[197] is to judge between day and night, the second is to judge between night and night, the third is to judge between day and day, the fourth is to judge all nights, and the fifth is to judge all days.[198] We judge between day and night when we distinguish the good from the bad. A person judges between night and night who knows how to distinguish the worse from the bad and the worst from the worse. Judging between day and day is to choose the better from the good and the best from the better. A person discerns all nights who evaluates each of the vices with a proper examination. Judging all days is to assess each virtue in accordance with its dignity.

Now let whoever merited to acquire these five talents of true discernment and profitable knowledge from the Lord's abundance strive to be productive with them and earn another five talents,[199] so that the image of truth, which was infused into their cognition by inspiring grace, may also be infused into their affect by human endeavor and cooperating grace.[200] Otherwise, it is better for them to have been unaware of the rule of truth than to despise it after learning of it.[201] Therefore, we earn a respectable profit from these acquired talents and, as it were, gain another five talents from them,[202] if we strive to form the quality of our affect in accordance with the rule of a learned discernment. Let us then strive to love what we know ought to be loved, and let us not love at all what is not worthy our love. But we should not be satisfied with the ascent to this first grade of virtue without also ascending to the second grade and to the third grade from the second. Let us then pursue with greater hatred what is worse among the evil, let us embrace with a deeper love what is better among the good, and let us be glad to have ascended to the third grade of virtue through the second. We can certainly love less what is less and love more what is better, but we absolutely cannot maintain the proper measure in either of these loves.[203] Likewise, it often happens that we also sin by a similar ignorance in reproving contrarieties. Let us strive then to ascend to the fifth grade through the fourth so that we may know how to preserve the proper measure of hate and love in all evil and good.

CHAPTER TWENTY-SEVEN. THE GRACE OF DISCERNMENT IS SOMETIMES GIVEN AND SOMETIMES REMOVED

Maybe you wonder how the aforementioned prophetic teaching agrees with this apostolic assertion.[204] How is it correct to say that every heart mourns and is blinded by the mourning, if there are people who can judge all days? Perhaps both are correct. After all, the Prophet did say that every heart mourns, but he did not say that every heart mourns all the time. There is *a time to weep and a time to laugh*[205] since indeed *weeping will linger until evening and happiness until morning.*[206] Evening is the time of sadness, and morning is the time of happiness. The former is the time of weeping, and the latter the time of laughing. The time of darkness is the time of mourning, and the time of light is the time of exultation. He knows this who said: *What sort of joy can I have who sit in darkness and see not the light of heaven?*[207] Why else then does every heart mourn unless because no heart has everlasting day in this life since it is not able to have the light of heaven present at all times? *The sun rises and sets, and it returns to its place,*[208] because the understanding of truth is sometimes given and sometimes removed, and after its removal the same grace as before is restored again.

As long as every heart sustains the necessary darkness of such alternating vicissitudes, what wonder is it then if every heart mourns? As long as we live on this earth, as long as we are on it, we necessarily sustain the vicissitudes of the times. In heaven there is day without night, and in hell there is night without day; on earth there is neither night without day nor day without night. And so in heaven there is joy without distress, and in hell there is sorrow without consolation; on earth there is neither sorrow without hope nor joy without fear. The place of unending laughter lies at top, and the place of unending weeping lies at the bottom; the time of laughing and of weeping lies in the middle. For *laughter will be mixed with sorrow, and mourning occupies the end of joy*.[209] Therefore, every heart needs to grieve and mourn until it completely escapes its darkness and *holds the seat of glory*,[210] and *its throne becomes as the day of heaven*.[211] What wonder is it then if a person is said to mourn who can judge all days given that he cannot always have the day?

Chapter Twenty-Eight. On the two grades of deliberation

If we reflect even more carefully on the nature of judgment and counsel, then we will find that counsel often wavers even when judgment stands firm and that judgment often considers an issue clearly even when counsel is clouded. Let us, as we said previously,[212] understand counsel here as heart. See then whether counsel can be clouded even when judgment was certain, so that the statement *every heart mourns* is true in spite of the fact that there are those who judge all days.[213]

Discussing what is good or evil in itself is different from deciding what is expedient or not expedient for someone. The first pertains to judgment, and the latter to counsel.[214] Just as all people cannot do all things, so *all things are not expedient for all people*.[215] What is the greater good in itself is often less expedient for some people, and what is the lesser good in itself is more expedient for other people. For it often happens that what is the height of damnation for some people is an occasion of salvation for other people; and what is the increase of crown for some people is the cause of ruin for other people. How many people do we see who were accustomed to or were able to stand firmly in a lower position but have fallen violently from a high position.[216] How many people do we see who used to walk idly and fall often on the plain of secular life but have now planted their feet firmly on the ascent of virtues and the advance of religion and hasten quickly on it. For that reason, a person *does not know what is profitable for himself in this life: in the days of his pilgrimage and in the time that passes like a shadow*.[217] This is certainly the reason why every heart mourns and the eye of counsel is blinded even in the person who judges all days.[218]

Do you finally wish to know clearly how many things judgment can accomplish that counsel cannot achieve at all? How many things, I ask, do we encounter that we confidently dare to affirm without doubt to be good, and how many countless things do we also encounter that we do not doubt to be truly bad? Find me just one person who can show me one thing that cannot become a cause of evil for someone. What, I ask, is so good that it cannot become an occasion for a fall, or what is so bad that it cannot be a reminder of precaution? Notice how every heart hesitates at every counsel, and how every counsel is blinded toward all foresight. As a result, the statement, *every heart mourns*, must be true in order to signify from that mourning the darkness it sustains. You certainly understand that it is easier to judge what is lawful or unlawful than to decide what is expedient or inexpedient. The first pertains to discernment, and the latter to deliberation; the first pertains to judgment, and the latter to counsel.[219]

The first knowledge is very different from the second; the talents of the first cognition are different from the talents of the second. Both are rare, both are precious, yet the second is much rarer than the first. And, though rare, they are still talents. For who would deny that from divine inspiration many people know how not only to determine what is useful but also to distinguish what is more useful from what is useful? And this is true even when they cannot be capable of all things and cannot wisely discern what is more expedient, what is less expedient, and what is not expedient at all. You thus know that you have received two very precious talents from the Lord's commission when you began to distinguish correctly between what is useful and not useful and from among what is useful to determine what is more useful than the others. When you have received these two talents of deliberation from the Lord's abundance, strive to be productive with them and profit from them so that you may externally express in your labor what was internally impressed in your cognition and, gaining two talents from two talents, you may be able to bring back a doubling of talents for the Lord's profits.

CHAPTER TWENTY-NINE. ON THE NORMS OF DISCERNMENT AND DELIBERATION, AND WHAT ARE TALENTS AND HOW ARE THEY INCREASED

You should notice that the first five talents [of discernment] should increase and multiply in the affect, and the [two] talents [of deliberation] should increase and multiply in action.[220] What was once impressed on the cognition as a result of the discernment of judgment needs to be carefully impressed afterwards in the affection as well. Let what was preformed in the cognition as a result of the deliberation of counsel be reformed in action according to the same rule of prudence. According to the earlier rule of prudence, we ought to love more the greater good; however, we should not do the same in practice, because the greater good is often impossible or less profitable. But, as we learn from the second rule of prudence, a person ought to do more in practice what is more expedient; however, what cannot be practiced or is not expedient is often better. Let us strive then to love more what is better but in such a way that we know when it is expedient to practice it less. Also let us practice more what is more expedient but less good in such a way that we love more what is less expedient but judged to be better. In this way the one and the same Lord gives some people five talents in the discernment of judgment, but he gives other people two talents in the deliberation of counsel.

CHAPTER THIRTY. WHY DOES DELIBERATION NOT HAVE FIVE GRADES JUST AS DISCERNMENT DOES?

Perhaps you are wondering why I did not indicate the five talents here with regard to the deliberation of counsel as I did before with regard to the discernment of judgment, when I could have done so.[221] But look more carefully and you will discover more quickly that of the three other talents one will be unprofitable to seek, the another will be impossible to own, and a third will be both unprofitable to seek and impossible to own.

[First,] among the talents that are clearly unprofitable, what profit is there in seeking and investigating which of them are more worthless? Obviously all of them should be removed from our considerations. And yet with the discernment of judgment we seek the worse from among the bad so that we may know what needs to be punished more and less, lest if we punish them less than they deserve now, then we leave them to be punished in the last day. [Second,] no one, I think, can comprehend the nature and extent of the benefit that each of the talents that are expedient bestows, nor has anyone ever received this talent of knowledge in this life, even though many people, inspired by the Lord, certainly distinguish what is unprofitable and choose what is more profitable. [Third,] among the talents that are unprofitable and not expedient at all, seeking and determining the property of each will be unprofitable and impossible, as it is clear from the previous two categories.

When we receive such talents from the Lord's abundance, the more mindful we are that we posses them because of another's gift, the more diligent we need to be productive with them so that we may return them to him with a profit. And so, whenever someone makes a right judgment or deliberates what is profitable, let him not attribute this to himself.

CHAPTER THIRTY-ONE. WE DO NOT ALWAYS HAVE PRESENT ILLUMINATING GRACE, AND WE NEVER HAVE PRESENT SUFFICIENT GRACE

Even one who has already merited the reception of such talents should not be so secure as if he cannot be deceived any longer. Just as only he, whom divine grace inspires and inspiration illumines, wisely discerns and prudently takes counsel for himself, so he can effectively achieve both only when inspiring grace is present. But who has, or can have, grace present at every moment in this life? *You visit him,* Job said, *at dawn and you suddenly test him.*[222] If [the Psalmist], who is distinguished among the prophets, had the light of divine revelation always present, then he certainly would not have proclaimed to the Lord: *Illumine my eyes;*[223] and: *Send forth your light and truth.*[224] And so, the divine ray of internal inspiration is sometimes poured forth and sometimes removed. For *darkness was set in place, and it became night: in it all the beasts of the woods will roam about.*[225] But at the command of the Lord *the sun rises again, and they are gathered together, and they will be assembled in their dens.*[226] Thus the sun sets and rises again,[227] and morning and evening result in a *time for weeping and a time laughing,*[228] because *weeping will linger until evening and happiness until morning.*[229] What wonder is it then if every heart mourns, because it cannot always have present the divine light, without which it perceives nothing clearly and discerns nothing rightly?

I dare say something more that no one, I think, dares to deny: even if people were to have grace present at all times, they still would not avoid the causes of mourning. In this sense people never actually have sufficient grace in this life, although they still have grace present at times. We can in fact make the same argument about the discernment of judgment as our previous discussion on free choice.[230] Just as in this life we never have grace sufficient for doing good, so we can never have grace sufficient for discerning truth.

Notice now, I ask, how great is the multitude of innumerable good things from the height of creation to its lowest part. Find me just one person among all of humanity who fully comprehends one of these good things and who dares say with certainty and affirm as truth that this is worth just so much, not more, not less, and that it is to be loved just so much, not more, not less. Even the person, who is said to judge all days,[231] cannot presume this, so that you should rightly wonder how someone can judge all days who can comprehend nothing completely. See how much darkness of uncertainty the human heart sustains, and how much of it it has to sustain as long as one is living in this life. Consequently, it was rightly said: *Every heart mourns*. Every heart certainly mourns on account of the darkness of mind, and it is darkened on account of the mourning of the mind. The more the heart mourns, the dimmer it becomes; and the dimmer it becomes, the more vehemently it mourns, because it becomes dim on account of the mourning, and it renews its mourning on account of its dimness.

We have made some observations above on the infirmity of free choice by discussing the faintness of the head,[232] and now we have learned here about the ambiguity of counsel by discussing the mourning of the heart. It still remains to hear and understand something about the unrest of desire by discussing the infirmity of the body.

CHAPTER THIRTY-TWO. ON THE DESIRE FOR EVIL

From the sole of the foot, the Prophet said, *up to the crown of the head, there is no soundness therein.*[233] As I said, I understand the carnal desire through the word "foot" and free choice through the word "head."[234] The sole is the bottom of the foot, and the crown is the top of the head. What is lower than that which is related to necessity, and what stands out higher than what is related to power? And so the sole of the foot is the necessity of lowest desire, and the crown of the head is the power of free choice. The sole of the foot is the necessity of concupiscence, and the crown of the head is volitional power (*potestas votiva*). The necessity of concupiscence pertains to the foot, but the capability of working pertains to the crown. The bottom of the foot is the necessity of desiring evil, and the top of the head is the capability of doing good. I am referring here to the good as a benefit and not as a merit. Merit pertains to health and not infirmity and should not be discussed in reference to such a crown: *From the sole of the foot up to the crown of the head, there is no soundness therein*. One could do so here, if perhaps the phrase "up to" is exclusive and not inclusive and only the "crown" is excluded from the law of the other members. But if only a person would have true good in power just as he truly has genuine evil in necessity!

CHAPTER THIRTY-THREE. THE WHOLE OF A HUMAN IS SUBJECT TO INFIRMITY

There is a good that pertains to merit, another good that pertains to guilt, and another kind of good that pertains neither to merit or guilt.[235] The good that pertains to guilt is more accurately called "evil" than "good," although those who freely engage in evil refer to it and love it as if it is good. But the good that does not pertain to merit or guilt is more accurately designated as "advantage." People have many such goods not only in freedom but very often in power as well, just as they often have many of the goods that pertain to guilt not only in the will but also in necessity. But people do not have any of the good that pertains to merit in free choice without divine aid. Concerning the difficulty of that good that pertains to merit, Jesus said: *Without me you can do nothing;*[236] concerning the capability of doing that good which does not pertain to merit or guilt, Jesus said: *If you know how to give good gifts to your children, even though you are evil, then how much more will your Father from heaven give the good Spirit to them that ask him!*[237] Concerning the necessity of that good which pertains to guilt, we read: *The evil which I do not desire, that I do.*[238]

Among these three kinds of good which we have distinguished, you can have one in power, a second in freedom, a third in the will, and a fourth in necessity. The good in power is what can be accomplished or neglected on account of the choice of the will. We have the good in freedom toward which we cannot be coerced by an alien force. And the good in the will is what you want to happen even if you cannot actually do it. And you have the good in necessity in regard to what you cannot resist even when you want to resist it.[239]

We are now able to bring together and join one after the other these four grades of distinctions, to distinguish the body of our interior man by its many members, and to order the manner of our examination upwards from the bottom of the foot or downwards from top of the head. But, not to linger too long on this matter, let us consider what the Prophet said here about such a body and what we should not overlook: *From the sole of the foot*, the Prophet said, *up to the crown of the*

head, there is no soundness therein.[240] If only the good that is capable
of merit pertains to soundness, then all that belongs to humans is subjected to infirmity because what is in power is incapable of merit, what
is in necessity is full of vice, and what is in the will and in freedom is
subject to both detriments. Therefore, *from the sole of the foot up to the
crown of the head, there is no soundness therein.* How does that which
has no value as merit, which is worthless in the judgment of retribution, and which cannot aid in the actual good—or rather what makes
people guilty and renders them liable to punishment because of genuine evil—pertain to good health? Therefore, *from the sole of the foot up
to the crown of the head, there is no soundness therein.* From the head
up to its crown infirmity seizes the whole body because power does not
expel necessity, does not satisfy the will, and does not liberate freedom
but entangles it even more. The more a person is capable of, the more
there is for which he must render an account. And so infirmity has
seized the whole body, and *from the sole of the foot up to the crown of
the head, there is no soundness therein.*

CHAPTER THIRTY-FOUR. HOW DISORDERED AFFECT IS OR HOW
UNRESTRAINED IT IS

Consider at length this analogy of our spiritual infirmity if you want
to understand it more fully. Surely you are listening to the names of the
members of the exterior man so that you may learn from what is known
what you do not know about the state of the interior man. Consider
then the nature and cause of the infirmity of the exterior man, and you
will see what you should think about spiritual infirmity. Just as we already discussed above,[241] the soundness of a body is the natural integrity of its temperament and the proportional symmetry of all the
humors. The infirmity of a body is the privation of that soundness and
corruption of that integrity. There are four humors from which every
body is composed, vegetated, regulated, nourished, and preserved.[242]
All of these humors coincide in every body according to a single law
under a fixed but dissimilar proportion in dissimilar bodies, and they
constitute different temperaments in different bodies. And so suitable
order and balanced measure need to be in every body according to the
capacity of nature, so that, as it was discussed, there may be proportional symmetry in them. And the body endures in its soundness as
long as each humor occupies its own proper place and preserves the
limit suitable to it.

Now what the four humors are in the body, the four principal affects are in the heart; and what sense (*sensus*) is in the flesh, understanding is in the mind. Common usage even allows "the sense (*sensum*) of the heart" to be utilized in the same way as "the sense (*sensum*) of the body," which is why we usually say that sentiment (*sententiam*) derives from the sense of the heart and not of the body. And so the four principal affects are love, hate, joy, and sorrow.[243] From these four affects all the other longings, desires, wishes, and affects draw their origin. Therefore, notice how many things we love or hate that we should not have loved or hated at all or very little. Notice also how many things that give rise to our disordered or immoderate joy or sorrow. And, just like the humors in the body, these affects in the heart generate various infirmities insofar as they disturb balanced order and measure. We have already noted above how dull the sense of the heart is.[244] Now let us see how sick the affect of the heart is.

Show me therefore just one object toward which you restrain your affect in a fixed and proper measure in such a way that you absolutely should not extend toward it any more, less or other than that measure. But how will the mind restrain its affect toward just one single object or according to the perfect law of equity as long as the intellect cannot understand fully any thing or determine the measure of its own dignity with a perfect definition? How can the mind become what it cannot know? If the fixed measure of a full and perfect love or any other affect is unknown, then how can its measure that cannot be known be preserved? And so if the affect of the mind is disordered in many things and entirely immoderate in all things according to the highest standard of equity, then you should not doubt or be amazed when you read: *From the sole of the foot up to the crown of the head, there is no soundness therein.*[245] We are deceived in our estimation at every hour and nearly at every moment; and, with the reins of equity having been torn asunder, we are unbridled in our desires. At no time is the standard and fixed measure preserved while the mind is always driven in different directions like a whirlwind by carnal impulse. *From the sole of the foot up to the crown of the head, there is no soundness therein.*[246] A happy time and awaited hour will come when our thinking is no longer deceived in its examination, when our affect is not unbridled in its desire. In the meantime we cannot achieve with our thoughts integrity of knowledge and perfection of virtue, nor can we preserve them with any effort of our mind.

CHAPTER THIRTY-FIVE. HOW A PERSON IS BROUGHT TO THE PROPER MEASURE OF INTEGRITY

This is the fullness of the promised denarius and the integrity of the true and supreme perfection that is promised to those working in the Lord's vineyard, but it is not bestowed until the end of the day after the work is finished.[247] The Lord's vineyard is the human conscience. This is the Lord's chosen vineyard in which he planted every true seed.[248] To cultivate this vineyard the Lord comes forth when he causes his will to become known through internal inspiration. The going forth of the Lord is his revelation. The repetition of this going forth is the increase of knowledge. The going forth multiple times is the revelation taking many shapes. The different hours are the various steps of progress. And so the Lord goes forth according to the progression of the day and the succession of the hours, because divine knowledge is augmented according to the advance of perfection and the promotion of virtues.

The cultivators of the vineyard are the thoughts and affects. Such cultivators have to work toward the cultivation of the vineyard because both need to work up a sweat in cleansing the conscience. The first cultivators need to work in investigating the truth and the second cultivators in practicing virtues. To dig deep and penetrate hidden mysteries pertains to the first cultivators, but to prune the excess of the branches and cut away the unprofitable habits pertains to the second cultivators. The labor of the first cultivators is the correction of errors, and the labor of the second cultivators is the pruning of vices. Those who labor in the vineyard and work up a sweat in cultivating it are brought in at different hours: daybreak, the third hour, the sixth hour, the ninth hour, and the eleventh hour. The light first begins to appear at daybreak. The day usually grows warm at the third hour and becomes hot at the sixth hour. At the ninth hour the sun clearly moves lower in the horizon and tempers the heat, and at the eleventh hour the heat gradually fades away with the light. What is the dawn of light unless the illumination of truth, and what is the beginning of heat unless the reception of goodness? The intensity of heat is the fervor of love, and the moderation of the heat is the detestation of vanity. But what else is the disappearance of heat and light other than the restraining of lust or even the dimness of carnal wisdom? And so the discernment of good and evil occurs at daybreak, the desire for genuine good occurs at the third hour, the desire for the supreme good at noon, the loathing of false good at the ninth hour, and the hatred or even oblivion of genuine evil occurs at the eleventh hour. Intellect is illuminated in the morning, consent is corrected at the third hour, affect is inflamed at the sixth hour, sense (*sensus*) of the body is restrained or even dulled at the ninth hour, and carnal appetite is cooled at the eleventh hour. Indeed if the sense of the body is not restrained from its own deviation, then the restlessness of the carnal appetite is not extinguished. But when the sense of the body is forcefully subdued by the vigor of abstinence and violently restrained with the rigor of discipline, then it begins to delight less and less in its usual pleasures and become more and more subdued with respect to its former delights. Now quenching of the appetites necessarily follows the dullness of the senses. The more human appetites and senses are restrained according to the measure of equity, the more quickly the denarius of retribution and the form of perfection are secured and draw near to the fullness of integrity. After all, for all to receive a denarius at the final hour is nothing other than to possess the form of perfection in all our senses in the end.

CHAPTER THIRTY-SIX. BY MEANS OF WHAT STEPS DO WE ADVANCE TO THE FULLNESS OF INTEGRITY?

The very first step is to seek counsel and, once found, to correct the will, and then to inflame the mind for the desire of heavenly things by practicing virtues. But, after the desire for eternal things, we should also curb our senses from what is lawful, so that we may be able to subdue our appetite for what is unlawful or, as much as possible, to extinguish it completely. Who can doubt that all these steps work together in the cultivation of the spiritual vineyard: rectitude of counsels, correction of the will, increased intensity of the desires for heavenly things, restrained senses, and subdued appetites?

Notice that the later the cultivators of the Lord's vineyard arrived, the less they worked. For the later the day of our progress grows, the practicing of virtues becomes more and more sweet; and the more the appetite of our desires is subdued, the weight of the day and heat is felt less and less. The more our love grows, the more our labor decreases. Indeed, the yoke and burden which seem intolerable at first become sweet and light through love.[249] You should also know that the more time we spend in the day of our progress and the closer we draw near to its end, then the purer and more perfect are our desires and wishes. That is why those workers who arrived later receive their denarius first because, with regard to those making progress, the things which come later always come closer to perfect integrity. The order of reward is begun with the last workers because, before a person is glorified in the other senses, the kindling for sin that rules principally over the appetite is first removed and the appetite is restrained according to the proper standard and measure of equity and is endowed with the denarius of integrity. Just as the will is never corrected without good counsel and the sense or appetite is never restrained and corrected without a corrected will, so it undoubtedly happens in the reverse order that the vice of appetites or of the senses is destroyed before the good will is ordered toward true peace. Our thinking always has something that it ought to accuse as long as the will finds a reason for being ashamed.

Now every cultivator of the vineyard, who perseveres in its cultivation, receives his denarius in the evening. What is evening unless the end of the day, the end of work, the hour of rest, and the time of retribution? All the workers receive their denarius in the evening because, after the end of work and at the time of reward, every human sensation is raised to the integrity of perfection, just as it was discussed.[250] Therefore, one and the same time is the end of our labor and the beginning of rest, the end of work and hour of our reward. For the work of cultivation is never finished and the restlessness of our conscience is never quenched except when the progress of our soul is brought to the end of perfection.

CHAPTER THIRTY-SEVEN. THE SAME FORM OF PERFECTION WILL RESIDE IN OUR THINKING AND AFFECT

What does it mean that one and the same measure of reward is paid to every worker? Nothing is increased for the first workers, and nothing is reduced for the last workers.[251] Who does not know that correct counsels in the cultivation of the vineyard precede both correct desires and correct labors? Whatever is desired or done without counsel does not work together for the cultivation of the vineyard but for its detriment. Thus, the labor of knowledge is in the vineyard before the labor of affect. As long as we live in this life, as long as we labor in the vineyard, there is certainly more that we can attain of the fullness of perfection by knowledge than what meanwhile we can impress fully on the affect and fulfill in action. Who can accomplish everything that he knows to be obligatory or proper? But when the time of reward has arrived, when the denarius of perfection will be paid to the Lord's workers as their reward, then nothing more will reside in counsel than in the desire, and nothing less will reside in affect than in knowledge. Without a doubt, after the reward is received, everyone will be able to accomplish and fulfill everything that they know to be obligatory or proper. The same form of perfection that will be in knowledge will absolutely and altogether be in love as well. Thus, the last workers receive the same denarius that the first workers also merited to receive.

But who are these workers who are first brought into the vineyard but paid last and who received this rebuke: *Take what is yours and go. Or is your eye evil because I am good*?[252] What sort of person would pant for the cleanliness of heart with such difficulty? What sort of person would devote so much of his effort in this cultivation if his conscience were not gnawing at him? The first worker of the vineyard is the faculty of thought, the accuser of the conscience. The more merciful and generous the Lord is to us, the more wicked and troubled the eye of such a worker is. The more grace we receive from the Lord, the more intensely we are afflicted with the sting of our gnawing conscience, as often as we sin. As long as our thoughts can find any imperfection in us, our conscience disturbs, troubles, and torments us when we see it. And so the labor of this worker is never finished until every imperfection is openly removed and the person is reformed to the fullness of integrity and presented with the denarius of perfection. But, after the consummation of the reward, this worker takes what is his own and departs, because, not finding what he rightfully condemned, the sting of reproof is quieted and fades away. O how excellent will be the perfection of knowledge at that time! O how great will be the consummation of virtue when estimation is not even slightly deceived and when no affect is anywhere unbridled! But what we expect then of every affect in everything we dare not presume now from any affect in anything. Therefore, notice how great our virtue will be in the future and how extensive our defect is now. O how great will the strength of man be then! O how extensive is his infirmity in the meantime! *From the sole of the foot up to the crown of the head, there is no soundness therein.*[253] Right now people have no confidence at all, unless presumptuously, that they can achieve or comprehend the highest measure of equity that then will be preserved and known in all things. I think you are certainly aware how wide the corruption of this human infirmity is spreading which dominates every affect in everything up until now, so that the

Prophet correctly proclaimed: *From the sole of the foot up to the crown of the head, there is no soundness therein.*[254]

Section Two

Chapter Thirty-Eight. On the three vices discussed thus far, and the three sins that will be discussed now

Let us now consider the next part of the verse: *The wound, the bruise, and the swelling sore—they are neither bandaged, nor treated with medicine, nor soothed with oil.*[255] We already described the three evils above, and now we are introducing three more evils: the wound, the bruise, and the swelling sore. The three evils treated above are produced, as it were, internally. The three evils introduced now are inflicted, as it were, externally. The faintness of head, mourning of the heart, and sorrow of the sick body arise inwardly from the defect of nature. The wound, the bruise, and the swelling sore occur externally on account of a supervening cause. Through the faintness of the head, as already discussed, we understand the weakness of free choice for the good;[256] through the infirmity of the body we understand the restlessness of the desire for evil;[257] and through the mourning of the heart we understand the darkness of the heart and uncertainty of the judgment to discern both good and evil. Impotence for good is understood in the faintness, lust for evil is understood in the vexation of infirmity, and ignorance of good and evil is understood in the cloud of mourning.

Who does not see that these three evils are so deeply rooted in people that, however much they look out for themselves or however cautiously they act, they cannot lack these evils that arise inwardly from the defect of nature? Are there any who are not slow at times in doing the good even when it is against their will? Does no one stumble at times in the darkness of ignorance even against their will? Who so thoroughly avoids the snares of lust that he does not come upon them even when he earnestly flees from them and vehemently resists them? But we suffer, as though from our own negligence or carelessness, those evils that we allow by our consent. So those that are allowed by consent are, so to speak, wounds inflicted on the nature of the soul. Those evils, which we suffer even reluctantly and cannot resist with any of our wisdom or effort, are innate to our nature rather than external inflictions.[258]

Now listen to how the Prophet describes the three evils that are inflicting people externally: *The wound, the bruise, and the swelling sore—they are neither bandaged, nor treated with medicine, nor soothed with oil.*[259] First, let us consider how the Prophet intended to distinguish the wound and the sore from one another. Perhaps the answer to our question is hinted in the fact that "swelling" modifies "sore," so that "sore" means something that swells and "wound" means something that lacks any swelling. A wound occurs when a body part is injured internally only insofar as the injury appears externally. A bruise occurs when a body part is damaged inwardly by being crushed and yet the injury does not appear externally like a wound. And a swelling sore occurs when a body part is crushed more extensively on the inside, and yet the injury appears in part on the outside like a wound.

Each of these injuries seems to have its own differences, and yet they clearly have this in common: they are inflicted externally from a supervening crushing, just as the first three evils arise inwardly on account of an internal corruption. Therefore, we generally and correctly ascribe the first three injuries that were treated in the first section only to vice, and we ascribe the next three injuries that are introduced now only to sins. In the third section we will ascribe the three antidotes to the remedy of both vices and sins. And so through the faintness of the head, through the mourning of the heart, and through the infirmity of the body we understand the three vices. Through the wound, the bruise, and the swelling sore we understand the three sins. And through the bandage, medicine, and oil we understand the three remedies.

CHAPTER THIRTY-NINE. WHAT IS A VICE AND WHAT IS A SIN

There is certainly a difference between an illness and a wound, just as there is undoubtedly a difference between a vice and a sin.[260] As we see something on the body, so we should also understand something about the heart, because the internal corruption spewing from a secret place is different from a visible injury inflicted externally. Evil that is experienced in thought alone against the will is different from evil that is committed out of deliberation with a willing agreement. The former occurrence is born, as it were, from within, and the latter is inflicted from without. A vice then is the weakness of natural corruption, and a sin is the depraved assent to a tempting infirmity. A vice is like a certain passion of nature, and a sin is a certain voluntary act of effort. A vice is the appetite for evil that usually precedes and provokes our consent, but a sin is the consent to evil that usually follows or accompanies the appetite. Certainly the sense of a depraved motion in the heart is different from consent to the depraved motion. That we sense this depraved motion is a vice; that we consent to it is sin.[261] And so a vice is in the sense and in affect (*in sensu et in affectu*); but sin is in consent alone or also in conduct (*effectu*). When what is true seems false to us and what is false seem to be true, this is a vice in the sense. When what is just seems bitter and what is unjust seems to be pleasant, this is a vice in affect. But when we put faith in a false opinion, the vice of our sense already crosses over into sin. When we assent to depraved desire, the vice of our affect crosses over into guilt. In this way vices change into sin and make the consenting person guilty. Thus the vice of the senses becomes the origin of errors, and the vice of the affects becomes the root of iniquities. But we mean here the senses of the heart not the body, and for that reason we do not hesitate to assert this opinion: the dullness of the senses and the disorder of the affects is the origin of every evil, as we said.[262] In this way a vice controls the sense and affect and becomes a cause for sin when it allures the consent or even crosses over into conduct. However, consent does not always lead to conduct. When conduct is hindered by necessity, the guilt of sin is achieved in the consent alone.

Notice how we have distinguished the differences between vice and sin, and according to this mode of distinction we have demonstrated three vices and three sins. Here are the three vices discussed above: aversion to the good, desire for evil, uncertainty in discerning good and evil. In the faintness of the head we have demonstrated how inactive people are to do the good, or rather how incapable they are of it; in the weakness of the body we have indicated how eager and restless people are for evil; and in the mourning of the heart we have shown how dull and bleary-eyed people are in discerning both good and evil. Here are the three vices: impotence, ignorance, and concupiscence. But I do not need to repeat the same discussion here because I already said above what needed to be said about these vices.

Chapter Forty. We commit sins in three ways

Three kinds of sins correspond to the three kinds of vices. We fall into some sins through infirmity, we incur other sins through error, and we commit other sins through iniquity alone.[263] We call the sins of infirmity what we cannot fully avoid even though we conduct ourselves steadily and wisely. We sin through error and ignorance when we commit an evil act because we think that it was good. Those who know something is evil and can avoid it but commit it purposely transgress from malice alone, because they do so only from love and desire for what is evil.

We are said to sin against the Father, Son, and Holy Spirit according to these three ways of sinning. Although power, wisdom, and goodness of the Father, Son, and Holy Spirit are one and the same, yet, according to some modes of expression found in certain places of the Scriptures, power seems to be assigned specifically to the Father, wisdom to the Son, and goodness to the Holy Spirit.[264] In that case then a person who commits a sin through infirmity is particularly opposed to the one who is supreme power; and a person who sins through ignorance is most opposed to the one who is supreme wisdom. And how can a person who commits a sin through malice alone be more opposed to the one who is supreme goodness? Accordingly a person who sins through infirmity seems to act specifically against the Father; a person who sins through ignorance seems to act specifically against the Son; and a person who sins through malice is specifically opposed to the Holy Spirit.[265]

A person who sins against the Holy Spirit is rightly not forgiven in this world or in the future, because full satisfaction is required from someone who sins through malice if he repents in the present life, but full damnation in the future is required from him if he does not repent. But those who sin through infirmity or ignorance have some excuse for their guilt just as they should have some remission in their punishment. Rightly there is more remission either in the present satisfaction or future damnation for those people whose guilt is eased through the excuse of inability or ignorance. However, those who have no excuse for their guilt rightly receive no remission in their punishment. Those then who perform penance for their voluntary sins in this life wonderfully receive remission without remission.[266] For they receive full remission for a committed sin without any remission of a condign satisfaction. Therefore, as it was said, sins against the Father are sins through inability; sins against the Son are sins through ignorance; and sins against the Holy Spirit are sins through malice.

CHAPTER FORTY-ONE. WHAT IS THE CHARACTERISTIC OF THESE SINS?

Let us listen to how the same teacher of truth describes these same evils in Isaiah when he said: *The wound, the bruise, and the swelling sore*. We understand "wound" to mean sin that is committed through infirmity alone; we understand "bruise" to mean sin that is contracted through error alone; we understand "swelling sore" to mean sin that is accomplished through iniquity.

Now if we understand "wound" to mean an injury that is externally visible but causes no internal swelling, then notice how correctly the Prophet describes the sin of infirmity as a wound. What else is an externally visible injury except guilt made clear without any pretense or contradiction? What else is an injury without swelling except guilt without pride or guilt with humility and shame? Such are those kinds of sins that we commit through infirmity as if unwillingly. We are ashamed of no sins more than these, we condemn no sins more than these. We usually deny the sins of ignorance rather than denounce them, and we are accustomed either to vaunt the sins of malice with impudence or defend our contumacy. Such [sinners] are described as those who are rebuked by Wisdom where it says: *They rejoice when they have done evil and boast in very wicked affairs.*[267]

A bruise occurs where the injury underlies the skin which prevents it from oozing its sanies. The sin of ignorance so covers itself under the concealment of its ambiguity lest it spews out into the open, and it disguises itself under the cover of a false opinion so the decay of its corruption does not ooze through the opening of confession.[268] Such minds that often submit to their own error and acquiesce to a false opinion are not even permitted to rest in their own darkness and so appear to be secure in themselves. But the alternating of various opinions and the fluctuation of multiple ambiguities drives the mind in different directions at different times and does not allow it to be at peace. Thus like a bruise it also torments a restless conscience through its anxiety and takes it to the blackness of terror.

The Prophet correctly describes the sin of malice that is not committed without contempt for God as a swelling sore.[269] How, unless through our contempt for God, can we commit sin which we can easily avoid and undoubtedly know to be sin? Such sins are rightly called sins of malice, because they are committed neither through ignorance nor through infirmity but only through an evil will. What else is the swelling in an injury from a blow except contumacy in perpetrating a crime and contempt for God in the transgression of his command? Therefore, as we have discussed, the sin of infirmity is correctly depicted through a wound which does not cause swelling; the sin of error is correctly depicted through a bruise which is hidden under the skin; and the sin of malignity is correctly depicted through the sore which causes swelling.

CHAPTER FORTY-TWO. ON THE THREEFOLD SIN OF ACTIONS, THOUGHTS, AND HABITS

Perhaps we can understand a wound as a corpse outside a house and a swelling sore as a corpse already rotting inside the tomb.[270] We can also understand a wound as a sin of action, a bruise as a sin of thought, and a swelling sore as a sin of habit. Note that just as a swelling sore is nothing other than a wound that becomes swollen, so a sin of habit is nothing other than an evil action that becomes a habit. Therefore, what else is a sin made clear through action except an open wound or a corpse carried out [of a house for burial]? And what else is a sin still latent in the thoughts except a bruise rotting under the skin or a corpse not yet leaving the lair of the house? Or what else is an evil habit already decayed through infamy except a sore swollen from decay or the members of a reeking corpse already putrefied?[271]

Let it concern no one that I discussed the injury of a wound before the injury of a bruise, because we must understand a wound as the sin of action and a bruise as the sin of thought. If the bruise was discussed first, the wound second, and the swelling sore third, then maybe it would seem to some that the mode of our corruption is more correctly ordered and distinguished by consistent stages of growth, so that the evil of action would be described after the evil of thought and the evil of habit after both. However, we must know that although a sin of action is greater in some respects, a sin of thought is still more dangerous in other respects. Although a sin of action is greater with respect to guilt, yet see whether perhaps a sin of thought is more difficult with respect to healing. The more embarrassed we are about a conspicuous sin, the more quickly we usually correct it. Guilt made clear through action is often either corrected through a rebuke or forsaken reluctantly after a punishment has been imposed. This is the reason why we read in the Gospel of Luke that the corpse of a boy who was being carried out of a house for burial was brought back to life before the corpse of a girl who was still found inside the house.[272] If then we correctly understand a wound as a sin of action and a bruise as a sin of thought, then what wonder is it if we find the wound first and the bruise second in the mystical reading, because a sin of thought seem to be more dangerous than a sin of action and because we approve the reason for its order based on an evangelical example? Now the swelling sore, designated as the evil of depraved habits, is treated in the last place as a kind of summit because it is more horrifying than all other sins with respect to guilt and more difficult with respect to healing.

CHAPTER FORTY-THREE. EACH OF THE AFOREMENTIONED SINS CAN BE UNDERSTOOD IN THREE WAYS

We can understand the sin that we reproach and yet do not forsake through the wound that is without swelling but also without any treatment as well; through the bruise we can understand the sin that we conceal through hypocrisy; and through the swelling sore we can understand the sin that we defend through contumacy. The injury of sin is thus concealed in three ways, it is covered over in three ways, and it is inflated in three ways. Sin is opened like a wound, it is concealed like a bruise, and it is inflamed like a swelling sore. An open wound is a conspicuous sin, but the wound of sin is manifested differently to oneself, to one's neighbor, or to God. It is manifested to oneself through thought, to one's neighbor through action, and to God through confession.[273] Insofar as we can, we conceal from God what we refuse to condemn through personal confession before him. Likewise the injury of sin is concealed in three ways and lies under the skin of concealment like a bruise. Our sin is concealed differently from ourselves, from God's eyes, or from our neighbors. Sin is hidden from us through error, from God through silence, and from our neighbor through deceit. Likewise the stain of sin becomes swollen in three ways and expands itself by means of inflammation like a swelling sore. Our sin decays in us through malice, and it swells before our neighbor through impudence and contrary to God through contumacy. A person first ruins himself through malice, destroys his neighbor through impudence, and fights against God through contumacy.

CHAPTER FORTY-FOUR. WHAT IS THE USUAL TRAIT OF SOME SINS

Although we seem to attribute these three general circumstances to every sin, because we usually find one and the same corrupting evil in different people or in the same person at different times—sometimes public, sometimes hidden, or sometimes swollen—, nevertheless it is a particular occurrence, or rather a familiar one, that some sins appear in the open with a certain liberty rather than by swelling, that other sins break out in great swelling of pride, and that other sins are never detected but always wish to be hidden. Who is unaware how sadness usually reveals itself totally in words, flows forth through complaint, and gushes forth in wails and groans as if oozing blood like a wound? But the evil of envy conceals itself in silence because the envious mind is embarrassed to show its vice,[274] and, for that reason, it envelops itself under the skin of deceit, lest it may be exposed to contempt and become vile to everyone if it spews forth into the open. And yet even this evil almost always, but reluctantly, makes itself known through noticeable evidence: it usually has a grim outlook, a bitter response, a pale countenance, and other signs of hidden weakness in such a way that it cannot entirely hide itself even though it may want to be hidden. But it makes itself clearly and outwardly known like a bruise, as was said, even though it, concealed under the skin of deceit, does not burst out through words. But anger rises in indignation at an inflicted injury and erupts outward through threats and insulting language like a swelling sore, while it is confined for the most part by shame and fear and spreads into the evil of revenge more extensively on the inside through the will than on the outside through word.

You are certainly considering, I think, how much sorrow is like a wound, how much envy is like a bruise, and how much anger is like a swelling sore. And we learn from the divine Scriptures how much or how these evils are to be feared. Of what sort is the evil of sorrow believed to be that, as the Apostle testifies, brings about death?[275] And we continually confirm what we should think about envy and anger from the testimony of sacred Scripture: *Anger kills the foolish man, and envy slays the child.*[276] Therefore, notice what great evils these are believed to be that bring about every death according to the testimony of Scripture.

Third Section

Chapter Forty-Five. On the three sins discussed thus far and the three remedies that will be discussed now

Now it can still be added to the increase of evil that mortal sins can be fully avoided with almost no skill or astuteness. Who, I ask, watches over himself with such great caution and vigilance that he never feels the bite of sorrow, envy, or anger? But if we cannot fully avoid these great evils, then why do we despise the remedy? Surely the contempt for the remedies is shown in this verse: *The wound, the bruise, and the swelling sore—they are neither bandaged, nor treated with medicine, nor soothed with oil.*[277] Three evils are mentioned first, and the three remedies are added after them. *The wound, the bruise, and the swelling sore.* Here we have the three evils, to which the three remedies of bandages, treatments, and fomentation are joined.

And perhaps it will seem to some that each remedy should be applied to each injury: bandages to a wound, treatments to a bruise, and fomentations to a swelling sore. But the grammar prohibits us from making this distinction of the words. The feminine form of "bandaged," rather than the neuter form, proves that it should not be referred to the neuter noun "wound." Similarly, because I read "treated" in the feminine not in the masculine, I do not see how it can refer only to the masculine noun "bruised." Therefore, because we read "bandaged," "treated," and "soothed" in the feminine, we must apply all of these remedies to the feminine noun "sore." However, nothing prevents us from applying each of the remedies to the other two injuries as well— the grammar does not prevent it, and the meaning of the statement does not oppose it. We understand the bandages as commandments, the treatment as warnings, and the fomentations as promises.

Chapter Forty-Six. On the three instructions

The likeness between chains and commandments is sufficiently fitting. We are restricted by chains, and our will is restrained by the divine commandments. We are drawn by chains, restricted by chains, and constricted by chains. Precepts are the chains that draw us, prohibitions are chains that restrict us, and admonishments are chains that constrict us. A precept concerns what must be done, a prohibition concerns what is not permitted to be done, and an admonishment is what is advantageous to do but could be omitted without guilt. Precepts often prod us to walk down the arduous path of good works; prohibitions often divert us away from where our desires hasten us; and admonishments constrict more tightly the aperture of or even the flux of our hearts because we often restrain our will from the use of what is licit.

And so the chains that draw us are these: *Love the Lord your God with your whole heart and your neighbor as yourself,*[278] and: *Honor your father and mother.*[279] The chains that restrict us are these: *Do not kill, do not commit adultery, and do not steal.*[280] The chains that constrict us are these: *If you are perfect, then go, sell all your possessions, and give to the poor,*[281] and what the Lord admonishes about virginity when he said: *He who can take it let him take it,*[282] about which the Apostle also said: *Now concerning virgins I do not have a precept of the Lord, but I give counsel. It is good for someone to be so;*[283] and elsewhere: *It is good for a man not to touch a woman.*[284] Therefore, by such chains we restrain the open wounds of our vices and the bruising of our soul, and we fortify ourselves from the outside as often as we hinder our noxious desires from action or even consent.

CHAPTER FORTY-SEVEN. ON THREE THREATS

It is not enough for the restoration of perfect health to utilize the chains of commandments to restrain the evil of depraved assent, unless we work hard to utilize the remedies of proper medical treatments to eradicate with equal concern the noxious humors of carnal affects and rottenness of our pleasures. Similar to what I said about the chains,[285] here are three kinds of medical treatments in the divine threats: the threat of rebuke, the threat of reprobation, and the threat of damnation. Regarding the first it was written: *God chastens those whom He loves, and He scourges every son whom he receives.*[286] Regarding the second it was written: *Therefore, he has mercy on whom he wills, and he hardens whom he wills.*[287] Regarding the third it was written: *Then he will say to those on his left: "Depart from me you who are cursed into the everlasting fire, which was prepared for the devil and his angels."*[288] This is the threat of reproof: *If you walk contrary to me and do not desire to hear me, then I will bring seven times as many plagues upon you for your sins;*[289] and immediately before that verse it was written: *I will bring seven times as many reproofs upon you for your sins, and I will break the pride of your stubbornness.*[290] This is the threat of hardening: *Behold I will harden the heart of Pharaoh.*[291] And this is the threat of damnation: *Their worm does not die, and their fire is not extinguished.*[292] The sap from herbs is certainly bitter,[293] but it is very effective for dehydrating the noxious humors of vices. What sort of person is so unrestrained that he does not strive to temper his lust? If only he pays careful attention and remembers that the Lord usually punishes sevenfold evil pleasures in some of his elect during this life. What sort of person is not very scared to persevere stubbornly with his perverse habits? Or what sort of person does not hasten to correct more quickly his depraved custom when he hears that some are given over to a reprobate sense[294] in this life and handed over irremediably to the stubbornness of their minds and the bond of sin, lest perhaps if they have not wanted to return to their senses when they still can, they cannot to do so any longer?

There still remains the third kind of threat in the remedy of such sicknesses—the most efficacious, powerful, and excellent remedy in comparison to all of the others. This is the remedy that usually heals most effectively the chronic illnesses of vices and restores hopelessly sick people nearly to full health. What sort of person can be found anywhere with a mind so irrational and stubborn that he is not terrified and not totally averse to purchasing the transitory charms of the flesh with everlasting torments? If only he carefully observes and continually notices how scanty or even momentary are all these pleasures of the flesh which pass right by, and how frightful or how dreadful the everlasting torments are which do not have nor can have an end. Therefore, notice that the restoration of our health is largely within our power if we strive to apply this kind of remedy to our sickness in a proper manner. *The wound, the bruise, and the swelling sore* which is *neither bandaged, nor treated with medicine.* Why are we astonished or what complaint do we have if a person cannot restore his health? Indeed, he rightly fails and perishes in his bruises, because he refused to apply the proper medical remedies on his illnesses even when he had an abundance of such medicines available. Or do you not know—you who despise the medicine of such healing—that according the insight of Wisdom healing will cause the greatest sins to cease?[295] But perhaps you dread the sap of the aforementioned herbs, seeing that it is bitter and very tart, and for that reason you become very scared to apply it on your wounds? But if the bitterness of the herbs seems very bitter to you, also notice that it is also a very efficacious remedy.

CHAPTER FORTY-EIGHT. ON THE THREE PROMISES

Receive three kinds of oil in the divine promises so that you may have something in which you can, when the opportune time comes, sooth the harshness of pain and sooth your members as they become more and more healthy or even nurture members already healed. And so the first kind of oil is the promise of forgiveness, the second is the promise of grace, and the third is the promise of glory. The merciful and gracious Lord is preeminent above malice,[296] and the Lord will bestow not only the forgiveness of sins but also grace and glory. Does this verse not seem to pertain to the first kind of oil that we called the promise of forgiveness? *If your sins are as scarlet, then they will be made as white as the snow; and if they are red as crimson, then they will be white as wool.*[297] That verse seems to pertain to the second kind of oil, that is, the promise of grace about which the Apostle said: *There are diversities of graces but the same Spirit, there are diversities of ministries but the same Lord, and there are diversities of works but the same God who works all in all. The manifestation of the Spirit is given to each as a benefit. To some the word of wisdom is given through the Spirit, to others the word of knowledge is given according to the same Spirit; to some faith in the same Spirit, to others grace of healing in one Spirit; to some the work of miracles, to others prophecy; to some the discernment of spirits, to others the diverse kinds of tongues; and to another interpretation of languages. But the one and same Spirit works all these, and he distributes them to each person as he wills.*[298] But if we understand the third kind of oil as the promise of glory, then does not what we read elsewhere in the same Apostle seem to pertain to it? *The glory of the heavens is different from the glory of the earth. The glory of the sun, the glory of the moon, and the glory of the stars are all different. Star even differs from star in glory, so also is the resurrection of the dead. What is sown in corruption will rise in incorruption. What is sown in dishonor will rise in glory. What is sown in weakness will rise in power. A natural body is sown; a spiritual body will rise.*[299]

CHAPTER FORTY-NINE. ON THE THREEFOLD POWER OF THE THREE PROMISES

Notice that you have three kinds of oil. Each is certainly not worthless or of mediocre value. They are all precious and necessary in their different functions, whether for healing wounds, for lighting,[300] or for seasoning food. The first oil is special and is more useful as an ointment; the second is more useful as a lamp; and the third is more useful as refreshment.[301] The first sooths more salubriously, the second burns more brightly, and the third tastes sweeter. The kind of oil that it is usually called the oil of joy in the Scripture seems to taste sweeter in comparison to the other oils.[302] What else is this oil except the participation in glory? But the oil, about which we read: *his unction teaches us about all things*,[303] seems to burn more brightly and illumine more effectively than all the other oils because just as we cannot maintain even slightly the way of truth without the illumination of grace, so under its guidance we certainly cannot lose the way of life or deviate anywhere. The kind of oil, about which you read: *the yoke decays at the presence of oil*,[304] seems to be more profitable than the others as a treatment for healing because the habit of sinning and servitude to sin are rubbed away with the divine mercy of forgiveness. But even though we have assigned to each of these oils a specific function, we can still recommend each kind of oil for daily use as beneficial and very effective to alleviate pain. How great could we find the bitterness of some pain that the great sweetness of divine promises cannot sooth it?

CHAPTER FIFTY. ON THE TRIPLE ALLEVIATION AGAINST TRIPLE PAIN

Some people suffer from the infliction of their injury and wounds, some people suffer from the faintness of their infirmity, and other people suffer from the fatigue of their tribulation and labor. The infliction of a wound is the perpetration of sin, the faintness of infirmity is the defect of virtue, and the fatigue of labor is the weariness of waiting that arises from the multitude of tribulations and the unbearable desire for the promised retribution. Pain arises from all these and afflicts the mind of people in many ways. But you have three kinds of oil countering the three pains. If you suffer from a wound and perpetration of sin, you have an oil of forgiveness that is offered by the Lord's promise. If you suffer from an infirmity, and if a defection of virtue has taken hold of you, you have the oil of promised grace. If you suffer from an affliction of fatigue, apply the oil of joy in the hope of promised grace. And so, if the pain of penitence afflicts your heart and the consciousness of sins besets you very severely, then accept the unction and receive consolation. For, regarding the Lord's voice, or rather the infusion of divine unction: *I live, says the Lord God, and I do not desire the death of the wicked, but that the wicked may turn from their way and live. Turn from your evil ways. Why will you die, O house of Israel?*[305] What, I ask, is the very intense bitterness of all contrition and penance that the infusion of this kind of divine unction cannot sooth? If you suffer from your faintness and defect, then persevere with your prayers[306] and do not stop until *you are clothed with power from on high* and are at peace and entirely recovered from all your pain or faintness,[307] that is, until you have been anointed with the most precious ointment of the evangelical urn:[308] *If you know how to give good gifts to your children, even through you are evil, then how much more will your Father from heaven give the good Spirit to them that ask him!*[309] But so that you may be more amazed, he *who gives and does not taunt*[310] leaves it up to each one's power to take up as much of the ointment as he wants when he says: *Every person who asks receives; and every person who seeks finds; and it will be open to the person who knocks.*[311] And so do not be scanty in your expenses or stingy in your payments. The more you pay, the more you abound: *You have received freely,* he said, *freely give.*[312] The infusion of grace and the outflow of such oil at the hands of the widow do not know how to stop unless there are no empty vases that can be filled.[313] If you are worn out amid tribulations or you are fatigued from excessive labor, then you have the anointing of glory with which you can sooth the pain of your fatigue when you accept from the maker of precious ointments what you hear: *The sufferings of this time are not worthy to be compared with the future glory which will be revealed to us.*[314] For what is momentary at present and light in our tribulations works in us an eternal weight of glory beyond measure in sublimity.*[315] Listen still to this maker of ointments offering the same kind of oil and anointing of glory: *When Christ, your life, shall appear, then you will also appear with him in glory.*[316]

CHAPTER FIFTY-ONE. THE DESIGNATION OF THE THREE PROMISES

The first kind of oil was that which the Samaritan poured on the wounds of the man who had fallen *among robbers, who also stripped him and, after wounding him, went away, leaving him half alive.*[317] The sinful woman healed the wounds of her sins and mitigated at last the excess of her pain with this kind of ointment so that she merited to hear from the Lord: *She is pardoned from many sins.*[318] Rich with this ointment, a gift of the Lord, she came to the feet of the Lord and liberally applied on the lowest parts of the Lord's body the unction of piety, which, as she was well aware, she had received from above, so that she, a sinner and penitent, might bestow the benefit of piety on sinners and penitents—such benefit, as she remembered, she too had received freely from the mercy of God. The wicked servant refused to pour this ointment of piety on the feet of the Lord even though he received this ointment in such great abundance from the Lord's gift. He is thus forced to return afterwards what he freely received earlier when he receives this rebuke: *Wicked servant, I pardoned you from all your debt, because you cried out to me. Should you not then have mercy on your fellow servant, just as I had mercy on you?*[319]

In my opinion the second kind of oil pertains to him who knew himself to be a debtor who replied to the one questioning him: *How much do you owe my lord? And he said: A hundred jars of oil.*[320] I ask that you notice that he, who does not deny that he owes a hundred jars of oil, had received the oil of grace in such a great abundance.[321] He was compelled to repay the debt of oil by the servant who vehemently admonished the debtors of his lord by saying: *Watch out that you do not receive the grace of God in vain.*[322] He was personally aware of his own debt of oil, and he was not ashamed to confess it when he said: *By the grace of God I am what I am.*[323] He demonstrated the extent of his labor to repay this debt of oil in the next part of this verse: *His grace in me was not in vain, but I have labored more abundantly than everyone else—yet, not I, but the grace of God with me.*[324]

Now, unless I am mistaken, the third kind of oil was what the five wise virgins had in abundance, and for that reason their lamps could not be extinguished, nor were they afraid of running out of oil. They run and hasten in the abundance of this oil and, while the foolish virgins stand outside, they enter with confidence into the joy of their Lord and recline in eternal joy at the wedding of the Lamb.[325] Christ has also received the fullness of this oil with which he had been fully anointed. About him the Prophet had truthfully asserted: *You have loved righteousness and hated iniquity; therefore, God, your God, anointed you with the oil of joy before your companions.*[326] It was right that this occurred before his companions and colleagues, not only before humans but also the angels, because *he was made so much better the angels, as he inherited a name more excellent than them.*[327] He was crowned with *glory and honor,*[328] and he received *the name that is above every name, so that at the name of Jesus every knee should bow, of those who are in heaven, on the earth, or under the earth.*[329] Worthy is the one who received the fullness of glory and who first had received the fullness of grace: *We see his glory, the glory as it were of the only begotten of the Father, full of grace and truth.*[330] Without a doubt the one *in whom dwells every fullness of divinity corporally*[331] really received every fullness according to every one of these kinds of oil designated above.[332] He is the font of mercy. From him flows the stream of all grace and in him resides the abyss of eternal and everlasting glory. Why, I ask, do we, who are still in need of this oil, labor? *We all receive from his fullness,*[333] if we so desire it. Let us ask for it and we will receive. The most precious kind of oil is what is called the oil of joy or glory;[334] he instructs us to ask and promises to give. *Ask*, he says, *and you will receive, so that your joy may be full.*[335] And so we have enough at hand because we receive at our petition when we completely desire it.

Chapter Fifty-Two. The designation of the multiple benefits of divine promises

We have three kinds of oil, all of which are as necessary as they are useful. The first oil counters the three kinds of injuries: the wound, the bruise, and the swelling sore. The second oil counters the three kinds of sorrows: the faintness of head, the mourning of heart, and the sickness of body. And the third oil counters the three kinds of fatigue of a healthy body: labor, poverty, and persecution. You have the oil of divine mercy, with which you sooth the wounds of sins; you have the oil of grace, with which you sooth the diseases of vices; and you have the oil of glory, with which you ease the fatigue of struggles. Just as an illness is different from a wound, so a vice is different from sin.[336] A vice is the privation of the natural good that is even apart from consent, and sin is the voluntary consent to the temptation of evil. A vice is the corruption of nature, and this corruption produces the inclination and longing for an evil to which people often refuse to consent. But sin is the perverse effort, through which people often consent voluntarily to an evil that they could easily resist. And so the first step is to heal the wounds of sins, the second is to cure the diseases of vices, and the third is to soothe the sorrows of fatigue. As previously discussed, we have the oil of mercy as a remedy for sins; we have the oil of grace as a treatment for vices; and we have the oil of glory as security against defects.[337] As a remedy for sins, you have a prophetic medicinal compound made from the first kind of oil: *Blessed are those whose iniquities are forgiven, and whose sins are covered.*[338] And wonderful is the ointment of mercy, which not only makes a sick person healthy but also a miserable person happy: *Blessed is the one to whom the Lord has not imputed sin.*[339] In addition to this, against the diseases of vices and corruption of nature accept another confection of ointment made from the oil of grace: *Blessed is the one who has the God of Jacob as his helper.*[340] Moreover, accept another unction made from the same oil of grace: *Blessed is the one whom you, O Lord, will instruct and teach concerning your law.*[341] Accept also this oil: *Blessed is the man who trusts in the Lord; the Lord will be his confidence.*[342] Blessed is the man who has the Lord as helper, teacher, and protector. Happy is he whom the Lord helps, instructs, and protects, that is, the Lord helps him to do the good, defends him from evil, and instructs him to discern both good and evil. To help, instruct, and defend is the whole of grace. The first counters the failure of strength, the second counters the failure of truth, and the third counters the failure of power—all of which counters the privation of the natural good. The first counters the debility of a faint head, the second counters the blindness of a mourning heart, and the third counters the anxiety of a sick body and the restlessness of burning desire.

Moreover, we have a third kind of oil and from it a triple confection of ointment that counters the three kinds of fatigue of a body already recovering. Against the fatigue of labor you have this oil: *Because you will eat from labors of your hands, you are happy, and it will be well with you.*[343] Against the affliction of poverty you have this oil: *Blessed are the poor in spirit, because the kingdom of heaven belongs to them.*[344] And against the tribulation of persecution you have this oil: *Blessed are those who endure persecution for the sake of righteousness, because the kingdom of heaven belongs to them.*[345] What sort of person, I ask, not only lacks sorrow but also joy during so many struggles of tribulations, although he learns the following from the testimony of sacred Scripture about which we dare not doubt: *Blessed is the man who endures temptation, because, when he has been proven, he will receive a crown of life, which God promised to them who love him.*[346] This is the reason why the apostles *went out from the presence of the council, rejoicing that they were considered worthy to suffer reproach for the name of Jesus.*[347] How accurate it is to call the third kind of oil the "oil of joy," for it causes people to rejoice about their tribulation! For who doesn't rejoice, or rather boast, in their infirmities and tribulations,[348] when they hope to receive as a reward for their struggle what *no eye has seen nor ear heard, neither has it ascended into the heart of man what God has prepared for those who love him?*[349]

We have said this about the different kinds of oils so that we may know what oils we have and what kind of useful or even necessary functions they serve. We should not be satisfied to have known about such kinds of oil and to have been able to distinguish their benefits from each other, unless we also strive to sooth our frail condition by using them according to the benefit and power of each, so that it seems that we are charged with the sentence of that divine reproof: *The wound, the bruise, and the swelling sore—they are neither bandaged, nor treated with medicine, nor soothed with oil.*[350]

NOTES

1. See Isa. 1.5–6.
2. "Charms of places" (*locorum amena*) is a classical topos, see Virgil, *Aeneid* 5.734 (Fairclough and Gool, Loeb 63:494); Cicero, *De oratore* II.29 (Sutton and Rackham, Loeb 348:418–19); Isidore of Seville, *Etym.* XIV.8.33 (Lindsay; tr. Barney, 299).
3. Cf. Hugh of St Victor, *Didasc.* V.5 (Buttimer, 103; tr. Harkins, VTT 3.156).
4. Cf. Richard of St Victor, *Decl. nonn. diff.* (Ribaillier, 212).
5. Cf. 2 Cor. 12:2; Richard of St Victor, *Sp. blasph.* (Ribaillier, 129); *Ad me clamat* (Ribaillier, 280).
6. This section is also found in *Misc.* VI.33 (PL 177.831D–6836D).
7. Isa. 1:5–6. See also Richard of St Victor, *Adnot. Ps.* 118 (PL 196.352C); *LE* X.11 (Châtillon, 389).
8. Cf. Ps. 102:14 (Vulg.).
9. Isa. 1:6.
10. Ps. 93:10 (Vulg.).
11. Cf. Richard of St Victor, *Vis. Ezek.* Prol. (Schröder, 372; PL 196.527C).
12. Cf. Richard of St Victor, *Erud.* I.25 (PL 196.1273C–1274D).
13. Cf. Hugh of Fouilloy, *De medicina animae* 1 (PL 176.1184A).
14. Cf. Gen. 4:7.
15. Cf. Job 28.18.
16. Cf. Ps. 118:25 (Vulg.).
17. Ps. 43:25 (Vulg.).
18. Cf. Gen. 1:26
19. Cf. *Misc.* VI.33 (PL 177.831C).
20. Cf. Bernard of Clairvaux, *Gratia* 9.28 (SBO 3:185–86).
21. Cf. Bernard of Clairvaux, *Gratia* 4.9 (SBO 3:172).
22. Prov. 3.13–15.
23. Cf. Matt. 13:44.
24. Cf. Job 28.18.
25. Job 28:12; see also Job 28:20.
26. Prov. 8:12.
27. See chap. 2.
28. Cf. Prov. 4:23; See also Richard of St Victor, *Quat. grad.* 23 (Dumeige, 149; tr. Kraebel, VTT 2.285).
29. Ps. 39:13 (Vulg.).
30. Hosea 7:11. See also Richard of St Victor, *Quat. grad.* 23 (Dumeige, 151; tr. Kraebel, VTT 2.285).
31. Cf. Deut. 32:28–29.
32. Prov. 2:10–11.
33. On carnal desire, see Richard of St Victor, *Quat. grad.* 14 (Dumeige, 139–41; tr. Kraebel, VTT 2.280–81); *XII patr.* 85 (Châtillon, 338; tr. Zinn, 133); *Missione* (PL 196.1028B–C).
34. Cf. Rom. 7:23.
35. On "the motion of the body" (*motus corporis*) and the "motion of sensuality" (*motus sensualitatis*), see Hugh of St Victor, *Sacr.* I.6.4 (PL 176.265C); cf. also *Misc.* I.22 (PL 177.489C–490B).
36. Cf. Bernard of Clairvaux, *Gratia* 2.3 (SBO 3:167–68); William of St Thierry, *Natura* II.78, 86 (Verdeyen, 130, 133).
37. Eccles. 5:7–8 (Vulg.).
38. Cf. Richard of St Victor, *Erud.* I.30 (PL 196.1281A–B); *Apoc.* V.9 (PL 196.837B).
39. See discussion in Ribaillier, "Richard de Saint-Victor: *De statu interioris hominis*," 18.
40. Cf. Hugh of St Victor, *Sacr.* II.14.6 (PL 176.561A; tr. Deferrari, 413); Richard of St Victor, *Erud.* I.3 (PL 196.1235D).
41. Cf. William of St Thierry, *Natura* I.23 (Verdeyen, 111).
42. Cf. Prov. 4:23; see chap. 4 above.

43 Cf. Augustine, *Trin.* XII.7.11 (Mountain and Glorie, 365).

44 Cf. Richard of St Victor, *Erud.* I.3 (PL 196.1236A).

45 Cf. 1 Kings 3:16.

46 Cf. Ps. 105:37.

47 Cf. Wisd. of Sol. 12:5–6.

48 Matt. 3:9. Cf. Richard of St Victor, *Pot. lig.* 3 (Ribaillier, 80).

49 Cf. Ezek. 37:4–5.

50 See chap. 2 above. Cf. Peter the Chanter, *Distinctiones Abel* (Vatican City, BAV Vat. lat. 1003, fol. 3va; Vatican City, BAV Vat. Lat. 1004, fol. 5v): "Human affects are called 'feet', because feet carry a person from place to place just as affects carry a person from one thought to another; because feet run off in different directions, thus *I have restrained my feet from every evil way* (Ps. 118:101); because feet trample on the ground, thus the Apostle regards all things as dung (cf. Phil. 3:8); and because feet sustain the body of good works, hence 'your affect gives a name to your work' (Ambrose, *De officiis* I.30.147 [Krabinger, 82; PL 16.66A]), and also 'what you want to do but cannot God counts it as a deed' (Augustine, *En. Ps.* 57.4 (Dekkers and Fraipont, CCL 39.711)" ("Affectus hominis pedes dicuntur, quia sicut pedes portant hominem de loco ad locum, ita affectus de una cogitatione ad aliam; quia huc et illuc discurrunt, unde *ab omni uia mala prohibui pedes meos*; quia terrena conculcant, unde Apostolus hec omnia arbitrans tanquam stercora; quia corpus bonorum operum sustentant, unde 'affectus tuus operi tuo nomen imponit', item 'quod uis et non potes Deus tibi pro facto reputat'").

51 On the troubles of carnal desire, cf. Richard of St Victor, *Quat. grad.* 14–15 (Dumeige, 141; tr. Kraebel, VTT 2.280–81).

52 Gen. 4:12. On the distinction between a wanderer (*vagum*) and a runaway/fugitive (*profugum*), cf. Richard of St Victor, *XII patr.* 39 (Châtillon, 202–203; tr. Zinn, 94–95).

53 Cf. Job 14:1–2.

54 "Affectus" and "affectio," which Richard uses interchangeably here, are difficult to translate. See general introduction above, VTT 4.58–59 n. 106. In chap. 34 below Richard discusses the affect and its disorder in more detail.

55 Eccles. 1:6.

56 See chap. 8.

57 On the meaning of "affect of the heart" (*cordis affectus*), cf. Richard of St Victor, *LE* II.2.14 (Châtillon, 229–30); *Misit Her.* (PL 141.283–86); Godfrey of St Victor, *Microcosmus* 105–106 (Delhaye, 116–18).

58 Cf. Bernard of Clairvaux, *SCC* 85.5 (SBO 2:310). See discussion in Ribaillier, "Richard de Saint-Victor: *De statu interioris hominis*," 18.

59 Cf. Richard of St Victor, *Quat. grad.* 16 (Dumeige, 141–43; tr. Kraebel, VTT 2.281–82); *Arca Moys.* III.22 (Aris, 81; PL 196.131C; tr. Zinn, 253).

60 Cf. 1 Cor. 15:52.

61 Cf. Gen. 1:26.

62 Eccles. 1:7.

63 cf. Bernard of Clairvaux, *Dilig.* VII.23 (SBO 3:138–39).

64 cf. Bernard of Clairvaux, *Dilig.* VII.18 (SBO 3:134–35).

65 Eccles. 1:7.

66 Prov. 14:13.

67 Cf. Richard of St Victor, *Exterm.*1.3 (PL 196.1075B).

68 Prov. 14:13.

69 Eccles. 1:7.

70 See chap. 2.

71 Isa. 1:5–6.

72 See chap. 2.

73 John 15:5. Cf. Richard of St Victor, *Erud.* I.30 (PL 196.1281C); *Exterm.* III.3 (PL 196.1105A);

Arca Moys. III.16 (Aris, 74; PL 196.125B; tr. Zinn, 244); Bernard of Clairvaux, *Gratia* 1 (SBO 3:165–66).

74   Rom. 9:16.
75   Eccles. 7:3.
76   Cf. Eccles. 1:18.
77   Ps. 37:4 (Vulg.).
78   Cf. Job 2:7.
79   Cf. Augustine, *En. Ps.* 37.5 (Dekkers and Fraipont, CCL 38.384–85).
80   Cf. Job 1:8.
81   James 1:14.
82   Cf. Job 7:1. Cf. also Augustine, *Jo. ev. tr.* 124.5 (Willems, 683–84).
83   See discussion in Ribaillier, "Richard de Saint-Victor: *De statu interioris hominis*," 17–18.
84   On this weakness of free choice, see *Summa sent.* III.8 (PL 176.101C); *Sent. divinit.* (Geyer, 34); Peter Lombard, *Sent.* II.24.3 (SB 4:453). At the Council of Sens (1140) the sixth of the condemned *capitula* of Peter Abelard's error read as follows: "free choice is sufficient on its own for something good" (*quod liberum arbitrium per se sufficiat ad aliquod bonum* [Denz.-Schön., 725]). See discussion in Luscombe, *The School of Peter Abelard*, 128–30.
85   1 Cor. 12:3.
86   Gen. 3:19.
87   Cf. Richard of St Victor, *Erud.* 1.30 (PL 196.1281D).
88   Cf. Augustine, *De correptione et gratia* 2 (PL 44.917); *Lib. arb.* I.35 (Green, 235); II.51 (Green, 271).
89   Cf. Bernard of Clairvaux, *Gratia* 2 (SBO 3:166–67); Hugh of St Victor, *Sacr.* I.6.4 (PL 176:265D).
90   See chap. 3.
91   Cf. Bernard of Clairvaux, *Gratia* 4.10 (SBO 3:173); VIII.24 (SBO 3:183–84).
92   Ps. 8:8–9 (Vulg.); cf. Gen. 1:26.
93   Deut. 32:24.
94   See discussion in Ribaillier, "Richard de Saint-Victor: *De statu interioris hominis*," 14–16.
95   Cf. Gen. 1:26.
96   Cf. Gen. 1:26.
97   Cf. Richard of St Victor, *Erud.* 1.30 (PL 196.1281A–B); *Trin.* VI.18 (Ribaillier, 253; tr. Evans, VTT 1.340).
98   Cf. Bernard of Clairvaux, *Gratia* 9.28 (SBO 3:185).
99   Cf. Augustine, *De peccatorum meritis et remissione* II.22.36 (Urba and Zycha, 107–108).
100 Cf. Wisd. of Sol. 5:18.
101 Cf. Wisd. of Sol. 5:21.
102 1 Pet. 5:8–9.
103 Ps. 103:21 (Vulg.).
104 Deut. 32:24.
105 Cf. Deut. 32:24.
106 Job 17:11.
107 Ps. 21:22 (Vulg.).
108 Job 5:2.
109 Ps. 6:8 (Vulg.).
110 Ps. 37:9 (Vulg.).
111 Cf. Ps. 112:7 (Vulg.).
112 Ps. 21:29 (Vulg.).
113 Cf. 1 Chron. 29:11.
114 Cf. Mal. 3:1; Dan. 7:13–14; Isa. 40:10.
115 Ps. 85:16 (Vulg.).
116 Cf. Richard of St Victor, *Super exiit* (Châtillon and Tulloch, 106); *Adnot. Ps.* 30 (PL 196.273–76); *Tract.* on Ps. 84 (PL 196.327–30; tr. Evans, VTT 4.175–76); *Diff. sac.* (PL 196.1054C).

117 Luke 18:27.
118 Cf. Matt. 8:9; Luke 7:8.
119 Cf. Rom. 6:12.
120 Gen. 41:44.
121 Ps. 2:6 (Vulg.).
122 Cf. Matt. 13:41.
123 1 Cor. 13:10.
124 Cf. 1 Cor. 15:26, 54.
125 Cf. Isa. 9:7.
126 Ps. 71:8 (Vulg.).
127 Jer. 23:6.
128 Cf. Jer. 46:27.
129 Gal. 5:17. Cf. Richard of St Victor, *Verbis ap.* (Ribaillier, 319).
130 Cf. Ps. 104:20 (Vulg.).
131 Luke 21:10.
132 Cf. Luke 11:17.
133 Isa. 19:2.
134 Isa. 19:2.
135 Isa. 9:20.
136 Cf. Richard of St Victor, *Erud.* 1.30 (PL 196.1287B).
137 Cf. Augustine, *De sancta uirginitate* 34 (Zycha, 273–75).
138 Cf. Isa. 19:2.
139 Cf. Isa. 19:2.
140 Cf. Luke 21:20.
141 Luke 11:17.
142 Matt. 24:6.
143 Cf. John 3:31.
144 Cf. Ps. 23:8 (Vulg.).
145 Cf. Matt. 10:34–35.
146 Matt. 10:36.
147 Cf. Luke 22:24.
148 On the opposition between mercy and justice, cf. Augustine, *En. Ps.* 50.7 (Dekkers and Frai-pont, CCL 39.603); Richard of St Victor, *Ad me clamat* 4 (Ribaillier, 260).
149 Cf. Ps. 77:54 (Vulg.).
150 Cf. 1 Sam. 15:28; Matt. 27:51.
151 Cf. Isa. 1:5.
152 Cf. 1 Cor. 15:53; Richard of St Victor, *Decl. nonn. diff.* (Ribaillier, 210).
153 Cf. 1 Cor. 4:7.
154 Cf. Richard of St Victor, *Erud.* 1.30 (PL 196.1281C).
155 Cf. Richard of St Victor, *Tract.* on Ps. 2 (PL 196.269D; tr. Evans, VTT 4.151).
156 See discussion in Ribaillier, "Richard de Saint-Victor: *De statu interioris hominis*," 26–27.
157 Cf. Bernard of Clairvaux, *Gratia* 4.10 (SBO 3:173).
158 Cf. Hugh of St Victor, *Sacr.* I.6.16 (PL 176.271D).
159 On cooperative grace, cf. Peter Lombard, *Sent.* II.26.1–2 (SB 4:470).
160 Cf. Rom. 7:15–20.
161 Cf. Job 9:3.
162 James 3:3.
163 1 John 1:8; cf. Richard of St Victor, *Decl. nonn. diff.* (Ribaillier, 204).
164 Cf. Richard of St Victor, *Tract.* on Ps. 28 (PL 196.296C).
165 Eccles. 7:21.
166 Cf. Augustine, *De peccatorum meritis et remissione* II.7 (CSEL 60.77–78); Richard of St Victor, *Decl. nonn. diff.* (Ribaillier, 206).

167 Cf. 1 Cor. 15:54.
168 Cf. Hugh of St Victor, *Sacr.* I.6.10 (PL 176.269D–270A).
169 Cf. Rom. 6:6; Augustine, *Enchiridion* 64 (Evans, 83–84).
170 Cf. Richard of St Victor, *Erud.* I.30 (PL 196.1281D); Bernard of Clairvaux, *Gratia* 4.9 (SBO 3:172–73).
171 Cf. Bernard of Clairvaux, *Gratia* 6.16 (SBO 3:177–78).
172 Cf. Bernard of Clairvaux, *Gratia* 7.21 (SBO 3:181–82).
173 See chap. 19.
174 Cf. Isa. 1:5.
175 See chap. 2, 4, 5, and 11.
176 Cf. Eccles. 1:18. See chap. 11.
177 Hosea 7:11. See chap. 4.
178 Cf. Prov. 3:5.
179 Eccles. 7:1.
180 Cf. Richard of St Victor, *Adnot. Ps.* 118 (PL 196.361B–C).
181 Isa. 5:20.
182 Ps. 61:10 (Vulg.).
183 Prov. 20:10, 23.
184 Lev. 19:36.
185 Cf. Ps. 77:54 (Vulg.).
186 Cf. Richard of St Victor, *Adnot. Ps.* 118 (PL 196.361D–362A).
187 Ps. 90:6 (Vulg.).
188 Cf. Matt. 4:16.
189 Cf. Gen. 1:2.
190 Cf. Ps. 42:3 (Vulg.).
191 Cf. Gen. 1:4.
192 Cf. Gen. 1:19.
193 Cf. Prov. 4:18.
194 Ps. 36:6 (Vulg.).
195 Rom. 14:5.
196 Cf. John 5:27
197 See chap. 25.
198 Cf. Richard of St Victor, *Adnot. Ps.* 143 (PL 196.381C–D).
199 Cf. Matt. 25:15–16.
200 Cf. *Summa sent.* III.7 (PL 176.99); Peter Lombard, *Sent.* II.26.1 (SB 4:436–37); Richard of St Victor, *Tract.* on Ps. 134 (PL 196.367D; tr. Evans, VTT 4.204–205).
201 Cf. 2 Peter 2:21.
202 Cf. Matt. 25:20.
203 Cf. Richard of St Victor, *Trin.* III.2 (Ribaillier, 136–37; tr. Evans, VTT 1.248); *Arca Moys.* III.23 (Aris, 82; PL 196.132B–C; tr. Zinn, 254); *XII patr.* 7 and 61 (Châtillon, 108–110, 266; tr. Zinn, 60, 118).
204 Cf. Isa. 1:5–6; Rom. 14:5.
205 Eccles. 3.4.
206 Ps. 29:6 (Vulg.).
207 Tob. 5:12 (Vulg.).
208 Eccles. 1:5.
209 Prov. 14:13.
210 1 Sam. 2:8.
211 Ps. 88:30 (Vulg.).
212 See chap. 2, 4, 5, 11, and 24.
213 Cf. Isa. 1:5–6; Rom. 14:5.
214 Cf. Bernard of Clairvaux, *Gratia* 4.11 (SBO 3:173–74).

215 Ecclus. 37:31; 1 Cor. 6:12; cf. 1 Cor. 10:22

216 Cf. Richard of St Victor, *Ad me clamat* 14 (Ribaillier, 275–76).

217 Eccles. 7:1.

218 Rom. 14:5.

219 Concerning discretion, see Richard of St Victor, *XII patr.* 67–69 (Châtillon, 314–18; tr. Zinn, 124–27); *Arca Moys.* III.7 and 23 (Aris, 64–65, 82; PL 196.117D, 132A–B; tr. Zinn, 232, 254); *Adnot. Ps.* 118 (PL 196.359B–363B); *Erud.* I.12 (PL 196.1248C); *Erud.* II.3 (PL 196.1301C); cf. also Bernard of Clairvaux, *SCC* 49.5 (SBO 2.75–76). Concerning deliberation, see *Arca Moys.* III.23 (Aris, 82–83; PL 196.132D–133A; tr. Zinn, 255); *Adnot. Ps.* 143 (PL 196.381D); *Erud.* 1.12 (PL 196.1248C).

220 See chap. 26 and 28.

221 See chap. 26 and 29. Cf. also Richard of St Victor, *Quat. grad.* 24 (Dumeige, 151; tr. Kraebel, VTT 2.285).

222 Job 7:18.

223 Ps. 12:4 (Vulg.).

224 Ps. 42:3 (Vulg.).

225 Ps. 103:20 (Vulg.).

226 Ps. 103.22 (Vulg.).

227 Cf. Eccles. 1:5.

228 Cf. Gen. 1:5; Eccles. 3:4.

229 Ps. 29:6 (Vulg.).

230 See chap. 12.

231 Rom. 14:5.

232 See chap. 12.

233 Isa. 1:6.

234 See chap. 2.

235 Cf. Bernard of Clairvaux, *Sermo de diversis* 16.1–3 (SBO 6:1.144–46); Hugh of St Victor, *Sacr.* I.4.19 (PL 176.242A–B).

236 John 15:5.

237 Cf. Luke 11:13; Matt. 7:11.

238 Rom. 7:19.

239 On the distinction between will (*velle*) and ability (*posse*), cf. Bernard of Clairvaux, *Gratia* 1.2 (SBO 3:166–67); William of St Thierry, *In epist. ad Rom.* IV.7.18 (ed. Verdeyen, 101); Peter Abelard, *Comm. in epist. Pauli ad Rom.* III.7 (Buytaert, 208.718–20); cf. also Richard of St Victor, *Exterm.* II.9 (PL 196.1095B–C).

240 Isa. 1:6.

241 See chap. 11.

242 Cf. Hugh of Fouilloy, *De medicina animae* 2 (PL 176.1184–85); William of St Thierry, *Natura* I.12–17 (Verdeyen, 107–109).

243 Cf. Augustine, *Civ. Dei* IV.3.2 (Dombart and Kalb, 416); *Conf.* X.14.22 (Verheijen, 166); *Jo. ev. tr.* 60.3 (Willems, 476); Bernard of Clairvaux, *Sententiae* 3.86 and 120 (SBO 6.2:124 and 222); Peter Lombard, *Sermo in Adventu Domini* (PL 171.366C–367A). Another division is found in Richard of St Victor, *XII patr.* 7 (Châtillon, 108; tr. Zinn, 60).

244 See chap. 31.

245 Isa. 1:6.

246 Isa. 1:6.

247 Cf. Matt. 20:1–10; Richard of St Victor, *LE* II.13.22 (Châtillon, 494).

248 Cf. Jer. 2:21.

249 Cf. Matt. 11:30.

250 See chap. 35.

251 Cf. Matt. 20:10.

252 Matt. 20:14–15.

253   Isa. 1:6.
254   Isa. 1:6.
255   Isa. 1:6.
256   See chap. 11–12.
257   See chap. 10.
258   See chap. 1.
259   Isa. 1:6.
260   Cf. Hugh of St Victor, *Sacr.* II.13.1 (PL 176.525A); Peter Abelard, *Scito te ipsum* 3 (Luscombe, 4).
261   Cf. Richard of St Victor, *Decl. nonn. diff.* (Ribaillier, 212); *Verbis ap.* (Ribaillier, 327).
262   See chap. 34.
263   Peter Lombard, *Sent.* II.22.4 (SB 4:414). See also Richard of St Victor, *Sp. blasph.* (Ribaillier, 122); *Decl. nonn. diff.* (Ribaillier, 212).
264   Cf. Hugh of St Victor, *Tribus diebus* (Poirel, passim; tr. Feiss, VTT 2.55–58, 61–102); *Eulogium* (PL 176.989A–B; tr. Feiss, VTT 2.126–27); Richard of St Victor, *Ad me clamat* 5 (Ribaillier, 262–63); *Super exiit* (Châtillon and Tulloch, 186); *Sp. Blasph.* (Ribaillier, 122); *Trin.* VI.15 (Ribaillier, 247–48; tr. Evans, VTT 1.335). See also Coolman, VTT 2.28–43.
265   Cf. Matt. 12.32.
266   On this phrase "remission without remission" (*remissio sine remissione*), see H. Weisweiler, *Eine neue Bearbeitung von Abelards* Introductio *und der* Summa sententiarum," *Scholastik* 9 (1934): 356.
267   Prov. 2:14.
268   Cf. Richard of St Victor, *Arca Moys* III.9 (Aris, 66; tr. Zinn, 234).
269   Cf. Richard of St Victor, *Diff. pecc.* (Ribaillier, 293).
270   For the dead man outside the house, see Luke 7:11–15. For the corpse inside the tomb, see Luke 8:49–56.
271   Cf. Richard of St Victor, *Decl. nonn. diff.* (Ribaillier, 206).
272   Cf. Luke 7:11–15; 8:49–56.
273   On the threefold sins, see Richard of St Victor, *Pot. lig.* 23 (Ribaillier, 106); *Sp. blasph.* (Ribaillier, 123); cf. *Summa sent.* III.16 (PL 176.113D); Peter Lombard, *Sent.* II.42.4 (SB 4:569).
274   "Livida mens" could either mean "bruised mind" or "envious mind."
275   2 Cor. 7:10.
276   Job 5:2.
277   Isa. 1:6.
278   Luke 10:27; cf. Matt. 22:37, 39; Mark 12:30–31; Deut. 6:5.
279   Exod. 20:12; cf. Deut. 5:16; Matt. 19:19; Rom. 13:9; James 2:11.
280   Exod. 20:13–15; cf. Deut. 5:17–18; Luke 18:20; Rom. 13:9; James 2:11.
281   Matt. 19:21.
282   Matt. 19:12.
283   1 Cor. 7:25–26.
284   1 Cor. 7:1.
285   See chap. 46.
286   Heb. 12:6.
287   Rom. 9:18.
288   Cf. Matt. 25:41.
289   Lev. 26:21.
290   Cf. Lev. 26:18–19.
291   Cf. Exod. 4:21; 7:3; 14:4.
292   Cf. Mark 9:43.
293   Certain sap is supposed to preserve the flesh from worms and decay at death. The sap is also supposed to restrain the lascivious desires of the flesh; cf. Honorius of Autun, *In cantica canitcorum* 4 (PL 172.426B). Consequently, the worm does not die (Mark 9:43) without the remedy of this sap.

294 Cf. Rom. 1:28.
295 Cf. Eccles. 10:4.
296 Cf. Ps. 85:15 (Vulg.); 110:4 (Vulg.); 144:8 (Vulg.).
297 Isa. 1:18.
298 1 Cor. 12:4–11.
299 1 Cor. 15:40–44.
300 Exod. 25:6; 35:8, 28; cf. Lev. 24:2; Num. 4:9, 16.
301 Cf. Bernard of Clairvaux, *SCC* 15.5 (SBO 1:85).
302 Ps. 44:8 (Vulg.).
303 Cf. 1 John 2:27.
304 Isa. 10:27.
305 Ezek. 33:11.
306 Cf. Richard of St Victor, *Decl. nonn. diff.* (Ribaillier, 206).
307 Luke 24:49.
308 Cf. Mark 14:3.
309 Luke 11:13; cf. Matt. 7:11.
310 Cf. James 1:5.
311 Matt. 7:8; Luke 11:10.
312 Matt. 10:8.
313 Cf. 2 Kings 4:1–7.
314 Rom. 8:18.
315 2 Cor. 4:17.
316 Col. 3:4.
317 Cf. Luke 10:30.
318 Cf. Luke 7:47.
319 Matt. 18:32–33.
320 Luke 16:5–6.
321 Cf. Richard of St Victor, *Adnot. Ps.* 118 (PL 196.353A–354A).
322 2 Cor. 6:1.
323 1 Cor. 15:10.
324 1 Cor. 15:10.
325 Cf. Matt. 25:2–10; Apoc. 19:7, 9.
326 Ps. 44:8 (Vulg.); Heb. 1:9.
327 Heb. 1:4.
328 Heb. 2:9.
329 Phil. 2:9–10.
330 John 1:14.
331 Col. 2:9.
332 See chap. 49.
333 John 1:16.
334 See chap. 1.
335 John 16:24.
336 See chap. 39.
337 See chap. 49.
338 Ps. 31:1 (Vulg.).
339 Ps. 31.2 (Vulg.).
340 Ps. 145:5 (Vulg.).
341 Ps. 93:12 (Vulg.).
342 Cf. Jer. 17:7.
343 Ps. 127:2 (Vulg.).
344 Matt. 5:3.
345 Matt. 5:10.

346   James 1:12.
347   Acts 5:41.
348   Cf. 2 Cor. 11:30; 12:5, 9.
349   1 Cor. 2:9; cf. James 1:12.
350   Isa. 1:6.

HUGH OF ST VICTOR

ON THE POWER OF PRAYER

INTRODUCTION AND TRANSLATION
BY HUGH FEISS OSB

INTRODUCTION

This treatise of Hugh of St Victor is very tightly focused on the question: How can one pray the words of Scripture with integrity when they express sentiments that one does not feel? This is a question that Christians often pondered, and like Hugh they usually focused their attention on praying the Psalms. This introduction will consider the author, recipient, date and title; the historical background and context of Hugh's treatment; his use of the rhetorical tradition to develop a typology of prayer; and his teaching on prayer.[1]

AUTHENTICITY, ADDRESSEE, DATE, AND TITLE

Hugh's authorship of this treatise has never been contested. The work and its prologue are listed in Abbot Gilduin's index (*Indiculum*) of Hugh's works as *Tractatus de virtute orandi*.[2] It is mentioned under the same title, but without the prologue, in another early catalogue of Hugh's works.[3] Many important early manuscript collections of Hugh's writings attributed this treatise to him by name. It was very popular. In his catalogue of manuscripts of Hugh's works, R. Goy lists 226 manuscripts, of which 104 are from the fifteenth century.[4]

The manuscripts generally indicate that the destinary of the covering letter is Th.[5] In a few manuscripts this is expanded to Theodericus

---

[1]   This introduction and translation have developed in stages over twenty-five years. In 1985 B. Dardis and I prepared an edition of *De virtute orandi*, collated from twenty-two manuscripts, with an introduction and notes. In *Oeuvres* 1 (1997), that Latin text was published with a translation by P. Sicard and an introduction by D. Poirel. The critical edition of the Latin text is now being completed by C. Evans, and his preliminary work has been taken into account here. This introduction and the notes to the translation are new, but they owe much to their predecessors, and especially to D. Poirel's introduction and notes.

[2]   J. de Ghellinck, "La table des matières de la première édition des œuvres de Hugues de Saint-Victor," *Recherches de science religieuse* 1 (1910): 281.

[3]   J. de Ghellinck, "Un catalogue des œuvres de Hugues de Saint-Victor," *Revue néo-scolastique de philosophie* 20 (1913): 230.

[4]   R. Goy, *Die Überlieferung der Werke Hugos von St. Viktor*, Monographien zur Geschichte des Mittelalters 16 (Stuttgart: Hiersemann, 1976), 404–48. Some of the more significant early manuscripts containing the work are Douai, BM 360 and 361; Paris, Bibliothèque de l'Arsenal 323; Paris, Bibliothèque Mazarine 717; Troyes, BM 301. There are at least forty other manuscripts that are not in Goy's list.

[5]   In the editions of 1526, 1648 and the PL, this was corrupted to "ch.", which was then expanded to "charissimo" ("dearly beloved"). This change had already occurred in several manuscripts.

or Theomar. It is tempting to identify Th. with Thietmar, the first superior of the monastery of canons regular at Hamersleben (1107–1138).
Several manuscripts include an addition at the end of prologue asking
the recipients to pray for Hugh's uncle. If, as seems likely, Hugh and his
uncle came to St Victor from Halberstadt, then this reference to his
uncle seems to strengthen the possibility that the covering letter was
addressed to someone who knew them, and Thietmar would be a good
candidate.[6]

There is no firm evidence about when the treatise was written. If it
was written for Thietmar, it must be dated before 1138, or at least before
news of his death could reach Hugh at St Victor.[7]

The titles assigned to Hugh's treatise in the manuscripts are quite
varied. The most frequently used is *De modo orandi*, then *De virtute
orandi, Libellus de oratione, De virtute orationis,* and *De studio orandi,*
most of which echo phrases in the cover letter and the first paragraph.
The best attested title seems to be *De virtute orandi,* although it is quite
possible that originally the work had no title.

SINCERE PRAYER: MIND AND VOICE IN HARMONY

According to W. Harmless, Augustine found that the Psalms
touched the ears of the heart and drew the one who heard them into
their sweet sound. They "were sung by the voice of Christ—by turns,

---

[6]   This addition is found in Paris, BnF MS lat. 16692 (Morimond, twelfth century): "Therefore,
      I pray first that for the love of Lord Jesus Christ in your prayer you commend the soul of
      my uncle to the Lord; then that you deign also to remember me to God especially since as
      it is necessary to pray for all so it is a duty to be discharged by all" ("Primum igitur precor
      propter amorem Domini Iesu Christi ut animam avunculi mei Domino precibus vestris
      commendetis, deinde ut mei quoque apud Deum memor esse dignemini, maxime cum hoc
      sicut omnibus petere necessarium, ita omnibus impendere debitum sit"). Unless otherwise
      noted, all translations are mine.
          This passage was edited first by J. Ehlers, *Hugo von St. Viktor. Studien zum Geschichts-
      denken und zur Geschichtsschreibung des 12.* Jahrhunderts, Frankfurter historische Abhand-
      lungen, 7 (Wiesbaden: Steiner, 1973), 29. Sicard, who includes this addition in his bilingual
      edition, conjectures that it was too personal to leave in the work when it began to circulate
      beyond the original recipients, so Gilduin or Hugh eliminated it (*Oeuvres* 1:163 n. 8). Part
      of the addition is also found in Wolfenbüttel, Herzog-August-Bibliothek, MS 50.4 Aug, 40
      (twelfth/thirteenth century, from St. Michael, Hildesheim). On Hugh's origins and his uncle
      see the literature cited in Feiss, VTT 2.185–88.
[7]   Sicard, *Oeuvres* 1:119, mentions a charter witnessed at Halberstadt in 1128 by a canon named
      Hugh. If this was Hugh of St Victor's uncle, who is known to have died at St Victor, then 1128
      would probably the terminus a quo.

the voice of the Risen Lord and the voice of His body, the Church on earth." Sometimes Christ's voice sighs, sometimes it laments, and sometimes it rejoices in hope. Augustine invited those who listened to his *Expositions of the Psalms* "to lay claim to the Psalms' emotional repertoire as a way to repair and renew their own damaged hearts."[8]

John Cassian recommended that, when troubled with distracting or unwholesome thoughts and feelings, the monk repeat constantly the psalm verse "O God, come to my assistance; O Lord, make haste to help me."[9] Having thus fixed his heart on God, he could make the Psalms his own, so that he experienced not the words but the feelings of the heart (*cordis affectus*) from which they arose and which they expressed.

> We find all these feelings expressed in the Psalms. Seeing the things that occur there as in a very pure mirror, we recognize them more effectively and so, taught by these feelings, we touch them not as something heard but as something perceived; we give birth to them from the internal feeling of our heart not as things commended to memory but as implanted in the very nature of things, so that we penetrate their meaning not by the text of the reading, but by our previous experience.[10]

---

8   W. Harmless, *Augustine in His Own Words* (Washington, DC: The Catholic University of America Press, 2010), 159, citing *En. Ps.* 41.9 (Dekkers and Fraipont, CCL 38.467); *En. Ps.* 42.1 (Dekkers and Fraipont, CCL 38.474); *En. Ps.* 96.2 (Dekkers and Fraipont, CCL 39.1354–55).

9   Ps. 69:2 (Vulg.); John Cassian, *Conferences* X.10 (Pichéry, SC 54:85–90; tr. Ramsey, 378–83).

10   *Conferences* X.11 (Pichéry, 2:93; tr. Ramsey, 385): "Omnes namque hos adfectus in Psalmis invenimus expressos, ut ea que incurrerint velut in speculo purissimo pervidentes efficacius agnoscamus et ita magistris adfectibus eruditi non ut audita, sed tamquam perspecta palpemus, nec tamquam memoriae conmendata, sed velut ipsi rerum naturae insita de interno cordis parturiamus adfectu, ut eorum sensus non textu lectionis, sed experientia praecedente penetremus;" see C. Stewart, *Cassian the Monk,* Oxford Studies in Historical Theology (New York: Oxford, 1998), 112–13. For similar ideas on praying the psalms with references to human feelings, see Athanasius, *Letter to Marcellinus,* 10–11 (PG 27.19B–24B; tr. R. Gregg, *Athanasius: The Life of Antony and the Letter to Marcellinus* [New York: Paulist, 1980], 107–11); Augustine, *En. Ps.* 30 (ed. Dekkers and Fraipont, CCL 38.212–13; PL 36.248); Cassiodorus, *Institutiones* I.4.3 (Mynors, 21; PL 70.1115CD); Cassiodorus, *In Psalmorum praefatio* 16 (PL 70.22CD); Gerhoh of Reichersberg, *Commentarius aureus in psalmos* (PL 193.634A–636A), who quotes Hugh's *Virtute orandi* 14. This way of interpreting the psalms in terms of feelings does not show up often in written commentaries, even of those who proposed it. According to J. M. Neale and R. F. Littledale, in his notations on the psalms in *Misc.* II.1–81 (PL 177.589–633) Hugh "has only left an exposition of the most obscure verses of the Psalter; but that is so truly valuable, as to make one regret that he did not extend his labors to the whole book. Perhaps, in proportion to its size, no commentary has yielded so much" (*A Commentary on the Psalms from Patristic and Medieval Writers,* 3rd ed. [London: Joseph Masters, 1874], 1:85). However, in these notes Hugh does not interpret the Psalms in the way he suggests in *Virtute orandi.* Hugh aimed at least to approximate the method of

Without specifying how, the *Rule of Benedict* taught that one should pray wisely and in the fear of God. Prayer should be made with pure devotion from a pure heart.[11] Because one prays the Divine Office in the presence of God and the angels, one should make sure that mind and heart are in harmony.[12] One makes a request to a powerful person with humility and reverence, so one should ask of God with humility and very pure devotion, not in abundance of words, but with purity of heart and tears of compunction.[13] Grimlac, a hermit who wrote about prayer early in the ninth century, echoes Benedict's teaching that that God listens not to the words, but to the devotion of a pure heart.[14] Alcuin's *De psalmorum usu* proposes eight thematic groupings of the psalms.[15]

In the "long twelfth century" (AD 1050–1215), there was a shift in Christian sensibility: prayer as a communal and charitable activity was less to the fore and the emphasis was increasingly placed on prayer as personal devotion. Of course, prayer for others continued in prayer for the dead and in, some places, the "oratio fidelium" (prayers of the faithful, bidding prayers, "prières du prone") at Mass,[16] but writers and

---

Virtute orandi in his *In Eccl.*, in which he endeavored to immerse himself in the sentiments of the biblical author so that the author's sentiments would penetrate his own heart and the hearts of his readers. He writes at the end of *In Eccl.* 1 (PL 175.133AB): "One needs to know that this book requires a new kind of exposition. Because the whole book aims at moving the feelings of the human heart, it is quite often necessary to speak about it in a conversational rather than an expository way. Hence it is sometimes necessary discuss at length even things that seem simple and obvious, so that the message of the words may touch the heart of the hearer more strongly and penetrate the heart more effectively" ("Sciendum est hunc librum novum quoddam expositionis genus requirere; quia cum totus ad commovendos affectus cordis humani intendat, saepius in eo quasi colloquendo quam exponendo sermonem formare oportet. Unde necesse est in iis etiam aliquando, quae plana et aperta videntur, diutius verbis immorari, ut ipsa locutionis inculcatio validius tangat et efficacius penetret cor audientis"). On this passage see H. de Lubac, *Medieval Exegesis: The Four Senses of Scripture* (Grand Rapids, MI: Eerdmans, 2009), 3:324–26.

11 *Rule of Benedict* 20.2–4 (Kardong, 206).

12 *Rule of Benedict* 19.1–4 (Kardong, 203); N. Bériou, ed., *Prier au moyen âge: Pratiques et expériences (v^e–xve siècles)*, Témoins de Notre Histoire 2 (Turnhout: Brepols, 1991), 135–37.

13 *Rule of Benedict* 20.1–3 (Kardong, 206–207). Kardong gives many references to similar a fortiori arguments in other early Christian authors and provides a helpful discussion of Benedict's views on psalmody and prayer (215–17). He mentions that Adalbert de Vogüé thinks that in these chapters of the *Rule of Benedict* "oratio" (prayer) refers not to communal psalmody, but to silent, private prayer, for which psalmody is a preparation.

14 *Regula solitariorum (Rule for Hermits)* 31, cited in Bérliou, 138.

15 Alcuin's *De psalmorum usu* (PL 101.465–69) proposes eight thematic groupings of the psalms, which correspond to spiritual situations. For another such grouping into 7 categories, see Bériou, 29.

16 Bériou, 71–72.

preachers emphasized prayer of recollection, which put the Christian alone in the presence of God, in an intimate dialogue of love and compunction.[17]

Among the reform movements of the eleventh and twelfth centuries this growing emphasis on interiority was accompanied by a certain amount of unease regarding liturgical prayer. Reformers were concerned about psalmody performed mechanically without the engagement of interior dispositions. Some warned against prayer that was long or beautiful but not sincere. Others saw extended liturgical prayer as too theatrical, leaving too little time or energy for personal prayer.[18]

After Hugh's time, Christians continued to give directives for prayer. For example, the *Speculum dominarum* by Durand of Champagne, confessor of Jeanne de Navarre († 1305), wife of Philippe le Bel, says that when we pray our liturgy of the hours there are three possible object of our attention: (1) saying the words correctly; (2) the sense of words; (3) the goal of our prayer, that is, God and what we ask of God in our prayer. This last is the best sort of attention in prayer.[19] According to Étienne de Bourbon's *Traité des diverses matières à prêcher* (ca. 1250), a diffuse treatise for preachers which therefore was directed ultimately toward the ordinary Christian, there are three main kinds of prayer: of the heart, of the voice, and of good works. Prayer of the heart, that is, mental prayer, takes the forms of contrition, compassion, affliction, devotion of heart, and insistence. Referring to the *Gloss* on 1 Tim. 2:1, Étienne divides prayer of the voice into deprecation, rogation, supplication, demand, intercession, devotion, praise, psalmody, thanksgiving, and jubilation.[20]

Much of the content of Hugh's treatise is traditional or found in writings of his contemporaries. He does not make use of Augustine's Christological interpretation of the Psalms. Apart from the reference to the Wedding at Cana (9.2), he does not refer to Christ; like Grimlac, Hugh speaks of prayer addressed to God.[21] However, like Augustine, Cassian, and much of the tradition after him, Hugh emphasizes the

---

[17]   Bériou, 14–15.

[18]   P. Henriet, *La parole et la prière au moyen âge: La Verbe efficace dans l'hagiographie monastique des XIᵉ et XIIᵉ siècles*. Bibliothèque du Moyen Âge 18 (Bruxelles: De Boeck, 2005), 164–67 (who gives many references). However, regarding Cluny, see J. Leclercq, "Culte liturgique et prière intime dans le monachisme au moyen âge," *La Maison-Dieu* 69 (1962): 39–55.

[19]   Bériou, 239–41.

[20]   Bériou, 288–91.

[21]   In his *Soliloquy on the Betrothal-Gift of the Soul*, the soul is betrothed to God, not to Christ.

importance of identifying with the feelings expressed by the Psalmist. Like Benedict, Grimlac and many others, to urge sincerity and humility when praying to God, he uses the analogy to making a request of a great personage. Although like others of his time Hugh emphasizes the interiority of the one praying, in his treatise he does not question the form or quantity of liturgical prayer. Although his use of verbs like "decantare" and "cantare" suggests public singing or recitation, his treatise does not refer specifically to public prayer. What he writes applies to any effort to pray the Scriptures, particularly the Psalms.

ARS ORANDI: A RHETORIC OF PRAYER

What is most original in Hugh's treatise is his application of the categories of rhetoric to prayer.[22] In Latin, "oratio," the word Hugh uses for "prayer" in the title of his work, had a range of meanings that centered on the idea of "persuasive speech." Classical Greek and Roman education trained the student for public life. "The arts of judicial, political, and panegyric oratory became central to the curriculum."[23] Cicero wrote extensively on "oratio," and his writings and the *Rhetorica ad Herennium,* sometimes attributed to him, had lasting influence. In this tradition an "oratio" was divided into six parts: introduction (*exordium*), statement of facts (*narratio*), division (*partitio*), proof (*confirmatio*), refutation (*reprehensio*), and conclusion (*conclusio*).[24] The exordium began the speech by disposing the hearers to listen (*captatio benevolentiae*), either directly (*principium*) or indirectly (*insinuatio*).[25] One gained the good will or favor of the hearers by the way one presented oneself, one's hearers, one's adversaries or the facts themselves.[26] Narration expounds the actual or purported facts.[27] "Oratio" can be

[22] On *ars orandi* as an identifiable genre of medieval literature, and William of Auvergne's development of it, see Poirel, *Oeuvres* 1:117–22.

[23] This and the next quotation are from P. Dronke, *The Medieval Poet and His World,* Storia e Letteratura 164 (Rome: Edizioni di Storia e Letteratura, 1984), 7. See also T. Haye, *Oratio: Mittelalterliche Redekunst in lateinischer Sprache,* Mittellateinische Studien und Texte 27 (Leiden: Brill, 1999), 1–16.

[24] Cicero, *De partitione oratoria* 8.27–17.60 (Rackham, Loeb 349:331–57); *De inventione* I.14.19–I.56.109 (Hubbell, Loeb 386:40–163); *Rhetorica ad Herennium* I.3.4 (Caplan, Loeb 403:8–11).

[25] *Rhetorica ad Herennium* I.3 (Caplan, Loeb 403:10–13).

[26] *Rhetorica ad Herennium* I.4.7–I.5.8 (Caplan, Loeb 403:12–15). See also Cicero, *De oratore* II.79.320–22 (Sutton and Rackham, Loeb 348:440–43); *De inventione* I.16.22 (Hubbell, Loeb 386:44–47).

[27] *Rhetorica ad Herennium* I.3.4 (Caplan, Loeb 403:8–9); I.8.12–I.10.16 (Caplan, Loeb 403:22–29); *De inventione* 19.27–21.30 (Hubbell, Loeb 386:44–47).

formulated in an ornate style, a plain style, or a style somewhere in between.[28] According to Cicero, "oratio" must be joined to wisdom if it is to serve the common good.[29]

Under the Roman Empire and in the Middle Ages, "the system of rules that had originally been devised for the orator became adapted to every aspect of literary composition," including poetry, drama, preaching and letter writing. In the thirteenth century John of Genoa wrote that "oratio" is fivefold: bound in meter, unbound in prose, addressed to someone in letters, back-and-forth in dialogues, narrative in historical accounts.[30]

Thus, although in the past some scholars thought that there was no development in theory and practice of rhetoric during the Middle Ages, that was not the case. Several traditions of rhetorical theory were handed on and developed during the Middle Ages, of which the most important derived from Cicero. This tradition, as applied to the art of letter-writing (*ars dictaminis*), divided letters into five or six parts into which Cicero had divided a speech: exordium (including both greeting [*salutatio*] and seeking favor [*captatio benevolentiae*]), background (*narratio*), statement of parts (*divisio*), proof (*confirmatio,* which in the *artes dictaminis* and in Hugh's treatise became the *petitio)*, attack on opponent's arguments (*refutatio*) and conclusion (*peroratio*). A treatise on letter-writing by one of Hugh's contemporaries distinguishes five main parts to a letter: salutation, seeking favor, narration, and petition (which may be supplicatory, didactic, menacing, hortatory, admonitory, advisory, reproving or merely direct), and conclusion. The author gives examples of how the order of the three central parts may be varied.[31]

In *The Power of Prayer*, Hugh uses this rhetorical tradition to treat a very specific form of "oratio," one addressed to God. In his prologue, itself a letter written according to the *ars dictaminis*,[32] he says he is

---

28   For example, *De optimo genere oratorum* 1 (Hubbell, Loeb 386:355).
29   *De inventione* I.1.1–I.4.5 (Hubbell, Loeb 386:2–13).
30   John of Genoa, *Catholicon,* cited by Haye, *Oratio,* 3.
31   Anonymous writer from Bologna, *Rationes dictandi,* tr. J. Murphy, *Three Medieval Rhetorical Arts* (Berkeley: University of California Press, 1971), 1–25.
32   Thus, Hugh's letter includes the requisite elements: (a) Salutation: "To his Lord and father, Th." Hugh puts the addressed first, because he is of higher station than Hugh; (b) Seeking favor: "Lord and father . . . receive this little gift of my love . . . the devotion with which I have offered it . . . Your charity;"(c) Narration: "I have sent . . . treatise on the power of prayer;" (d) Petition: "going to ask for prayer . . . give a gift in return."

writing a brief composition (*dictatum brevem*). He aims to show two
things: (1) in what ways the mind of someone in prayer[33] is moved by
compunction while saying the words of his prayer; (2) why passages
from Scripture which are not petitionary in form are offered as prayers
for salvation. These two aims structure his treatise:

(A) How the mind of someone in prayer is aroused to compunction and
devotion.
(1) The two wings of prayer: meditation on God's mercy and human misery (1–2).[34]
    (a) misery (3)
    (b) mercy (4)
(2) Devotion (4–5)
(3) Three kinds of prayer (6)
    (a) Supplication (7.1)
        1) seeking favor (7.2); commend one's person/cause; praise
        one prayed to; disparage opponent
        2) insistence (7.3); remind the one addressed about his per-
        son or the speaker's or about the speaker's cause
        3) pure prayer (7.4)
        4) with nouns only, verbs only, or both nouns and verbs (7.5)
    (b) Request: imploring, asking, or simply requesting (8)
    (c) Suggestion (9.1)
        1) with fear (9.1)
        2) with confidence (9.2)
        3) with contempt (9.3)
(B) Why non-petitionary scriptural passages can be employed in prayers
for salvation
(1) Using Scripture in prayer (10.1)
        (a) objection (10.1–2)
        (b) differences between prayer to the all-knowing God and
        to human beings (11.1)
        (c) devotion is the heart of prayer (11.2)
        (d) all forms of prayer can include seeking favor (12.1–12.3)
        (e) sincerity in seeking favor; stirs up or expresses devout
        feelings (13)
        (f) examples from the Psalms (14)

---

[33] "orantis": more generally, someone making a persuasive speech verbally or in writing, but
here applied to one addressing God.
[34] The numbers in parentheses refer to the paragraphs divisions of Hugh's treatise.

In analyzing the kinds of prayer Hugh makes use of many categories from the rhetorical tradition, although he tweaks their order and meaning. Under supplication he lists four ways of seeking favor (*captatio benevolentiae* [7.2]), which he draws from the rhetorical tradition. Emphasizing one's wretchedness (3) and praising the goodness of the one addressed (4) were two of these that fitted easily into Christian prayer. Disparaging one's opponent seems to apply less easily, but Hugh has no trouble finding examples in the Psalms. Hugh uses other terms from classical rhetoric: insistent reminding (*exactio*); a narrative (*narratio*) into which a petition is inserted (8); suggestion (*insinuatio*), a narrative without an explicit petition, which is particularly appropriate when one is speaking to God who knows what one needs already (9). The influence of classical rhetoric's judicial application is evident in Hugh's references to the petitioner's case or cause (*causa*). The three motivations for using suggestion (*insinuation*)—fear, confidence and contempt—are also found in the rhetorical tradition (9.3).

The Argument

In the first sentence of his treatise Hugh introduces two key concepts, zeal (*studium*) and feeling (*affectus*). Both are aroused by meditation on one's wretchedness (*miseria*) and God's mercy (*misericordia*) (1). Reading the Psalms and other Scriptural passages leads to meditation, which leads to knowledge, which gives birth to compunction, which gives birth to devotion, which perfects prayer. Devotion, the heart of prayer, is "a turning to God with loving and humble feeling:" humble from consciousness of one's weakness, loving from consideration of divine kindness. Such a turning presupposes faith, hope and love (5). The rest of Hugh's treatise explores the ways words (*voce*) arouse devotion in prayer: (a) supplication, three forms of which are seeking favor (*captatio benevolentiae*) before making a request, insistence, and pure prayer (7); (b) request or narration with an overt request, three forms of which are urgent, moderate, and simple (8); (c) suggestions or the narration with an implied petition, the three forms of which are with fear, confidence, and contempt (9). God already knows what we need, and so one can pray to God without a narration or petition; a devout supplication from the heart is enough (11.2). Seeking favor (*captatio benevolentiae*) is found in the other forms of supplication as well. (12.1). Whenever we praise God, our heart is saying one thing, that it reverences and loves God and entrusts itself to him. It may do this by praising God, calling attention to our need, or disparaging our enemies. So, in praying the Psalms or other Scriptures, we should consider what feeling they serve and try to rouse our hearts to that feeling, which will help us know the words better, which in turn will increase our devotion (12.3).[35] Thus, Hugh locates the heart of prayer in the affective nature of human beings: "in the feelings of filial love is all the power of prayer" ("In affectibus pietatis est omnis virtus orandi" [14.1]). Then, Hugh goes on to give examples of various feelings of piety: those expressing praise: love, awe, joy; those expressing wretchedness: humility, sadness, fear; those accusing adversaries: indignation, zeal, assurance (14.2–3). All of these are found in the Psalms (14.4–9).

SIGNIFICANT THEMES

From Mediation to Prayer

Hugh's treatise begins in the reading and recitation of biblical texts. He suggests a form of meditation on these readings that will lead to sincere prayer. Like others of his time, Hugh distinguished several moments in the spiritual life: reading (*lectio*), meditation, prayer (*oratio*), action (*operatio*), and contemplation. These are not stages as much as interwoven threads or components. However, there is a logical progression from reading that brings knowledge, to meditation that ponders the implications of that knowledge, to prayer for a deeper understanding or help and guidance to act on what the Scriptures teach, and to contemplation that is the fruit of prayer and virtue expressed in action.[36] Hugh wrote treatises on reading, meditation, and here on prayer.[37]

---

[35] *Virtute orandi* 11.2: "Quaecumque ergo sunt verba orantis absurda non sunt, si tantummodo ad hoc competenter proferri possint, ut vel orantis affectum ad amorem Dei excitent, vel quod amplius est si iam amore eius flagrat excitatum demonstrent" ("Whatever the words of the one praying, they are not absurd if only they can be uttered suitably to arouse the one praying to feel love of God, or what is greater, if he already burns with love of Him, they show his intensity").

[36] *Didasc.* III.10 (Buttimer, 59.15–21; tr. Harkins, VTT 3.125–26); V.9 (Buttimer, 109–10; tr. Harkins, VTT 3.161–62); *Meditatione* (Baron, 46.16–19; tr. Van Liere, VTT 4.387–92); Pseudo-Hugh, *Expositio super Regulam S. Augustini* 1 (PL 176.885A), 9 (PL 176.911D–912A). See Feiss, VTT 2.308–309 n. 20.

[37] *Didasc.* and *Mediatione.*

Misery and Mercy

In identifying the misery of human beings and the mercy of the Creator as the two wings of prayer, Hugh touched on an idea close to the heart of biblical religion. Yves Congar writes:

> There is no motive for prayer more authentic, none more surely answered than an appeal to God's mercy in view of the wretchedness of men. The relationship which religion implies receives here its perfect expression: on our side, nothing and absolute need; of God's, the utmost royalty and divine power.[38]

One of the Hymns from Qumran reads:

> I thank you, Lord, because you saved my life from the pit . . . The depraved spirit you have purified from great offence so that he can take a place with the host of the whole ones.[39]

Benedetto Calati describes medieval monasticism as suffused with a profound "sense of reverential fear joined to confidence; the full knowledge of one's own misery joined to an enlightened optimism regarding the prompt response of God's grace."[40] Hugh makes frequent use of this contrast and play on words: "miseria/misericordia."[41]

Devotion and Feeling

In Hugh's estimation, the heart of prayer is devotion. Devotion is a turning toward God with sentiments of love and humility. Humility is aroused by awareness of one's wretchedness; love arises from thinking

---

[38] *The Revelation of God,* tr. A. Manson and L. C. Sheppard (NY: Herder and Herder, 1968) 49, translated from *Les voies du Dieu Vivant* (Paris: Éditions du Cerf, 1962) and originally published as, "La miséricorde, attribut souverain de Dieu," *La vie spirituelle* 106/482 (April, 1962): 380.

[39] 1QH II.19–24, cited in J. Levison, *Filled with the Spirit* (Grand Rapids, MI: Eerdmans, 2009), 203.

[40] Cited by B. Baroffio, "Preghiera personale e preghiera liturgica," *Dizionario degli Istituti di Perfezione* 7 (1983): 614. Two examples of such early medieval prayer are to be found in Bériou, 26, 28.

[41] Hugh of St Victor, *Quat. volunt.* (PL 176.644D–645A); *Lament.* (PL 175.314AB); *Misc.* I.74 (PL 177.509A); II.45 (PL 177.611D–612A); II.51 (PL 177.617D–618B); II.58 (PL 177.622B); II.63 (PL 177.623A); Pseudo-Hugh of St Victor, *Tractatus de Trinitate et de reparatione hominis* (ed. R. Baron, "Hugues de St. Victor, *Tractatus de Trinitate et de reparatione hominis* du ms. Douai 365," *Mélanges de science religieuse* 18 [1961]: 112); Pseudo-Hugh of St Victor, "Que sit summa scientiae" (ed. Baron, "Textes spirituels inédits de Hugues de Saint-Victor," *Mélanges de science religieuse* 13 [1956], 168); *Sent. quest.* 29 (Lottin, 205).

about God's mercy. Devotion was a term used in pre-Christian Rome for the dedication of a person to the gods or to the service of the emperor. A devout person was faithful, submissive, respectful and obedient. The early Christian writers adopted the term to designate liturgical actions and the interior sentiments of faith, piety and fervor that ought to animate liturgical rites. In a wider sense, devotion was the fundamental outlook, arising from heartfelt faith, which expressed itself in sentiments and acts of divine service.[42]

Several twelfth-century authors also emphasized or analyzed devotion. A brief exemplum about a Cistercian lay brother uses the word "devotion" eight times.[43] St Bernard of Clairvaux described devotion as the divine gift of fervor, which is fueled by meditation on sin. For Guigo I, the fifth prior of the Grand Chartreuse, devotion is the fundamental attitude of the Christian toward God; it is almost identified with love. Its works are reading, meditation, prayer, contemplation, and liturgical action. Hugh's particular contribution was to explore its connection to prayer.[44]

According to Hugh's treatise, loving devotion toward God can be expressed in nine feelings (*affectus*), which both express and deepen understanding. As he divided prayer into three kinds, each with three subdivisions, so he divides the feelings into three kinds, each with three subdivisions: (a) those expressing praise: love, awe, joy; (b) those expressing wretchedness: humility, sadness, fear; (c) those accusing adversaries: indignation, zeal, assurance. The three main divisions are derived from the three ways in which one seeks favor in an "oratio." The nine subdivisions are derived from traditional lists of feelings (love, joy, sadness, fear), from feelings that Hugh invoked in discussing the nature of prayer to God (humility and wretchedness), and feelings he connected with disparaging one's adversaries in seeking to gain favor.[45]

---

[42]   For this and the following paragraph see J. Châtillon, "Devotio," *DS* 3 (1957): 702–716.

[43]   Konrad, *Exordium magnum cisterciense* IV.13 (Griesser, 238–39), cited in Bériou, 98–101.

[44]   There is a fine discussion of devotion in St Francis de Sales, *Introduction to the Devout Life* I.1 (tr. J. Ryan [Garden City, NY: Doubleday, 1955], 33–37).

[45]   On *affectus, see* VTT 2, subject index, "Feeling(s)." See also, Augustine, *En. Ps.* 30.2.3.1 (Dekkers and Fraipont, CCL 38.1856): "Et si orat psalmus, orate; et si gemit, gemite; et si gratulatur, gaudete; et si sperat, sperate; et si timent, timete" ("If the psalm prays, pray; if it groans, groan; if it rejoices, rejoice; if it hopes, hope; if it fears, fear"). Hugh envisages a deepening of prayer, in which the meaning of the words and the feeling reinforce each other.

THE KINDS OF PRAYER

Prompted by 1 Tim. 2:1, which mentions supplications, prayers, intercessions and thanksgiving,[46] Christians have distinguished different kinds of prayer.[47] John Cassian commented on the different kinds of prayer named in 1 Tim. 2:1 in the ninth of his *Conferences* and arranged them in a progression. The fourth, thanksgiving, is proper to those who, having laid a foundation of compunction, humility and recollection, consider with a pure mind God's mercies and are "rapt by their fervent heart to that fiery prayer which can be neither grasped nor expressed by human speech."[48] But at any stage of spiritual development one may make pure and intense prayers, filled with love.[49] All four kinds of prayer can be subsumed in perfect prayer "formed by the contemplation of God alone and through the fervor of love, by which the mind, having been dissolved and flung into love of him, speaks most familiarly to God as to its own father with a particular filial love."[50] Thus a pure heart and mind, filled with love, utter pure prayer, intense and wordless.[51] We hear a clear echo of this teaching in the third and highest kind of supplication, described by Hugh, in which the intensity of one's love causes one to forget any petition and to rejoice totally in God.

[46] In the Vulgate these are "obsecrationes," "orationes," "postulationes," "gratiarum actiones."
[47] E.g., Origen, *On Prayer* 14. (PG 11.459–64; tr. O'Meara, ACW 19 [1954], 53–57). For other authors see Poirel, *Oeuvres* 1:166 note 26. In the ST II–II.83.17, St Thomas Aquinas, commenting on 1 Tim 2:1, quotes Cassian and echoes Hugh. Aquinas says that three things are necessary in prayer ("oratio," the ascent of the mind to God): (1) the praying person approaches God (2) with a petition ("postulatio," which has three forms: "postulatio" (which asks for something specific), "supplicatio" (in which what is asked is unspecified), and "insinuatio" (which includes a narration), (3) which God grants because of his holiness and the petitioner's gratitude.
[48] John Cassian, *Conferences* IX.15.1 (Pichéry, SC 54:51; tr. Ramsey, 339): "mente purissima retractantes ad illam ignitam et quae ore hominum nec conprehendi nec exprimi potest orationem ferventissimo corde raptantur."
[49] John Cassian, *Conferences* IX.15.2–3 (Pichéry, SC 54:52–53; tr. Ramsey, 339).
[50] John Cassian, *Conferences* IX.18.1 (Pichéry, SC 54:55; tr. Ramsey, 340): "contemplatione dei solius et caritatis ardore formatur, per quem mens in illius dilectionem resoluta atque reiecta familiarissime deo velut patri proprio peculiari pietate conloquitur." Cassian then expounds the Lord's Prayer (*Conferences* IX.18–24).
[51] Stewart, *Cassian the Monk*, 108. In addition to Stewart's study, which treats extensively Cassian's teaching on prayer, see M. Alexandre, "La prière de feu chez Jean Cassien," in *Jean Cassien entre l'orient et l'occident*, ed. C. Badilita and A. Jakab (Paris: Beauchesne/Bucharest: Polirom, 2003), 169–203.

EDITIONS

Opera Hugonis de Sancto Victore. Ed. Josse Clichtove (Paris: Henricus Stephanus, 1506), 63r–71r.

Opera omnia Hugonis de Sancto Victore. (Paris: Iosse Bade and Jehan Petit, 1526), 2:150v–154v.

Opera omnia Hugonis de Sancto Victore (Rouen: Joannis Berthelin, 1648), 2:238–44.

PL 176.977A–988A.

Ed. Hugh Feiss, *Oeuvres* 1:126–60.

TRANSLATIONS

French
Patrice Sicard, *Oeuvres* 1:127–61.

Monique Duchet-Suchaux and Jean Longère, *Prier au moyen âge*, 305–307 (par. 2–5).

German
Paul Wolff, *Die Viktoriner: Mystische Schriften.* Vienna: Thomas-Verlag Jakob Hegner, 1936. Pp. 65–70 (par. 1–5, 10.1–11.2).[52]

---

[52]   The same author published *Mystiche Schriften: mit einem Anhang über Augustins Einfluß auf die Mystik der Viktoriner* (Trier: Paulinus-Verl., 1961), which I have not seen; it may contain the *De virtute orandi.*

ON THE POWER OF PRAYER

Prologue

To his Lord and father, Th.[1] [from] Hugh. I pray that you receive this little gift of my love with benevolence equal to the devotion with which I know I have offered it.[2] I have sent to Your Charity a brief treatise on the power of prayer, although it is written in an unpolished style.[3] In it you have distinguished the various modes by which the mind[4] of the one praying is enkindled through compunction amid the words of the prayers. It is also shown why in our prayer, when we are asking for the salvation of others or ourselves, we utter Scriptures that do not have the form of a petition. I have therefore written about prayer in order to ask for your prayer. The more perfectly you have already tasted prayer's sweetness[5] by the protracted zeal of your piety, the more willingly you should accept the gift and give a gift in return.

The End of the Prologue.

The Beginning of the Treatise on the Power of Prayer

1. We can consider with what effort and feeling[6] we should pray to God from the standpoint both of our misery and of his mercy. For what would more effectively spur a person to zeal for prayer than the misery and loss that come from the great evils that oppress and enslave him? And what could draw one more joyfully to actually pray than the mercy of one's Creator, which one experiences so often amid one's evils. One's need compels the human mind not to be lazy about praying, and the love of God (*pietate*) incites it not to pray fearfully or anxiously.[7] These two wings,[8] namely, the misery of humanity and the mercy of the Creator, lift prayer up, because when the mind ceaselessly rouses itself to devotion by alternating consideration of these two, it is lifted up by an impetus of spiritual desire and takes flight.

2. Thus, holy meditation is necessary for prayer, since prayer cannot be completely perfect if meditation does not accompany or precede it. Those who neglect to consider their evils are easily misled through

ignorance to ask for nothing or for something other than they should, or they surely grow lukewarm through slothfulness by asking less worthily than they should. Therefore, if we wish to pray to God wisely and usefully, it is first necessary that we exercise our mind in continual meditation and learn by consideration of our misery[9] for what we need to ask, and by consideration of the mercy of our God with what desire we should ask it.

3.1. Let us think about how short our life is, how treacherous the way is, and how uncertain death is.[10] Let us think about how we came into this life wailing, how we pass through it in sorrow, and how we are going to leave it in mourning. Even if something sweet or pleasant should beckon us when we meet it on the course of this life, let us think what bitter things are mixed in with it. How deceptive, how suspect, how unstable, how passing is anything that love of this world engenders or anything that temporal appearance and beauty promise. There are some evils with which we are born and from which in the course of time we are freed by the hidden grace of God or obvious effort. Others come into this life with us and never leave us before our death. Other evils grow in us over time and leave again over time. But others we incur after our birth and do not eliminate before our death.

3.2. Who could enumerate all the evils of this life? Not to mention the evils that commonly oppress all people, how are we to reckon up the secret dangers of which each person is conscious within himself?[11] If anyone should want to think about the evils he has done from the start of his life and those he has undergone, let him set before his eyes the past times and days of his life, and let him consider carefully how many useless labors he bore, how often he wore himself out uselessly for love of this life, how often he found disappointing results in laborious undertakings, and after prolonged running never achieved peace. Then he will know what estimate he can make about this life. When he considers the hardship of this life, let him also give thought to the agreeableness and sweetness of his heavenly home and ponder what he has found, what he has lost, where he lies, and whence he has fallen, so that he may understand from both how much he ought to grieve in this exile. For thus Solomon says: *Whoever adds knowledge adds sorrow.*[12] For the more a person understands his evils, the more he sighs and groans.

4. Finally, it remains for us, as we recall our evils, to remember also the mercy of God. For we seek his mercies for the future with greater confidence if we think about how he has been merciful to us in the past.

Let us call to mind the good things which he has granted:[13] he kindly rescued us when we were frequently in dangers; he could never be overcome by our sins and so not be merciful; he warned those who were forgetful of him[14] about him; he recalled those who had turned away from him; he received kindly those coming to him; he forgave penitents; he guarded the persevering; he held up those who were standing; he lifted up the fallen; he changed evil delights into bitterness, but to those who were burdened in a curative way with bitterness he again granted his consolations; finally, he who never failed to correct sinners or to guard the just restored calm and perfect peace to those who had been purified by tribulations.

5.1. Whoever has occupied his mind before the time of prayer with meditations of this kind does not perchance come to prayer either unprepared or half-heartedly.[15] Constant meditation gives birth to knowledge; knowledge once engendered repels ignorance and gives birth to compunction; compunction once born puts sloth to flight and gives birth to devotion. Devotion in its turn perfects prayer. Knowledge is when a person is enlightened to know himself. Compunction is when from a consideration of its evils the heart is touched with interior sorrow. Devotion is a loving and humble feeling (*affectus*)[16] toward God, which is engendered from compunction. For the mind, terrified by the extent of its evils and lacking confidence in its own powers, turns toward God. And the more it sees that outside of God nothing is left for it in which it can trust, the more ardently its seeks his protections.

5.2. Therefore, devotion is turning toward God with loving (*pio*) and humble feeling:[17] humble from awareness of one's weakness; loving from consideration of the divine forbearance. It has in itself the three principal virtues: faith, hope and charity. A person would not turn toward God in devotion if he did not believe that he could be saved by Him and hoped that He wished to have mercy. Finally, unless he loved Him more than his evils, he would not flee them and opt for refuge in him. Therefore, he believes, hopes and loves (*diligit*). He believes in his power, hopes in his mercy, loves (*amat*) his protection. Therefore, prayer is nothing else than devotion of the mind, that is, turning toward God with a loving and humble feeling, supported by faith, hope and charity. However, because the mind is enkindled through devotion in many ways, and likewise because devotion of the mind is expressed by the voice in various ways, we must distinguish one by one some kinds of prayer so that we can more clearly point out its power.

6. There are three kinds of prayer: supplication, request, and suggestion.[18] Supplication is humble and devout prayer (*precatio*) without a specific request. Request is a narrative that includes[19] a specific petition. Suggestion is a signifying of one's wish made by narration alone without a petition.

7.1. There are three forms of supplication: seeking favor, insistence, and pure prayer.

7.2. Seeking favor[20] is what happens before a demand in order to dispose and incline the mind of the hearer. This we do in three ways. The first is when we say something that commends our person or cause, by relating our merit or weakness or something else that can serve to recommend our cause or person to him to whom we are offering our petition. The second mode of seeking favor is when in praise of the one to whom we are praying we offer something by which we signify that in our mind he is dear and acceptable, so that we may deserve his love in response to our own. The third mode of seeking favor is when we say something through which in the mind of our hearer the cause or person of our adversary is disparaged, so that he seems worthy of hatred rather than love.[21] Seeking favor occurs in these three ways. Divine Scripture very often makes use of this form of supplication. We use it whenever we sing the praises of God, when we tell of our weakness, whenever we speak of the malice of our adversaries, and in general when before making a petition we say something worthy of God's ears and suitable to our necessity.

7.3. Insistence[22] is what usually occurs after a demand has been made, when we frequently remind our hearer in what I may call an annoying and pushy way so he will not forget our petition.[23] Memory seems to be refreshed in three ways: namely, when we repeat something about his person, our person, or our case, so we may make fresh in his mind ourselves or our cause and petition. This form of supplication seems as pleasing and praiseworthy to God as it is annoying to people.

7.4. Pure prayer[24] is when from an abundance of devotion the mind is so enkindled that when it turns to ask something of God it forgets even its petition because of the greatness of His love; and while it vehemently desires to enjoy the love of him whom its sees and wants to rest totally in him now, it spontaneously sets aside its concern regarding that for which it came. This form of prayer has only one variety, and just as it is therefore unique in a way that the others are not, so it is more precious to God than all others. But among these three forms of supplication, seeking favor has the lowest place, insistence the middle rank, and pure prayer the supreme and most excellent one, because seeking favor has fear, insistence has confidence, and pure prayer has perfect love.[25]

7.5. One should also know that sometimes supplication occurs only through nouns, such as "My Mercy," "My Refuge," "My Support, "My Liberator," "My God," and "My Helper;"[26] sometimes only through verbs, such as "take heed," "have mercy," "pardon," "attend to," and "act;"[27] and sometimes through nouns and verbs, such as this: *Lord, hear with your ears my words, understand my shout. Pay attention to the sound of my prayer, my King and my God.*[28] That form of supplication which occurs only through nouns is as full of an inner abundance of love as it is imperfect in external expression. For feeling has this property: the greater and more fervent it is within, the less it can be displayed outwardly in words.[29] That form of supplication that is expressed only by verbs shows less devotion than the former, but greater devotion than that which is expressed by nouns and verbs together, that is, fully articulated. Therefore, that which occurs by nouns alone seems to pertain to pure prayer, that which is expressed by verbs alone to insistence, and that which is expressed by nouns and verbs together to seeking favor, in such a way that the more pure prayer turns into jubilation[30] and approaches God, the more quickly it arrives and the more effectively it obtains its request.

8. Request[31] is a narrative that includes a specific petition, such as this: *A clean heart create in me, O God, and an upright spirit renew within me.*[32] It occurs in three ways: by imploring, by asking and simply by requesting. Imploring[33] is when a very urgent necessity pushes one to apply oneself more devoutly to prayers. In more moderate causes we ask, and in the least pressing we simply request.[34] These three therefore have their differences: to implore is most excellent, to ask is intermediate, and simply to request is the least.

9.1. Suggestion[35] is to make one's will known without a petition through narration alone. This also happens in three ways: with fear, with confidence and with contempt. It happens with fear when the cause we are pleading is great, or the person we are asking is great, such as this: *Lord, if you had been here, my brother would not have died.*[36] She wished to ask the Lord to raise up her dead brother, but because of the magnitude of her cause and out of reverence for the person, she was fearful, so she chose to suggest rather than to request. *Lord,* she said, *if you had been here, my brother would not have died.* She spoke in such a way that her desire would be understood, but her boldness would not be rebuked so that if she was not heard she would not suffer the disgrace of being rejected, and if she were heard she would gain the result she wanted.

9.2. Suggestion comes from assurance when we are confident because either our cause is easy or the person is benevolent, and therefore we neglect to express our desire openly, because we hope to be able to obtain it by suggestion alone. Such was the case when his mother said to the Lord at the wedding when the wine was running short: *They do not have wine.*[37] She did not say, "I ask that you supply the lack of drink by creating or transforming wine," because she judged that it was owed to the privilege of maternal reverence that she should not suffer a refusal from her Son whatever she hinted that she wanted. And indeed this would have been correct if she had asked him for something of the sort that he could do according to the nature that he had received from her. Now, however, in a way she is rightly rebuked, because from that nature which she had not given she required obedience in a miracle. He says to her: *What is it to me and to you, woman?*[38] For to perform a miracle belongs to divine, not human power. And therefore when his mother asks Christ the man for a miracle, he, not as man but as God, accuses her as a woman, not as his mother, of presumption. For if it was necessary, Mary should have humbly asked Christ for the miracle as a woman, rather than have required it of him as a mother from a Son.[39]

9.3. Suggestion occurs with contempt when the cause is trivial or the person who is asked is humble. That is completely excluded from prayer to God. However among men, especially the proud and powerful, it is exercised with great energy.[40]

9.4. As we have shown above, so also in these three we find a distinction. Suggestion from confidence befits the perfect; suggestion from fear befits beginners; suggestion from contempt befits the wicked.

9.5. Next we must add the remaining things we proposed to consider regarding prayer.

10.1. Certain ones are usually upset that when in our prayers we want to ask God for our salvation or the salvation of others, we are accustomed to chant[41] psalms that do not have words of petition or do not pertain to our petition. And they also adduce a similar incongruity in regard to other Scriptures, which we regularly use in our prayers, when they are such that they do not have the form of prayer or they are not in harmony with the cause that we are pleading. "What benefit is there," they say, "in including in prayer these words in which we find either nothing that we need to ask from God or something else than what we need? If someone has come into God's presence as if to make a request and suddenly turns away to repeat other things which seem to have no connection to the matter, he does not pray but rather mocks God and provokes him to anger." They say, "Look, we wish to ask God for forgiveness of our sins. How does it benefit us in that regard if we chant, *Why do the nations rage,*[42] or *Pay attention, my people,*[43] or some other Psalm of that sort? Is it not ridiculous that we believe that we are praying when we sing such things?" Perhaps some say this and think that there is no benefit whenever we mix such things with our prayers.

10.2. But if anyone will look carefully at the kinds of prayer mentioned above, he will easily recognize how powerful these words are in these prayers. For this kind of prayer is often found even more effective in obtaining what one asks than that in which we pray by expressing clearly what we are asking.[44] And although, as we said, this can be understood clearly enough from the things that we recalled above,[45] will the truth not be more evident if it is especially demonstrated here?

11.1. There is this difference when we pray to a human being and when we pray to God. A human being cannot know what we need unless taught it by another. God, however, knows what we need even before he is asked.[46] When a request is made to a human being, he learns through our narration what we want, and through our supplication he is prompted to grant what we ask. But in prayer made to God narration is not necessary, unless perhaps a person narrates in order to better understand his own petition so that, alerted by his narration, he may consider what he asks and prompted by consideration of his petition may pray more devoutly.[47]

11.2. Clearly as far as God is concerned, supplication alone suffices, because, as we said, God does not need to be instructed in order to know; rather, he is to be asked so that he may grant.[48] But in no other way can God be more quickly inclined toward granting than if the mind of the one asking turns toward him with a feeling of complete devotion. Whatever the words of the one praying are, they are not absurd if only they can be uttered suitably either to arouse the one praying to feel love of God, or, what is greater, if he already burns with love of Him, they show his intensity. However, they show this not to teach God hidden things about us that he does not know, but so that when we express outwardly our interior desire, by these very words of ours we may be inflamed to greater love. Devotion of the heart alone

could suffice for God, if prayer was not formed into words also to enkindle the mind of the one praying to greater devotion. For, as we said,
if a narration is inserted into a petition, God is not instructed but the
one praying is admonished to consider what he asks so that he may
pray more devoutly. If it is supplication alone because it signifies that
there is devotion within in the heart, it enkindles the mind to greater
devotion. Therefore we should not exclude from our prayers those
words that even if they do not unfold our petition nevertheless very
beneficially enkindle the feeling of the mind to love of God and loving
devotion.

11.3. But because human feeling is aroused to love of God in various
ways, it is now agreeable to distinguish those ways one by one and once
they are distinguished to show them through examples.

12.1. But first it should be known that almost this entire form of
prayer, which as some think should be completely excluded from the
exercise of prayer, pertains to seeking favor. Although above we counted
seeking favor as a kind of supplication, according to a broader usage
we frequently seek favor not only by supplication but also by request
and insistence.[49] When we seek favor we procure the benevolence of
the listener. This occurs in three ways: either when we say something
in his praise, or when we call to mind some aspect of our misery, or
also when we bring before him something that serves to put down our
enemies.[50]

12.2. Let us say, then, that all those Scriptures, which in the opinion
of some should not be employed in prayer, can and should be usefully
and fittingly recited in the context of our prayer requests because they
arouse in us a feeling of burning devotion. Either they arouse our heart
to love of him by setting forth the praise of God, or they humble us in
his sight by recalling our misery, or they gain us a useful solicitude and
a greater confidence before him by enlarging on the wickedness of our
adversaries. We know the praise of God in his power and goodness,
our misery in that we are fragile sinners, the wickedness of our adversaries because they are well versed in destroying and irreverent in op-
pressing. Therefore, if in order to exercise our minds and increase our
good devotion, while praying we recall the praise of God for his goodness and power, or our misery in our weakness and guilt, or the wickedness of our adversaries in their tyranny, we do nothing senseless and
through the pious feeling that the very words arouse in us we are praying in all of this.

12.3. Let me summarize all these things briefly: whenever we re-count the praise of God, whatever are the words, however lengthy, what does our heart say in all these things interiorly if not one thing, namely, it loves him in being in awe of him and is in awe of him in loving him?[51] Similarly, when in prayer we treat our misery before him, whatever the words, however lengthy, what does our heart say in all these if not this one thing: that we confess that we seek his mercy and place all our confidence in him? The closer such devotion is to humility the more pleasing it is to God. Likewise when we indict the wickedness of our adversaries in our prayers before God, whatever the words, however lengthy, what else do we implore through all these except the just judg-ment of God for our liberation, so that he may snatch us away from those by whose tyranny we are unjustly oppressed and whose wicked-ness we justly oppose? And because we gladly leave to the divine judg-ment to take vengeance on our enemies and to judge our case, what is there that we should not justly ask for from God in exchange for this humility and devotion. Therefore, let each one, when in prayer he sings psalms or any other Scriptures, carefully consider what feeling they serve, and let him expend every effort to rouse his heart to that feeling to which he sees what he is saying most relates,[52] because if he has the feeling of the words which he speaks, through that very feeling he will know better the power of the words and grasp their understanding, and through the understanding of the words he will enkindle his feel-ing to greater devotion.[53]

13.1. Our human way of acting, although corrupt, shows us by a kind of imitation of virtue how much the good disposition[54] of the heart pleases God.[55]

13.2. Certainly we see how flatterers pretend to be devoted toward those from who they expect something. They often make it a point of meeting them when they are going along. When they are in a crowd they honor them with pompous greetings. They prepare the way for them when they want to pass through; they order others to give way; and they proclaim that their lords are coming. They set up chairs for them in the center place; they spread out cushions; they throw them-selves at their feet. They recount from the ancient histories the great deeds of their ancestors, and if they do not find in them something to praise, they twist the deeds of ancestors to their praise. They not only say that they are devoted and trustworthy, they swear it. They try mightily to seem what they do not want to be.

13.3. Do you not think they could be justly reproached if they were what they are not but pretend to be? If it were bad to be such, why would they try so hard to seem such? Moreover, if they were such as they pretend to be and are not, they would be truly praiseworthy. Other people often refuse their request for no other reason than because they are known not to be what they pretend to be.

13.4. If therefore they are justly repulsed in their petitions because they are known not to be what they pretend to be, then let us strive to show God that we really are what they pretend to be, so that we may deserve to receive what we ask of God. Let us show outwardly with words that we have an interior feeling of devotion toward God. Let us not only show it, but let us have what we show, lest if we only show it we be not true lovers but flatterers. Because we cannot deceive God by outward show, it is ourselves we may deceive. Moreover, just as those previous flatterers offer counterfeit devotion and through it wish to gain the favor of those they are petitioning, so also let us all come before the face of God with our prayers; and, in order to merit obtaining what we ask, let us offer not counterfeit devotion but genuine charity.

13.5 Let us bless the friends of our Lord; let us be indignant toward his enemies. Let us praise his power, magnify his loving-kindness, wonder at his wisdom, extol his generosity, speak well of his fairness. Likewise let us tell him about our misery and indicate our need; let us reveal our weakness to him; let us confess to him our guilt; let us offer him our obedience. Let us say and believe that there is no other through whom we can be rescued, through whom we hope to be freed. Likewise let us show him the wickedness, cruelty, evil, and tyranny of our adversaries, the demons and evil people; let us show him that those who persecute us are opposed to him; that those who oppose him are our enemies; that we hate what he hates; that we love what he loves; that for his sake we prefer to suffer the hatreds of his enemies rather than to have peace with them in opposition to him.

13.6 Therefore, all Scriptures of this sort that are suitable for seeking favor—whether that happens through supplication, or through request, or through insistence—are not to be considered inappropriate to use in prayer, because, although some of their narrations do not include a petition, nevertheless they all have virtuous feelings, which they enkindle in us, through which those who pray are answered more quickly than through verbal petition.

14.1. Therefore, because all the power of prayer is in feelings of piety, let us enumerate some of them and give examples[56] (there are countless feelings so we cannot list them all), so that we can gather from some of them what is praiseworthy and acceptable to God in all of them.

14.2. There is a feeling of love when the mind, either seeing or remembering what it loves, is suddenly seized by the fire of love. There is the feeling of wonder when, contemplating something new and striking, the mind is stunned. There is the feeling of joy, when, seeing something acceptable and pleasing, it is filled with some kind of happiness.[57] There is the feeling of humility when from consideration of its weakness it is spontaneously kept from vainglory. There is the feeling of sadness when from a consideration of its evils the mind in some way pines away and grows weak. There is a feeling of fear when it is shaken by a consideration of looming punishments. There is the feeling of indignation when it is inflamed to hatred of its adversaries because of the very magnitude of their wickedness. There is the feeling of zeal when by love of justice it is enkindled to a desire for punishment. There is a feeling of healthy assurance when from some new and singular confidence it is moved more than usual to seek reparation.

14.3. Of these feelings, the first three pertain particularly to that kind of Scriptures which expresses praise, because the feeling of love arises from remembrance of goodness, the feeling of wonder arises from remembrance of power and strength, and the feeling of joy arises from remembrance of some favorable outcome or happy deed. The three following feelings pertain to that kind of Scriptures which recalls unhappiness and misery, because the feeling of humility arises from remembrance of one's own weakness, the feeling of sorrow arises from remembrance of present and past evils, and the feeling of fear from foreseeing future evils. The last three feelings connect more to that form of Scriptures in which there is inveighing and accusation against adversaries, namely, indignation against their vileness, zeal against their injustice, greater assurance regarding the mercy of God because of their wickedness.

14.4. Here are examples of each. From the feeling of love one chants the Psalm, *I will love you, Lord.*[58] From the feeling of wonder, one sings the Psalm, *O Lord, Our Lord.*[59] From the feeling of joy one sings the Psalm, *All peoples.*[60] In all of these there is praise. From the feeling of humility one sings the Psalm, *In you, Lord, I have hoped.*[61] From the feeling of sorrow, one sings the Psalm, *How long will you forget, O Lord?*[62] From the feeling of fear, one sings the Psalm, *Lord, do not in anger.*[63] And in all these there is entreaty mixed with complaint. From the feeling of indignation one sings the Psalm, *Why do you glory in wickedness?*[64] From the feeling of zeal one sings the Psalm, *God of vengeance.*[65] From the feeling of healthy assurance, one sings the Psalm, *Judge me, Lord, for I.*[66]

14.5. One should know, though, that not all psalms have this property that one feeling extends throughout the text,[67] but often the psalm passes from one feeling into another according to which the minds of those praying are usually touched in different ways. To explain how this can be understood in each of the psalms requires treatment in a longer work. However, we wish to show this in some of them by way of example.

14.6. For example, I have begun to think about what great happiness it is to be with God, likewise what great misery it is to live in this world, and finally what a great disaster it is to be tortured forever in hell. From this meditation, I am suddenly drawn by love of the heavenly homeland, and led by his love I pass on to these words: *Blessed the man who has not gone away at the counsel of the wicked.*[68] If we examine the meaning of the whole text of the Psalm from the viewpoint of the intimate feeling of compunction, what do we find it saying throughout but this: Happy are those who have never departed from God; happy are those who have always remained with God; happy are those who have stayed faithful and devoted in his service? For unhappy and miserable are those who have gone away from him, who have chosen not to remain with him, or who have not afterwards returned to him. Thanks to him insofar as I have remained steadfast; shame on me insofar as I have gone away. Now insofar as I am near, I do not wish to be distanced, and insofar as I am at a distance, I wish to return. Would that I may reach him, would that I may never depart from him! Help me, my God! This, then, is the feeling of love arising from praise.

14.7. Here is the example of another feeling. I have thought to myself how great the power of God is, and then I begin to wonder at the madness of people who are mortal yet have no fear about opposing his will. By this wonder I am compelled to exclaim and declare: *Why do the nations rave?*[69] And this is wonder mixed with indignation: we wonder at the madness; we are indignant at the presumption. Or again in ourselves, when we see the frequent and insistent assaults of vices without and we rely on the help of God within, we reprove the nuisance of our temptations with a kind of indignation, saying: *Why do the nations rave?*[70] And the whole Psalm leads to this: strengthened through the power of God, we make light of unusual adversities, and we assume that the nearer we are to God, the stronger are we against our enemies.

We await their speedy downfall; we oppose the magnificence of God to their pride that it may be broken. With all reverence we submit our mind to obey him, wondering always at his power over us, despising the insolence of those beneath us. This is the feeling of wonder, mixed with indignation, rising from praise.

14.8. The flow of the following Psalm is not woven of one feeling, but often passes from one feeling to another. For example, finding myself in trouble, I start thinking how I always trusted in the mercy of God, but because I see myself in some way abandoned by him from a feeling of sorrow I cry out these words: *Lord, why are those who assail me multiplied? Many arise against me. Many say to my soul: "There is no salvation for him in his God."*[71] Once again passing from the feeling of sorrow to the feeling of healthy confidence, I say: *But you, Lord, are my support.*[72] Thus, I may relieve sorrow by confidence, and I may chasten confidence with sorrow.

14.9. And who could enumerate in speech all the virtues of the Psalms, those fiery feelings of holy compunction by which the mind is enkindled in prayer[73] and offers to God a most pleasing sacrifice on the altar of the heart?[74]

NOTES

1   This is probably Thietmar (d. 1138), prior of the Augustinian canons of Hamersleben, discussed in the introduction.

2   Hugh expresses similar sentiments in the introductions or covering letters to several of his works: *Assumpt.* (PL 177.1209–10); *Laude car.* (PL 176.969D–971D; tr. Harkins, VTT 2.159); *Arrha* (PL 176.951–53; tr. Feiss, VTT 2.205); *Quinque sept.* (Baron, 118.272–73; tr. Benson, VTT 4.361); *Virtutibus* (Baron, 250).

3   It was common in the Middle Ages to preface a work with disclaimers about its poor style; e.g., Hugh of St Victor, *Sacr.* Pref. (PL 176.173–74; tr. Evans, VTT 3.261). However, apart from this "humility topos," classical and medieval rhetoric distinguished three levels of style: simple, moderate and ornate.

4   "animus": Throughout, both "animus," which occurs often in this text, and "mens" will be translated as "mind."

5   The idea of sweetness will be discussed in the notes to Book V of Richard of St Victor's *Archa Moysis* in VTT 5.

6   "affectus" (a fourth declension noun, and so the form "affectus" may be either singular or plural): a state of body or mind, affection, love, desire, fondness, feeling, or good-will. Among the Victorines it usually means a specific affect or emotion, rather than affection or feeling in the abstract, which they more often designate by "affectio," although they sometimes use the words interchangeably, which is how these words were used in classical Latin. "Affectus" is not easy to translate. "Disposition" conveys an affect that is a bit too weak and too permanent. "Emotion" seems anachronistic. "Feeling" conveys the elasticity of the Latin term, but seems too emotive. "Affect" would be another option. Here, unless otherwise noted, "affectus" will be translated as "feeling." In his French translation of *Virtute orandi* in *Oeuvres* 1, Sicard translates "affectus" as "amour," "affection," and "sentiment." For more on *affectus*, see VTT 1.100 n. 61; VTT 2.85–87. Here, by connecting "affectus" with effort (*studium*), Hugh makes it clear that "affectus" is more than spontaneous impulse. Poirel nicely observes that Hugh's central idea in the work is that devotion is refracted in different *affectus* (*Oeuvres* 1:163 n. 10).

7   On the pair misery/mercy (*miseria/misericordia*), see Poirel, *Oeuvres* 1:163 n. 11.

8   For the image of two wings of prayer, see Ambrose, *Expositio Psalmi* 118.22.5 (Petschenig, 491); Augustine, *En. Ps.* 42.8 (Dekkers and Fraipont, CCL 38.481); Bernard of Clairvaux, *Sermo in Epiph.* 3.6.4 (SBO 4:307). In *Misc.* II.22 (PL 177.600B) Hugh writes that the two wings of God are mercy and charity.

9   The misery of man is a commonplace that Hugh explores especially in his *Homilies on Ecclesiastes* and *On Vanity*. According to Poirel (*Oeuvres* 1:164 n. 15), Herman of Reun incorporates this passage into his *Sermo* 7. Before becoming pope in 1198, Innocent III wrote a widely copied treatise *De miseria humanae conditionis* (PL 217.701–746C; tr. M. Dietz, *On the Misery of the Human Condition* [Indianapolis: Bobbs-Merrill, 1969]).

10   This sentence was widely cited: Richard of St Victor, *Apoc.* 1 (PL 1196.693D; tr. Kraebel, VTT 3.353); Charter (AD 1317) of Nicholas of Regensburg (ed. T. Ried, *Codex Chronologico-Diplomaticus Episcopatus Ratisbonensis* [Regensburg: Schaupf, 1816], 2:737). There is a somewhat similar passage in St Columban, *Instructio* 5 (ed. Walker, *Sancti Columbani Opera*, [Dublin: Institute for Historical Studies, 1957], 85–86).

11   In the previous paragraph Hugh distinguished four kinds of evils according to when in life they begin and end. Now he distinguishes between those common to all and those proper to each, a distinction which corresponds to the distinction between goods common to all, to some, and to each that he made in his *Arrha* (e.g., tr. Feiss, VTT 2.211) and *Eulogium* (e.g., tr. Feiss, VTT 2.125–26). The distinction between evils committed and evils undergone derives from St Augustine, e.g., *Lib. arb.* I.1 (Green, 211; tr. Pontifex, 35).

12   "Qui addit scientiam addit dolorem": cf. Eccles. 1:18: "Et qui addit scientiam addit et laborem" ("Whoever adds knowledge adds work as well").

13 Hugh does this in the "confessio" in *Arrha* 62–63 (Sicard, 273–76; tr. Feiss, VTT 2.224–25).

14 Here and in the next clause one can also take these reflexive pronouns as referring to people who were self-forgetful or turned away from themselves, but the following clauses show that these pronouns refer to God. A person reading the sentence in Latin might at first think of both possibilities.

15 Poirel observes that these two faults, one cognitive, the other affective, are remedied by the knowledge and compunction which come from meditation (*Oeuvres* 1:164 n. 21).

16 In *Oeuvres* 1:132, Sicard translates this definition of "devotion" as "un mouvement d'amour vers Dieu, affectueux et humble" ("a movement of tender and humble love toward God").

17 Conversion or a turning toward God is a central biblical idea; in neoplatonic philosophy it referred to the turning of each level of emanation to contemplate the level above it. Poirel refers to Pseudo-Dionysius' use of *epistrophe* for the return to God (*Oeuvres* 1:164 n. 24).

18 "Supplicatio": in classical Latin a day set aside for public prayer. "Postulatio": demand, request, claim, complaint. "Insinuatio": literally, to place in one's bosom; to bring to or in by a circuitous way; to ingratiate; recommend; penetrate. Disregarding the technical, philosophical meanings of the terms, Hugh calls these three kinds (*species*) and in the next paragraph distinguishes three forms (*genera*) of supplication.

19 Reading "inserta;" the PL and *Oeuvre 1* have "incerta."

20 "captatio": Like "oratio" ("prayer") and "insinuatio" ("suggestion")" "captatio [benevolentiae]" is a term used in rhetoric. See, e.g., Cicero, *Rhetorica ad Herennium* I.4.6 (Caplan, Loeb 403:12–13); I.6.9–10 (Caplan, Loeb 403:16–21); Cicero, *De inventione* I.16.23–17.25 (Hubbell, Loeb 386:46–51).

21 The reference to adversaries comes from the judicial roots of "oratio." An orator spoke to a judge against an adversary. The speech, especially "captatio benevolentiae," praised the judge, expanded on the need of the speaker, and disparaged his adversary.

22 "exactio": a judicial term for forcing payment of a tax or debt. Here Hugh keeps the notion of forcefulness.

23 Cf. Luke 18:1–8.

24 For "pure prayer," a term drawn from John Cassian, see the introduction.

25 On the relation between love and fear in the Hugh and the other Victorines, see the subject index to VTT 2, "Love, fear and." Here, because his treatise is structured in threes, between love and fear Hugh adds a third intermediate affective state, "confidence." For similar distinctions see *Summa sent.* III.17 (PL 176.115); Peter Lombard, *Sent.* III.24.4.4 (SB 5:192–93); Thomas Aquinas, *ST* II-II.19.2 (Caramello, 93).

26 Ps. 143:2 (Vulg.): "misericordia mea et refugium meum, susceptor meus et liberator meus, protector meus;" cf. Ps. 17:3 (Vulg.): "Dominus firmamentum meum et refugium meum et liberator meus. Deus meus adjutor meus . . . protector meus . . . et susceptor meus" ("The Lord, my firmament and my refuge and my liberator, my God, my help . . . my protector . . . and my support"). Hugh comments on Psalm 17:3 in *Misc.* II.26 (PL 177.601AC).

27 Ps. 24:16 (Vulg.): "respice in me et miserere mei" ("look upon me and have mercy on me") and Dan. 9:19: "exaudi Domine, placare Domine, attende et fac" ("listen, pardon, attend to, and act").

28 Ps. 5:2–3.

29 For the idea that the more intense a feeling is, the less it can be put into words, see Augustine, *En. Ps.* 30.2.3.10 (Dekkers and Fraipont, CCL 38.220); John Cassian, *Conferences* IX.25 (Pichéry, SC 54:62; tr. Ramsey, 345–46).

30 "jubilationem": "jubilatio," "jubilus," and "jubilum" were quasi-technical terms for the melismatic melodies extending the final "a" of alleluia. More generally, the terms refer to wordless expression of joy. See, e.g., Augustine, *En. Ps.* 32.2.1.8 (Dekkers and Fraipont, CCL 38.254); *En. Ps.* 150.8 (Dekkers and Fraipont, CCL 40.2196); John Cassian, *Conferences* XXI.26.2 (Pichéry, SC 64:101; tr. Ramsey, 739); Pseudo-Hugh of St Victor, *De officiis ecclesiasticis* 2.15 (PL 177.417A).

31 "postulatio": Apart from 1 Tim. 2:1, this word appears one other time in the Bible: Ps. 118:170 (Vulg.).

32 Ps. 50:12

33 "obsecratio": I Tim: 2:1, and twenty other places in the Vulgate.

34 "rogatio": Ecclus. 4:4 is the only occurrence of the word in the Latin Bible.

35 "insinuatio": In *De inventione* I.14.20 (Hubbell, Loeb 386:42–43) Cicero defines this term a: "discourse which works itself into the mind of the hearer covertly through dissembling and circumlocution" ("insinuatio est oratio quadam dissimulatione et circumitione obscure subiens auditoris animum"); cf. *De inventione* I.17.23–25 (Hubbell, Loeb 386:46–51); *Rhetorica ad Herennium* 1.6 (Caplan, Loeb 403:16–21).

36 John 11:21.

37 John 2:3.

38 John 2:4.

39 As Poirel observes (*Oeuvres* 1:168 n. 41–42), this rather odd interpretation of the story of the miracle at Cana (John 2:1–12) illustrates the importance Hugh's treatise gives to sentiments. Hugh's explanation of Jesus' rebuke is found also in Augustine, *Jo. ev. tr.* 8.9 (Willems, 88–89) and Bede, *Homiliarum evanglii libri* I.14 (Hurst, 97). The Christology here seems to concentrate one-sidedly on the two natures of Christ and not on his single person of whom Mary was the mother.

40 Hugh did not need to include "suggestion with contempt," but it rounds out the series of nine. Its inclusion also shows his dependence on classical rhetoric.

41 "decantare": words for singing are very difficult to translate. Here "decantare" will regularly be translated as "chant." Hugh is evidently thinking mainly of the Liturgy of the Hours, which consisted primarily of Psalms.

42 Ps. 2:1. As was the custom in the Middle Ages, Hugh refers to the Psalms by their opening words. Poirel, *Oeuvres* 1:169 n. 45, observes that in the *De tribus rerum circumstantiis* Hugh recommends that one begin by learning the number and first words of each psalm as a first step toward memorizing the Psalter; see W. M. Green, "Hugh of St. Victor *De tribus maximis circumstantiis gestorum*," *Speculum* 18 (1943): 489–90.

43 Ps. 77:1 (Vulg.).

44 See Jerome, *Epist.* 7.6 (Hilberg, 31; tr. Wright, Loeb 262:27): "Epistulae brevitas conpellit tacere, desiderium vestri cogit loqui. Praeproperus sermo; confusa turbatur oratio; amor ordinem nescit" ("The brevity of a letter compels me to be silent; my longing for you compels me to speak. My words are hurried, my discourse confused and poorly arranged; but love does not know order").

45 In short, any text that addresses God with titles implying praise can serve as an *oratio*, even if it does not express an overt request.

46 Matt. 6:8.

47 "narratio" and "petitio": these terms were discussed in the introduction.

48 Augustine, *En. Ps.* 102.10 (Dekkers and Fraipont, CCL 39.1460): "Intelligamus quod Dominus et Deus noster non voluntatem nostram sibi velit innotescere, quam non potest ignorare, sed exerceri in orationibus desiderium nostrum, quo possimus capere quod praeparat dare" ("Let us understand that our Lord and God does not wish to inform him what we want, which he cannot not know, but to rehearse our desire, by which we can receive what he is prepared to give"). See also *Epist.* 130.8 (Goldbacher, CSEL 44.59).

49 In this broad sense, seeking favor (*captatio benevolentiae*) is not a subdivision of "supplication," but includes the other two main categories of prayer—request and suggestion—because they also are ways of seeking favor.

50 These are the forms of "captatio benevolentiae" in the narrower sense in which it is a subspecies of supplication (see 7.1; 14.3).

51 "admirans amat et amando admiratur": one might expect "admirando amat et amando admiratur." As I have translated the former the meaning is the same as the latter.

52 In addition to the texts cited in the introduction regarding the need for heart and mind to
be in harmony, see Augustine, *Praeceptum* II.3 (Verheijen, 1:421; tr. Mary and Bonner, 112);
Epist. 130.8 (Goldbacher, CSEL 44.59).

53 Augustine, *En. Ps.* 30.23.1 (Dekkers and Fraipont, CCL 38.213). "Et si orat psalmus, orate; et
si gemit, gemite; et si gratulatur, gaudete; et si sperat, sperate; et si timet, timete"("If the Psalm
prays, pray; if it groans, groan; if it rejoices, rejoice; if it hopes, hope, and if it is afraid, be
afraid"). For classifications of the psalms according to the feelings they express, see Alcuin,
De psalmorum usu (PL 101.465–69); see also Bériou, 29.

54 "affectus cordis bonus": to translate this as "*good feeling* of the heart" conveys the wrong
connotations. Hugh is thinking specifically of devotion.

55 The subdivisions of paragraph 13 here differ slightly from both the Latin and the French in
Oeuvres 1:150. This section of Hugh's treatise is somewhat ponderous. To show that praying
the Psalms that do not directly express our petitions is not hypocritical, Hugh observes that
hypocrites would not pretend to be devoted if devotion were not important. In human affairs,
devotion is not rejected in itself, but only when it is insincere. If those who pray the Psalms
are filled with devotion, they are not hypocrites, but they are doing what hypocrites only
pretend to do.

56 See Alcuin, *De psalmorum usu* (PL 101.465–69).

57 Richard of St Victor, *Arca Moys.* V.5–18 (Aris, 129–48; tr. Zinn, 316–42) identifies three causes
of ecstasy (*mentis excessus*): great devotion, great wonder, and great joy. These correspond
quite closely to the first three "affectus" in Hugh's list of nine "affectus." Moreover, Hugh's list
of nine "affectus" lines up closely with the sequence of "affectus" that Richard of St Victor
uses to structure part of *On the Twelve Patriarchs*. Here are Hugh's nine "affectus" with Richard's in parentheses: "dilectio" ("amor"), "admiratio," "congratulatio" ("gaudium"), "humili-
tas," "moeror" ("dolor"), "timor" ("timor"), "indignatio" ("odor"), "zelus" ("zelus"),
"presumptio" (Richard adds "spes," "pudor").

58 Ps. 17:1 (Vulg.).

59 Ps. 8:1.

60 Ps. 46:1 (Vulg.).

61 Ps. 30:1 (Vulg.).

62 Ps. 12:1 (Vulg.).

63 Ps. 6:1.

64 Ps. 51:3 (Vulg.).

65 Ps. 91:1 (Vulg.).

66 Ps. 25:1 (Vulg.).

67 "seriem": Hugh uses this word for "text" or "document," but also as in 14.8 for the flow of
thought in a text. The same word appears in Hugh of St Victor, *Cant. BM* Prol. (Jollès, 26;
tr. Harkins, VTT 4.427).

68 Ps. 1:1.

69 Ps 2:1.

70 Ps. 2:1.

71 Ps. 3:2–3.

72 Ps. 3:4.

73 John Cassian, *Conferences* IX.26 (Pichéry, SC 54:72; tr. Ramsey, 346).

74 Augustine, *Civ. Dei* X.3 (Dombart and Kalb, CCL 47.275; tr. O'Meara, 375). "Ei sacrificamus
hostiam humilitatis et laudis in ara cordis igne feruidam caritatis ("On the altar of our heart
we sacrifice to him a sacrifice of humility and praise warmed with the fire of love"); Hugh of
St Victor, *Lament.* (PL 175.876D): "Anima nostra . . . debet esse . . . sacerdos . . . quia Deo
iugiter offerre debet devotionem suam" ("Our soul . . . must be . . . a priest . . . because it must
offer its devotion to God continually").

HUGH OF ST VICTOR

ON THE FIVE SEVENS

INTRODUCTION AND TRANSLATION
BY JOSHUA C. BENSON

INTRODUCTION

Hugh likely composed *On the Five Sevens* between the years 1130/1 and 1137, a time of great theological activity for the master of St Victor, when he was also composing his theological synthesis: *On the Sacraments of the Christian Faith.*[1] Its authenticity is assured by its presence in the *Indiculum*—the list of Hugh's works drawn up by the abbot Gilduin after Hugh's death.[2] What has remained a challenge for scholars is locating the genre of *On the Five Sevens.* Since this question can aid our understanding of the text's purpose and place within Hugh's corpus, we will examine the question of the text's genre after reviewing its content.

As its epistolary preface relates, the *Five Sevens* is a careful coordination of five sets of seven items that Hugh culls from Scripture and the patristic and medieval tradition. The text begins by enumerating what we call the seven deadly sins, or in Hugh's terminology "the seven capital or principal vices."[3] Set against these sins, Hugh coordinates the seven petitions of the *Our Father.* These lead to the seven gifts of the Holy Spirit (taken from Isaiah 11:2), which are an "antidote" to the seven deadly sins. The "health" of seven virtues are offered next, though they are not the seven virtues we might expect. Rather than offer the four cardinal and three theological virtues, Hugh offers the seven 'macarisms' of the beatitudes from Matthew 5:3–10.[4] The final set of seven is the "joy" of the seven beatitudes, which are here the rewards of the beatitudes that follow upon their macarisms (i.e., 'kingdom of heaven' is the joy of the first beatitude).

The material in *On the Five Sevens* may be easily correlated with material found in Hugh's other works. He details seven deadly sins in

---

[1]   For these dates see Poirel, *Hugues de Saint-Victor*, 36–47. On Hugh's life and works in English, see P. Rorem, *Hugh of St. Victor* (Oxford: Oxford University Press, 2009).

[2]   See the introduction to the Latin edition by R. Baron in *Six opuscules spirituels*, SC 155 (1969), 30–1. Baron's use of the *Indiculum* as a measure of authenticity is supported by the more recent work of D. Poirel on the *Indiculum* in *Livre de la nature et débat trinitaire au XIIᵉ siècle, Le De tribus diebus de Hugues de Saint-Victor*, BV 14 (Turnhout: Brepols, 2002), 75.

[3]   Hugh of St Victor, *Quinque sept.* II (Baron, 102; tr. Benson, VTT 4.362).

[4]   A 'macarism' is the first half of each beatitude that articulates the reason the person is blessed (i.e., *poor in spirit* is the macarism of the first beatitude).

precisely the same way in his *On the Sacraments of the Christian Faith.*[5] *On the Seven Gifts of the Holy Spirit*, also translated in this volume, continues to meditate on those gifts precisely as medicine, the image also used to describe them in *On the Five Sevens.*[6] *On the Lord's Prayer* describes the seven deadly sins and their relationship to the petitions of the *Our Father.*[7] The brief *Virtues and Vices* suggests many parallels to *On the Five Sevens*: its epistolary opening, its use of a medical motif for the interaction of the vices and virtues, its identical list of the vices, and its closing image of how the vices conspire in a precise order to rob, beat, exile, seduce, and enslave a human person.[8] Certain parallels to the structure and movement of *On the Five Sevens* may also be found in *Ark of Noah*, especially in the way Hugh 'concatenates' or interconnects virtues in a chain of action.[9] Hugh also discusses the beatitudes in *Ark of Noah*, but there he lists eight, not seven.[10]

On the Five Sevens also influenced later writers, including the *Expositio moralia in Abdiam* and *Summa sententiarum.*[11] Though the work was certainly influential in the coming years, one notable borrowing and transformation of Hugh's classifications occurs in Bonaventure's *Collations on the Gifts of the Holy Spirit*. In the first collation Bonaventure describes a series of not five but seven sevens and goes on to describe three of them more fully in the following collation.[12] Bonaventure's

---

5   See Hugh of St Victor, *Sacr.* II.13.1 (PL 176.525–26; tr. Deferrari, 374–76).

6   See below Benson, VTT 4.371–72.

7   See PL 175, 774–89.

8   See *Virtutibus* (Baron, 250–55). Note that the text has not been definitively ascribed to Hugh. Goy lists it among the "probably authentic works" of Hugh; see his *Die Überlieferung der Werke Hugos von St. Viktor*, 480.

9   Concantenation is a technical term used to describe how sins or virtues can build upon one another. The term has its source in the work of John Cassian. See R. Newhauser, "The Capital Vices as Medieval Anthropology," in *Laster im Mittelalter / Vices in the Middle Ages*, ed. C. Flüeler and M. Rohde (Berlin: Walter de Gruyter, 2009), 105–23 at 112. Instances of concantenation occur at least in *Archa Noe* III.2 and 11 (Sicard, 55–56 and 71–80; tr. a Religious of C.S.M.V., 94–95 and 108–17).

10 See *Archa Noe* III.9 (Sicard, 69–70; tr. a Religious of C.S.M.V., 106–107).

11 See the discussion of these works in M. Bloomfield, *The Seven Deadly Sins: An Introduction to the History of a Religious Concept with Special Reference to Medieval English Literature* (East Lansing: Michigan State University Press, 1967), 84–85. Note however that Bloomfield assumes that Hugh of St Victor wrote the *Expositio moralia in Abdiam*, the authenticity of which is rejected by scholars today. See also R. Newhauser, *The Treatise on Vices and Virtues in Latin and the Vernacular*, Typologie des sources du Moyen Âge occidental 68 (Turnhout: Brepols, 1993), 120.

12 The seven sevens are the seven sacraments, seven actions of justice and seven works of mercy (in relationship to the grace that cures us from evil); the seven habits of the virtues and seven gifts of the Holy Spirit (in relationship to the grace that strengthens us in the

inspiration seems to come from Hugh, though it could have come from more proximate sources already influenced by Hugh's work. Before further examining the contents of *On the Five Sevens*, we will consider different ways of describing the genre of the text, which can shed more light on its content and its place within Hugh's corpus.

Perhaps the most natural way to consider *On the Five Sevens* is as a treatise on vices and virtues.[13] This is a genre with a long history. It emerges out of Egyptian monasticism and the work of Evagrius Ponticus (d. 399) who described eight areas of sinfulness. Evagrius and the conception of eight sins were then passed on to the West by John Cassian (d. 433) in a formalized but not necessarily rigid pattern: GLAITAVS—*gula, luxuria, avaritia, ira, tristitia, acedia, vanagloria, superbia* (gluttony, lust, avarice, wrath, sadness, sloth, vainglory, pride). Further innovation and development then occurred in Gregory the Great's *Moralia in Job*, which transformed the list into seven sins whose root is pride (*superbia*): *inanis gloria, invidia, ira, tristia, avaritia, ventris ingluvies (gula), luxuria* (vainglory, envy, wrath, sadness, avarice, gluttony, lust). Gregory's list was to dominate the medieval period (especially since Peter Lombard employed it in his *Sentences*), though its very construction allowed for interplay between lists of seven or eight sins.[14] "However," R. Newhauser relates, "one can say that at the latest by the twelfth century the most commonly accepted number of the vices had stabilized at seven, perhaps earliest in Hugh of St Victor's *De quinque septenis*."[15] Roughly from this point, envy (*invidia*) is fixed among the seven and pride is incorporated in the list, rather than as a source standing outside the list of seven. During the thirteenth century the genre flourished among the great theological masters, mendicant

---

good); the seven beatitudes and seven gifts of the glorified body (in relationship to the grace that is completed in glory). See *Collationes de septem donis Spiritus Sancti*, Opera Omnia 5, ed. PP. Collegii a S. Bonaventura (Quaracchi: Collegium S. Bonaventurae, 1891), 461a–b and 462–63. The text exists in a translation: *Collations on the Seven Gifts of the Holy Spirit* (St. Bonaventure: The Franciscan Institute, 2008). Note the textual problems of the edition itself: J. Hamesse, "La deuxième reportation des *Collationes de septem donis Spiritus Sancti* de saint Bonaventure," *Bulletin de philosophie médiévale* 19 (1977), 59–64; "New perspectives for critical editions of Franciscan texts of the Middle Ages," *Franciscan Studies* 56 (1998), 169–87.

13   The following description of this genre is heavily indebted to R. Newhauser, *The Treatise on Vices and Virtues* (Turnhout: Brepols, 1993).

14   Peter Lombard lists seven sins following Gregory in *Sent.* I.2 (SB 4.570; tr. Silano, 210).

15   Newhauser, *The Treatise on Vices and Virtues*, 190.

and secular, as witnessed in the works of the Franciscan John of La Rochelle and the secular, William of Auvergne.[16]

Works within this genre were often brief, but they could be quite long. The genre sought to offer a "system of moral constructs analyzed in a discursive manner by means of a structure placing the members and sub-members of the system in hierarchic relationship to each other."[17] The uses to which such a work could be put were various, but they were often used as texts that aided self-reflective moral analysis. This means that such texts could be used in the context of religious formation, instruction, and ultimately within the context of the sacrament of confession. The brief and carefully structured nature of these texts also allowed for them to be easily memorized. Accordingly, many of these texts employed some sort of mnemonic structure that could aid the memory: motifs of a ladder or steps, a journey, medicine, a tree, combat between the vices and virtues, and even the beast with seven heads from the Apocalypse are all common.[18]

On the Five Sevens fits neatly into this genre. Hugh seems to have largely followed the list of sins compiled by Gregory, though he has clearly incorporated pride into the list itself; he lists and coordinates hierarchically all the items he will describe; he 'concatenates' the sins and virtues—explaining how one sin or virtue can be connected to another; he uses a broad medical analogy to connect all five sets of seven together.

Why would Hugh have composed such a work? As is the case with some of Hugh's other writings, it seems he composed the work at the request of others, as the epistolary opening and closing indicate.[19] But what purpose did the unknown addressee have in mind? Here we may follow the text's editor, R. Baron, and speculate further on the genre of the text. R. Baron argues that *On the Five Sevens* is connected to the second part of Hugh's *Instruction of Novices.*[20] *On the Five Sevens* would

---

16   See Newhauser, *The Treatise on Vices and Virtues*, 124–35. Newhauser also tracks the development of the genre in vernacular treatises.

17   Newhauser, *The Treatise on Vices and Virtues*, 58.

18   See Newhauser, *The Treatise on Vices and Virtues*, 157–66.

19   Hugh's *Sacr.* was also written at the request of others. See *Sacr.* I.Preface (PL 176.174; tr. Evans, VTT 3.261; tr. Deferrari, 1).

20   See Baron, SC 155:31; Ibid., "Hugues de Saint-Victor: Contribution à un nouvel examen de son œuvre," *Traditio* 15 (1959): 276–77. Of course, works for the instruction of novices are a genre with a long and complex history. The editors of the text briefly note the *Conlationes* of John Cassian as an ancient Latin antecedent, as well as John Climacus's *Scala Paradisi* as an ancient Greek antecedent. There are naturally eleventh-century antecedents as well. See

therefore constitute something of a third part of the *Instruction of Novices*. We could easily imagine how it would fit into this type of work and why someone may have requested it. The *Instruction of Novices* promises to give instruction in three things: knowledge, discipline, and goodness. Hugh concatenates the three towards the close of the prologue, which gives the rationale for his choice of this series: "One passes through knowledge to discipline, through discipline to goodness, through goodness to beatitude."[21] However, the text never really treats goodness; all that is offered in closing is that one should pray for it.[22] We could imagine how *On the Five Sevens* could fulfill the promise to treat goodness on the way to beatitude and further imagine that someone in charge of the formation of new canons might want to know how Hugh would have completed his promised intentions at the outset of *Instruction of Novices*.

As interesting as the possibility may be that *On the Five Sevens* completes Hugh's thoughts on the formation of novices, the ancient list of Hugh's works drawn up by Gilduin does not place the work alongside *Instruction of Novices*. Instead, we are offered a third way to consider *On the Five Sevens* by Gilduin's *Indiculum*: it is a work of tropological or moral exegesis. We should recall here that moral exegesis occupied the third movement in Hugh's description of the senses of Scripture in *On the Sacraments of Christian Faith*. There he defined the senses in this fashion: "History is the narration of things accomplished that is contained in the first meaning of words. Allegory occurs when through what is said to have been done something else done in the past, present, or future is signified;" and finally, of importance here: "Tropology occurs when through what is said to have been done something that ought to be done is signified."[23] Further, in the *Didascalicon* Hugh notes regarding the twofold fruits of reading (i.e., knowledge and morals) that "The whole of Sacred Scripture is directed to this [twofold] end."[24] The moral interpretation of Scripture thus occupies a crucial place in Hugh's thought and we might profitably consider that what we call

---

Poirel, *Oeuvre 1*, 7–9. However, C. Jaeger—who offers a lengthy discussion of the text—suggests the following: "The fundamental ideas of the *De institutione* are indebted more to the secular traditions of antiquity and the cathedral schools of the eleventh century than to monastic and canonical traditions" (*The Envy of Angels: Cathedral Schools and Social Ideals in Medieval Europe, 950–1200* [Philadelphia: University of Pennsylvania Press, 1994], 262).

[21]   Hugh of St Victor, *Inst. nov.* Prol. (Sicard, 20.55–57).
[22]   Hugh of St Victor, *Inst. nov.* 21 (Sicard, 98. 1229–30).
[23]   Hugh of St Victor, *Sacr.* I.Prol.4 (PL 176.184–85; tr. Evans, VTT 3.264).
[24]   Hugh of St Victor, *Didasc.* V.6 (Buttimer, 104; tr. Harkins, VTT 3.157).

'spirituality,' Hugh would have more naturally understood as moral exegesis.[25]

Our knowledge of Gilduin's index of Hugh's works comes down to us in two forms. J. de Ghellinck's reconstruction of the *Indiculum* followed its presentation in Oxford, Merton College MS 49.[26] Through further research involving numerous manuscripts, D. Poirel has offered a new reconstruction of the *Indiculum*.[27] In both presentations, the *Indiculum* records *On the Five Sevens* situated firmly between the *Instructions on the Decalogue* and *On the Word of God*. Each of these texts can easily be thought of as works of moral exegesis. The former text works through the Ten Commandments (and like the overall thrust of *On the Five Sevens*, also dwells on their order).[28] The latter text is an amazing meditation that tracks scriptural passages regarding God's speech, and thus his Word, until it lands and reflects at length on Hebrews 4:12–13: *The word (sermo) of God is living and effective*, etc. This passage allows Hugh to move from reflections about the Word of God to its impact upon the human soul.[29] *On the Five Sevens*, in terms of both its placement in the *Indiculum* and its content, fits within the context of Hugh's moral exegesis.

In summary then there are at least three ways to view the genre of *On the Five Sevens*, and all three can function together: there is every reason to think of the text as a treatise on the vices and virtues and at the same time, to believe that such a work was ultimately a work of moral exegesis, certainly meant to serve the self-reflective moral analysis of Hugh's brothers in religion and possibly meant to more directly serve those in formation. We may now turn to a brief analysis of the text itself.

In the opening of the work, Hugh lays out the five sets of seven that the treatise will cover. They may be more easily considered with the aid of the following table:

---

[25]   See Rorem's remarks on this in *Hugh of St. Victor*, 119 and following. For further on Hugh's exegesis, see F. Harkins, *Reading and the Work of Restoration: History and scripture in the Theology of Hugh of St. Victor* (Toronto: Pontifical Institute of Medieval Studies, 2009).

[26]   De Ghellinck, "La table des materières," 270–89; 385–96.

[27]   Poirel, *Livre de la nature*, 61–75.

[28]   See Hugh of St Victor, *Decalogum* (PL 176.9–15).

[29]   See Hugh of S. Victor, *Verbo Dei* (Baron, 60–81).

Vices	Petitions	Gifts	Virtues	Beatitudes
Pride	Hallowed be thy name	Fear of the Lord	Poverty of Spirit, Humility	Kingdom of heaven
Envy	Thy kingdom come	Piety	Meekness, Kindness	Possession of the land
Anger	Thy will be done	Knowledge	Compunction, Sorrow	Consolation
Sadness	Give us this day our daily bread	Fortitude	Hunger for justice, Good desire	Fullness of justice
Avarice	Forgive us our trespasses	Counsel	Mercy	Mercy
Gluttony	And lead us not into temptation	Understanding	Purity of heart	Vision of God
Lust	Deliver us from evil	Wisdom	Peace	Sonship of God

With the series of sevens mapped out, Hugh now presses on to discuss the seven capital vices. He expresses both the gravity and interconnectedness of the vices by asserting that they are the "sources of the dark abyss, the head waters of the rivers of Babylon," which leech out into the whole world. Playing on the word "Babylon" Hugh connects the dark abyss of vice to the captive people Israel, weeping beside the rivers of Babylon in Psalm 136:1 (Vulg.). In a powerful way, perhaps, the sinner is shown to be captive to sin and is left weeping, remembering God's grace or covenant (i.e. Zion from the Psalm) that they have deserted. These vices, Hugh continues, "corrupt the whole integrity of nature and produce the seeds of every evil."[30] The seriousness of sin, its destructive power, and the way sins interconnect with each other should grab the reader's attention: what is to follow is no trite description of qualities we do not like in other people, but a description of the destructive force of moral evil. As he makes his way into the body of his presentation of the vices, Hugh first concatenates the vices and their destructive effects by describing how they assail the human person. He then proceeds to describe each vice in further detail, always following

[30]   Hugh of St Victor, *Quinque sept.* II (Baron, 102–4; tr. Benson, VTT 4.362).

the careful order he has initially laid out. The conclusion to the section prepares for the discussion of the *Our Father* that is to follow by observing that there is no way for those who have become captive slaves to regain their freedom unless the Savior intervenes. If we then connect this concluding image to the Psalm verse at the beginning of the discussion, we can imagine that without the Savior's aid, we shall only be able to weep beside the waters of Babylon. We are captives in need of rescue.

Horrified by what we have become, we should be ready to pray, ready to cry out to the Savior—and so Hugh begins to introduce the seven petitions of the *Our Father* that will be set against the seven vices. Hugh is confident in the power of these petitions because they flow from the one who taught us to pray, and the one who promised that he would "heal our wounds and lift the yoke of our captivity."[31] The Savior will bring us back from the streams of Babylon. Hugh next offers a different and very brief concatenation of the vices, which lands him at another Scriptural image for the person's state thanks to sin. This time, he draws on Psalm 68:3 (Vulg.): *I stick fast in the mire of the deep*, which leads him to conclude that when we are stuck in the mire, our only recourse is to call out to God—just as the Psalmist does in Psalm 39. Now that he has made us aware of the need for God's assistance, Hugh will detail the assistance the petitions of the *Our Father* provide us.

Whereas in the prior section Hugh simply dwelt on the vices themselves, in this section he addresses the petitions of the *Our Father* and their relationship to the gifts that God gives us in response to our cries for help, the virtue that the gift creates in us, and the beatitude that crowns the process. In this way, Hugh covers the other four series of sevens by showing how their concatenation heals the vices to which each series of petitions, gifts, virtues and beatitudes corresponds. The goal of the whole work, as the final series indicates, is nothing less than the reformation of the image of God in us, as our minds approach inner joy. While we may wish to see Hugh's concatenation of vices and virtues as naïve, a deeper truth stirs in the text: our sins do not occur in isolation and our sins never simply affect just ourselves. Likewise, our healing occurs not through our own effort, but through God's gracious assistance, implored not merely by our cries, but by the cry of a prayer he has already formed for us, in response to which he will give us the gift of his own healing spirit.

---

[31]   Hugh of St Victor, *Quinque sept.* III (Baron, 108; tr. Benson, VTT 4.364).

The translation that follows has been made from the Latin edition of Roger Baron referenced in the footnotes to this introduction. I have reproduced the numbered divisions of his edition. The translation has benefited from his French translation also included in the edition. There is an English translation of Migne's edition: Joachim Wach, "Hugo of St. Victor on Virtues and Vices," *Anglican Theological Review* 31 (1949): 25–33, at 25–30.

ON THE FIVE SEVENS

Brother, I have found five sevens in Sacred Scripture that I first want to distinguish from each other, if I can, just as you asked, by enumerating each one. Afterwards, I want to demonstrate the correspondence which exists between them by comparing them to each other.

I.

In the first place there are seven vices: the first is pride; the second envy; the third anger; the fourth sadness; the fifth avarice; the sixth gluttony; the seventh lust.

In the second place the seven petitions contained in the Lord's Prayer are set against these vices: the first, whereby it is said to God: *Hallowed be thy name*; the second: *Thy kingdom come*; the third: *Thy will be done on earth as it is in heaven*; the fourth: *Give us this day our daily bread*; the fifth: *Forgive us our trespasses as we forgive those who have trespassed against us*; the sixth: *And lead us not into temptation*; seventh: *Deliver us from evil.*[1]

In the third place the seven gifts of the Holy Spirit follow next.[2] First, the spirit of the fear of the Lord; second, the spirit of piety; third, the spirit of knowledge; fourth, the spirit of fortitude; fifth, the spirit of counsel; sixth, the spirit of understanding; seventh, the spirit of wisdom.

Next, in the fourth place come the seven virtues. First, poverty of spirit, that is, humility; second, meekness or kindness; third, compunction or sorrow; fourth, hunger for justice or good desire; fifth, mercy; sixth, purity of heart; seventh, peace.[3]

Finally, in the fifth place the seven beatitudes are arranged: First, the kingdom of heaven; second, the possession of the land of the living; third, consolation; fourth, fullness of justice; fifth, mercy; sixth, the vision of God; seventh, to be a child of God.[4]

First, we distinguish these, so that you may understand that these vices are a kind of sluggishness of soul, or like wounds in the interior man, but that interior man is, as it were, a sick patient; the doctor is God; the gifts of the Holy Spirit are the antidote; the virtues are health; the beatitudes are the joy of happiness.

II.

There are seven capital or principal vices, and all evils arise from them. They are the sources of the dark abyss, the head waters of the rivers of Babylon, and after they have flowed out into the whole earth, they pour out iniquity drop after drop. Of those rivers the Psalmist chanted in the person of the faithful people, saying: *By the rivers of Babylon, there we sat and wept, when we remembered Zion. On the willows, in the midst of Babylon, we hung up our instruments.*[5] To the extent we think it sufficient for the present work, we will speak about these seven destructive vices that corrupt the whole integrity of nature and at the same time produce the seeds of every evil.

There are seven of them. Three of them rob a person; the fourth beats the person who has been robbed; the fifth casts out the person who has been beaten; the sixth seduces the person who has been cast out; the seventh subjects the person who has been seduced to slavery. Pride takes God away from a person; jealousy takes away his neighbor; anger takes him away from himself; sadness beats the person who has been robbed; avarice banishes the person who has been beaten; gluttony seduces the person who has been banished; lust subjects the person who has been seduced to servitude. Now let us go over these again and explain each one in order.

We said that pride takes God away from a person. Pride is love of one's own excellence, when the mind loves the good that it has all on its own, i.e., without the one from whom it received the good. O pestilent pride, what are you doing? Why do you urge the stream to separate itself from the spring? Why do you urge the ray to turn itself from the sun? Why, if not that the former may dry up when it ceases to be filled, and the latter may become dark when it turns away from the one providing the light. When both of them stop receiving what they do not yet have, they immediately lose even what they have. Surely you do this because you teach people to love the gift apart from the giver. In this way whoever falsely claims for himself part of the good that was given by the giver loses the whole good that is in the giver. So it happens that he cannot have what he has in a beneficial way, as long as he does not love it in him from whom he has it. For just as every good is truly from God, so no good can be usefully possessed apart from God. But rather he loses the very thing that he has, because he does not love it in him and with him from whom he has it. Whoever knows only how to love the good that he has in himself must, when he sees in another a good that he does not have, be tormented the more bitterly by his own imperfection, the more he does not love him in whom all good resides.

And for that reason jealousy always follows pride. For if someone does not fix his love on where all good resides, then the more misguidedly he revels in his own good, the more seriously he is tormented by the good of another. The jealousy, which pride begets from itself, is very justly considered his punishment for self-exaltation. Because it refuses to love the good common to all, rightly it is now consumed with envy regarding the good of another. Certainly, the success of someone else's happiness would not burn him, if he possessed through love the one in whom all good resides. And he would not judge the good of another as foreign to himself, if he loved his own good there, where he possessed both his own good and the good of another. Therefore, the more he now revels in himself through pride against his Creator, the further he falls beneath his neighbor through envy; and the more he wrongly lifts himself up here, the more he is truly cast down there.

But once the corruption starts it cannot stop here. As soon as jealousy was born from pride, it begets anger from itself. Indeed a miserable mind is now angry at itself for its own imperfection, because it does not rejoice in the good of another through charity. Even what he has begins to displease him, since he recognizes in another what he cannot have. Therefore whoever could possess everything in God through charity loses through jealousy and anger what he tried to have apart from God through pride, because after he loses God through pride, he loses his neighbor through jealousy and himself through anger.

Therefore, because everything has been lost and nothing remains in which the unhappy conscience may rejoice, it is weighed down because of sadness, and the conscience that would not lovingly rejoice in the good of another is justly tortured by its own evil. Therefore after pride, jealousy and anger which despoil a person, the sadness that beats the person stripped bare follows next.

Avarice then follows after. Avarice casts out the beaten person, because, after interior joy has been lost, it forces him to look for consolation outside himself.

Next comes gluttony, which seduces him who has been cast out. For this vice, like a tempter close at hand, lures the mind panting after external things to excess through the natural appetite.

Finally lust arrives, which forces the seduced mind to servitude. For after the flesh has been inflamed through overindulgence, the weakened and exhausted mind cannot vanquish the flame of sensuality that comes over it. Therefore the mind so disgracefully subdued is a slave to a very cruel master; and unless the loving kindness begged from the Savior intervenes, there will be no way for its lost liberty to be restored to the captive slave.

III.

And so the seven petitions follow against the seven vices. By them we pray that the one who taught us to pray might come to our aid. To those of us who pray he promised that he would give the good Spirit to heal our wounds and lift the yoke of our captivity. But before we explain these petitions, we first want to show by another comparison how much corruption the aforesaid vices produce in us, because the more dangerous the weakness is shown to be, the more necessary the medicine is proven to be.

Pride puffs up the heart. Jealousy dries it up. Anger cracks it to pieces. Sadness crushes it and pulverizes it, so to speak. Avarice scatters it. Gluttony infects it and moistens it, so to speak. Lust tramples it and turns it into mud. The miserable person can now say: *I am stuck in the deep mire, there is no sure standing. I have come into the depth of the sea and the tempest has overwhelmed me.*[6] Any time the mind has been stuck in the deep mire and engulfed in the mud of defilement and impurity, it can only be pulled out if it cries out to God and asks for his help. The Psalmist speaks of this when he says: *I have waited patiently for the Lord, and he was attentive to me. And he heeded my prayers and brought me out of the pit of misery and the mire of dregs.*[7] He therefore taught us to pray so that our whole good may be from him and so that we may understand that what we ask for and what we receive when we ask, is not something we deserve, but his gift.

The first petition is against pride, whereby we say to God: *Hallowed be thy name.*[8] We ask this so that he enables us to fear and venerate his name in order that we may be subject to him through humility, just as we were defiant and rebels because of pride. In response to this petition, he gives the spirit of fear of the Lord as a gift, so that as the Spirit comes into the heart it creates in it the virtue of humility that heals the illness of pride. Then the humble person can reach the kingdom of heaven, which the arrogant angel lost by exalting himself.

The second petition is against jealousy, whereby it is said: *Thy king-dom come.*[9] The kingdom of God is indeed our salvation, because God is said to rule in us when we are subject to God. So now we adhere to him through faith, but later through sight. Therefore whenever we ask that the kingdom of God may come, we surely seek the salvation of all. Accordingly, when we ask for the common salvation of all, we show that we repudiate the vice of envy. The spirit of piety is given in response to this petition, so that it stirs the heart to kindness when it comes to it. In this way we arrive at the same possession of eternal inheritance that we desire others to reach.

The third petition is against anger, whereby it is said: *Thy will be done on earth as it is in heaven.*[10] Whoever says, "thy will be done," does not want to quarrel. Rather, he indicates that he is pleased with whatever God's will determines for him or for others according to the decision of God's good pleasure. The spirit of knowledge is given in response to this petition, so that it gives instruction and salutary compunction to the heart when it comes to it. As a result we know that the evil we suffer comes from our own fault and that whatever good we have comes from God's mercy. Accordingly, we learn not to be angry with the Creator over whatever evil we suffer or good we lack, but to exhibit patience in all things. Therefore, the anger and indignation of the mind are best mitigated by the compunction of the heart, which is born interiorly from humility through the work of the spirit of knowledge. By contrast anger kills the fool.[11] When the mind is agitated and blinded in adversities by the vice of impatience, it does not recognize either that it has deserved the evil it suffers or that it has received by grace the good it has. The reward of consolation follows this virtue, that is, compunction or sorrow, so that whoever willingly afflicts himself with lamentations here before God deserves to find there true joy and happiness.

The fourth petition is against sadness, whereby it is said: *Give us this day our daily bread.*[12] Sadness is a weariness of the mind combined with grief, when the mind, in some way wasted and embittered by its own vice, no longer desires internal goods. Thus, with all its vigor died off, the mind is not cheered up by the desire for spiritual rest. We need to call upon the Lord's mercy to heal this vice, so that he, with his constant loving kindness, may bring the food of internal refreshment near to the soul run down by its own weariness. As a result, enticed by the taste of what is present, it begins to love what it does not know how to desire when [his loving kindness] is absent. The spirit of fortitude is given in response to this petition, so that it lifts up the fainting soul. Thus the soul recovers the strength of its former vigor and recuperates from the defect of its own weariness back to the desire of internal taste. Therefore the spirit of fortitude creates a hunger for justice in the heart, so that while it is deeply stirred here by the desire of piety it may obtain there as a reward the complete satisfaction of beatitude.

The fifth petition is against avarice, whereby it is said: *Forgive us our trespasses as we forgive those who trespass against us.*[13] It is fair that one who decides not to be greedy in requiring the payment of a debt should not be anxious about repaying his own debt. So therefore, when the vice of avarice is removed from us by the grace of God, we are taught by the proposed condition for salvation how we should be absolved from our debt. Therefore, the spirit of counsel is given in response to this petition. It teaches us to extend mercy freely to those who sin against us in this age so that in the future when we will have to render an account for our sins, we may deserve to find mercy.

The sixth petition is against gluttony, whereby it is said: *And lead us not,* that is, do not permit us to be led, *into temptation.*[14] This is the temptation whereby the allurement of the flesh often tries to lead us into excess through the natural appetite. This temptation secretly subjects us to pleasure while it openly flatters us about what we need. Certainly we are never led into this temptation, if we strive to sustain our nature within the limits of what is needed. This is the case as long as we always remember to guard our appetite against the allurement of pleasure. In order for us to achieve this the spirit of understanding is given in response to our petition, so that the internal refreshment of God's word may restrain the exterior appetite and so that the mind strengthened by spiritual food may not be broken by physical need nor overcome by carnal delight. The Lord, while he was hungry, responded to his tempter who gave deceptive advice about the nourishment of physical bread: *A man does not live by bread alone, but by every word that comes from the mouth of God.*[15] In this way he clearly demonstrated that when the mind is refreshed interiorly by that bread, it is not very concerned whether it suffers physical hunger for a while. Therefore, the spirit of understanding is granted against gluttony. However, when that spirit comes to the heart it cleanses and purifies the heart. With the knowledge of the Word of God, as if with a certain salve, that spirit heals the interior eye and renders it so luminous and clear that it becomes penetrating enough to contemplate the very glory of God. Therefore, the spirit of understanding as a remedy is opposed to the vice of gluttony. Purity of heart is born from this spirit of understanding, and purity of heart deserves the vision of God, as it is written: *Blessed are the pure of heart, for they shall see God.*[16]

The seventh petition is against lust, whereby it is said: *Free us from evil.*[17] A servant rightly asks for freedom. Therefore, the spirit of wisdom is granted in response to this petition. It restores lost freedom to the captive. Aided by grace the captive escapes from the yoke of unjust rule which he could not do by his own powers. For wisdom (*sapientia*) derives from the word "taste" (*sapor*). When the mind is touched by the taste of internal sweetness, it gathers itself completely within through its desire. Then it cannot be scattered away in the outward pleasure of the flesh because it has within itself the whole in which it delights. Therefore, interior sweetness is fittingly opposed to outward pleasure, so the more the mind begins to taste and enjoy the interior sweetness, the more freely and willingly it despises the outward pleasure. Finally, the mind at peace in itself rests entirely within by love, as long as it seeks nothing outside. Therefore, the spirit of wisdom, when it touches the heart with its own sweetness, calms the outward intensity of concupiscence and creates inner peace when it has quieted concupiscence, so that we are fully and perfectly reformed in the image of God when our whole mind is drawn into internal joy. Thus it is written: *Blessed are the peacemakers, for they shall be called children of God.*[18]

I have now answered your request, brother, not as I should have, but as best I could at this time. Receive this poor gift about the five sevens for which you asked, and when you have considered it, remember me. May the grace of God be with you. Amen.

NOTES

1   Matt. 6:9–13.
2   See Isa. 11:2.
3   See Matt. 5:3–10.
4   See Matt. 5:3–10.
5   Ps. 136:1 (Vulg.).
6   Ps. 68:3 (Vulg.).
7   Ps. 39:2 (Vulg.).
8   Matt. 6:9.
9   Matt. 6:10.
10 Matt. 6:10.
11 Cf. Job 5:2.
12 Matt. 6:11.
13 Matt. 6:12.
14 Matt. 6:13.
15 Matt. 4:5.
16 Matt. 5:8.
17 Matt. 3:13.
18 Matt. 5:9.

HUGH OF ST VICTOR

*ON THE SEVEN GIFTS
OF THE HOLY SPIRIT*

INTRODUCTION AND TRANSLATION
BY JOSHUA C. BENSON

INTRODUCTION

On the Seven Gifts of the Holy Spirit was written during the same fecund period as Hugh's *On the Sacraments of Christian Faith* and his *On the Five Sevens* (also translated in this volume), likely between the years of 1130/1 and 1137. R. Baron, the editor of the work, notes that the text was once attributed to Bernard of Clairvaux.[1] Hugh's authorship is confirmed, however, from its presence in the *Indiculum*—the list of Hugh's works drawn up by abbot Gilduin after Hugh's death. In the version of the *Indiculum* published by J. de Ghellinck, *On the Seven Gifts* appears at the very end of the second volume.[2] This could place the work, as we saw in the introduction to *On the Five Sevens*, within Hugh's moral exegesis. The work's content certainly bears out this classification. D. Poirel's work on the corpus of Hugh would also support this classification, though at least one important manuscript (Paris, Bibl. Mazarine 717) does not contain the work, and another (Paris, BnF 14303) places it much closer to *On the Five Sevens* than other manuscripts: the two works are there only separated by *On the Lord's Prayer*.[3] The Patrologia Latina would take a much further step in linking *On the Five Sevens* and *On the Seven Gifts* together when it published them as one continuous work.[4] Looking further at the relationship of the two texts can help us understand the unique content of *On the Seven Gifts*.

We could immediately note that the two texts bear an obvious relationship to each other: both texts lay out the same order of the gifts of the Holy Spirit taken from Isaiah 11:2, and both texts employ the analogy of a medicine working on a disease for the relationship between sin and the gifts. Yet the two texts are also strikingly different and were certainly meant to be separate works. Above all, we can be confident that they were meant to be separate because they are (as far as I can discern) always separate in the manuscripts. Further, *On the Five Sevens* has a clear epistolary opening and closing which would

---

[1] R. Baron, *Six opuscules spirituels*, SC 155:38.
[2] J. de Ghellinck, "La table des materières," 270–89, 385–96.
[3] See D. Poirel, *Livre de la nature*, 47, 49.
[4] PL 175.405–414.

preclude the easy insertion or removal of *On the Seven Gifts*. These two factors already clarify that the two texts are indeed separate works. However, returning again to the question of genre can further allow us to distinguish the works and allow us an avenue into the positive content of *On the Seven Gifts*. The introduction to *On the Five Sevens* in this volume notes that it might be naturally classified as a treatise on vices and virtues because of its method of concatenation, that is, offering interconnected lists of vices and virtues that build on one another. *On the Seven Gifts*, by contrast, does not concatenate the gifts beyond the fact that it lists them in the traditional order; nor does it interconnect the gifts with any of the other series of sevens found in *On the Five Sevens*. Thus, rather than an extension of or appendix to *On the Five Sevens*, *On the Seven Gifts* concerns in its own way the interaction of grace and sin in the human soul. Rather than a concatenation of terms, it is an exhortation to open oneself to the grace of the Spirit and an analysis of the initial effects the grace of the Spirit brings about in us. These effects, as the text shows us, sometimes have unexpected consequences and Hugh is perhaps preparing his readers for the pitfalls to avoid in their own self-reflective analysis of what it means to experience God's grace. How should we ask for grace? What is it that is given? How should we deal with the tension-filled experience of recognizing our sin in the light of God's healing grace? Questions like these seem to occupy Hugh in this little work, rather than the task of mapping-out and coordinating the gifts themselves. In this way, then, the title of the work is somewhat misleading. We may now look more closely at the text itself.

The first part of the text does not properly concern the gifts of the Spirit, but rather the posture we must take in asking for God's grace. The lemma that guides Hugh's discussion is Luke 11:13. Consequently, Hugh explains that we must be like children who ask good things from our Father. Our proper posture is childlikeness—our proper vision of God is of a generous, loving Father. If we seek and desire his heavenly gifts—the gift of the Spirit—all other things will be given us besides. Though we may feel unworthy to ask the Father for his Spirit because our sin has made us so sick, we should not fear: the Father will give us the Spirit to heal us. No matter how great our corruption, we cannot corrupt the healing balm of the Spirit. Indeed, though we are not worthy of the Spirit, the coming of the Spirit makes us so.

In the second part of the text, Hugh relates that the seven gifts will heal the seven vices, though he has not actually described these vices in the text. He then lists the seven gifts as seven spirits, which, as he explains, are not seven different spirits but seven ways the one Spirit bestows himself upon us. In fact, it is the Spirit's very unity that, when received into us, forms us for different works and heals us of the different illnesses of sin. This brief second section leads into Hugh's third section, where he describes why the reception of God's grace can be such a painful experience. He uses two basic metaphors: the reception of light by sore eyes and clear eyes; the reception of medicine by a sick person. In both cases Hugh's intention is to account for the fact that when we are not fully receptive to the Spirit due to sin, we perceive his coming as painful. Yet, the very torment of our soul is an indication that healing is under way and regardless of our sin, the Spirit will come to illuminate us. Hugh details this illumination in the fourth section. The Spirit gives us light and life, which cause us to see and perceive the evil within us. Through the Spirit we recognize that we have suffered evil through our own fault and will suffer a further future evil, punishment. This causes us to be sorrowful and then fearful over the evil we have committed and the punishment we shall receive. Fear is key here (and we can imagine that Hugh is dwelling on it so long because it is the first of his gifts) because it makes us sorry for a fault we have committed, for which we may never feel sorry, since the fault we have committed arises from its pleasure. This causes a problem that Hugh analyzes further: how could we be sorry for a fault that caused pleasure or something good? The answer is that we become sorry by recognizing the punishment, which transforms our understanding of even what was pleasurable in the fault we committed. At last we are able to recognize that this pleasure was in fact an evil. All of this is caused by the light of the Spirit, which because of the evil it reveals in us, can cause us to fear it as well as the evil it illuminates. Yet, we need the fear that the Spirit's light causes, for without it we cannot recognize our fault or the punishment we deserve. Further, this punishment is both evil because it torments us, and not evil because it frees us by allowing us to recognize the evil in the fault we have committed. Hugh is recognizing the potentially disruptive force of the Spirit in human life—a force we need, but could misunderstand if we do not become acquainted with the way we perceive his healing presence. Hugh abruptly concludes by affirming that the Spirit who gives us freedom through moral illumination, is the same as the Spirit who will later give us joy through his sweetness.[5] Brief as it is, *On the Seven Gifts* is a penetrating analysis of the working of grace in the human soul—a text of obvious use to Hugh's fellow canons in both their own moral self-analysis and in their pastoral duties.

The translation has been made from R. Baron's Latin edition, noted in the footnotes above. The translation has benefited from the French translation also included in his edition. Migne's Latin edition, which conflates *On the Seven Gifts* and *On the Five Sevens*, was the basis for the English translation of J. Wach, "Hugo of St. Victor on Virtues and Vices," *Anglican Theological Review* 31 (1949): 25–33, at 30–33.

---

[5]   The abrupt, though coherent, conclusion causes one to wonder if Hugh intended to compose a longer work but never had the time. I am aware of no scholarly speculation on the text's integrity.

ON THE SEVEN GIFTS OF THE HOLY SPIRIT

I.

It is written: *For if you, being evil, know how to give good gifts to your children, how much more will your heavenly Father give the good Spirit to them that ask him.*[1] Therefore the heavenly Father will give the Spirit to his children who ask him. Those who are children seek nothing else. Those who do seek something else are hired servants, not sons. Those who seek silver, who seek gold, who seek the transitory, who seek things of earth seek the service of slavery, not the spirit of freedom. What is sought is what is given. If you seek the physical, you receive nothing more than what you seek. If you seek the spiritual, what you seek is given and what you do not seek is added: spiritual things are given, carnal things are added. *Seek first the kingdom of God, and all these things will be added unto you.*[2]

Therefore, when you are ready to petition the Father, the Father who is in heaven, seek heavenly gifts, not earthly ones: not a physical substance, but a spiritual grace. For he will give the good Spirit to them that ask him; he will give his own Spirit to heal your spirit; he will give the Holy Spirit, and he will heal the spirit of sinners. The one spirit is sick, the other is the medicine. Therefore, if you want the one spirit to be healed, seek the other Spirit. If you are asking for the sake of your spirit, ask the Spirit. Do not be afraid to apply the medicine to the illness. The illness does not corrupt the medicine, but the medicine disrupts the illness. The illness does not infect the medicine, but the illness is destroyed by the medicine. Therefore, do not be afraid to invite the Holy Spirit of God into your sinful spirit, because you are a sinner and unworthy of his fellowship. This does not happen because you are worthy but to make you worthy. The Spirit will come to you to make his dwelling in you.[3] For when the Spirit comes, he will not discover a dwelling, but he will come to make it. First the Spirit will build, later he will dwell. First the Spirit will heal, later he will illuminate. The first is done for health, the later for joy.

If then you are a son and you ask your father, be confident and do not fear. God hears, a Father answers. Just as it is impossible for him not to hear because he is God, so it is impossible for him not to answer because he is pious. Therefore he will give to you what you ask if you ask rightly, and your prayer will not be in vain if it was worthy of a response. You asked for your illness to be healed, and you will receive the medicine. Your vices, your illness; the Spirit of God, your health. Against the illness of pride the spirit of fear will be given to you as a medicine to heal the corruption that is conceit and restore the health that is humility.

II.

Each vice has its medicine. There are seven vices and seven spirits. There are as many medicines as there are illnesses. What are the seven spirits? They are the seven gifts of the Spirit: the gifts are the spirits, and the spirits are the gifts. The gift of the Spirit is the Spirit. The Spirit gives himself. The one Spirit bestows himself in seven ways. There is one Spirit and seven spirits because the Spirit is given in seven ways and inspired in seven ways. There are seven inspirations and one Spirit. One medicine cures seven illnesses. Hence, there is one and seven: one nature, seven works; one substance, a sevenfold effect.

The first spirit is the spirit of fear; the second is the spirit of piety; the third is the spirit of knowledge; the fourth is the spirit of fortitude; the fifth is the spirit of counsel; the sixth is the spirit of understanding; the seventh is the spirit of wisdom.[4] *But one and the same Spirit works all these things.*[5] He is fear. He is piety. He is knowledge. He is fortitude. He is counsel. He is understanding. He is wisdom. He who is one in himself does all these things for you: by receiving him who is not diverse you are formed for diverse works.

III.

He who is always one and the same in himself is multiplied in you. For he who is your love is himself your fear. *Jacob swore to Laban by the fear of his father Isaac.*[6] For he who completes is the one who also begins. First he comes to you to make you fearful; but he comes in the end to make you loving. The light is the same that pricks bleary eyes and delights clear eyes: it does different things because it finds different things. Yet the Spirit is one in himself. He would also be one in you if he found you one. If you have a healthy eye, you perceive the light without pain. But if the eye is sick, light comes as an annoyance. Yet it is better that the light actually comes this way, because if you are not tormented, you are not illuminated.

Two opposites are fighting, the medicine and the illness. The medicine fights for you, the illness against you. If the medicine did not resist the illness, health would not follow. If the illness did not resist the medicine, pain[7] would not be felt. The battle of opposites is your punishment; yet do not blame the medicine but the illness. Attribute to one of them the sorrow caused by both; the medicine wants to profit you, the illness intends to injure you. For that reason, the illness alone causes pain,[8] not health; the medicine alone provides health, not pain. But when they are both present, the pain is the conflict of opposites: one wants to enter in order to benefit; the other does not want to leave in order to harm. But the illness indeed must be accused in this pain, not the medicine, because what causes torment is from the illness. If there were no torment, there would be health and no pain.

And so the Spirit comes and he inspires and infuses himself within you. Because you have his contrary, you do not immediately submit to him, but you oppose him, so that he does not peacefully enter into you. Nevertheless he comes and illuminates you, so that you may see in yourself what you had before but did not see; and therefore you did not see it, because you did not pay attention.

IV.

When the Spirit comes, you are illumined and vivified: illumined so that you may see, vivified so that you may sense. For you sense and have presentiment, you see and foresee. You see one thing and foresee another; you sense one thing and have a presentiment of another. You see evil and foresee evil. You see the present evil, you foresee a future evil. You sense guilt, you have a presentiment of punishment. Before the Holy Spirit came to you, you were blind and did not see, and you were dead and did not sense. You did not see because you were not looking, and you did not sense because you were not paying attention. But after the good has returned, you are aroused by its taste and illumined so that you might recognize evil: first the evil that you endured, i.e., guilt; then also the evil that you merited because of the first and in proportion to the first, i.e., punishment. At its arrival the good taught two things: to sense the present evil and to foresee future evil.

At this point the medicinal punishment arises. When you have sensed the evil that you suffer, you begin to be sorrowful so that you amend yourself; and when you are illumined of the evil that you deserve, you begin to be afraid so that you take precaution. For unless you were sorrowful, you would not amend yourself; and unless you were afraid, you would not take precaution. Therefore, you are illumined first in order to see your guilt, second in order to fear your punishment, and finally, after being filled with fear, in order to grieve over your guilt and correct it. Perhaps you would not be sorry, unless you were afraid. For if no one saw the punishment that was frightful, they would not grieve over the guilt that gave them pleasure. The punishment that will follow after the guilt is shown to you, so that the guilt that gives pleasure in its experience may at least give displeasure in its retribution. As a result you begin to acknowledge that what seems to be sweet in it is also evil, because what is perceived with bitterness from it and after it is very evil. Therefore you are illumined and you are moved, because you see what terrifies you and possess what is causing you sorrow. If you were not illumined, you would not have been tormented, because you would not see what you should fear. However, if there was nothing in you that should be consigned to the flames, the fire would seem to be without pain, and you would receive illumination without sensing the affliction.

The punishment frightens, the guilt causes fear. All of this results from the light that comes upon you by which the punishment is displayed in order to be seen and the guilt is sensed in order to be recognized. Nevertheless, there is a difference between the means of sight and the object of sight. There is a difference between the means of illumination and what is illuminated. The means of illumination nourishes you, what is illuminated frightens you. Nevertheless the fear is regarded as the light, because you were not afraid until you were illumined. Nevertheless it is better that the terror comes, because the guilt is not corrected unless the punishment frightens you. The light benefits you as long as it shows you the cause of your torment, because in this way it corrects your wicked delight. Therefore you are illumined in such a way that you are afraid. The first light is awful. Rather the darkness is awful that is seen through the light, because what cannot be sensed without sorrow, cannot be seen without terror, especially by the one who recognizes that he deserved it, so that he senses what he sees threatening him and what he cannot avoid.

At that moment when danger is foreseen, fear is born which includes the pain. It is an evil because it torments, not because it frees: an evil, I say, that is not an evil. For every punishment is an evil, but not every punishment is evil. For what is useful and beneficial to something is good even if it is not good in itself. For that reason a lesser punishment comes so that a greater punishment is avoided. This is good, although it comes from what is not good. For through punishment we are freed from punishment, and it is better to sense for a time what is troublesome, so that what is intolerable must not be sensed forever.

He who is your true good accomplishes your good out of what is not your good. A different good will be achieved for you later that comes not only through him but from him. For first he accomplishes your freedom from your pain, later he accomplishes your joy from his own sweetness. Nevertheless He is one and the same in both works. In the first work he is the one who acts; in the other he is both the one who acts and the source from which he acts.

NOTES

1   Luke 11:13.
2   Matt. 6:33.
3   See John 14:23.
4   See Isa. 11:2.
5   1 Cor. 12:11.
6   Gen. 31:53.
7   The Latin "poena" can refer to "satisfaction," "pain" or "punishment." I have translated it as "pain" or "punishment" depending upon the context.
8   Rather than "punishment" the Latin reads "peace" (*pacem*). This emended reading is supported by the juxtaposition of "health" and "punishment" in the next sentence.

HUGH OF ST VICTOR

ON MEDITATION

INTRODUCTION AND TRANSLATION
BY FRANS VAN LIERE

INTRODUCTION

Hugh of Saint Victor entered the abbey of Saint Victor possibly around 1115. Sometime in the 1120s, he was put in charge of the students at the abbey, and made master of the school at Saint Victor, a position he retained until his death in 1141.[1] Among the works that were collected by Abbot Gilduin shortly after the death of Hugh in 1141, we find a short didactic work on meditation, *De meditatione*, or *De generibus meditationum et quae sit utilitas eorum* (*On the kinds of meditation and their usefulness*), translated here into English for the first time.[2] The work was widely copied throughout the Middle Ages. It shares some stylistic characteristics as well as content with Hugh's other works, specifically the *Didascalicon* (III.7), which describes the relationship between reading and meditation; parts of his commentary on Ecclesiastes, in which he explains the differences between meditation (which is a discursive thought process) and contemplation (which involves a more immediate intellectual grasp);[3] and the possibly spurious works *De contemplatione et eius specibus* and *De modo dicendi* (*sic*, for *discendi*) *et meditandi*, which is largely a *doublure* of parts of the *Didascalicon* (III.13 and 7).[4] Scholars have previously examined Hugh's concept of meditation in relation to reading,[5] but by comparison Hugh's ideas on the relationship between meditation and the examination of one's own moral conduct, which is perhaps the most interesting aspect of this work, have received little attention.

Hugh starts his treatise with a brief definition of meditation. Meditation, for Hugh, is a thought process, by which what already exists in one's consciousness (*cognitio*) is transferred into the mind. It is a frequent

[1] J. Taylor, *The Origin and Early Life of Hugh of St. Victor*, Texts and Studies in the History of Medieval Education 5 (Notre Dame: Notre Dame University Press, 1957).
[2] De Ghellinck, "La table des matières," 270–89, 385–96.
[3] Hugh of St Victor, *In Eccl.*1 (PL 175.116–18).
[4] Goy, *Die Überlieferung der Werke Hugos von St. Viktor*, 479–80 and 487.
[5] I. Illich, *In the Vineyard of the Text: A Commentary to Hugh's Didascalicon* (Chicago: University of Chicago Press, 1993), 51–65; B. Stock, *After Augustine: The Meditative Reader and the Text*, Material Texts (Philadelphia: University of Pennsylvania Press, 2001), 8–23; M. McWhorter, "Hugh of St Victor on Contemplative Meditation," *Heythrop Journal* (2011), http://onlinelibrary.wiley.com/ doi: 10.1111/j.1468-2265.2011.00738.x.

reflection, or as he formulates in his commentary on Ecclesiastes, a concentrated consideration, investigating the manner in which something is (*modum*), its cause (*causa*), and its reason (*ratio*), or, as in *Didasc.*, its utility (*utilitas*). As Grover Zinn points out, the purpose of meditation was "to make the knowledge obtained by thought morally and spiritually effective."[6] This readies the mind for grasping these truths through contemplation (*contemplatio*).[7] Meditation thus is a process of intellectual discernment and thought ordering. To cite Zinn again:

> Order in thought is more than a question of intellectual tidiness for our Victorine canon. It is an existential concern touching the very core of life, whether in the classroom, cloister, or choir. Through the proper ordering of thought in the mind, a beginning of order and stability in life may be effected.[8]

There are three kinds of meditation, Hugh says: on creatures (in the division given in *Didasc.*, Hugh first lists the meditation on "works"), on Scripture (*Didasc.* lists "commandments" here), and of moral conduct (*mores*, which also could be translated as "manners"). Hugh discusses all three in order, spending considerably more time on the last point, however. Considering that the first two were treated at length in his *On the three days*, a prolonged meditation of God's creation,[9] and his *On Sacred Scripture*, an introduction to the meditation on Scripture,[10] it should not surprise that he keeps both at a minimum here.

The meditation on creation, Hugh says, arises out of admiration of the marvelous disposition of creation. This admiration leads one to question what caused it to be this way (*causa*), which in turn leads one to investigate the reason (*ratio*) of creation. This in turn will lead to discovery of the divine realities that are the ultimate cause and reason for these works of creation. Meditation on Scripture, Hugh says, has its

---

6   Zinn, "De Gradibus Ascensionum," 61–79, here 74.
7   Hugh, *In Eccl.*1 (PL 175.116–17). See also Illich, *In the Vineyard of the Text*, 51–53, and I. van 't Spijker, "Hugh of Saint Victor's Virtue: Ambivalence and Gratuity," in *Virtue and Ethics in the Twelfth Century*, edited by I. Bejczy and R. Newhauser (Leiden: E. J. Brill, 2005), 75–94, here 91–92.
8   G. Zinn, "Hugh of Saint Victor and the Art of Memory," *Viator: Medieval and Renaissance Studies* 5 (1974): 211–34, here 220.
9   Introduction and translation by H. Feiss in VTT 1.49–102. The exact date of composition of *De meditatione* is not known. However, Van den Eynde convincingly argues that it is to be dated between that of the *Disdasc.* and *Tribus diebus*: D. van den Eynde, *Essai sur la succession et la date des écrits de Hugues de Saint-Victor* (Rome: Pontificium Athenaeum Antonianum, 1960), 116.
10   Introduction and translation by F. A. van Liere in VTT 3.203–52.

origin in the reading (*lectio*) of Scripture. Hugh offers here a brief in-
troduction to the *lectio divina*, the meditative reading of Scripture.
Reading will cause meditation, and this is done in a three-fold manner:
according to history, according to allegory, and according to tropology.
Hugh follows here the division he also presented in his *Didascalicon*,
On Sacred Scripture, and *On the sacraments of the Christian faith*.[11]
Meditation on Scripture will lead to prayer, Hugh says, when we lift up
the things we meditate on toward God; action, when we transform our
meditation into works; and contemplation, when we contemplate the
truths that Scripture presents to us. In the rest of the treatise, almost
half its length, Hugh offers some guidelines for the meditation on
moral conduct, or manners. As Stephen Jaeger has pointed out, the two
were intrinsically connected in the thought of the Victorines. The two
concepts were very much part of the same "congruence of inner world
and outer appearance that found a good, perhaps ideal context in the
lives and customs of canons regular, with their stress on humanity,
charity, and irreproachable appearance in external things."[12] Hugh's
treatise here offers some great insights into the twelfth-century art of
introspection and psychological self-examination.

The brief and punctuated style of Hugh's *On Meditation* is a clear
indication of the didactic purpose of the text; it almost reads like a draft
or a dictation for the benefit of a student. Its goal was to place meditation
within the overall educational goals of the school of Saint Victor: to bring
the admiration of the created world, the reading of Scripture, and the
discernment of one's own moral conduct to spiritual fruition, so that
one's entire life could be reformed and restored into the image of God.

The text translated here can be found in Baron's edition of Hugh's
Six opuscules spirituels, which also presents a French translation.[13] An
earlier edition can be found in Migne's *Patrologia Latina*, PL
176.993–98.

[11] *Didasc.* III.5 (tr. Harkins, VTT 3.150–51); *Script.* 3 (tr. Van Liere, VTT 3.214–15); *Sacr* . 4 (tr.
      Evans, VTT 3.264).
[12] C. S. Jaeger, "Humanism and Ethics at the School of Saint Victor," *Mediaeval Studies* 55
      (1993): 79.
[13] Hugues de Saint Victor, *Six opuscules spirituels*, ed. R. Baron, SC 155 (Paris: Éditions du Cerf,
      1969), 45–59.

ON MEDITATION

Meditation is a frequent reflection investigating the manner, the cause, and the reason of each thing. The manner investigates what it is, the cause why it exists, and the reason how it exists. There are three kinds of meditations: on creatures, on Scriptures, and on moral conduct. The first arises out of admiration, the second out of reading, and the third out of prudence.

I. Meditation on Creatures.[1]

In the first kind of meditation, admiration raises inquiry, inquiry investigation, and investigation discovery. Admiration is associated with arrangement, inquiry with the cause, and investigation with the reason. Arrangement is that in heaven all is equal, and on earth there is height and depth. This engenders admiration. Cause is that the earth exists for the earthly life, and heaven for the heavenly life. This engenders questioning. Reason is that the earthly life resembles the earth, and the heavenly life heaven. This engenders investigation.

II. Meditation on Scripture.

1. In reading we have to consider the following. Reading offers material to know the truth, meditation assimilates it, prayer lifts it up, action organizes it, and contemplation rejoices in it. Meditation on the Scriptures is how we ought to know. For example, it is written: *Avoid evil and do good.*[2] After reading comes meditation. Why does he first say, *Avoid evil,* and afterwards, *do good*? The cause tells us that, unless evils recede first, no goods can come near. Reason tells us that first bad plants are weeded out, and then good crops can be planted. Again, why does he say, *Avoid evil*? Because you encounter it on the way. Again, *Avoid,* for, where we cannot resist by strength, we have to avoid by counsel and reason. Again, we avoid evil by evading the matter of sin, and thus we ought to avoid riches to evade pride, abundance to evade

intemperance, carnal beauty to evade lust, and the love of possessions to evade envy and strife. That is what "avoiding" means.

Again, just as it is prescribed to avoid all evil, so it is commanded to do all good. And just as he is guilty who does not decline from all evil, so too is everyone who does not do all good. But if that is the case, then who is not guilty? Thus we are commanded to avoid all evil, but some good things are necessary, and others voluntary. Necessary are those goods that are prescribed by a command or a vow. If something more is done than what is needed, it is recompensed, but if not, it is not faulted.

2. Furthermore, meditation on reading means to reflect on how those things exist that are known to exist and how those things should be done that are known to be done. For meditation is the reflection on the plan of how to put into practice what we know, because it is no use to know something unless we put it into practice.

3. Furthermore, meditation on reading is a threefold examination according to history, allegory, and tropology. It is according to history when we either seek or admire the reason for the things that are done, which is perfect in its times, places, and suitable arrangement. In this respect, consideration of divine judgments is a good exercise for one who meditates, for at no time these judgments failed to be righteous and just, and through them what should have happened and what was just was rendered to each. According to allegory meditation endeavors to order past events by looking at their signification of future events, because this order was arranged by a wonderful reason and providence, as was necessary to shape an understanding and the formation of faith. According to tropology meditation endeavors to identify what fruit certain sayings bring forth, and to discern what they suggest ought to be done or what they teach should be avoided, what the reading of Scripture propounds for teaching, for exhortation, for consolation, or to strike fear;[3] what illumination it gives for the understanding of virtue, what food it gives to affection, and what instruction it gives on the rule of conduct for the path of virtue.

III. MEDITATION ON MORAL CONDUCT.

1. The meditation on moral conduct can be according to affects, thoughts, and works.

Regarding affects, we have to consider whether they are right and sincere, that is, with regard to what they should be and how they should be. For to love what one should not love is evil, and similarly it is evil to love what one ought to love in a manner one should not love it. Thus an affect is good when it is directed towards what it should be directed to, and in the manner that it should be. Amnon loved his sister, and this affect was appropriately directed, but because he loved in an evil manner, it was not as it should have been.[4] Thus an affect can be directed to the right object, but not in the right manner. But it can never be in the right manner, unless it is also directed towards the right object. In that it is directed to the right object, it is right, and in that it is in the right manner, it is sincere.

Regarding thoughts we have to reflect on whether they are pure and well-ordered. They are pure when they neither originate from evil affections, nor generate evil affections. They are well-ordered when they occur rationally, that is, in their own time. For it is not without fault to think about even good things at their improper time, such as to think about prayer during reading, or about reading during prayer.

Regarding works we have to consider first whether they are done with a good intention. A good intention is one that is simple and right: simple without malice, and right without ignorance. The one without malice is full of zeal, but the one in ignorance lacks *in knowledge*.[5] Thus the intention needs to be both right through discernment and simple through kindness. The second thing to consider in works is whether what was begun with the right intention also is brought to an end with the fervor of perseverance, so that neither perseverance grows numb, nor love grows tepid.

2. Furthermore, meditation on moral conduct is touching on a twofold consideration, namely, inside and outside; outside with respect to reputation, and inside with respect to conscience. Outside pertains to what is profitable and what is proper: proper to serve as example, and profitable for merit; merit for ourselves, and an example for others. Inside pertains to conscience, so that our conscience may be pure and not suffer reproach, either because it is too lazy to do good or because it presumes to do evil. That conscience is pure which is neither accused rightly about something in the past, nor is it rejoicing wrongly about something in the present.

3. Furthermore, meditation on moral conduct is engaged in consideration to discern all movements that originate in the heart, whence they come and where they go. Whence they come concerns their ori-

gin; where they go concerns their end. For every movement comes from somewhere and goes somewhere. Thus the movements of the heart sometimes have a manifest origin, sometimes a hidden one; and the origin that is manifest is sometimes manifestly good, sometimes manifestly evil. The origin that is manifestly good is from God, but the origin that is manifestly evil is either from the devil or from the flesh. These three are the authors of all suggestions, and all desires that occur invisibly in the heart proceed from these. Likewise, when they are hidden they are sometimes good and hidden, sometimes evil and dubious. When they are good they are from God, and when they are evil they are from the devil or from the flesh.

What is manifest, whether good or evil, is judged by its first origin, but what is dubious in origin is tested by its end. The end reveals what is hidden in origin, and, for that reason, he who cannot judge his movements by their origin should investigate their end and final result. Those that are doubtful or uncertain either are hidden goods or evils. And those that are evil, as is said, are either from the devil or from the flesh. And those that are evil either way are not different from each other in that they are evil, but they differ in that those from the flesh very often arise out of necessity, but those from the devil very often arise contrary to reason. What is suggested by the devil is often as foreign to human reason as it is from the human person, as, for example, when someone who has just eaten suffers hunger, or someone who shortly before has drunk is thirsty, or someone who wakes up from a good long rest is burdened by sleepiness. In this way the devil's works can be discerned, because they are contrary to man, and contrary to human reason. But the works of the flesh and its suggestions are very often caused by a preceding necessity, but because they exceed limit and measure, they grow into excess, just as, for instance, when someone desires too much food after experiencing hunger, or one does not keep measure in eating food after a period of abstinence.

4. Furthermore, the meditation on moral conduct is practiced by a three-fold kind of judgment. It first needs to judge between night and day, second between day and day, and third it needs to judge each day.[6] To judge between night and day is to divide evil from good. To judge between day and day is to discern between what is good and what is better. To judge each day is to esteem each individual good on its own merits.

5. Furthermore, the meditation on moral conduct considers the end and direction of every manner of life. The end is where it is aimed, and

the direction is how it is achieved most easily. Everyone who aims for something guides his course in a certain direction, and everyone who proceeds in a more direct way arrives there faster. Some works are good even if there is much motion but very little progress. Other good works produce copious fruit with little labor. We have to consider and choose those that have the greatest benefit. For those that bring the greatest benefit are better, and each work has to be judged by its fruit.[7] Many people, who do not have this discernment, work very hard but make very little progress, because they have an eye focused only externally on the appearance of the work, and not internally on the fruit of virtue. They rejoice in their great deeds, rather than in their exercise of useful deeds; and they love those deeds that make them the center of attention, rather than the ones that can improve them.

6. Furthermore, the meditation on moral conduct first considers what one's duty is either on account of a commandment or on account of a vow, and it judges that those deeds to be done first have merit when done, but are faulted when left undone. Those things should first be done that cannot be omitted without guilt. After this if there is something to be added on top of that by voluntary action, it should be done in such a way that it does not infringe on one's duty. Some people want to accomplish what is not their duty, and they are unable to accomplish what is their duty. Others, even though they value their duty, add some voluntary impediments, willing to do what is not within their duty.

7. Furthermore, the meditation on moral conduct considers two evils especially to be avoided in a good work, namely frustration (*afflictio*) and obsessiveness (*occupatio*). Frustration brings bitterness (*amaritudo*), and obsessiveness brings dissolution (*dissipatio*). Through frustration, one's sweetness of mind becomes embittered. By obsessiveness, one's stillness of mind (*tranquillitas*) becomes scattered. Frustration happens when one burns with impatience because one cannot accomplish certain tasks. Obsessiveness happens when one gets carried away by lack of self-control (*intemperantia*) in the tasks one is able to accomplish. In order that one's spirit not be badly embittered, one's incapability needs to be patiently sustained; but in order that one does not become badly obsessed, one should not exert one's capability beyond its measure.

8. Furthermore, the meditation on moral conduct determines the rule of conduct by another consideration. It shows that it is no good to desire impatiently what does not happen, nor to lose interest in the good things that do. For he who always desires what does not happen

and has no interest in those that do, does not enjoy the present things, nor is he satisfied with the future things. What he begins he abandons before it is accomplished, and what he has started he takes on prematurely. For that reason, it is good to be content with one's good and to increase the present good by doing more good, and not to abandon it for future goods. It belongs to shallowness (*levitas*) to exchange one good for another, but it belongs to virtue to put them in action, and those who throw away the old for the new run a different course from those who ascend from low to high. He who always seeks change is easily bored, but he who seeks perfection is zealous. But he advances most rightly who is so desirous for what is better, that he is not bored with what is good, but sustains the former until he apprehends the latter in its own time.

NOTES

1   These chapter headings are suggested in the French translation of Baron.
2   Ps. 36:27 (Vulg.).
3   Cf. 2 Tim. 3:16.
4   See 2 Sam. 13:1–14.
5   Rom. 10:2.
6   Rom. 14:5.
7   Cf. Matt. 7:16.

RICHARD OF ST VICTOR

EXPOSITION ON THE LORD'S PRAYER

INTRODUCTION AND TRANSLATION
BY FRANS VAN LIERE

INTRODUCTION

Richard of St Victor's *Book of Notes* was probably composed some time in the 1150s. It can be best characterized as a reading course in theological instruction for the students at the school of Saint Victor. It offers a concise Victorine program for study, as was also laid out, for instance, in the *Didascalicon* of Hugh of St Victor.[1] It lists the divers "artes," the books that should be read in the study of these "artes," and it gives an introduction on how to read the sacred texts. After this, it gives an overview of the geography of the world and the course of history, which in the pedagogical program of Saint Victor often served as the framework for a further study of theological doctrine and spiritual truths, which was offered in the second part of the book, called the *Allegories on the New Testament*. This second part also contained Richard's *Exposition of the Lord's Prayer*, translated here.

In the manuscript tradition, Richard's *Exposition* exists in two versions. The first, presumably older version, shows the work as a series of seven separate sermons on the seven petitions of the Lord's Prayer, while the second shows the work as a unified treatise, preceded by a prologue. In its latter version, the work has been ascribed spuriously to Hugh of St Victor, Peter Abelard (who also wrote his own exposition of the same subject),[2] Henry of Hesse and, more frequently, to Peter Comestor. Only four manuscripts mention Richard as the author of the treatise in their colophon; no fewer than twenty-nine manuscripts, by contrast, ascribe the work to the Parisian bishop Maurice of Sully, who had strong connections to Saint Victor and retired there as a canon. R. Goy concludes that, since the earlier version is explicitly ascribed to Richard, the work is indeed Richard's; it was not until its later stage that the work was mixed in with the sermon collections of Maurice of Sully.[3]

---

[1]   Coulter, "Richard of Saint-Victor," in VTT 3.295.

[2]   C. Burnett, "*Expositio orationis dominicae*: Peter Abelard's Exposition of the Lord's Prayer," *RBen*. 9 (1985): 60–72.

[3]   Goy, *Die handschriftliche Überlieferung*, 81–98. On the ascription to Peter Abelard, see J. Barrow, C. Burnett, and D. Luscombe, "A Checklist of the Manuscripts Containing the Writings of Peter Abelard," *Revue d'histoire des textes* 14–15 (1984–1985): 265–67. On the as-

As was said, Richard's *Exposition of the Lord's Prayer* is a set of seven sermons on the seven petitions of the Lord's Prayer, preceded by a short prologue. In this prologue, Richard points out that prayer is one of the most beneficial actions of Man toward God, and that Christ, in the Lord's Prayer, provided a model of how to pray. However, Richard says, if prayer is done without a pure conscience and humility of heart, God does not hear it. One recurring theme in this set of sermons is the call for clerical reform. In the mid-twelfth century at the Abbey of Saint Victor, Church reform was a hot political issue, and it could be fairly contentious. The early half of the twelfth century had seen a continuous effort by a reform party, including the Victorines, to reform the secular clergy of Paris cathedral to the regular life. In the mid 1140s, when the monastery of Mont Ste Geneviève was placed under the administration of the canons of Saint Victor, this reform movement seemed to have gained a decisive victory.[4] This call to reform may be the background of some of Richard's severe criticisms of "unreformed" clergy in his *Exposition*. In the sermon on the first petition, he mentions clergy who do not blush to approach the altar and handle the sacraments while living in a state of sin. In the sermon on the fourth petition ("Give us this day our daily bread"), he deplores the fact that many of the ordained clergy are not offering to the laity any "spiritual bread," that is, education in sacred doctrine. They feed on the flock, while the sheep go hungry, Richard says. Even worse, many of the laity are misled by teachers who go around sowing the seeds of false doctrine. It leaves the laity no other choice than to seek this spiritual nourishment within themselves, or to go to "learned priests that are living saintly in other places, . . . and ask humbly of them to be taught by them the counsel of their souls." It is interesting to note in this context that in the latter half of the twelfth century the canons of Saint Victor increasingly assumed pastoral responsibilities within the growing student population of the Paris schools.[5] With its emphasis on Christian living and reform,

cription to Maurice of Sully, who was part of the Victorine circle, see J. Longère, *Les sermons latins de Maurice de Sully, évêque de Paris († 1196): Contribution à l'histoire de la tradition manuscrite*, Instrumenta Patristica 16 (Steenbrugis: In Abbatia S. Petri; Dordrecht: Kluwer Academic Publishers, 1988), 309, 319–25.

4   R. Bautier, "Origines et premiers développements de l'abbaye Saint-Victor," in *L'abbaye parisienne de Saint-Victor au Moyen Age*, ed. J. Longère, BV 1 (Turnhout: Brepols, 1991), 23–52.

5   J. Longère, "La fonction pastorale de Saint-Victor à la fin du XIIe et au début du XIIIe siècle," in *L'abbaye parisienne de Saint-Victor au Moyen Age*, ed. J. Longère, BV 1 (Turnhout: Brepols, 1991), 302.

the sermon illustrates that, for Richard, Christian prayer and Christian living were intrinsically connected.

The Latin edition of the texts translated here into English for the first time can be found in Jean Châtillon's edition of Richard's *Book of Notes*.[6] Another edition can be found in Migne, with the works of Hugh (PL 175.767–74) and Peter Abelard (PL 178.611–18); it is also included in Cousin's edition of Peter Abelard's works.[7]

6   Richard of St Victor, *Liber exceptionum. Texte critique avec introduction, notes et tables*, ed. J. Châtillon, TPMA 5 (Paris: J. Vrin, 1958), 381–85 and 447–55. I wish to thank Fr. Hugh Feiss for his helpful suggestions on this translation.
7   *Petri Abaelardi Opera*, ed. V. Cousin (Paris: A. Durand, 1849–1859), 1:596–603.

EXPOSITION ON THE LORD'S PRAYER

Of all the things that human weakness can do to please the Creator or placate Him, prayer is the most beneficial, if it is done with a pure conscience and humility of heart. I say "with a pure conscience and humility of heart" for a reason, for if the conscience is polluted by a dirty stain of depraved will or work, or if our heart is filled with vain self-glory, our prayer is not received by God, and our inner stirring (*animus*) is not heard. For the prayer of one who averts his ear so as not to hear the Law will be detestable. Hence the mediator between God and mankind, the man Jesus Christ, looking after human salvation and mercifully providing for it, instituted a form of prayer, together with other words of most sacred teaching, and taught us how we ought to pray to the Father, saying: *When you pray, you shall not be as the hypocrites who love to stand and pray in synagogues and on the corners of the squares.*[1] *And when you are praying, do not speak with many words, as the heathens do. For they believe that they will be heard because of their verbosity.*[2] *But you shall pray thus: Our Father, who art in heaven,* etc.[3] In this Lord's Prayer, we can discern seven petitions. The first petition is: *Our Father, who art in heaven, hallowed be Your name.* The second is: *Your kingdom come.* The third petition is: *Your will be done; as it is in heaven, so also on earth.* The fourth petition is: *Give us today our daily bread.* The fifth petition is: *Forgive us our debts, as we forgive our debtors.* The sixth petition is: *Lead us not into temptation.* The seventh petition is: *Deliver us from evil.*

1. THE FIRST PETITION OF THE LORD'S PRAYER

Our Father who art in heaven, etc.[4] See, most beloved ones, on almost all days, but especially on feast days, the clergy and the people, men and women, come together in our churches, and all of them clothe themselves in their best clothes in the sight of the people, and all together enter into the house of God, secure as children of God, bow their knees, beat their breasts, raise their hands, open their mouths and offer prayers, saying, *Our Father.* But this cannot be said without major grief:

how many go in to the house of God to pray to God, and how few will be heard! How many call God in that prayer "Father" who are not his children, but children of the father of whom is written, *You are of your father the devil.*[5] They are not the children of God, because they have lost grace; they are children of the devil, because he has given birth to them and he raises them in guilt. They are children of the devil, as we often say in other sermons (*sententiae*), all the unclean, keepers of concubines, adulterers, misers, slanderers, money lenders,[6] and depraved with whatever other damnable sin, who say to their brother: "fool"; who look at a woman to desire her,[7] and all those who are separated from God, perhaps not by an evil deed, but certainly by an evil desire. And, what is much worse, what is more to weep about, not only common, uncouth and unlettered lay people, but even a great number of priests of our time, who are anointed with sacred oil, who are daily adorned with sacred vestments and approach the sacred altar, who ought to handle the sacrament of the body and blood of our Lord with the cleanest of hands, and placate God with dedicated prayers for themselves and for those entrusted to them,[8] they themselves are involved in the most sordid of vices and polluted by the stains of sin. But what is much worse, not only are they soiled with such sins as are many lay people, but even much worse; and they are placed there, not to the edification, but to the scandal and ruin of the people, and become bywords, and objects of ridicule and contempt for all. But these priests must know that daily, when they chant to God at the first hour, they either curse themselves, or pronounce the testimony of divine condemnation against themselves when they chant: *Cursed are they who fall away from Your commandments.*[9] Whoever, then, brethren, calls God in the Lord's Prayer "Father" and whoever desires to be heard by Him, should live in such a way that God would recognize him to be His son by grace, who is the Father of all by nature. Otherwise, when he will be judged, he will go condemned, and his prayer will be reckoned as a sin.

Our Father, who art in heaven. Whoever says "Father" desires benevolence; whoever says "our" excludes pride; whoever says "who art in heaven" shows reverence. Whoever says "Father" desires benevolence, because he calls him loving; whoever says "our" excludes pride, because he does not pray arrogantly for himself alone as being special, but also as common together with others; who says "who art in heaven" shows reverence, because he announces that He does not preside merely over the lowest but even over the highest. *Hallowed be Your name.* There are many names for God; which name do we ask to be sanctified when we pray "Hallowed be Your name"? The name of God is faith in God, by which he is known to believers. *Hallowed be Your name*; sanctified be faith in you, which is the knowledge of you. For is the notion (*numen*)[10] of the Lord not sanctified and holy? For all the Scriptures call out, all sound together: *Hallowed be Your name*. The name of the Lord is indeed holy, but in the hearts of some it can be even more greatly hallowed. It can be hallowed in the hearts of pagans, in whom it is not yet sanctified by faith; it can be hallowed in the hearts of Jews, in whom it is not yet sanctified by the completion of faith; it can be hallowed in the hearts of false Christians, in whom it is not yet sanctified by love; it can also be more greatly hallowed in the hearts of the elect by a greater confirmation of faith and a greater love of God and neighbor. For the more perfectly anyone believes in God and loves him, the more greatly he sanctifies the name of the Father in him and shows it as sanctified. *Our Father who art in heaven, hallowed be Your name*: May Your name be hallowed in the hearts of pagans, may it be hallowed in the hearts of Jews, so that the former may believe in you, and the latter believe in you more perfectly, and so that both may love you; may it be hallowed in the hearts of false Christians, so that, as they have knowledge of you by faith, they also may have love for you by experience (*affectus*). May it even be hallowed in the hearts of the elect by a greater clarity of knowing and a greater sweetness in loving. *Our Father who art in heaven, hallowed be Your name.*

2. THE SECOND PETITION

Your kingdom come.[11] What is it we ask when we say *Your kingdom come?* Does not God have a kingdom? Is God not king? If he is not a king, or does not have a kingdom, why then does the Psalmist say, *God is king of the whole earth; wisely sing psalms to him?*[12] Thus God is king, and he has a kingdom. Why then do we ask that his kingdom may come? When we ask that his kingdom may come, we do not ask that it may come where it is, but where it is not yet; or that it may be more clearly manifested where it is not yet manifest. There are yet many to be born who are predestined to be in his kingdom, and those who are predestined are not yet manifested in all things to be of his kingdom. Thus, *Your kingdom come*, O heavenly Father, so that those predestined to your kingdom from among those born through the nature of the flesh may both be reborn by the grace of baptism, and be justified, and that through the clarity of justice they may be revealed to all as children of Your kingdom. May *Your kingdom* also *come*, so that at the end of time, on the day of judgment, at the general resurrection, the grain may be separated from the chaff,[13] the fish from the snakes, the sheep from the goats,[14] the wheat from the weeds,[15] and may Your Church, which is Your kingdom, at Your calling, cross from the pressure of the present world into the glory of the heavenly fatherland. Again: *Your kingdom come*, so that as you now reign in the justified, you may soon reign in those to be justified, and so that as you reign in those who already are good, you may reign also in those who still are bad, after you have driven out the power of the demons. *Your kingdom come.*

3. THE THIRD PETITION

Your will be done, as it is in heaven, so also on earth.[16] We know that in heaven not one of the saints or angels deviates from the will of God, and no one contradicts him. How can it then happen that the will of God happens on earth just as it does in heaven, namely such that no one on earth transgresses either by ignorance, or by human frailty, while there is not a child of one day old on earth without sin, and we all *offend in many things?*[17] But we have to know that "as" is not said of quantity but of quality, and it denotes similitude, not equality. If someone builds a small house according to the form and arrangement of a larger house, we will not say about the smaller house "this one is as large as (*tanta*) the larger one," but we will say "this one is like (*talis*) the other one": 'like' in similitude, not 'as large as' in quantity. Thus, *Your will be done*, O Father, *as it is* done *in heaven* by the angels and by the saints who are already glorified by the first robe,[18] *thus likewise on earth* by the people who will be justified and glorified, so that, as the former do Your will in heaven, the latter may do it on earth, if not in equal measure, certainly in the same way, that is, if not in the measure of their perfection, then certainly in the imitation of their perfection. *Your will be done* not only in the elect by the manifestation of their good works, but also in the reprobate, by the ordering of their evils. Even though You are not the author of the evils, you are still their disposer, and even though there are many evils under Your power, you still leave nothing unordered, and thus Your will is done in all things: in the good things by Your doing, and in the bad things by Your ordaining. *Your will be done; as it is in heaven, so also on earth*, so that as in heaven the cherubim, seraphim, thrones, dominions, powers, virtues, principalities, angels, archangels, and also the patriarchs, prophets, apostles, martyrs, confessors, virgins, and all of the souls of the elect, freed from the chains of their bodies and glorified with you, do Your will, thus on earth all bishops, priests and all the clergy, all kings, princes and all the people, male, female, great, small, good, and also the evil ones converted from evil to good, do Your will, according to the grace bestowed by You and according to their own capability. *Your will be done*, not only in rational creatures by knowing and loving You, but also in irrational creatures, by their existing and procreating. And *Your will be done* not only in sensible things by the fecundity of propagation, but also in insensible and living things by the sprouting of what grows; hence *Your will* shall *be done* not only in the things that are now living, but also in things that are existing in whatever manner that is pleasing to you. And similarly, *Your will be done; as it is in heaven, so also on earth*, that is, as it is done in those who are already justified, so may it be done by those who are to be justified. And similarly, *Your will be done; as it is in heaven, so also on earth*, that is, just as reason assisted by Your grace dictates something to be done, thus may the flesh carry out those dictates without contradiction and defect. *Your will be done; as it is in heaven, so also on earth.*

4. THE FOURTH PETITION

Give us today our daily bread.[19] God has made mankind out of a double substance, namely corporeal and spiritual. Since mankind, then, is composed of these two substances, it needs a double bread: one for the body, and one for the spirit. The bread for the body is corporeal, and that for the spirit is spiritual. The body feeds on grain from the fields; the spirit feeds on sacred doctrine. The corporeal bread we ask of God, for unless God gives rain and makes the earth spring forth seeds, we cannot have this bread. The spiritual bread we also ask of God, for unless God gives it, we do not have it. Biological fathers distribute the corporeal bread to themselves and their sons; the spiritual bread spiritual fathers, that is the prelates and teachers [of the Church], need to distribute. Hence *how it is required among the distributors, that a man is found faithful.*[20] For in our time, *who is a faithful and prudent servant, whom the Lord has put in charge of his family, so that he may give them food at the right time,*[21] faithfully and prudently; faithfully with respect to God, prudently with respect to the people; faithfully with respect to God, namely so that he may distribute the word of God with such faith, such fear, such solicitude, such promptness, and such diligence, as God commands it; and prudently with respect to the people, so that he may educate all of them each according to his capacity?

But what cannot be called to mind without great sadness, as Saint Gregory says,[22] is that the world is full of priests, but even if there is one who hears a good word, there is none who will say it. What will certain modern-day priests do and say on the day of judgment, when they finally come to the day of calamity? They have received the priestly order, but they do not blush to live inordinately; they love to sit at the crossroads with people who are entrusted to them, who are entirely unlearned, corrupted by bad morals, in order to speak and listen to useless or even pernicious words, judge haughtily, and they not only disparage the living but even the dead. They ask for the revenue of the churches that are committed to them, when appropriate or not; they desire offerings with all the greed of their heart; and what they often shamelessly denounce with their mouth, they receive with both hands when it comes their way. Some attend parties and drinking bouts, get involved in adulterous affairs and sexual immorality, and *many things are done by them* that, as the Apostle says, *are too sordid to mention.*[23] They clothe themselves with the wool of the Lord's flock, and are fed with its milk, but the sheep die from want and hunger for the word of God.[24] Time goes by, and the cycle of the liturgical year is completed, but not one word comes from their mouths, by which the flock that is committed to them is educated, rebuked concerning evil, called back to the good, and conformed to him. But thinking that they are daily applying themselves in the service of God, they howl and hiss the words of God's praise, and by the sound of their voice and the movement of their bodies, they offend rather than edify those who hear and see them. Lord, feed Your own flock;[25] may Your unction teach them about all things, so that Your Spirit may infuse them by internal inspiration with the doctrine that the mute mouth of such priests does not distribute to them. Those priests should think about the prophetic warnings that were pronounced against them, by which is said: *And as it shall be with the people, so with the priest.*[26] And again: *The priests did not say: Where is the Lord? And those who held the law knew me not.* And in another place, we find written about such people: *Mute dogs cannot bark, and impudent dogs do not know when they have had enough.*[27]

Hence let no one expect that such priests will give them the bread of sacred doctrine, for these priests do not know how to teach, or they are ashamed to, or they disdain it. What then will they do with the sheep that are entrusted to them? These sheep have to consider learned priests that are living saintly in other places, and go to them, and ask humbly to be taught by them the counsel of their souls. There are also certain pseudo-preachers who are sowed like weeds in the field of the Lord by the devil,[28] who fill the entire world with their phylacteries,[29] and who with lying words bless the unlearned people that are burdened with various sins, *saying peace, peace, while there is no peace.*[30] But what does Scripture say? *My people, the same ones who bless you also seduce you, and they destroy the path of your steps.*[31] And again: *Those who bless and those who are blessed will fall headlong.*[32]

Give us today, O Father, *our daily bread;* the corporeal and spiritual bread. The corporeal bread, to make the earth germinate, bear and ripen fruit, and bring it to fullness; the spiritual bread, so that you may inspire the prelates and teachers of Your Church to be diligent in faithfully and prudently distributing to us the doctrine that was handed over to them. And if they do not care to break this bread with us, feed us Yourself, by the hidden inspiration of Your spirit, so that through You we may grasp internally this bread, of which we were externally defrauded by their lack of communication. *Give us today our daily bread.*

5. THE FIFTH PETITION

Forgive us our debts, as we forgive our debtors.[33] How fearful in many ways, how dangerous in many ways, is this prayer, brothers. For many, this prayer brings on more loss than gain, more damnation than lucre. For there are some who, hardened by a great and long malice of spite and hatreds, desire to strangle and dismember with their own hands those who have become their debtors by any kind of injury, and harm them in all possible ways and confound them, and do not want to receive any kind of satisfaction or achieve reconciliation, either out of fear of God or by the entreaties of people. About these people, it is written: *Their grapes are the grapes of wrath, and their cluster is exceedingly bitter. Their wine is the gall of dragons, and an incurable venom of vipers.*[34] But in this state, they still confidently flock to church, and say in the presence of God at the altar, praying: *Our Father, forgive us our debts, as we forgive our debtors.*

But what miserable foolishness, what unfortunate presumption, to provoke the wrath of God against oneself with prayers! *Man reserves wrath for man, but from God he asks mercy.*[35] There are certain imperfect people, to whose imperfection, as Saint Augustine says,[36] God's mercy reaches out and grants that they forgive their debtors their debts, at least at the moment when these debtors ask for it as a favor to be given to them, as a lord is read to have done to his wicked servant, as it is written: *Wicked servant, I have forgiven you all your debt, because you asked me to.*[37] But whoever is asked by a debtor to forgive a debt owed for some injury, and spurns to do it, asks in vain from the Lord for his sin's debt to be forgiven, or rather, in the eyes of the judge he makes this debt heavier rather than lighter. Even though it is conceded to the imperfect to ask for what is theirs, and receive satisfaction from the injuries they suffered, and to be asked for indulgence by their debtors, if it so happens that none of these occurs, by all means they have to check the wrath of their own heart and drive the darkness of hatred out of themselves. They have to be mindful of what is written: *God's justice does not work by the wrath of man.*[38] And again: *Whoever hates his brother is a murderer,*[39] *and no murderer has a part in the kingdom of Christ and God.*[40] But it belongs to the perfect to forgive their debtors, all things to all people, with a pure heart, a joyful mien, without any kind of restitution, without satisfaction for injuries, and without any kind of asking, and above that, they give what is properly theirs and show the consideration of charity. Let everyone provide for himself in this prayer, *forgive us our debts as we forgive our debtors*, so that he may be eager to provide to others such a remission as he desires from God. If not, in my opinion he should be silent and refrain from saying this prayer: *Forgive us our debts, as we forgive our debtors.*

Forgive, then, Father, *our debts, as also we forgive our debtors*, and if you see that because of some weakness or out of mischief we cannot forgive as we should, give us the grace to forgive according to Your will and thus deserve Your forgiveness. Give that we may so love people that we do not love their errors, that we may so love the nature in them and not their guilt, that we may love them for what they are and not for what they have done wrong. *Forgive us our debts, as we forgive our debtors.*

6. The sixth petition

And lead us not into temptation.[41] Since it is written: *God is not the tempter of evils; he does not tempt anyone, but every person is tempted by his own concupiscence, being drawn away and allured.*[42] What then is it we ask for when we say, *Lead us not into temptation?* The meaning is this: *Lead us not into temptation*, not that you should never permit us to be tempted, but that you should never permit us to be overcome by temptations, and grant that we are tested by temptations, but not condemned by them. Temptations benefit the just in many ways, for by the victory over temptations we arrive at the crown, as the Apostle attests, saying, *Blessed is the man who endures temptation, because when he has been tested he shall attain the crown of life, which God has promised to them that love Him.*[43] And in the beginning of that same letter: *Consider it every joy, brethren, when you fall into divers temptations, knowing that by proving your faith* (which happens by temptations) *patience is produced.*[44] And about patience, it is written: *In your patience you shall possess your souls.*[45] There are four kinds of temptations, as we already have said in another place:[46] one temptation is light and hidden, another light and out in the open, another grave and hidden, and yet another grave and out in the open. There are three things that tempt us: our flesh, the world, and the devil. Our flesh tempts us by gluttony and luxury; the world tempts us by prosperity and adversity: by prosperity to deceive us, and by adversity to break us; the devil assaults us in all these ways and tries to induce us to every evil. Father, *lead us not into temptation*, so that you may not permit us *to be tempted more than we are able, but give with temptation also success, that we may be able to bear it.*[47] *Lead us not into temptation.*

7. The seventh petition

Deliver us from evil.[48] There are many evils to which the human condition is subjected, and whose pressure by itself can hardly be avoided. We can generally distinguish among six different kinds: there is evil of the body, and evil of the soul; there is the evil of guilt, and the evil of punishment, and, finally, the evil of this age, and the evil of the coming age. When we pray, *Deliver us from evil*, we pray that we may be liberated from all these and from all others that are understood by them and contained under them. As if we said: *Deliver us from* every *evil*, Father; from the evil of the body, from the evil of the soul, from the evil that is guilt, and the evil that is punishment, from the evil of this age and that of one to come. Deliver us from all evil, for unless you deliver us, we cannot be delivered without you, not from a single evil, not from the least. You, therefore, Father, *deliver us from evil.*

8. AMEN CONCLUDES ALL THE AFOREMENTIONED PETITIONS

Amen[49] is translated "truly," and it concludes all the petitions of the preceding prayer. *Amen*, as if we say: O, *our Father who art in heaven*, may all things for which we prayed above truly happen in us and in others. Truly may *Your name be hallowed*; truly may *Your kingdom come*; truly may *Your will be done; as it is in heaven, so also on earth*; truly may You *give us today our daily bread*; truly may You *forgive us our debts as we forgive our debtors*; truly may You *not lead us into temptation*; truly may You *deliver us from evil.* This prayer, O brethren, must continually be meditated upon, and continually be said aloud, as our Savior himself taught us, and by which he ordered us to pray to the Father. No prayer is more sublime than this, and none more useful. There are some people, who, like the Gentiles, are proud that they use a lot of words,[50] read many Psalters, recite the various Hours, and say lengthy prayers all the time. And while with the mouth they pray to the Lord, with the heart they often stray to all the ends of the earth. May people of this sort think about Scripture which says, *These people honor me with their lips, but their heart is a long way away from me.*[51] We do not belittle with these words the skill and perseverance of holy prayer and persevering devotion; indeed we very much praise them, as long as the prolixity of prayer is accompanied by the fervor of internal devotion.

NOTES

1   Matt. 6:5.
2   Matt. 6:7.
3   Matt. 6:9–13.
4   Matt. 6:9.
5   John 8:44.
6   Eph. 5:5; 1 Cor. 6:9–10.
7   Matt. 5:22, 28.
8   Cf. Lev. 9:7.
9   Ps. 118:21 (Vulg.).
10 Richard plays here on the words "numen" (the notion of the divine; a sense of divine presence) and "nomen" (name).
11 Matt. 6:10.
12 Ps. 46:8 (Vulg.)
13 Matt. 3:12; Luke 3:17.
14 Matt. 25:32–33.
15 Matt. 13:30.
16 Matt. 6:10.
17 James 3:2.
18 Apoc. 6:11.
19 Matt. 6:11.
20 1 Cor. 4:2.
21 Matt. 24:45.
22 Gregory the Great, *Hom. ev.* I.17.3 (Étaix, 118; PL 76.1139D).
23 Eph. 5:12.
24 Ezek. 34:3.
25 John 21:16.
26 Isa. 24:2.
27 Isa. 56:10–11.
28 Matt. 13:25, 39.
29 Matt. 23:5.
30 Jer. 8:11.
31 Isa. 3:12.
32 Isa. 9:16.
33 Matt. 6:12.
34 Deut. 32:32–33.
35 Ecclus. 28:3–4.
36 Dubious attribution.
37 Matt. 18:32.
38 James 1:20.
39 1 John 3:15.
40 Eph. 5:5.
41 Matt. 6:13.
42 James 1:13–14.
43 James 1:12.
44 James 1:2–3.
45 Luke 21:19.
46 See Richard of St Victor, *LE* 7.13 (Châtillon, 323–24).
47 1 Cor. 10:13.
48 Matt. 6:13.
49 Matt. 6:13.
50 Matt. 6:7.
51 Isa. 29:13; Matt. 15:8; Mark 7:6.

HUGH OF ST VICTOR

EXPOSITION
ON THE CANTICLE OF MARY

INTRODUCTION AND TRANSLATION
BY FRANKLIN T. HARKINS

INTRODUCTION

The *Exposition on the Canticle of Mary* is a spiritually rich and theologically profound verse-by-verse commentary on the *Magnificat*, the song of the Virgin found in Luke 1:46–55. The commentary, which circulated in medieval manuscripts under the titles *Expositio* or *Explanatio super Canticum Mariae*, is one of three major Marian works produced by Hugh of St Victor. The other two are *On the Assumption of the Virgin* (*Pro Assumptione Virginis*) and *On the Virginity of Blessed Mary* (*De beatae Mariae virginitate*).[1] Damien van den Eynde dates all three of these works to the period 1130/31–1137, thereby situating them after the composition of such works as the *Didascalicon on the Study of Reading*, *On the Three Days*, *On the Ark of Noah*, and the *Little Book on the Formation of the Ark*, but prior to *On the Sacraments of the Christian Faith*, *The Praise of the Bridegroom*, the *Soliloquy on the Betrothal-Gift of the Soul*, and *On the Power and Will of God*.[2] In Paris, Mazarine 726, a mid-twelfth-century manuscript likely produced and used at St Victor, the *Exposition on the Canticle of Mary* immediately follows *On the Sacraments of the Christian Faith* and precedes *On the Assumption of the Virgin*, *The Praise of the Bridegroom*, and *On the Vanity of the World*.[3] This, together with the fact that Hugh appears to have written the *Exposition on the Canticle* before his other two major Marian works, suggests the importance not only of this commentary in the Victorine's larger corpus, but also of the canticle itself to the liturgical and spiritual life of St Victor.

As was the liturgical custom for secular clergy and monks alike in the medieval West, the Victorine canons regular would have prayed the *Magnificat* each evening at Vespers.[4] In his prologue, Hugh situates

---

[1]   A Latin edition and French translation of each of these works, together with a Marian homily entitled *Egredietur virga* and a brief sentence entitled *Maria porta*, appears in *Oeuvre* 2.
     I would like to thank Angela Kim Harkins, Frans van Liere, and the other members of the VTT editorial board for their very helpful comments on both this introduction and the translation that follows.

[2]   See D. van den Eynde, *Essai sur la succession*, 92–93, 119–23, 170, 189–90; and *Oeuvre* 2:8–9.

[3]   See G. Ouy, *Les manuscrits de l'abbaye de Saint-Victor. Catalogue établi sur la base du répertoire de Claude de Grandrue (1514)* (Turnhout: Brepols, 1999), 2:259–60.

[4]   J. Black, "The Divine Office and Private Devotion in the Latin West," in *The Liturgy of the*

his *Exposition* within the context of the Divine Office when he declares: "Behold, the Canticle of Mary, which the Church repeats with so renowned and regular—indeed, daily—sacred proclamation throughout the world. Who does not know that it contains the greatest mysteries of spiritual understanding?" That Hugh's fellow canons and students seemed to have asked him to comment on Mary's Canticle intimates that, although they surely knew that her song contains such profound mysteries, they needed some exegetical guidance in accessing what the Victorine master describes as the "higher understanding" of apparently ordinary words. With great caution Hugh embarks upon this commentary, probably first delivered orally in chapter, maintaining that moving responsibly from a pedestrian text to the spiritual realities signified by such a customary letter presents the "greatest difficulty that I find in Sacred Scripture".[5]

There is the further danger of attempting to interpret by means of human words Mary's utterly ineffable experience of God's power, presence, and grace at the Annunciation, as Hugh explains:

> Immediately, the Holy Spirit came to the Virgin and filled her most holy home with the grace of every virtue through the coming of the Son of God. There is no doubt that the Virgin herself received the extraordinary and indescribable pleasure of supernatural delights and everlasting sweetness when that eternal light, with all the splendor of its majesty, descended upon her and when what the whole world cannot contain established itself in her womb. Who can say what she, being filled with such a plentiful and excellent manifestation of the divine presence, saw or what she experienced? I boldly proclaim that she herself was not able to explain fully what she experienced.[6]

Yet her own words in the *Magnificat* are absolutely trustworthy in revealing truth precisely because they came forth from Mary's contemplative union with the highest Truth Himself. Echoing Augustine's analogy between human speech and the divine Incarnation, Hugh explains that, like the eternal Word whom the Virgin miraculously conceived and birthed in time, every word constituting her song of praise should be carefully contemplated by virtue of the fact that it was "brought forth from such a profound conception." Hugh's understand-

---

Medieval Church, 2nd ed., ed. Thomas J. Heffernan and E. Ann Matter (Kalamazoo, Mich.: Medieval Institute Publications, 2005), 41–64, here 54.

5   See the prologue below.

6   *Cant. BM.* on Luke 1:46.

ing that every word that Mary uttered in her *Magnificat* carries meaning, that is, the song's omnisignificance, is grounded in the Virgin's own inconceivable contemplative experience of the God whom she conceived. "For nothing is without a reason," the Victorine master explains, "because everything that she said emanated from that most secret light of highest Truth to which the mind of the Virgin clung excellently."[7]

The *Magnificat* provides a fitting scriptural canvas, then, on which we see Hugh at work as an able exegete who understands the intricacies and challenges of textual signification, as a canon regular whose daily life is shaped by the liturgy, as a teacher who is aware of the instructional and formational needs of his students, as a spiritual master who is attuned to contemplative and mystical realities, and as a scholastic theologian who is alive to the pressing questions in the schools of his day and who employs their methods in an attempt to answer them. In short, here we catch a glimpse of the holistic vision of St Victor and its most renowned twelfth-century master.

Modern readers may be surprised by how characteristically (at times, even high) scholastic the *Exposition* appears, particularly in Hugh's concern for conceptual and linguistic precision, in his drawing of numerous distinctions, and in the speculative nature of the questions that he poses and seeks to answer. Among the noteworthy distinctions that aid Hugh in shedding light on the scriptural text are that between or among: "soul" and "spirit" (vv. 46–47), "Lord" and "Savior" (vv. 46–47), three types of divine consideration (v. 48), four modes of servitude (v. 48), "humility" and "humiliation" (v. 48), four kinds of fear (v. 50), and three ways of being written in the Book of Life (v. 51). This first distinction, that between "soul" and "spirit," leads Hugh to discuss the important scholastic question of the number of souls that constitute the human person. More specifically, he seeks to refute "the error of certain thinkers" who maintain that in every human there exist two souls, one rational and one sensible. Hugh describes their line of reasoning in this way:

> Therefore, since it is evident that a rational soul is infused only in a formed body, and since it is also clear that the body, before it receives the human form, is moved and grows and is led to this very form by the vital motion that is inherent in it, they think that it must be conceded without objection that before the human body receives a rational

---

[7]   *Cant. BM.* on Luke 1:46–47.

soul, it has a sensible soul by which it lives, moves, and develops, and from which it receives its form.[8]

They affirm this so certainly, the Victorine explains, that they believe that if the rational soul were not infused during the process of conception and formation, a brute beast would be born in human form from human parents! Although Hugh, in good politically correct medieval fashion, does not disclose the names of contemporary proponents of this position, the broader intellectual context within which Hugh and his adversaries are working is that of reconciling the Augustinian view that God created and infused a single rational soul into each human body with the Aristotelian view that multiple souls (namely, the vegetative, the sensitive or sensible, and the rational) constitute the human person. Whereas Aristotle's works on nature, science, and ethics—including *On the Soul* (*De anima*)—would not be translated into Latin and transmitted to the West until at least a decade after Hugh penned his *Exposition*, the Victorine is certainly aware of the Philosopher's teaching on the soul and the potential difficulties it raises for the traditional Christian view that "there exists in the human one and the same soul that both gives life to the body and itself lives through understanding."[9]

That Hugh's treatment of this question significantly influenced subsequent scholastic discussions of the rational human soul is perhaps best seen by briefly considering Richard Rufus of Cornwall, who produced his commentary on the *Sentences* of Peter Lombard between 1246 and 1250, a little over a century after the Victorine's *Exposition*.[10] In commenting on distinction 17 of Book II, Rufus presents the conflicting views of the philosophers and the theologians on the nature of the human soul: whereas the former maintain that there are three substances but one soul in the human, the theologians contend that the soul is one substance with three powers. Rufus's compromise position, for which he claims to have found support in Hugh of St Victor's *Ex-*

---

[8]   *Cant. BM.* on Luke 1:46–47.

[9]   *Cant. BM.* on Luke 1:46–47. For an overview of the new translations of Aristotle and his Arabic commentators that were made during the period between 1140 and 1300, see T. Noone, "Scholasticism," in *A Companion to Philosophy in the Middle Ages*, ed. Jorge J. E. Gracia and T. Noone (Malden, Mass.: Blackwell, 2003), 55–64, esp. 59.

[10]   The following summary of Rufus's discussion depends on R. Dales, *The Problem of the Rational Soul in the Thirteenth Century* (Leiden: Brill, 1995), 56–60. An edition of the section of Rufus's *Sentences* commentary discussed here appears in D. Callus, "Two Early Oxford Masters on the Problem of the Plurality of Forms. Adam of Buckfield—Richard Rufus of Cornwall," *Revue néo-scholastique de philosophie* 42 (1939): 411–45.

position on the Canticle of Mary, is that a single soul with all three powers (viz., vegetative, sensible, and rational) comes from without and is infused in the human embryo, in which preexist vegetative and sensible powers that come forth from matter. Rufus seems to have learned from Hugh that movement and growth of the embryo prior to its reception of the form of the rational soul need not necessarily be attributed to a soul or substance separate from the rational soul.[11]

A second set of high scholastic questions that Hugh anticipates here in his *Exposition* derives from his commentary on verse 49, *Because the Mighty One has done great things for me*. Hugh understands Mary, in calling God "the Mighty One," as simply confessing His power, but not presuming to inquire into it, "since no one can know the degree of this power, which is most truly known to be immeasurable."[12] The Victorine understands Mary, in refusing to move beyond such a simple confession, as setting an example of intellectual humility for Peter Abelard and other of his contemporaries who "think they can rationally examine the divine works and bring His power within measurable limits."[13] Because such adversaries have exceeded the proper bounds of human epistemology vis-à-vis God, Hugh responds to them with two questions: (1) whether God can in any way do something other than what He does without His foresight (*prouidentia*) being either changed or nullified; and (2) whether God can do something better than He does it. Concerning this second question, in light of the arguments of his opponents who claim that the universe cannot be better than it is, Hugh draws two important distinctions: namely, that between particular creatures considered in themselves and the universe of all things; and that between "better" understood as possessing greater goodness and "better" understood as the ability to receive the greater goodness that is lacking. To claim that particular creatures cannot possess greater goodness is to equate these creatures with their Creator, which Hugh obviously rejects. To claim that the entire universe lacks the ability to receive greater goodness pertains to present deficiency, not to final consummation. Hugh concludes, then, that although God Himself cannot be better than He is, everything He made can become better if He who is supremely powerful wills it.[14]

11   *Cant. BM.* on Luke 1:46–47.
12   *Cant. BM.* on Luke 1:49.
13   *Cant. BM.* on Luke 1:49.
14   *Cant. BM.* on Luke 1:49.

About two decades after Hugh's *Exposition*, Peter Lombard, in distinction 44 of Book I of his *Sentences*, asked this same question and answered it in a way strikingly similar to that of the Victorine master.[15] The Lombard's text, in turn, shaped how thirteenth-century theological masters like Albert the Great, Bonaventure, and Thomas Aquinas approached and answered the question. A brief consideration of each of these theologians on the forty-fourth distinction of the Lombard's first book will hopefully bring Hugh's angle and influence into sharper relief.

Albert the Great, who lectured on the *Sentences* before becoming a master of theology at Paris in the spring of 1245, begins his comments on distinction 44, as elsewhere, by dividing the Lombard's text in order to nail down precisely what he is asking and how he is answering.[16] Albert makes clear in his *divisio textus* that in this distinction Peter Lombard is actually posing three different questions related to the manner of divine omnipotence vis-à-vis creation, namely: (1) whether God was able to make *the world* better than He made it; (2) whether God was able to make what He made *in a better way*; and (3) whether God is *now* able to make what He was *once* able to make.[17] In treating the *what* of God's creative power, Albert reiterates a crucial distinction found in Hugh's *Exposition* and subsequently explained in greater detail by both Bonaventure and Aquinas, namely, that between the goodness of the individual creatures that God has made and the goodness of the orderly arrangement of the whole world.[18] Unlike Hugh, though, Albert maintains that God could not make the universe better than He made it. Specifically, in taking up what he describes as "the very difficult question" of whether God was able to make the goodness that results from the order of the entire world better, the first authority that Albert invokes in the *sed contra* is Genesis 1:31, "God saw everything that He

---

15 See *Sent.* I.44.2–3 (tr. Silano, 1.238–39).

16 On the dating of Albert's commentary on the *Sentences*, see J. Weisheipl, "The Life and Works of St. Albert the Great," in *Albertus Magnus and the Sciences: Commemorative Essays 1980*, ed. J. A. Weisheipl, OP (Toronto: Pontifical Institute of Mediaeval Studies, 1980), 13–51, here 21–23. Although Albert likely lectured on the *Sentences* upon his arrival in Paris (*ca.* 1243–1244), the record of those lectures that we have in the Borgnet edition is clearly an *ordinatio* that was not completed until after 25 March 1249.

17 *Comm. in I Sent.* d. XLIV divisio textus, in *B. Alberti Magni Opera Omnia*, vol. 26, ed. S. C. E. Borgnet (Paris: Ludovicum Vives, 1893), 388.

18 Albert's second article asks, of individual things, "whether God was able to make those things that He made better," whereas article 3 asks "whether God was able to make the goodness that results from the order of the world better than He made it" (*Comm. in I Sent.* d. XLIV aa. 2–3 [ed. Borgnet, 388]).

had made, and indeed it was very good." Immediately thereafter, he teaches: "The Gloss says that each [created] thing was good in itself, but taken all together they are the best: but the best cannot be made better."[19]

In his discussion of this question at the level of the world, Bonaventure is concerned with whether God could have made a better world (1) with regard to the *substance, essence, or being* of its integral parts, what Aquinas will call its "essential goodness," and (2) with regard to the *order* of its parts.[20] First, on the substance of the world's integral parts, Bonaventure explains that what he describes as "an excess of substantial or essential goodness" in a thing (i.e., what is meant by "better" in the question at hand) can be understood in two ways: either with regard to the nobility and status of the thing's essence, or with regard to its being as concerns addition or increase. To use Bonaventure's own examples: we say that a human is better than an ass because its essence is more noble; but we say that eight ounces of gold is better than one ounce not because eight ounces have a more noble form or essence than one, but rather because they have more of the substance of gold and so more goodness and economic value.[21]

If one asks whether God was able to make a better world and he or she understands an excess of essential good in the first way, namely, that the world would consist of better and more noble essences, Bonaventure answers negatively. This is so because if the same world that now exists had been able to be made better, it would not be this world but another. "Just as if this one who was made a human had been made an ass, he would not be who he is," Bonaventure explains. Here the

---

[19]   *Comm. in I Sent.* d. XLIV a. 3 sed contra: Super illud Genes. 1, 31 (ed. Borgnet, 393): "*Vidit Deus cuncta fecerat: et erant valde bona*: dicit Glossa, quod bona erant in se, sed in universo optima: optimo autem non potest melius fieri."

[20]   Bonaventure treats these in question 1 and question 3, respectively, of article 1 of his commentary on distinction 44. In his own lectures on the *Sentences*, Aquinas drew on the commentaries of both Albert the Great and Bonaventure. Bonaventure began lecturing on the *Sentences* in 1250, two years prior to Aquinas. See C. Cullen, *Bonaventure* (Oxford: Oxford University Press, 2006), 11; and J. Wawrykow, *The Westminster Handbook to Thomas Aquinas* (Lousville: Westminster John Knox Press, 2005), 135.

[21]   *In Sent. I*, d. XLIV, a. 1 q. 1 corpus (*S. Bonaventurae Opera Theologica Selecta*, vol. 1, ed. Pp. Collegii S. Bonaventurae [Quarrachi: Collegium S. Bonaventurae, 1934], 621): "Dicendum quod excessus bonitatis substantialis in rebus potest attendi dupliciter: aut quantum ad essentiarum nobilitatem et gradus, et sic dicitur, quod species hominis melior est et nobilior specie asini; aut quantum ad esse, prout concernit additionem sive augmentum, sicut dicitur, quod marca auri melior est uncial, non quia nobiliorem habet formam uel essentiam, sed quia plus habet de auri substantia ac per hoc de bonitate et valore."

hypothetical created thing would, of course, display a *reduction* of essential good with regard to the nobility of its essence, but his point is the same. If one asks the question and understands an excess of essential good in the second way, Bonaventure answers affirmatively. Indeed, he teaches that God was able to make not only another world but even this world better in the sense of an increase of being. If God had made a larger or greater world, it would not have been another world, Bonaventure teaches, "just as He could have made this boy as big as a giant, having more substance and strength [than he now has], but he still would not have been a different person than he is."[22]

When Bonaventure turns to consider this question from the perspective of the *order* of the world's parts, his opening objection quotes Genesis 1:31 and the same gloss on it that appears in Albert. Like Albert, Bonaventure invokes both the sacred text and its gloss (telling us that the latter originates with Augustine) to support the claim that God was not able to make a more perfectly ordered world than the one He made.[23] He proceeds to explain that both with regard to the order of parts in the whole (*in toto*) and with regard to the order of parts toward their end (*in finem*), God has ordered the things of this world in the best way. Bonaventure explains the perfect ordering of things thus:

> The whole world is, as it were, the most beautiful song, which flows along with the best harmonies, with some parts following others until things are perfectly ordained toward their end . . . Thus, the order of things in the whole world shows wisdom, and the order of things to their end shows goodness, but in the relationship of one thing to another the greatest wisdom and the greatest goodness are shown.[24]

[22]   *In Sent. I*, d. XLIV, a. 1 q. 1 corpus (ed. Pp. Collegii S. Bonaventurae, 621): "Quando ergo quaeritur, utrum Deus potuerit mundum facere meliorem quantum ad substantiam partium; sit tu intelligas de excessu quantum ad primum modum, quod mundus constaret ex melioribus et nobilioribus essentiis, dico quod idem mundus, qui est nunc, non potuit fieri melior, quia non esset iste, sed alius; sicut, si iste qui factus est homo, fuisset factus asinus, non esset ille qui est. Quia tamen posse eius non est arctatum nec limitatum, non video quare non potuisset mundum facere meliorem hoc genere melioritatis. Si autem intelligas quantum ad secundum modum, sic dico quod non solum alium, verum etiam hunc potuit facere meliorem, sicut et maiorem. Et si fecisset non esset alius; sicut posset facere quod iste puer esset ita magnus ut gigas, et plus haberet de substantia et virtute, et tamen non esset alius quam est."

[23]   *In Sent. I*, d. XLIV, a. 1 q. 3 obj. a (ed. Pp. Collegii S. Bonaventurae, 624).

[24]   *In Sent. I*, d. XLIV, a. 1 q. 3 corpus (ed. Pp. Collegii S. Bonaventurae, 625): "Similiter optime ordinatae sunt res in finem, salvo ordine universi, quia universum est tamquam pulcherrimum carmem [sic], quod decurrit secundum optimas consonantias, aliis partibus seccedentibus aliis, quousque res perfecte ordinentur in finem . . . sic ordo rerum in universe in se ostendit sapientiam, et ordo ad finem bonitatem, sed in comparatione unius ad alterum ostenditur summa sapientia et summa bonitas . . ."

In the opening article of the first question of his *Scriptum* on distinction 44 of Book I, Thomas Aquinas frames the question in individual rather than universal terms: "whether God was able to make *any creature* better than He made it."[25] In article 2 he proceeds to inquire, as Bonaventure does, whether God could have made the whole world better, but his initial concern is with the individual things of creation. Thomas's tack here is, like Bonaventure's, philosophical: specifically, his solution hangs on the distinction, derived from Aristotle and borrowed from his teacher Albert, between essential and accidental goodness.[26] Because being is twofold and because being and goodness are intimately linked, Thomas explains, each thing can be thought to possess an essential goodness and an accidental goodness. Rationality, for example, is constitutive of the essential goodness of the human person, whereas health and knowledge are aspects of his or her accidental goodness.[27] If we have in mind a thing's accidental goodness when we ask whether God could have made that thing better than He made it, then we must answer in the affirmative, Thomas maintains, as God was able to confer greater goodness on each particular thing. If, on the other hand, we have in mind a thing's essential goodness, determining the question requires a further distinction, namely, that between the thing in question (according to species) and another or a different thing (according to species). Aquinas explains:

> Because if something is added to [a thing's] essential goodness, it would not be the same thing but another thing: since, according to the Philosopher in *Metaphysics* VIII.10, just as with numbers adding or subtracting one changes the original figure, so too with the classification [of creatures] adding or subtracting a distinguishing characteristic changes the species. For example, if the ability to reason were added to the description of a cow, it would no longer be a cow but another species, namely, a human; if the power of perception were taken away, it would remain alive [but] in the way that trees live. Hence, just as God cannot make something that is threefold remain threefold when a fourth element is added—although He can thereby make a greater

---

25 *Scriptum in I*, d. XLIV, q. 1, a. 1 (ed. Mandonnet, 1015): "Utrum Deus potuerit facere aliquam creaturam meliorem quam fecerit." Aquinas delivered his lectures on the *Sentences* at Paris in 1252–1256. See Wawrykow, *Westminster Handbook*, 135.

26 Cf. Albert, *Comm. in I Sent.* d. XLIV a. 2 corpus (ed. Borgnet, 392), who distinguishes between "substantial goodness" and "accidental goodness."

27 *Scriptum in I*, d. XLIV, q. 1, a. 1 corpus (ed. Mandonnet, 1016).

number—He cannot make this [created] thing remain the same if it has more or less essential goodness.[28]

Thomas teaches, in short, that God can make a creature better with regard to its accidental goodness, but not with regard to its essential goodness without making it a creature of a different species.

Although Albert, Bonaventure, and Thomas approach the question of whether God can do something better than He does it in somewhat different ways and draw somewhat different conclusions, each of them accepts the basic orientation to the question established in Hugh's *Exposition* and distinction 44 of Book I of the *Sentences*. The Victorine's distinction between individual creatures and the universe or world remains central to thirteenth-century discussions. Bonaventure's distinction between the world with regard to the substance of its integral parts and the world with regard to the order of its parts represents, for example, a significant modification and development of Hugh's original distinction. So too the Franciscan's two ways of understanding an excess of substantial goodness builds on the Victorine's twofold view of the meaning of "better." Thomas's distinction between essential and accidental goodness similarly represents a further nuancing of Hugh's brief treatment of particular creatures considered per se. Finally, although our thirteenth-century theologians draw conclusions that appear to diverge from that of the *Exposition* on Luke 1:49, they do so toward an end which they share in common with Hugh, namely, that of maintaining the supreme power of God. Indeed, they undoubtedly agreed with Hugh when he affirmed: "He who can do everything that is possible is supremely powerful; and He is not less powerful because He cannot do impossible things, for to be able to do impossible things is not to be powerful, but rather to be powerless".[29]

There exist two printed editions of Hugh's *Exposition* on *the Canticle of Mary*: (1) that of J. P. Migne in the *Patrologia Latina* (PL 175.413B–432B); and (2) that of E.-M. Denner in "Serva secretum, custode com-

---

[28]   *Scriptum in I*, d. XLIV, q. 1, a. 1 corpus (ed. Mandonnet, 1016): "Quia si adderetur ad bonitatem essentialem aliquid, non esset eadem res, sed alia: quia, secundum Philosophum, in VIII *Metaph.*, text. 10, sicut in numeris unitas addita, vel subtracta semper variat speciem; ita in definitionibus differentia addita vel subtracta; verbi gratia, si definitioni bovis addatur rationale, jam non erit bos, sed alia species, scilicet homo; si subtrahatur sensibile, remanebit vivens vita arborum. Unde sicut Deus non potest facere quod ternarius manens ternarius habeat quatuor unitates, quamvis quolibet numero majorem numerum facere possit, ita non potest facere quod haec res maneat eadem, et majorem bonitatem essentialem habeat, vel minorem."

[29]   *Cant. BM.* on Luke 1:49.

missum, absconde creditum," *Sacris Erudiri* 35 (1995): 133–220, here 200–20, which edition she made according to the twelfth-century manuscript Grenoble BM 246, ff. 44vb–51va. Denner's edition is reprinted, with a facing-page French translation by Bernadette Jollès, in *Oeuvre* 2.24–99. The translation that appears below, made from Denner's edition, is, to my knowledge, the first complete translation of this work into English.

EXPOSITION ON THE CANTICLE OF MARY

PROLOGUE

The greatest difficulty that I find in Sacred Scripture is this: sometimes where the occasion compels us to search for noble and sublime words, the letter [of the text] seems to offer us nothing beyond language that is customary and undistinguished. In fact, I think it is less difficult for the mind of the reader to grasp the realities proposed in extraordinary and marvelous words (however powerful and concealed in figures of speech they may be) than it is to move the reader to a higher understanding of the words that at first sight he may have found ordinary and insignificant.

Behold, the Canticle of Mary, which the Church repeats with so renowned and regular—indeed, daily—sacred proclamation throughout the world. Who does not know that it contains the greatest mysteries of spiritual understanding? For even if we pass over what alone could suffice to commend the authority of this canticle—namely, that with very good and exceedingly reasonable cause ecclesiastical tradition has held this song, above all others found in Sacred Scripture, in such reverence—who would doubt that blessed Mary, recently filled with such fullness and grace of the Holy Spirit who came upon her, would not have been able to offer some small reply in praise of her Savior that would not exceed the capacity of earthly minds? Thus, it is quite evident that Mary, erupting with a new joy that is unusual for human minds from such fullness and with such devotion, rejoicing in her Jesus, proclaimed her extraordinary delight at the imminent advent of the eternal God with unusual praise and singular celebration.

Nevertheless, when we move sequentially through the text of her Canticle, we find certain things set forth on the surface of the narrative in such a way that it seems that nothing more should be sought in them. And yet, although these things may be holy and true, it can be doubted whether they are sufficient for such great mysteries and sacraments. Consequently, I am rather afraid to embark upon an exposition of this Canticle, lest I either introduce issues that are unrelated to the text or overlook those that properly belong to it. And so, paralyzed by the possibility of being charged with either negligence or rashness, instead of pleasing you, I run the risk of displeasing you, though you yourselves have requested this commentary from me. My exposition includes several marginal comments which, if they are interwoven with the others, could perhaps seem less suitably joined with them. But I know the real reason you have asked for this commentary, and so I comply with the desire of those asking me insofar as I am able.

On the Canticle of Mary

My soul magnifies the Lord.[1] If we are willing to pay careful attention to the circumstance of the thing done, it becomes clearer how much consideration these words deserve. For a holy interpretation moves more suitably toward lucidity when the reader comes to know by whom the sacred narrative (*relatio mistica*) has been conveyed, or for what reason the author was driven or able or willing to narrate such things. Let us see, therefore, how it happened that blessed Mary said the things that are recounted here. It is written in the Gospel of Luke that *the angel Gabriel was sent by God into the city of Nazareth in Galilee to a virgin betrothed to a man named Joseph from the house of David, and the virgin's name was Mary*,[2] to proclaim the extraordinary advent of the Son of God in the flesh. *When the angel had come to her, he venerated the virgin with unusual reverence and said: Hail Mary, full of grace, the Lord is with you; blessed are you among women. When Mary had heard this*, not without great amazement, *she was troubled by the words of the angel and pondered what sort of greeting this might be.*[3] But the angel, explaining the reason for so excellent a greeting and so much veneration, comforted the holy Virgin and soothed her with sweet words, saying: *Do not fear, Mary, for you have found grace with God. Behold, you will conceive in your womb and bear a son, and you will call him Jesus. He will be great and will be called the Son of the Most High, and the throne of David his father will be given to him. And he will reign over the house of Jacob forever, and his kingdom will have no end.*[4] But Mary said, *How will this happen since I have not known a man?*[5] Immediately the angel explained the cause and mode of such an ineffable mystery (*ineffabilis sacramenti*): *The Holy Spirit will come upon you and the power of the Most High will overshadow you. And therefore the child who will be born from you will be holy, and he will be called the Son of God.*[6] And, in order to remove any ambiguity of meaning for the believer, the angel clearly reveals the efficacy of the divine power by adding another miracle to this unparalleled wonder, saying: *And behold, your relative Elizabeth has also conceived a son in her old age, and this is the sixth month for her who was called barren; for nothing will be impossible for God.*[7] Then the Virgin, full of faith and exultation and with great rejoicing, responded: *Here I am, the servant of the Lord; let it be done to me according to your word.*[8] Immediately, the Holy Spirit came to the Virgin and filled her most holy home with the grace of every virtue through the coming of the Son of God. There is no doubt that the Virgin herself received the extraordinary and indescribable pleasure of supernatural delights and everlasting sweetness when that eternal light, with all the splendor of its majesty, descended upon her and when what the whole world cannot contain established itself in her womb. Who can say what she, being filled with such a plentiful and excellent manifestation of the divine presence, saw or what she experienced? I boldly proclaim that she herself was not able to explain fully what she experienced.

In the midst of such wonderful deeds, how could the human tongue have remained silent unless that very same Spirit, who had filled the Virgin until she burned with the vigor of abundance, had restrained her by means of the sweetest embrace? For already at that time the Wisdom of God in that blessed soul [of Jesus] proclaimed: *The Spirit blows where it wills, and you hear its voice but you do not know from where it comes or where it goes.*[9] "For you," it is as if he said, "have suddenly received the Holy Spirit within you, but your knowledge did not anticipate the Spirit's advent such that you either sought the Spirit before it came, directed it as it came, or understood it once it entered you. Suddenly the Spirit flowed into you and bestowed itself freely to you: it came without seeking you, it poured itself into you without warning. You secured the Spirit's infusion, but you did not stretch yourself out toward the depth of its immeasurable greatness. And so you do not know from where it comes because, although you can feel how much has been given to you, you cannot investigate out of how much it has been given. If, therefore, you could not anticipate the Spirit's coming into you, you should not presume to go ahead [of it] to advance it toward others by yourself, because you do not know where the Spirit goes, just as you are ignorant of from where it comes. Protect what is hidden; guard what has been entrusted to you; shelter what has been granted to you. It is not for you to know the times or the hours that the Father has ordained in His power. He alone knows when and by whom and how He will reveal the hidden mysteries of His greatness: as for you, only be prepared to obey the one commanding you, to serve the one directing you." Restraining herself with such a realization, Mary wisely chose to remain silent until the liberal giver of the gift deigned, in His wisdom, to become the author of the revelation.

But because she, having been taught by the same Holy Spirit, had learned not only to safeguard her own good gifts through humility but also to rejoice with others in their gifts through charity, she soon arose and—with an abundance of grace—hurried to feast at a banquet of lesser grace. She traveled through the mountains of Judea to see and congratulate Elizabeth, and as she journeyed she reflected on the trustworthy things that she had heard and she accepted them with appropriate exultation. But she who, so devout, ran to celebrate the good gifts proclaimed to another, rightly deserved to hear her own good gifts proclaimed by others, so that God's glory might also be visible in the one who was not envious of another's exaltation.[10] Hence Elizabeth, full of the Holy Spirit, realized how excellent and how great the one who had come to her was. And she explained the extent to which she judged herself unworthy of Mary's visit when she said: *How has this happened to me, that the mother of my Lord should come to me? For as soon as I heard the sound of your greeting, the child in my womb jumped for joy. And blessed*, she said, *are you who has believed that what the Lord has spoken to you will be accomplished.*[11]

Then Mary said: *My soul magnifies the Lord.* She was not able to contain herself any longer when the Spirit, whom she felt to be abundantly overflowing among such great secrets in her heart, became determined to burst through the gate of Mary's mouth. At that time, therefore, her mouth opened in order to reveal the Spirit and, bringing forth the good word which she had conceived, exclaimed in praise of the Savior: *My soul magnifies the Lord.* Let no one, then, think that these words should be taken lightly. For they were brought forth from such a profound conception that without a profound investigation no one can appropriately penetrate them. Oh how I hope that we, who seek the hidden truths of these words, might advance under the guidance of that Spirit by which Mary was filled to conceive the Word of the Father and deserved to magnify the Father of the Word with a word of exultation!

She said, therefore: *My soul magnifies the Lord. And my spirit exults in God my Savior.*[12] Truly beloved and unique one, having been introduced by the King to your spouse in a wine cellar—intoxicated by the abundance of His house and having drunk heavily from the fountain of life that was in His presence—you have loudly proclaimed the memory of His sweet abundance and you have exulted in His justice. You have seen and you have tasted: you have seen His majesty; you have tasted His sweetness. For that reason what you drank inwardly you have outwardly offered to others to drink. *My soul magnifies the Lord.* See what she said: *My soul magnifies. And my spirit exults.*

Two and two: soul and spirit, magnifies and exults. The soul magnifies, the spirit exults. And again two: Lord and Savior; two words, one reality—but nevertheless two: Lord and Savior. "Lord" denotes power, "Savior" denotes mercy. Let us consider, then, the distinction between these words. First the soul magnifies the Lord, then the spirit exults in the Savior. Mary did not say "my soul exults," nor "my spirit magnifies." Rather, she said "my soul magnifies" and "my spirit exults." And she did not say "magnifies the Savior" and "exults in the Lord," but rather "magnifies the Lord" and "exults in the Savior." First, let us see why she distinguishes between "magnifies" and "exults," and why she said "magnifies" first and then "exults." For nothing is without a reason, because everything that she said emanated from that most secret light of highest Truth to which the mind of the Virgin clung excellently. She was not able to say anything different [from what she said]—she who did not speak by thinking (*meditando*), but by experiencing (*gustando*); she who was taught not by discursive thought, but by a devoted mind clinging to the sole font of Wisdom through contemplation. She said: *My soul magnifies, and my spirit exults.*

There are two things, of course, that the blessed spirits of the angels and of humans drink in at the font of the Good by eternal contemplation, namely the incomprehensible majesty of God and His ineffable goodness: one of these produces pious fear, the other brings forth love. They worship the Lord on account of His majesty and they love Him on account of His goodness, lest either love without reverence be dissolute or reverence without love be damnable. For those who are in awe (*admirantes*) of Him love Him and those who love Him are in awe of Him, so that love might blaze inextinguishably through awe (*per admirationem*) and awe might burn sweetly in love. On account of this reverence it has been said that *the pillars of heaven tremble before Him,*[13] for without a doubt not even the heavenly hosts can behold such majesty without being awestruck. But the trembling of the blessed spirits does not disturb their tranquility; rather, it is the unceasing and vivifying purpose of [their] everlasting contemplation. For, because they are never capable of fully comprehending Him whom they see perfectly, they always look intently beyond themselves, watching vigilantly—as if with awe (*per admirationem*)—lest at any time they should grow bored with what they are able to comprehend. The more penetratingly they gaze upon Him, the more ardently they love Him because to see God Himself is to taste Him, and what is seen is sweetness. But the more perfectly true sweetness is experienced, the more longingly it is desired because if what is perceived is truly sweet, it will necessarily be sweeter if it is perceived to a greater degree.

The mind of Mary had been raised, therefore, to this light of contemplation, and she expressed the sweetness of the heavenly fatherland as marvelously as she comprehended it ineffably. For, when she magnified the Lord, she revealed that by an inner vision she had clearly beheld that the majesty of the eternal divinity should be venerated and revered by all. And when she stated that she exulted in her Savior, she showed that she had perceived the taste of internal sweetness. Hence she declared both, namely the Lord and Savior, so that she might show that God should be rightly feared for the power by which He rules over all of His creatures—even those who do not love Him—and so that she might demonstrate that God is worthy of love for the goodness by which He mercifully saves some. Truly, because *all your ways, Lord, are mercy and truth*,[14] perfect praise confesses the Lord and Savior since truth is designated by "the Lord" and mercy is designated by "Savior." For truth pertains to the Lord and mercy pertains to the Savior. Because He governs all of his works with such great and such perfect justice that even what is found in them to have been done contrary to justice does not remain disordered, and because what was done wrongly can neither escape His judgment nor oppose the laws of His eternal providence, in truth He preserves the course of His justice. But because He brings certain unjust things into life for no special reason and then restores them to salvation, in His judgment He moderates justice by means of the lenience of mercy. For this reason, we magnify the Lord and we exult in the Savior, because the justice of the Judge is venerable and the mercy of the Savior is sweet. Therefore, Mary said: *My soul magnifies the Lord, and my spirit exults in God my Savior.*

Why does the soul magnify and the spirit exult? It may be that the same thing was repeated with a different word, for in a human the soul is the same as the spirit, although "soul" denotes one thing and "spirit" something else: for "spirit" is said according to substance and "soul" according to vivification [i.e., that which makes alive].[15] Nevertheless, because an occasion has presented itself, I think that we should here recall the error of certain thinkers on this point. For there are those who contend that in every human there are two souls: one rational, and one sensible and without reason like the souls of brute beasts.[16] They try to prove this opinion with certain rational arguments and authorities. For they say that the rational soul (*animam*) is infused into the womb only after the body has been formed, just as we read regarding the first human that his body was formed first and then life was breathed into his nostrils. And in the Law Moses says, *If anyone strikes a pregnant woman and she miscarries: if the one aborted had been formed, the murderer should give life for life (animam pro anima); but if the one aborted had not been formed, he should be punished with a fine.*[17] Even certain holy fathers asserted this in their treatises. Therefore, since it is evident that a rational soul is infused only in a formed body, and since it is also clear that the body, before it receives the human form, is moved and grows and is led to this very form by the vital motion that is inherent in it, they think that it must be conceded without objection that before the human body receives a rational soul, it has a sensible soul by which it lives, moves, and develops, and from which it receives its form. [They hold this] to such an extent that if, in the process of conception and formation, the rational soul were not given at the same time as that soul which from its first conception is irrational, a brute beast would be born in human form from a human; and it would be no different from other irrational creatures except that it would have drawn its substance from human seed. For, since the power to vivify the creature at the very time of the seed's arrival naturally belongs to the seed of brute beasts, it seems degrading to deny this to the human seed, since it is more excellent in nature [than the seed of beasts]. After all these arguments, they add as evidence in their defense that we frequently find in the Catholic Scriptures that "soul" and "spirit" are designated with both nouns in a single person; and that in the daily prayer of the Church, when we faithfully perform the rite of burial, we entrust the "soul" and the "spirit" of the deceased to the Lord. In this way, then, they wish to prove that every human has two souls, one by which it lives, the other by which it understands; and that among the elect both will be blessed in the future—one, that is, the sensible soul, through the incorruptibility of the body; the other, the rational soul, through the vision of the Creator. Similarly, among the damned both will be tormented— one, that is, the sensible soul, by corporeal fire; the other, that is, the rational soul, by a bad conscience.

But the Catholic faith does not accept this sort of assertion. Rather, it most truthfully bears witness that there exists in the human one and the same soul that both gives life to the body and itself lives through understanding. And neither is it necessary to say that if a human body is not given a rational soul before it is formed, even if it moves and grows before it assumes a human form, this happened due to some kind of soul, since we also manifestly see that plants and herbs move and have growth without a soul (unless one should want to call that growing and natural movement a soul. But that force, although one could call it a soul in one sense, should not be called "soul" in the sense that it is sensible or makes an animal.) The idea that we should call a human body that comes into being without a rational soul a beast is absurd and totally contrary to reason. Rather, we should say that the human body would neither live nor come into being unless it had been made alive by the rational soul. For what they declare to be shameful, namely that human seed is believed to be less powerful in vivifying even according to natural conception than the seeds of all other animals and so ineffective that it is of no consequence, is in fact evident, since we see that almost all brute beasts far surpass the human in their powers of perception. Indeed, this very fact more truly demonstrates that human seed can only be given life and receives its ability for sense perception from the rational soul, because surely it was right that a greater capacity for sense perception should be given to brute beasts, to whom no capacity for understanding had been given; and, on the other hand, the more the human suffers a greater defect in his bodily senses, the more evident his necessity of exercising reason should be. We find a number of times in Sacred Scripture that the two words "spirit" and "soul" designate one and the same person, but this has been done not to signify different substances, but rather different properties of the same substance. For one and the same spirit is called "spirit" with respect to itself and "soul" with respect to the body. Hence, those spirits that were created in the beginning to stand firm in their innocence and that do not mingle with bodies [viz., angels] can be called "spirits" but not "souls" because they have a spiritual nature but not a corporeal mode of existence. On the other hand, the spirits of brute beasts, because beasts are essentially bodies and their spirits do not have being apart from corporeal vivification, are more properly called "souls" than "spirits." But the human soul, because it has being both in the body and outside the body, is properly called both "soul" and "spirit." It is called "soul" inasmuch as it is the life of the body; it is called "spirit" inasmuch as it is a spiritual substance endowed with reason.

Therefore, in this life the soul is destroyed so that the spirit might be made well (*saluus*), since this life is despised for the sake of God so that afterwards eternal life might be granted by God. But as much as we lose according to substance, we receive the very same. Therefore, in the Gospel the Lord by no means taught us to destroy the soul (*animam*) in order to receive a healthy spirit (*spiritum saluum*); rather, He said that the very same soul should be lost in the present life so that it might be restored to health in the life to come.[18] By this He certainly signified that whoever for the sake of God voluntarily despises this life, which is now constituted by the vivification of the body by the soul and is temporally mortal, will in the future receive not only the eternal life and immortality of the soul but also of the body. Hence, holy Church, which believes most faithfully in the resurrection of the flesh, prays not only for the spirits but also for the souls of its faithful. The Church asks especially that, at the appearance of the just when there will be that beatitude resulting from the vision of God by those who are pure in heart, its faithful might take up as immortal and incorruptible for the glory of eternal life through the resurrection of the flesh what they now lay down as corruptible through the death of the flesh. We have certainly digressed in discussing the distinction between "soul" and "spirit," but perhaps it is still useful. Now let us return to the order of our narrative as we have received it.

We ask, then, what such a distinction of words signifies in itself: whether it suggests something to us that Mary says that her soul, not her spirit, magnifies the Lord; and that she reveals that her spirit, not her soul, exults in its Savior. And perhaps someone might think that to thoroughly examine each word in this way and to refuse to pass by the least important things without proper consideration should be attributed to curiosity more than diligence. I know that in Scripture there are many things said in this way in order to arouse the emotions, things either expressed in vivid language or repeated forcefully. This is the case in this text also, in the hope that whoever [might read it] would say that there is nothing unfitting here. And so it says, "My soul magnifies and my spirit exults" as if to say: "From my soul and my spirit, that is, from my whole heart and from my whole will, I praise God, and with my entire being I exult in His salvation, which I now see has been prepared for the human race. For now I see that on my behalf He assumed what I believe should be offered for me; and so let me now confess my Savior who, since He had not previously offered the sacrifice of his own flesh, now coming in time assumed flesh and offered it as a sacrifice. Therefore, the Savior, who is the Savior not only now but from eternity, has now come through the assumption of flesh in order to save. But from eternity He ordained to bestow the salvation that He would make known at the appropriate time."

Without a doubt it is fittingly said according to the distinction of words that the soul magnifies God and the spirit exults in its Savior. For often in Scripture it is customary to designate certain emotions and the tenderness of mind by the soul. Therefore, when Mary asserts that she magnifies God from her soul, she shows that she worships God not with any hint of servile fear, but rather with the feeling of love. And again, when she affirms that her spirit exults in her Savior, she clearly indicates that she is referring not to a this-worldly salvation in which the flesh rejoices, but rather to the eternal salvation having been prepared beforehand among spiritual goods in which the spirit exults. Because that blessed soul had conceived the sweetness of pious fear, she declared that she magnified the Lord not with the terror of a slave but with the love of a daughter. To be sure, the feeling and devotion of one who loves are expressed, as we have said, in the soul, because to praise from the soul is nothing other than to adore with feeling and to honor with love. And because Mary had drunk in the assurance of eternal salvation from that font of fatherly kindness, she exulted in her Savior with her spirit.

And we should not silently pass over the fact that when Mary mentioned the name "Lord," she added nothing to it; but when she uttered "Savior" she did not simply say "Savior" but rather "my Savior." For Almighty God, by the power with which He governs His entire creation, is the Lord of all; but by the fatherly kindness with which He restores only some but not all to life, He is not the Savior of all. For His lordship provides equally for all, but His goodness sets only some apart for salvation. Therefore, His dominion is spoken of as applying to no one in particular; but individually the elect alone glory in the salvation that God gives them as their very own merited gift. This is why in Sacred Scripture God wished to be called the God of some in particular, because He who bestowed existence on all gave His very self as a reward only to the good so that they might have a blessed existence. He said, *I am the God of Abraham, the God of Isaac, and the God of Jacob,*[19] as if to say: "Whereas others have only being from me, these were chosen through grace by me, from whom they have being, so that they might be blessed. I have given my very self to them and I wish to be called their God because I am theirs, whom they have received through grace, whom they neither could receive through nature nor merit [to receive] on account of their fault. But now they have taken possession of me and, behold, I am their inheritance, their God and Savior, *the God of Abraham, the God of Isaac, and the God of Jacob!*" Rightly, therefore, the blessed Virgin, who understood that she had been elected in a unique way since she had received grace in a unique way, as if reassured by a certain privilege of divine election, confidently with joy and exultation called upon Him as Savior whom she had conceived as son for the salvation of the world.

Because He has considered the humility of His handmaid.[20] This is the reason for her exultation, because He has considered the humility of His handmaid, as if to say: "Rightly I rejoice in Him because it is He from whom my rejoicing comes. Because I rejoice in His grace, that in which I rejoice is from Him; and because I love His gifts on account of Him, I rejoice in Him." We should distinguish between two things: certain people rejoice neither from God nor in God, for those who rejoice in bodily pleasure or who, according to Solomon, *delight in doing evil and rejoice in the most wicked acts*[21] rejoice neither from God nor in God. Because they rejoice in an evil act, it is certainly clear that their rejoicing does not come from God. On the contrary, because they rejoice from evil with a view toward evil and establish their delight in malice, they do not rejoice in God at all. There are others who squander the gifts of grace they have received and convert things given to them for the salvation of their souls to carnal use and worldly glory. Receiving the gifts of God, they delight and rejoice that they have what God has given, not so that they might be aided by these gifts to attain to God, but so that they might be shown to surpass others in the acquisition of grace. These people, although they seem to have that in which they rejoice from God, by no means rejoice in God because they love what they have received from God neither in God nor on account of God. On the other hand, those who, having received grace itself, completely convert what they receive from Him to the love of God, certainly are proven to rejoice from God and in God. And so, whenever we feel some joy in our mind, we must carefully examine it to ensure that what lifts up the mind with delight has neither arisen from evil, nor, having arisen from the good, purposefully driven the mind toward evil. Therefore, Mary, in order to show that her joy was perfect, made clear that it had neither arisen from nor turned toward vanity; rather, she revealed that she loved in God the gifts of God and rejoiced in her Savior on account of the grace that she had received beforehand, saying: *My spirit exults in God my Savior, because He has considered (respexit) the humility of His handmaid.*

In Sacred Scripture the consideration of God (*respectus Dei*) is understood in three ways, namely, according to knowledge, according to grace, and according to judgment. Concerning the consideration by divine knowledge the Apostle says: *All things are bare and open to His eyes.*[22] Therefore, by means of knowledge God considers all things. But by means of grace He does not consider all, for concerning the consideration by grace it is written: *The eyes of the Lord are upon the just and His ears are open to their prayers.*[23] Those do not deserve this consideration [by grace] to whom in the end He says: *I do not know you.*[24] Concerning the consideration by judgment it is written: *The eyes of the Lord gaze upon the good and the evil.*[25] And again: *His eyes are upon the ways of humans and He considers all their steps. There is no dark corner and no shadow of death where those who work iniquity might hide.*[26] Therefore, for God to consider by means of knowledge is for Him to be ignorant of nothing that exists; for Him to consider by means of grace is to weigh out the gifts of mercy; and for Him to consider by means of judgment is to determine each person for punishment or for glory according to his works. But because this passage concerns the consideration by grace, let us look more carefully at how God considers the human person by means of grace. The very word "consideration" indicates a certain expression such that "to consider" seems to denote something more than "to see." For "to consider" is to visit the lowly and forsaken first. For instance, God is said to withdraw from a person when through the severity of His judgment He takes away the gifts of His grace; but when, being kindly disposed, He restores through His mercy what was taken away, He again turns Himself back to him by means of the consideration of grace. Rightly, then, Mary bears witness that the Lord considered the humility alone in her, because He restored in her through humility the favor of God that human nature in its first parents lost through pride. For since in her the Word of the Father assumed the substance of flesh which He united to Himself, in mercy He considered the very nature that He had earlier abandoned as something to be elevated.

Therefore, God considered the humility of Mary, to whom on account of the merit of humility He gave the ability to conceive His own Son in her flesh and from her flesh to give birth to true God and true man, the Savior of all humans whom Christ Himself determines. Next, noting the degree of her humility, Mary adds "of His handmaid." Because she humbly recognized herself as the handmaid that she was, she sublimely merited to be the mother that she was not. But because we said that Mary calling herself "handmaid" expressed the degree of her humility, we must distinguish among the kinds of servitude so that it might be clear how this word "humility" commends [a person]. There are four different modes of servitude: according to creation, according to necessity, according to fear, and according to love. According to creation all things ought to be obliged to divine servitude. A work is indebted to its maker on account of its creation so that it might obey His arrangements and follow His decrees in order that, just as it was created by Him, it might also make progress only under Him and according to Him. According to necessity perverse wills are said to serve God when they strive to oppose His commands. But they are forced into His ineffable arrangement of things such that they are able to bring nothing to fruition without His permission. So those who wish not to be subject to God's precepts unwillingly serve His arrangement [of all things]. The third servitude is that of fear, which occurs when we fulfill the divine commands not out of love but rather out of fear. The fourth servitude is when we voluntarily obey God's commands because we love Him who commands [them]; and in our service we do not seek another reward apart from this very one: that, walking according to His ways, we might be strong enough to finally arrive at Him. For this is to do on account of God what He commands: to do what He commands in order to arrive at Him.

Of the four kinds of servitude, it seems to me that the one especially commended in this passage is servitude according to creation. Indeed, our parents in paradise were unwilling to offer their Creator this servitude when, puffed up with pride, they disdained to live under Him by whom they had been created, and in a perverse way they wished to be equal to Him in majesty who were not His equals according to nature. Fittingly, then, grace answered this offense. In her pride, Eve, not considering herself a creature of God and a work of God, wished to be equal to God. But Mary, humbly placing herself under her Creator, called herself a "handmaid." Therefore, Eve was abandoned and Mary was chosen: God despised proud Eve, but considered humble Mary; and what the proud woman lost the humble one recovered.

Therefore, she says: *He considered the humility of His handmaid*. He considered the humility; He considered the humiliation. He considered the humility by rewarding the humble one. He considered the humiliation by exalting the humiliated one. Humility and humiliation are two different things: humility is inward in the power of the mind, whereas humiliation is outward in rejection by human opinion. The servants of God sometimes have humiliation along with humility; sometimes they have humility but not humiliation; but they never have humiliation without humility. Those who are humble in God's eyes and despicable in the eyes of humans have humility with humiliation. Those who do not appear despicable outwardly to humans but nevertheless inwardly maintain the inviolable merit of humility before God have humility without humiliation. The world has been crucified to the former and they have been crucified to the world, because through humility they hate the world and through humiliation the world hates them. But the world has not been crucified to the latter, although they have been crucified to the world, because inwardly by virtue of their humility they despised the human glory that they had received, though had not sought, outwardly. Therefore, Mary, who was humble in the eyes of God and abject in the eyes of humans on account of God, bears witness in both of these ways that she was considered by God, because her humility was made acceptable in the eyes of God and her humiliation was transformed into glory in the eyes of humans. Hence, it follows:

Behold, from this day all generations will call me blessed.[27] Until that day she had carried the shame of barrenness in the eyes of humans because she preferred the integrity of virginity to the marriage bed. Whereas in an earlier carnal generation she had put up with a kind of condemnatory judgment, from that time forward every generation has praised her greatly with a well-deserved blessing because of all women she alone was granted both to bear the fruit of fertility and to retain the integrity of virginity. For God considered her humility and took away her humiliation, and for that reason she says: "*From this day all generations will call me blessed.* All generations that have lost beatitude—of which they have been robbed by the fruit of the forbidden tree—will be restored to health by the fruit of my womb. And all will call me blessed, so that having put up with the shame of barrenness in a past generation is already an insignificant thing because I will be called blessed by every future generation on account of the fruit of my fertility." She said "from this day" as if to say to Elizabeth: "Because by your mouth God has revealed the mighty deeds that He has worked in me, from this day forward He will greatly exalt these same deeds by disclosing them to all generations."

Because the Mighty One has done great things for me, and holy is His name.[28] It was a great thing that a virgin conceived a son without the seed of a man. It was a great thing that she carried in her womb the Word of God the Father clothed in His own flesh. It was a great thing that, while she confessed that she was a handmaid, she became the mother of her own Creator. But all these things, however great they are, are nevertheless not impossible for Him by whom they were done, because He is the Mighty One. Therefore He did great things because He is mighty, and uniquely great things because He is uniquely mighty. For this reason she did not say, "He is able to do this or that," but rather "the Mighty One" so that you might understand as omnipotent the one who is called mighty absolutely because He is able to do all things. She confessed Him to be mighty but said nothing more because, although it can be believed that His power exists, its nature and degree cannot be comprehended. Therefore, she merely confessed His power but did not presume to inquire into it, since no one can know the degree of this power, which is most truly known to be immeasurable.

So let those who think that they can rationally examine the divine works and bring His power within measurable limits glory in their own understanding. For when they say, "He is powerful to this point but no further," what is this other than to confine His power, which is infinite, and to restrict it? Indeed, they say: "God cannot do anything other than what He does, nor better than what He does. For if He can do something other than what He does, He can do what He did not foresee; and if He can do what He did not foresee, God can work without foresight (*preuidentia*). Because God does everything that He foresaw that He was going to do, He does not do anything that He did not foresee. If, therefore, His providence (*prouidentia*) can neither be changed so that something other than what He foresaw happens nor be nullified so that what He foresaw does not happen at all, it is necessary that everything that He foresaw happens and that nothing happens that He did not foresee. It is certain, moreover, that whatever happens was foreseen, and there is no doubt that whatever was foreseen happens. If it is impossible for anything outside of providence to happen, it is necessary that everything that was foreseen happens and it is in no way possible for something other than what happens to happen. Furthermore, if God can do whatever He does better than He does it, He does not act well in that He does not do what He does in the best way. For He would do better if He were to do what He does in a better way. Indeed, to do something and not want to do it better is to act badly, even for someone who is doing a good thing. But a holy mind cannot allow this to be said of God. So from this line of reasoning it seems to follow that God, who acts in such a way that He does not do badly whatever He does, cannot do better than He does."[29]

Some people are led by positions and arguments of this sort to say that God is so restricted and bound by the limit and law of His own works that He can neither do anything other than what He does nor do it better than He does. In doing so, they who extend this power to some particular thing that truly has an actual limit and deny that it goes any further are clearly found guilty of restricting that infinite and im-measurable power of the divinity within a boundary and limit. For it is certain that everything that has been made possesses its own fixed boundary and proper limit according to number, weight, and measure. If the power of the Creator is understood, then, according to the mea-sure and mode of His works, this power is undoubtedly shown to be restricted by a boundary and limit. Therefore, lest we appear either to deny without reason a commonly held view that arguments seem to support, or, being completely gullible, to accept as true something that is false without examining it, we must respond briefly—in proportion to our short treatment here—to the things that have been said.

First we must consider whether God can in any way do something other than what He does without His providence being either changed or nullified. It is apparent that everything that happens was foreseen from eternity as going to be, since from eternity the thing itself was going to be, even though it does not exist from eternity. And we say that it is possible for what was going to be not to happen; but if what was going to happen should not happen, and if it is possible for it not to happen, it would have never been going to be nor would it have been foreseen. This is so because what will happen is always going to be and was always foreseen. Therefore, no change in or nullification of provi-dence is found here because, just as it was foreseen and will happen, so too if it had not been foreseen it would not have happened. "But it was already foreseen," they say. "It was foreseen correctly because it is going to be." They continue: "Although providence can be neither changed nor nullified, an outcome can be hindered so that what was going to be might not happen. But if the outcome of an event, which is able to happen, were hindered, providence would be either changed or nulli-fied, which is not at all possible." But we respond to this by saying that if an outcome, which is able to happen, were changed, providence would be neither changed nor nullified because that is not at all possible. Rather, [we maintain that] what never was going to be had never been foreseen; and providence would have consisted in the fact that it would not happen, just as now it actually consists in the fact that it would happen. So providence is not changed in such a way that one thing existed after another, but rather in such a way that the other thing never existed at all. Therefore, God can do something other than what He does. But He Himself would not be different by doing it. Rather, whether He does the same or something else, He Himself is always the same.

Now it remains for us to discuss whether God can do something better than He does it. Here our famous scrutinizers—who, by careful examination, failed in their investigation—assert that they offer something new; and indeed it is something new, but not as true as new! They say that particular creatures, considered in themselves, lack perfection, but that the universe of all things has been formed according to such perfection of goodness that it cannot be better than it is. So I demand first an answer to this question: when they say that the universe of all things cannot be made better than it is, how should we understand what they say, namely, that it cannot be better? Is it that it cannot be better because it is supremely good, such that it lacks no perfection of goodness? Or is it that it cannot be better because it cannot receive the greater goodness that it lacks? But if it is said to be supremely good such that it lacks no perfection of goodness, the work of the Creator is already made entirely equal to the Creator Himself; and either what is below is extended beyond its boundary, or what is highest is restricted within an immense area. Each of these is impossible and equally unfitting. If, however, the universe cannot be better because it cannot receive the greater goodness that it lacks, this inability pertains to present deficiency, not to final consummation. And it can be better if it becomes capable of greater goodness, because He who made it can give it this capacity. Therefore, it cannot be better in itself but it can be better in God, because the universe itself is not powerful, but God is powerful; yet the degree to which He is powerful cannot be specified. Consequently, God Himself cannot be better, but everything that He made can be better if He who is powerful wills it. He Himself could have made what He made better, not by correcting things made badly, but by making things made well even better. He would not do this in order to make Himself better, but in order that—by working continually and remaining steadfast in the same work—what He made might become better. Therefore, He who can do everything that is possible is supremely powerful; and He is not less powerful because He cannot do impossible things, for to be able to do impossible things is not to be powerful, but rather to be powerless.

For that reason Mary says: *Because the Mighty One has done great things for me, and holy is His name.* She does not say He has done great things "through me" or "in me," but she says He has done great things "for me." For God worked in her for the salvation of all, and by this privilege of election God uniquely ordained her to His glory. She said "great things" but did not add what kind they were because, although all the works of God surpass the capacity of human sense perception, it is clear that the sacrament of redemption and the mystery of the Incarnation of the Word are ineffable beyond them all. For nothing more wonderful has ever happened than that God became human, and incomprehensible nature united corporeal substance to itself in such a way that it was neither smaller in this substance since it was infinitely immense in itself, nor smaller in itself since it was whole and entire in that substance. Therefore, these things that were done in Mary for the salvation of all and for Mary for her unique glory are great and ineffably great. For this reason she says: *Because the Mighty One has done great things for me, and holy is His name.*

Holy is His name in itself, and it is made holy in us as we are made holy in His name. What is His name? His fame is His name; knowledge of Him and faith in Him constitute His name. His name is holy among the saints because the saints glorify and praise His name. But evil-doers blaspheme His name: *And my name is blasphemed among the nations because of you.*[30] Therefore, because He has done great things His name has been made holy. While the Word is miraculously born in flesh, the glory of God is revealed among humans through the Word. He says: *Father, I made your name known to humans and I glorified you on earth.*[31] And therefore: *the Mighty One has done great things, and holy is His name.*

And His mercy is from generation to generation for those who fear Him.[32] Mary says, "He has done [great things] for me." But He has not done [great things] for her alone apart from others; rather, He has done them for her alone in a particularly excellent way. Nevertheless, His mercy is from generation to generation for those who fear Him. No one is excluded from grace, but in every nation he who fears God and acts justly is accepted by Him. "From generation to generation," that is, in every generation. Regarding this grace, nothing distinguishes one person from another except the fear of God. Whether one is Greek, barbarian, or Scythian, male or female, slave or free: if one fears God, one will be saved. *His mercy is from generation to generation for those who fear Him.*

And here we should not neglect the things that must be said concerning fear. Sacred Scripture distinguishes among four kinds of fear: servile, worldly, initial, and filial. Servile fear is when someone who retains an evil will refrains from evil in order to avoid punishment (*pena*). Worldly fear is when someone who retains a good will refrains from good in order to avoid punishment. Initial fear is when someone, in order to avoid punishment, eliminates perverse thoughts in addition to evil deeds. Filial fear is to cling steadfastly to the good because you do not want to lose it. Of these four kinds of fear, two are evil—namely, servile and worldly—and two are good—namely, initial and filial. Servile fear dreads the punishment imposed by humans, and it is sufficient to cause someone to cease from evil deeds because, wishing to please humans, it serves outward appearances but does not fear the guilt of conscience. Worldly fear, however, does not seek to please humans; rather, fearing to displease them, it pretends to be what it is not: it is so false in denying the truth that another deception arises in hiding the falsehood. And both of these kinds of fear offend against the truth: the one because it fearfully denies what it is; the other because it perversely pretends to be what it is not. But initial fear, because it works hard to avoid the punishment that God threatens, sees that it is not at all sufficient to refrain from forbidden deeds themselves; for it is not enough for the approval of Him who looks on the heart that actions are virtuous unless the very meditation of the heart also appears pure and undefiled before His eyes. Because it fears displeasing Him who sees everything, it recognizes that it is necessary for perfect innocence in His presence to clean everything; and this fear is called initial because, through a good will, it is both the beginning of virtue and the end of vice. But it is not yet perfect because, while one thing is done and another is aimed at, the good is still not loved for its own sake. Then charity approaches and enters through that fear which, while it reveals that we ought to flee danger, makes us in a certain way reach for and long for help. The heart, therefore, turns toward God so as to flee in a certain way from Him to Him, that is, while it avoids Him as angry, it is eager to have Him favorable. Then follows filial fear, which is born from charity and succeeds it, so that to fear Him is now nothing other than to refuse to abandon the good having been tasted in charity. Some degree of hardship (*aliquid pene*) accompanies this fear as long as we walk in inconstancy, and the mutable state of our present life can move in either direction. But when there will be no mutability, then there will be no pain (*nulla pena*) from the uncertainty of imperfection; and then there will be fear in a certain sense without fear because we will be fixed in stability and we will not cease to show reverence to the Creator. Therefore, *His mercy is from generation to generation for those who fear Him.* And not only for those who fear Him with perfect charity, but even for those beginning to fear Him and converting to Him through imperfect understanding, *His mercy is from generation to generation for those who fear Him.* And then Mary begins to explain more fully the mercy that is offered to those who fear Him and to reveal, by means of a clear narrative, the very order and mode of human redemption, saying:

He has shown power in His arm; He has scattered the proud with the intention of His heart.[33] This is the mercy that God offers to those who fear Him, that He sent His Word into this world through assumed flesh so that through Him with mighty power He might vanquish the powers of the air and redeem the human race from their rule.[34] For these are the proud whom He has scattered, driving them out of human hearts and plundering their spoils; He has dispersed that power by which they previously ruled over humans. Mary says, *He has shown power in His arm* because by the humanity of His Son He defeated the devil. Thus, *He has shown power in His arm*: His arm is His Son. *Power in His arm* because, through what was made, what was made by Him was redeemed in Him.[35] He has shown power, He has shown weakness; and weakness itself was power because by it the devil was defeated and humans broke free from his power.

He has shown power in His arm; He has scattered the proud with the intention of His heart. What does "with the intention of His heart" mean? With the intention of His heart He has scattered them; with His profound purpose He has scattered them. Profound was the purpose according to which God became human for the sake of humanity and He, being innocent, suffered in order to redeem the guilty. In all these actions His intention was profound, and the devil was not able to foresee it. But a hook captured Leviathan[36] and the wisdom of God struck down the proud. [This is] *the mystery*, the Apostle says, *kept secret from eternity*,[37] known only to God, *which none of the rulers of this world knew; because if they had known it, they never would have crucified the Lord of glory.*[38] This is the meaning of "with the intention of His heart": He was turning this [mystery] over in His mind (*in corde suo*); indeed,

He was not only turning it over in His mind, but also keeping it there, and the devil did not know about it. *The princes of Tanis are fools, the wise counselors of Pharaoh have given foolish advice. Where are your wise men now? Let them announce to you and reveal what the Lord of hosts has planned against Egypt. The princes of Tanis have become fools, the princes of Memphis have gone astray: they have deceived Egypt, the cornerstone of the nations. The Lord has stirred up a spirit of confusion among them.*[39] And with this *He has scattered the proud with the intention of His heart* and *He has shown power in His arm*, because through the Incarnation of His Son He powerfully defeated the demons and wisely tripped them up.

He has shown power in His arm; He has scattered the proud with the intention of His heart. We are also able, not inappropriately, to understand the proud as the Jews, who were boasting that they are from the stock of Abraham and were presuming on his righteousness and therefore had not submitted to the righteousness of God. By the power shown in His arm God has scattered these proud [Jews] because, through the advent of His Son in flesh, He taught that no one can be justified by the works of the Law, but only by faith which is from God. He has scattered the Jews—who tried to defend the works of the Law against the righteousness of God and proudly disparaged the humble advent of Christ—from His grace in which they seemed to stand. But God has taken to Himself the Gentiles, who were confessing their sins and preferring the righteousness of God.

Hence, it is fittingly added: *He has cast down the powerful from their throne and has exalted the humble.*[40] He has cast down the powerful from their throne because He has abandoned the Jews, who seemed to be sons of the kingdom. And He has exalted the humble, namely, the Gentiles, because He has brought the nations, who had been abandoned, through humble confession into the inheritance of His kingdom and into a relationship as adopted sons. Or, according to a better interpretation, He has cast down the powerful because He has driven a selfish spirit from human hearts; and He has exalted the humble because He has restored those humiliated people whom He had earlier abandoned on account of their pride. Therefore, *He has shown the power in His arm; He has scattered the proud with the intention of His heart. He has cast down the powerful from their throne and has exalted the humble.* But I see that there is still another point that we can add to what has been said concerning the scattering of the proud. For if we understand the phrase "with the intention of His heart" according to the meaning established earlier, it is clear that it happened according to the deep and unsearchable purpose of God that the Jews, who had been chosen first, were subsequently rejected, and the Gentiles, who previously had been rejected, were afterwards chosen. Therefore, it happened according to His profound and inscrutable purpose that God subjected all things to sin in order that He might show mercy to all. And for this reason the Apostle, astonished by this profound reality, exclaimed: *O the depth of the riches of the wisdom and knowledge of God, whose judgments are incomprehensible and whose ways are unsearchable.*[41] We, therefore, can contemplate this reality in the phrase "with the intention of His heart."

Even if we wish to interpret this phrase in a different way, we should not look down upon this interpretation. For the intention of the heart of God is that long-lived and everlasting arrangement of His inner and hidden plan of predestination. It is the Book of Life, in which have been written the names of those who are saved and who are inscribed for life in Jerusalem.[42] This intention, therefore, is that Book. And what is written there will endure, as if it were preserved in the mind through memory, and it will not be blotted out. And so it is said here: *He has scattered the proud with the intention of His heart.* The psalmist expressed the same reality with different words when he said: *May they be blotted out of the Book of the living.*[43] But the foreknowledge of divine predestination does not change; so in these scriptural passages to be blotted out or to be scattered does not mean to cease to be where one once was, but rather never to have been there. Thus, the psalmist rightly added: *but let them not be written with the just.*[44]

We must understand, however, that someone is said to be written in the Book of Life in three ways: according to foreknowledge, according to origin, and according to action. According to foreknowledge, they have been written into the Book of Life who have been predestined to life and who are never blotted out, because no one from among those who have been predestined for salvation is permitted to perish, though for a time he may be allowed to stray from the way of truth like one who is going to perish. According to origin, they have been written into the Book of Life who walk in righteousness for a time; and sometimes these people become worthy of salvation if they remain righteous all the way to the end. But they are blotted out when they forsake the righteousness in which they began and when, by straying, they turn back to errors from the way of truth along which they had begun to advance. Finally, according to action, or rather according to human opinion, they are said to have been written in the Book of Life whose works appear so excellent according to human judgment that they seem worthy to be written in the Book of Life. On the other hand, when they forsake the good works that they were appearing to perform, they are judged to be blotted out of the Book of Life. The people who are blotted out of the Book of Life, to the extent that they do not merit to be written in it, are the ones who were never written there according to foreknowledge, although they seem to be written there for a time either according to the origin of righteousness or according to the judgment of human opinion. The rational creature, in its angelic and human manifestations, had been written in the Book of Life at creation in order to receive the honor of the celestial homeland and the supernal inheritance. But through the pride by which he wished to equate himself perversely with his Creator, the rational creature has been thrown down and deprived of his honor. This is why now, indeed, *He has scattered the proud with the intention of His heart*, when He permitted those who were puffed up with pride against Him to fall away from internal stability, casting them out by their own earthly desires. *He has scattered the proud with the intention of His heart. He has cast down the powerful from their throne and has exalted the humble.* First He cast the proud angel out of heaven and the proud human out of paradise, and afterwards He restored the human, through humble repentance, to his former glory. But He also daily casts down and humbles the proud by withdrawing His grace from them; and subsequently, by restoring this previous grace, He exalts these same people who were humbled. The following words pertain to this reality:

He has filled the hungry with good things and has sent the rich away empty.[45] Mary calls those "hungry" who recognize that they are in need of true goodness. By "rich" she wishes to signify those who are proud and puffed up and imagine that they surpass others in the gifts of grace. Therefore, just as the humble merit the reception of a greater grace by thinking of themselves humbly, so too the proud and puffed up deserve to lose the things they have received.

He has lifted up Israel, His servant.[46] As a physician lifts up a patient, He has lifted up His servant Israel, that is, His people. He has lifted up His servant Israel, that is, the humble and innocent, so that He might heal the sick, ransom the captive, justify the wicked, and save the just. He has lifted up Israel, but not the Israel that He found; rather, in order that He might constitute Israel. *He has lifted up Israel, His servant.*

Being mindful of His mercy:[47] which formerly He had promised, but had delayed for a long time. Now at last, however, He offered it.

Just as He spoke to our fathers, to Abraham, and to his descendants forever.[48] He is compassionate in promising it and truthful in offering it, because He promised it without obligation and He offered it without deceit. *Just as He spoke to our fathers, to Abraham, and to His descendants forever.*

NOTES

1 Luke 1:46.
2 Luke 1:26–27.
3 Luke 1:28–29.
4 Luke 1:30–33.
5 Luke 1:34.
6 Luke 1:35.
7 Luke 1:36–37.
8 Luke 1:38.
9 John 3:8.
10 Hugh's point here concerns the "fittingness" of God having done things the way He did them. It was altogether appropriate that Elizabeth proclaimed the divine gifts given to Mary precisely because Mary willingly ran to celebrate the lesser gifts given to Elizabeth. And the divine glory was revealed to an even greater extent by the fact that Elizabeth was not envious of the greater grace given to Mary.
11 Cf. Luke 1:43–45.
12 Luke 1:46–47.
13 Job 26:11.
14 Ps. 24:10.
15 This distinction predates Hugh and can be found, e.g., in Gennadius of Marseilles, *De ecclesiasticis dogmatibus*, written *ca.* 600 (ch. 20; PL 58.985B).
16 Although we cannot be altogether certain whom Hugh has in mind here, the tradition of postulating either two (or three) souls or two (or three) powers of a single soul in the human is witnessed in such twelfth-century thinkers as Gerhoch of Reichersberg, *Exposition on Ps. 102:2* (PL 194.609C–D), and Peter of Poitiers, *Sentences* II.20 (PL 211.1026A). This tradition resulted from medieval western thinkers working to reconcile the Augustinian and pseudo-Augustinian view that God created and infused a single rational soul into each human body, on the one hand, with the Aristotelian view that three souls (namely, vegetative, sensitive or sensible, and rational) are constitutive of the human person, on the other. On the ancient background to this tradition and its thirteenth-century manifestations, see Dales, *The Problem of the Rational Soul*, 4–12. For the influence of Hugh on the subsequent scholastic tradition, see our discussion in the introduction to the present translation above.
17 Exod. 21:22–23 (Vulg.).
18 Cf., e.g., Matt. 10:39 and 16:25; Mark 8:35; Luke 9:24 and 17:33; and John 12:25.
19 Matt. 22:32; cf. Exod. 3:6.
20 Luke 1:48a.
21 Prov. 2:14.
22 Heb. 4:13.
23 1 Pet. 3:12.
24 Matt. 25:12.
25 Prov. 15:3.
26 Job 34:21–22.
27 Luke 1:48b.
28 Luke 1:49.
29 Those whom Hugh has in view here, who glory in their own understanding of the divine works, appear to be Peter Abelard and his students. See, e.g., Peter Abelard, *Theologia Scholarium* III (Buytaert and Mews, 499–549), as well as A. Mignon, *Les origines de la scolastique et Hugues de Saint-Victor* (Paris: Lethielleux, 1895), 1.139–42, and J. Jolivet, *Abélard ou la philosophie dans le langage*, Vestigia 14 (Fribourg, Suisse: Éditions universitaires; Paris: Éditions du Cerf, 1994), 175–78.
30 Rom. 2:24; cf. Isa. 52:5 and Ezek. 36:20–22.

31   Undoubtedly quoting from memory, Hugh here fuses John 17:6 and 17:4.

32   Luke 1:50.

33   Luke 1:51.

34   The "powers of the air" (*aerias potestates*) to whom Hugh here refers are demons. Cf. Eph. 2:2.

35   With echoes of the prologue of John's Gospel, Hugh's meaning here is that through the assumed humanity of the Son humankind, which was made by Him, was restored or redeemed.

36   Cf. Job 40:20.

37   Rom. 16:25; cf. Eph. 3:9 and Col. 1:26.

38   1 Cor. 2:8.

39   Isa. 19:11–14. Cf. Eph. 3:8–10.

40   Luke 1:52.

41   Rom. 11:33.

42   That is, the New Jerusalem or the heavenly city. See, e.g., Apoc. 21–22 and Heb. 12:22.

43   Ps. 68:29a.

44   Ps. 68:29b.

45   Luke 1:53.

46   Luke 1:54.

47   Luke 1:54.

48   Luke 1:55.

ADAM OF ST VICTOR

SEQUENCES ON THE VIRGIN MARY

INTRODUCTION AND TRANSLATION
BY HUGH FEISS OSB

INTRODUCTION

Adam of St Victor (active in Paris from early in the twelfth century until his death at St Victor about 1146) celebrated Mary in a number of his sequences.[1] In the two sequences translated here, *Salve Mater Salvatoris/vas* (= S), for the Nativity of Mary, and *Ave, Virgo Singularis/Mater* (= A), for the Assumption or its octave, Adam is writing for feasts for which there is no explicit information in the Bible. To praise and honor Mary on these feasts he does not refer to extra-canonical descriptions of Mary's birth or assumption into heaven, but instead he salutes Mary (Salve, Ave) using a rich tradition of imagery, derived

---

[1] In her edition and translation (Adam de Saint-Victor, *Quatorze proses du XII⁴ siècle à louange de Marie*, Sous la Règle de saint Augustin 1 [Turnhout: Brepols, 1994]), B. Jollès presents fourteen sequences that she judges to be authentic compositions of Adam devoted to the Blessed Virgin. In the *Les séquences d'Adam de Saint-Victor, Étude littéraire (poétique et rhétorique): Textes et traductions, commentaries*, BV 20 (Turnhout: Brepols, 2008), 866–67, J. Grosfillier avows that all fourteen of these are likely authentic works of Adam. He comments on eleven of them, including five he places in a category he calls "Marian Sequences." He assigns five others to Christmastime and categorizes the eleventh, which is for the Feast of the Purification or Presentation, as transitional. The two sequences presented here are edited and translated by both authors, and both sequences are included in Grosfillier's "Marian Sequences." In the text, references will be given to them as A and S, and to the line numbers that are assigned to them by both Jollès and Grosfillier. In her *Gothic Song: Victorine Sequences and Augustinian Reform in Twelfth-Century Paris* (New York: Cambridge University Press, 1993), M. Fassler approaches the sequences associated with St Victor from a musicological perspective. She finds that the Victorines used the same melody for different sequences, a practice that created links of resonance between different texts, in the cause of the church reform that the Victorines espoused. She does not treat either S or A at length. She notes that the melody of S was used more often at Notre Dame than at St Victor and that the uniquely Victorine melody for A was used at St Victor for only one other sequence (181–82, 314–15). In chapter 14, devoted to Marian sequences at St Victor ("Mary and the microcosm," 321–40), Fassler argues that the Marian sequences with music by the Victorines are later compositions. The first aim of the Victorine repertory was to celebrate Christ, the apostles, the early church, and the *vita apostolica* as a model for the twelfth-century Church. She concludes from the musical evidence that "the veneration of Mary was not of major importance during the first half of the twelfth century" (321). "Hugh of St Victor did not write extensively about Mary, but what he did have to say served as a springboard for later ideas found in Victorine sermons and sequences" (328–29). She suggests that Godfrey or Richard may have been responsible for the increased emphasis on Mary at St Victor after the mid-twelfth century. Grosfillier (698 n. 9) is not convinced by Fassler's arguments. One might note that in *Oeuvre* 2 Jollès compiled a 300-page bilingual collection of Marian works by Hugh of St Victor.

from the Bible and applied to Mary by his predecessors and contemporaries.[2] The two sequences he presents are interesting for both their theological contents and their poetics.

THEOLOGY

In these two sequences, Adam concentrates on Mary's unique role as Virgin Mother of Jesus Christ (A 25–32). Mary is the Mother of the Savior (A 2, S 1, S 21), the Mother of the Word (S 7, cf. S 60, S 76, A 29), the Mother of Piety (S 57), and the Mother of those who sing Adam's sequences (A 23, A 47–48). In conceiving Christ, Mary remains a virgin, and in giving birth to him she is spared the pains of childbirth, which were part of the legacy of Eve (A 37–40). Mary was chosen for her role from eternity (S 2, A 33). She is incomparable (*singularis*), exalted above all the saints and angels (S 38–39, S 44–52, S 64–66; A 41–48). Mary excels all others in virtue (S 47–48). Among her virtues, Adam singles out charity and perpetual chastity (S 40–41, S 53–56). Adam asks Mary, whom he calls (S 20) "Mediatrix" (female mediator) or "Restauratrix" (female restorer) (S 20),[3] to commend those who pray to her to her Son (S 68, A 7–8, 55–60), and he ends both sequences with a direct prayer to Christ, asking to be conformed to his glory (S 76–80).[4]

In *Salve Mater Salvatoris/vas*, Christ is Solomon (S 37), Wisdom, who carved out Mary as his throne (S 5–6). Mary is addressed and described with a number of metaphors. First of all she is a vessel, foreseen and chosen, full of honor and grace, and cut out by the hand of Wisdom (S 2–6). The vessel metaphor highlights Mary's capacity to receive the incarnate Word into her virginal womb. Other metaphors in the sequence do the same: she is a closed door and a cellar (S 13–15, cf. A 35–36), and a paradise (S 31). She is a hall in which dwells the whole Trinity (S 58–59), a place where the Word received hospitality (S 60–62). Corresponding to these metaphors of enclosure are refer-

---

2   Jollès, *Quatorze*, 12–25. Hugh of St Victor and his successors at St Victor developed a rich theological basis for the spiritual (doctrinal, moral, mystical) interpretation of Scripture, which insisted that such interpretation be rooted in the literal sense. Jollès, *Quatorze*, 73, writes that *Ave, virgo singularis/mater* is probably the richest in symbolism of all Adam's Marian sequences, but all of that symbolism in biblical in origin.

3   Grosfillier, 716.

4   For the theology of Adam's Marian sequences, see Jollès, *Quatorze*, 25–38.

ences to Christ ("the anointed") whom she enclosures: he is ointment, fragrances, and spices (S 14–18); she is redolent with his sweet scents (S 16–18).[5]

The other dominant cluster of metaphors in *Salve Mater Salvatoris/ vas* presents Mary in botanical metaphors. She is a flower blooming on a thorn bush, but without thorns herself. She is the glory of the thorn bush, which is the human race (S 8–10). Or, to change the metaphor, all others have been scratched by a thorn that Mary never touched (S 11–12).[6] She is the myrtle of temperance, the rose of long-suffering, sweet-smelling nard (S 22–24), and an uncut Cedar of Lebanon, giving off a sweet scent (S 32–33). Again, she is a humble, unplowed valley, which bears fruit. Here her defining virtues are humility and virginity. That fruit that Mary bore, or Mary from whom that fruit was born, is a flower of the field and lily of the valley (S 25–30).

In *Ave, Virgo salutaris/mater*, the dominant metaphor is of Mary, Star of the Sea (A 3, S 63), who guides Christians through the storms of life (A 4–8), past the Sirens of pleasure, the dragon, dogs, and pirates. We live on earth amid a fearful storm, in which we fear we will perish (A 9–24). In the end Adam prays to Christ, who is son of Mary yet coequal to the Father (29–32). Christ, the fruit of Mary's womb (A 65), is a mild judge, who gave cause for hope on the cross (A 61–64). Adam prays to Him to take the tiller and bring us to a safe haven (A 65–72). He asks that Christ be leader, way, and safe-conduct to heaven (A 66–68). In addition to the nautical metaphors, in *Ave, Virgo salutaris/mater* Adam refers to Mary as a flower, a vine and an olive true, who without any graft, bears fruit (49–52). She is a light, brighter than the sun (53–54).

POETICS

Ave Virgo, singularis/mater is notable for it repeated references to Virgil's *Aeneid* in lines 13–20. Grosfillier[7] points out the remarkable poetry of lines like A 9–12, noting the repetitions of vowels in the first two lines, and the variations on the verb, *curro*, in the second two.

---

[5]   Grosfillier, 713–15.
[6]   Grosfillier, 712–13.

Sevit mare, fremunt venti,
fluctus surgunt turbulenti,
navis currit, sed currenti
tot occurrunt obvia.

Salve mater Salvatoris/vas resembles a litany in its frequent invocations of Mary with "Salve," "Tu, and "O." Only strophe 9, a kind of lyrical interlude, does not begin with one of these words of address. The repetition of the word "vas" ("vessel") in opening strophe establishes Mary as a receptacle of grace and of the incarnate God.[7] The third through sixth strophes establish Mary as a paradise, virgin ground, who re-establishes the innocence that Eve lost. She is a fountain in a garden from which flow the scents of divine gifts. Then the seventh and eighth strophes present Mary's unique glory, to which her humility brought her, and which are the conditions appropriate to Mary's unique mission.

TRANSLATIONS

These translations were made from the text as given in the editions of Grosfillier and Jollès. They are included in a bilingual, Latin-English edition of a large collection of sequences and other texts attributed to and about Adam: *The Liturgical Poetry of Adam of St Victor from the Text of Gautier*, tr. and ed. D. S. Wrangham (London: Kegan Paul, Trench, 1881), 2:173–77 and 2:218–25. I checked my translation against his, and against the bilingual edition of J. Mousseau in Dallas Medieval Texts (Leuven: Peeters, 2013) and the French translations of J. Grosfillier and B. Jollès. In the notes I give a sampling of the sources and parallel texts identified by Jollès and Grosfillier.

---

[7]   Grosfillier, 709–712.

AVE, VIRGO SINGULARIS / MATER

Sequence for the feast of the Assumption

1.

    Hail,[1] incomparable[2] Virgin,
    mother of our Savior.[3]
    Called "star of the sea,"[4]
    you never wander.[5]
5   Do not let us shipwreck
    on the sea of this life,[6]
    but always intercede for us
    with your Savior.[7]

2.

    The sea lashes, the winds roar,
10   the turbulent waves surge,
    the ship sails, but runs
    into so many obstacles.
    Here are the sirens of pleasure,[8]
    the dragon,[9] dogs,[10] and pirates.
15   All of them threaten death[11]
    to those nearly desperate.[12]

3.

    Raging waves toss the fragile boat
    from deep troughs heavenward.[13]
    The mast bends, the sail flaps,
20   the sailor stops working.[14]
    Our fleshly self[15] wearies[16]
    in these evil circumstances.
    May you, our spiritual mother,[17]
    free us—we are perishing.[18]

4.

25　You, perfumed in heavenly dew,[19]
　　in whom is preserved chastity's flower,[20]
　　brought to the world
　　a new flower[21] in a new way.
　　The Word, coequal[22] with the Father,
30　entering your virginal body,
　　became embodied for us[23]
　　in the shaded shelter[24] of your womb.

5.

　　He, the powerful ruler of all things,
　　foresaw and chose you.[25]
35　When he filled your holy womb,
　　he did not break modesty's enclosure,[26]
　　Unlike what the first mother experienced,
　　when you were giving birth,
　　delivering the Savior,
40　you felt no labor pain.[27]

6.

　　O Mary, as befits
　　the dignity of your merits,
　　you are raised uniquely
　　above the choirs of angels.[28]
45　Today is a happy day
　　when you go up toward heaven.
　　Look with a mother's love
　　on us here below.

7.

　　Holy root, living root,[29]
50　flower, vine,[30] and olive tree,[31]
　　which no engrafting power
　　has helped to fructify,
　　light of the earth, splendor of heaven,
　　you excel the sun in splendor.
55　commend[32] us to your Son
　　so he will not judge us strictly.[33]

8.

In the sight of the supreme King,[34]
be mindful of the tiny flock.[35]
Though it transgressed the law given it,[36]
60   it is still confident of pardon.
The Judge, meek and kindly,[37]
deserving of unending praise,
gave the guilty a pledge of hope
when he became a sacrifice on the cross.

9.

65   Jesus, fruit of a holy womb,[38]
be for us a way, a leader,
amid the waves of the world,
a safe-conduct[39] to heaven.
Take the tiller, command the ship,
70   You who calm the fierce storm,[40]
as befits your kindness,
give us a quiet harbor.[41]

SALVE MATER SALVATORIS / VAS

SEQUENCE FOR THE FEAST OF THE NATIVITY OF MARY

1.

Hail, mother of the Savior,[42]
chosen vessel,[43] vessel of honor,[44]
vessel of heavenly grace.[45]
A vessel foreseen from eternity,
5   a remarkable vessel,[46] cut out
by the hand of wisdom.[47]

2.

Hail, holy mother[48] of the Word,
flower from thorn, without thorn,[49]
flower, the thorn bush's glory.
We are the thorn bush, we are

bleeding from the thorn of sin,[50]
but you know no thorn.[51]

3.

    Closed door, fountain of gardens,[52]
    a cellar that guards the ointments,
15   cellar of perfumes,[53]
    you surpass the fragrances of
    cinnamon sticks, and of
    myrrh, frankincense, and balsam.[54]

4.

    Hail, honor of virgins,
20   woman who restores[55] humankind,
    by giving birth[56] to the Savior.
    Myrtle[57] of temperance,
    rose of patience,[58]
    fragrant nard.[59]

5.

25   You, humble valley,[60]
    uncultivatable[61] earth
    that bears fruit.[62]
    Flower of the field, incomparable,
    lily of the valleys,[63]
30   Christ has proceeded from you.[64]

6.

    You, heavenly paradise,[65]
    and uncut cedar of Lebanon,[66]
    sending forth a sweet scent.
    You possess the fullness
35   of brightness and beauty,
    of sweetness and scent.[67]

7.

You are the throne of Solomon,[68]
no throne equals you
in art or material.
40 Pure white ivory prefigures
the mysteries of your chastity,
deep yellow gold, your charity.[69]

8.

You carry an incomparable palm;
you have no equal on earth
45 nor in the court of heaven.
Glory of the human race,
you have privileged virtues
exceeding all others.

9.

The sun is brighter than the moon,
50 the moon brighter than the stars,[70]
so Mary is worthier
than all other creatures.
The chastity of the Virgin is
a light that knows no eclipse;
55 her immortal charity is
an inextinguishable ardor.

10.

Hail, mother of piety,[71]
and noble hall[72]
of the entire Trinity,[73]
60 You prepare a special
resting-place[74] for the majesty
of the Word incarnate.

11.

O Mary, star of the sea,[75]
incomparable in dignity,

ranked above all
the ranks of the heavens.[76]
Set above the heights of heaven,
commend[77] us to your Son.
Let not terrors and wiles
70　　of enemies trip us up.[78]

12.

Cinched up[79] for battle,
we are safe in your protection.[80]
May the force of the shrewd,
tenacious enemy yield to your virtue,
75　　his treachery to your providence.
Jesus, Word of the supreme Father,
keep safe the servants[81] of your mother.
Set free the guilty, by your grace[82]
save them and configure us
80　　to your bright glory.[83]

NOTES

1   "Ave": recalling the angel's greeting to Mary in Luke 1:28.

2   "singularis": a term often applied to Mary in Victorine sequences and other medieval writings (see Jollès, *Quatorze*, 58 n. 1).

3   "salutaris": a term used in the Vulgate (e.g., Ps 64:6) for "salvation." Here Adam invokes Luke 1:47 where the word is used to mean "savior."

4   The expression "stella maris" occurs several times in Adam's sequences. Jerome, *Nom. heb.* (De Lagarde, 137; PL 23.842) suggests this meaning for "Miriam," and Isidore, *Etym.* VII.10 (Lindsay; tr. Barney *et al.*, 170) mentions it. Two examples among many of its use are the antiphon, *Alma redemptoris mater* (*Liturgia horarum iuxta ritum Romanum* [Vatican City: Libreria Editrice Vaticana, 1977], 540) and Bernard of Clairvaux, *Laud. BVM* 2.17 (SBO 4:34–35).

5   Jollès (*Quatorze*, 58 n. 4) writes that Seneca referred to a planet as a "stella erratica." By contrast, Adam thinks of Mary as the polestar that was a guide for nighttime navigation.

6   The idea that life is a dangerous voyage had its origin in pagan authors. Hugh of St Victor applies the metaphor to the Church in *Archa Noe* 5 (Sicard, 23; PL 176.629D–630A): "Ipsa ecclesia archa est, quod summus Noe, id est Dominus noster Jesus Christus, gubernator et portus inter procellas hujus vitae regens per se ducit ad se" ("The Church itself is an ark, which the Supreme Noah, that is Our Lord Jesus Christ, the helmsman and port, ruling amid the storms of this life, leads through himself to himself"). Hugh takes up the theme again in *Vanitate* and *Quid vere* (see VTT 2.172–74), as does Richard of St Victor in *LE* II.10.4 (Châtillon, 381–85 = *Serm. cent.* 4 (PL 177.907D–911A). There Richard cites lines 9–24, 65–72 of this sequence and refers to its author as "egregius versificator" ("a renowned poet"). Bernard of Clairvaux applies the metaphor to the individual soul in *Laud. BVM* 2.17 (SBO 4:34–35).

7   Grosfillier, 399 n. 8, interprets this to mean "your [Son, the] Savior."

8   Isa. 13:22: "et sirenae in delubris voluptatis." The Sirens appear in *Physiologus* 12, as cited by R. Baxter, *Bestiaries and their Users in the Middle Ages* (Stroud: Sutton Pub.; London: Courtauld Institute, 1998), 35: "Isaias propheta dicit: Sirena et daemonia saltabunt in Babylonia," The Sirens also have an entry in medieval bestiaries such as *The Book of Beasts: a Facsimile of Ms Bodley 764* (Oxford: Bodleian Library, 2008), fol. 74v–75r.

9   Ps. 73:14 (Vulg.); Apoc. 12:9; 13:16–17; 20:2.

10   Deut. 23:8; Ps. 21:17 (Vulg.); Phil. 3:2; Apoc. 25:15. Grosfillier (399 n. 14, 704–705) suggests that lines 13–14 allude to the sea-dragon Scylla and her dogs described by Virgil, *Aeneid* III.427–32 (Fairclough and Goold, Loeb 63:401–402): "Scylla . . . postrema immani corpore pistrix / delphinum caudas utero commissa luporum . . . et caeruleis canibus resonantia saxa" ("Scylla . . . below, she is a huge sea monster, with dolphins' tails joined to a belly of wolves . . . and rocks that echo with her sea-greens dogs").

11   "Mortem paene desperatis / haec intentant omnia": Lines 15–16 allude to Virgil, *Aeneid* I.91 (Fairclough and Goold, Loeb 63:268–69): "Praesentemque viris intentant omnia mortem" ("all things threaten the sailors with instant death").

12   Ps. 106:23, 2–26; Ecclus. 24:8; cf. Richard of St Victor, *LE* II.10.12.21–22 (Châtillon, 400.21 = *Serm. cent.* 12; PL 177.925B).

13   "Post abyssos nunc ad caelum / furens unda fert phaselum": cf. Virgil, *Aeneid* I.103 (Fairclough and Goold, Loeb 63:268): "velum adversa ferit, fluctusque ad sidera tollit" ("[the storm] strikes against the sail, and raises the waves to the stars").

14   For lines 19–20 compare Virgil, *Aeneid* V.867 (Fairclough and Goold, Loeb 63:530): "Cum pater amisso fluitantem errare magistro / sensit et ipse ratem nocturnis rexit in undis" ("when the father found it drifting, her pilot lost, he himself took charge of the boat on the waves of night"). Cf. Richard of St Victor, *LE* II.10.4 (Châtillon, 382.12 and 383.5–6, 9–10 = *Serm. cent.* 4, *Ave maris stella* [PL 177.908A, 909AB]; tr. Van Liere, VTT 4.480–81), where the ship is the faith of believers, the mast is hope, the sail is charity. On the sailors ceasing to work, see Ps. 106:23.

15 "homo noster animalis": In 1 Cor. 2:14 this refers to a person left to his own resources without God's help. More generally "homo animalis" means a human being as an animate (ensouled; from "anima" ["soul"]) physical being, sometimes with the connotation of being animalistic.

16 Ps. 106:26 (Vulg.).

17 Adam may be the first to called Mary "our spiritual mother." Perhaps he does so here for poetic, rather than clearly theological reasons. Augustine uses the expression in relation to the church; see *Ep.* 34.3 (PL 33.132).

18 I Cor. 1:18; 10:10.

19 A metaphor for Mary's virginal conception of Christ, recalling the story of Gideon's fleece (Judg. 6:38). The image was also applied to Christ as the dispenser of grace.

20 Bernard of Clairvaux, *SCC* 47 (SBO 2:62–66), which is on Song of Songs 2.1.

21 The idea of Christ as a flower derives from Num.17:8 (Aaron's rod) and Isa. 11:1 (a flower from the root of Jesse). However, flowers can, as in line 50, refer to Mary herself, who is sometimes seen as a flower sprung from a thorn bush.

22 See Adam's sequence, *Qui procedis* (Grosfillier, 338.71).

23 Jollès calls attention to the dense theology of lines 29–31 (*Quatorze*, 64 n. 15).

24 "umbraculo": cf. Luke 1:35.

25 "praevidit et elegit": see parallels in other authors given in Jollès, *Quatorze*, 64–65 n. 16; 254 n. 14.

26 Song of Songs 4:12. See the Ambrosian Christmas hymn, *Intende qui regis Israel* 4: "claustrum pudoris permanet" ("the enclosure of modesty remained"). For this hymn, see www.preces-latinae.org/thesaurus/Hymni/VeniRedemptorG.html (accessed 8/24/2011).

27 The idea that Mary was spared labor pains goes back at least to St Ambrose and is found in the Christmas liturgy; see Jollès, *Quatorze*, 65 n. 17. Grosfillier, 702–703, goes further and sees a reference to the idea of Mary's *virginitas in partu*, which I do not find explicit in Adam's text.

28 "supra choros angelorum / sublimaris unice": Mary's exaltation above the choirs of angels is evoked in the liturgy for the Assumption, e.g., in the third antiphon for first Vespers: "Exaltata est Virgo Maria super omnes caelos" (*Liturgia horarum*, 4:1056) and the second antiphon for Lauds: "Exaltata est Virgo Maria super choros angelorum" (*Liturgia horarum*, 4:1064). See also Bernard of Clairvaux, *Laud. BVM* I.7 (SBO 4:19.3–4); Richard of St Victor, *Serm. cent.* 47 (PL 177.1026D).

29 See the Marian antiphon, *Ave Regina coelorum*: "salve radix, salve porta, / ex qua mundo lux est orta" (*Liturgia horarum*, 4:490). In the Middle Ages, the text read: "salve radix sancta." Usually Mary is seen not as a root, but as a branch or twig (*virga*) springing from the root of Jesse (Isa. 11:1). See Jollès, *Quatorze*, 86–87 n. 15; Hugh of St Victor, *Egredietur* (Jollès, 2:280); Richard of St Victor, *Comp. Christi* (PL 196.1031–32).

30 The image of a vine is more often applied to Christ; see Richard of St Victor, *Serm. cent.* 55 (PL 177.1062A).

31 Ecclus. 24:19; Richard of St Victor, *LE* II.10.12.32–33 (Châtillon, 400.29–401.38 = *Serm. cent.* 12; PL 177.925BC); *Serm. cent.* 47 (PL 177.1028A).

32 "adsigna": one ancient manuscript reads "commenda," which is a more common verb in this context (Jollès, *Quatorze*, 68 n. 21).

33 There is a similar blend of fear and confidence before Christ the Judge in Anselm, *Oratio* 6 and *Oratio* 7 (Schmitt, 3:15–25).

34 1 Kings 24:3; Tob. 3:24; Ps. 97:6 (Vulg).

35 Luke 12:32: "Nolite timere pusillus grex" ("Fear not, little flock").

36 James 2:9, 11.

37 Acts 10:42; Ps. 85:5.

38 Luke 1:42.

39 This translation may be a bit too free. Grosfillier, 703, thinks Adam has in mind Christ, now free from the underworld, assembling (*conductus*) the souls of the dead and leading them to heaven.

40 In returning to the image of human life as a difficult voyage on a stormy sea, Adam no longer invokes Mary as intercessor as he did in strophes 1–3; he now invokes Christ as Savior. In *De paenitentia* 4.6 (Borleffs, 327), Tertullian spoke of penitence as a plank that carries the sinner to the harbor of divine mercy ("amplexare ut naufragus alicuius tabulae fidem. Haec te peccatorum fluctibus mersum prolevabit et in portum divinae clementiae protelabit"). See the text from Hugh of St Victor's *Archa Noe* cited in conjunction with strophe 2 above.

41 Cf. Ps. 106:30.

42 Anselm, *Oratio* 7 (Schmitt, 3:19.32–33; tr. B. Ward, *The Prayers and Meditations of Saint Anselm* [Baltimore: Penguin, 1973], 116.53); Bernard of Clairvaux, *Laud. BVM* II.16 (SBO 4:21–22).

43 Acts 9:15; Rom 9.2–23.

44 2 Tim. 2:21.

45 The angel greeted Mary as "full of grace" (Luke 1:28). On the development of this theme, see Jollès, *Quatorze*, 204 n.2.

46 The word "vas" (vessel) occurs five times in this strophe. It can mean a piece of equipment or an instrument.

47 This strophe draws on the Wisdom writings: Wisd. of Sol. 6:17 (providence); Prov. 8:23 (from eternity); Prov. 9:1 (Wisdom cuts out); Ecclus. 24:14. See also Deut. 2:34. See Bernard of Clairvaux, *Sermo* 52 (SBO 6/1:275.6–8): "Haec itaque Sapientia quae Dei erat, et Deus erat, de sinu Patris ad nos veniens, *aedificavit sibi domum*, ipsam scilicet matrem suam virginem Mariam, in qua *septem columnas excidit*" ("This Wisdom, which was of God, and was God, coming from the bosom of the Father to us, built a home for himself, namely his mother, the Virgin Mary, in whom he cut out seven columns").

48 "salve Verbi sancta parens": "salve, sancta parens" is a phrase from Sedulius, used as the entrance verse in Common for Masses of the Blessed Virgin Mary in the Roman liturgy. For other references to the Word ("Verbum"), see lines 60, 76.

49 Songs of Songs 2:2: "Sicut lilium inter spinas" ("like a lily among thorns"); Richard of St Victor, *Serm. cent.* 65 (PL 177.1102D), on the Nativity of the Blessed Virgin. Regarding this image, see Grosfillier, 725–26.

50 Gen. 3:18.

51 This line indicates that Mary was without sin, but it need not refer specifically to the idea of her Immaculate Conception.

52 Ezek. 44:2; Song of Songs 4:12; 4:15; Jerome, *Adv. Jovinianum*, I.31 (PL 23.265CD); Bernard, *Sermo in Nat. BVM* (SBO 5:280.23–24); Adam of St Victor, *Lux advenit veneranda*, 5 (Jollès, *Quatorze*, 166.34): "haec est ille fons signatus / hortus clausus" ("she is that sealed fountain, an enclosed garden").

53 Isa. 39:2; Song of Songs 1:3,5; 2:4; 3:6; 4:4,10; Hugh of St Victor, *Assumpt.* (Jollès, 2:126–28; PL 177.1213D–1214A); *Egredietur* (Jollès, 2:274–76); Richard of St Victor, *Serm. cent.* 47 (PL 177.1026CD).

54 Ps. 44:9 (Vulg.); Songs of Songs 3:6; 4:6,11,14; Apoc. 18:13; Richard of St Victor, *Serm. cent.* 47 (PL 177. 1029AB).

55 "restauratrix": some manuscripts read "mediatrix" (see Jollès, 210 n. 11).

56 "puerpera": the same word is used in *Ave mater singularis/ mater* 5 (Grosfillier, 401.40; tr. above).

57 Isa. 41:19; 55:13. Gregory the Great, *Hom. ev.* I.20.13 (Étaix, 165; PL 76.1166D–1167A), where he says that myrtle stands for the virtue of temperance, which Gregory explains as compassion for the sufferings of others; see also his *Mor.* XVIII.20 (Adriaen, CCL 143A.907.21–30).

58 Ecclus. 24:18. The red rose was associated with martyrdom, a radical act of "patientia" (from "pati," to undergo).

59 Song of Songs 1:11; Bernard of Clairvaux, *Serm. 4.7, In Assumpt.* (SBO 5:249); Bernard of Clairvaux, *SCC* 42.6 (SBO 2:36).

60   Song of Songs 2.1; Bernard of Clairvaux, *SCC* 47.7.3–4 (SBO 2:65–66); Augustine, *En. Ps.* 120.1 (Dekkers and Fraipont, CCL 40.1787.2–15) applies the phrase to humankind, which can only appeal to God in humility.

61   "non arabilis": Isa. 45:8; Ps. 66:7 (Vulg.); Grosfillier, 71 cites a passage from Tertullian, *De carne Christi* XVII.3–4 (Kroymann, 904): "Virgo erat adhuc terra nondum opere compressa, nondum sementi subacta."

62   Grosfillier (417 n. 27) and Jollès (212–13 n. 14) think "fruit" makes a transition to metaphors about Christ, to whom they apply lines 28–29. Nevertheless, the two lines may well refer to Mary.

63   Grosfillier discusses the symbolism of the lily (723–25); it was referred to Christ, to Mary, to the Church, or to the individual soul.

64   Song of Songs 2:1.

65   Song of Songs 4:13.

66   Ecclus. 2:21: "quasi libanus non incisus vaporavi" ("like an uncut Lebanon cedar I gave off scent"). See Richard of St Victor, *Serm. cent.* 55 (PL 177.1061BC); Achard of St Victor, *Sermo* 13.11 (Châtillon, 145; tr. Feiss, *Works*, 221–23; tr. Feiss, VTT 4.98).

67   Richard of St Victor, *Serm. cent.* 34 (PL 177.980D).

68   1 Kings 10:18, 20. In describing Mary's death in its entry for the Feast of the Assumption the *Golden Legend* (tr. W. Ryan [Princeton, NJ: Princeton University Press, 1993], 2:79) has Christ recite part of a response that was used for the liturgy of the feast: "Veni electa mea et ponam in te thronum meum, quia concupivit rex speciem tuam. Specie tua et pulchritudine tua, intende, prospere procede et regna" ("Come my chosen one and I will place my throne on you, because the king has desired your beauty. With your comeliness and beauty, set forth, proceed with good fortune, and reign"). In *LE* II.7.4 (Châtillon, 317–18), Richard of St Victor identifies the Church as Christ's throne. On this see Grosfillier, 719–20.

69   1 Kings 10:18; Richard of St Victor, *LE* II.7.1.39–40 (Châtillon, 314).

70   1 Cor. 15:41.

71   According to Jollès, *Quatroze*, 216–17 n. 21, Thomas of Cantimpré, who was a Victorine before becoming a Dominican, related that when Adam was composing this strophe, the Blessed Virgin Mary appeared to him and expressed her gratitude. "Mother of piety" could also be read, "Mother of Pity." Adam frequently uses the words "pietas" and "pius" (see Feiss, VTT 2.72–73 and n. 197). "Pietas" and "misericordia" are used interchangeably; see Grosfillier, 721.

72   "triclinium": Jollès, *Quatorze*, 217 and n. 23, explains the meaning of this term with reference to a Roman dining-room and its furniture, but she leaves it untranslated. Grosfillier, 419.58 renders it "lit d'accueil." In VTT 2.220, in translating its occurrence in Hugh of St Victor's *Arrha* 53, I rendered it "dining hall" for the reasons given in VTT 2.231 n. 39. Alain of Lille cites lines 57–59 in *Distinct. dict.* (PL 210.979D–980A).

73   Hugh of St Victor, *Assumpt.* (Jollès, 122): "Tota ergo Trinitas venit ad Virginem" ("So the whole Trinity comes to the Virgin"). See Grosfillier, 722.

74   "hospicium": a place of reception or resting. See Notker, *Congaudent angelorum chori* cited by Jollès, 218 n. 25: "Quae domino caeli / praebuit hospitium / sui sanctissimi corporis" ("She who offered the hospitality of her most holy body to the Lord of heaven"). See also Leo the Great, *In nativ. Dom.* 2.2 (Chavasse, 92): "claustrum pudoris et sanctitatis hospitium" ("a enclosure of modesty, a resting-place of holiness").

75   See Adam of St Victor, *Ave Virgo singularis / mater* 1 (Grosfillier, 399.3; tr. above); *O Maria, stella maris* 1 (Jollès, 192.1–2); *In natale Salvatoris* 11 (Jollès, 140.13)

76   See lines 51–52 above.

77   "commenda": see *Ave Virgo singularis / mater* 7 (Grosfillier, 402.55; tr. above).

78   Ps. 16:13; Prov. 4:16.

79   Ps. 17:40.

80   Bernard of Clairvaux, *Laud. BVM* II.17 (SBO 4:34–35).

81 Ps. 85:2 (Vulg.); Anselm of Canterbury, *Oratio* 6 (Schmitt, 3:16.48–50): "Pie domine, parce servo matris tuae . . . Bona mater, reconcilia servum tuum filio tuo" ("Kind Lord, spare the servant of your mother . . . Good mother, reconcile your servant to your Son").

82 "gratis": Augustine, *Jo. ev. tr.* III.9 (Willems, 24) explains: "ex eo quia tantum donum indigni accepimus, gratia vocatur. Quid est gratia? Gratis data" ("It is called grace because we receive so great a gift although we are unworthy. What is grace? What is given gratis").

83 Phil. 3:21; Rom.8:28; 1 John 3:2; 2 Cor. 3:18. Grosfillier, 723, observes that the sequence ends on an anagogic (heavenward) note.

RICHARD OF ST VICTOR

SERMON "AVE MARIS STELLA"

INTRODUCTION AND TRANSLATION
BY FRANS VAN LIERE

INTRODUCTION

According to the seventeenth-century biographer Jean de Toulouse, Richard of St Victor was born in Scotland, but modern-day scholars think that England was more likely the country of his origin. He entered the abbey of Saint Victor sometime in the 1140s, became subprior in 1159, and prior in 1162. The latter he remained until his death in 1173. Richard's title "magister" suggests that he held a position of authority that was associated with his function as a teacher in the school at Saint Victor.[1] Preaching would have been one of the duties within that function.[2] We know of a large number of sermons by the hand of Richard of Saint Victor; the best known collection is his *One-hundred sermons*, which was also included in Richard's *Book of Notes*, and which was transmitted also under the name of Hugh of Saint Victor. According to R. Goy, there is no doubt about Richard's authorship.[3] The fourth sermon in this series is the sermon *Ave maris stella*, translated here.

Preaching was a basic form of instruction at Saint Victor. In his sermons, Richard addresses his audience most often as "fratres carissimi" ("dear brethren") indicating that these sermons were intended for the instruction of the community of canons. The *collatio* that is prescribed in the *Liber ordinis* probably included some instruction in the form of a sermon.[4] Even though some of Richard's *One-hundred*

---

[1]   See Châtillon, "Richard de Saint-Victor," *DS* 13 (1988), 593–98 and Coulter, *Per visibilia ad invisibilia*, 20–23.

[2]   According to the *Liber ordinis*, preaching was done by the abbot, who could delegate the duty to a brother of his choosing. See J. Châtillon, "Sermons et prédicateurs victorins de la seconde moitié du XIIᵉ siècle," *AHDLMA* 32 (1965): 7–60. See also Longère, "La fonction pastorale de Saint-Victor," 291–313, here 298–99. On Richard as preacher, see H. Old, *The Reading and Preaching of the Scriptures in the Worship of the Christian Church: The Medieval Church* (Grand Rapids, MI: Eerdmans, 1998), 3:306–22.

[3]   Goy, *Die handschriftliche Überlieferung*, 379–80; J. Châtillon, "Le contenue, l'authenticité, et a date du *Liber exceptionum* et des *Sermones centum* de Richard de Saint-Victor," *Revue du moyen âge latin* 4 (1948): 23–52, 343–66. On the ascription to Hugh, also see R. Baron, "Hugues de Saint Victor," 260–62.

[4]   See Longère, "La fonction pastorale de Saint-Victor," 291–313, here 295. Saint Victor was in this respect not all that different from other twelfth-century monastic foundations; see

sermons seem to have been intended for specific occasions (sermons one and two are entitled "On the dedication of a church," sermons six through eight are for the feasts of unspecified saints or Apostles; nine is for the feast of the conception of Mary, twenty-four for the feast of the Nativity of our Lord), most of them have more generic thematic titles ("One the fear of God," "On spiritual health," etc.). The sermons are not organized by any particular order of the liturgical year or any order of a scriptural sequence.

Richard's sermon on *Ave maris stella* was probably intended for the feast of Annunciation, on March 25. Some manuscripts give it the title "In festo Beatae Mariae," although it does not say what feast specifically. The hymn *Ave maris stella* was sung at Saint Victor on the feast of Annunciation,[5] but the hymn *Ave virgo singularis* by Adam of Saint Victor, with which the sermon concludes, was intended for the feast of Assumption. The subject of the sermon, however, was not specifically Marian in character, except for the last paragraph, where Richard admonishes his audience to often salute and invoke Mary, while "crossing the sea of this world." Instead, the sermon is an extended treatment of the image of the ship as allegory of the Christian life. The Christian life is seen as a journey across the sea of this world.[6] The length of the ship's hull is compared to the history of the Christian faith, starting with one narrow board (Abraham), widening to comprise the ship's hull (the entire Christian Church), and again narrowing to the sternpost (the Church at the time of the tribulation of the Last Judgment). One could compare the use of this image to Hugh's mental image of the Ark of Noah, where the stretched-out keel of the ship also represents the progression of the Church throughout history.[7] While the ship itself stands for faith, the mast is hope, the sail is love, the ropes are the virtues, the oars are good deeds, the weather vane and the rudder stand for spiritual discernment, and the anchor is humility. The boards of the ship stand for Sacred Scripture, which can be read sequentially in its historical sense, but which are connected to each other in a parallel fashion as well: just as the planks of a ship are connected one layer over another, the two Testaments are connected through a spiritual reading that is

---

B. Kienzle, "The Twelfth-Century Monastic Sermon," in *The Sermon*, ed. B. Kienzle, Typologie des sources du Moyen Âge occidental 81–83 (Turnhout: Brepols, 2000), 271–323.

5   According to the ordinal of St Victor, Paris, BnF lat. 14506, fol. 304v. I wish to thank Christopher Evans for providing this reference.

6   Coulter, *Per visibilia ad invisibilia*, 27.

7   Hugh of Saint Victor, *Libellus* (tr. Weiss, 41–70, here 43).

dictated by the authority of the Fathers, who are symbolized by the nails that hold the planks together. The sailors' food stands for reading and meditation, and, finally, just as sailors sing shanties, thus Christians continuously sing the praises of God.

The Latin edition of the texts translated here into English for the first time (except for the translation of the hymn by Adam of Saint Victor, for which several translations exist),[8] can be found in J. Châtillon's edition of Richard's *Book of Notes*.[9] Another edition is in Migne's *Patrologia latina*, under the name of Hugh of Saint Victor (PL 177.907–911).

---

[8] Adam of Saint Victor, *The liturgical poems of Adam of Saint Victor*, tr. D. S. Wrangham (London: Kegan Paul, Trench, & Co., 1881), 2:173–77; J. Mousseau, *Adam of Saint Victor's Sequences*, Dallas Medieval Texts (Leuven: Peeters, 2013).

[9] Richard of St Victor, *Liber exceptionum; texte critique avec introduction, notes et tables*, ed. J. Châtillon, TPMA 5 (Paris: J. Vrin, 1958), 381–85 and 447–55.

SERMON "AVE MARIS STELLA"

1. "Hail, star of the sea."[1] The present world, dearest brethren, is the sea. Just like the sea, it stinks, it swells, and it is false and unstable. It stinks on account of luxury, it swells on account of pride, it is false on account of its bitterness, and unstable on account of its idle curiosity. Thus, brethren, we ought to have a ship, and all that pertains to a ship, if ever we want to traverse such a dangerous sea without risk. We ought to have a ship, with a mast, a sail, and two beams between which the sail is extended above and below, and a vane, which we can call a weather cock (*gallus*),[2] observing the wind. We need ropes, oars, a rudder, an anchor, and food. We also should have nets, so that we may catch some fish. Now see what all these things mean. The ship signifies faith, which had its beginning in Abraham, who was the first person to believe,[3] as it were with one piece of wood, and was still very narrow in Isaac and Jacob. But later, the ship widened, with the propagation of the ten tribes, and the more the number of believers grew, the more the ship of faith widened. And later, after the crossing of the Red Sea, when the children of Israel took up the Law of God, and later when they multiplied in the Promised Land, it became even wider. And finally, with the coming of Christ, and after he suffered for the human race, and after the sound of apostolic preaching was heard throughout the world, after the fullness of the Gentiles started to come in, the ship widened even more. But in the time of Antichrist, after the love of many had grown cold[4] and the false believers were excluded, it became again narrower, and just as Abraham, on the prow of faith, was the first wood, similarly the last righteous person in its stern will be the last piece of wood. Certainly, whoever has crossed the sea of the present world safely, and whoever has evaded its dangers, and whoever has come safely into the port of salvation, they all have sailed the ship of faith and crossed over. *By faith Abel offered to God a sacrifice exceeding that of Cain, by which he obtained a testimony that he was just, God giving testimony to his gifts; and by it he being dead yet speaks. By faith Enoch* pleased *God and he was translated. By faith Noah framed the ark in order to save his house. By faith he who is called Abraham, obeyed* [the command] *to go out into a place which he was to receive. By faith Sarah,*

being barren, received strength to conceive. By faith Isaac blessed each of his sons.[5] *By faith Joseph, when he was dying, mentioned the exodus of the children of Israel, and gave instructions concerning his bones. By faith Moses, when he was born, was hid. By faith Moses, when he was grown up, denied that he was the son of Pharao's daughter. By faith he celebrated the Passover. By faith* the children of Israel *passed through the Red Sea; by faith the walls of Jericho fell down. And what more shall I yet say? For there is not enough time for me to tell of* the saints of old, *who by faith conquered kingdoms, wrought justice, obtained promises.* Some of them *stopped the mouths of lions,* like Daniel, and some *quenched the violence of fire,* like the three young men, some *recovered strength from weakness,* like Job and Hezekiah, and some *became valiant in battle,* like Joshua and Judah Maccabee, some *women received their dead raised to life again,* as by Elijah and Elisha. *But others were racked, not accepting deliverance,* as the seven brothers who suffered, as we read in the book of Maccabees. Others *were stoned,* as Jeremiah in Egypt, and Ezechiel in Babylon, or *cut asunder,* as Isaiah, some *were put to death by the sword,* as Uriah and Josiah; some *wandered about in sheepskins,* as Elijah and others. *And all these* and many others traversed the dangers of this world, because they were found to be *approved by faith.*[6]

2. The boards of this ship are the sentences of Sacred Scripture, and the Old Testament gives us some boards and the New Testament some others to build it. The nails, by which these boards are held together, that is, by which these sentences are connected, represent the authority of the saints, by whom those things that are contained in sequence in both Testaments correspond to each other. These boards are felled by reading and hewed into shape by meditation. The mast, which stands up high, signifies hope, by which we are lifted up to heaven, by seeking and understanding, as it is written: *Seek the things that are above, not those things that are on earth. Seek those things that are above, where Christ is sitting at the right hand of God* the Father.[7] The sail is love, which extends in front, to the right, and to the left; in front by the desire of future things, to the right by the love of one's friends, and to the left by the love of one's enemies. The two beams, the higher and lower, signify reason and feeling: reason above and feeling below. Love should be held firmly above by reason and be fixed in place, but below it should not only be held by feeling but also be moved by it, for by feeling it will be moved to good deeds. Thus it is similar with a real boat, for the beam above is immovable, while the beam below can be moved. The weather vane signifies the discernment of spirits, since for this reason a weather

vane, or something like it, is put on top of the mast, so that one may discern what wind is blowing or from which direction it is blowing. About this weather cock, that is, the probing of spirits, it is written: *Probe the spirits, whether they are from God.* And again: *To some is given the discernment of spirits.* The ropes are the virtues: humility, patience, compassion, modesty, chastity, continence, constancy, meekness, goodness, prudence, fortitude, justice, and temperance. These ropes, that is, virtues, always have to be stretched with use, so we can fasten the mast of our hope by their use. For no mast of hope can have a firm foundation if the exercise of the virtues is absent. Then follow the oars, which come out of the ship and are put in the water, by which good works are signified, which proceed from faith, and reach into the water, that is, to our neighbors. For the waters are those people who come into the world with their birth, flow toward mortality, and vanish through death. We ought to have these oars not only to our right, in order to do good to those who do good to us, but also to the left, so that we may do good to those who do evil to us, as it is written: *Do good to those who hate you,*[8] and: *If your enemy is hungry, feed him; if he is thirsty, give him drink.*[9] The rudder, by which the ship is steered, signifies the discernment which leads us on a straight course, so that we are not lost to the right by prosperity or shipwrecked to the left by adversity. Our anchor is humility, which is sent into the deep, by which our ship is stabilized, so that our ship is not shattered and does not sink into the deep by the blowing of the wind of diabolical suggestions and the turbulent sea of our thoughts. Thus the ship of our faith needs to be stabilized and held firm by humility, so that in the time of temptation it has a firm place, even as it cannot run its free course. We ought to have food by the reading of Scripture. The evil do not desire this food, as it is written: *Their soul abhorred all manner of food, and they drew nigh even to the gates of death.*[10] It is distributed to the good, as it is written: *He sent his word, and healed them; and he delivered them from their destructions.*[11] The nets signify preaching. These nets we should throw out without ceasing, and pull up people who are submersed in the flow of this present world, and, after the scales of their sins are removed, prepare them for our Lord Jesus Christ. And just like sailors, we ought to continually sing shanties, with the melodies of God's praise, as the Psalmist says: *I will bless the Lord at all times, his praise shall be always in my mouth.*[12] And after all these things, we need wind, which signifies the inspiration of the Holy Spirit, so that by Her we are directed to the port of rest, the saving physician, the promised land, the eternal home.

3. Thus we ought to have, dearest brethren, faith for a ship, hope for a mast, love for a sail, the probing of spirits for a weather vane, the exercise of virtues for ropes, the practice of good works for oars, discernment for a rudder, humility for an anchor, the reading of the Scriptures for food, preaching for nets, and we have to sing shanties for the jubilation of God's praise. But the Lord will give wind by the inspiration of his Holy Spirit, for *every good gift and every perfect gift, is from above, coming down from the Father of lights*.[13] These lights are gifts: the Father the author of lights, the granter and dispenser of gifts. The 'good gift' signifies the gifts of nature, and the 'perfect gift' the gifts of grace. He, then, will give us an advantageous wind, that is, the Holy Spirit, who will give us the other gifts, whether those that are by nature, or those that are given to us by grace. But, in order that we, dearest brethren, may safely traverse that sea, let us often greet the star of the sea, that is blessed Mary, and call on her in salutation, saying: "Hail, star of the sea." Like sailors, we also pour out our prayers to the blessed Mary and her Son. For many are our impediments, as the excellent poet testifies, saying:

"The sea is seething, winds are blowing,
turbulent the waves are rising,
the ship is running, but its running
many counter-currents meets.

Voluptuously luscious mermaid,
dragon, dog, and wily pirate,
to those who nearly desperate
already are, they threaten death.

Now into the deep, then up to heaven,
by wild waves our boat is driven,
The mast wavers and the sail is riven;
The sailor works in vain.

Surrounded by these evils,
human nature almost falters,
Holy Mother, you can save us,
lest we go down in the waves.

Jesus, fruit of that womb holy,
be our life, midst this world's folly,
Be our guide and show our way
to the realms of heaven above.

Seize the helm, direct the ship,
calm the storm that's raving,[14]
Bring us into a safe haven,
by your power alone,"[15]

who lives and reigns with God.

NOTES

1   *Liber Hymnarius* (Solesmes: Abbaye Saint-Pierre de Solemnes, 1983), 259–60, and *Liber Usualis*, edited by the Benedictines of Solemnes (Tournai: Desclée and Co., 1938), 1262.

2   Richard here probably has in mind a weather vane in the shape of a rooster, which is more common on buildings than on a ship.

3   Prudentius, *Psychomachia*, 1.1, ed. H. J. Thomson, Loeb Classical Library (Cambridge: Harvard University Press, 1949–1953), 1. Prudentius here uses the Latin word "via" to mean person.

4   Cf. Matt. 24:12.

5   In a note to the edition, J. Châtillon points out that the author here conflates Heb. 11:20 and 21.

6   Heb. 11:4–5, 7, 11, 21–24, 28–30, 32–35, 37, and 39.

7   Col. 3:1–2.

8   Matt. 5:44.

9   Rom. 12:20.

10   Ps. 106:18 (Vulg.).

11   Ps. 106:20 (Vulg.).

12   Ps. 33:2 (Vulg.).

13   James 1:17.

14   Mark 4:39.

15   Adam of St Victor, *Sequentiae* (Grosfillier, 399–400; tr. Feiss, VTT 4.459–60). My translation is indebted to that of Wrangham (see n. 9 in introduction).

GODFREY OF ST VICTOR

SERMON ON THE NATIVITY OF THE BLESSED VIRGIN

INTRODUCTION AND TRANSLATION
BY HUGH FEISS OSB

INTRODUCTION

The introduction to the selection from Godfrey of St Victor's *Microcosm* translated in VTT 2.301–341 included a sketch of his life and a list of his writings. This sermon, like his two hymns that are also translated in this volume, should be added to that list of his works. Although the sermon and the hymns do not seem to have circulated beyond the walls of the Abbey of St Victor, they are works notable in themselves and for what they tell us of Godfrey and his milieu.[1] For example, that Godfrey would give a sermon on a feast day could indicate that he was an esteemed member of the community at the time he gave it. The style of the sermon is traditional, but his explicit use of the rhetorical technique of "emphasis" is not. Godfrey's logically precise treatment of the question on where the Church without spot or wrinkle is offers evidence of a mind trained in dialectic. His references to efficient and material causes and his use of the term "principium" show some receptivity to philosophical ideas. The sermon is long and complex, and though Godfrey may have reworked it after delivering it, it suggests an audience of cultivated "brothers." Some of his ideas are innovative and must have been thought-provoking to his audience.

Outline

The sermon divides into three parts, corresponding to the historical, allegorical and tropological meaning of Mary's birth:

(A) The Literal Meaning (1–10): The Twofold Birth of Mary, Mother of Grace.

    (1) Mother of Grace, First in Dignity and Time (1–6).
    (2) Mary the Shoot (and Wisp of Incense), Christ the Sprout (7–9).
    (3) The Twofold Birth of the Church; Mary's Reception of Grace of Baptism (10).

---

[1] This sermon was edited and discussed by J. Beumer, "Die Parallele Maria-Kirche nach einem ungedruckten Sermo des Gottfried von St. Viktor," *RTAM* 27 (1960): 248–66. The translation that follows is based on this edition. I have numbered the paragraphs.

(B) The Allegorical Meaning (11–15).

    (1) Mary and the Church: Virgin Spouses of the King, Mothers, without Spot or Wrinkle (11).

    (2) Where is the Church without Spot or Wrinkle of Serious Sin to be Found? (11–15).

        (a) Not in the church building or in Christians generally, nor in the Church or in a region (12–13).

        (b) Not only in heaven (14–15), but also on earth.

        (c) In the dispersed gathering of holy souls united in striving toward God (15).

(C) The Tropological Meaning (16–18).

    (1) The Three Meanings of the Virgin Spouse of the King and Mother (16).

    (2) Let Us Be What We Are Called: Virgin Spouse of the King and Mother (17).

    (3) Especially Insofar as We Wear the Habit of Religious.

Sources

As the notes show in this sermon Godfrey draws heavily on Sacred Scripture, especially the Psalms, Matthew, and the Song of Songs. For Godfrey Christ is clearly the key to the Scriptures, as is evident, for example, when he combines Isaiah 9 and Titus 3:5 (2). However, he is steeped in a rich tradition within which he reads and interprets the Bible. His scriptural interpretation draws on the *Glossa ordinaria*, Augustine, and Hugh and Richard of St Victor.[2] Moreover, his sermon

---

[2]   Beumer found very few comparisons between Mary and the Church in the writings of Godfrey's contemporaries ("Die Parallele," 261–66). He cites three twelfth-century sermons for the Assumption. In a sermon that Hugh of St Victor preached on Song of Songs 4:7, *Tota pulchra es, amica mea* ("You are wholly beautiful, my friend"), he explains that Mary is Christ's friend or beloved by her physical virginity (*intacta*) and his mother because she is fruitful (*fecunda*). The Virgin Mary brought forth Christ, and from Christ on the cross was born the virgin Church, who like Mary is his friend and mother (PL 177.1211). Isaac of Stella (d. ca. 1169) explained that the one Body of Christ exists in heaven and on earth. Both Mary and the Church are both one mother and many, one virgin and many. What the Word of God says about the spouse of the Word, the mother, daughter and sister of Christ, the fruitful virgin, can apply universally to the Church, especially to Mary, and singularly to the faithful soul (PL 194.1863A–B). Serlo of Savigny (d. 1158) declared that as Mary was assumed, so too will the Church be assumed. Mary is the head and principal member of the Church. As Christ dwelt in Mary corporeally, so he dwells in the Church spiritually. Like Mary, the Church is Christ's mother and friend (ed. B. Tissier, *Biblotheca Patrum Cisterciensium*

was a homily delivered on the Feast of the Nativity, 8 September, of an unknown year. He is clearly drawing on liturgical texts from the Bible, and on other texts as well, such as the hymn *Ave maris stella*. He uses traditional topoi, such as "rescue from the shipwreck of the turbulent or falling world," "the aging world" and "Eva-Ave." He uses a technical term of classical rhetoric and refers to Aristotle's efficient and material causes.

STYLE

J. Beumer rightly notes the impressive style of the sermon: "Such a high achievement was scarcely to be expected from a theologian of the twelfth century."[3] The sermon is well-organized, clearly and carefully formulated, devout and rhetorically polished. The sermon begins and ends with a use of the rhetorical strategy of "emphasis," understatement or exaggeration to focus the reader's attention. The idea that Christ, not only gives grace, but is grace, enables us to consider the angel's greeting, "Hail, full of grace," in a new light. By placing this rhetorically charged statement at the beginning and end of the sermon, Godfrey creates an inclusio, which underlies the theological point that it is by divine grace given in Christ that Mary is "the Mother of Grace."

THEOLOGICAL HIGHLIGHTS

Almost every paragraph in the sermon broaches a topic of theological interest. Mary is Mother of Grace because of her intercession, but more so because she so brought Christ into the world. Christ may be called "Grace," for he is given to the world gratis and gives to the world gratis every grace (2). While others may be spiritual mothers of the Word and of grace, Mary is also uniquely his mother bodily and personally (3). The generation of Divine Wisdom is threefold: once in eternity and twice in time, in Mary and in Christ's other mothers (4).

[Bonofonte: A. Renesson, 1664], 6:115). The content of Godfrey's sermon has some things in common with each of these passages, but he develops those shared ideas in a broader and deeper way.

[3] Beumer, "Die Parallele," 257: "Alles in allem genommen, muss man wohl das Urteil wagen, dass eine solche Leistung kaum von einem Theologen des 12. Jahrhunderts in dieser Höhe zu erwarten war."

Mary is the mother first in dignity (3–4) and in time (5–6). As he did in the *Microcosm*,[4] Godfrey distinguishes between nature and grace (5). He elaborates on the comparison between Mary and Eve, seeing Eve as spouse and mother to Adam, in a way that parallels Mary's place as spouse and mother to Christ. He makes the striking assertion that Mary is head of the Church, then goes on to explain this statement in a doctrinally orthodox way that distinguishes clearly between her headship as first member and that of Christ as ruler and authority; he is its efficient cause, she its material cause (5–6). In the process he employs philosophical terms like "principle," "matter," and "efficient cause" in a fairly technical way (6).

Having developed the notion of Mary as Mother and Spouse and head of the Church, Godfrey turns to the metaphors of vine, stalk, shoot and twig or wisp of smoke. Using the latter image Godfrey applies Song of Songs 3:6 to Mary (8). The Church had a twofold birth; it was born in Mary, reborn from the pierced side of Christ. If she was not baptized earlier, Mary was certainly baptized by fire and the Holy Spirit's Annunciation (10).

Allegorically, that is, with reference to doctrine, and in reality Mary stands for the Church, because both are virgin spouses of the king, without spot or wrinkle, and mothers as well. Both are to provide escape from the shipwreck of this stormy and aging world. Christ sanctified Mary even before she was born (11). Godfrey wonders where one can locate the bride without spot or wrinkle and finally decides this bride is constituted by those in the Church, who, though dispersed throughout the world, are united by their dependence on God in genuine faith and devotion (13–15). By their profession, religious should be among these virgin brides of the king and mothers without spot or wrinkle; Godfrey and his hearers should strive to be what they are called (17–18).

Some of these points deserve special notice. Godfrey's mariological teachings have received the most attention. As Beumer observes, Godfrey twice touches on Mary's sinlessness. Having distinguished between birth and rebirth, Godfrey writes that Mary received the grace of baptism at the Annunciation when, if she had any blemishes of sin, they were washed away, and from then on she had no further blemishes (10). He also compares Mary to Jeremiah who was sanctified from his mother's womb. This does not assert the Immaculate Conception of Mary,

---

4   See, e.g., Feiss, VTT 2.306–307.

but her sanctification from when she was in the womb, that is, either while she was in the womb or at the moment she left it (11).[5] Though Beumer seems to think Godfrey did not endorse the doctrines of Mary's sinlessness and Immaculate Conception, I think rather that Godfrey was deliberately leaving both questions open.

Godfrey's describes Mary as "the first Mother of Grace" (2–6) and "head of the Church" (5–6). Godfrey has thought carefully about these appellations: he uses them both for rhetorical effect and as springboards to reflection. In both cases, he is very careful to show that Mary is subordinate to Christ. Mary is "Mother of Grace" as an intercessor, but she is "Mother of Grace" for a much deeper reason: she conceived and bore Christ, who can rightly be called "Grace." Christ is "Grace" for two reasons. He came into the world as the free gift of divine love. As head of his Body he has measureless grace that he distributes generously to all his members. Mary is head of the Church, not as a bishop might be said to head of a local church, but insofar as she was the first member of the Church, its temporal beginning.[6] Christ is head by being the efficient cause of the Church; she is the initial part of the material which constitutes it, because she us the first living stone Christ lays down in building the Church.

Mary is the first Mother of Grace, not just in time, but also in dignity, because she gave birth to Christ not just spiritually but also in his body and person. However, there are many "second" spiritual mothers of either gender who, having become brothers and sisters of Christ through rebirth (3), conceive the divine Word from heaven in their souls by listening, learning, and meditating, and then give birth to the word in their teaching, preaching and acting (3–4). They are the virgin

5   Cf. Beumer, "Die Parallele," 258. He refers to Pseudo-Richard of St Victor, *Cant.* 26 (PL 196.482C–483D), commenting on Song of Songs 4:7 ("Tota pulchra es, amica mea, et macula non est in te" ["You are wholly beautiful, my friend, and there is no spot in you"]): "... mundata in utero, et deinde in sanctitate munditia confirmata, fomite peccati primo in ea sopito, ut non peccaverit, et tandem exstincto, ut peccare deinceps non potuerit" ("[She was] cleansed in the womb, and then, when her cleanness was confirmed in holiness, the spark of sin was dormant in her, so that she did not sin, and finally it was extinguished, so that from then on she could not sin").

6   St Thomas treats Christ's grace as head of the Church in *ST* III.8.1–7 (Caramello, 4:71–79). Christ is the "universal" principle of the whole Church ("universale principium totius Ecclesiae," a. 1, obj. 3) and its head (a. 1), but others like bishops can be called "heads of the church(es)" in a subordinate and limited way (a. 6). The soul of Christ received grace in the highest way and that grace is essentially the same grace which he bestows to justify others (a. 5).

spouses of the king and mothers[7] who form on earth the Church without spot or wrinkle (16–17). Christ abides in the soul, and in expressing the charity that abides in them Christians are mothers.[8]

Godfrey's focus is not on Mary as intercessor (2, 18), but on her role as exemplar (first mother) of the Church and of individual Christians (second mothers). Having developed his theology of Mary and the Church as virgin spouses of Christ and mothers, Godfrey calls his brothers, presumably the canons regular of St Victor and those associated with them, to be virgin spouses of Christ and mothers. His description of second mothers as those who conceive the Word by listening (to his sermon, for example!), learning, and meditating, and then give birth to the Word through teaching, preaching and action (3), expresses the blend of action and contemplation that was the spiritual ideal of the canons of St Victor.[9]

---

[7] In her first letter to Agnes of Prague, Clare of Assisi writes in a similar fashion: "You have merited to be called a sister, spouse, and mother of the Son of the Father" (tr. R. Armstrong and I. Brady, *Francis and Clare: The Complete Works* [New York: Paulist Press, 1982], 193).

[8] B. McGinn, *The Flowering of Mysticism*, The Presence of God: A History of Western Christian Mysticism 3 (New York: Crossroad, 1998), 67–68; see also B. McGinn, *The Harvest of Mysticism in Medieval Germany*, The Presence of God: A History of Western Christian Mysticism 4 (New York: Crossroad, 2005), 119 n. 165.

[9] See, e.g., S. Chase, *Contemplation and Compassion: The Victorine Tradition*, Traditions of Christian Spirituality Series (Maryknoll, NY: Orbis Books, 2003); P. Sicard, *Théologies victorines* (Paris: Parole et Silence, 2008), 57–106. Godfrey's prayer in par. 4 expresses this idea in terms of conceiving and giving birth.

SERMON ON THE NATIVITY OF THE BLESSED VIRGIN

1. To celebrate gratefully and devoutly the sacred and saving birth of the first Mother of Grace befits all the second mothers of that same grace and their second sons and daughters.

2. We rightly say that the most blessed Virgin, whose temporal birth we celebrate today, is the Mother of Grace, not only because she is able and willing to obtain by the intervention of her merits and prayers every grace for us from the Father of graces and the fountain of mercies, but also for a far more excellent reason, namely because she, pure, brought forth into the world ineffably the one who can be called with emphasis, that is, expressively,[1] grace itself. We customarily say emphatically, that is, expressively, *My God, my Mercy;*[2] *Lord, my Refuge;*[3] *the Lord is my light and my salvation,*[4] and similar things. So, in the same form we can say especially to our Lord Christ, *My Lord, my Grace.* A first reason is that he has been given gratis to the world, that is, by divine charity alone, not because of any prior merits of the world, as it is written: *A child is born for us, a son is given to us,*[5] *for he has saved us not because of works of justice that we have done, but according to his mercy.*[6] A second reason is that he gives gratis to the world all grace, which he has principally, as the head of his body, and without measure and which he distributes generously to all his members. Grace and truth come to be and are distributed through Christ:[7] truth comes to be, grace is distributed.

3. It is most correct that we call the Blessed Virgin not only the Mother of Grace, but also the first Mother of Grace. She is first both in dignity and in time. In dignity, because she merited giving birth not only spiritually but also bodily to the Word of God divinely sent into her. Other holy and chaste virgins have merited to conceive and give birth to the divine Word breathed into their souls spiritually from heaven: to conceive by listening, learning, and meditating; to give birth by teaching, preaching, and action.[8] For that reason, we give them the name of "second mothers" of the same Word and of grace, as it is written, *For whoever does the will of my Father, who is in heaven, is my brother, sister, and mother.*[9] Brother or sister in either gender when she or he is born; mother in either gender when she or he gives birth.[10]

This, I say, of the other holy virgins, but this unique, singular, incomparable virgin brought forth for the salvation of the world the one Word of God wholly poured into her through the working of the Holy Spirit not only, as we said, spiritually but also bodily and personally[11] in an ineffable way, which could never happen to any of the others.

4. O mother truly excelling in a singular way in childbirth; O mother utterly singular in the mode of giving birth.[12] O living Wisdom of God, who proceeds and proceeded from the mouth of the Most High eternally[13] and in time entered not only into the heart of the Virgin spiritually, but also into her body corporeally. Who can enable my miserable, blind and squalid soul to become worthy to conceive you even spiritually for the illumination of its blindness and for cleaning its filthiness and to give birth to you for the edification of itself and its neighbors?[14] O divine Wisdom, your generation is threefold: the first is eternal from the eternal Father alone without a mother; the second is temporal, only from this singular and temporal mother of whom we spoke, without a father; the third is also temporal but from many holy mothers of either sex without a male father, among whom, O kind Wisdom, I ask your grace to deign also to number even me. Deservedly, therefore, the Blessed Virgin is named the Mother of Grace who is first in dignity.

5. No less can she also be called the first Mother of Grace in time. Since there are two kinds of people, the carnal and the spiritual, the wicked and the good, likewise of these same kinds of people there are two kinds of mothers, nature and grace, guilt and pardon. As among the mothers of nature the first in time is Eve, so among the mothers of grace the first in time is found to be her to whom was uttered the angelic "Ave," which is the name of "Eva" spelled backwards.[15] The former was the first to give birth for the world carnally to a carnal[16] human being; the latter was the first to give birth spiritually for God to a spiritual human being. The former was the first to give birth to guilt and damnation; the latter was the first to give birth to pardon and salvation. The former was the first door for those entering into this world; the latter was the first door for those entering into heaven. The former was the first door of hell; the latter was the first window of heaven.[17] The former had the first Adam in some way as both spouse and son; in a contrasting way the latter had the second Adam as both spouse and son. The former had her Adam as a spouse by the flesh, her son by carnality:[18] her spouse by carnal intercourse, and her son of carnality by the beginning of guilt. The latter, by contrast, had her Adam as a spouse in her mind, as a son by the flesh: a spouse by spiritual joining,

a son by carnal[19] generation, and in a wondrous kind of way first as spouse, then as son, a spiritual spouse, a corporeal son. Finally, the former was the head and principle[20] of the whole family of the world, and the latter was the head and principle of the entire Church of God. From the former is the time and the law of nature; from the latter the time and law of grace had their origin.

6. Rightly, therefore, the Blessed Virgin is called the first Mother of Grace and the head of the Church in time also. Although before her many holy and chosen souls pertained by faith and predestination to the Church that was sometime going to be, none before her started and founded it, beginning in the present, as did she who was its first member and head. Nor is it an obstacle that according to the teaching of Sacred Scripture we learn that the blessed fruit of her womb, the Lord Jesus, is the head of the Church, for she is head in one way and he in another: she in time, he in authority; she by being the beginning, he by being its foremost ruler.[21] She is also head materially as its first part and matter; he is head causally as its first efficient cause.[22] This should not lead anyone to imagine that the Church is two-headed or a two-headed monster, for someone is not said to be a quadruped or to have four feet because it has feet of the body, and also feet of the mind.[23]

7. Therefore, today, the Virgin Mary, a shoot[24] going forth from the stalk of David, begins the vine of the Lord beginning to be planted in her, and she does so as its first and not undistinguished sprout. For something consisting of parts is rightly said to begin when its first part takes substantial shape. So, certainly, a house first is said to have been founded when the first stone is set in the foundation. So, also, a vine is rightly said to be first planted when its first sprout is planted (*defoditur*) in the earth.[25]

8. He is that noble sprout, she is the green and flowering shoot which the holy prophet, having once perceived it through the Spirit, foretold, saying: *A shoot shall go forth from the root of Jesse*, etc.[26] I say a straight shoot, a slender shoot, a delicate shoot, the shoot that the Holy Spirit in the Song of love sees going up from the desert and in wonder says: *Who is this who ascends through the desert like a wisp of smoke*[27] *from incenses of myrrh and frankincense and every powder of the perfumer.*[28] By a wondrously suitable comparison, he says she is a wisp of smoke rising through the desert, because beginning from the desert of Judea and ascending from the desert of the Gentiles from so small a sprig it wondrously grew into the tree of the Church, so great, bushy and fruitful. Or, certainly, he spoke of a "wisp" and "ascending

through the desert" because from the time she was born by God's will she was always kept far from the earthly and base desires of the world and like a straight shoot raised herself to heaven and through the desert, that is, through a celibate[29] life far from the disturbances of the world, she did not cease ascending until she reached beyond the heavens, until she merited to become the queen[30] of heaven, that is, to be exalted above the choirs of angels. Also, how beautifully he said, "wisp of smoke," wishing to signify by a hidden mystery that she would be, as we said, the first sprig of the Church, which Church is signified by the name "smoke," for this reason, namely, that just as smoke at one and the same time is partly released into the breezes of air and partly still being born from the burning material, so surely the holy Church is always rapt into heaven in its dying members and partly always reborn anew ardently[31] from the fire of the Holy Spirit in aromatic material, that is, in the souls of holy repute who succeed them. Whence he also added: "from incenses." O holy shoot, truly aromatic shoot, which both from its branches and from itself pours forth into the heavens the sweetest smoke and smell not only of myrrh and frankincense, that is, of the mortification of the flesh and devout prayer, but also emits all kinds of sweetness of every colored powder, that is, of all virtues reduced as it were to dust by the pestle of humility. For as aromatic spices[32] and medicinal drugs first have strength as a medical preparation when they are reduced to powder, so all virtues that send off a sweet scent and are curative of spiritual sickness first lead to perfection when through the virtue of humility they are considered as nothing. In the Blessed Virgin this virtue of humility so prevailed over all her great merits that she, so to speak, crushed all her other virtues through it and judged them to be dust.[33]

9. O blessed stalk, or holy root, from which such a thin stalk came forth, which at first was very small and then grew into a great vine, a chosen vine, the Lord's vine, a vine so great, so extensive that it extended[34] it branches all the way to the sea and its tendrils to the river, and even from the river to the ends of the earth, and its shade covered the mountains and its branches the cedars of God. And if all who passed on the way harvested it, and if the wild boar from the forest destroyed it, and if each wild beast fed on it,[35] and if they strove as much as they could to pull it up by the roots,[36] none of them prevailed against it,[37] but amid straits and tribulations it grew up more and more and produced and produces fruit in its time.[38] Therefore, today let the whole of Mother Church exult and rejoice, because not only does she cele-

brate the temporal birth of one Mother Virgin,[39] but also in one Mother Virgin she recalls her own birth. For although today is born the one Virgin Mary, in that one and with that one all are born, that is to say, the Church.

10. It is not an obstacle that one reads that Eve was formed from the side of the sleeping Adam, in which it is mystically understood that the Church was formed from the side of Christ dying on the cross,[40] and so it seems to have begun not from this day but from the time of the Lord's passion. This, I say, is not an obstacle. For today there began by being born what then began by being reborn: today through generation and then through regeneration; today began to be what then began to be holy. Thus, certainly, there is a twofold birth for each of the faithful, one carnal, the other spiritual, one unto life, and the other unto holy life. Therefore, I do not say that today the Church was reborn, but that it is rightly believed that the Church was born when the first person of the Church is born. For the blessed Virgin is believed to have been first among all the persons eventually to be reborn through the grace of baptism, who alone are properly and specifically called persons or members of the Church. For one should not believe that she, who, as it were, merited being the fount and bearer of grace, did not receive the grace of baptism in a supreme way. We believe that she obtained this grace completely, if not at some other time then at the time when the Holy Spirit came upon her and the power of the Most High overshadowed her and she conceived this very Grace in her womb.[41] O how truly did the Spirit who came upon her baptize her in spirit and in fire.[42] Thus it comes about that she is cleansed, so that she is both washed clean from past blemishes, if there were any, and from then on she could be blemished with no contagion of sin.[43] We say these things because we have no certain authority by which it can be determined whether she was sacramentally baptized, although she was still alive when that general law of rebirth was promulgated by the institution of the Supreme Authority (*principis*) which states: *Unless someone has been reborn,* etc.[44]

11. However, it is not only according to the letter that today the Virgin being born began the Church being born, but she also signifies the same Church mystically by the fact, name and time of her birth. In fact, she is a virgin and so is it. She is without spot and wrinkle, and it too is without spot and wrinkle.[45] She is spouse of the king, and so is it the spouse of the king; she is a mother, and so is it a mother; she is the first mother, it is the second mother. Indeed, it is second mothers, for

the one is mothers, many mothers; the one Church, many churches, just as one people is many peoples and vice versa. By name also, or by interpretation of the name, because she is Maria, that is, way of the sea (*maris via*), and it is Maria, that is, way of the sea. For each is a true way, through which one escapes the shipwreck of this changing world.[46] Each is a true star at the pole, that is, fixed immovably at the highest pivot of things, which, if he focuses on it, directs each man sailing through the sea of this world to the port of eternal salvation. She also signifies it expressly (*expresse*) by the time of her nativity. For the Virgin Mary is born in the autumn season, when the world is growing old; the virgin Church is born in the autumn of the world, where the world is inclining toward old age.[47] The Virgin Mary was born when the sun was occupying the sign of Virgo;[48] the virgin Church was born when Christ, the sun of justice, was preparing a dwelling for himself in the Virgin. He did not first inhabit her when he entered into her corporeally; rather he sanctified her from (*ex*) the womb as a chosen vessel for himself. Who does not believe that he, who is known to sanctify prophets and lesser chosen ones from the womb, sanctified his mother from (*ex*) the womb? How would he not sanctify his only mother Mary from (*ex*) the womb, when he also sanctified from the womb Jeremiah, who was not his only prophet? He says, *Before I formed you*, etc.[49]

12. But now, dearest brothers, let us turn our sermon toward ourselves and let us investigate, if we can, what is this Church, which we commend so highly, which we preach as a virgin, as incorrupt, as without spot or wrinkle, as spouse and mother of the king, which finally we presume to compare to such a great virgin and mother. For what is she—is she these walled buildings in which we are enclosed? Yes she is, not in reality, but by signification.[50] For these lofty buildings, clean, whitened inside and out, signify the Church of God, lofty in virtues, cleansed from vices, chaste in mind and body, constructed of living stones.[51] What then? Is it the whole gathering of the Christian people? It is certainly not that by possession of virtue, but by sharing in the sacraments; not by the divine will,[52] but by name; not by merit, but by number.[53] *For many are called, but few are chosen.*[54] What then? Is it perhaps that Church that commonly is spoken of as at Rome or at Jerusalem, Gallic or Hispanic or something else. What shall I say, brothers? I do see and recognize in these the name "Church," but I do not see or recognize the reality of the name, either because it is hidden or because is completely absent. What then? Which of these, which are commonly called churches, is a spotless virgin, worthy to be called

king's spouse without stain or wrinkle, I mean, without the stain of sinful guilt and the wrinkle of double mindedness,[55] which that Church, which is truly the spouse of God, necessarily must be without? And now I am not speaking of the stain of venial sins,[56] from which even the true spouse of God cannot be free in this life.

13. For shame! I say, how many spots there are in the moon,[57] that is, in what is popularly called the Church, even those which will never be removed. Travel through lands, seas, cities, villages, the streets, squares, castles, cloisters, houses, and corners—everywhere there are stains, everywhere there are wrinkles. To pass over the worst, everywhere there are deceptions, cheatings, lies, perjuries, slanders, hypocrisies, hatreds, avarice, uncleanness, envy, and pride. Alas, what, how many and how great, how filthy and indelible the spots, how great and how palpable the wrinkles!

14. What, then, can we say, brothers? Where will we find what we seek: the Church, the virgin spouse and mother of the king, wholly beautiful, wholly immaculate, to whom the spouse says in the Canticle: *You are wholly beautiful, my friend, and there is no spot in you,*[58] "wholly," I say, even in your lesser (*inferioribus*) members? Or, perhaps, is the name empty, a name without any reality?[59] We have indeed found the time of her birth, but we have not been able to find the place where she dwells. Therefore, either she is hidden, or she has been lifted up from our midst, or she has been taken up from her place. Or by chance has she who was born today with the Virgin been taken with the Virgin into heaven? Woe to us, if she has been transferred to heaven and is not also on earth.

15. I know, indeed, I know that her dwelling is in heaven; her way of life (*conversatio*) is among the holy angels of God. But I hope that she is not only in heaven, but also on earth. For I have heard that her portion is still twofold, one reigning in heaven, the other fighting on earth. I do not seek the one reigning in heaven, but I seek the one fighting on earth. I am confident about the one that reigns in heaven; but I am extremely concerned about the one that is still fighting on earth. Do you still wish to know, brothers, what and where is this virgin spouse of the king and mother? Unless I am mistaken, it is certainly (that we may show it exactly according to its place on the way) the dispersed gathering or gathered dispersion of holy souls striving toward God in true faith and united commitment. "Dispersed" in place, "collected" in aim; a dispersal of places, but not a variety of commitments; gathered in commitments, not identity of places.[60] You will not

find many (I say "many" in comparison to the wicked) of this kind in one place, but you will find them one in commitment. For this is the scarcity of grains lying hidden under the abundance of straw that will not be manifested before it is winnowed in the Lord's air at the end.[61] Or, certainly, if one wants to consider this morally, it is each faithful soul depending on God with sincere faith and devotion.[62]

16. For as we learn from the Sacred Scriptures, this virgin spouse of the king and mother is threefold. First there is that singular blessed woman, who is born today, the virgin spouse of the king and mother, Mary. Second there is more generally that blessed virgin spouse of the king and mother, which equally begins to be today the Church. Thirdly, there is that special blessed who is born daily, the virgin spouse of the king and mother, the faithful soul.[63] The first is spoken of historically; the second, allegorically; the third, tropologically. The first is singular, the second universal, and the third particular. The first is one in one, the second is all in one, and the third is also one in one.

17. Dearly beloved brothers, thinking about these things, let us strive to be what we are said to be. We are called the virgin spouse of the king and mother Church; let us be the virgin spouse of the king and mother Church: virgin through disgust at defilement and through preservation of chastity; spouse of the king through the devotion of faith and love; mother through wholesome teaching and holy action. Let no one fool himself, let no one deceive himself, let no one foolishly flatter himself, because people number us in the present Church. What good does it do me to be numbered in the Church by human beings, if it does not also happen that I am actually placed there by the heavenly Examiner of merits? What does it profit an animal if a blind man numbers him among human beings, which if he saw it he would not do. Dearly beloved, not thus will an animal be a human being or a human being an animal. In discerning the merits of people we are all blind. Who is deserving of grace or hate, we do not see. Only the heavenly and infallible Examiner already sees the qualities and merits of each, and if he does not yet divide their places, he will eventually gather the good and the bad from the net[64] of our unsorted Church and choose some and cast out others, dividing the lambs from the kids by location.[65] Let us not think about deceiving (*fallere*) the Infallible One, but as we said, let us strive to be what we are said to be, not to be said to be what we are not. Otherwise woe on us, and double woe! First because we are not what we are said to be, and secondly because we are said to be what we

are not, because through hypocrisy we usurp an honor not owed us. For falsified identity is a twofold iniquity.

18. Brothers, I say this especially on our account, we who rightly put forward a special appearance, who wear the habit of perfection in our outer person, lest it happen secular people turn the Gospel back on us: *Be on guard against false prophets who come to you in the clothing of sheep, but are inwardly ravenous wolves; by their fruits you will know them.*[66] Truly because we cannot be what we should be without the grace of God, let us implore that singularly blessed Mother of Grace, whose glorious nativity is celebrated today, and also that more singularly blessed only-begotten Son, called "grace," that by the intercession of the one and the concession of the other, we may, cleansed of every spot and wrinkle, merit to become sharers in the reality as we are of the name. May he deign to grant this, etc.

NOTES

1   "emphatice" and "expressive": the two words are equivalent; "emphatice" is a word taken from Greek that is attested in a few Christian writers of late antiquity; "expressive" occurs in Pseudo-Hugh of St Victor, *Quaestiones in epistolas Pauli ad Rom.* 13 (PL 175.435A). At the end of his sermon Godfrey will use the expression "per emphasim" to refer to Christ as "grace," thus forming an inclusio. "Emphasis" (= "significatio") is a technical term of classical rhetoric, difficult to define, which refers to giving emphasis or calling attention to something by an unexpected addition or subtraction. It is discussed in R. Lanham, *A Handlist of Rhetorical Terms*, 2nd ed. (Berkeley: University of California Press, 1991), 138–40. Lanham cites a definition given in *Ad Herenniun* 4.54.67.

2   Ps. 58:18 (Vulg.).

3   Ps. 17:3 (Vulg.); 143:2 (Vulg.). Grammatically, in this quotation, "Lord" ("domine") is in the vocative case (for direct address), whereas in the quotation from Ps 26:1 that follows, "The Lord" ("dominus") is in the nominative.

4   Ps. 26:1 (Vulg.); cf. 2 Tim. 1:10.

5   Isa. 9:6, a passage used in the Introit for the Mass for Christmas Day.

6   Titus 3:5.

7   John 1:17.

8   See my introduction to the selection from Godfrey's *Microcosm* in VTT 2.308–309.

9   Matt. 12:50.

10   It is difficult to know who the subject of "is born" (*gignitur*) is. (a) The subject could be Christ, and so the meaning is that when he is born from Mary physically and spiritually or from someone else spiritually, a believer becomes (anew) his brother and sister. If the subject is the believer, it could mean either (b) when they are born spiritually, believers become Christ's brothers and sisters, or (c) reversing the order of the clauses, when they give birth to Jesus spiritually, believers become his mother, then when he has been born they become his brothers and sisters.

11   "personaliter": Godfrey seems to mean that Mary gave birth to a physical human being who was personally the Word.

12   "modo pariendi": Godfrey may be referring to the theory (*virginitas in partu*) that Mary gave birth to Christ in a miraculous way.

13   Here Godfrey cites Ecclus. 24:3, which provided the first part of the "O antiphon" for Dec 17: "O Sapientia, quae ex ore Altissimi prodisti" ("O Wisdom, who proceeded from the mouth of the Most High").

14   Godfrey intersperses a brief prayer, which anticipates the later application of the sermon to the individual Christian and particularly to the canons regular (or possibly some other religious group Godfrey was addressing). The next sentence is also addressed to the Word in the second person and the paragraph ends with another brief prayer.

15   In the Latin Bible, Gabriel's greeting to Mary at the Annunciation began with "Ave," "Hail!" In Latin the name for Eve is Eva. Hence, the words constitute a palindrome. The theme of Mary as the New Eve (though not the palindrome Ave-Eva) appears already in the *Adversus haereses* of Irenaeus of Lyon (*ca.* 175) V.19.1; 20.2; 21.1, included in the Roman Catholic Liturgy of Hours, Office of Readings for Friday of the Second Week of Advent (*Liturgia horarum iuxta ritum romanum* [Vatican City: Libreria Editrice Vaticana, 1977] 1:197–98). The palindrome appears in the early Marian hymn, "Ave maris stella," (*Liturgia horarum*, 1:1034) which includes several other images [Maria = star of the sea (11); door of heaven (5)] found in Godfrey's sermon:

Ave, maris stella / Dei mater alma / atque semper virgo / felix coeli porta

Sumens illud "Ave" / Gabrielis ore, / funda nos in pace, / mutans Evae nomen.

Hail, star of the sea / God's nurturing mother / ever virgin / happy gate of heaven.

Receiving that "Ave," / from Gabriel's mouth / establish us in peace / transforming Eve's name.

16   "carnaliter," "carnalem": literally "fleshly," from "caro" (flesh). The rest of this paragraph em-
     ploys the multiple connotations of "caro" and the words formed from it. As in English, it has
     a neutral meaning: "body," "bodily," and also a pejorative meaning, which is most evident in
     the adjective "carnal." In order to convey this dual connotation, I have translated "carnalis,"
     "carnalitas," and "carnaliter" as "carnal," "carnally," and "carnality," which may give a more
     pejorative tone than the Latin original. The negative connotation of "caro" and its derivatives
     comes primarily from St Paul, who contrasted "flesh," all that remains of the old, unregener-
     ate self that tugs the Christian toward sin, with "spirit," the impulses that lead the baptized
     self, the new creation, toward God. On this see J. Dunn, *The Theology of Paul the Apostle*
     (Grand Rapids, MI: Eerdmans, 1998), 472–82. Godfrey is very careful to distinguish human
     nature and sin. Eve gives birth physically to a physical human being, and she gives birth to
     sin and damnation; that is, Eve brought physical children into the world through physical
     birth, and she also brought sin into the world through her sin in which she enticed Adam to
     participate. In the same way, Mary gave birth spiritually to Christ, a "spiritual" being, and in
     giving birth to him she gave birth to the source of pardon and salvation. Eve was the door to
     earth and to hell; Mary was the door and window of heaven. Eve had Adam as a spouse to
     whom she was joined by sexual intercourse; she had Adam as her son, insofar as she engen-
     dered sin in him. Throughout his *Microcosm* Godfrey has a very positive regard for the hu-
     man body ("flesh"), and in chapter 225 (Delhaye, 245–47; tr. Feiss, VTT 2.334–35) he writes
     very positively of the physical love of married couples.

17   "fenestra celi": It is possible that the image of a window may have been suggested by Song of
     Songs 2:9, and/or by the window in the ark of Noah (Gen. 6:16; 8:6). Godfrey draws the
     comparison: Eve is to Mary as door-to-the world is to door-to-heaven; then he writes that
     Eve is to Mary as door-to-hell is to window-to-heaven. This last comparison is not very
     enlightening; Godfrey may have written himself into a corner.

18   The idea here seem to be that Eve gave birth to sin in Adam, by conveying to him the serpent's
     evil suggestion.

19   This is an example of a neutral use of "carnalis."

20   "principium": "origin," "foundation," "principle," connoting not just the first in a line (say of
     people waiting for a bus), but first in a way that those who come after depend on it (like a
     blood line of border collies).

21   "principaliter": an adverb derived from "principium," connoting "first in a commanding
     fashion."

22   Here Godfrey refers to two of the four causes of Aristotelian philosophy (the other two are
     formal and final).

23   That the feelings ("affectus") were the feet of the soul was a commonplace of medieval
     thought. For example, explaining the allegorical meanings of Jesus' washing of the disciples'
     feet at the Last Supper, Anthony of Padua wrote: "pedes, affectus eorum" ("their feet [signify]
     their feelings") (*Sermo in cena Domini* 1.3 [Costa *et al.*, 3:170]); Pseudo-Richard of St Victor,
     Nahum 83 (PL 196.751A): "Animae vero pedes illius sunt affectiones. Sicut enim corpus por-
     tatur pedum officio, sic anima movetur ad diversa affectionum studio" ("The feet of the soul
     are its feelings. As the body is carried through the good offices of the feet, so the soul is moved
     by the impetus of feelings toward different things"); Anonymous Victorine, *Sermo* 8.4 (Châtil-
     lon, *Sermones inediti*, 285.104–105): "Unde David: 'Et statuit supra petram pedes meos.' Pedes
     vocat affectiones" ("Hence, David [writes]: 'And he set my feet upon a rock.' He calls feelings
     feet"). In a note to this passage, Châtillon refers to the following passages from St Augustine:
     Jo. ev. tr. 56.4 (Willems, 468.7–8); *En. Ps.* 94.2 (Dekkers and Fraipont, CCL 39.1331.21–32);
     Sermo ad catechumenos, De cantico novo 4 (PL 40.681). For this image see J. Callahan,
     Augustine and the Greek Philosophers (Villanova: Villanova University Press, 1967), 47–74.

24   Like many medieval authors, Godfrey makes use of the wordplay "virgo" (virgin) – "virga"
     (sprout); in this sentence he adds alliteration by the use of "vinea" (vine). This imagery derives
     from Isa. 11:1, "Et egredietur virga de radice Jesse" ("A shoot will spring up from the root of

Jesse"), a passage which is the basis for the Jesse Tree image in Christian art and which Godfrey quotes a few lines below.

25 Godfrey has been working with the metaphor of the root of Jesse from which comes Mary, a tender shoot (*virga, virgula*) of which Christ emerges as a sprig (*surculus*). Here Godfrey seems to use a slightly different metaphor. A vine begins to be planted when a slip is planted in the ground. "Defodio" means to dig down, dig up, bury.

26 Isa. 11:1.

27 "virgula": a diminutive of "virga," small shoot or thin column of smoke.

28 Song of Songs 3:6. The subject of this quotation is feminine. Richard of St Victor introduces this same verse in his *Arca Moys.* V.5 (Aris, 129; tr. Zinn, 317). There he explains that ecstasy may occur in three ways: through intense devotion, wonder, and exultation. The first way Richard explains by the image of melting wax and Song of Songs 3:6; the second by the image of lightning and Song of Songs 6:9 and the third by inebriation and Song of Songs 8:5. In *Arca Moys.* V.6–7 (Aris, 130–31; Zinn, 317–20), Richard explains that in the first way, the soul so burns with love that it ascends to heaven by longing, as smoke ascends from fire. Song of Songs 3:6 speaks of a thin column of smoke, one that is graceful and straight. So the Christian's longing should be unified by a right intention. The myrrh is contrition of the flesh; the incense is devotion of the heart; the powders of the perfumer are the consummation of all the virtues. All these virtues are present because charity is the consummation of the virtues, and where there is full charity there the other virtues are present. The soul rises up from the desert, from herself.

29 "Celibem vitam": strictly speaking "celebs" in Latin, like "celibate," means unmarried. Mary was married, but virginal, and that no doubt is the way Godfrey was using the word here.

30 "Regna": either Godfrey is coining a word "queen" (= *regnatrix, regina*), or he is using the plural form "kingdoms of heaven," which seems odd and would yield, "she became the kingdoms of heaven." "Regna" does not appear in these dictionaries: DuCange, Lewis and Short, Blaise, or Niermeyer. The simplest solution is that Godfrey or his copyist forgot to write a letter: reg<i>na.

31 "Ardente": ordinarily this would be a present singular ablative participle, but it seems here to be an adverb, the equivalent of "ardenter."

32 "Species": which according to Lewis and Short can mean "spices" or "drugs" in Late Latin. The word is repeated in both phrases, but I translate it as "spices" in the first and "drugs" in the second.

33 Many features of Godfrey's allegorical interpretation of Song of Songs 3:6 are present in the *Glossa ordinaria*: the Church arises through the desert of Jews and Gentiles; the desert symbolizes withdrawing from worldly allurements; the column of smoke is the fire of love; the smoke simultaneously rising from the burning material and dispersing in the sky is symbolic of the Church whose members are both on earth and in heaven; myrrh signifies mortification of concupiscence, frankincense, offering to God the promises of one's heart; grinding the incenses into dust is humility that keeps one from pride in one's virtues See *Glossa ordinaria, pars 22: In Canticum Canticorum,* ed. M. Dove, CCCM 170 (1997), 206–209. This version of the *Gloss* makes no mention of Mary.

34 From here to the end of the sentence is a close paraphrase of Ps. 79:10 with the two clauses reversed.

35 The preceding part of this sentence is a close paraphrase of Ps. 79:13–14 (Vulg.).

36 Ezek. 17:9.

37 Matt. 16:18.

38 Ps. 1:3 (Vulg.).

39 "mater Virgo": the emphasis here is on mother, and to convey that it seemed better to translate the two words in the order Godfrey has them, though it sounds unusual.

40 *Glossa ordin.* on Eccles. 17:5. (ed. princeps 2:760). "*Creavit ex ipso.* Sicut de latere Ade dormientis formata est Eva, sic de latere Christi in cruce morientis exiuit sanguis et aqua, de

quibus formatur Ecclesia" ("*He created from him.* Just as Eve was formed from the side of the sleeping Adam, so blood and water, from which the Church is formed, flowed from the side of Christ dying on the cross").

[41] Luke 1:35. Godfrey's concern in this paragraph is in what sense Mary was baptized. He skirts some other questions, which were still open at his time. Thus, here he alludes to the earlier phrase in the angel's greeting, "full of grace" (Luke 1:28), but leaves open the question of whether Mary was full of grace before or only after the angel's greeting. His notion that Christ was grace itself is theologically profound.

[42] Matt. 3:11; Luke 3:16.

[43] Godfrey leaves open the question of whether Mary was sinless her whole life long. He may have been thinking specifically of original sin. The doctrine of the Immaculate Conception was being debated during his lifetime and continued to be debated for several centuries afterwards.

[44] John 3:3, 5.

[45] Eph. 5:27.

[46] See Hugh of St Victor, *Quid vere* 5 (Baron, 96–99; tr. Feiss, 180); *Vanitate* 2 (PL 176.731BC); *Archa Noe* 2.1 (Sicard, 34.48–49); Horace, *Carm.* III.3.7–8 (Bailey, 70), echoed by Cyprian, *Ad Demetrianum* 20 (PL 4.559B); *Ad Donatum* 14 [PL 4.220]); Bruno, *Letter to the His Carthusian Brothers* (ed. M. Laporte, *Lettres des premiers Chartreux* I, SC 88:82); C. Smith, *Metaphor and Comparison in the* Epistulae ad Lucillum *of L. Anneas Seneca* (Baltimore: J. H. Furst, 1910), 124–26.

[47] The theme of the aging world (*mundus senescens*) was a common one among patristic and medieval Christian writers: Cyprian, *Ad Demetrianum* 3 (PL 4.546–47); Augustine, *Serm.* 81.8 (PL 38.504–505); *Serm.* 163.4 (PL 38.891); see De Lubac, *Catholicism*, 267 n. 70.

[48] Virgo is the sixth astrological sign; it is assigned four weeks in the autumn. The Feast of Mary's Nativity occurs on September 8.

[49] Jer. 1:5.

[50] "Per significationem": This can be, and here probably is, the Latin equivalent of the "per emphasim" discussed in n. 1 above. In any case, the idea is that the stone church is only a symbol of the real Church made up of the baptized.

[51] "Vivis ex lapidibus": Ps. 125:7 (Vulg.); 1 Peter 2:5; hymn for the Dedication of a Church, "Urbs beata Ierusalem dicta pacis visio / quae construitur in caelis vivis ex lapidibus" (*Liturgia horarum*, 1:1011); Honorius of Autun, *Expositio in Psalmos* (PL 172.284B); Bernard of Clairvaux, *Sermo in dedicatione ecclesiae* 1.6 (SBO 5.374.5).

[52] "Numine": from "numen," nod, and hence divine will. Presumably Godfrey thought Christians who lacked virtue and merit and so would not be saved were nevertheless in the Church by the divine will. Hence, I have translated "numine" by "predestination," in parallel to the next sentence, "many are called, but few are chosen."

[53] The series of contrasts that Godfrey gives here was a classic one. In his edition and translation of Radulphus Ardens, *The Questions on the Sacraments*, Medieval Law and Theology 3 (Toronto: Pontifical Institute of Medieval Studies, 2010), 247, C. Evans cites the following examples: Pseudo-Jerome, *Expositio euangelii secundum Marcum* 14 (Cahill, 60): "Iudas Iscariotes unus de duodecim, unus numero, non unus merito; unus nomine, non unus numine; unus corpore, non unus animo;" *Glossa ordin.* Prol. on Ps. (ed. princeps 2:458; PL 113.844C): "Item de Ecclesia tribus modis: aliquando secundum perfectos, aliquando secundum imperfectos, aliquando secundum malos: qui sunt in Ecclesia corpore, non mente; numero, non merito; nomine, non numine"; Bernard of Clairvaux, *Sent.* 3.113 (SBO 6.2.199): "Hi sunt inter bonos corpore, veste non mente, habitu non affectu, nomine non numine"; Peter Lombard, *II ad Cor.* 7.1 (PL 192.53): "Vel de his qui sunt intus, id est in Ecclesia corpore non mente, nomine non numine"; Peter the Chanter, *Verbum abbreviatum* (*textus conflatus*) 1.25 (Boutry, 204): "Etsi sacramentaliter Eucharistiam sumat, qui de Ecclesia sunt nomine sed non numine;" Radulphus Ardens, *Speculum uniuersale* 8.59 (Evans, 108); *Hom. de com-*

muni sanctorum 1 (PL 155.1491A): "Falsi Christiani, qui in Ecclesia ista militante sunt, numero, non merito, nomine, non numine;" *Hom. de tempore* 2.43 (PL 155.2096C): "In Ecclesia, numero, non merito, nomine, non numine."

54 Matt. 20:16; 22:14.

55 "dupplicitatis": cf. the "duplex" person of James 1:8; 4:8.

56 "venialium"" by contrast to the "criminalis culpae" of the previous sentence. "Crimen" has the connotation of serious or mortal sin.

57 For moon spots, see P. Toynbee, "Dante's Theories as to the Spots on the Moon," in *Dante, Studies and Researches* (London: Methuen, 1902), 78–86. Godfrey refers to them in his *Sermon in generali capitulo* (Riedlinger, 189).

58 Song of Songs 4:7. One Eastertime Godfrey gave a sermon on this verse to a general chapter (*Sermo gen. cap.*, Riedlinger, 188–93). Godfrey asks: Who is the bride who is spotless, and so more than human? He says the verse applies well to Mary, but the Holy Spirit was not speaking about Mary. It applies to the Church and individuals in heaven, but they are not so much brides (*sponsae*) as wives (*uxores*). Everyone on earth sins. So, it seems the bride without spot is neither in heaven nor on earth. Godfrey finds a way out of this dilemma by saying the Bridegroom is referring to the graces that Christ gives to the newly baptized innocent, to the just who are advancing toward God, as well as to the blessed in heaven. The first state is the extermination of evil, the second the advance of good, the third the consummation of the good (cf. Richard of St Victor, *Exterm.* I.3–4 [PL 196.1075A–1076B], 2.13 [PL 196.1101AB]). Those advancing should try to keep the garment of innocence beautiful. To help Godfrey and his hearers to do this, St Augustine is father and mother by the twofold grace of understanding and doing, contemplation and action. They are beautiful in their state of life; they should be beautiful in their persons as well.

59 This is an allusion to the theories of nominalism that were discussed in the schools of Paris when Godfrey was a student.

60 Godfrey here repeatedly uses the words "dispersa/dispersio" and "collecta/collectio," but in at the end of the sentence he uses some odd words to achieve rimed prose: "dispersa locorum, non votorum varietate; collecta votorum, non locorum idemptitate." The translation is somewhat free.

61 Matt. 3:12; Luke 3:17.

62 This understanding of the "Church without spot or wrinkle" is very much like Augustine's understanding of the "City of God," constituted by those who acquiesce to divine revelation, adhere to Christ and live a virtuous life. More briefly, the "City of God" is made up of those who love God and neighbor. As Godfrey does in par. 16, Augustine emphasizes that human beings cannot know whether another human being is genuinely virtuous and so who is a member of the "City of God." For a brief sketch of Augustine's views, see E. Fortin, "*De Civitate Dei*," in *Augustine through the Ages*, ed. A. Fitzgerald (Grand Rapids, MI: Eerdmans, 1999), 196–202; and Augustine, *Gn. litt.* 11.15.30 (Zycha, 347–48; tr. Hill, 439–40).

63 For these categories, singular, special, general, see Hugh of St Victor, *Arrha* 31–32 (Sicard, 250; tr. Feiss, VTT 2.214–15).

64 Matt. 13:47–48.

65 Matt. 25:33.

66 Matt. 7:15–16.

GODFREY OF ST VICTOR

TWO HYMNS

INTRODUCTION AND TRANSLATION
BY HUGH FEISS OSB

INTRODUCTION

GODFREY'S MANUSCRIPT

The ancient library of St Victor contained a manuscript of Godfrey of St Victor's works with the shelf mark JJ15 (Paris, Mazarine 1002). In it the table of contents prepared by Claude de Grandue lists nineteen of Godfrey's sermon (fols. 1r–143r), his *Fountain of Philosophy* (fols. 145r–221r), the *Preconium Augustini* (fols. 221v–231v), and two hymns of his, the *Canticle of the Blessed Virgin and Mother Expanded through Godfrey's Effort* (fols. 232r–235r) and his *Plaint of the Blessed Virgin and Mother at the Passion of the Lord* (fols. 235r–237r).[1] This manuscript contains two self-portraits of Godfrey.[2] Gilbert Ouy and Françoise Gasparri have determined that the manuscripts of Godfrey's works are written or corrected in his own hand.[3] These two hymns are written partially in Godfrey's own hand and partially (the beginning of the *Planctus*) in that of a collaborator. These two pieces are accompanied by music.[4]

---

[1] G. Ouy, *Les manuscripts de l'abbaye de Saint-Victor*, 2:277. The manuscript of Godfrey's works has been bound with another manuscript which contains excepts from Hugh of St Victor's *Homilies of Ecclesiastes*, Achard of St Victor's *On the Distinction of soul, spirit and mind* (here wrongly attributed to Richard of St Victor), and [Pseudo-] Hugh's *Notes on Romans and Corinthians*. In the manuscript Godfrey wrote out the lines of both hymns continuously as though they were prose. He used only one form of punctuation throughout, whether for minor pauses or major breaks. The latter he indicates by following them with a capital letter. In her edition Gasparri transcribes the text exactly as Godfrey wrote it. In the translation I have divided the lines into the short sections that are defined by the musical scheme. I have based my translation on Gasparri's transcription, but I corrected a couple of readings based on a microfilm of Paris, Mazarine 1002.

[2] F. Gasparri, "Observations paléographiques sur deux manuscripts partiellement autographes de Godefroid de Saint-Victor," *Scriptorium* 36 (1982): 47–58. See the frontispiece to VTT 2 and H. Feiss, "Preaching by Word and Example," in *From Knowledge to Beatitude: St. Victor, Twelfth-Century Scholars, and Beyond. Essays in Honor of Grove A. Zinn, Jr.* (Notre Dame: University of Notre Dame Press, 2013).

[3] F. Gasparri, "Textes autographes d'auteurs victorins du xiie siècle," *Scriptorium* 35 (1981): 277–84; G. Ouy, "Manuscrits entièrement ou partiellement autographes de Godefroid de Saint-Victor," *Scriptorium* 36 (1982): 29–42; F. Gasparri, "Observations," 43–50.

[4] F. Gasparri, "Godefroid de Saint-Victor: Une personnalité peu connue du monde intellectuel et artistique parisien au xiie siècle," *Scriptorium* 39 (1985): 60.

The Canticle of the Blessed Virgin and Mother Expanded by Godfrey's Effort

Form and Style

The rhyme schemes within the units Godfrey marks off with capital letters vary for unit to unit and can be quite complex. The opening unit of the poem is "Unius numinis sed trium no*minum*; mea magnificat anima Do*minum*, quia letificat filios ho*minum*; impetus fluminis de fonte flu*minum*," which is then followed by the word "Et," whose capital letter indicates a new sentence. In this opening unit there are four clauses, all of them ending in "–minum." So, I have written it as a four-line stanza. The first three lines are an expansion on Mary's words; the final line a metaphorical description of the Son, who springs from the Father, the Fountain of the Godhead rushing down into Mary, as the Angel foretold: "The Holy Spirit will come upon you and the power of the Most High will overshadow you" (Luke 1:35).

Another example occurs in the units that I have translated as stanzas 7 and 8:

> Millitat in milite pro milite.
> dimicat cum demone pro homine.
> vetus preda tollitur.
> victus predo cadit.
> captivator capitur.
> captivus evadit.
> per me salus mundi salo.
> per me malus caret malo.
> boni fit plantatio.

Godfrey's rhyme schema here is a, a, b, c, b, c, d, d, d.[5] A glance at the Latin reveals more of Godfrey's literary dexterity. The first two units are exactly parallel: militat/dimicat, in milite/cum demone, pro milite/pro homine. The next two units alliterate on *v* and *p*, and play on the words "preda" and "predo" ("plunder" and "plunderer"). Something

---

5   Another pattern occurs in the last stanza. The first half of it begins with four words in "–elis" and ends with a word in "–a." "Recordatur ut fidelis. servi sui Israhelis. et ad vocem Gabrielis. misso filio de celis. sumit hunc in gloria," that is, a, a, a, a, b. This parallels and ties into the second half, which has c, c, c, c, b: "Implet quod per ora vatum. patribus est revelatum. Abrahe semen beatum. de quo datum fero natum. cui laus in secula." The end of each of the two units (b, b) is anagogic, pointing to the heavenly outcome of what God is going to do in Mary.

similar happens in the next two units as the "captor" is captured and the "captive" escapes.

Stanza 8 displays other aspects of Godfrey's virtuosity. The parallelism and alliteration of the two lines beginning with "per me," is broken with the final line which rhymes with the preceding two but provides closure by evoking the result of this struggle: a garden of goodness, a new Eden.

It is clearly impossible to convey much of Godfrey's literary skill in an English translation. I have divided his poem into stanzas and lines, guided by his punctuation, capitalization, and rhymes. Such a rendering is an interpretation, one that falls far short of Godfrey's poetic text.

Theological Elaboration

As a glance at the notes make clear, in this *Canticum* Godfrey follows strictly the order of the *Magnificat*, the prayer Mary uttered after Elizabeth greeted her (Luke 1:46–55). This was a technique of biblical exposition that Hildegard of Bingen used in her sermons and elsewhere in her writings, but whereas she expanded the biblical words to tell a different story "that stems from and runs in parallel to the biblical text,"[6] Godfrey stays close to the literal meaning of Mary's prayer as he elaborates on it in poetical ways. For the most part, his expansions are not just repetitions; they provide theological elaboration and Scriptural background for what Mary says.

The Lord whom she exalts is the Trinity. Although she is the recipient of a singular privilege, all the Daughters of Sion are her companions (*consodales*), fellow servants (*conancillule*) and fellow spouses (*consponsales*).[7] It appears these unusual compound words are meant

---

6   B. Kienzle, *Hildegard of Bingen and Her Gospel Homilies*, Medieval Women: Texts and Contexts (Turnhout: Brepols, 2009), 127 (see 115–36 for further elaboration on Hildegard's technique).

7   In his commentary on the Song of Song, William of Newberg uses similar compound words beginning "co-," when he has Mary say to Christ: "Therefore, on the third day your flesh will flower again (*reflorescet caro tua*), and your bed will be flowery, namely, that bed on which your flesh will rest through the Triduum in hope. But your bed, is it not also mine? For without a doubt, I will have died and have been buried with you through my maternal affection (*per maternum ero tibi commortua et consepulta affectum*). Therefore, 'our bed is flowery', that is your flesh having blossomed again will bloom with the flowers of the new resurrection" (William of Newburgh, *Explanatio sacri epithalamii in matrem sponsi* II [1:15–16], ed. J. Gorman, *A Commentary on the Canticle of Canticles* (12ᵗʰ C.), Spicilegium Friburgense 6 [Fribourg: Universitätsverlag, 1960], 109–10, cited by R. Fulton, *From Judgment to Passion* [New York: Columbia University Press, 2002], 457).

to invite the reader to be a fellow mother, sufferer, servant and spouse with Mary. Like the choirmaster in the abbey, she leads them in spiritual songs, which unite them in heart and voice.[8] Such a song is the one that Godfrey, a musician and poet, has here composed. Mary's motherhood comes at the end of a long history which begins with Eve and climaxes in the becoming human of the Almighty, an act of comfort and help, mercy and grace. The humble are exalted; the well fed are sent away empty because they did not provide food for beggars. In Mary God's promise to Abraham, from whose seed Mary's Son is born, is fulfilled.

Godfrey and Hugh of St Victor on the Canticle of Mary

Elsewhere in this volume there is a translation of Hugh of St Victor's brief *Explanation* of Mary's *Magnificat*. The two works are very different. In the *Explanation* Hugh writes as a commentator on a text spoken by another. He writes in prose. His work includes what he himself recognizes as theological digression on topics like the identity of soul and spirit,[9] and the operation of divine power, providence, and mercy.[10] He makes distinctions such as those between humility and humiliation,[11] four different kinds of fear,[12] four kinds of servitude to God,[13] and nature, guilt and grace.[14] As he nears the end of the text, his comments become very short.[15] He includes few of the evocative images of Marian

---

8   On music as expressive of harmony in Adam of St Victor, see the introduction to VTT 2.72.

9   Jollès, 40–51 (PL 175.418C–420C; tr. Harkins, VTT 4.428–52). Hugh explains that (1) soul and spirit are one in essence (Jollès, 40–47; tr. Harkins, VTT 4.432–36); (2) the soul expresses the fervor of its love for God, whereas the spirit exults in the hope of salvation from God (Jollès, 48–51; tr. Harkins, VTT 4.436); (3) "Lord" refers primarily to God the Creator of all, and "Savior" to God who comes to bring the elect to glory (Jollès, 51–53; tr. Harkins, VTT 4.436–37). Origen and Ambrose, who wrote the earliest extant commentaries on the *Magnificat*, note the distinctions soul/spirit and Lord/Savior, but do not expound them in the same way that Hugh does. See Clara Burini de Lorenzi, "Il 'Magnificat' (Lc. 1, 46–55) nella interpretazione di Origene e di Ambrogio," *Augustinanum* 50 (2010): 101–103, 108–11.

10   Jollès, 34–39 (PL 175.417A–418C; tr. Harkins, VTT 4.431–32): "Dominus et salutaris: Dominus potentiam notat, salutaris misericordiam" (Jollès, 34 [PL 175.417A]; tr. Harkins, VTT 4.431); Jollès, 64–75 (PL 175.425A–427C; tr. Harkins, VTT 4.441–45); Jollès, 80–81 (PL 175.428D–429A; tr. Harkins, VTT 4.446–47).

11   Jollès, 60–63 (PL 175.424AB; tr. Harkins, VTT 4.439–40).

12   Jollès, 76–77 (PL 175.427D–428A; tr. Harkins, VTT 4.445–46).

13   Jollès, 58–59 (PL 175.423BC; tr. Harkins, VTT 4.439).

14   Jollès, 52–53 (PL 175.421D; tr. Harkins, VTT 4.436–37).

15   Jollès, 7, notes this and refers to P. Sicard, *Hugues de Saint-Victor*, 255–56 n. 37.

typology and devotion.[16] He does refer several times to themes of his *Soliloquy on the Betrothal Gift of the Soul.*[17]

There are few parallels to Hugh's *Explanation* in Godfrey's poem. Godfrey highlight's Mary singular gift and call (3) and joins power and mercy (4–5), but these themes are suggested by the text itself. There seems to be no clear evidence that Godfrey was influenced by Hugh's work, but since the genres and aims are quite different that does not mean that Godfrey did not know Hugh's commentary.

THE PLAINT OF THE BLESSED VIRGIN AND MOTHER AT THE PASSION OF HER SON

Date and Authorship

To understand the dilemmas surrounding the interconnected questions of date and authorship of the *Planctus ante nescia*, it will be helpful to summarize its history and the scholarly literature on it.

The *Planctus ante nescia* appears in the second passion play in the *Carmina burana*, and various editions of that play have been published. P. Dronke, who has studied the play closely, dated the it to ca. 1180, and the *planctus* to the 1140s. The reason for the dating of the *planctus* is that it was cited anonymously in a letter from Bec in the mid-twelfth century.[18]

---

[16]   Jollès, 56–57 (PL 175.423D–424A; tr. Harkins, VTT 4.438): Eve's pride contrasted to Mary's humility; Jollès, 62–63 (PL 175.424D; tr. Harkins, VTT 4.440): the fruit of the ancient tree; Jollès, 34–35.141–43 (PL 175.416D; tr. Harkins, VTT 4.430–31): in one sentence only imagery from the Song of Songs "vere dilecta, et unica, et in illam vinariam a rege sponso tuo introducta, ab ubertate domus ejus inebriata" ("truly beloved, the only one, led into that vineyard by the king, your spouse, inebriated by the richness of his house").

[17]   Jollès, 50–53 (PL 175.421C; tr. Harkins, VTT 4.436–37): God gives all people being, but only some receive beatitude; Jollès, 52–53 (PL 175.422A; tr. Harkins, VTT 4.437–38): Mary loves God's gift on account of God, not the other way around; Jollès, 74–75.692–93 (PL 175.427D; tr. Harkins, VTT 4.444–45); cf. Jollès, 34–35 (PL 175.416D; tr. Harkins, VTT 4.430–31); Jollès, 64–65.555–56 (PL 175.424C; tr. Harkins, VTT 4.441): Mary received a singular and unique grace: "mihi . . . fecit non tamen soli singulariter, sed uni excellenter" ("Me . . . he made not alone singly, but uniquely excellent). These might be taken as an indication that Hugh's *Explanation* was written about the same time as his *Soliloquy*, and so perhaps near the end of Hugh's life. On dating the work, see Jollès, *Oeuvres* 2:8–9.

[18]   "Laments of the Maries: From the Beginnings to the Mystery Plays," in P. Dronke, *Intellectuals and Poets in Medieval Europe*, Storia e letteratura 183 (Rome: Edizioni di Storia e Letteratura 1993), 457–89, at 457–58, 464. In his later study of the second *Camina burana* passion play P. Dronke saw no reason to revise his earlier dating of this *planctus*; see *Nine Medieval*

The "Florilegium of Peter Daniel" (Paris, BnF lat. 4880 [sec. xiii]) contains the text of the *planctus*, preceded by an anonymous prologue that says that the work was written by a aged religious who had entered a monastery at an early age and was accustomed to stay alone in church after Matins to meditate on the sorrows of Mary. He decided to write a poem describing Mary's anguish at Calvary to arouse others to compunction. Mary appeared to him and said that such an undertaking exceeded human capacities. She alone could say what she suffered, and so she dictated to him this "heavenly, sweet song." Delhaye, who transcribed this prologue and the text of the *planctus* that follows it, judged the prologue to be a pious fiction, since in the *Fons philosophiae*, Godfrey indicates that he spent years in the schools of Paris studying (and perhaps teaching) before he entered St Victor.[19]

There was a flurry of scholarly interest in the *Planctus ante nescia* in the last decade of the nineteenth century. G. M. Dreves included the *planctus* in his collection, *Cantiones et muteti* (1895). He edited it from two manuscripts: Codex Taurinensis [Torino] E. V. 20 (*ca.* 1200) and Prague, XII D a; and he attributed it to Godfrey of St Victor.[20] In an article in the *Revue de Chant Grégorien* (1896–1897) J. Pothier transcribed the text of the *planctus*, provided the music in modern Gregorian chant notation, and supplied a French translation. He referred to Paris, Mazarine 942 and 1002; Evreux, BM 2 and 39; Rouen, BM A 506. He noted that some manuscripts attribute the work to St Anselm or St Bernard.[21] U. Chevalier included the *planctus* in his *Repertorium hymnologicum* (1897) and listed a number of manuscripts: Evreux, BM 2, fol. 4; Evreux, BM 39, fol. 1; Oxford, Bodlein MS Add. A44, fol. 80v; Paris, Mazarine 942, fol. 234; Paris, BnF lat. 3639, fol. 185; Paris, BnF lat. 4880; Paris, BnF lat. 15163, fol. 220; Rouen, BM 364, fol. 16; Rouen, BM 666, fol. 95, as well as some early printed versions.[22]

F. Gennrich discussed and edited the text and music in his 1932 study of the forms of medieval songs.[23] He attributed it to Godfrey of

---

Plays, Cambridge Medieval Classics 1 (New York: Cambridge University Press, 1994), 185. On pages 230–33 he edits and translates the *planctus* as it appears in the passion play.

[19] P. Delhaye, *Microcosmus*, 251–59.

[20] *Analecta hymnica medii aevi*, vol. 20 (Leipzig, 1895; Johnson Reprint, 1961).

[21] J. Pothier, "Planctus B. Marie Virginis," *Revue du Chant Grégorien* 5 (1896–1897): 17–21.

[22] U. Chevalier, *Repertorium hymnologicum*, vol. 2 (Louvain/Brussels, 1897) at #14950.

[23] F. Gennrich, *Grundriss einer Formenlehre des mittelalterlichen Liedes als Grundlage einer musikalischen Formenlehre des Liedes* (Halle: Max Niemeyer, 1932), 143–48. He reported that the text was found with metric neums in Rouen, BM 666 (A 506), fol. 94v and Evreux, BM

Breteuil, Subprior of St Victor († 1196). F. Gasparri, who has studied
the paleographical evidence for the life and work of Godfrey of St Victor, observed that this *Planctus beate Virginis et matris in passione Domini* is one of four musical works copied at the end of the collection of
Godfrey's works in Paris, Mazarine 1002, fols. 235r–237r, on folios
which were originally blank. The other three poems and the last part
of the *planctus* are in Godfrey's handwriting. Having studied the manuscript and transcribed the Latin texts, she concluded that the
evidence

> argues in favor of spontaneous writing, near to the actual composition,
> rather than merely texts transmitted by ordinary copying. In any case,
> it seems difficult not to consider Godfrey as the author of these four
> musical pieces, which have definitely been established to be auto-
> graphs, both the texts and the melodies, which seem to have been
> copied at the same time.[24]

These scholars are unanimous in attributing the *Planctus ante nescia*
to Godfrey of St Victor. This consensus is based in part on attributions
of the work to Godfrey in the manuscripts in which the work appears.
P. Dronke is inclined to agree with this attribution, but observes that
there is a problem:

> My slight remaining hesitation about the authorship is connected with
> the generally accepted date of Godfrey's birth, *ca.* 1125–1130. If this is
> correct, he must have been extremely young when he composed *Planc-
> tus ante nescia*, whereas its extraordinary verbal artistry suggests to me
> a poet at the summit of his powers.[25]

At this point, it is necessary to recall the few biographical facts about
Godfrey, the student and writer. If his *Fountain of Philosophy* contains
reliable biographical information on his academic career, he was a stu-
dent of the arts in Paris around 1140–1150 and then studied Sacred
Scripture in the 1150s before entering St Victor. Godfrey dedicated the
Fountain of Philosophy to Stephen of Tournai, abbot of St Geneviève

---

39, fol. 2r, and that the text had been printed by Dreves and Blume, *Ein Jahrtausend lateinischer Hymnendichtung* (Leipzig, 1909), 2:283f.

[24] "Godefroid de Saint-Victor: une personalité," 65: "Ce qui plaide en faveur d'une écriture
spontanée, proche de la composition elle-même, plutôt que de textes simplement transmis
par un vulgaire travail de copie. Il semble en tout cas difficile de ne pas considérer Godefroid
comme l'auteur de ces quatre pièces musicales dont le caractère autographe est désormais
définitivement établi, tant pour le texte que pour la mélodie, qui semblent avoir été tracés
simultanément."

[25] *Intellectuals and Poets*, 464 n. 9.

from 1176 to 1192, and a marginal note in one manuscript dates the work to 1178. Godfrey's works exist almost exclusively in manuscripts that he wrote or which were prepared under his own supervision. The manuscript in which the *planctus* appears (Paris, Mazarine 1002) is one of these. These manuscripts were written when he was at the end of his literary career and of his life, sometime after he wrote the *Fountain of Philosophy*, and so in the 1180s or 1190s. Of his works, only the *Planctus inter nescia* and one of his sermons are known to have had wide circulation, or perhaps any circulation at all.[26]

Even if one does not accept the accuracy of the autobiographical account in the *Fountain of Philosophy*, all indications are that Godfrey lived between 1130 and 1196 (±5 years). If the letter from Bec that cites the poem is from around 1150, Godfrey must have written the *planctus* when he was a young man, which as Dronke observes, seems surprising. In that case, the copy of it in Paris, Mazarine 1002 was written at least 30 or 40 years after the composition of the *planctus*. The story about a religious who wrote the poem in his old age after entering religious life at any early age seems wrong on both counts. It is odd also that of Godfrey's works only the *planctus* enjoyed wide circulation, though its literary and musical excellence make its popularity understandable.

The question of the date and authorship of the *Planctus ante nescia* will only be resolved, if it can be resolved by a close study of the manuscript evidence for the poem and a careful reconsideration of the chronology of Godfrey's life.[27] At this point, all one can say is that the poem has been thought to have been written by him and that it may well be that he did write.

Planctus

Planctus, the first word of the lament, indicates its genre. Several forms of lament (*planctus*) appeared during the early Middle Ages, e.g., dirges for dead royalty, or those that were sung by the women at the tomb in the *Visitatio sepulchri* dramas. The author of a *planctus* puts himself or herself in the place of a historical or fictional person and

---

[26]   See the introduction to the *Fountain of Philosophy* in VTT 3.373–87.

[27]   In addition to the reference in the previous note, see also the introduction in VTT 4 to Walter of St Victor's sermon *On the Feast of the Purification*, where it is suggested that another element in Godfrey's biography, the supposed conflict with Walter of St Victor, may need reconsideration.

expresses that person's feelings at a time of loss or sorrow. It is a personal and highly dramatic genre. Abelard wrote six laments. In the twelfth-century laments of the Virgin Mary emerged as the pre-eminent form. The *Stabat mater dolorosa*, probably composed by a late thirteenth-century Franciscan, is the best known Marian *planctus*.[28]

Narrative Structure

In the *Planctus ante nescia* Mary first tells the reader about her great sorrow that her Son, the light of the world, is being crucified (I). Then she addresses Christ on the Cross (III–IV), uttering nine "O's," the first three of them addressed to Christ, the rest to the reader (V–VI). Then Mary addresses "death", asking that she be allowed to die instead of her Son or with him" (VII–IX). Finally, she addresses the Jews, whom she had said in (I) deprive the world of its light and her of her Son (X–XIV). Readers are rendered attentive and compassionate by the two sections (I, V–VI) that Mary addresses to him, evoking Jesus' sufferings and her own. The reader listens as Mary addresses other actors in the Passion story: Jesus, Death and the Jews, those who crucified Jesus and their descendants. The prominence given to Jewish complicity in Christ's death and the epithets applied to them are jarring to a twenty-first century reader. Godfrey does have Mary call the Jewish people to recognize that Jesus died for them and is ready to pardon them (XII–XIII), and she asks them to grieve for her as she grieves for them (XIV).

Poetry and Perspective

P. Dronke faulted the *Stabat mater dolorosa* for devoting sixty lines of rich and hypnotic rhyming to just two thoughts: "The mother watched the crucifixion sorrowing," and "let me mourn with you." He also found the poem's concluding plea for help at the last judgment

[28] P. Dronke, *Poetic Individuality in the Middle Ages: New Departures in Poetry, 1000–1150*, 2nd ed. (London: Westfield College, University of London Committee for Medieval Studies, 1986), 26–31, who distinguishes six forms of *planctus*; J. Stevens, "Planctus," in *The New Grove Dictionary of Music and Musicians*, ed. S. Sadie (Washington, DC: Macmillan, 1980), 20:847–48; S. Sticca, *The Planctus Mariae in the Dramatic Tradition of the Middle Ages*, tr. J. Berrigan (Athens: University of Georgia Press, 1988). One celebrated medieval *Planctus Mariae* is that by Ogier of Locedio (1136–1214), which was formerly attributed to St Bernard. On it see Sticca, *Planctus*, 105–106. It originally formed part of a larger work, which is translated by D. Jenni, *Ogier of Locedio: Homilies: In Praise of God's Holy Mother; On Our Lord's Words to His Disciples at the Last Supper*, CS 70 (Kalamazoo: Cistercian Publications, 2006); the *Planctus Mariae* is on pages 142–56.

"petty and selfish."[29] The *Stabat mater dolorosa* and Godfrey's *planctus* are about the same length. However, there are differences, three of which stand out.

The *Stabat mater dolorosa* is written in three-line stanzas with the same meter (trochaic tetrameter) and rhyme scheme throughout (a, a, c; b, b, c), Here are the first two stanzas with a widely known English translation:

Stábat máter dólorósa	At the cross her station keeping
Júxta crúcem lácrimósa	stood the mournful mother weeping
Dúm pendébat Fílius.	close to her son to the last.
Cúius ánimám geméntem	Through her heart, his sorrow sharing,
Cóntristátám et doléntem	all his bitter anguish bearing
Pértransívit gládius.	now at length the sword has passed.

By contrast Godfrey's poem has a very complex structure, which Gennrich and earlier scholars termed a "double cursus." His *planctus* of 120 lines divided into 14 stanzas[30] incorporates a number of different poetic meters and rhyme schemes and many different musical lines in which the poetry and the melody are interwoven in complex ways. The first stanza illustrates this:

(1) Plánctus ánte néscia (2) plánctu lássor ánxia (3) crúcior dolóre. (4) Órbat órbem rádio (5) mé Judéa fílio (6) grándi dulcóre.

The music for lines (1) and (4) is identical, as is the music for lines (2) and (5). The music for (1) and (4) differs from that for (2) and (5) only in the last syllable. The music for (3) and (6) is identical, but differs from the music for (1) and (4), and (2) and (5).

The third stanza has the same rhyme scheme (a, a, b) but a different poetic rhythm and musical melody:

(15) Flos flórum, (16) dux mórum, / (17a) vénie (17b) véna
(18) Quam grávis, (19) in clávis, / (20a) ést tibi (20b) péna
(21) Proh dólor, (22) hinc cólor, (23a) éffugit (23b) óris
(24) Hinc rúit, (25) hinc flúit, (26a) únda cru(26b)óris

The meter for all four lines is the same. The music for all four lines is also identical except for the final two syllables. (17), (20), (23) and

---

29 P. Dronke, *The Medieval Lyric*, 2nd ed. (New York: Cambridge University Press, 1977), 62–63. Whatever its limitations, the *Stabat mater dolorosa* has been set to music hundreds of times and sung or heard by millions.

30 Gennrich has 121 lines, but he has no line 101. I have corrected this by renumbering the last 20 lines.

(26) begin the same, but the final two syllables of (17) and (23) are paired, and differ from the final two syllables of (23) and (26), which are also paired.

The final stanza of the lament, in which Mary addresses the Daughters of Sion, is written such a way that the final two lines are set off as a conclusion, which states the invitation implicit throughout the *plantus*.

> (117a) Ín hoc sólo (117b) gáudeo (118a) quód pro vóbis (118b) dóleo.
> (119) Vícem quéso réddite. (120) Mátris dámpnum plángite.

The poetic rhythm of the (117) – (118) is parallel to that of (119) – (120). Musically, however, (117a) and (118a) are identical, but (117b) and (118b) are not. (119) and (120) are identical neither which each other or with (117) and (118).

A second notable difference is that, whereas the *Stabat mater dolorosa* is written from the standpoint of the devout reader, who describes what he sees and entreats Mary to let him share in her sufferings, Godfrey, as we have seen, writes from Mary's standpoint: he describes what she experiences at the cross and says to Jesus, Death and the Jews. Whereas at the end of the *Stabat mater dolorosa* the narrator asks Mary to be his defense on judgment day, at the end of Godfrey's hymn Mary asks the Daughters of Sion to grieve for her loss as she grieves for theirs.

Third, although like the *Stabat mater dolorosa* Godfrey's poem is an invitation to feel compassion for Mary and to share in her compassion for her Son, Mary describes details of passion as she sees and experiences them. Godfrey seeks to impress memories[31] and to stir up meditation in a reader (or rather a performer and listener, since his *planctus* is a hymn) by words and by images (Christ's wounds as springs dug in his body which slake thirst and wash away sin; Christ as healing medicine; the contrast between the brutal hand of the one crucifying Jesus and Jesus own gentleness in pain). He also includes enigmatic statements that cause a reader to think and question: In what sense is Mary, mother and woman, both so happy and so miserable? Is the "flower of flowers" Christ (the bud sprung from the shoot growing from the stump of Jesse) or is it the cross; and if it is Christ, how is the penalty nailed to him? What does it mean to say that love made his body booty?

---

[31]   R. Fulton, *From Judgment to Passion*, 254–65.

GODFREY AND TWELFTH-CENTURY MARIAN DEVOTION

Godfrey lived during a century that saw the emergence of new kinds of devotion to Mary. The feasts of her nativity and assumption into heaven celebrated events that were matters of devotion, events that were not discussed in the Scripture, which provided a challenge for preachers. These readings and antiphons for these feasts drew heavily on the Song of Songs. During the twelfth century, Honorius Augustodunensis, Rupert of Deutz, Philip of Harvengt, and William of Newburgh produced the first commentaries on the Song of Songs in which Mary was identified as the bride.[32] Preachers like the Victorines pondered the text and antiphons, producing works such as Hugh of St Victor's *Praise of the Bridegroom*,[33] which applies one of the antiphons for the Feast of the Assumption to the union of the soul with the God who loves her in an unconditional and singular way, and the Marian sermons and poetic hymns produced in this volume. In the latter Mary was imagined as a real person in the drama[34] of bringing the Word and Son of God to birth in the world, a story of nursing, nurture and love leading to the cross where Christ looked compassionately on Mary who looked compassionately upon him, her heart pierced with a sword of love. Godfrey's sermon and poems, too intense not to reflect his own devotional immersion in the story and images he presents, invite the reader to enter into the story, to give birth to the Word, to be compassionate toward Christ, Mary and all who suffer, to incorporate themselves "into history, specifically into that history narrated in the text of Scripture, a history, as Augustine would have it, of love told with love, longing adapted to the understanding of the beloved."[35] With Mary one enters into

> the mystery of a love so absolutely complete that was nothing beyond it, nothing of body or spirit, humanity or divinity, creation or generation, in which it did not participate. It was a love that was itself the very perfection of empathy beyond the experience of the meditant who might know Christ only through contemplation, beyond the experience of the communicant who might know Christ in body only through bread, beyond the experience of the flagellant who might know Christ only in pain. For, after all, . . . Mary had known—and still knew—

---

[32]   Fulton, *From Judgment to Passion*, 244–404.
[33]   PL 177:987–94; tr. Feiss, VTT 2.113–36.
[34]   Fulton, *From Judgment to Passion*, 265–80.
[35]   Fulton, *From Judgment to Passion*, 465.

Christ in all of these ways, with this difference: she alone knew what it had been to carry God in her womb.[36]

Godfrey invites those who hear or listen to his words and music to impress upon their memories images of this great love, as it was expressed and experienced by Mary, so that in their bodily lives they might express and experience it also, and respond as Mary did offering to God a Song of praise and love.[37]

---

[36] Fulton, *From Judgment to Passion*, 464.

[37] Fulton, *From Judgment to Passion*, 170–92, sees this as a key idea of Anselm of Canterbury's Christology: Christ gave Himself as the only recompense human beings could give to God for their sins; those who are in Christ can only impress the memory of what He did for them on their memories and offer Him love and praise. Anselm, addressing Mary standing in agony under the cross, said the same of the Christian's debt to Mary: "Mary, how much we owe you, Mother and Lady, by whom we have such a brother! What thanks and praise can we return to you?" (*Oratio 7*, Schmitt, *Opera* 3:24: tr. B. Ward, *Prayers and Meditations of Saint Anselm* [Baltimore: Penguin, 1973] 124, cited by Fulton, *From Judgment to Passion*, 192). Godfrey's emphasis on grace in the sermon on the Nativity of Mary makes the same point (tr. Feiss, VTT 4.491–504).

THE CANTICLE OF THE BLESSED VIRGIN AND MOTHER
EXPANDED BY GODFREY'S EFFORT

1   My soul exalts the Lord,[1]
one in godhead, three in names,[2]
for He gives joy to the sons of men,
the rush of a river from the spring of rivers.

2   My spirit exults[3]
in the Father's Only-begotten Who is my salvation—[4]
mine in a singular way since He comes to be from me—
because I see that in Him salvation has arisen for the Gentile.

3   Ah! Daughters of Sion,[5] my intimates,
my fellow servants, betrothed with me,[6]
sing spiritual songs with me to the spouse.
As I lead, sing with me similar melodies.[7]

4   The Creator, seeing humankind under the ancient penalty
long ago worn down by the demon,
rises up ready to act mercifully and mightily
to fight the enemy on behalf of humanity.[8]

5   An amazing mode of saving the one in misery:
immutable power wishes to become a human being.
The Lord sees the humility of His handmaid,[9]
from me the Mightiest takes up weakness.

6   He comforts humankind through a human being,
He comes to the aid of a virgin through a virgin.[10]
He is born a human being for humanity; the virgin gives birth
on her own account.[11]
Whatever He is going to do, nothing is queried of God.[12]

7   He fights in the fighter for the fighter;
He struggles with the demons for humankind.
The old plunder is taken away; the plunderer falls vanquished.
The captor is captured; the captive escapes.

8   Through me salvation from the sea of the world,[13]
through me the apple tree lacks evil,[14]
and becomes a seeding for good.
For this reason every generation

will call me a woman blessed,[15]
created on their behalf.

9   He who could did the great things He wanted.
His holy name[16] that lay hidden He made known to all nations.
His mercies and his graces are
from generation to generation to those who fear Him.[17]

10   With his outstretched hand[18] he did powerful things[19];
In the powerful little one he shattered pride.

11   One by one He scattered[20] unbelieving Jews,
lying[21] Pharisees, to the ends of the world.

12   Those exalted in ruling, lofty in teaching,
He brought down to earth and removed from office.

13   The king of humility exalted the humble,[22]
and sated the hungry with bread,
the bread of fullness and satiety,[23]
and gratis He filled the empty with the good things of life.

14   He sent away the rich[24] whose tables were full;
their elegant luncheons and exquisite dinners
now are made disgusting and destitute
because they did not do good to beggars.

15   He remembered as faithful
his servant Israel,[25]
And when, at Gabriel's word,
He sent His Son down from heaven,
He raised him in glory

He fulfilled what had been revealed
to the fathers through the mouths of the prophets,
the blessed seed of Abraham[26]
from which comes the baby I bear,
to whom be glory through the ages.

THE PLAINT OF BLESSED MARY, VIRGIN AND MOTHER, ON THE PASSION OF HER SON

I.   I, who before knew no lament,[27]
Am troubled, wearied with lament;
tormented with sorrow.
Judea deprives the world of its light,
5   and me of my sweet
Son of joy.

II.   My Son, unique sweetness,
singular joy,
look on your weeping mother,
10   give her solace.
Your wounds torment
my breast, mind and eyes,
What mother and woman,
so happy and so miserable?[28]

III.   Flower of flowers,
moral guide,
channel of forgiveness,
How heavy to you
is the penalty
20   in the nails![29]
Alas, the sorrow;[30]
hence color
drained from your mouth.[31]
Hence a wave
25   of blood rushes,
hence it flows.

IV.   O how lately given,
how quickly you leave me!
O how worthily born,
30   how meanly you die!
O what love
made spoils of your body?[32]
O how bitter the recompense
of the sweet pledge!

V.   O the loving
grace
of the one dying thus!
O the zeal,[33]

O the crime,
40   of the envious people!
O the fierce
right hand
of the crucifier!
O gentle
45   amid its pains
the mind of the one suffering!

VI.   O the true word
of just Simeon;
of the sword he promised
50   I feel the pain!
Moans, sighs,
and tears outside
are tokens of an
interior wound.

VII.   Death, spare my Son,
not me;
Only you[34] can
heal me only,
Blessed one, let death
60   separate me from you[35]
if only you, my Child,
are not crucified.

VIII.   What a crime, what atrocities,
a savage race has committed!
65   Without fault he suffers
chains, rods, wounds,
spittings, thorns, and the rest.
Please spare my son;
crucify his mother,
70   or nail us to the tree
of the cross together;
it is terrible that he die alone.

IX.   Most sorrowfully return
his body, even if lifeless,
75   so that the crucified one,
so shrunken, may grow
by kisses and embraces.
Would that I might so grieve
that I perish from grief,

80		for to die without dying
		is a worse sorrow
		than perishing quickly.
	X.	Why are you stunned, O wretched race,[36]
		that the earth moves,
85		the stars are clouded over,
		the sick mourn?[37]
		You deprive the sun of the light.
		How would it shine?
		You deprive the sick of the medicine.
90		How would he get well?[38]
	XI.	You free the homicide.
		You hand Jesus over to punishment.[39]
		Wickedly you maintain peace.
		Discord will come.[40]
95		Taught by the weight of hunger, massacre,
		and plagues, you will know
		that Jesus died for you,
		and that Barabbas lives.
	XII.	Blind race, doleful race,
100		do penance
		when Jesus bends
		to pardon you.
		May the streams of the springs
		that you dug[41] profit you.
105		They slake the thirst of all,
		and they wash away all sins.
	XIII.	Weep daughters of Sion,[42]
		grateful for such great grace.
		The Young Man's sufferings
110		for your sins
		are delights to him.
		Rush to his embrace
		while he hangs on the tree.
		By stretching out his arms
115		He prepared himself for mutual embraces
		with those who love him.
	XIV.	In this alone do I rejoice,
		that for you[43] I grieve.
		Please, return the favor;
120		weep for a mother's loss.

NOTES

1   Luke 1:46.

2   The use of "names" here could imply Trinitarian modalism, where "Father," "Son," and "Spirit" are just different names of the same divine person, but that is surely not Godfrey's intention. In the *Fountain of Philosophy* 785–804 (Michaud-Quantin, 62–63; tr. Feiss, VTT 3.414–15 with n. 121), Godfrey mentions that he could not fathom the theology of the Trinity and so turned his attention to Christology.

3   Luke 1:47a.

4   Luke 1:47b.

5   The phrase "Daughter(s) of Sion" is quite common in the Scriptures: e.g., Ps. 9:15 (Vulg.); Song of Songs 3:11; Isa. 1.8 (and often); Lam. 1:6 (and often); Zeph. 3:14; Zech 2:10; Matt. 21:5; Luke 23:28; John 12:15. The Song of Songs most often uses the equivalent "Daughters of Jerusalem." Cf. Luke 23:28 which may have been Godfrey's inspiration here.

6   In the first two lines of this stanza, Godfrey adds the prefix "co(n)-" to several words in a way reminiscent of Paul's use of "syn-" ("with") compounds; cf. Dunn, *The Theology of Paul*, 401–404.

7   These lines reflect Godfrey's interest in music: "mecum sponso canite cantus spiritales. Precino. Succinite. modulos equales." They are also self-referential: Godfrey has set these lines to music, and he invites the reader to sing with him. The prefix in "pre-cino" suggests a leader in singing; the prefix (sub) in "suc-cinite" connotes "with." It might be that "equales modulos" means parallel organum, where two voices sang the same melody at an interval of a fourth or fifth. As Gasparri observes ("Godefroid de Saint-Victor," 58), in the first of his self-portraits in Paris, Mazarine 1002, Godfrey inscribes, "aspicio cantans, aspiciensque cano" ("singing/proclaiming I gaze, gazing I proclaim/sing"), a self-description that suggests both a preacher and a musician. The second self-portrait, at the beginning of the *Fountain of Philosophy* in the same manuscript, describes the form that Godfrey's teaching took: "prosaice, rythmice, metrice, melice," adverbs that suggest a range of compositions: in prose ("prosaice," but "prosa" also means "sequence"); in rhythmic poetry ("rythmice:" in by contrast to the metered poetry of classical Latin); in verse ("metrice")"; in song, ("melice"; "melificare" means "to write in verse, compose a song").

8   This is an example of "Christus victor" Christology, in which Christ is viewed as a warrior or knight fighting against the devil on behalf of humanity. The violence of the metaphor is softened by "misericorditer."

9   Luke 1:48a.

10   In stanza 5 Godfrey wrote that the Creator wished to become a human being ("homo fieri"). Here he writes "consulit homini per hominem, subvenit virgini per virginem." In the first phrase the ambiguity of "homo" is in play: he became a "human being" on behalf of "humankind" or on behalf of "a human being." The phrase "he comes to the aid of a virgin through a virgin" evokes ancient theme of the Virgin Mary undoing the damage that the Virgin Eve did. See Irenaeus, *Adv. haer.* III.22 (PG 7:959C–960A; tr. R. Grant, *Irenaeus of Lyons*, The Early Church Fathers [New York: Routledge, 1997], 141). In Genesis 3, the account of the Fall precedes the statement, *The man had relations with his wife Eve, and she conceived and bore Cain* (Gen. 4:1).

11   "homo sibi nascitur, virgo sibi parit": The idea seems to be that human being is born on behalf of humanity; a virgin (Mary) gives birth on behalf of a virgin (Eve).

12   It is not strictly true that Mary did not question God (Luke 1:34). Godfrey's point is probably that Mary raises no objections to whatever God is going to do.

13   Although this unit does not begin with a capital letter, the rhyme scheme seems to require that it begin a new sentence.

14   "malus": malus (fem.) means "apple tree." This play on words (malo = evil) refers to Gen. 3, though there the word for tree is "lignum" and the kind of "fructus" is not specified.

15 Luke 1:48b.

16 Luke 1:49.

17 Luke 1:50.

18 In Luke 1:51 the phrase is "in brachio suo." Godfrey has "extenso brachio," a phrase used to evoke God's power in the Old Testament; e.g., Deut. 4:34, 5:15; 7:1; 11:2; Jer. 27:2; 32:17, 21; Ezek. 20:33, 35. The same adjective, "extensus," occurs in the title where it is translated "expanded."

19 Luke 1:51a.

20 "dispersit": he scattered; Luke 1:51b.

21 "pseudolus": liar, the title of a play by Plautus.

22 Luke 1:52.

23 Luke 1:53.

24 Luke 1:53.

25 Luke 1:54.

26 Luke 1:55.

27 "planctus": lament, complaint from "plangere" to beat, wring one's hands, lament.

28 This is a very ambiguous sentence in Latin. At first glance "your" seems to modify "eyes," but it seems to fit better with "wounds." The second half does not seem to be closely connected to the first half grammatically.

29 Reading "in clavis" with Gennrich, in place of "inclavis" in Gasparri.

30 "Pro dolor": Since "dolor" is in the nominative, "pro" must be an exclamation of lamentation (commonly spelled "proh"), not the preposition. Gennich has "proh"; Gasparri has "pro," as is found in the manuscript.

31 I take this clause to mean that "color drained from your mouth," i.e., you turned deathly pale; it could mean blood flowed from Christ's mouth and thus parallel the next line in meaning as well as structure (see the Latin text in the introduction).

32 Gasparri correctly transcribes "O quis amor corporis / tibi fecit spolia," which is difficult to translate and interpret. The translation takes "quis," which ordinarily is an interrogative pronoun, as an interrogative adjective and construes "tibi" as a dative of reference with adjectival force ("the body which is for you"). The idea seems to be that Christ's love for humankind prompted him to allow himself to be become spoils for his enemy, the devil, whose unjust instigation of Jesus' death cost the devil whatever dominion he had over humankind.

33 "zelus": zeal or envy. It seems to refer forward to the "envious people." Gennrich reads "relus," which may indicate confusion of the Gothic "r" for the "z" in Paris, Mazarine 1002, fol. 235v.

34 In place of Gasparri's "tu," Gennrich has "tunc" (then), perhaps because the bottom-stroke of the superscripted musical note was taken as an abbreviation siglum.

35 "beate": one could translate this as a adverb, "blessedly" instead of as a vocative. Gennrich has "separer a te" instead of Gasparri's "separet a te," and that is how I have translated it.

36 This could refer to Jews (cf. line 24, "envious people") or to the human race as a whole or to the Jewish people as representative of the human race in its wickedness. In *The Fountain of Philosophy*, lines 537–48 (tr. Feiss, VTT 3.406–407), Godfrey has a remarkable passage about the continuities and connections between the two peoples, Jews and Christians.

37 Matt. 27:51; Luke 23:44–45.

38 Christ performed a number of healing miracles in which he cured sick people of diseases. By the Middle Ages the idea of Christ the Physician ("medicus") and medicine was a commonplace of Christian thinking. See, e.g., Ignatius of Antioch, *Eph.* 7.2 (K. Lake, Loeb 24 [1977], 1.180–81); Walter of St Victor, *Sermo* 13.5 (Châtillon, 136.112); *Sermo* 14.8 (Châtillon, 128.202); *Sermo* 16.1 (Châtillon, 136.21–22); *Sermo* 16.2 (Châtillon, 137.42–43). See also D. Knipp, *'Christus Medicus' in der frühchristlichen Sarkophagskulptur*, Vigiliae Christianae, Supplements, 37 (Leiden: Brill, 1998).

39 Mark 15:7–15.

40 The reference here is probably to the peace that was forged between Pilate and Herod at the

time of Christ's trial (Luke 23:13), or perhaps to Caiaphas' declaration that it was expedient that one man die for the people (John 11:49–50; 18:14).

[41]   A reference to the wounds inflicted on Jesus' hands, feet and side.

[42]   As transcribed by Gasparri, the next lines are extremely difficult to translate:

> Flete Syon filie. / tante grate gratie. / *invenis* [Gennrich:
> *munere*] angustie / sibi sunt delicie /
> pro vestris offensis.
> In amplexus ruite / dum pendet in stipite. / Mutuis
> amplexibus / *separat* amantibus. /
> brachiis protensis.

Godfrey's manuscript (Paris, Mazrine 1002, fol. 237r) clearly reads "iuvenis," not "invenis." It may seem unusual to refer to Christ as "iuvenis" (a person between the ages of about 17 and 45), but that is what he was, and in IV.27–28 Mary indicated as much when she exclaimed, "O how lately given, how quickly you leave me!" R. Pepin called my attention to a reference to Christ as a "juvenem pulcherrimum" in the twelfth-century life of Hamo of Savigny, *Vita B. Hamonis Saviniacensis* 8 (ed. E. P. Sauvage, *Analecta Bollandiana* 2 [1883], 512). Moreover, for Gasparri's "separat," Gennrich has "parat se," and Paris, Maz. 1002, fol. 237r has "se parat." I have followed the manuscript's reading. Gasparri's reading might yield something like "He parts his arms, stretched out for mutual embraces."

[43]   "vobis": plural "you."

WALTER OF ST VICTOR

SERMON 6:
ON THE FEAST
OF THE PURIFICATION

INTRODUCTION
BY HUGH FEISS OSB

TRANSLATION
BY VANESSA BUTTERFIELD

INTRODUCTION

WALTER OF ST VICTOR AND HIS WORKS

According to John of Thoulouse, a canon of St Victor (d. 1659), Walter of St Victor was from England. He entered St Victor during the abbacy of Gilduin (1114–1155). He served as subprior for at least some of the time Richard was prior (1162–1173), and became prior at Richard's death. Walter died August 20 probably in 1179 or 1180.[1]

Against the Four Labyrinths of France

Among modern scholars, there are two reasons why Walter has a rather bad reputation. The first of these is a work he wrote, but did not circulate, called *Against the Four Labyrinths of France* (*Contra quatuor labyrinthos franciae*). In the estimate of its editor, P. Glorieux, Walter's work was a bad act that produced a bad book.[2] In it Walter attacks stridently what he regards as the heretical teachings of Peter Abelard, Peter Lombard, Peter of Poitiers, and Gilbert of Poitiers. Glorieux faults both the hostile spirit in which the book was written and its execution, which lacks originality, logical rigor, and fair evidence. The other reason for the low esteem in which Walter is held is P. Delhaye's conjecture that hostility from Walter led to Godfrey of St Victor's being sent away

---

[1] Châtillon, *Sermones inediti* (CCCM 30.3). R. Berndt gives the same biographical markers in his article on Walter in the *Lexikon des Mittelalters* (Stuttgart: J. B. Metzler, 1999), 8:2000–2001.

[2] P. Glorieux, "Le *Contra quatuor labyrinthos Franciae* de Gauthier de Saint-Victor," *AHDLMA* 19 (1953): 187–95 (introduction), 195–335 (text); P. Glorieux, "Mauvaise action et mauvais travail: Le *Contra quautor labyrinthos Franciae*," *RTAM* 21 (1954): 179–93. Châtillon refers also to J. de Ghellinck, *Le mouvement théologique du XIIᵉ siècle*," 2ⁿᵈ ed. (Bruges: Éditions "De Tempel," 1948), 260–63. Glorieux believes Walter either acted in bad faith or was very stupid; he suggests he was blinded by animosity ("Mauvaise action," 183–84). It is hard not to see in these hard judgments on Walter a reflection of the author's concern about twentieth-century "intégristes" (see Glorieux, "Mauvaise action," 182). It should be noted that like the works of Godfrey of St Victor Walter's *Contra quatuor labyrinthos Franciae* scarcely circulated beyond the walls of St Victor and perhaps not even within them (Glorieux, "Mauvaise action," 182–83). On the subject of Christ's knowledge, Walter and Godfrey do not seem to have been far apart; see H. Santiago-Otero, "Gaulterio y Godofredo de San Victor; su tesis acerca del conocimiento de Cristo hombre," *Divinitas* 18 (1974): 168–79.

from St Victor for a prolonged period, during which, happily, he found time to write his *Microcosmus*.[3] Delhaye offers two reasons for his conjecture. First, he cites Walter's denunciation, derived from Jerome, of those who wish to drink the cup of Christ and the cup of demons, that is, mix Christian learning and the learning of unbelievers. This could be a reference to the prefatory letter to Abbot Stephen of Sainte-Geneviève that Godfrey attached at the beginning of his *Fons philosophiae*. Secondly, Walter denounces Seneca as a particularly pernicious pagan philosopher, whereas Godfrey praises him highly.[4] Delhaye may be correct in seeing a conflict between Godfrey and Walter, who wrote at almost the same time (in the late 1170s) and place, but it is a stretch to conjecture that Walter had a part in exiling Godfrey from St Victor. There are many other possible reasons why Godfrey may have ended up away from St Victor, perhaps at a dependent priory of the abbey.[5]

[3] Delhaye, *Le* Microcosmus *de Godefroy de Saint-Victor*, 30–32, 243–51.

[4] For Seneca, see Godfrey of St Victor, *Fons* (tr. Feiss, VTT 3.402–403.410–412; 420–21 n. 57). On the mixed cup, see Godfrey, *Fons philosophiae, Epistola . . . ad abbaem sancta Genevese* 6–10 (Michaud-Quantin, 33; tr. Feiss, VTT 3.389): "Calicem plenum mixto . . . detinavi . . . Continet autem mixtum dupplicter, vel materie scilicet, vel artificii varietate" ("I am sending you a mixed drink . . . It contains a twofold mixture by the variety of its content and its style"). Compare this with Walter's statement in the *Contra quat.* (Glorieux, 273): "Unde et ieronymus: que pars fideli cum infideli? 'Que coniunctio lucis ad tenebras? Qui consensus christo ad belial? Quid faciet cum psalterio oratius, cum evangeliis maro, cum apostolis cicero. Non scandalizatur frater si te viderit in idolio recumbentem? Et licet omnia sunt munda mundis et nichil reiciendum quod cum gratiarum actione percipitur, tamen simul bibere non debemus calicem Christi et calicem demoniorum'" ("Hence, Jerome wrote: What share does the believer have with the unbeliever? 'What connection does light have with darkness? What agreement is there between Christ and Belial [2 Cor. 6:14]? What will Horace do with the Psalter, Virgil with the Gospels, Cicero with the apostles? Is not your brother scandalized if he sees you reclining at an idol [1 Cor. 8:10]? And although all things are clean to the clean [Titus 1:15] and nothing is to be rejected that is received with thanksgiving [1 Tim. 4:4], still we must not drink both the chalice of Christ and the chalice of the demons' [1 Cor. 10:21])." [*Letter* 22, To Eustochium, *Select Letters of St. Jerome*, tr. F. A. Wright, Loeb Classical Library (Cambridge, MA: Harvard University Press, 1975), 124–25]. See also K.-D. Nothdurft, *Studien zum Einfluss Senecas auf die Philosophie und Theologie des zwölften Jahrhunderts*, Studien und Texte zur Geistesgeschichte des Mittelalters 7 (Leiden: Brill, 1963), 44, 71 (Godfrey), 78–80 (Walter).

[5] Godfrey was not the only Victorine who was unhappy with being assigned away from the abbey. In a letter to Abbot Ernisius, Jonas, a canon of St Victor and a miserable exile (*miser exsul ac peregrinus*) in a region of unlikeness (*regione dissimilitudinis*), begged to return to the Abbey from the Victorine house in Cherbourg (PL 196.1388BD).

Sermons

The sermons of Walter of St Victor show him in a strikingly different light. Scholars have identified twenty-one sermons that can be firmly attributed to him, and six others may well be his.[6] Although some scholars see the same harshness in his sermons that they find in the *Against the Four Labyrinths of France*, Châtillon's judgment, based on his edition, is that this is unfair to Walter. In them Walter draws on the writings and ideas of Hugh, Richard and Achard, and on other theologians of his time, including the *Sententiae* and *Collectanea in epistolas Pauli* of Peter Lombard, who is the primary object of his criticism in the *Against the Four Labyrinths of France*.

Walter several times downplays his oratorical ability; his disclaimers seem to be sincere, more than just a perfunctory nod to humility.[7] In fact, however, he was a skilled preacher. Châtillon concludes his appraisal of Walter's preaching thus:

> His language and style lack neither warmth nor elegance; his exegesis remains sober; and if he sometimes raises his voice a little . . . he is primarily concerned to provide his brothers with a spiritual teaching, nourished by theology and constantly based on Scripture, whose quality no one can deny.[8]

It should be noted that most of Walter's sermons were preached on important feast days, presumably at a community Mass or in the chapter room. The occasions for the twenty-one sermons firmly ascribed to him are these:

Sermon 21: Advent
Sermon 12: Christmas[9]
Sermons 4, 7, and 18: Epiphany
Sermons 5 and 6: Purification
Sermon 1: Palm Sunday

---

[6] Châtillon, *Sermones inediti* (CCCM 30.5–8).

[7] *Serm.* 2.1 (Châtillon, 19.10–11); *Serm.* 12.1 (Châtillon, 104.4–25); *Serm.* 15.1 (Châtillon, 129.12–14).

[8] *Sermones inediti* (CCCM 30.10): "Sa langue et son style ne manquent ni de chaleur ni d'élégance, son exégèse reste sobre, et s'il lui arrive parfois d'élever un peu la voix, comme on le lui a si sévèrement reproché, il reste avant tout préoccupé de procurer à ses frères un enseignement spirituel, nourri de théologie et constamment fondé sur l'Écriture, dont on ne peut contester la qualité."

[9] In *Serm.*15.2 (Châtillon, 130.30–32) Walter lists the six special solemnities of the Savior: Annunciation, Christmas, Circumcision, Epiphany, Easter, and Ascension. He evidently considered the Purification a feast of Mary.

Sermons 2 and 9: Easter
Sermons 15 and 16: Ascension
Sermons 3 and 8: Pentecost
Sermon 10 and probably 13: Assumption[10]
Sermon 14: Nativity of Mary
Sermon 11 and 19: All Saints
Sermons 17 and 20: Common Sermons

These same feasts were the occasion for many of Richard of St Victor's *Sermones centum* and the thirty-two surviving sermons of Godfrey of St Victor.[11] Delivering these sermons seems to have been part of Walter's duties as a major official of the abbey.

The contrast between the Walter of the *Against the Four Labyrinths of France* and the Walter of the sermons may perhaps be explained by the difference in genre and by his age. If as John of Thoulouse reports, Walter joined St Victor under Abbot Guilduin, it is quite possible that Walter was an old man when he wrote out his criticisms of the four theologians. If he entered as a young man in 1120, he was in his seventies by the time he wrote down those notes. He could have been tired, sick, even mentally troubled. On the other hand, if he entered in 1150 as a young man, he would have been only fifty and presumably at the height of his powers. However, since he served as subprior between 1162 and 1173 an earlier entry into the abbey seems likely. A second reason for the contrast is that Walter's criticism of the four labyrinthine theologians occurred in private notes; they never circulated, and he never finished his text. Did he die first; have a stroke; lose interest; calm down? We don't know. As a counter narrative to Delhaye's speculations on Walter's role in Godfrey's exile, we might think of Godfrey, in his role as *armarius* (sacrist and archivist), collecting the recently deceased Walter's parchments and preserving them in the archives as an act of duty, fraternity or even reconciliation.

---

[10]   See Châtillon, *Sermones inediti* (CCCM 30.115 n. 1).

[11]   P. Delhaye, "Les sermons de Godefroy de Saint-Victor," *RTAM* 21 (1954): 194–210. See also Godfrey of St Victor, *Sermon on the Nativity of the Blessed Virgin* (tr. Feiss, VTT 4.531–50). That Godfrey preached on these important feasts makes one wonder if he did not hold an office that required him to preach on important feasts. He is known to have been *armarius* (archivist and sacrist), but did that include preaching duties? Perhaps, during the time he was assigned away from the abbey, Godfrey preached his sermons to his fellow canons regular at a dependent priory. However, one of his sermons is to a general chapter, so it must have been preached where the general chapter was held.

SERMON 6: ON THE FEAST OF THE PURIFICATION

A Three-Dimensional Feast

Walter preached this sermon on a feast with a complex history. Right at the beginning he recognizes that the feast has different names that emphasize different aspects of the events being recalled. It is the feast of Mary's purification and of the presentation of her first-born son to the Lord.[12] It is also the Feast of Candlemas ("Chandeleur" in medieval France). Candles were blessed on this day and carried in the procession to recall that Christ is, as Simeon declared in the gospel of the feast, "the light of revelation to the nations and the glory of your people Israel."[13] Walter frames his sermon around the three clauses of Luke 12:35–36: *Let your loins be girded, and your lamps burning, and be like men awaiting their Lord.* Walter ties these words to the idea of a three-stage procession or progression, from purification, through enlightenment, to union or meeting. Richard of St Victor laid out the same three-step progression in his *Super exiit edictum* or *The Three Processions.*[14] In his treatise Richard goes on to speak of two more liturgical processions (Palm Sunday = progress; Ascension = contemplation or perfection).[15] Referring to the third name for the feast, Walter describes goal of Christian progress as the meeting (*ypapanti*) of the purified and enlightened Christian with his Lord.

Outline

(A) Introduction

  (1) The Text: "Let your loins be girded, / and your lamps be burning, / and be like men awaiting their master" (Luke 12:35–36).
  (2) Purification, Candlemas, Ypapanti = purgation, enlightenment, meeting or perfection. (Par. 1)

---

[12] Luke 2:21–23. On the Old Testament background for these two themes, see L. T. Johnson, *The Gospel of Luke*, Sacra Pagina 3 (Collegeville, Minn.: Liturgical Press, 1991), 54.

[13] Luke 2:32.

[14] J. Châtillon and W.-J. Tulloch, eds., *Richard de Saint-Victor, Sermons et opuscules spirituels inédits*. Vol. 1: *L'édit d'Alexandre ou Les Trois Processions*, tr. J. Barthélemy (n. pl.: Desclée De Brouwer, 1951).

[15] Châtillon, *L'édit*, l–lxxix.

(B) Let your loins be girded: Be free of all stain of the flesh and spirit.

(1) Of the flesh.
    (a) Lust (Par. 2)
    (b) Pollution of the eyes,[16] ears and lips (Par. 3)

(2) Of the spirit (Par. 4)
    (a) Anger
    (b) Desire
    (c) Reason
    (d) Confession

(C) Let your lamps be burning.

(1) Heat and light: love and knowledge (Par. 5)
(2) Wax, wick, and light: Christ's body, soul and divinity in Simeon's arms (Par. 6)

(D) Be like men awaiting their master: desire for the Lord (fear) Jesus (mercy) (Par. 7).
(E) Recapitulation: Avoid evil, do good, seek eternal life (Par. 8).
(F) Purified, illuminated, and perfected by grace, one is able to purify, illuminate and perfect others (Par. 9).

Procession: Purification, Advance, Perfection

Walter's schema for the Christian life is drawn from Pseudo-Dionysius, whose *Celestial Hierarchy* he quotes in Latin translation in par. 9.[17] This is itself significant. Walter is evidence that the study of Pseudo-Dionysius begun by Hugh of St Victor continued at the abbey; it would reach its apogee in the work of Thomas Gallus in the early thirteenth century.[18]

---

[16] In *Serm.* 12.6 (Châtillon, 108.153–109.160) Walter invokes Hugh of St Victor's theme of the three eyes. Cf. Hugh of St Victor, *In hier. cael.* 3 (PL 175.976A); *Sacr.* I.10.2 (Berndt, 225; PL 176.329C–330A; tr. Deferrari, 167).

[17] In *Serm.* 18.10–13 (Châtillon, 154.332–160.333) he mentions zeal for prayer, reading, and meditation, which formed part of a common Victorine mapping of the spiritual life. On that scheme, see Feiss, VTT 2.87, 308–309 n. 2, 333.

[18] At the initiative of Cardinal Gaula Bicchieri, Thomas Gallus (d. 1246) was sent from St Victor to Vercelli in 1219 to begin a new Victorine monastery there. He wrote many works on the Bible and on Pseudo-Dionysius. For biography and bibliography see http://:en.wikipedia.org/wiki/Thomas_Gallus, and *Mystical Theology: The Glosses by Thomas Gallus and the Commentary of Robert Grosseteste on De Mystica Theologia*, ed. and tr. McEvoy, Dallas Medieval Texts and Translations 3 (Leuven: Peeters, 2003).

Walter begins with purification from lust, a vice that touches both body and soul. Avoidance, asceticism, and fear of hell are ways to ward off sexual temptations. We should avoid listening to worldly, empty, griping, harmful and slanderous talk, and we should also avoid speaking in those ways.

Turning to the purification of the interior life, Walter invokes the tripartite soul of Plato, endowed with the virtues or capabilities of anger, desire and reason, each of which can be exercised in good or bad ways. It is noteworthy that he uses anger and desire (*concupiscentia*) in positive and well as negative ways. Reason must regulate and direct the other two impulses; reason should see that they are ordered and moderated, though Walter does not invoke that definition of virtue found often in Victorine authors.[19] Using a Pseudo-Dionysian term, Walter speaks of grace as an originating or principal (*principalis*) purification, that is, the efforts of asceticism and rational control are rooted in grace.

Purification must precede illumination. In the second stage, light and heat, faith and love, knowledge of truth and love of virtue grow and work hand in hand.[20] Knowing is inseparable from experience, which brings savory knowledge, and both kinds of knowledge are required of teachers. Illumination comes to those who desire to see the face of God, who pray, "Come, Lord Jesus." By referring to Christ as fearful and merciful and to Christ's three "substances" signified by wax, wick, and light, Walter makes sure his audience does not lose sight of Christ. Elsewhere he says, "his life is our teaching, his action is our reading."[21]

The eschatological tension of the Christian journey is very pronounced in Walter's sermon. Although elsewhere he describes contemplation or mystical union with Christ,[22] in this sermon he is content to state that perfection follows illumination.

At the end of his sermon, Walter takes the same turn that Richard did at the end of the *Four Degrees of Violent Love*[23] and Achard at the

---

[19] See, e.g., Hugh of St Victor, *Subst. dilect.* 4–12 (tr. Butterfield, VTT 2.144–46); Feiss, VTT 2.54–55, 96–97, 309–11.

[20] On this pervasive theme in Victorine writings, see, e.g., Walter of St Victor, *Serm.* 11.9 (Châtillon, 101.291–98); *Serm.* 20.2 (Châtillon, 172.33–49); Feiss, VTT 2.83–84, 251–52.

[21] *Serm.* 15.4 (Châtillon, 131.80–82).

[22] *Serm.* 11.10 (Châtillon, 101.318–20): "The pure of heart, who are at peace with themselves, cling to God and become one Spirit with God;" *Serm.* 13.7 (Châtillon, 120.171–73): "Contemplation of heavenly wisdom and taste of interior sweetness fill the believer;" *Serm.* 4.10 (Châtillon, 39.208–212) and *Serm.* 15.1 (129.9–10): "spiritual inebriation."

[23] *Quat. grad.* 41–47 (Dumeige, 170–77; tr. Kraebel, VTT 2.293–306).

end of *Sermon 15*.[24] Using the language of Pseudo-Dionysius, he speaks of the canon regular's task—after he himself has been purified, illuminated and perfected—to purify, illumine and perfect others. However, that task is for this life only. Walter's final prayer is that God, the supreme illumination and perfection, may lead us, cleansed, illuminated, and perfected in every goodness, to the kingdom of light.

The Translation and Notes

This sermon is translated from the only printed edition ever made of it, in Jean Châtillon's *Galteri a Sancto Victore et quorumdam aliorum: Sermones inediti triginta sex*, CCCM 30 (Turnhout: Brepols, 1975). The translation reproduces most of the notes in Châtillon's edition and adds a few. He explained that the purpose of his notes was to indicate the sources of the biblical, liturgical and patristic citations and allusions. In some cases he also explained some theological terms and expressions and indicated similar ideas in other authors. Those are the aims of most of the notes to this translation as well, most of which are derived from Châtillon's edition. We have also added a few notes on Latin words in order to clarify the meaning or explain the translation. We are grateful to Christopher Evans, the editor of this volume, and to the editorial board of Victorine Texts in Translation for their help.

---

[24]   *Serm.* 15.35–37 (Châtillon, 239–42; tr. Feiss, 346–50).

SERMON 6: ON THE FEAST OF THE PURIFICATION

1. *Let your loins be girded, and your lamps be burning and be like men awaiting their master*, etc.[1] Today's festive solemnity is called by different names in three languages. In the Latin language it is called the Purification; in the French language the name has an association with candles,[2] and in Greek it is referred to as the Ypapanti of the Lord, that is, the meeting with the Lord.[3] These three names signify three degrees of virtues, three increments of spiritual progress, namely, purgation, enlightenment, and meeting or perfection,[4] as will be apparent in what follows. To these degrees of virtues the Lord's words with which I began can be beautifully adapted: *Let your loins be girded*, etc. To purification pertains *Let your loins be girded*; to enlightenment pertains *And your lamps be burning*; and to meeting pertains *And be like men awaiting their master*. Therefore in its names this solemnity warns us and exhorts us to say something on this solemnity, according to our small measure, about the aforesaid three virtues, namely, cleansing, enlightenment, and meeting.

2. *Let your loins be girded.*[5] By these words the Lord and Master teaches us what is especially necessary for us to celebrate the Feast of the Purification. What is it to celebrate the Feast of the Purification if not to rejoice about purification? Who is able to rejoice about purification unless he has been previously purified *from all stain of the flesh and the spirit*,[6] but especially from the stain of lust? In fact, among all impurities none is greater than this. Hence the Apostle declares: *Every [other] sin a man commits is outside of the body; however, he who fornicates sins against his own body.*[7] Other sins pollute the soul, but this sin also pollutes the body. Hence, it is proper to apply greater care and diligence to the cure of this sin. Nor should we wait until this impulse arises; rather, it is proper and useful to anticipate it. Aware of this, the Lord says: *Let your loins be girded.*[8] However, when it arises against us and begins to oppress us, then we should not only restrain its jaws with the bit and bridle of abstinence,[9] or even scourge it with the rod and staff of vigilance[10] and other heavenly disciplines, but also conquer it with the ax and hammer of divine fear,[11] saying with the Apostle, *Those who do such things will not possess the kingdom of God;*[12] and *practice*

holiness, without which no one will see God.[13] Indeed, all who have this hope, that is, of seeing God, make themselves holy just as he is holy, knowing that they cannot have union with the Holy without holiness.[14] However, as long as it sets before us a momentary and pleasurable delight, let us set against it eternal anguish, according to what has been written: In every time of your life *remember your end, and into eternity you will not sin.*[15] Nothing restrains the soul from consent to sin more than the recollection and recalling to mind of eternal punishment. Therefore, it is proper, as has been said, to be more zealous about curing this disease, for this part of our nature is weaker, more afflicted, and more infected by the serpent's venom. For this reason the enemy and persecutor of our race is said to have *strength in his loins.*[16] So how can his *strength* be *in his loins,*[17] unless because our infirmity is his strength? Accordingly, the seat of our particular infirmity is where his strength is said to dwell. Therefore, if we want to overcome this and destroy it completely, let us crucify every forbidden impulse and diseased desire, so that the enemy dies in this crucifixion.

3. After we have been purified from this pollution, it is certainly fitting that we be cleansed from the pollution of other members of the body,[18] especially the eyes, ears, and lips. We are defiled by the pollution of the eyes as often as death from inordinate carnal desire[19] has occasion from vanity to enter through the windows of our eyes.[20] Therefore, as often as the beauty of a woman or something else that usually punishes us with matter for sinning presents itself, we should not fix our eyes on it because fixing the eyes is an abomination to the Lord.[21] Instead we should avert them so they will *not see the vanity*[22] through which they may drink in death.

We are defiled from the pollution of the ears as often as we yield them to secular words, empty words, harmful and slanderous words; as often as we willingly listen to those words whose utterance *creeps like a malignant cancer,*[23] whose *discourses corrupt good habits.*[24] Its great pollution is indeed a corrupter of good habits. These are the people about whom the apostle John says, *They are of the world, and they speak about the world, and the world listens to them.*[25] These people *are of the world*; in fact, they are the world, that is, lovers of the world; and *they speak about the world*, that is, about mundane and empty things; and the *world*, that is lovers of the world, *listens to them.* Therefore, the world listens to the world speaking about the world, that is, vain people spinning vain tales about vanity. If, therefore, we do not want to be corrupted by the conversations of such people, if we want to preserve the integrity of good habits unharmed, let us flee such people as corrupters of the soul.

By all means we need to be cleansed from pollution of the lips. Death, which enters through the windows of the eyes and ears, wants to go out through the door of the mouth, not to leave, but to kill others. If it should happen that it has entered, do not let it go out to destroy others, but rather let death die while it is still inside and inwardly waste away and vanish. The apostle James speaks about this pollution: *The tongue is fire, a world of wickedness which, having been kindled by Gehenna, inflames the wheel of our birth.*[26] He calls the devil "Gehenna," which was made for the devil, who always burns and makes burn, first by the fire of inordinate desire and afterwards by the fire of hell. By this, therefore, the inflamed tongue inflames the wheel of our birth. By the "wheel" is understood our mutability and our inclination to sin. Therefore, it is said to be "of our birth" because it is inborn in us, innate and original. We acquire it from our origin and birth so we are called *children of wrath.*[27] Therefore, this wheel of our birth, inflamed by the tongue that is inflamed by hell,[28] turns, and is moved round by such great force that it is easier to tame any beast than to restrain this wheel.[29] About these people over whom this wheel, having thus moved, prevails, the Lord says, *Offspring of vipers, how are you able to speak good things, when you are evil?*[30] By "vipers" are understood the malevolent, the envious, *murmurers, disparagers, hateful to God,*[31] filled with venom. In fact, through the offspring of vipers, those who freely listen to such people are made like them by listening, as though poisoned because begotten from those poisoned. Therefore, lest the poison of the tongue kill us, let no evil speech proceed from our mouth.

4. After we have been perfectly purified *from every pollution of the flesh,* for us to celebrate the Feast of the Purification, it is also necessary that we be cleansed from every *pollution of the spirit.*[32] There are three pollutions of the spirit. The pollution of every interior human being pertains either to the corruption of anger, to the corruption of desire (*concupiscentiae*), or to the corruption of reason—anger directed at evil; desire toward the good, and reason to be set over, rule and govern the others.[33] It rules over anger so that it may never move against the good, but also so that having moved against evil it might not be excessive. It rules over desire that it might never extend its hand toward a forbidden tree, that is, that it might never desire evil. Through the sin of our first parents anger was so corrupted that it rises up against good rather than against evil. Desire is certainly inclined toward evil, but

sluggish in regard to the good. Reason is subject to ignorance and deception. One should be aware that name "anger" signifies both the virtue and its corruption; and "desire" is used to refer both to the natural virtue and its corruption. The corruption of reason itself is not called reason, but ignorance and deception. For curing this threefold corruption and renewing the threefold virtue, the sacrifice of a fundamental[34] purification is necessary, namely, heavenly grace. It is called the principal purification because without it all offerings and sacrifices are invalid and cannot have any effect. It is called an offering because it is first offered to us, and then by us; first it is offered to us by God for purification, then it is offered to God by us for propitiation. Therefore, this principal (*principalis*) offering of propitiation purifies anger from all malice, cleanses desire from all impurity, and heals reason of all error and ignorance. It subdues anger, restrains concupiscence, illuminates reason, and thus heals the whole person. Therefore, what remains except that we always recognize our weakness and always confess our need for the grace of God? He confessed his own weakness and the grace of God who said, *Have mercy on me, Lord, for I am weak;*[35] he confessed the grace of God and his own impurity who said, *Lord, if you want, you can cleanse me;*[36] and those disciples of the Lord revealed their own weakness and implored divine aid, when they said, *Lord, deliver us, we perish.*[37] Therefore, if we in this way are *purified from all pollution of the flesh and spirit,*[38] we will be worthy for the light and capable of divine splendor and transcendent glory (*superprincipalis claritatis*).[39] However, he who is not cleansed from all malice and impurity will not have been able to be deservedly illuminated. For the Lord says, *Do not give what is holy to dogs,* and *do not scatter your pearls before swine.*[40] Who are the dogs? They are evildoers who gnaw away the truth with a tooth of malice. The swine are understood to be unclean people, living like swine. Therefore, if we want to be illuminated, it is necessary that we be cleansed first. The Lord teaches this, saying, *Let your loins be girded, and your lamps be burning.*[41] He did not say, "Let your lamps be burning and your loins be girded," but the other way around, because purification precedes illumination, not illumination purification.

5. *Let your loins be girded, and your lamps be burning.*[42] Your lights ought to burn not only with the splendor of divine knowledge, but also with the fervor of divine love.[43] The lights of some seem to shine and not to warm; such are the lights of those who have puffed-up knowledge but not edifying love.[44] The lights of some seem to burn hot but

not to shine; such are the lights of those who have *zeal for God, but not in accord with knowledge.*[45] Those whose lights shine and do not give off heat are similar to the moon which is bright and cold. They are night and the children of night, darkness and the children of darkness. Everything that they see they see darkly, as though it were under a veil[46] and in a night vision. For them the *Sun of justice* has not yet arisen, as he has for *people fearing God.*[47] The Lord Jesus speaks to them in parables, *so that seeing they might not see, and hearing they might not hear.*[48] Those whose lights not only shine but also give off heat are like a shining and burning sun. They are a light in the Lord, and sons of light, and sons of the day; they are *God-fearing* and for them *the Sun of Justice has risen*[49] and illuminates and inflames them invisibly within. He illuminates by knowledge of truth; he inflames them with the love of virtue. These are the ones whose *minds the Lord opens* so that they may understand the *Scriptures;*[50] these are those who contemplate *the glory of the Lord with their face uncovered.*[51] Most holy is the teaching of those who alone teach what they understand (*sapiunt*), convey what they perceive, and see what they taste and experience. The visible lights that the faithful carry today symbolize these shining and burning lamps. The faithful desire to accomplish that command of the apostle: *Glorify and carry God in your body.*[52] Even more, the visible lamps signify that true light which illuminates invisible lamps.

6. Fittingly, therefore, on this solemnity the faithful carry kindled lights in their hands; they desire to be made sharers of that happy joy of blessed Simeon, who today receives the *boy Jesus in his arms.*[53] Of course, we cannot carry him in the same way; nor is it helpful for us to do so. Therefore, we do what we are able to do; we hold burning wax candles in his memory and in recollection of him; in them his likeness is expressed. For in a wax candle there are three things: wax, a wick, and light. So, too, in Christ there are three substances: flesh, soul, and divinity.[54] The wax is a figure of the flesh; the wick, which is in the middle between the wax and light, is a figure of the soul; the material light is a figure of divine light.[55]

These signs signify the same faith that is taught by these words: *A man was born in her, and the Most High, himself, established her;*[56] and *His name will be called Emmanuel, that is, God is with us;*[57] and *The word was made flesh;*[58] and *The savior of my face, and my God.*[59] Indeed it is beautiful that the Solemnity of Purification is not enacted without light and fire. For without the light of faith *it is impossible to please God.*[60] About the light of love it is written: *For love covers a multitude of sins*.[61] This fire truly purifies and consumes; it not only purifies from corruption, but also from every imperfection.

7. *Let your limbs be girded and your lamps be burning, and be like men awaiting their master*.[62] Who are the men awaiting their master to whom we should be similar? They are the good servants, *the servants who are keeping watch*,[63] desiring above all to hear *the voice* of their master knocking *at the door*.[64] Certainly the wicked and unfaithful servants do not keep watch. In fact, since *they have become intoxicated* they sleep;[65] they do not await their master nor do they desire to hear his *voice* knocking *at the door*.[66] Instead, they tremble, unprepared and conscious of wickedness. Let us, therefore, be like the good and faithful servants, like him who said, *When shall I come and appear before the face* of the Lord?[67] He was also like *the men awaiting their master*,[68] who said, *I desire to be released and to be with Christ*.[69] He greatly desired his master; in order to see him he desired or even longed to die. He was similar to *men awaiting their master*,[70] and said, *Come, Lord Jesus*.[71] He did not simply say, *Come, Lord*, but added, *Jesus*, for "Lord" is a name of fear, but "Jesus" is a name of sweetness, goodness, total grace and mercy.[72] Indeed, whose spirit is not joyful, does not rejoice and dance for joy when he hears the name of Jesus? You who already came in the flesh to redeem us, come a second time to glorify us.[73] That joyful voice, that desirable *voice sounds in my ears*:[74] *Well done, good and faithful servant, enter into the joy of your master*.[75] *Come, Lord Jesus*:[76] John placed these words at the end of the canon, that is, at the conclusion of all of sacred scripture.[77] He expressed the desire of all the saints and the perfection of those who are prepared to hurry to meet *on the way Christ in the air*.[78] This perfection and meeting pertain to the Ypapanti of the Lord.[79]

8. *Let your loins be girded, and your lights be burning, and be like men awaiting their master*.[80] Let me speak briefly and generally about the meaning of the words. Avoid evil and do good, and do both with a good intention and with a good end, that is, to say, on account of future beatitude. Indeed what is *Let your loins be girded*, if not to avoid evil? And what is *And let your lights be burning*, if not to strive for good works? And what is *And be like men awaiting their master*, if not this: In everything which you do, whether mortifying sins or devoting yourself to virtues, seek eternal life and do everything for obtaining it. These three degrees of virtues are symbolized in the adornment of Ezekiel's temple. One reads of a Cherubim with two faces drawn between two palms; on one the face of a man, and on the other the face of a lion.[81]

The face of the man, who alone is rational among animals, stands for prudent knowledge through which evil things are shunned. The face of the lion, which is the bravest of all animals, symbolizes the strength of love through which all good things are done. The palm refers to the triumph of eternal reward. Therefore, why does the face of man look toward one palm and the face of the lion toward the other palm, if not because in all things we do, either by overcoming sins or by accomplishing good, we ought always to look toward the palm of eternal reward. Therefore, likewise, the face of a man refers to *Let your loins be girded*; the face of the lion to *Let your lights be burning*; the palm to *Be like men awaiting their master.*[82]

9. *Let your loins be girded and your lights be burning and be like men awaiting their master.*[83] By these three steps we ascend unto the likeness of God.[84] I do not say that the divine nature, eternal beatitude, is cleansed, because it does not need to be cleansed to be clean and pure, since it is purification itself and of such a kind that it is above every purification. Divine nature is full of eternal light, indeed it is light itself, such that it is light above all light and illumination above all illumination. It is perfect and nothing is lacking to it so that it is the highest perfection.

Therefore, those who have been purified, illuminated, and perfected already by the grace of God are similar to and conformed to God, having through grace what God has through nature,[85] possessing according to participation what God possesses according to favorable plentitude.[86] However, they are God's co-workers[87] who have made such progress that they are not only cleansed, but cleanse others, they not only illuminated but also illuminate others, and they are not only perfected but perfect others in holiness.[88] Nothing is more divine than this;[89] nothing is more sublime. Thus, those who cleanse others should have perfect purification so that by the greatness of their own purification they may cleanse others.[90] Similarly, it is fitting for illuminators of others, who ought to illuminate all, to have knowledge of all things. Furthermore, through the supereminence of holiness they ought to carry the light of their wisdom so that, as it were, they are shining in loftiness and pouring out their light from above.[91] In the same way it is expedient, or even necessary, for the perfecters of others to have every perfection.[92] How can anyone who has an imperfection make all others perfect? If anybody who is not cleansed presumes to cleanse others, he is told, *Physician, heal yourself,*[93] and *Hypocrite, first cast out the beam from your own eye, then you will see to cast out the splinter from the eye of your brother.*[94] He who carries the beam in his own eye does not see, so if he reaches out his hand to *cast out the splinter from the eye of his brother*, he will sooner pluck out his eye than cast out the splinter. Such were the *Pharisees* who brought the *woman seized in adultery* to Jesus so that she might be stoned.[95] But the Wisdom of God, in whom is perfect justice, did not judge it fair that these men who ought to have been stoned should have stoned the woman who was to be stoned. He said, if anybody is *without sin*, let him be *the first to throw a stone* at her.[96] He did not deny that she should be stoned, because in truth she was worthy of stoning, but he was unwilling that such men should punish such a woman, that guilty men should punish the guilty woman, that sinful men should punish the sinful woman. It should be recognized that God cleanses, illuminates, and perfects all who deserve to be cleansed, illuminated, and perfected. Some he cleanses, illuminates, and perfects directly himself, with no one serving as an intermediary. Then through those who have been cleansed, illuminated, and perfected, he cleanses, illuminates, and perfects others. For example, he cleansed, illuminated, and perfected the apostles through himself; and then when they were cleansed, illuminated, and perfected, and sent into the world, they cleansed, illuminated, and perfected others. May he who himself is the supreme purification, illumination, and perfection, cleanse, illuminate, and perfect us, may he lead us, well cleansed, illuminated, and perfected in every goodness, to the kingdom of light. Amen.

NOTES

1   Luke 12:35–36.
2   John Beleth, *Rationale divinorum officiorum* 81 (PL 202.86B). For background on the feast, currently known as the Feast of the Presentation of the Lord, see J. Pascher, *Das liturgische Jahr* (Munich: Max Hueber, 1963), 612–23.
3   Sicard of Cremona, *Mitrale* 7 (PL 213.243A).
4   On the threefold distinction of the Christian journey into purification, illumination and perfection/union, or beginners, advancing, and perfect, see Pseudo-Dionysius, *De coel. hier*, 3.2 and 7.3 (PG 3.165BC and 209 C); Hugh of St Victor, *In hier. cael.* 4 and 6–7 (PL 175.992CD, 998B–1001C, 1033–1034B, 1060A–1069C); *Didasc.* V.8–9 (Buttimer, 108–111; tr. Taylor, 130–33; tr. Harkins, VTT 3.160–62); Richard of St Victor, *Apoc.* III.6 (PL 196.784A); *LE* II.10.19 (Châtillon 411.8–14) = *Serm. cent.* 19 (PL 177.935A); *Tract.* on Ps. 28 (PL 196.301C, 302B); *Serm. cent.* 53 (PL 177.1054D); *Archa Moys.* 3.11 (Aris, 69; PL 196.121BD; tr. Zinn, 238); Pseudo-Richard of St Victor, *Cant.* Prol. (PL 196.409B–410A); Walter of St Victor, *Serm.* 20.2 (Châtillon, 172.38–49); Anon. of St Victor, *Serm.* 2.1 (Châtillon, 245.24–27); Bernard of Clairvaux, *SCC* 3 (SBO 1:14–17; tr. Walsh, 16–20); M. B. Pennington, "Three Stages of Spiritual Growth according to St Bernard," *Studia Monastica* 11 (1969): 315–26; William of St Thierry, *Ep. ad Fratres de Monte Dei* 1.5.12 (Déchanet, SC 223:176–90; PL 184.315C–316B). Hugh of Balma's *Theologia mystica* (ed. F. Ruello and J. Barbet, *Théologie mystique*, SC 408–409 [1995]) is one of many books of spirituality which is divided in the purgative, illuminative and unitive ways.
5   Luke 12:35.
6   2 Cor. 7:1.
7   1 Cor. 6:18. Walter gives a strong argument for the unique invasiveness or pervasiveness of sins of lust, but he joins the tradition of the seven deadly sins, following upon the eight thoughts of Evagrios, and treats sins of lust and gluttony as the first and perhaps easiest to conquer. Pride is the last and hardest. See, e.g., Evagrios of Pontus, "On the Vices Opposed to the Virtues," and "On the Eight Thoughts," and "The Monk: A Treatise on the Practical Life," in Evagrios of Pontus, *The Greek Ascetic Corpus*, tr. R. Sinkewicz, Oxford Early Christian Studies (New York: Oxford University Press, 2006), 60–114, e.g., pp. 68–69; John Cassian, *Conferences* 5 (Pichery, SC 42.188–217; tr. Ramsey, 177–209, e.g., 178–79); C. Stewart, *Cassian the Monk*, Oxford Studies in Historical Theology (New York: Oxford, 1998), 62–84, especially 65–66.
8   Luke 12:35.
9   Ps. 31:9 (Vulg.).
10   Ps. 22:4 (Vulg.).
11   1 Kings 6:7; Achard of St Victor, *Serm.* 13.24–27 (Châtillon, 155–66; tr. Feiss, *Works*, 236–41; tr. Feiss, VTT 4.107–110).
12   Gal. 5:12.
13   Heb. 12:14; Walter of St Victor, *Serm.* 11.9 (Châtillon 100.275); *Serm.* 14.5 (Châtillon 125.125).
14   Lev. 11:44; 19:2; 20:7; 1 Pet. 1:16.
15   Ecclus. 7:40.
16   Job 40:11.
17   Job. 40:11.
18   1 Cor. 7:1.
19   "carnalis concupiscentia:" later in his sermon Walter will use "concupiscentia" in a neutral sense to mean "desire." Here, however, he clearly means inordinate desire (English: concupiscence).
20   Gregory the Great, *Mor.* XXI.2.4 (Adriaen, CCL 143A.1065–1067; PL 76.1890; tr. *Morals on the Book of Job*, 2/3–4:515–17).
21   Prov. 3:32.
22   Ps. 118:37 (Vulg.).

23 2 Tim. 2:17.

24 1 Cor. 15:33.

25 1 John 4:5.

26 James 3:6; "the wheel of our birth" (*rotam nativitatis nostrae*), that is, the course of our life.

27 Eph. 2:3.

28 James 3:6.

29 James 3:7–8.

30 Matt. 12:34.

31 Rom. 1:29–30.

32 2 Cor. 7:1.

33 This tripartite distinction of the soul stems from Plato, *Republic*, 439d–440e, 548c, *Phaedrus*, 246a, *Timaeus* 69c; see B. McGinn, *The Foundations of Mysticism*, The Presence of God: A History of Western Mysticism 1 (New York: Crossroad, 1991), 28. See Tertullian, *De anima*, 16 (PL 2.673AC); for Evagrios and Cassian, see McGinn, *Foundations*, 147–49, 219; Jerome, *Com. in Evangelium Matthaei* 2.13.23 (Hurst and Adriaen, 109.899–910); Isaac of Stella, *Epistola de anima* (PL 194.1877B): "Est igitur anima rationalis, concupiscibiis, irascibilis, quasi quaedam sua trinitas; et hoc totum, et nihil amplius, aut minus; et tota haec trinitas, quaedam animae unitas, et ipsa anima" ("The soul is rational concupiscible and irascible, like a kind of trinity; it is all this, and nothing more, nothing less; and this whole trinity, is a kind of unity of the soul, even the soul itself"); R. U. Smith, Jr., "Saint Bernard's Anthropology: Traditional and Systematic," *Cistercian Studies Quarterly* 46 (2011): 419–21.

34 "principalis": this is a word from Pseudo-Dionysius freighted with overtones. It is not easy to translate or understand. Here I translate it as "fundamental." At other times "principal" or "originating" seems a better rendering. I will translate "superprincipalis" as "transcendent" in par. 4.

35 Ps. 6:3 (Vulg.).

36 Matt. 8:2; Luke 5:12; Mark 1:40.

37 Matt. 8:25.

38 2 Cor. 7:1.

39 Pseudo-Dionysius, *De cael. hier.* (tr. John Scotus, PL 122.1037C); Hugh of St Victor, *In hier cael.* II (PL 175.933C–934B; 941D–943A); Walter of St Victor, *Serm.* 15.6 (Châtillon, 134.171–75); *Serm.* 20.6 (Châtillon, 175.129); Anonymous Victorine, *Serm.* 5.7 (Châtillon, 268.179): "superprincipalem claritatem in paterno lumine" ("transcendent brightness in the light of the Father"); *Serm.* 8.6 (Châtillon, 287.162–63).

40 Matt. 7:6.

41 Luke 12:35.

42 Luke 12:35.

43 On fire as burning and bright, see Walter of St Victor, *Serm.* 3.2 (Châtillon, 27.41–43): "Spiritus sanctus, qui est ignis invisibilis, in igne visibili apparuit, ut ignem divini amoris in cordibus fidelium suorum infunderet et splendore divinae cognitionis mentes illustraret" ("The Holy Spirit, who is invisible light, appeared in visible fire [on Pentecost] to pour the fire of divine love in the hearts of his faithful and to illumine their minds with the splendor of divine thought").

44 Cf. 1 Cor. 8:1; Hugh of St Victor, *In hier. cael.* 7 (PL 175.1061B): "illuminatio proprie ad illam cognitionem peritinet quae scientiam aedificat" ("illumination properly pertains to that thought which builds up knowledge").

45 Rom. 10:2.

46 Gen. 6:2.

47 Mal. 4:2.

48 Luke 8:10; Jer. 5:1; Ezek. 12:2; Matt. 13:14; Mark 4:12.

49 Mal. 4:2.

50 Luke 24:45.

51   2 Cor. 3:18.

52   1 Cor. 6:20.

53   Luke 2:27–28.

54   Hugh of St Victor, *Sapientia* (PL 176.847C); Achard of St Victor, *Serm*. 13.34 (Châtillon, 167.25–26; tr. Feiss, 252–52); Bernard of Clairvaux, *Consid*. 5.9.20 (SBO 3:484.1–3); Peter Lombard, *Sent*. III.6 (SB 5:573–82).

55   For this comparison between Christ and a lighted candle, see Pseudo-Hugh of St Victor, *Misc*. VII.9 (PL 177.873A); Richard of St Victor, *Serm. cent*. 91 (PL 177.1183A).

56   Ps. 86:5 (Vulg.). The Psalm says that a human being has been born in Zion, and the Most High established her (= Zion). In *En. Ps*. 86.7–8 (Dekkers and Fraipont, CCL 39.1205) St Augustine refers the passage to Christ who was God before us and became man for us. Christ created the mother from whom he was born.

57   Isa. 7:14.

58   John 1:14.

59   Ps. 42:6 (Vulg.).

60   Heb. 11:6.

61   1 Pet. 4:8.

62   Luke 12:35–36.

63   Luke 12:37.

64   Apoc. 3:20.

65   John 2:10.

66   Apoc. 3:20.

67   Ps. 41:3 (Vulg.).

68   Luke 12:36.

69   Phil. 1:23.

70   Luke 12:36.

71   Apoc. 22:20.

72   Bernard of Clairvaux, *SCC* 15.1 (SBO 1:83.2; tr. Walsh, 105–106).

73   Titus 2:14.

74   Song of Songs 2:14.

75   Matt. 25:21.

76   Apoc. 22:20.

77   Achard, *Serm*. 3.1 (Châtillon, 43.1–2; tr. Feiss, 111).

78   1 Thess. 4:16.

79   See above par. 1.

80   Luke 12:35–36.

81   Ezek. 41:18–19.

82   Luke 12:35–36.

83   Luke 12:35–36.

84   This paragraph follows closely Pseudo-Dionysius, *De cael. hier*. 3.2 (tr. John Scotus, PL 122.1045BC); Hugh of St Victor, *In hier. cael*. 4 (PL 175.991BC, 997D–999C).

85   Hugh of St Victor, *In hier. cael* (PL 175.998D).

86   Achard of St Victor, *Serm*. 13.14 (Châtillon, 148; tr. Feiss, *Works*, 225–26; tr. Feiss, VTT 4.100–101).

87   1 Cor. 3:9.

88   Hugh of St Victor, *In hier. cael*. (PL 175.998B).

89   Pseudo-Dionysius, *De cael. hier*. 3.2 (tr. John Scotus, PL 122.1045B); Hugh of St Victor, *In hier. cael*. (PL 175.991B, 997B–998A).

90   Pseudo-Dionysius, *De cael. hier*. (tr. John Scotus, PL 122.1045C); Hugh of St Victor, *In hier. cael*. (PL 175.991CD, 1000B, 1000D–1001A).

91   Hugh of St Victor, *In hier. cael*. (PL 175.1001AB).

92   Hugh of St Vcitor, *In hier. cael*. (PL 175.1001C).

93   Luke 4:23.

94   Matt. 7:5.
95   John 8:3, 5.
96   John 8:7.

BIBLIOGRAPHY

Primary Sources

Achard of St Victor. *De discretione animae, spiritus et mentis*. Ed. Germain Morin, "Un traité faussement attribué à Adam de Saint-Victor." In *Aus der Geisteswelt des Mittelalters*. BGPTMA, Supplementband 3/1, 251–62. Münster: Aschendorff, 1935. Ed. Nicholas Häring, "Gilbert of Poitiers, Author of the 'De discretione animae, spiritus et mentis' commonly attributed to Achard of Saint Victor." *Mediaeval Studies* 22 (1960): 148–91. Tr. Hugh Feiss, *On the Distinction of Soul, Spirit and Mind*. In *Achard of Saint Victor: Works*. CS 165:353–74. Kalamazoo, Mich.: Cistercian Publications, 2001.

_____. *De unitate Dei et pluralitate creaturarum*. Ed. and tr. Emmanuel Martineau, *L'unité de Dieu et la pluralité des créatures*. Saint-Lambert des Bois: Authentica, 1987. Tr. Hugh Feiss, *On the Unity of God*. In *Achard of St Victor: Works*. CS 165:375–480. Kalamazoo, Mich.: Cistercian Publications, 2001.

_____. *Sermons inédits*. Ed. Jean Châtillon, TPMA 17. Paris: J. Vrin, 1970. Tr. Hugh Feiss, *Sermons*. In *Achard of St Victor: Works*. CS 165:59–351. Kalamazoo, Mich.: Cistercian Publications, 2001.

Adam of St Victor. *Sequentiae*. Ed. Guido Maria Dreves and Clemens Blume, *Analecta Hymnica Medii Aevi* 54–55. Leipzig: O. R. Reisland, 1922. Ed. Jean Grosfillier, *Les sequences d'Adam de Saint-Victor: Étude littéraire (poétique et rhétorique). Textes et traductions, commentaires*. BV 20. Turnhout: Brepols, 2008. Ed. E. Misset and Pierre Aubry, *Les proses d'Adam de Saint-Victor, texte et musique*. Paris: H. Welter, 1900. Ed. and tr. Bernadette Jollès, *Quatorze proses du xiie siècle à la louange de Marie*. Sous la Règle de saint Augustin 1. Turnhout: Brepols, 1994. Ed. and tr. Digby Wrangham, *The liturgical poetry of Adam of St. Victor*. 3 vols. London: Kegan Paul, Trench, & Co., 1881. Tr. Juliet Mousseau,

Adam of Saint Victor's Sequences. Dallas Medieval Texts and Translations. Leuven: Peeters, 2013.

Adelard of Bath, *Quaestiones naturales*. Ed. and tr. Charles Burnett, *Adelard of Bath: Conversations with his nephew, On the same and the different, Questions on natural science, and On birds*. Cambridge: Cambridge University Press, 1988.

Aelred of Rievaux. *Opera omnia*. Ed. A. Hoste and C. H. Talbot. CCCM 1. Turnhout: Brepols, 1971.

Alain of Lille. *In distinctionibus dictionum theologicalium*. PL 210.685A–1012D.

Albert the Great. *B. Alberti Magni Ratisbonensis episcopi, ordinis Praedicatorum, Opera omnia*. 38 vols. Ed. Auguste Borgnet, Êmile Borgnet, Jacques Quétif, and Jacques Échard. Paris: Apud Ludovium Vivès, 1890–1895.

Alcher of Clairvaux. *De spiritu et anima liber unus*. PL 40.779–832. Tr. Erasmo Leiva and Benedicta Ward, *Treatise on the Spirit and Soul*. In *Three Treatises on Man*, ed. Bernard McGinn. CS 24, 181–288. Kalamazoo, Mich.: Cistercian Publications, 1977.

Alcuin. *De psalmorum usu liber*. PL 101.465B–508D.

Alexander Neckam. *Alexander Nequam: Speculum speculationum*. Ed. Rodney M. Thomson. Auctores Britannici Medii Aevi 11. Oxford: The Oxford University Press, 1988.

Anselm of Canterbury. *Opera omnia*, 6 vols. Ed. Franz von Sales Schmitt. Edinburgh: T. Nelson, 1938–1961.

_____. *The Prayers and Meditations of Saint Anselm*. Tr. Benedicta Ward. Harmondsworth: Penguin, 1973.

Ambrose of Milan. *Expositio Psalmi CXVIII*. Ed. Michael Petschenig. CSEL 62. 1913.

_____. *De officiis ministrorum libri III*. Ed. George Krabinger. Tubingae: Henry Laupp, 1857. PL 16.23A–184B.

Anselm of Laon. *Anselms von Laon systematische Sentenzen*. Ed. Franz P. Bliemetzrieder. Beiträge zur Geschichte der Philosophie des Mittelalters. Texte und Untersuchungen 18, 2/3. Münster: Aschendorff, 1919.

Anthony of Padua. *S. Antonii Patavini Sermones dominicales et festivi ad fidem codicum recogniti*. 3 vols. Ed. Beniamino Costa, Leonardo Frasson, and Giovanni Luissetto. Padua: Centro studi antoniani: Edizioni Messaggero, 1979.

Athanasius of Alexandria. *The Life of Antony and the Letter to Marcellinus*. Tr. Robert C. Gregg. New York: Paulist Press, 1980.

Augustine of Hippo. *Confessionum libri tredecim.* Ed. Lucas Verheijen. CCL 27. Turnhout: Brepols, 1981. Tr. Maria Boulding, *Confessions.* Hyde Park: New City Press, 1997.

——————. *De ciuitate Dei.* Ed. Bernhard Dombart and Alfons Kalb. CCL 47–48. Turnhout: Brepols, 1955.

——————. *De correptione et gratia.* PL 44.915–45.

——————. *Enarrationes in Psalmos.* Ed. Eligius Dekkers and Jean Fraipont. CCL 38–40. Turnhout: Brepols, 1956.

——————. *Enchiridion ad Laurentium de fide spe et caritate.* Ed. Ernest Evans. CCL 46. Turnhout: Brepols, 1969.

——————. *Epistulae.* Ed. Alois Goldbacher. CSEL 34, 44, 57–58. Vienna: Tempsky, 1895–1923.

——————. *De Genesi ad litteram.* Ed. Joseph Zycha. CSEL 28.1. Vienna: Tempsky, 1894.

——————. *De Genesi contra Manichaeos.* Ed. Dorothea Weber. CSEL 91. Vienna: Verlag der österreichischen Akademie der Wissenschaften, 1998.

——————. *In Iohannis euangelium tractatus CXXIV.* Ed. Radbod Willems. CCL 36. Turnhout: Brepols, 1954.

——————. *De libero arbitrio.* Ed. William M. Green. CCL 29. Turnhout: Brepols, 1970. Tr. Mark Pontifex, *The Problem of Free Choice.* ACW 22. Westminster, MD: Newman, 1955.

——————. *De peccatorum meritis et remissione.* Ed. Carol Urba and Joseph Zycha. CSEL 60. Vienna: Tempsky, 1913.

——————. *Praeceptum.* Ed. Luc Verheijen, *La Règle de saint Augustin.* 2 vols. Paris: Études augustiniennes, 1967. Tr. Agatha Mary and Gerald Bonner, *Saint Augustine: The Monastic Rules.* Hyde Park, NY: New City Press, 2004.

——————. *De sancta uirginitate.* Ed. Joseph Zycha. CSEL 41. Vienna: Tempsky, 1900.

——————. *Sermones.* PL 38, 39.

——————. *Sermones.* Ed. Michel Denis, "Sancti Augustini sermones post Maurinos reperti." In *MA* 1. Rome: Tipografia Poliglotta Vaticana, 1930. Tr. Edmund Hill. *Sermons (51–94) on the New Testament.* WSA III/3. New York: New City Press, 1991.

——————. *Tractatus in epistolam Ioannis I.* Ed. Paul Agaësse. SC 75. Paris: Éditions du Cerf, 1961.

Bede. *Homiliarum evanglii libri II.* Ed. David Hurst. CCL 122. Turnhout: Brepols, 1955.

Benedict of Nursia. *Rule*. Tr. Terrence Kardong, *Benedict's Rule: A Translation and Commentary*. Collegeville: Liturgical Press, 1996.

Bernard of Clairvaux. *Bernard of Clairvaux: Selected Works*. Translation and forward by G. R. Evans. Introduction by Jean Leclercq. Preface by Ewert Cousins. The Classics of Western Spirituality. New York: Paulist Press, 1987.

_____. *On Grace and Free Choice*. Tr. Daniel O'Donovan. Kalamazoo, Mich.: Cistercian Publications, 1988.

_____. *Sancti Bernardi Opera*. 9 vols. Ed. Jean Leclercq, Charles H. Talbot, and Henri Rochais. Rome: Editiones Cistercienses, 1957–1977.

Bernard of Silvestre. *De mundi universitate libri duo*. Ed. Carl S. Barach and Johann Wrobel, *Bernardi Silvestris De mundi universitate libri duo*. Frankfurt a.M.: Minerva, 1964.

Boethius. *De Consolatione philosophiae*. Ed. Ludwig Bieler. CCL 94. Turnhout: Brepols, 1984.

_____. *In Isagogen Porphyrii commenta*. Ed. Georg Schepss. CSEL 48. Vienna: F. Tempsky, 1906.

_____. *The Theological Tractates; The Consolation of Philosophy*. Ed. and tr. H. F. Stewart, E. Rand and I. Tester. Loeb Classical Library. Cambridge, Mass.: Harvard University Press, 1952.

Bonaventure. *Opera Omnia*. 10 vols. Ed. PP. Collegii a S. Bonaventura. Quaracchi: Collegium S. Bonaventurae, 1882–1902. Tr. Robert Karris, *Collations on the Seven Gifts of the Holy Spirit*. St. Bonaventure: The Franciscan Institute, 2008.

The Book of Beasts: a Facsimile of Ms Bodley 764. Introduction by Christopher de Hamel. Oxford: Bodleian Library, 2008.

Bruno. *Lettres des premiers Chartreux* I. Ed. Maurice Laporte. SC 88. Paris: Éditions du Cerf, 1962.

Pseudo-Bruno. *Expositio in Psalmos*. PL 152.637B–1420C.

Cassiodorus. *Institutiones*. Ed. R. A. B. Mynors. Oxford: Clarendon Press, 1961. Ed. Wolfgang Bürsgens, *Institutiones divinarum et saecularium litterarum/Einfürung in die geistlichen und weltlichen Wissenschaften*. Fontes Christiani. Freiburg: Herder, 2003. PL 70.1105–50.

_____. *In psalmorum praefatio*. PL 70.9A–23A.

Cicero. *De inventione. De optimo genere oratorum. Topica*. Tr. H. M. Hubbell. Loeb Classical Library 386. Cambridge, Mass.: Harvard University Press, 1949.

_____. *De oratore, De partitione oratoria.* Tr. Edward W. Sutton and Harris Rackham. Loeb Classical Library 348–49. Cambridge, Mass.: Harvard University Press, 1942.

_____. *Rhetorica ad Herennium.* Tr. Harry Caplan. Loeb Classical Library 403. Cambridge, Mass.: Harvard University Press, 1954.

Clare of Assisi. *Francis and Clare: The Complete Works.* Tr. Regis Armstrong and Ignatius Brady. New York: Paulist Press, 1982.

Codex Chronologico-Diplomaticus Episcopatus Ratisbonensis, vol. 2: *A saeculo xiv ad finem saeculi xvi.* Ed. Thomas Ried. Regensburg: Schaupf, 1816.

Columban. *Sancti Columbani Opera.* Ed. G. S. M. Walker. Dublin: Institute for Historical Studies, 1957.

Council of Vienne (1311–1312). Ed. Heinrich Denzinger and Adolf Schönmetzer, *Enchiridion Symbolorum, Definitionum et Declarationum de Rebus Fidei et Morum*, 895. 36th ed. Barcinone: Herder, 1976. Tr. *Decrees of the Ecumenical Councils* I, ed. Norman Tanner, 336–401. Washington, DC: Georgetown University Press, 1990.

Cyprian of Carthage. *Epistolae.* PL 4.191A–438C.

_____. *Liber ad Demetrianum.* PL 4.544B–564B.

Dhuoda of Uzès. *Liber manualis.* Ed. Pierre Riché. SC 225. Paris: Éditions du Cerf, 1975. Tr. Marcella Thiebaux, *Dhuoda, Handbook for Her Warrior Son. Liber Manualis.* New York: Cambridge University Press, 1998.

Pseudo-Dionysius. *Liber de caelesti Ierarchia.* Tr. John Scotus Erigena. PL 122.1035A–1070C.

Evagrios of Pontus. *The Greek Ascetic Corpus.* Tr. Robert E. Sinkewicz. Oxford Early Christian Studies. New York: Oxford University Press, 2006.

Expositio in epistolas Pauli. Ed. Rolf Peppermüller, *Anonymi Auctoris Saeculi XII: Expositio in epistolas Pauli (ad Romanos-II ad Corinthios 12).* Münster: Aschendorff, 2004.

Francis de Sales. *Introduction to the Devout Life.* Tr. John K. Ryan. Garden City, NY: Doubleday, 1955.

Gennadius of Marseilles. *De ecclesiasticis dogmatibus.* PL 58.979C–1000B.

Gerhoh of Reichersberg. *Expositionis in Psalmos continuatio.* PL 194.9A–998B.

Gilbert of Poitiers. *Expositio in epistolas Pauli.* Lisbon, Biblioteca Nacional Fundo Alcobaça XCVII/178, fols. 1r–117r (sec. xiv).

_____. *Expositio in Psalterium.* Cambridge, Queens' College Ms 5, fols. 1r–169r (sec. xii); Klosterneuburg, Stiftsbibliothek 815, fols. 1r–144v (sec. xii); Lisbon, Biblioteca Nacional Fundo Alcobaça LVIII/436, fols. 1r–204r (sec. xiv); Valenciennes, BM 44, fols. 1r–173r (sec. xii); Vorau, Stiftsbibliothek 261, fols. 1r–261v (sec. xii).

Glossa ordinaria. Ed. Karlfried Froehlich and Margaret T. Gibson, *Biblia latina cum glossa ordinaria. Facsimile reprint of the* editio princeps: *Adolph Rusch of Strassburg 1480/81.* 4 vols. Turnhout: Brepols, 1992. PL 113–114.

Glossa ordinaria in Canticum Canticorum. Ed. Mary Dove. CCCM 170. Turnhout: Brepols, 1997.

Glossa ps-Pictavensis super libros quatuor Sententiarum (Pseudo-Peter of Poitiers Gloss). Bamberg, Staatsbibliothek Msc. Patr. 128, fols. 27r–58r (Bk 1; sec. xiii); London, British Library, Royal 7.F.XIII, f. 4r–58v (sec. xiii); Naples, Biblioteca Nazionale, cod. VII C 14, fols. 2r–70v (sec. xiii); Paris, BnF lat. 14423, fols. 41r–119r (sec. xiii).

Godfrey of Winchester. *Epigrammata.* Ed. Thomas Wright, *The Anglo-Latin Satirical Poets and Epigrammatists of the Twelfth Century* II. Rerum Britannicarum Medii Aevi Scriptores or Chronicles and Memorials of Great Britain and Ireland During the Middle Ages. London: Longman & Co., 1872.

Godfrey of St Victor. *Fons philosophiae.* Ed. Pierre Michaud-Quantin. Analecta mediaevalia Namurcensia 8. Louvain: Nauwelaerts/ Namur: Godenne, 1956. Tr. Edward Synan. *The Fountain of Philosophy.* Toronto: Pontifical Institute of Mediaeval Studies, 1972.

_____. *Microcosmus.* Ed. Philippe Delhaye. Lille: Facultés catholiques, 1951. Partially tr. Hugh Feiss, *Microcosm (par. 203–27).* VTT 2.301–41.

_____. *Sermo in generali capitulo.* Ed. Helmut Riedlinger. In *Die Makellosigkeit der Kirche in den Lateinischen Hoheliedkommentaren des Mittelalters.* BGPTMA 38/3, 188–193. Münster: Aschendorff, 1958.

_____. *Sermo de Natiuitate beate Marie.* Ed. Johannes Beumer, "Die Parallele Maria-Kirche nach einem ungedruckten Sermo des Gottfried von St. Viktor." *RTAM* 27 (1960): 248–66. Tr. Hugh Feiss, *Sermon on the Nativity of the Blessed Virgin.* VTT 4.491–504.

Gregory the Great. *Dialogues.* Ed. Adalbert de Vogüé. SC 260 and 265. Paris: Éditions du Cerf, 1979–1980.

—————. *Homiliae in Euangelia.* Ed. Raymond Etaix. CCL 141. Turnhout: Brepols, 1999. Tr. David Hurst, *Forty Gospel Homilies: Gregory the Great.* CS 123. Kalamazoo, Mich.: Cistercian Publications, 1990.

—————. *Moralia in Iob.* Ed. Marcus Adriaen. CCL 143, 143A, 143B. Turnhout: Brepols, 1979–1985; Ed. Robert Gillet and tr. André de Gaudemaris, *Morales sur Job.* SC 32–32bis. Paris: Éditions du Cerf, 1989. PL 75.515–1162. Tr. Members of the English Church, *Morals on the Book of Job.* 3 Vols. Library of the Fathers of the Church. Oxford: J. Parker, 1844–1850.

Grimlaicus. *Regula solitariorum (Rule for Hermits).* Tr. Andrew Thorton. Collegeville, Minn.: Cistercian Publications, 2011.

Hilary of Poitiers. *Tractatus super psalmos.* Ed. Antonius Zingerle. CSEL 22. 1891.

Honorius of Autun. *Expositio in cantica canticorum.* PL 172.347C–496C.

—————. *Selectorum psalmorum expositio.* PL.172.269B–312B.

Horace. *Q. Horati Flacci Opera.* Ed. D. R. Shackleton Bailey. 3rd ed. Stuttgart: Teubner, 1995.

Hugh of Balma. *Theologia mystica.* Ed. Francis Ruello and Jeanne Barbet. SC 408–409. Paris: Éditions du Cerf, 1995.

Hugh of Fouilloy. *De medicina animae.* PL 176.1183A–1202C.

Hugh of St Victor. *Adnotationes elucidatoriae in Pentateuchon.* PL 175.29–114.

—————. *De archa Noe, Libellus de formatione arche.* Ed. Patrice Sicard. CCCM 176. Turnhout: Brepols, 2001. Tr. a Religious of C.S.M.V., *Ark of Noah.* In *Hugh of Saint-Victor: Selected Spiritual Writings,* 45–153. New York: Harper and Row, 1962. Tr. Jessica Weiss, "A Little Book About Constructing Noah's Ark." In *The Medieval Craft of Memory. An Anthology of Texts and Pictures,* ed. Mary Carruthers and Jan M. Ziolkowski, 41–70. Philadelphia: University of Pennsylvania Press, 2002.

—————. *De arrha animae.* Ed. and tr. Patrice Sicard *et al.,* *Oeuvre* 1:226–83. Ed. Karl Müller, *Hugo von St. Viktor, Soliloquium de arrha animae und De vanitate mundi.* Kleine Texte für Vorlesungen und Übungen 123, 1–26. Bonn: Marcus und Weber, 1913. Tr. F. Sherwood Taylor, *The Soul's Betrothal-Gift.* Westminster, England: Dacre Press, 1945. Tr. Kevin Herbert, *Soliloquy on the Earnest Money of the Soul.*

Medieval Philosophical Texts in Translation 9. Milwaukee: Marquette University Press, 1956. Tr. Hugh Feiss, *Soliloquy on the Betrothal-Gift of the Soul*. VTT 2.183–232.

_____. *Pro assumptione Virginis*. Ed. Bernadette Jollès, *L'œuvre de Hugues de Saint-Victor*, 2:112–61. Sous la Règle de saint Augustin. Turnhout: Brepols, 2000.

_____. *De beatae Mariae virginitate*. Ed. Bernadette Jollès, *L'œuvre de Hugues de Saint-Victor*, 2:182–253. Sous la Règle de saint Augustin. Turnhout: Brepols, 2000.

_____. *Super canticum Mariae*. Ed. Bernadette Jollès, *L'œuvre de Hugues de Saint-Victor*, 2:24–91. Sous la Règle de saint Augustin. Turnhout: Brepols, 2000. Tr. Franklin T. Harkins, *Exposition on the Canticle of Mary*. VTT 4.427–52.

_____. *Commentariorium in hierarchiam caelestem*. PL 75.923–1154.

_____. *Didascalicon: De studio legendi*. Ed. Charles Henry Buttimer. The Catholic University of America, Studies in Medieval and Renaissance Latin 10. Washington, DC: The Catholic University Press, 1939. Tr. Jerome Taylor. *The Didascalicon of Hugh of St. Victor: A Medieval Guide to the Arts*. Records of Civilization, Sources and Studies 64. New York: Columbia University Press, 1968. Tr. Michael Lemoine. *Hugues de Saint-Victor: L'art de lire; Didascalicon*. Sagesses Chrétiens. Paris: Éditions du Cerf, 1991. Tr. Thilo Offergeld, *Didascalicon de studio legendi: Studienbuch*. Fontes Christiani 27. Freiburg: Herder, 1997. Tr. Franklin T. Harkins, *Didascalicon on the Study of Reading*. VTT 3.81–201.

_____. *Super "Egredietur uirga."* Ed. Bernadette Jollès, *L'œuvre de Hugues de Saint-Victor*, 2:270–86. Sous la Règle de saint Augustin. Turnhout: Brepols, 2000.

_____. *In Salomonis Ecclesiasten homiliae*. Grenoble, BM 247, fols. 136v–138r (excerpt; sec. xii); New Haven, Library T. E. Marston 248, fols. 229r–272v (sec. xiii); Oxford, Bodleian Library, Laud. Misc. 370, fols. 164r–229v (sec. xii); Troyes, BM 496, fols. 73r–174r (sec. xii); Troyes, BM 1388, fols. 50r–127v (sec. xii); PL 175.113–256.

_____. *Eulogium sponsi et sponsae (De amore sponsi ad sponsum)*. PL 176.987–94. Tr. Hugh Feiss, *The Praise of the Bridegroom*. VTT 2.113–36.

——————. *Institutiones in Decalogum.* PL 176.9–15.

——————. *De institutione novitiorum.* Ed. Patrice Sicard, *L'œuvre de Hugues de Saint-Victor*, 1:18–114. Sous la Règle de saint Augustin. Turnhout: Brepols, 1997.

——————. *Super Lamentationes.* PL 175.255–322.

——————. *De laude caritatis.* Ed. Patrice Sicard, *L'œuvre de Hugues de Saint-Victor*, 1:182–207. Sous la Règle de saint Augustin. Turnhout: Brepols, 1997. Tr. Joseph McSorley, *Hugh's Praise of Love*. Patterson, NJ: Saint Anthony Guild Press, 1941. Tr. Franklin T. Harkins, *On the Praise of Charity*. VTT 2.149–68.

——————. *De meditatione.* Ed. Roger Baron, *Six opuscules spirituels*. SC 155:44–59. Paris: Éditions du Cerf, 1969. Tr. Frans van Liere, *On Meditation*. VTT 4.387–93.

——————. *Miscellanea* I and II. PL 177.469–588.

——————. *De oratione dominica.* PL 175.774–89.

——————. *De quatuor voluntatibus.* PL 176.841–46.

——————. *Quid vere diligendum sit.* Ed. Roger Baron, *Six opuscules spirituels*. SC 155:94–99. Paris: Éditions du Cerf, 1969. Tr. Vanessa Butterfield, *What Truly Should be Loved?* VTT 2.169–82.

——————. *De quinque septenis.* Ed. Roger Baron, *Six opuscules spirituels*. SC 155:100–19. Paris: Éditions du Cerf, 1969. Tr. Joshua Benson, *On the Five Sevens*. VTT 4.361–68.

——————. *De sacramentis christianae fidei.* Cambridge, Trinity College West 363, fols. 1r–193v (sec. xii); Cambridge, Trinity College West 1478, fols. 1r–271 (sec. xii); Douai, BM 361, fols. 1r–139 (sec. xii); Douai, BM 362/I, fols. 1r–109 (sec. xii); New Haven, Library T. E. Marston 248, fols. 1r–141v (sec. xiii). PL 176.173A–618B. Ed. Rainer Berndt, *Hugonis de Sancto Victore De sacramentis Christiane fidei.* Corpus Victorinum: Textus historici 1. Münster: Aschendorff, 2008. Tr. Roy Deferrari, *On the Sacraments of the Christian Faith (De sacramentis) of Hugh of Saint Victor.* The Medieval Academy of America Publications 58. Cambridge: The Medieval Academy of America, 1951.

——————. *De sacramentis legis naturalis et scriptae dialogus.* Berlin, Staatsbibliothek Preussischer Kulturbesitz Lat. 744, fols. 82rb–97rb (sec. xiii); Florence, BML S. Marco 476, fols. 1ra–8va; Grenoble, BM 390, fols. 87r–95v (sec. xii); Laon,

BM 463, fols. 77v–86r (sec. xii); Paris, BnF 14303, fols. 160vb–171vb (Abbey of St Victor; sec. xiii); PL 176.17C–42B.

_____. *De sapentia Christi*. PL 176.845–56.

_____. *De scripturis et scriptoribus sacris*. PL 175.9–28. Tr. Frans van Liere, *On Sacred Scripture and its Authors*. VTT 3.213–48.

_____. *Selected Spiritual Writings*. With an introduction by Aelred Squire. Tr. by a Religious of C.S.M.V. London: Harper & Row, 1962.

_____. *Sententiae de divinitate*. Ed. A. Piazzoni, "Ugo di San Vittore 'auctor' delle '*Sententiae de divinitate*.'" *Studi medievali*, 3rd series, 23 (1982): 861–955. Tr. Christopher P. Evans and Hugh Feiss, *Sentences on Divinity*. VTT 1.111–77.

_____. *De septem donis Spiritus sancti*. Ed. Roger Baron, *Six opuscules spirituels*. SC 155:120–33. Paris: Éditions du Cerf, 1969. Tr. Joshua Benson, *On the Seven Gifts of the Holy Spirit*. VTT 4.375–80.

_____. *De substantia dilectionis*. Ed. Roger Baron, *Six opuscules spirituels*. SC 155:82–93. Paris: Éditions du Cerf, 1969. Tr. Vanessa Butterfield, *On the Substance of Love*. VTT 2.137–48.

_____. *De tribus diebus*. Ed. Dominique Poirel. CCCM 177. Turnhout: Brepols, 2002. Tr. Hugh Feiss, *On the Three Days*. VTT 1.61–102.

_____. *De vanitate mundi*. Douai, BM 364, fols. 85–103 (*ca.* 1159); Douai, BM 365, fols. 3v–20r (sec. xii); Grenoble, BM 390, fols. 147r–161v (sec. xii); Laon, BM 463, fols. 70v–77v (sec. xii); Paris, Mazarine 717, fols. 124r–135v (Abbey of St Victor; sec. xii/xiii); Paris, BnF lat. 14506, fols. 111r–126v (Abbey of St Victor, sec. xiii); PL 176.703–39.

_____. *De Verbo Dei*. Ed. Roger Baron, *Six opuscules spirituels*. SC 155:60–81. Paris: Éditions du Cerf, 1969.

_____. *De virtute orandi*. Ed. Hugh Feiss, *L'œuvre de Hugues de Saint-Victor* 1:126–61. Sous la Règle de saint Augustin. Turnhout: Brepols, 1997. Tr. Hugh Feiss, *On the Power of Prayer*. VTT 4.331–47.

Pseudo-Hugh of St Victor. "Quae sit summa scientiae." Ed. Roger Baron, "Textes spirituels inédits de Hugues de Saint-Victor." *Mélanges de science religieuse* 13 (1956): 157–78.

_____. *Tractatus de Trinitate et de reparatione hominis.* Ed. Roger Baron, "Hugues de St. Victor, *Tractatus de Trinitate et de reparatione hominis* du ms. Douai 365." *Mélanges de science religieuse* 18 (1961): 111–22.

Pseudo-Haymo. *Glossae psalterii continuae.* Troyes, BM 904, fol. 1ra–159ra. PL 116.191A–696A.

Ignatius of Antioch. *Apostolic Fathers.* Tr. Kirsopp Lake. Loeb Classical Library 24. Cambridge, Mass.: Harvard University Press, 1977.

Innocent III. *De miseria humanae conditionis.* PL 217.701B–746C. Tr. Margaret Mary Dietz, *On the Misery of the Human Condition.* Library of Liberal Arts 132. Indianapolis: Bobbs-Merrill, 1969.

Irenaeus of Lyons. *Adversus haereses.* PG 7.437–1224.Tr. Robert M. Grant, *Irenaeus of Lyons.* The Early Church Fathers. New York: Routledge, 1997.

Isaac of Stella. *Epistola de anima.* PL 194.1875B–1890A. Tr. Bernard McGinn, *The Letter of Isaac of Stella on the Soul.* In *Three Treatises on Man,* ed. Bernard McGinn. Cistercian Fathers Series 24, 155–77. Kalamazoo, Mich.: Cistercian Publications, 1977.

Isidore of Seville. *Etymologiarum Sive Originum Libri XX.* Ed. W. M. Lindsay. Oxford: Clarendon Press, 1911. Tr. Stephen A. Barney *et al., Etymologies.* New York: Cambridge University Press, 2006.

Jacobus de Voragine. *Golden Legend.* 2 vols. Tr. William Granger Ryan. Princeton, NJ: Princeton University Press, 1993.

Jerome. *Adversus Jovinianum libri duo.* PL 23.205–338A.

_____. *Epistulae.* Ed. Isidorus Hilberg. CSEL 54, 55, 56. 1910–1918. Tr. Frederick A. Wright, *Select Letters of St. Jerome.* Loeb Classical Library 262. Cambridge, Mass.: Harvard University Press, 1975.

_____. *Liber interpretationis Hebraicorum nominum.* Ed. Paul de Lagarde. CCL 72.58–161. Turnhout: Brepols, 1969.

_____. *Commentarium in Evangelium Matthaei.* Edited by David Hurst and Marcus Adriaen. CCL 77. Turnhout: Brepols, 1969.

Pseudo-Jerome. *Breviarium in Psalmos.* Troyes, BM 88, fol. 1ra–184rb. PL 26.821C–1278C.

_____. *Expositio evangelii secundum Marcum.* Ed. Michael Cahill. CCL 82. Turnhout: Brepols, 1997.

John Beleth. *Rationale divinorum officiorum*. PL 202.13A–166C.

John Cassian. *Collationes patrum XXIV*. Ed. Michael Petschenig. CSEL 13. Vienna: C. Geroldi filium, 1886. Ed. Eugène Pichery. SC 42, 54, 64. Paris: Éditions du Cerf, 1955–1959. Tr. Boniface Ramsey, *The Conferences*. ACW 57. New York: Paulist Press, 1997.

John of Salisbury. *Metalogicon*. Ed. J. B. Hall. CCCM 98. Turnhout: Brepols, 1991. Tr. Daniel D. McGarry. *The Metalogicon of John of Salisbury: A Twelfth-Century Defense of the Verbal and Logical Arts of the Trivium*. Los Angeles: University of California Press, 1955.

Konrad, Abbot of Eberbach. *Exordium magnum cisterciense sive Narratio de intitio cisterciensis ordinis*. Ed. Bruno Griesser. CCCM 138. Turnhout: Brepols, 1997.

Liber Hymnarius: cum invitatoriis et aliquibus responsoriis. Solesmes: Abbaye Saint-Pierre de Solemnes, 1983.

Liber ordinis Sancti Victoris Parisiensis. Ed. Luc Jocqué and Ludo Milis. CCCM 61. Turnhout: Brepols, 1984.

Liber Usualis. Ed. Benedictines of Solemnes. Tournai: Desclée and Co., 1938.

Leo the Great. *Sermons*. Ed. René Dolle. SC 22, 22bis, 49, 74, 200. Paris, Éditions du Cerf, 1949–1973.

—————. *Tractatus septem et nonaginta*. Ed. Antoine Chavasse. CCL 138, 138A. 1973.

Liturgia horarum iuxta ritum romanum. 4 vols. Vatican City: Libreria Editrice Vaticana, 1977.

Magister Martin. *Conpilatio questionum theologie*. Paris, BnF lat. 14526, ff. 60–144 (sec. xiii); Paris, BnF lat. 14556, fols. 267–364 (sec. xiii); Toulouse, BM 209, fols. 1r–235v (sec. xiii); Troyes, BM 789, fols. 1–134 (sec. xiii).

Magister Udo. *Sententie*. Salzburg, Stiftsbibliothek Sankt Peter a.V.35, fols. 1r–165v (sec. xii); Vatican City, BAV Pal. lat. 328, fols. 1r–68v (sec. xii/xiii); Vienna, ONB 1050, fols. 114r–173v (sec. xii/xiii).

Ogier of Locedio. *Homilies: In Praise of God's Holy Mother; On Our Lord's Words to His Disciples at the Last Supper*. Tr. D. Martin Jenni. CS 70. Kalamazoo, Mich.: Cistercian Publications, 2006.

Origen. *Prayer; Exhortation to Martyrdom*. Tr. John J. O'Meara. ACW 19. Westminster, MD: Newman Press, 1954.

Peter Abelard. *Commentaria in epistolam Pauli ad Romanos.* Ed. Eloi M. Buytaert. CCCM 11. Turnhout: Brepols, 1969.

————. *Scito te ipsum.* Ed. and tr. David E. Luscombe, *Peter Abelard's Ethics.* Oxford: Clarendon Press, 1971.

————. *Theologia 'Scholarium.'* Ed. Eloi M. Buytaert and Constant J. Mews. CCCM 13. Turnhout: Brepols, 1987.

————. *Petri Abaelardi Opera.* Edited by Victor Cousin. Paris: A. Durand, 1849–1859.

Peter the Chanter. *Distinctiones Abel.* Graz, Universitätsbibliothek 724, fols. 1r–187v (sec. xiii); Vatican City, BAV Vat. lat. 1003, fols. 3r–69v (sec. xiii); Vatican City, BAV Vat. lat. 1004, fols. 5r–81v (sec. xiii).

————. *Verbum adbreviatum (textus conflatus).* Ed. Monique Boutry. CCCM 196. Turnhout: Brepols, 2004.

Peter Damian. *Die Briefe des Petrus Damiani.* Ed. Kurt Reindel. Monumenta Germaniae historica. Briefe der deutschen Kaiserzeit. 4 Vols. München: Monumenta Germaniae Historica, 1983–1993.

Peter Lombard. *Collectanea in omnes Pauli epistolas.* PL 191.1297A–1696C.

————. *In totum Psalterium commentarii.* PL 191.55A–1296C.

————. *Sententiarum libri IV.* SB 4–5. Grottaferrata: Editiones Collegii S. Bonaventurae Ad Claras Aquas, 1971–1981.

Peter of Poitiers. *Sententiarum libri quinque.* PL 211:791A–1280D. Ed. Philip Moore and Marthe Dulong, *Sententiae Petri Pictaviensis,* 2 vols. Publications in Mediaeval Studies 7 and 11. Notre Dame, IN: University of Notre Dame Press, 1943–1950 (Books 1–2).

Plato. *Euthyphro, Apology, Crito, Phaedo, Phaedrus.* Tr. Harold Fowler. Loeb Classical Library 36. Cambridge, Mass.: Harvard University Press, 1990.

————. *Republic.* Tr. Paul Shorey. Loeb Classical Library 236, 276. Cambridge, Mass.: Harvard University Press, 1953–1956.

————. *Timaeus.* Tr. Robert G. Bury. Loeb Classical Library 234. London: W. Heinemann, 1929.

Prepositinus. *Summa.* Einsiedeln, Stiftsbibliothek 230 (Msc. 498), pp. 1–234; Paris, BnF lat. 14526, fols. 1r–59v; Vienna, ONB 1409, fols. 1r–81v; Vienna, ONB 1501, fols. 1–85.

Prudentius. *Psychomachia.* Tr. H. J. Thomson. Loeb Classical Library 387, 398. Cambridge, Mass.: Harvard University Press, 1949–1953.

Radulphus Ardens. *In Epistolas et Evangelia dominicalia homiliae.* PL
         155.1667A–2118D.

_____. *In Epistolas et Evangelia sanctorum homiliae.* PL
         155.1301D–1626B.

_____. *The Questions on the Sacraments: Speculum uniuersale*
         8.31–92. Ed. and tr. Christopher P. Evans. Medieval Law
         and Theology 3. Toronto: Pontifical Institute of Medieval
         Studies, 2010.

Rationes dictandi. Tr. James J. Murphy, *Three Medieval Rhetorical Arts.*
         Berkeley: University of California Press, 1971.

Pseudo-Remi d'Auxerre. *Expositio psalmorum.* PL 131.133D–844C.

Richard of St Victor. *In Apocalypsim.* PL 196.683–95.

_____. *Ad me clamat ex Seir.* Ed. Jean Ribaillier, *Opuscules
         théologiques.* TPMA 15:256–80. Paris: J. Vrin, 1967.

_____. *De arca Moysi. De arca mystica; De contemplatione;
         Benjamin major.* Ed. Marc-Aeilko Aris. *Contemplatio.
         Philosophische Studien zum Traktat Benjamin Maior des
         Richard von St. Victor.* Fuldaer Studien 6, 4–148. Frankfurt:
         Josef Knecht, 1996. PL 196.63–190. Tr. Grover A. Zinn. *The
         Twelve Patriarchs, The Mystical Ark, and Book Three on the
         Trinity.* The Classics of Western Spirituality, 149–370. New
         York: Paulist Press, 1979.

_____. *Carbonum et cinerum.* Ed. Jean Châtillon, *Trois opuscules
         spirituels de Richard de Saint-Victor,* 253–63. Paris: Études
         augustiniennes, 1986.

_____. *Causam quam nesciebam.* Ed. Jean Châtillon, *Trois
         opuscules spirituels de Richard de Saint-Victor,* 201–21.
         Paris: Études augustiniennes, 1986.

_____. *De Comparatione Christi ad florem et Mariae ad virgam.*
         PL 196.1031–32.

_____. *Declarationes nonnullarum difficultatum Scripturae.* Ed.
         Jean Ribaillier, *Opuscules théologiques.* TPMA 15:201–214.
         Paris: J. Vrin, 1967.

_____. *De differentia peccati mortalis et venialis.* Ed. Jean Ribaillier,
         Opuscules théologiques. TPMA 15:291–93. Paris: J. Vrin,
         1967.

_____. *De differentia sacrificii Abrahae a sacrificio Beatae Mariae
         Virginis.* PL 196.1043–60.

_____. *De duodecim patriarchis (Benjamin Minor).* Ed. Jean

Châtillon, *Les douze patriarches ou Beniamin minor*. SC 419. Paris: Éditions du Cerf, 1997. Tr. Grover Zinn, *Richard of Saint Victor: The Twelve Patriarchs, The Mystical Ark, Book Three of the Trinity*, Classics of Western Spirituality, 51–147. New York: Paulist Press, 1979.

_____. *De Emmanuele*. PL 196.601–66.

_____. *De eruditione hominis interioris*. PL 196.1229–1366.

_____. *De exterminatione mali et promotione boni*. Paris, BnF lat. 17469, fol. 49r–72v (sec. xii). PL196.1073–1116.

_____. *In illa die*. Ed. Jean Châtillon, *Trois opuscules spirituels de Richard de Saint-Victor*, 123–52. Paris: Études augustiniennes, 1986.

_____. *De illo verbo Ecclesiastici "Eleemonsina patris non erit in obliuionem."* Ed. Jean Ribaillier, *Opuscules théologiques*. TPMA 15:295–96. Paris: J. Vrin, 1967.

_____. *Liber exceptionum*. Ed. Jean Châtillon. TPMA 5. Paris: J. Vrin, 1958.

_____. *Misit Herodes rex manus*. PL 141.277–306.

_____. *De missione Spiritus sancti sermo*. PL 196.1017–32.

_____. *Nonnullae allegoriae tabernaculi foedoris*. PL 196.191–202.

_____. *De quatuor gradibus violentae caritatis*. Ed. Gervais Dumeige, *Ives, Épître à Séverin sur la charité; Richard de Saint-Victor, Les quatre degrés de la violente charité*. TPMA 3:126–77. Paris: J. Vrin, 1955. Tr. Andrew B. Kraebel, *On the Four Degrees of Violent Love*. VTT 2.261–300.

_____. *De potestate ligandi et solvendi*. Ed. Jean Ribaillier, *Opuscules théologiques*. TPMA 15:77–110. Paris: J. Vrin, 1967.

_____. *Selected Writings on Contemplation*. Tr. Clare Kirchberger. London: Faber and Faber, 1957.

_____. *Sermo in die pasche*. PL 196.1059–1074.

_____. *Sermones centum*. PL 177.899–1210.

_____. *Sermo in ramis palmarum*. PL 196.1059–1067.

_____. *De spiritu blasphemiae*. Ed. Jean Ribaillier, *Opuscules théologiques*. TPMA 15:121–29. Paris: J. Vrin, 1967.

_____. *De statu interioris hominis post lapsum*. Ed. Jean Ribaillier, "Richard de Saint-Victor: *De Status Interioris Hominis*." AHDLMA 42 (1967): 61–128. Tr. Christopher P. Evans, *On the State of the Interior Man*. VTT 4.251–314.

_____. *Super exiit edictum sive De tribus processionibus*. Ed. Jean Châtillon and Willaim-Joseph Tulloch, *Sermons et opuscules spirituels inédits: L'édit d'Alexandre ou Les trios processions*. N. pl: Desclée de Brouwer, 1951.

_____. *Tractatus super quosdam Psalmos* (= *Mysticae adnotationes in Psalmos*), PL 196.265–404. Partially ed. Barthélemy Hauréau, *Notices et extraits de quelques manuscrits latins de la Bibliothèque Nationale*, vol. 1:112–14, 116–17, 118–19. Paris: C. Klincksieck, 1890. Tr. Christopher P. Evans, *Tractates on Certain Psalms*. VTT 4.147–240.

_____. *De Trinitate*. Ed. Jean Ribaillier, *De Trinitate: text critique avec introduction, notes et tables*. TPMA 6. Paris: J. Vrin, 1958. Ed. Gaston Salet, *La Trinité*. SC 67. Paris: J. Vrin 1959. Tr. Christopher P. Evans, *On the Trinity*. VTT 1.209–382.

_____. *De tribus personis appropriatis in Trinitate*. Ed. Jean Ribaillier, *Opuscules théologiques*. TPMA 15:182–87. Paris: J. Vrin, 1967.

_____. *In visionem Ezechielis*. Ed. Jochen Schröder, *Gervasius von Canterbury, Richard von Saint-Victor und die Methodik der Bauerfassung im 12. Jahrhundert*, vol. 2:372–553. Veröffentlichung der Abteilung Architekturgeschichte des Kunsthistorischen Instituts der Universität zu Köln 71. Cologne: Kleikamp, 2000. PL 196.527–606.

Pseudo-Richard of St Victor. *In Cantica Canticorum explanatio*. PL 196.405A–534A.

Robert of Melun. *Abbreviationes* (Books I and II). London, British Library, Royal 7.F.XIII, fols. 59r–122v (sec. xiii).

_____. *Quaestiones de epistolis Pauli*. Ed. Raymond Martin, *Oeuvres de Robert de Melun*, Tome II, Spicilegium Sacrum Lovaniense 18. Louvain: "Spicilegium Sacrum Lovaniense" Bureaux, 1938.

_____. *Sententiae*. Innsbruck, Universitätsbibliothek Codex 297, fols. 101r–213v (sec. xiii) (= Sententiae Bk. I). Ed. Raymond Martin, *Oeuvres de Robert de Melun*. Tome III.1–2, Spicilegium Sacrum Lovaniense 21, 25. Louvain: "Spicilegium Sacrum Lovaniense" Bureaux, 1947–1952 (= *Sententiae* I.1.1–6); tr. N. Van Baak, *Sentences (selections)*, VTT 3.445–72. Ed. Richard Heinzmann, *Die Unsterblichkeit der Seele und die Auferstehung des Leibes; eine problemgeschichtliche Untersuchung der frühscholastischen Sentenzen- und Summenliteratur von*

> *Anselm von Laon bis Wilhelm von Auxerre,* BGPTMA 40.3 (Münster: Aschendorff, 1965), 86–102 (= *Sententiae* I.2.1, 5–8, 16–37). Ed. Raymond Martin, "*L'immortalité de l'âme d'après Robert de Melun*," *Revue néo-scolastique de philosophie* 41 (1934): 139–45 (= *Sententiae* I.2.9–15).

Sententiae Atrebatenses. Ed. Odon Lottin. In *Psychologie et morale aux XIIᵉ et XIIIᵉ siècles,* Vol. 6: *Problèmes d'histoire littéraire.* Gembloux: J. Duculot, 1959. Pp. 403–40.

Sententiae divinitatis. Ed. Bernhard Geyer, *Die Sententiae divinitatis: Ein Sentenzenbuch der gilbertschen Schule; Aus den Handschriften zum ersten Male herausgegen und historisch untersucht.* BGPTMA 7/2–3. Münster, Aschendroffsche, 1967.

Sicard of Cremona. *Mitrale.* PL 213.13A–434A.

Simon of Tournai. *Institutiones in sacram paginam.* Burgo de Osma, Biblioteca de la Catedral de Osma, cod. 147, fols. 1ra–44ra (sec. xiii); London, BL Royal 9.E.XII, fols. 11va–46va (sec. xiii); Oxford, Merton College 132, fols. 105ra–162va (sec. xiii); Paris, Bibliothèque Arsenal 519, fols. 1ra–75ra (sec. xiii); Paris, BnF lat. 14886, fols. 1va–72va (sec. xiii).

Stephen Langton. *Glossa super maior glossatura Lombardi.* Paris, BnF lat. 14443, fols. 253–433 (sec. xiii); Salzburg, Stiftsbibliothek Sankt Peter a.X.19, pp. 1–224 (sec. xiii).

Summa sententiarum. Douai, BM 363, fols. 1r–52v; Douai, BM 364, fols. 1r–50v; Klosterneuburg, Stiftsbibliothek 312, fols. 1r–80v; PL 176.41–174.

Tertullian. *De anima.* PL 2.641D–752B.

⸻. *De carne Christi.* Ed. Emil Kroymann. CCL 2. Turnhout: Brepols, 1954.

⸻. *De paenitentia.* Ed. Jan Willem Philip Borleffs. CCL 1. Turnhout: Brepols, 1954.

Thomas Gallus. *Mystical Theology: The Glosses by Thomas Gallus and the Commentary of Robert Grosseteste on* De Mystica Theologia. Ed. and tr. James McEvoy. Dallas Medieval Texts and Translations 3. Leuven: Peeters, 2003.

Thomas Aquinas. *Summa theologiae.* Ed. Pietro Caramello. 3 vols. Turin: Marietti, 1952–1956. Tr. Fathers of the English Dominican Province. *Saint Thomas Aquinas Summa Theologica.* 5 vols. New York: Benziger Bros., 1948.

Walter of St Victor. *Contra quatuor labyrinthos Franciae.* Ed. Palémon Glorieux, "Le *Contra quatuor labyrinthos Franciae* de Gauthier de Saint-Victor." *AHDLMA* 19 (1953): 187–335.

_____. *Sermones inediti triginta sex.* Ed. Jean Châtillon. CCCM 30. Turnhout: Brepols, 1975.

Warner of St Victor. *Gregorianum.* PL 193.23A–462A.

William of Conches. *Dragmaticon philosophiae.* Ed. Italo Ronca. CCCM 152. Turnhout, Brepols, 1997. Tr. Italo Ronca and Matthew Curr, *William of Conches: A Dialogue on Natural Philosophy (Dragmaticon Philosophiae).* Notre Dame, IN: University of Notre Dame Press, 1997.

William of Newburgh. *Explanatio sacri epithalamii in matrem sponsi.* Ed. John C. Gorman, *A Commentary on the Canticle of Canticles (12th C.).* Spicilegium Friburgense 6. Fribourg: Universitätsverlag, 1960.

William of St Thierry. *Expositio super Epistolam ad Romanos.* Ed. Paul Verdeyen. CCCM 86. Turnhout: Brepols, 1989.

_____. *Lettre aux frères du Mont-Dieu: Lettre d'or.* Ed. and tr. Jean Déchanet. SC 223. Paris: Éditions du Cerf, 1985.

_____. *De natura corporis et animae.* Ed. Paul Verdeyen. CCCM 88. Turnhout: Brepols, 2003. Tr. Benjamin Clark, *William of St Thierry: The Nature of the Body and Soul.* In *Three Treatises on Man,* ed. Bernard McGinn. CS 24, 103–52. Kalamazoo, MI: Cistercian Publications, 1977.

Virgil. *Eclogues. Georgics. Aeneid I–VI.* Tr. Henry Rushton Fairclough and G. P. Goold. Loeb Classical Library 63. Cambridge, Mass.: Harvard University Press, 1999.

Secondary Sources

Alexandre, Monique. "La prière de feu chez Jean Cassien." In *Jean Cassien entre l'orient et l'occident,* ed. Cristian Badilita and Attila Jakab, 169–204. Paris: Beauchesne; Bucharest: Polirom, 2003.

d'Alverny, Marie-Thérèse. *Alain de Lille: Textes inédits.* Paris: J. Vrin, 1965.

Baroffio, Bonifacio. "Preghiera personale e preghiera liturgica." *Dizionario degli Istituti di Perfezione* 7 (1983): 580–719.

Baron, Roger. "Hugues de Saint-Victor: Contribution à un nouvel examen de son œuvre." *Traditio* 15 (1959): 223–97.

_____. *Science et Sagesse chez Hugues de Saint-Victor*. Paris: P. Lethielleux, 1957.

_____."La situation de l'homme d'après Hugues de St. Victor." In *L'homme et son destin d'après les penseurs du Moyen Âge*. Actes du premier congrès de philosophie médiévale. Louvain: Nauwelaerts, 1960. Pp. 431–36.

_____. "Spiritualité médiévale: le traité de la contemplation et ses espèces." *Revue d'ascétique et de la mystique* 39 (1963): 137–51.

Barrow, Julia, Charles Burnett, and David Luscombe. "A Checklist of the Manuscripts Containing the Writings of Peter Abelard." *Revue d'histoire des textes* 14–15 (1984–1985): 183–302.

Bautier, Robert Henri. "Origines et premiers développements de l'abbaye Saint-Victor." In Longère, *L'abbaye parisienne de Saint-Victor*, 23–52.

Baxter, Ron. *Bestiaries and their Users in the Middle Ages*. Stroud: Sutton Pub.; London: Courtauld Institute, 1998.

Bériou, Nicole, Jacques Berlioz, and Jean Longère. *Prier au Moyen Âge: pratiques et expériences (v^e-xve siècles)*. Témoins de Notre Histoire. Turnhout: Brepols, 1991.

Berndt, Rainer. "Walter von St-Victor." In *Lexikon des Mittelalters* 8.2000–2001, ed. Robert Auty. Stuttgart: J. B. Metzler, 1999.

Bertaud, Émile and André Rayez. "Échelle spirituelle." In *DS* 4, ed. M. Viller, F. Cavallera, J. De Guibert, 62–86. Paris: G. Beauchesne et ses fils, 1960.

Bertola, Ermenegildo. "Di alcuni trattati psicologici attributi ad Ugo da S. Vittore." *Rivista di Filosofia Neoscolastica* 51 (1959): 436–55.

_____. "Di una inedita trattazione psicologica intitolata: *Quid sit anima*." *Rivista di Filosofia Neo-Scolastica* 58 (1966): 573–77.

Black, Jonathan. "The Divine Office and Private Devotion in the Latin West." In *The Liturgy of the Medieval Church*, ed. Thomas J. Heffernan and E. Ann Matter, 45–71. Kalamazoo, Mich.: Medieval Institute Publications, 2005.

Blaise, Albert. *Lexicon latinitatis medii aevi: praesertim ad res ecclesiasticas investigandas pertinens = Dictionnaire latin-français des auteurs du moyen-âge*. CCCM. Turnhout: Brepols, 1975.

Bloomfield, Morton. *The Seven Deadly Sins: An Introduction to the History of a Religious Concept with Special Reference to Medieval*

English Literature. East Lansing: Michigan State University Press, 1967.

Bonnard, Fourier. *Histoire de l'abbaye royale et de l'ordre des chanoines réguliers de Saint-Victor de Paris. t. 1: Première periode (1113–1500)*. Paris: Arthur Savaète, 1904.

Bouman, Cornelius. "Immaculate Conception in the Liturgy." In *The Dogma of the Immaculate Conception*, ed. Edward D. O'Connor, 113–59. Notre Dame, IN: University of Notre Dame Press, 1958.

Bouyer, Louis. *The Spirituality of the New Testament and the Fathers*. Tr. Mary Ryan. New York: Desclee Company, 1963.

Bruce, Scott G. "'Lurking with Spiritual Intent': A Note on the Origin and Functions of the Monastic Roundsman (Circator)." *RBen*. 109 (1999): 75–89.

Burini de Lorenzi, Clara. "Il 'Magnificat' (Lc. 1, 46–55) nella interpretazione di Origene e di Ambrogio." *Augustinanum* 50 (2010): 101–111.

Burnett, Charles W. "*Expositio orationis dominicae*: Peter Abelard's Exposition of the Lord's Prayer." *RBen*. 9 (1985): 60–72.

Bynum, Caroline Walker. *Docere Verbo et Exemplo*: An Aspect of Twelfth-Century Spirituality. Missoula, MT: Scholars Press, 1979.

_____. *Jesus as Mother: Studies in the Spirituality of the High Middle Ages*. Los Angeles, CA: University of California Press, 1982.

Callahan, John F. *Augustine and the Greek Philosophers*. Villanova, PA: Villanova University Press, 1967.

Callus, Daniel A. "Two Early Oxford Masters on the Problem of the Plurality of Forms. Adam of Buckfield—Richard Rufus of Cornwall." *Revue néo-scolastique de philosophie* 42 (1939): 411–45.

Cacciapuoti, Pierluigi. *Deus existentia amoris: Carità e Trinità nell'itinerario teologico di Riccardo di San Vittore (d. 1173)*. BV 9. Turnhout: Brepols, 1998.

Casey, Michael. *Athirst for God: Spiritual Desire in Bernard of Clairvaux's Sermons on the Song of Songs*. CS 77. Kalamazoo, Mich.: Cistercian Publications, 1988.

Chase, Steven. *Contemplation and Compassion: The Victorine Tradition*. Traditions of Christian Spirituality Series. Maryknoll, NY: Orbis Books, 2003.

Châtillon, François. "Hic, ibi, interim." *Revue d'ascetique et mystique* 25 (1949): 194–99.

Châtillon, Jean. "Achard de Saint Victor et le 'De discretione animae, spiritus et mentis.'" *AHDLMA* 31 (1964): 7–35.

_____. "Le contenu, l'authenticité, et la date du *Liber exceptionum* et des *Sermones centum* de Richard de Saint-Victor." *Revue du Moyen Âge latin* 4 (1948): 23–52, 343–66.

_____. "*Cor et cordis affectus.*" In *DS* 2.2, ed. Charles Baumgartner, 2288–2300. Paris: G. Beauchesne et ses fils, 1953.

_____. "La crise de l'Église aux xie et xiie siècles et les origines des grandes fédérations canoniales." *Revue d'histoire de la spiritualite* 53 (1977): 3–46.

_____. "The *De laude liberi arbitrii* of Frowin of Engelberg and Achard of St Victor." *American Benedictine Review* 35 (1984): 314–29.

_____. "Devotio." In *DS* 3, ed. Charles Baumgartner, 702–15. Paris: G. Beauchesne et ses fils, 1957.

_____. "Richard de Saint-Victor." In *DS* 13, ed. Marcel Viller, F. Cavallera, and J. de Guibert, 593–654. Paris: G. Beauchesne et ses fils, 1987.

_____. "Sermons et prédicateurs victorins de la seconde moitié du xiie siècle." *AHDLMA* 32 (1965): 7–60.

_____. *Théologie, spiritualité et métaphysique dans l'œuvre oratoire d'Achard de Saint-Victor.* Études de philosophie médiévale 58. Paris: J. Vrin, 1969.

Chenu, M.-D. "*Imaginatio*: note de lexicographie philosophique." *Miscellanea Giovanni Mercati* II, 593–602. *Studi e Testi* 22. Vatican City: Biblioteca Apostolica Vaticana, 1946.

_____. *Nature, Man, and Society in the Twelfth Century.* Tr. Jerome Taylor and Lester K. Little. Chicago: The University of Chicago Press, 1968.

_____. "*Spiritus*: Le vocabulaire de l'âme au xiie siècle." *Revue des sciences philosophiques et théologiques* 41 (1957): 209–32.

Chevalier, Ulysse. *Repertorium hymnologicum*, 6 vols. Louvain; Brussels, 1892–1921.

Choquette, Imelda. "*Voluntas, Affectio* and *Potestas* in the *Liber De Voluntate* of St. Anselm." *Mediaeval Studies* 4 (1942): 61–81.

Congar, Yves. *I Believe in the Holy Spirit.* Tr. David Smith. New York: Crossroad Pub. Co., 1997.

——————. *The Revelation of God.* Tr. A. Manson and L. C. Sheppard. London: Darton, Longman & Todd; New York, Herder and Herder, 1968.

Constable, Giles. *"Love and Do What You Will": The Medieval History of an Augustinian Precept.* Morton W. Bloomfield Lectures IV. Kalamazoo, Mich.: Medieval Institute Publications, Western Michigan University, 1999.

Coolman, Boyd Taylor. *The Theology of Hugh of Saint Victor: An Interpretation.* Cambridge: Cambridge University Press, 2010.

Coulter, Dale M. *Per visibilia ad invisibilia: Theological Method in Richard of St. Victor (d. 1173).* BV 19. Turnhout: Brepols, 2006.

Cullen, Christopher M. *Bonaventure.* Great Medieval Thinkers. Oxford: Oxford University Press, 2006.

Dales, Richard C. *The Problem of the Rational Soul in the Thirteenth Century.* Leiden: E. J. Brill, 1995.

Delhaye, Philippe. *Le* Microcosmus *de Godefroy de Saint-Victor: étude théologique.* Mémoires et trauaux 57. Lille: Facultés catholiques, 1951.

——————. "Les perspectives morales de Richard de Saint-Victor." *Mélanges offerts à René Crozet.* Ed. Pierre Gallais and Yves-Jean Riou, 855–61. Poitiers: Société d'Études Médiévales, 1966.

——————. "Les sermons de Godefroy de Saint-Victor." *RTAM* 21 (1954): 194–210.

Den Bok, Nico. *Communicating the Most High.* BV 7. Turnhout: Brepols, 1996.

Dixon, Thomas. *From Passions to Emotions: The Creation of a Secular Psychological Category.* Cambridge: Cambridge University Press, 2003.

Dreyer, Elizabeth Ann. "*Affectus* in St. Bonaventure's Description of the Journey of the Soul to God." PhD diss., Marquette University, 1982.

Dreves, Guido Maria and Clemens Blume. *Ein Jahrtausend lateinischer Hymnendichtung: eine Blütenlese aus den Analecta Hymnica mit literarischen Erläuterungen.* Leipzig, 1909.

Dronke, Peter. *Intellectuals and Poets in Medieval Europe.* Storia e letteratura 183. Rome: Edizioni di Storia e Letteratura, 1993.

——————. *The Medieval Lyric.* 2nd ed. New York: Cambridge University Press, 1977.

——————. *The Medieval Poet and His World.* Storia e Letteratura 164.

Rome: Edizioni di Storia e Letteratura, 1984.

_____. *Nine Medieval Plays.* Cambridge Medieval Classics 1. New York: Cambridge University Press, 1994.

_____. *Poetic Individuality in the Middle Ages: New Departures in Poetry, 1000–1150.* 2nd ed. London: Westfield College, University of London Committee for Medieval Studies, 1986.

Dumeige, Gervais. *Richard de Saint-Victor et l'idée chrétienne de l'amour.* Paris: Presses universitaires de France, 1952.

Dunn, James D. G. *The Theology of Paul the Apostle.* Grand Rapids: Wm. B. Eerdmans Pub. Co., 1998.

Ebner, Joseph. *Die Erkenntnislehre Richards von St. Victor.* BGPTMA 19.4. Münster: Aschendorff, 1917.

Ehlers, Joachim. *Hugo von St. Viktor: Studien zum Geschichtsdenken und zur Geschichtsschreibung des 12. Jahrhunderts.* Frankfurter historische Abhandlungen 7. Wiesbaden: Steiner, 1973.

Evans, Gillian R. *Old Arts and New Theology: The Beginnings of Theology as an Academic Discipline.* Oxford: Clarendon, 1980.

Feiss, Hugh. "*Circatores* from Benedict of Nursia to Humbert of Romans." *American Benedictine Review* 40 (1989): 346–79.

_____. "*Circatores* in the *Ordo* of St. Victor." In *The Medieval Monastery,* ed. Andrew McLeish, 53–58. Medieval Studies at Minnesota 2. St. Cloud: North Star, 1988.

_____. "Learning and the Ascent to God in Richard of St. Victor." STD diss., Rome: Pontifical Athenaeum of Sant' Anselmo, 1976.

_____. "The Ordo of St. Victor in Ireland." In *Ordo Canonicus,* series altera 4, 56–87. Neustift: Studium Vitae Canonicae, 1988.

_____. "Three Victorine Texts in Frowin of Engelberg's *De laude liberi arbitrii.*" *Studia Monastica* 50 (2008): 203–219.

Fortin, Ernest L. "*De Civitate Dei.*" In *Augustine through the Ages,* ed. Allan D. Fitzgerald, 196–202. Grand Rapids: Wm. B. Eerdmans Pub. Co., 1999.

Fulton, Rachel. *From Judgment to Passion: Devotion to Christ and the Virgin Mary, 800–1200.* New York: Columbia University Press, 2002.

Fumagalli, Maria. *Le Quattro sorelle, il re e il servo.* Milan: Cisalpino-goliardica, 1981.

Gambero, Luigi. *Mary in the Middle Ages: The Blessed Virgin Mary in the Thought of Medieval Latin Theologians.* Tr. Thomas Buffer. San Francisco: Ignatius Press, 2000.

Gasparri, Françoise. "Godefroid de Saint-Victor: Une personnalité peu connue du monde intellectuel et artistique parisien au xiie siècle." *Scriptorium* 39 (1985): 57–69.

_____. "Observations paléographiques sur deux manuscrits partiellement autographes de Godefroid de Saint-Victor." *Scriptorium* 36 (1982): 43–50.

_____. "Textes autographes d'auteurs victorins du xiie siècle." *Scriptorium* 35 (1981): 277–84.

Ghellinck, Joseph de. "Un catalogue des œuvres de Hugues de Saint-Victor." *Revue néo-scolastique de philosophie* 20 (1913): 226–32.

_____. *Le mouvement théologique du xiie siècle.* 2nd ed. Bruges: Éditions "De Tempel," 1948.

_____. "La table des materières de la première édition des œuvres de Hugues de Saint-Victor." *Recherches de Sciences Religieuses* 1 (1910): 270–89, 385–96.

Gennrich, Friedrich. *Grundriss einer Formenlehre des mittelalterlichen Liedes als Grundlage einer musikalischen Formenlehre des Liedes.* Halle: M. Niemeyer Verlag, 1932.

Gilson, Etienne. *History of Christian Philosophy in the Middle Ages.* New York: Random House, 1955.

_____. *The Philosophy of St. Bonaventure.* Tr. Illtyd Trethowan. Paterson, N.J.: St. Anthony Guild Press, 1965.

_____. *The Spirit of Medieval Philosophy.* Tr. A. H. C. Downes. New York: Scribner, 1940.

Glacken, Clarence C. *Traces on a Rhodian Shore: Nature and Culture in Western Thought from Ancient Times to the End of the Eighteenth Century.* Berkeley: University of California Press, 1973.

Glorieux, Palémon. "*Mauvaise action et mauvais travail:* Le *Contra quautor labyrinthos Franciae* de Gauthier de Saint-Victor." *RTAM* 21 (1954): 179–93.

Goy, Rudolf. *Die Überlieferung der Werke Hugos von St. Viktor. Ein Beitrag zur Kommunikationsgeschichte des Mittelalters.* Monographien zur Geschichte des Mittelalters 16. Stuttgart: A. Hiersemann, 1976.

_____. *Die handschriftliche Überlieferung der Werke Richards von Sankt Viktor im Mittelalter.* BV 18. Turnhout: Brepols,

2005.

Green, William H. "Hugh of St. Victor *De tribus maximis circumstantiis gestorum.*" *Speculum* 18 (1943): 484–93.

Gross-Diaz, Theresa. *The Psalms Commentary of Gilbert of Poitiers: From Lectio Divina to the Lecture Room*. Brill's Studies in Intellectual History 68. New York: E. J. Brill, 1996.

Hamesse, Jacqueline. "La deuxième réportation des *Collationes de septem donis Spiritus Sancti* de saint Bonaventure." *Bulletin de philosophie médiévale* 19 (1977): 59–64.

_____. "New perspectives for critical editions of Franciscan texts of the Middle Ages." *Franciscan Studies* 56 (1998): 169–87.

Hance, Nicholas. "Cosmic Connections." *Way* 50/3 (July 2011): 97–107.

Harmless, William J. *Augustine in His Own Words*. Washington, DC: The Catholic University of America Press, 2010.

Harkins, Franklin T. *Reading and the Work of Restoration: History and Scripture in the Theology of Hugh of St. Victor*. Toronto: Pontifical Institute of Medieval Studies, 2009.

Haye, Thomas. *Oratio: Mittelalterliche Redekunst in lateinischer Sprache*. Mitellateinsiche Studien und Texte 27. Leiden: E. J. Brill, 1999.

Heimsoeth, Heinz. *The Six Great Themes of Western Metaphysics*. Tr. Ramon J. Betanzos. Detroit: Wayne State University Press, 1994.

Heinzmann, Richard. *Die Unsterblichkeit der Seele und die Auferstehung des Leibes; eine problemgeschichtliche Untersuchung der frühscholastischen Sentenzen- und Summenliteratur von Anselm von Laon bis Wilhelm von Auxerre*. BGPTMA 40.3. Münster: Aschendorff, 1965.

Henriet, Patrick. *La parole et la prière au moyen âge: La Verbe efficace dans l'hagiographie monastique des XIe et XIIe siècles*. Bibliothèque du moyen âge 18. Bruxelles: De Boeck, 2005.

Ilkhani, Mohammad. *La philosophie de la création chez Achard de Saint-Victor*. Bruxelles: Ousia, 1991.

Illich, Ivan. *In the Vineyard of the Text. A Commentary to Hugh's Didascalicon*. Chicago: University of Chicago Press, 1993.

Jaeger, C. Stephen. *The Envy of Angels: Cathedral Schools and Social Ideals in Medieval Europe, 950–1200*. Philadelphia: University of Philadelphia Press, 1994.

_____. "Humanism and Ethics at the School of Saint Victor."

Mediaeval Studies 55 (1993): 53-79.

Javelet, Robert. *Psychologie des auteurs spirituels du xiie siècle.* Epinal, Vosges: Javelet, 1959.

_____. "Thomas Gallaus et Richard de Saint-Victor mystiques." *RTAM* 29 and 30 (1962 and 1963): 206-33 and 88-121.

Johnson, Luke Timothy. *The Gospel of Luke.* Sacra Pagina 3. Collegeville, MN: Liturgical Press, 1991.

Jolivet, Jean. *Abélard ou la philosophie dans le langage.* Vestigia 14. Fribourg, Suisse: Éditions Universitaires; Paris: Éditions du Cerf, 1994.

Kienzle, Beverly Mayne. *Hildegard of Bingen and Her Gospel Homilies.* Medieval Women: Texts and Contexts. Turnhout: Brepols, 2009.

_____. "The Twelfth-Century Monastic Sermon." In *The Sermon,* ed. Beverly Mayne Kienzle, 271-323. Typologie des sources du Moyen Âge occidental 81-83. Turnhout: Brepols, 2000.

Kornexl, Lucia. "Ein benedikitinischer Funktionsträger und seine Name: Linguistische Überlegungen und um den *circa.*" *Mittellateinisches Jahrbuch* 31 (1996): 39-60.

Kleinz, John. *The Theory of Knowledge of Hugh of St. Victor.* Washington, D.C.: The Catholic University of America Press, 1944.

Knipp, David. *Christus Medicus in der frühchristlichen Sarkophagskulptur: ikonographische Studien der Sepulkralkunst des späten vierten Jahrhunderts.* Supplements to Vigiliae Christianae 37. Leiden: E. J. Brill, 1998.

Knuuttila, Simo. *Emotions in Ancient and Medieval Philosophy.* Oxford: Clarendon Press, 2004.

Landgraf, Artur M. *Dogmengeschichte der frühscholastik.* Vol 1: *Die Gnadenlehre.* 2 pts. Regensburg: Friedrich Pustet, 1952-1953.

_____. *Introduction à l'histoire de la littérature théologique de la scolastique naissante.* Tr. Albert M. Landry and Louis B. Geiger. Montreal: Institut d'études médiévales, 1973.

Lanham, Richard A. *A Handlist of Rhetorical Terms.* 2nd ed. Berkeley: University of California Press, 1991.

Lasić, Dionysius. *Hugonis de S. Victore theologia perfectiva: eius fundamentum philosophicum ac theologicum.* Studia Antoniana 7. Rome: Pontificium Athenaeum Antonianum, 1956.

Leclercq, Jean. "Culte liturgique et prière intime dans le monachisme au moyen âge." *La Maison-Dieu* 69 (1962): 39-55.

_____. *Études sur le vocabulaire monastique du Moyen Âge.* Studia Anselmiana philosophica theologica 48. Rome: "Orbis Catholicus," Herder, 1961.

_____. "La spiritualite des chanoines reguliers." In *La vita commune del clero nei secoli XI e XII: atti della Settimana di studio, Mendola, settembre 1959.* Milan: Società editrice Vita e pensiero, 1962. Pp. 117–41

_____. "Les psaumes 20–25 chez les commentateurs du haut Moyen Âge." In *Richesses et déficiences des anciens psautiers latins.* Collectanea Biblica Latina 13, 213–29. Rome: Libreria Vaticana, 1959.

_____. "Nouveau témoin du 'conflit des filles de Dieu'." *RBen.* 58 (1948): 110–124.

_____. "Spiritualitas." *Studi medievali* 3 (1962): 279–96.

Levison, John R. *Filled with the Spirit.* Grand Rapids, Mich.: Wm. B. Eerdmans Publishing Co., 2009.

Longère, Jean, ed. *L'abbaye parisienne de Saint-Victor au Moyen Âge: communications présentées au XIIIe Colloque d'humanisme médiéval de Paris (1986–1988).* BV 1. Turnhout: Brepols, 1991.

_____. "La fonction pastorale de Saint-Victor à a fin du XIIe et au debut du XIIIe siècle." In Longère, *L'abbaye parisienne de Saint-Victor,* 291–313.

_____. *Les sermons latins de Maurice de Sully, évêque de Paris (†1196). Contribution à l'histoire de la tradition manuscrite.* Instrumenta Patristica 16. Steenbrugis: In Abbatia S. Petri; Dordrecht: Kluwer Academic Publishers, 1988.

Lottin, Odon. *Psychologie et morale aux XIIe et XIIIe siècles.* 6 Vols. Gembloux: J. Duculot, 1957–1960

Lubac, Henri de. *Catholicism: Christ and the Common Destiny of Man.* Tr. Lancelot C. Sheppard and Elizabeth Englund. San Francisco: Ignatius, 1988.

_____. *Exégèse médiévale. Les quatre sens de l'Écriture.* Théologie. Études publiées sous la direction de la Faculté de théologie S.J. de Lyon-Fourvière, 41, 42, 49. Paris: Aubier, 1959–1964. Tr. Mark Sebanc and E. M. Macierowski, *Medieval Exegesis: The Four Senses of Scripture.* 3 vols. Grand Rapids, Mich.: Wm. B. Eerdmans Pub. Co., 1998–.

Luscombe, David E. *The School of Peter Abelard.* Cambridge: University Press, 1970.

Marmion, Declan. *A Spirituality of Everyday Faith: A Theological Investigation of the Notion of Spirituality in Karl Rahner.* Louvain: Peeters Press, 1998.

Martin, Raymond. "Les idées de Robert de Melun sur le péché originel." *Revue des sciences philosophiques et théologiques* 7 (1913): 700–25.

_____. "L'immortalité de l'âme d'après Robert de Melun." *Revue néo-scolastique de philosophie* 41 (1934): 128–45.

McGinn, Bernard. *The Flowering of Mysticism (1200–1350).* The Presence of God: A History of Western Christian Mysticism 3. New York: Crossroad, 1998.

_____. *The Harvest of Mysticism in Medieval Germany (1300–1500).* The Presence of God: A History of Western Christian Mysticism 4. New York: Crossroad, 2005.

_____. *The Foundations of Mysticism.* The Presence of God: A History of Western Mysticism 1. New York: Crossroad, 1991.

_____. *The Growth of Mysticism: Gregory the Great through the 12th Century.* The Presence of God: A History of Western Christian Mysticism 2. New York: Crossroad, 1994.

Meyer, Ann. *Medieval Allegory and the Building of the New Jerusalem.* Rochester, NY: D. S. Brewer, 2003.

McWhorter, Matthew. "Hugh of St Victor on Contemplative Meditation." *Heythrop Journal* (2011), http://onlinelibrary.wiley.com/doi: 10.1111/j.1468-2265.2011.00738.x.

Michaud-Quantian, Pierre. "La classification des puissances de l'âme au XIIᵉ siècle." *Revue du moyen âge latin* 5 (1949): 15–34.

Mignon, Armand. *Les origines de la scolastique et Hugues de Saint-Victor,* vol. 1. Paris: Lethielleux, 1895.

Miles, Margaret R. "Leaning toward Enlightenment." *Harvard Divinity Bulletin* 38 (2010): 67–68.

Moore, Philip. *The Works of Peter of Poitiers.* Notre Dame, IN: University of Notre Dame, 1936.

Mulligan, Robert. "*Ratio Superior* and *Ratio Inferior*: the Historical Background." *The New Scholasticism* 29.1 (1955): 1–32.

Neale, John M. and Richard F. Littledale. *A Commentary on the Psalms from Patristic and Medieval Writers.* 3rd ed. London: Joseph Masters, 1874.

Neuheuser, Hans Peter. "Domus dedicanda, anima sanctificanda. Rezeption des Ivo von Chartres und Neuprägung der hochmittelalterliches Kirchweihtheologie durch Hugo von St. Viktor." *Ecclesia Orans* 18 (2001): 373–96; 19 (2002): 7–44.

Newhauser, Richard. "The Capital Vices as Medieval Anthropology." *Laster im Mittelalter / Vices in the Middle Ages*, ed. Christoph Flüeler and Martin Rohde, 105–23. Berlin: Walter de Gruyter, 2009.

——————. *The Treatise on Vices and Virtues in Latin and the Vernacular*. Typologie des sources du Moyen Âge occidental 68. Turnhout: Brepols, 1993.

Noone, Timothy B. "Scholasticism." In *A Companion to Philosophy in the Middle Ages*, ed. Jorge J. E. Gracia and Timothy B. Noone, 55–63. Malden, Mass.: Blackwell, 2003.

Nothdurft, Klaus Dieter. *Studien zum Einfluss Senecas auf die Philosophie und Theologie des zwölften Jahrhunderts*. Studien und Texte zur Geistesgeschichte des Mittelalters 7. Leiden: E. J. Brill, 1963.

Old, Hughes Oliphant. *The Reading and Preaching of the Scriptures in the Worship of the Christian Church. Vol. 3: The Medieval Church*. Grand Rapids: Wm. B. Eerdmans Publishing Co., 1998.

O'Malley, John W. *Four Cultures of the West*. Cambridge: Harvard University Press, 2004.

Ostler, Heinrich. *Die Psychologie des Hugo von St. Victor*. BGPTMA 6.1. Münster: Aschendorff, 1906.

Ottaviano, Carmelo. *Riccardo di S. Vittore: La vita, le opera, il pensiero*. Memorie della R. Academia Nazionale dei Lincei. Classe di scienze morali, storiche e filologiche, serie VI, vol. IV, fasc. V. Rome: Dott. Giovanni Bardi, tipografo della R. Accademia nazionale dei Lincei, 1933.

Ouy, Gilbert. *Les manuscripts de l'abbaye de Saint-Victor. Catalogue établi sur la base du répertoire de Claude de Grandrue (1514)*. 2 vols. BV 10. Turnhout: Brepols, 1999.

——————. "Manuscrits entièrement ou partiellement autographes de Godefroid de Saint-Victor." *Scriptorium* 36 (1982): 29–42.

Pascher, Joseph. *Das liturgische Jahr*. Munich: Max Hueber, 1963.

Pennington, M. Basil. "Three Stages of Spiritual Growth according to St. Bernard." *Studia Monastica* 11 (1969): 315–26.

Pinckaers, Servais. "Recherches de la signification veritable du terme 'spéculatif.'" *Nouvelle revue théologique* 81 (1959): 673–95.

Poirel, Dominique. *Hugues de Saint-Victor.* Paris: Éditions du Cerf, 1998.

_____. *Livre de la nature et débat trinitaire au XIIᵉ siècle, Le "De tribus diebus" de Hugues de Saint-Victor.* BV 14. Turnhout: Brepols, 2002.

Pothier, J. "Planctus B. Marie Virginis." *Revue du chant grégorien* 5 (1896–1897): 17–21.

Principe, Walter. "Toward Defining Spirituality." *Studies in Religion* 12/2 (1983): 127–41.

Ralston, Michael E. "The Four Daughters of God in *The Castell of Perseverance.*" *Comitatus: Journal of Medieval and Renaissance Studies* 15 (1984): 25–44.

Reypens, L. "Ame (son fond, ses puissances, et sa structure d'après les mystiques)." In *DS* 1, ed. Marcel Viller, 433–69. Paris: G. Beauchesne et ses fils, 1937.

Rivière, Jean. *Le dogme de la rédemption au début du moyen âge.* Bibliothèque thomiste 19. Paris: J. Vrin, 1934.

Robilliard, J. "Les six genres de contemplation chez Richard de Saint Victor et leur origine platonicienne." *Revue des sciences philosophiques et théologiques* 28 (1939): 229–33.

Rorem, Paul. *Hugh of St. Victor.* Oxford: Oxford University Press, 2009.

Saarinen, Risto. *Weakness of the Will in Medieval Though: From Augustine to Buridan.* Leiden: E. J. Brill, 1994.

Santiago-Otero, Horacio. "Gaulterio y Godofredo de San Victor; su tesis acerca del conocimiento de Cristo hombre." *Divinitas* 18 (1974): 168–79.

Sheldrake, Philip. *Spirituality and History.* New York: Crossroad, 1992.

Shuffelton, George. *Codex Ashmole 61: A Compilation of Popular Middle English Verse.* Kalamazoo, Mich.: Medieval Institute Publications, 2008.

Sicard, Patrice. *Diagrammes médiévaux et exégèse visuelle: Le Libellus de formatione arche de Hugues de Saint-Victor.* BV 4. Paris: Brepols, 1993.

_____. *Hugues de Saint-Victor et son école.* Turnhout: Brepols, 1991.

_____. *Théologies victorines: études d'histoire doctrinale médiévale et contemporaine.* Paris: Parole et Silence, 2008.

Singer, Werner Ziltener, and Christian Hostettler. *Thesaurus proverbiorum medii aevi* = *Lexikon der Sprichwörter des romanisch-germanischen Mittelalters*, vol. 3. Berlin: W. de Gruyter, 1995.

Sirovic, P. Franz. *Der Begriff "Affectus" und die Willenslehre beim Hl. Bonaventura: Eine analytische-synthetische Untersuchung.* Mödling bei Wien, Druck: Missionsdruckerei St. Gabriel, 1965.

Smalley, Beryl. *The Study of the Bible in the Middle Ages.* Oxford: Blackwell Publishing, 1952. 3rd ed., 1983.

Smith, Charles Sidney. *Metaphor and Comparison in the* Epistulae ad Lucillum *of L. Anneas Seneca.* Baltimore: J. H. Furst, 1910.

Solignac, Aimé. "Sagesse." In *DS* 14, ed. D. Derville, P. Lamarche, and A. Solignac, 103–107. Paris: G. Beauchesne et ses fils, 1990.

_____. "Spiritualité." In *DS* 14, ed. D. Derville, P. Lamarche, and A. Solignac, 1142–60. Paris: G. Beauchesne et ses fils, 1990.

Stevens, John. "Planctus." In *The New Grove Dictionary of Music and Musicians* 20, ed. Stanley Sadie, 847–48. Washington, DC: Macmillan, 1980.

Stewart, Columba. *Cassian the Monk.* Oxford Studies in Historical Theology. New York: Oxford, 1998.

Sticca, Sandro. *The Planctus Mariae in the Dramatic Tradition of the Middle Ages.* Tr. Joseph R. Berrigan. Athens: University of Georgia Press, 1988.

Stock, Brian. *After Augustine. The Meditative Reader and the Text.* Material Texts. Philadelphia: University of Pennsylvania Press, 2001.

Talbot, Charles H. *Ailred of Rievaulx: De Anima.* Nendeln/Liechtenstein: Kraus, 1976.

Taylor, Jerome. *The Origin and Early Life of Hugh of St. Victor: An Evaluation of the Tradition.* Notre Dame, Ind.: University of Notre Dame Press, 1957.

Tinsley, Lucy. *The French Expression for Spirituality and Devotion: A Semantic Study.* Studies in Romance Languages and Literatures 47. Washington, DC: Catholic University of America Press, 1953.

Toynbee, Paget. *Dante, Studies and Researches.* London: Methuen, 1902.

Van den Eynde, Damien. "Complementary Note on the Early Scholastic *Commentarii in Psalmos.*" *Franciscan Studies* 17 (1957): 121–72.

————————. *Essai sur la succession et la date des écrits de Hugues de Saint-Victor.* Spicilegium Pontificii Athenaei Antoniani 13. Rome: Pontificium Athenaeum Antonianum, 1960.

————————. "Literary Note on the Earliest Scholastic *Commentarii in Psalmos.*" *Franciscan Studies* 14.2 (1954): 149–54.

Van 't Spijker, Ineke. "Exegesis and Emotions: Richard of St. Victor's *De Quatuor Gradibus Violentae Caritatis.*" *Sacris erudiri* 36 (1996): 147–60.

————————. "Hugh of Saint Victor's Virtue: Ambivalence and Gratuity." In *Virtue and Ethics in the Twelfth Century,* ed. István P. Bejczy and Richard G. Newhauser, 75–94. Leiden: E. J. Brill, 2005.

Von Ivánka, Endre. "Zur Überwindung des neuplatonischen Intellektualismus in der Deutung der Mystik: intelligentia oder principalis affectio." *Scholastik* 30 (1955): 185–94.

Wach, Joachim. "Hugo of St. Victor on Virtues and Vices." *Anglican Theological Review* 31 (1949): 25–33.

Wawrykow, Joseph P. *The Westminster Handbook to Thomas Aquinas.* Louisville: Westminster John Knox Press, 2005.

Wéber, Edouard-Henri. *La personne humaine au xiiie siècle.* Paris: J. Vrin, 1991.

Weisheipl, James A. "The Life and Works of St. Albert the Great." In *Albertus Magnus and the Sciences: Commemorative Essays 1980,* ed. James A. Weisheipl, 13–51.Toronto: Pontifical Institute of Mediaeval Studies, 1980.

Winston, David. *The Wisdom of Solomon.* Anchor Bible. Garden City, NY Doubleday, 1979.

Weisweiler, Heinrich. "*Eine neue Bearbeitung von Abelards* Introductio *und der* Summa sententiarum." *Scholastik* 9 (1934): 346–71.

Wolff, Paul. *Die Viktoriner: Mystische Schriften.* Vienna: Thomas-Verlag Jakob Hegner, 1936.

Zinn, Grover A. "De Gradibus Ascensionum: The Stages of Contemplative Ascent in Two Treatises on Noah's Ark by Hugh of St. Victor." In *Studies in Medieval Culture V,* ed. John R. Sommerfeldt, 61–79. Kalamazoo: Medieval Institute Press, 1975.

————————. "Hugh of Saint Victor and the Art of Memory." *Viator. Medieval and Renaissance Studies* 5 (1974): 211–34.

————————. "The Regular Canons." In *Christian Spirituality: Origins to the Twelfth Century.* Ed. Bernard McGinn and John Meyendorff, 218–27. New York: Crossroad, 1996.

INDEX OF SCRIPTURE REFERENCES

OLD TESTAMENT

New Testament

INDEX OF ANCIENT AND MEDIEVAL AUTHORS

VICTORINE AUTHORS

ACHARD OF ST VICTOR

GODFREY OF ST VICTOR

Hugh of St Victor

PSEUDO-RICHARD OF ST VICTOR

ROBERT OF MELUN

WALTER OF ST VICTOR

WARNER OF ST VICTOR

WRITINGS ASSOCIATED WITH ST VICTOR

EARLY AND MEDIEVAL CHRISTIAN AUTHORS

CLASSICAL AUTHORS

SUBJECT INDEX